Lecture Notes in Artificial Int

Edited by J. G. Carbonell and J. Siekman

T0250753

Subseries of Lecture Notes in Computer Science

Jean-François Boulicaut
Floriana Esposito   Fosca Giannotti
Dino Pedreschi (Eds.)

Machine Learning: ECML 2004

15th European Conference on Machine Learning
Pisa, Italy, September 20-24, 2004
Proceedings

 Springer

Series Editors

Jaime G. Carbonell, Carnegie Mellon University, Pittsburgh, PA, USA
Jörg Siekmann, University of Saarland, Saarbrücken, Germany

Volume Editors

Jean-François Boulicaut
INSA Lyon
LIRIS CNRS FRE 2672, 69621 Villeurbanne Cedex, France
E-mail: jean-francois.boulicaut@insa-lyon.fr

Floriana Esposito
University of Bari
Department of Computer Science
Via Orabona 4, 70126 Bari, Italy
E-mail: esposito@di.uniba.it

Fosca Giannotti
Science and Technology Institute
Knowledge Discovery and Delivery (KDD)
Via G. Moruzzi 1, 56124 Pisa, Italy
E-mail: Fosca.Giannotti@isti.cnr.it

Dino Pedreschi
University of Pisa
Department of Computer Science
Via F. Buonarroti 2, 56125 Pisa, Italy
E-mail: pedre@di.unipi.it

Library of Congress Control Number: 2004111517

CR Subject Classification (1998): I.2, F.2.2, F.4.1, H.2.8

ISSN 0302-9743
ISBN 3-540-23105-6 Springer Berlin Heidelberg New York

Springer is a part of Springer Science+Business Media

springeronline.com

Typesetting: Camera-ready by author, data conversion by Olgun Computergrafik
Printed on acid-free paper   SPIN: 11322788   06/3142   5 4 3 2 1 0

Preface

The proceedings of ECML/PKDD 2004 are published in two separate, albeit intertwined, volumes: the Proceedings of the 15th European Conference on Machine Learning (LNAI 3201) and the Proceedings of the 8th European Conferences on Principles and Practice of Knowledge Discovery in Databases (LNAI 3202). The two conferences were co-located in Pisa, Tuscany, Italy during September 20–24, 2004.

It was the fourth time in a row that ECML and PKDD were co-located. After the successful co-locations in Freiburg (2001), Helsinki (2002), and Cavtat-Dubrovnik (2003), it became clear that researchers strongly supported the organization of a major scientific event about machine learning and data mining in Europe.

We are happy to provide some statistics about the conferences. 581 different papers were submitted to ECML/PKDD (about a 75% increase over 2003); 280 were submitted to ECML 2004 only, 194 were submitted to PKDD 2004 only, and 107 were submitted to both. Around half of the authors for submitted papers are from outside Europe, which is a clear indicator of the increasing attractiveness of ECML/PKDD.

The Program Committee members were deeply involved in what turned out to be a highly competitive selection process. We assigned each paper to 3 reviewers, deciding on the appropriate PC for papers submitted to both ECML and PKDD. As a result, ECML PC members reviewed 312 papers and PKDD PC members reviewed 269 papers. We accepted for publication regular papers (45 for ECML 2004 and 39 for PKDD 2004) and short papers that were associated with poster presentations (6 for ECML 2004 and 9 for PKDD 2004). The global acceptance rate was 14.5% for regular papers (17% if we include the short papers).

The scientific program of ECML/PKDD 2004 also included 5 invited talks, a wide workshop and tutorial program (10 workshops plus a Discovery Challenge workshop, and seven tutorials) and a demo session.

We wish to express our gratitude to:

- the authors of the submitted papers;
- the program committee members and the additional referees for their exceptional contribution to a tough but crucial selection process;
- the invited speakers: Dimitris Achlioptas (Microsoft Research, Redmond), Rakesh Agrawal (IBM Almaden Research Center), Soumen Chakrabarti (Indian Institute of Technology, Bombay), Pedro Domingos (University of Washington, Seattle), and David J. Hand (Imperial College, London);
- the workshop chairs Donato Malerba and Mohammed J. Zaki;
- the tutorial chairs Katharina Morik and Franco Turini;
- the discovery challenge chairs Petr Berka and Bruno Crémilleux;

- the publicity chair Salvatore Ruggieri;
- the demonstration chairs Rosa Meo, Elena Baralis, and Codrina Lauth;
- the members of the ECML/PKDD Steering Committee Peter Flach, Luc De Raedt, Arno Siebes, Nada Lavrač, Dragan Gamberger, Ljupčo Todorovski, Hendrik Blockeel, Tapio Elomaa, Heikki Mannila, and Hannu T.T. Toivonen;
- the members of the Award Committee, Michael May and Foster Provost;
- the workshops organizers and the tutorialists;
- the extremely efficient Organization Committee members, Maurizio Atzori, Miriam Baglioni, Sergio Barsocchi, Jérémy Besson, Francesco Bonchi, Stefano Ferilli, Tiziana Mazzone, Mirco Nanni, Ruggero Pensa, Simone Puntoni, Chiara Renso, Salvatore Rinzivillo, as well as all the other members of the KDD Lab in Pisa, Laura Balbarini and Cristina Rosamilia of L&B Studio, Elena Perini and Elena Tonsini of the University of Pisa;
- the great Web masters Mirco Nanni, Chiara Renso and Salvatore Rinzivillo;
- the directors of the two research institutions in Pisa that jointly made this event possible, Piero Maestrini (ISTI-CNR) and Ugo Montanari (Dipartimento di Informatica);
- the administration staff of the two research institutions in Pisa, in particular Massimiliano Farnesi (ISTI-CNR), Paola Fabiani and Letizia Petrellese (Dipartimento di Informatica);
- Richard van de Stadt (www.borbala.com) for his efficient support to the management of the whole submission and evaluation process by means of the CyberChairPRO software;
- Alfred Hofmann of Springer for co-operation in publishing the proceedings.

We gratefully acknowledge the financial support of KDNet, the Pascal Network, Kluwer and the Machine Learning journal, Springer, the Province of Lucca, the Province of Pisa, the Municipality of Pisa, Microsoft Research, COOP, Exeura, Intel, Talent, INSA-Lyon, ISTI-CNR Pisa, the University of Pisa, the University of Bari, and the patronage of Regione Toscana.

There is no doubt that the impressive scientific activities in machine learning and data mining world-wide were well demonstrated in Pisa. We had an exciting week in Tuscany, enhancing further co-operations between the many researchers who are pushing knowledge discovery into becoming a mature scientific discipline.

July 2004

Jean-François Boulicaut,
Floriana Esposito,
Fosca Giannotti,
and Dino Pedreschi

ECML/PKDD 2004 Organization

Executive Committee

Program Chairs	Jean-François Boulicaut (INSA Lyon)
	Floriana Esposito (Università di Bari)
	Fosca Giannotti (ISTI-CNR)
	Dino Pedreschi (Università di Pisa)
Workshop Chairs	Donato Malerba (University of Bari)
	Mohammed J. Zaki (Rensselaer Polytechnic Institute)
Tutorial Chairs	Katharina Morik (University of Dortmund)
	Franco Turini (University of Pisa)
Discovery Challenge Chairs	Petr Berka (University of Economics, Prague)
	Bruno Crémilleux (University of Caen)
Publicity Chair	Salvatore Ruggieri (University of Pisa)
Demonstration Chairs	Rosa Meo (University of Turin)
	Elena Baralis (Politecnico of Turin)
	Ina Lauth (Fraunhofer Institute for Autonomous Intelligent Systems)
Steering Committee	Peter Flach (University of Bristol)
	Luc De Raedt (Albert-Ludwigs University, Freiburg)
	Arno Siebes (Utrecht University)
	Nada Lavrač (Jozef Stefan Institute)
	Dragan Gamberger (Rudjer Boskovic Institute)
	Ljupčo Todorovski (Jozef Stefan Institute)
	Hendrik Blockeel (Katholieke Universiteit Leuven)
	Tapio Elomaa (Tampere University of Technology)
	Heikki Mannila (Helsinki Institute for Information Technology)
	Hannu T.T. Toivonen (University of Helsinki)
Awards Committee	Michael May (Fraunhofer Institute for Autonomous Intelligent Systems, KDNet representative)
	Floriana Esposito (PC representative)
	Foster Provost (Editor-in-Chief of Machine Learning Journal, Kluwer)
Organizing Committee	Maurizio Atzori (KDDLab, ISTI-CNR)
	Miriam Baglioni (KDDLab, University of Pisa)
	Sergio Barsocchi (KDDLab, ISTI-CNR)
	Jérémy Besson (INSA Lyon)
	Francesco Bonchi (KDDLab, ISTI-CNR)
	Stefano Ferilli (University of Bari)
	Tiziana Mazzone (KDDLab)
	Mirco Nanni (KDDLab, ISTI-CNR)
	Ruggero Pensa (INSA Lyon)
	Chiara Renso (KDDLab, ISTI-CNR)
	Salvatore Rinzivillo (KDDLab, University of Pisa)

ECML 2004 Program Committee

Hendrik Blockeel, Belgium
Marco Botta, Italy
Henrik Boström, Sweden
Jean-François Boulicaut, France
Ivan Bratko, Slovenia
Pavel Brazdil, Portugal
Nello Cristianini, USA
James Cussens, UK
Ramon Lopes de Mantaras, Spain
Luc De Raedt, Germany
Luc Dehaspe, Belgium
Josè del R. Millan, Switzerland
Sašo Džeroski, Slovenia
Tapio Elomaa, Finland
Floriana Esposito, Italy
Peter Flach, UK
Johannes Fürnkranz, Germany
Joao Gama, Portugal
Dragan Gamberger, Croatia
Jean-Gabriel Ganascia, France
Fosca Giannotti, Italy
Attilio Giordana, Italy
Haym Hirsh, USA
Thomas Hofmann, USA
Tamas Horvath, Germany
Thorsten Joachims, USA
Dimitar Kazakov, UK
Roni Khardon, USA
Joerg Kindermann, Germany
Yves Kodratoff, France
Igor Kononenko, Slovenia
Stefan Kramer, Germany
Miroslav Kubat, USA
Stephen Kwek, USA
Nada Lavrač, Slovenia
Charles Ling, Canada

Donato Malerba, Italy
Heikki Mannila, Finland
Stan Matwin, Canada
Dunja Mladenic, Slovenia
Katharina Morik, Germany
Hiroshi Motoda, Japan
Remi Munos, France
Richard Nock, France
David Page, USA
Georgios Paliouras, Greece
Dino Pedreschi, Italy
Bernhard Pfahringer, New Zealand
Enric Plaza, Spain
Juho Rousu, UK
Celine Rouveirol, France
Tobias Scheffer, Germany
Michele Sebag, France
Giovanni Semeraro, Italy
Arno Siebes, The Netherlands
Robert Sloan, USA
Gerd Stumme, Germany
Henry Tirri, Finland
Ljupčo Todorovski, Slovenia
Luis Torgo, Portugal
Peter Turney, Canada
Maarten van Someren, The Netherlands
Paul Vitanyi, The Netherlands
Sholom Weiss, USA
Dietrich Wettschereck, UK
Gerhard Widmer, Austria
Marco Wiering, The Netherlands
Ruediger Wirth, Germany
Stefan Wrobel, Germany
Thomas Zeugmann, Germany
Tong Zhang, USA
Blaž Zupan, Slovenia

PKDD 2004 Program Committee

Elena Baralis, Italy
Michael Berthold, Germany
Elisa Bertino, USA
Hendrik Blockeel, Belgium
Jean-François Boulicaut, France
Christopher W. Clifton, USA
Bruno Cremilleux, France
Luc De Raedt, Germany
Luc Dehaspe, Belgium
Sašo Džeroski, Slovenia
Tapio Elomaa, Finland
Floriana Esposito, Italy
Martin Ester, Canada
Ad Feelders, The Netherlands
Ronen Feldman, IL
Peter Flach, UK
Eibe Frank, New Zealand
Alex Freitas, UK
Johannes Fürnkranz, Germany
Dragan Gamberger, Croatia
Minos Garofalakis, USA
Fosca Giannotti, Italy
Christophe Giraud-Carrier, Switzerland
Bart Goethals, Finland
Howard Hamilton, Canada
Robert Hilderman, Canada
Haym Hirsh, USA
Frank Hoeppner, Germany
Se Hong, USA
Samuel Kaski, Finland
Daniel Keim, Germany
Jorg-Uwe Kietz, Switzerland
Ross King, UK
Yves Kodratoff, France
Joost Kok, The Netherlands
Stefan Kramer, Germany
Laks Lakshmanan, Canada
Nada Lavrač, Slovenia
Donato Malerba, Italy
Giuseppe Manco, Italy
Heikki Mannila, Finland
Stan Matwin, Canada
Michael May, Germany

Rosa Meo, Italy
Dunja Mladenic, Slovenia
Katharina Morik, Germany
Shinichi Morishita, Japan
Hiroshi Motoda, Japan
Gholamreza Nakhaeizadeh, Germany
Claire Nedellec, France
David Page, USA
Dino Pedreschi, Italy
Zbigniew Ras, USA
Jan Rauch, Czech Rebuclic
Christophe Rigotti, France
Gilbert Ritschard, Switzerland
John Roddick, Australia
Yucel Saygin, Turkey
Michele Sebag, France
Marc Sebban, France
Arno Siebes, The Netherlands
Andrzej Skowron, Poland
Myra Spiliopoulou, Germany
Nicolas Spyratos, France
Reinhard Stolle, USA
Gerd Stumme, Germany
Einoshin Suzuki, Japan
Ah-Hwee Tan, Singapore
Ljupčo Todorovski, Slovenia
Hannu Toivonen, Finland
Luis Torgo, Portugal
Shusaku Tsumoto, Japan
Franco Turini, Italy
Maarten van Someren, The Netherlands
Ke Wang, Canada
Louis Wehenkel, Belgium
Dietrich Wettschereck, UK
Gerhard Widmer, Austria
Ruediger Wirth, Germany
Stefan Wrobel, Germany
Osmar R. Zaiane, Canada
Mohammed Zaki, USA
Carlo Zaniolo, USA
Djamel Zighed, France
Blaž Zupan, Slovenia

ECML/PKDD 2004 Additional Reviewers

Fabio Abbattista
Markus Ackermann
Erick Alphonse
Oronzo Altamura
Massih Amini
Ahmed Amrani
Anastasia Analiti
Nicos Angelopoulos
Fabrizio Angiulli
Luiza Antonie
Annalisa Appice
Josep-Lluis Arcos
Eva Armengol
Thierry Artieres
Maurizio Atzori
Anne Auger
Ilkka Autio
Jérôme Azé
Vincenzo Bacarella
Miriam Baglioni
Yijian Bai
Cristina Baroglio
Teresa Basile
Ganesan Bathumalai
Fadila Bentayeb
Margherita Berardi
Bettina Berendt
Petr Berka
Guillaume Beslon
Philippe Bessières
Matjaz Bevk
Steffen Bickel
Gilles Bisson
Avrim Blum
Axel Blumenstock
Damjan Bojadžiev
Francesco Bonchi
Toufik Boudellal
Omar Boussaid
Janez Brank
Nicolas Bredeche
Ulf Brefeld
Wray Buntine
Christoph Büscher
Benjamin Bustos
Niccolo Capanni
Amedeo Cappelli

Martin R.J. Carpenter
Costantina Caruso
Ciro Castiello
Barbara Catania
Davide Cavagnino
Michelangelo Ceci
Alessio Ceroni
Jesús Cerquides
Eugenio Cesario
Silvia Chiusano
Fang Chu
Antoine Cornuéjols
Fabrizio Costa
Gianni Costa
Tom Croonenborghs
Tomaz Curk
Maria Damiani
Agnieszka Dardzinska
Tijl De Bie
Edwin D. De Jong
Kurt De Grave
Marco Degemmis
Janez Demšar
Damjan Demšar
Michel de Rougemont
Nicola Di Mauro
Christos Dimitrakakis
Simon Dixon
Kurt Driessens
Isabel Drost
Chris Drummond
Wenliang Du
Nicolas Durand
Michael Egmont-Petersen
Craig Eldershaw
Mohammed El-Hajj
Roberto Esposito
Timm Euler
Theodoros Evgeniou
Anna Maria Fanelli
Nicola Fanizzi
Ayman Farahat
Sebastien Ferre
Stefano Ferilli
Daan Fierens
Thomas Finley
Sergio Flesca

François Fleuret
Francesco Folino
Francesco Fornasari
Blaz Fortuna
Andrew Foss
Keith Frikken
Barbara Furletti
Thomas Gärtner
Ugo Galassi
Arianna Gallo
Byron Gao
Paolo Garza
Liqiang Geng
Claudio Gentile
Pierre Geurts
Zoubin Ghahramani
Arnaud Giacometti
Emiliano Giovannetti
Piotr Gmytrasiewicz
Judy Goldsmith
Anna Gomolinska
Udo Grimmer
Matthew Grounds
Antonella Guzzo
Amaury Habrard
Stephan ten Hagen
Jörg Hakenberg
Mark Hall
Greg Hamerly
Ji He
Jaana Heino
Thomas Heitz
Frank Herrmann
Haitham Hindi
Ayca Azgin Hintoglu
Joachim Hipp
Susanne Hoche
Pieter Jan 't Hoen
Andreas Hotho
Tomas Hrycej
Luigi Iannone
Inaki Inza
François Jacquenet
Aleks Jakulin
Jean-Christophe Janodet
Nathalie Japkowicz
Tony Jebara

Tao-Yuan Jen
Tao Jiang
Xing Jiang
Yuelong Jiang
Alípio Jorge
Pierre-Emmanuel Jouve
Matti Kääriäinen
Spiros Kapetanakis
Vangelis Karkaletsis
Andreas Karwath
Branko Kavšek
Steffen Kempe
Kristian Kersting
Jahwan Kim
Minsoo Kim
Svetlana Kiritchenko
Richard Kirkby
Jyrki Kivinen
Willi Kloesgen
Gabriella Kókai
Petri Kontkanen
Dimitrios Kosmopoulos
Mark-A. Krogel
Jussi Kujala
Matjaž Kukar
Kari Laasonen
Krista Lagus
Lotfi Lakhal
Stéphane Lallich
Gert Lanckriet
John Langford
Carsten Lanquillon
Antonietta Lanza
Michele Lapi
Dominique Laurent
Yan-Nei Law
Neil Lawrence
Gregor Leban
Sau Dan Lee
Gaëlle Legrand
Edda Leopold
Claire Leschi
Guichong Li
Oriana Licchelli
Per Lidén
Jussi T. Lindgren
Francesca A. Lisi
Bing Liu
Zhenyu Liu
Peter Ljubič

Marco Locatelli
Huma Lodhi
Ricardo Lopes
Pasquale Lops
Robert Lothian
Claudio Lucchese
Jack Lutz
Tuomo Malinen
Michael Maltrud
Suresh Manandhar
Alain-Pierre Manine
Raphael Marée
Berardi Margherita
Elio Masciari
Cyrille Masson
Nicolas Méger
Carlo Meghini
Corrado Mencar
Amar-Djalil Mezaour
Tatiana Miazhynskaia
Alessio Micheli
Taneli Mielikäinen
Ingo Mierswa
Tommi Mononen
Martin Možina
Thierry Murgue
Mirco Nanni
Phu Chien Nguyen
Tuan Trung Nguyen
Alexandru Niculescu-Mizil
Siegfried Nijssen
Janne Nikkilä
Blaž Novak
Alexandros Ntoulas
William O'Neill
Kouzou Ohara
Arlindo L. Oliveira
Santiago Ontañón
Riccardo Ortale
Martijn van Otterlo
Gerhard Paass
Ignazio Palmisano
Christian Panse
Andrea Passerini
Jaakko Peltonen
Lourdes Pena
Raffaele Perego
José Ramón Quevedo Pérez
Fernando Perez-Cruz
Georgios Petasis

Johann Petrak
Sergios Petridis
Viet Phan-Luong
Dimitris Pierrakos
Joël Plisson
Neoklis Polyzotis
Luboš Popelínský
Roland Priemer
Kai Puolamäki
Sabine Rabaseda
Filip Radlinski
Mika Raento
Jan Ramon
Ari Rantanen
Pierre Renaux
Chiara Renso
Rita Ribeiro
Lothar Richter
Salvatore Rinzivillo
François Rioult
Stefano Rizzi
Céline Robardet
Mathieu Roche
Pedro Rodrigues
Teemu Roos
Benjamin Rosenfeld
Roman Rosipal
Fabrice Rossi
Olga Roudenko
Antonin Rozsypal
Ulrich Rückert
Salvatore Ruggieri
Stefan Rüping
Nicolas Sabouret
Aleksander Sadikov
Taro L. Saito
Lorenza Saitta
Luka Šajn
Apkar Salatian
Marko Salmenkivi
Craig Saunders
Alexandr Savinov
Jelber Sayyad Shirabad
Francesco Scarcello
Christoph Schmitz
Joern Schneidewind
Martin Scholz
Tobias Schreck
Ingo Schwab
Mihaela Scuturici

ECML/PKDD 2004 Tutorials

Evaluation in Web Mining
Bettina Berendt, Ernestina Menasalvas, Myra Spiliopoulou

Symbolic Data Analysis
Edwin Diday, Carlos Marcelo

Radial Basis Functions: An Algebraic Approach (with Data Mining Applications)
Amrit L. Goel, Miyoung Shin

Mining Unstructured Data
Ronen Feldman

Statistical Approaches Used in Machine Learning
Bruno Apolloni, Dario Malchiodi

Rule-Based Data Mining Methods for Classification Problems in the Biomedical Domain
Jinyan Li, Limsoon Wong

Distributed Data Mining for Sensor Networks
Hillol Kargupta

ECML/PKDD 2004 Workshops

Statistical Approaches for Web Mining (SAWM)
Marco Gori, Michelangelo Ceci, Mirco Nanni

Symbolic and Spatial Data Analysis: Mining Complex Data Structures
Paula Brito, Monique Noirhomme

Third International Workshop on Knowledge Discovery in Inductive Databases (KDID 2004)
Bart Goethals, Arno Siebes

Data Mining and Adaptive Modelling Methods for Economics and Management (IWAMEM 2004)
Pavel Brazdil, Fernando S. Oliveira, Giulio Bottazzi

Privacy and Security Issues in Data Mining
Yücel Saygin

Knowledge Discovery and Ontologies
Paul Buitelaar, Jürgen Franke, Marko Grobelnik, Gerhard Paaß, Vojtech Svátek

Mining Graphs, Trees and Sequences (MGTS 2004)
Joost Kok, Takashi Washio

Advances in Inductive Rule Learning
Johannes Fürnkranz

Data Mining and Text Mining for Bioinformatics
Tobias Scheffer

Knowledge Discovery in Data Streams
Jesus Aguilar-Ruiz, Joao Gama

Table of Contents

Posters

Author Index

Random Matrices in Data Analysis

Dimitris Achlioptas

Microsoft Research, Redmond, WA 98052, USA
optas@microsoft.com

Abstract. We show how carefully crafted random matrices can achieve distance-preserving dimensionality reduction, accelerate spectral computations, and reduce the sample complexity of certain kernel methods.

1 Introduction

Given a collection of n data points (vectors) in high-dimensional Euclidean space it is natural to ask whether they can be projected into a lower dimensional Euclidean space without suffering great distortion. Two particularly interesting classes of projections are: i) projections that tend to preserve the interpoint distances, and ii) projections that maximize the average projected vector length.

In the last few years, distance-preserving projections have had great impact in theoretical computer science where they have been useful in a variety of algorithmic settings, such as approximate nearest neighbor search, clustering, learning mixtures of distributions, and computing statistics of streamed data.

The general idea is that by providing a low dimensional representation of the data, distance-preserving embeddings dramatically speed up algorithms whose run-time depends exponentially in the dimension of the working space. At the same time, the provided guarantee regarding pairwise distances often allows one to show that the solution found by working in the low dimensional space is a good approximation to the solution in the original space.

Perhaps the most commonly used projections aim at maximizing the average projected vector length, thus retaining most of the variance in the data. This involves representing the data as a matrix A, diagonalizing $A = UDV$, and projecting A onto subspaces spanned by the vectors in U or V corresponding to the largest entries in D. Variants of this idea are known as Karhunen-Loève transform, Principal Component Analysis, Singular Value Decomposition and others.

In this paper we examine different applications of random matrices to both kinds of projections, all stemming from variations of the following basic fact: if R is an $n \times n$ random matrix whose entries are i.i.d. Normal random variables, $N(0, 1)$, then the matrix $\frac{1}{\sqrt{n}} R$ is very close to being orthonormal.

2 Euclidean Distance Preservation

A classic result of Johnson and Lindenstrauss [7] asserts that any set of n points in $\mathbb{R}^d$ can be embedded into $\mathbb{R}^k$, with $k = O(\log n)$, so that all pairwise distances are maintained within an arbitrarily small factor. More precisely,

J.-F. Boulicaut et al. (Eds.): ECML 2004, LNAI 3201, pp. 1–7, 2004.
© Springer-Verlag Berlin Heidelberg 2004

Lemma 1 ([7]). *Given* $0 < \epsilon \leq 1$ *and an integer* n, *let* k *be a positive integer such that* $k \geq k_0 = (12/\epsilon^2) \log n$. *For every set* P *of* n *points in* $\mathbb{R}^d$ *there exists* $f : \mathbb{R}^d \to \mathbb{R}^k$ *such that for all* $u, v \in P$

$$(1 - \epsilon)||u - v||^2 \leq ||f(u) - f(v)||^2 \leq (1 + \epsilon)||u - v||^2 .$$

Perhaps, a naive attempt to construct an embedding as above would be to pick a random set of k coordinates from the original space. Unfortunately, two points can be very far apart while differing only along one original dimension, dooming this approach. On the other hand, if (somehow) for all pairs of points, all coordinates contributed "roughly equally" to their distance, such a sampling scheme would be very natural. This consideration motives the following idea: first apply a random *rotation* to the n points, and then pick the first k coordinates as the new coordinates. The random rotation can be viewed as a form of insurance against axis alignment, analogous to applying a random permutation before running Quicksort.

Of course, applying a random rotation and then taking the first k coordinates is equivalent to projecting the n points on a uniformly random k-dimensional subspace. Indeed, this is exactly how the original proof of Lemma 1 by Johnson and Lindenstrauss proceeds: to implement the embedding, multiply the $n \times d$ data matrix A with a random $d \times k$ orthonormal matrix. Dasgupta and Gupta [5] and, independently, Indyk and Motwani [6] more recently gave a simpler proof of Lemma 1 by taking the following more relaxed approach towards orthonormality.

The key idea is to consider what happens if we multiply A with a random $d \times k$ matrix R whose entries are independent Normal random variables with mean 0 and variance 1, i.e., $N(0, 1)$. It turns out that while we do not explicitly enforce either orthogonality or normality in R, its columns will come very close to having both of these properties. This is because, as d increases: (i) the length of each column-vector concentrates around its expectation as the sum of d independent random variables; (ii) by the spherical symmetry of the Gaussian distribution, each column-vector points in a uniformly random direction in $\mathbb{R}^d$, making the $k \leq d$ independent column-vectors nearly orthogonal with high probability.

More generally, let R be a random matrix whose entries are independent random variables with $\mathbf{E}(r_{ij}) = 0$ and $\text{Var}(r_{ij}) = 1$. If $f : \mathbb{R}^d \to \mathbb{R}^k$ is given by

$$f(x) = \frac{1}{\sqrt{k}} x R ,$$

it is easy to check that for any vector $x \in \mathbb{R}^d$ we have $\mathbf{E}(||f(x)||) = ||x||$. Effectively, the squared inner product of x with each column of R acts as an independent estimate of $||x||^2$, making $||f(x)||^2$ the consensus estimate (sum) of the k estimators. Seen from this angle, requiring the k vectors to be orthonormal simply maximizes the mutual information of the k estimators. For good dimensionality reduction, we also need to minimize the variance of the estimators.

In [1], it was shown that taking $r_{ij} = \pm 1$ with equal probability, in fact, slightly reduces the number of required dimensions k (as the variance of each column-estimator is slightly smaller). At the same time, and more importantly, this choice of r_{ij} makes f a lot easier to work with in practice.

3   Computing Low Rank Approximations

Given n points in $\mathbb{R}^d$ represented as an $n \times d$ matrix A, one of the most common tasks in data analysis is to find the "top k" singular vectors of A and then project A onto the subspace they span. Such low rank approximations are used widely in areas such as computer vision, information retrieval, and machine learning to extract correlations and remove noise from matrix-structured data.

Recall that the top singular vector of a matrix A is the maximizer of $\|Ax\|_2$ over all unit vectors x. This maximum is known as the L_2 norm of A and the maximizer captures the dominant linear trend in A. Remarkably, this maximizer can be discovered by starting with a random unit vector $x \in \mathbb{R}^d$ and repeating the following "voting process" until it reaches a fixpoint, i.e., until x stops rotating:

– Have each of the n rows in A vote on candidate x, i.e., compute $y = Ax \in \mathbb{R}^n$.

– Compose a new candidate by combining the rows of A, weighing each row by its enthusiasm for x, i.e., update $x \leftarrow \dfrac{A^T y}{\|A^T y\|} \in \mathbb{R}^d$.

The above idea extends to $k > 1$. To find the k-dimensional invariant subspace of A, one starts with a random subspace, i.e., a random $d \times k$ orthonormal matrix, and repeatedly multiplies by $A^T A$ (orthonormalizing after each multiplication). Computing the singular row-vectors of A, i.e., the eigenvectors of $B = A^T A$, is often referred to as Principal Component Analysis (PCA). The following process achieves the exact same goal, by extracting the dominant trends in A sequentially, in order of strength: let A_0 be the all zeros matrix; for $i = 1, \ldots, k$:

– Find the top singular vector, x_i, of $A - A_{i-1}$, via the voting process above.
– Let $A_i = A_{i-1} + A x_i x_i^T$, i.e., A_i is the optimal rank i approximation to A.

To get an idea of how low rank approximations can remove noise, let G be an $n \times d$ random matrix whose entries are i.i.d. $N(0, \sigma^2)$ random variables. We saw earlier that each column of G points in an independent, uniformly random direction in $\mathbb{R}^n$. As a result, when n is large, with high probability the $d \leq n$ columns of G are nearly orthogonal and there is *no* low-dimensional subspace that simultaneously accommodates many of them. This means that when we compute a low rank approximation of $A + G$, as long as σ is "not too large" (in a sense we will make precise), the columns of G will exert little influence as they do not strongly favor any particular low-dimensional subspace. Assuming that A contains strong linear trends, it is its columns that will command and receive accommodation.

To make this intuition more precise, we first state a general bound on the impact that a matrix N can have on the optimal rank k approximation of a matrix A, denoted by A_k, as a function of $\|N_k\|$. Recall that $\|A\|_F = \sqrt{\sum_{i,j} A_{ij}^2}$.

Lemma 2. *For any matrices A and N, if $\widehat{A} = A + N$ then*

$$\|A - \widehat{A}_k\|_2 \leq \|A - A_k\|_2 + 2\|N_k\|_2 \quad and$$

$$\|A - \widehat{A}_k\|_F \leq \|A - A_k\|_F + \|N_k\|_F + 2\sqrt{\|N_k\|_F \|A_k\|_F} \ .$$

Notice that all error terms above scale with $\|N_k\|$. As a result, whenever N is poorly approximated in k dimensions, i.e., $\|N_k\|$ is small, the error caused by adding N to a matrix A is also small.

Let us consider the norms of our Gaussian perturbation matrix.

Fact 1 *Let G be a random $n \times d$ matrix, where $d \leq n$, whose entries are i.i.d. random variables $N(0, \sigma^2)$. For any $\epsilon > 0$, with probability $1 - 1/\mathrm{poly}(n, \epsilon)$,*

$$\|G\|_2 = \|G_k\|_2 < (2 + \epsilon)\sigma\sqrt{n} \quad and \quad \|G_k\|_F < (2 + \epsilon)\sigma\sqrt{kn} \ .$$

Remarkably, the upper bound above for $\|G\|_2$ is within a factor of 2 of the *lower bound* $\sigma\sqrt{n}$ on the L_2 norm of *any* $n \times d$ matrix with mean squared entry σ^2. In other words, a random Gaussian matrix is nearly as unstructured as possible, resembling white noise in the flatness of its spectrum. On the other hand, $\|A\|_2$ can be as large as $\sigma\sqrt{dn}$ for an $n \times d$ matrix A with mean squared entry σ^2.

This capacity of spectral techniques to remove Gaussian noise is by now very well-understood. We will see that the above geometric explanation of this fact can actually accommodate much more general noise models, e.g. N_{ij} that are not identically distributed and, in fact, whose distribution depends on A_{ij}. In the next section, this generality will enable the notion of "computation-friendly noise", i.e., noise that enhances (rather than hinders) spectral computations.

Fact 1 also suggests a criterion for choosing a good value of k when seeking low rank approximations of a $n \times d$ data matrix A:

$$\|A - A_k\|_2 \sim \sigma\sqrt{n}, \text{ where } \sigma^2 \text{ is the mean squared entry in } A - A_k.$$

In words: we should stop when, after projecting onto the top k singular vectors, we are left with a matrix, $A - A_k$, whose strongest linear trend is comparable to that of a random matrix of similar scale.

3.1   Co-opting the Noise Process

Computing optimal low rank approximations of large matrices often runs against practical computational limits since the algorithms for this task generally require superlinear time and a large working set. On the other hand, in many applications it is perfectly acceptable just to find a rank k matrix C satisfying

$$\|A - C\| \leq \|A - A_k\| + \delta \ ,$$

where A_k is the optimal rank k approximation of the input matrix A, and δ captures an appropriate notion of "error tolerance" for the domain at hand.

In [2], it was shown that with the aid of randomization one can exploit such an "error allotment" to aid spectral computations. The main idea is as follows.

Imagine, first, that we squander the error allotment by obliviously adding to A a Gaussian matrix G, as in the previous section. While this is not likely to yield a computationally advantageous matrix, we saw that at least it is rather harmless. The first step in using noise to aid computation is realizing that G is innocuous due precisely to the following three properties of its entries:

independence, zero mean, small variance.

The fact that the G_{ij} are Gaussian is *not* essential: a fundamental result of Füredi and Komlós [4] shows that Fact 1 generalizes to random matrices where the entries can have different, in fact arbitrary, distributions as long as all N_{ij} are zero-mean, independent, and their variance is bounded by σ^2.

To exploit this fact for computational gain, given a matrix A, we will create a distribution of noise matrices N that *depends on* A, yet is such that the random variables N_{ij} still enjoy independence, zero mean, and small variance. In particular, we will be able to choose N so that $\widehat{A} = A + N$ has computationally useful properties, such as sparsity, yet N is sufficiently random for $\|N_k\|$ to be small with high probability.

Example: Set $N_{ij} = \pm A_{ij}$ with equal probability, independently for all i, j.

In this example, the random variables N_{ij} are independent, $\mathbf{E}[N_{ij}] = 0$ for all i, j, and the standard deviation of N_{ij} equals A_{ij}. On the other hand, the matrix $\widehat{A} = A + N$ will have about half as many non-zero entries as A, i.e., it will be about twice as sparse. Therefore, while $\|A\|_2$ can be proportional to $\sqrt{dn}$, the error term $\|N\|_2$, i.e., the price for the sparsification, is only proportional to $\sqrt{n}$.

The rather innocent example above can be greatly generalized. To simplify exposition, in the following, we assume that $A_{ij} \in [-1, +1]$.

- **Quantization:** For all i, j, independently, set $\widehat{A}_{ij}$ to $+1$ with probability $(1 + A_{ij})/2$, and to -1 with probability $(1 - A_{ij})/2$. Clearly, for all i, j, we have $\mathbf{E}[N_{ij}] = \mathbf{E}[\widehat{A}_{ij} - A_{ij}] = 0$, while $\mathrm{Var}(N_{ij}) \le N_{ij}^2 \le 4$.
- **Uniform sampling:** For any desired fraction $p \in (0, 1]$, set $\widehat{A}_{ij} = A_{ij}/p$ with probability p, and 0 otherwise. Now, $\mathrm{Var}(N_{ij}) = A_{ij}^2(1 - p)/p \le 1/p$, so that the error grows only as $1/\sqrt{p}$ as we retain a p-fraction of all entries.
- **Weighted sampling:** For all i, j, independently, set $\widehat{A}_{ij} = A_{ij}/p_{ij}$ with probability p_{ij}, and 0 otherwise, where $p_{ij} = pA_{ij}^2$. This way we retain even fewer small entries, while maintaining $\mathrm{Var}(N_{ij}) = 1/p - A_{ij}^2 \le 1/p$.

Reducing the number of non-zero entries and their representation length causes standard eigenvalue algorithms to work faster. Moreover, the reduced memory footprint of the matrix $\widehat{A}$ enables the handling of larger data sets. At a high level, we perform data reduction by randomly perturbing each data vector so as to simplify its representation, i.e., sparsify and quantize. The point is that the perturbation vectors we use, by virtue of their independence, do not fit in a small subspace, acting effectively as "white noise" that is largely filtered out.

4   Kernel Principal Component Analysis

Given a collection $\mathcal{X}$ of training data $x_1, \ldots, x_n \in \mathbb{R}^d$, techniques such as linear SVMs and PCA extract features from $\mathcal{X}$ by computing linear functions of $\mathcal{X}$. However, often the structure present in the training data is not a linear function of the data representation. Worse, many data sets do not readily support linear operations such as addition and scalar multiplication (text, for example).

In a "kernel method" the idea is to map $\mathcal{X}$ into a space $\mathcal{H}$ equipped with inner product. The dimension of $\mathcal{H}$ can be very large, even infinite, and therefore it may not be practical (or possible) to work with the mapped data explicitly by applying $\Phi : \mathcal{X} \to \mathcal{H}$. Nevertheless, in many interesting cases it is possible to efficiently evaluate the dot products $\langle \Phi(x_i), \Phi(x_j) \rangle$ via a positive definite kernel k for Φ, i.e., a function k so that $k(x_i, x_j) = \langle \Phi(x_i), \Phi(x_j) \rangle$. Algorithms whose operations can be expressed in terms of inner products can thus operate on $\Phi(\mathcal{X})$ implicitly, given only the *Gram* matrix

$$K_{ij} := k(x_i, x_j) \ .$$

Given n training data points, the Kernel PCA (KPCA) method [8] begins by forming the Gram matrix K above and computing the ℓ largest eigenvalues, $\lambda_1, \ldots, \lambda_\ell$, and corresponding eigenvectors, $e_1, \ldots, e_\ell$ of K, for some appropriate choice of $\ell \le n$. Then, given an input point x, the method computes the value of the ℓ nonlinear feature extractors, corresponding to the inner product of the vector $k(x) = (k(x, x_1), k(x, x_2), \ldots, k(x, x_n))$ with each of the eigenvectors. These feature-values can be used for clustering, classification etc.

While Kernel PCA is very powerful the matrix K, in general, is dense making the input size scale as n^2, where n is the number of training points. As kernel functions become increasingly more sophisticated, e.g. invoking dynamic programming to evaluate the similarity $k(x_i, x_j)$ of two strings x_i, x_j, just the cost of $\Theta(n^2)$ kernel evaluations to construct K rapidly becomes prohibitive.

The uniform sparsification and quantization techniques of the previous section are ideally suited for speeding up KPCA. In particular, "sparsification" here means that we actually only construct a matrix $\widehat{K}$ by computing $k(x_i, x_j)$ for a uniformly random subset of all input pairs x_i, x_j and filling in 0 for the remaining pairs. In [3], it was proven that as long as K has strong linear structure (which is what justifies KPCA in the first place), with high probability, the invariant subspaces of $\widehat{K}$ will be very close to those of K.

Also, akin to quantization, we can replace each exact evaluation of $k(x_i, x_j)$ with a more easily computable unbiased estimate for it. In [3], it was shown that for kernels where: i) $\mathcal{X} \subseteq \mathbb{R}^d$, and, ii) $k(x_i, x_j)$ depends only on $\|x_i - x_j\|$ and/or $x_i \cdot x_j$, one can use random projections, as described in Section 2 for this purpose. Note that this covers some of the most popular kernels, e.g., radial basis functions (RBF) and polynomial kernels.

5   Future Work

Geometric and spectral properties of random matrices with zero-mean, independent entries are the key ingredients in all three examples we considered [1–3]. More general ensembles of random matrices hold great promise for algorithm design and call for a random matrix theory motivated from a computational perspective. Two natural directions are the investigation of matrices with limited independence, and the development of concentration inequalities for non-linear functionals of random matrices.

We saw that sampling and quantizing matrices can be viewed as injecting "noise" into them to endow useful properties such as sparsity and succinctness. The distinguishing feature of this viewpoint is that the effect of randomization is established without an explicit analysis of the interaction between randomness and computation. Instead, matrix norms act as an interface between the two domains: (i) matrix perturbation theory asserts that matrices of small spectral norm cannot have a large effect in eigencomputations, while (ii) random matrix theory asserts that matrices of zero-mean, independent random variables with small variance have small spectral norm. Is it possible to extend this style of analysis to other machine-learning settings, e.g. Support Vector Machines?

Acknowledgments

Many thanks to Robert Kleinberg, Heikki Mannila, and Frank McSherry for reading earlier drafts and providing helpful suggestions.

References

1. Dimitris Achlioptas, *Database-friendly random projections: Johnson-Lindenstrauss with binary coins*, JCSS **66** (2003), no. 4, 671–687.
2. Dimitris Achlioptas and Frank McSherry, *Fast computation of low rank matrix approximations*, JACM, to appear.
3. Dimitris Achlioptas, Frank McSherry and Bernhard Schölkopf, *Sampling techniques for kernel methods*, NIPS 2002, pp. 335–342.
4. Zoltán Füredi and János Komlós, *The eigenvalues of random symmetric matrices*, Combinatorica **1** (1981), no. 3, 233–241.
5. Sanjoy Dasgupta and Anupam Gupta, *An elementary proof of the Johnson-Lindenstrauss lemma*, Technical report 99-006, UC Berkeley, March 1999.
6. Piotr Indyk and Rajeev Motwani, *Approximate nearest neighbors: towards removing the curse of dimensionality*, STOC 1998, pp. 604–613.
7. William B. Johnson and Joram Lindenstrauss, *Extensions of Lipschitz mappings into a Hilbert space*, Amer. Math. Soc., Providence, R.I., 1984, pp. 189–206.
8. Bernhard Schölkopf, Alex J. Smola and Klaus-Robert Müller, *Nonlinear component analysis as a kernel Eigenvalue problem*, Neural Computation **10** (1998), no. 5, 1299–1319.

Data Privacy

Rakesh Agrawal

IBM Almaden Research Center, San Jose, CA 95120, USA

There is increasing need to build information systems that protect the privacy and ownership of data without impeding the flow of information. We will present some of our current work to demonstrate the technical feasibility of building such systems:

Privacy-preserving data mining. The conventional wisdom held that data mining and privacy were adversaries, and the use of data mining must be restricted to protect privacy. Privacy-preserving data mining cleverly finesses this conflict by exploting the difference between the level where we care about privacy, i.e., individual data, and the level where we run data mining algorithms, i.e., aggregated data. User data is randomized such that it is impossible to recover anything meaningful at the individual level, while still allowing the data mining algorithms to recover aggregate information, build mining models, and provide actionable insights.

Hippocratic databases. Unlike the current systems, Hippocratic databases include responsibility for the privacy of data they manage as a founding tenet. Their core capabilities have been distilled from the principles behind current privacy legislations and guidelines. We identify the technical challenges and problems in designing Hippocratic databases, and also outline some solutions.

Sovereign information sharing. Current information integration approaches are based on the assumption that the data in each database can be revealed completely to the other databases. Trends such as end-to-end integration, outsourcing, and security are creating the need for integrating information across autonomous entities. In such cases, the enterprises do not wish to completely reveal their data. In fact, they would like to reveal minimal information apart from the answer to the query. We have formalized the problem, identified key operations, and designed algorithms for these operations, thereby enabling a new class of applications, including information exchange between security agencies, intellectual property licensing, crime prevention, and medical research.

References

1. R. Agrawal, R. Srikant: Privacy Preserving Data Mining. ACM Int'l Conf. on Management of Data (SIGMOD), Dallas, Texas, May 2000.
2. R. Agrawal, J. Kiernan, R. Srikant, Y. Xu: Hippocratic Databases. 28th Int'l Conf. on Very Large Data Bases (VLDB), Hong Kong, August 2002.
3. R. Agrawal, A. Evfimievski, R. Srikant: Information Sharing Across Private Databases. ACM Int'l Conf. on Management of Data (SIGMOD), San Diego, California, June 2003.

J.-F. Boulicaut et al. (Eds.): ECML 2004, LNAI 3201, p. 8, 2004.

Breaking Through the Syntax Barrier: Searching with Entities and Relations

Soumen Chakrabarti

IIT Bombay
soumen@cse.iitb.ac.in

Abstract. The next wave in search technology will be driven by the identification, extraction, and exploitation of real-world entities represented in unstructured textual sources. Search systems will either let users express information needs naturally and analyze them more intelligently, or allow simple enhancements that add more user control on the search process. The data model will exploit graph structure where available, but not impose structure by fiat. First generation Web search, which uses graph information at the macroscopic level of inter-page hyperlinks, will be enhanced to use fine-grained graph models involving page regions, tables, sentences, phrases, and real-world-entities. New algorithms will combine probabilistic evidence from diverse features to produce responses that are not URLs or pages, but entities and their relationships, or explanations of how multiple entities are related.

1   Toward More Expressive Search

Search systems for unstructured textual data have improved enormously since the days of boolean queries over title and abstract catalogs in libraries. Web search engines index much of the full text from billions of Web pages and serve hundreds of millions of users per day. They use rich features extracted from the graph structure and markups in hypertext corpora.

Despite these advances, even the most popular search engines make us feel that we are searching with mere strings: we do not find direct expression of the entities involved in our information need, leave alone relations that must hold between those entities in a proper response. In a plenary talk at the 2004 World-wide Web Conference, Udi Manber commented:

> If music had been invented ten years ago along with the Web, we would all be playing one-string instruments (and not making great music).

referring to the one-line text boxes in which users type in 1–2 keywords and expect perfect gratification with the responses.

Apart from classical Information Retrieval (IR), several communities are coming together in the quest of expressive search, but they are coming from very different origins.

Databases and XML: To be sure, the large gap between the user's information need and the expressed query is well-known. The database community has been traditionally uncomfortable with the imprecise nature of queries inherent in IR.

J.-F. Boulicaut et al. (Eds.): ECML 2004, LNAI 3201, pp. 9–16, 2004.

The preference for precise semantics has persisted from SQL to XQuery (the query language proposed for XML data). The rigor, while useful for system-building, has little appeal for the end-user, who will not type SQL, leave alone XQuery.

Two communities are situated somewhere between "uninterpreted" keyword search systems and the rigor of database query engines. Various sub-communities of natural language processing (NLP) researchers are concerned with NL interfaces to query systems. The other community, which has broad overlaps with the NLP community, deals with information extraction (IE).

NLP: Classical NLP is concerned with annotating grammatical natural language with parts of speech (POS), chunking phrases and clauses, disambiguating polysemous words, extracting a syntactic parse, resolving pronoun and other references, analyze roles (eating with a spoon vs. with a friend), prepare a complete computer-usable representation of the knowledge embedded in the original text, and perform automatic inference with this knowledge representation. Outside controlled domains, most of these, especially the latter ones, are very ambitious goals. Over the last decade, NLP research has gradually moved toward building robust tools for the simpler tasks [19].

IE: Relatively simple NLP tasks, such as POS tagging, named entity tagging, and word sense disambiguation (WSD) share many techniques from machine learning and data mining. Many such tasks model unstructured text as a sequence of tokens generated from a finite state machine, and solve the reverse problem: given the output token sequence, estimate the state sequence. E.g., if we are interested in extracting dates from text, we can have a positive and a negative state, and identify the text spans generated by the positive state. IE is commonly set up as a supervised learning problem, which requires training text with labeled spans.

Obviously, to improve the search experience, we need that

- Users express their information need in some more detail, while minimizing additional cognitive burden
- The system makes intelligent use of said detail, thus rewarding the burden the user agrees to undertake

This new contract will work only if the combination of social engineering and technological advances work efficiently in concert.

2   The New Contract: Query Syntax

Suitable user interfaces, social engineering, and reward must urge the user to express their information need in some more detail. Relevance feedback, offering query refinements, and encouraging the user to drill down into response clusters are some ways in which systems collect additional information about the user's information need. But there are many situations where direct input from the user can be useful. I will discuss two kinds of query augmentation.

Fragments of types: If the token *2000* appears in grammatical text, current technology can usually disambiguate between the year and some other number, say a money amount. There is no reason why search interfaces cannot accept a query with a type hint so as to avoid spurious matches. There is also no reason a user cannot look for persons related to SVMs using the query `PersonType NEAR "SVM"`, where `PersonType` is the anticipated response type and *SVM* a word to match. To look for a book in SVMs published around year 2000, one might type `BookType (NEAR "SVM" year~2000)`. I believe that the person composing the query, being the stakeholder in response quality, can be encouraged to provide such elementary additional information, provided the reward is quickly tangible. Moreover, reasonably deep processing power can be spent on the query, and this may even be delegated to the client computer.

Attributes, roles and relations: Beyond annotating query tokens with type information, the user may want to express that they are looking for "a business that repairs iMacs," "the transfer bandwidth of USB2.0," and "papers written in 1985 by C. Mohan." It should be possible to express broad relations between entities in the query, possibly the placeholder entity that must be instantiated into the answer. The user may constrain the placeholder entity using attributes (e.g. MacOS-compliant software), roles and relations (e.g., a student advised by X). The challenge will be to support an ever-widening set of attribute types, roles and relations while ensuring ongoing isolation and compatibility between knowledge bases, features, and algorithms.

Compared to query syntax and preprocessing, whose success depends largely on human factors, we have more to say about executing the internal form of the query on a preprocessed corpus.

3   The New Contract: Corpus and Query Processing

While modest changes may be possible in users' query behavior, there is far too much inertia to expect content creators to actively assist mediation in the immediate future. Besides, questions preprocessing can be distributed economically, but corpus processing usually cannot.

The situation calls for relatively light processing of the corpus, at least until query time. During large scale use, however, a sizable fraction of the corpus may undergo complex processing. It would be desirable but possibly challenging to cache the intermediate results in a way that can be reused efficiently.

3.1   Supervised Entity Extraction

Information extraction (IE), also called named entity tagging, annotates spans of unstructured text with markers for instances of specified types, such as people, organizations, places, dates, and quantities.

A popular framework [11] models the text as a linear sequence of tokens being generated from a Markov state machine. A parametric model for state transition and symbol emission is learned from labeled training data. Then the model is evaluated on test data, and spans of tokens likely to be generated by desired states are picked off as extracted entities.

Generative models such as hidden Markov models (HMMs) have been used for IE for a while [7]. If $\mathbf{s}$ is the (unknown) sequence of states and $\mathbf{x}$ the sequence of output features, HMMs seek to optimize the joint likelihood $\Pr(\mathbf{s}, \mathbf{x})$.

In general, $\mathbf{x}$ is a sequence of feature vectors. Apart from the tokens themselves, some derived features found beneficial in IE are of the form: Does the token

- Contain a digit, or digits and commas?
- Contain patterns like DD:DD or DDDD or DD's where D is a digit?
- Follow a preposition?
- Look like a proper noun (as flagged by a part-of-speech tagger[1])?
- Start with an uppercase letter?
- Start with an uppercase letter and continue with lowercase letters?
- Look like an abbreviation (e.g., uppercase letters alternating with periods)?

The large dimensionality of the feature vectors usually corners us into naive independence assumptions about $\Pr(\mathbf{s}, \mathbf{x})$, and the large redundancy across features then lead to poor estimates of the joint distribution.

Recent advances in modeling conditional distributions [18] directly optimize $\Pr(\mathbf{s}|\mathbf{x})$, allowing the use of many redundant features without attempting to model the distribution over $\mathbf{x}$ itself.

3.2   Linkage Analysis and Alias Resolution

After the IE step, spans of characters and tokens are marked with type identifiers. However, many string spans (called *aliases*) may refer to a single entity (e.g., *IBM, International Business Machines, Big Blue, the computer giant* or www.ibm.com). The variations may be based on abbreviations, pronouns, anaphora, hyperlinks and other creative ways to create shared references to entities. Some of these aliases are syntactically similar to each other but others are not.

In general, detecting aliases from unstructured text, also called *coreferent resolution*, in a complete and correct manner is considered "NLP complete," i.e., requires deep language understanding and vast amounts of world knowledge. Alias resolution is an active and difficult area of NLP research. In the IE community, more tangible success has been achieved within the relatively limited scope of **record linkage**.

In record linkage, the first IE step results in structured tables of entities, each having attributes and relations to other entities. E.g., we may apply IE techniques to bibliographies at the end of research papers to populate a table of papers, authors, conferences/journals, etc. Multiple rows in each table may refer to the same object. Similar problems may arise in Web search involving names of people, products, and organizations.

The goal of record linkage is to partition rows in each table into equivalence classes, all rows in a class being references to one real-world entity. Obviously, knowing that two different rows in the author table refer to the same person (e.g., one may abbreviate the first name) may help us infer that two rows in the paper table refer to the same real-world paper.

A veriety of new techniques are being brought to bear on record linkage [10] and coreferent resolution [20], and this is an exciting area of current research.

---

[1] Many modern part-of-speech taggers are in turn driven by state transition models.

3.3   Bootstrapping Ontologies from the Web

The set of entity types of interest to a search system keeps growing and changing. A fixed set of types and entities may not keep up. The system may need to actively explore the corpus to propose new types and extract entities for old and new types. Eventually, we would like the system to learn how to learn.

Suppose we want to discover instances of some type of entity (city, say) on the Web. We can exploit the massive redundancy of the Web and use some very simple patterns [16,8,1,13]:

"cities" { "," } "such as" NPList2
NP1 { "," } "and other cities"
"cities" { "," } "including" NPList2
NP1 "is a city"

Here { } denotes an optional pattern and NP is a noun phrase. These patterns are fired off as queries to a number of search engines. A set of *rules* test the response Web pages for the existence of valid instantiations of the patterns. A rule may look like this:

NP1 "such as" NPList2 AND
        head(NP1)="cities" AND
        properNoun(head(each(NPList2)))
⇒   instanceOf(City,head(each(NPList2)))

KNOWITALL [13] makes a probabilistic assessment of the quality of the extraction by collecting co-occurrence statistics on the Web of terms carefully chosen from the extracted candidates and pre-defined *discriminator phrases*. E.g., if X is a candidate actor, "X starred in" or "starring X" would be good discriminator phrases. KNOWITALL uses the *pointwise mutual information* (PMI) formulation by Turney [24] to measure the association between the candidate instance I and the discriminator phrase D: $\mathrm{PMI}(I, D) = |\mathrm{Hits}(D + I)|/|\mathrm{Hits}(I)|$.

Apart from finding instances of types, it is possible to discover subtypes. E.g., if we wish to find instances of *scientists*, and we have a seed set of instances, we can discover that physicists and biologists are scientists, make up new patterns from the old ones (e.g. "scientist X" to "physicist X") and improve our harvest of new instances.

In Sections 3.5 and 3.6 we will see how automatic extraction of ontologies can assist next-generation search.

3.4   Searching Relational Data with NL Queries

In this section and the next (§3.5), we will assume that information extraction and alias analysis have led to a reasonably clean entity-relationship (ER) graph. The graphs formed by nodes corresponding to authors, papers, conferences and journal in DBLP, and actors/actresses, movies, awards, genres, ratings, producers and music directors in the Internet Movie Database (IMDB) are examples of reasonably clean entity-relationship data graphs. Other real-life examples involve e-commerce product catalogs and personal information management data, with organizations, people, locations, emails, papers, projects, seminars, etc.

There is a long history of systems that give a natural language interface (NLI) to relational engines [4], but, as in general NLP research, recent work has moved from highly engineered solutions to arbitrarily complex problems to less knowledge-intensive and more robust solutions for limited domains [21]. E.g., for a table `JOB(description,platform,company)` and the NL query *What are the HP jobs on a UNIX system?*, the translation to SQL might be `select distinct description from JOB WHERE company = 'HP' and platform = 'UNIX'`. The main challenge is to agree on a perimeter of NL questions within which an algorithm is required to find a correct translation, and to reliably detect when this is not possible.

3.5   Searching Entity-Relationship Graphs

NLI systems take advantage of the precise schema information available with the "corpus" as well the well-formed nature of the query, even if it is framed in uncontrolled natural language. The output of IE systems has less elaborate type information, the relations are shallower, and the questions are most often a small set of keywords, from users who are used to Web search and do not wish to learn about any schema information in framing their queries.

Free-form keyword search in ER graphs raises many interesting issues, including the query language, the definition of a "document" in response to a query, how to score a document which may be distributed in the graph, and how to search for these subgraphs efficiently.

Multiple words in a query may not all match within a single row in a single table, because ER graphs are typically highly normalized using foreign key constraints. In an ER version of DBLP, paper titles and author names are in different tables, connected by a relation `wrote(author,paper)`. In such cases, what is the appropriate unit of response? Recent systems [6,3,17] adopt the view that the response should be some minimal graph that connects at least one node containing each query keyword.

Apart from type-free keyword queries, one may look for a single node of a specified type (say, a paper) with high proximity to nodes satisfying various predicates, e.g., keyword match ("indexing", "SIGIR") or conditions on numeric fields (`year<1995`). Resetting random walks [5] are a simple way to answer such queries. These techniques are broadly similar to Pagerank [9], except that the random surfer teleports only to nodes that satisfy the predicates. Biased random walks with restarts are also related to effective conductance in resistive networks. In a large ER graph, it is also nontrivial to *explain* to the user why/how entities are related; this is important for diagnostics and eliciting user confidence. Conductance-based approaches work well [14]: we can connect $+1$ V to one node, ground the other, penalize high-fanout nodes using a grounded sink connected to every node, and report subgraphs that conduct the largest current out of the source node.

Recent years have seen an explosion of analysis and search systems for ER graphs, and I expect the important issues regarding meaningfulness of results and system scalability to be resolved in the next few years.

3.6   Open-Domain Question Answering

Finally, the Web at large will continue to be an "open-domain" system where comprehensive and accurate entity and relation extraction will remain elusive. No schema of entities and relationships can be complete at any time, even if they become more comprehensive over time. Moreover, even a cooperative user will not be able to remember and exploit a universal "type system" in asking questions. Instead, search systems will provide some basic set of *roles* [15] that apply broadly. Questions will express roles or refinements of roles, and will be matched to probabilistic role annotations in the corpus.

In open-domain QA, question analysis and response scoring will necessarily be far more tentative. Some basic machine learning will reveal that the question *When was television invented?* expects the type of the answer (atype) to be a *date*, and that the answer is almost certainly only a few tokens from the word *television* or its synonym. In effect, current technology [22,2,12,23] can translate questions into the general form

```
find x from corpus where x InstanceOf(Atype(question))
    and x RelatedTo GroundConstants(question)
```

Here `Atype(question)` represents the concept of time, and we are looking for a reference to an entity x which is an instance of time. (This is where a system like KNOWITALL comes into play.) In the example above, *television* or *TV* would be in `GroundConstants(question)`.

Checking the predicate `RelatedTo` is next to impossible in general. QA systems employ a variety of approximations. These may be as crude as linear proximity (the number of of tokens separating x from `GroundConstants(question)`. Linear proximity is already surprisingly effective [23]. More sophisticated systems[2] attempt a parse of the question and the passage, and verify that x and `GroundConstants(question)` are related in a way specified by (a parse of) the question. As might be expected, there is a trade-off beteen speed and robustness on one hand and accuracy and brittleness on the other.

4   Conclusion

Many of the pieces required for better searching are coming together. Current an upcoming research will introduce synergy as well as build large, robust applications. The applications will need to embrace bootstrapping and life-long learning better than before. The architecture must isolate feature extraction, models, and algorithms for estimation and inferencing. The interplay between processing stages makes this goal very challenging. The applications must be able to share models and parameters across different tasks and across time.

References

1. E. Agichtein and L. Gravano. Snowball: Extracting relations from large plain-text collections. In *International Conference on Digital Libraries (DL)*, volume 5. ACM, 2000.
2. E. Agichtein, S. Lawrence, and L. Gravano. Learning search engine specific query transformations for question answering. In *WWW Conference*, pages 169–178, 2001.
3. S. Agrawal, S. Chaudhuri, and G. Das. DBXplorer: A system for keyword-based search over relational databases. In *ICDE*, San Jose, CA, 2002. IEEE.

---

[2] Visit, e.g., http://www.languagecomputer.com/

4. I. Androutsopoulos, G. D. Ritchie, and P. Thanisch. Natural language interfaces to databases–an introduction. *Journal of Language Engineering*, 1(1):29–81, 1995.

5. A. Balmin, V. Hristidis, and Y. Papakonstantinou. Authority-based keyword queries in databases using ObjectRank. In *VLDB*, Toronto, 2004.

6. G. Bhalotia, A. Hulgeri, C. Nakhe, S. Chakrabarti, and S. Sudarshan. Keyword searching and browsing in databases using BANKS. In *ICDE*, San Jose, CA, 2002. IEEE.

7. D. M. Bikel, R. L. Schwartz, and R. M. Weischedel. An algorithm that learns what's in a name. *Machine Learning*, 34(1–3):211–231, 1999.

8. S. Brin. Extracting patterns and relations from the World Wide Web. In P. Atzeni, A. O. Mendelzon, and G. Mecca, editors, *WebDB Workshop*, volume 1590 of *LNCS*, pages 172–183, Valencia, Spain, Mar. 1998. Springer.

9. S. Brin and L. Page. The anatomy of a large-scale hypertextual web search engine. In *Proceedings of the 7th World-Wide Web Conference (WWW7)*, 1998.

10. W. Cohen and J. Richman. Learning to match and cluster entity names. In *SIGKDD*, volume 8, 2002.

11. T. G. Dietterich. Machine learning for sequential data: A review. In T. Caelli, editor, *Structural, Syntactic, and Statistical Pattern Recognition*, volume 2396 of *Lecture Notes in Computer Science*, pages 15–30. Springer-Verlag, 2002.

12. S. Dumais, M. Banko, E. Brill, J. Lin, and A. Ng. Web question answering: Is more always better? In *SIGIR*, pages 291–298, 2002.

13. O. Etzioni, M. Cafarella, D. Downey, S. Kok, A.-M. Popescu, T. Shaked, S. Soderland, D. S. Weld, and A. Yates. Web-scale information extraction in KnowItAll. In *WWW Conference*, New York, 2004. ACM.

14. C. Faloutsos, K. S. McCurley, and A. Tomkins. Connection subgraphs in social networks. In *Workshop on Link Analysis, Counterterrorism, and Privacy*, SIAM International Conference on Data Mining, 2004.

15. D. Gildea and D. Jurafsky. Automatic labeling of semantic roles. *Computational Linguistics*, 28(3):245–288, 2002.

16. M. Hearst. Automatic acquisition of hyponyms from large text corpora. In *International Conference on Computational Linguistics*, volume 14, pages 539–545, 1992.

17. V. Hristidis, L. Gravano, and Y. Papakonstantinou. Efficient IR-style keyword search over relational databases. In *VLDB*, pages 850–861, 2003.

18. J. Lafferty, A. McCallum, and F. Pereira. Conditional random fields: Probabilistic models for segmenting and labeling sequence data. In *ICML*, 2001.

19. R. J. Mooney. Learning semantic parsers: An important but under-studied problem. In *AAAI Spring Symposium on Language Learning: An Interdisciplinary Perspective*, pages 39–44, Mar. 2004.

20. V. Ng and C. Cardie. Improving machine learning approaches to coreference resolution. In *ACL*, volume 40, 2002.

21. A. Popescu, O. Etzioni, and H. Kautz. Towards a theory of natural language interfaces to databases. In *Intelligent User Interfaces*, pages 149–157, Miami, 2003. ACM.

22. J. Prager, E. Brown, A. Coden, and D. Radev. Question-answering by predictive annotation. In *SIGIR*, pages 184–191. ACM, 2000.

23. G. Ramakrishnan, S. Chakrabarti, D. A. Paranjpe, and P. Bhattacharyya. Is question answering an acquired skill? In *WWW Conference*, pages 111–120, New York, 2004.

24. P. D. Turney. Mining the Web for synonyms: PMI-IR versus LSA on TOEFL. In *ECML*, 2001.

Real-World Learning
with Markov Logic Networks

Pedro Domingos

Department of Computer Science and Engineering
University of Washington
Seattle, WA 98195, USA
pedrod@cs.washington.edu
http://www.cs.washington.edu/homes/pedrod

Machine learning and data mining systems have achieved many impressive successes, but to become truly widespread they must be able to work with less help from people. This requires automating the data cleaning and integration process, handling multiple types of objects and relations at once, and easily incorporating domain knowledge. In this talk, I describe how we are pursuing these aims using Markov logic networks, a representation that combines first-order logic and probabilistic graphical models. Data from multiple sources is integrated by automatically learning mappings between the objects and terms in them. Rich relational structure is learned using a combination of ILP and statistical techniques. Knowledge is incorporated by viewing logic statements as soft constraints on the models to be learned. Application to a real-world university domain shows our approach to be accurate, efficient, and less labor-intensive than traditional ones.

This work, joint with Parag and Matthew Richardson, is described in further detail in Richardson and Domingos [1], Richardson and Domingos [2], and Parag and Domingos [3].

References

1. Richardson, M., & Domingos, P.: *Markov Logic Networks*. Technical Report, Department of Computer Science and Engineering, University of Washington, Seattle, Washington, U.S.A. (2004).
   http://www.cs.washington.edu/homes/pedrod/mln.pdf.
2. Richardson, M., & Domingos, P.: Markov logic: A unifying framework for statistical relational learning. In *Proceedings of the ICML-2004 Workshop on Statistical Relational Learning and its Connections to Other Fields*, Banff, Alberta, Canada (2004). http://www.cs.washington.edu/homes/pedrod/mus.pdf.
3. Parag, & Domingos, P.: Multi-relational record linkage. In *Proceedings of the KDD-2004 Workshop on Multi-Relational Data Mining*, Seattle, Washington, U.S.A. (2004). http://www.cs.washington.edu/homes/pedrod/mrrl.pdf

J.-F. Boulicaut et al. (Eds.): ECML 2004, LNAI 3201, p. 17, 2004.
© Springer-Verlag Berlin Heidelberg 2004

Strength in Diversity: The Advance of Data Analysis

David J. Hand

Department of Mathematics, Imperial College, 180 Queen's Gate,
London SW7 2AZ, UK
d.j.hand@imperial.ac.uk

Abstract. The scientific analysis of data is only around a century old. For most of that century, data analysis was the realm of only one discipline - statistics. As a consequence of the development of the computer, things have changed dramatically and now there are several such disciplines, including machine learning, pattern recognition, and data mining. This paper looks at some of the similarities and some of the differences between these disciplines, noting where they intersect and, perhaps of more interest, where they do not. Particular issues examined include the nature of the data with which they are concerned, the role of mathematics, differences in the objectives, how the different areas of application have led to different aims, and how the different disciplines have led sometimes to the same analytic tools being developed, but also sometimes to different tools being developed. Some conjectures about likely future developments are given.

1 Introduction

This paper gives a personal view of the state of affairs in data analysis. That means that inevitably I will be making general statements, so that most of you will be able to disagree on some details. But I am trying to paint a broad picture, and I hope that you will agree with the overall picture.

We live in very exciting times. In fact, from the perspective of a professional data analyst, I would say we live in the *most* exciting of times. Not so long ago, analysing data was characterised by drudgery, by manual arithmetic, and the need to take great care over numerical trivia. Nowadays, all that has been swept aside, with the burden of tedium having been taken over by the computer. What we are left with are the high-level interpretations and strategic decisions; we look at the summary values derived by the computers and make our statements and draw conclusions and base our actions on these. It is clear from this that the computer has become *the* essential tool for data analysis.

But there is more. The computer has not merely swept aside the tedium. The awesome speed of numerical manipulation has permitted the development of entirely new kinds of data analytic tools, being applied in entirely new ways, to entirely new kinds, and indeed sizes, of data sets. The computer has given us new ways to look at things. The old image, that data analysis was the realm of the boring obsessive, is now so diametrically opposite to the new truth as to be laughable.

J.-F. Boulicaut et al. (Eds.): ECML 2004, LNAI 3201, pp. 18–26, 2004.

This paper describes some of the history, some of the tools, and something of how I see the present status of data analysis. So perhaps I should begin with a definition. *Data analysis is the science of discovery in data, and of processing data to extract evidence so that one can make properly informed decisions.* In brief, data analysis is *applied philosophy of science*: the theory and methods, not of any particular scientific discipline itself, but of *how to find things out.*

2 The Evolution of Data Analytic Disciplines

The origins of data analysis can be traced back as far back as one likes. Think of Kepler and Gauss analysing astronomical data, of Florence Nightingale using plots to demonstrate that soldiers were dying because of poor hygiene rather than military action, of Quetelet's development of 'social mechanics', and the fact that world's oldest statistical society, the Royal Statistical Society, was established in 1834. But these 'origins' really only represent the initial stirrings: it wasn't until the start of the 20th century that a proper scientific discipline of data analysis really began to be formed. That discipline was statistics, and for the first half of the 20th century statistics was the only data analytic game in town. Until around 1950, statistics *was* the science of data analysis. (You will have to permit me some poetic leeway in my choice of dates: 1960 might be more realistic.)

Then, around the middle of the 20th century, the computer arrived and a revolution began. Statistics began to change rapidly in response to the awesome possibilities the computer provided. There is no doubt that, had statistics been born now, at the start of the 21st century, rather than 100 years ago at the start of the 20th, it would be a very different kind of animal. (Would we have the *t*-test?.) Moreover, although statistics was the intellectual owner of data *analysis* up until about 1950, it was never the intellectual owner of *data* per se, and in the following decades other changes occurred which were to challenge the position assumed by statistics. In particular, another discipline grew up, whose primary responsibility was, initially, the storage and manipulation of data. From data manipulation to data analysis was then hardly a large step. Statistics was no longer the only player.

Nowadays, of course, computer science has grown into a vast edifice, and different subdisciplines of it have developed as specialised areas of data analysis, all overlapping with each other and overlapping with their intellectual parent, statistics. These subdisciplines include machine learning, pattern recognition, and data mining, and one could arguably include image processing, neural networks, and perhaps even computational learning theory and other areas also. I cannot avoid remarking that Charles Babbage, typically regarded as one of the fathers of computing with his *analytical engine*, would have been fascinated by these developments: he was also one of the founders of the Royal Statistical Society. Of course, these various data analytic disciplines are not carbon copies of each other. They have subtly different aims and emphases, and often deal with rather different kinds of data (e.g. in terms of data set size, correlations, complexities, etc.). One of my aims in this talk is to examine some of these differences. Moreover, if the computer has been the strongest influence leading to the development of new data analytic technologies, application areas have always been and continue to have a similar effect. Thus we have psychometrics, bioinformatics, chemometrics, technometrics, and other areas, all addressing the same sorts of problems, but in different areas. I shall say more about this below.

3   Data

I toyed briefly with the idea of calling this talk 'analysing tomorrow's data' since one of the striking things about the modern world of data analysis is that the data with which we now have to deal could not have been imagined 100 years ago. Then the data had to be painstakingly collected by hand since there was no alternative, but nowadays much data acquisition is automatic. This has various consequences.

Firstly, astronomically vast data sets are readily acquired. Books on data mining (e.g. [2],[3]), which is that particular data analytic discipline especially concerned with analysing large data sets, illustrate the sorts of sizes which are now being encountered. The word *terabyte* is no longer unusual. When I was taught statistical data analysis, I was taught that first one must familiarise oneself with one's data: plot it this way and that, look for outliers and anomalies, fit simple models and examine diagnostics. With a billion data points (one of the banking data sets I was presented with) this is clearly infeasible. Other problems involve huge numbers of variables, and perhaps relatively few data points, posing complex theoretical as well as practical questions: bioinformatics, genomics, and proteomics are important sources of such problems.

Secondly, one might have thought that automatic data acquisition would mean better data quality, since there would be no subjective human intervention. Unfortunately, this has not turned out to be the case. New ways of collecting data has meant new ways for the data collection process to go wrong. Worse, large data sets can make it more difficult to detect many of the data anomalies.

Data can be of low quality in many ways: individual values may be distorted or absent, entire records may be missing, measurement error may be large, and so on. As discussed below, much of statistics is concerned with *inference* - with making statements about objects or values not seen or measured, on the basis of those which have been. Thus we might want to make statements about other objects from a population, or about the future behaviour of objects. Accurate inferences can only be made if one has accurate information on how the data were collected. Statisticians have therefore predicated their analyses on the assumption that the available observations were drawn in well-specified ways, or that the departures from these ways were understood and could be modelled. Unfortunately, with many of today's data sets, such assumptions often cannot be made. This has sometimes made statisticians (quite properly) wary of analysing such data. But the data still have to be analysed: the questions still need answers. This is one reason why data mining has been so successful, at least at first glance. Data miners have been prepared to examine distorted data, and to attempt to draw conclusions about it. It has to be said, however, that often that willingness has arisen from a position of ignorance, rather than one of awareness of the risks that were being taken. Relatively few reports of the conclusions extracted from a data mining exercise, for example, qualify those conclusions with a discussion of the possible impact of selectivity bias on the data being analysed. This is interesting because, almost by definition, data mining is secondary data analysis: the analysis of data collected for some other purpose. The data may be of perfect quality for its original purpose (e.g. calculating your grocery bill in the store), but of poor quality for subsequent mining (e.g. because some items were grouped together in the bill).

A third difference between many modern data analysis problems and those of the past is that nowadays they are often dynamic. Electronics permit data to be collected as things happen, and this opens the possibility of of making decisions as the data are collected. An example is in commercial transactions, where a customer can supply information and expects an immediate decision. In such circumstances one does not have the luxury of taking the data back to one's laboratory and analysing it at leisure. Speech recognition is another example. This issue has led to new kinds of analytic tools, with an emphasis on speed and not merely accuracy. No particular area of data analysis seems to have precedence for such problems, but the computer science side, perhaps especially machine learning clearly regards such problems as important.

Although every kind of data analytic discipline must contend with all kinds of data, there is no doubt that different kinds are more familiar in different areas. Computational areas probably place more emphasis on categorical data than on continuous data, and this is reflected in the types of data analytic tools (e.g. methods for extracting association rules) which have been developed.

4 The Role of Mathematics

Modern statistics is often regarded as a branch of mathematics. This is entirely inappropriate. Indeed, the qualitative change induced by the advent of the computer means that statistics could equally be regarded as a branch of computer science.

In a sense statistics, and data analysis more generally, is the opposite of mathematics. Mathematics begins with assumptions about the structure of the universe of discourse (the axioms) and seeks to deduce the consequences. Data analysis, on the other hand, begins with observations of the consequences (the data) and seeks to infer something about the structure of the universe. One consequence of this is that one can be a good mathematician without understanding anything about any area to which the mathematics will be applied – one primarily needs facility with mathematical symbol manipulation – but one cannot be a good statistician without being able to relate the analysis to the world from which the data arose. This is why one hears of mathematics prodigies, but never statistics prodigies. Analysis requires understanding.

There are other differences as well. Nowadays a computer is an essential and indispensable tool for statistics, but one can still do much mathematics without a computer. This is brought home to our undergraduate students, taking mathematics degrees, with substantial statistical components, when they come to use software: statistical software packages such as Splus, R, SAS, SPSS, Stata, etc., are very different from mathematical packages such as Maple and Mathematica. Carrying out even fairly basic statistical analyses using the latter can be a non-trivial exercise.

David Finney has commented that it is no more true to describe statistics as a branch of mathematics than it would be to describe engineering as a branch of mathematics, and John Nelder has said *'The main danger, I believe, in allowing the ethos of mathematics to gain too much influence in statistics is that statisticians will be tempted into types of abstraction that they believe will be thought respectable by mathematicians rather than pursuing ideas of value to statistics.'*

There is no doubt that the misconception of statistics as mathematics has been detrimental in the past, especially in commercial and business applications. Data mining, in particular took advantage of this - its very name spells glamour and excitement, the possibility of gaining a market edge for free. But there are also other examples where the image of statistics slowed its uptake. For example, experimental design (that branch of statistics concerned with efficient and cost effective ways to collect data) was used in only relatively few sectors (mostly manufacturing). Reformulations of experimental design ideas under names such as the Taguchi method and Six Sigma, however, have had a big impact. If anything ought to convince my academic colleagues of the power of packaging and presentation, then it should be these examples.

5   Several Cultures Separated by a Common Language

The writer George Bernard Shaw once described England and America as *'two cultures divided by a common language'*, and I sometimes feel that the same applies to the various data analytic disciplines. Over the years, I have seen several intense debates between proponents of the different disciplines. Part of the reason for this lies in the different philosophical approaches to investigation. Statistics, perhaps because of its mathematical links, places a premium on proof and mathematical demonstration of the properties of data analytic tools. For example, demonstrating mathematically that an algorithm will always converge. Machine learning, on the other hand, places more emphasis on empirical testing. Of course there is overlap. Most methodological statistics papers include at least one example of the methods applied to real problems, and most machine learning papers describe the ideas in mathematical terms, but there is a clear difference in what is regarded as of central importance.

Another reason for the debates has been that many of the ideas were developed in parallel, by researchers naturally keen to establish their priority and reputation. This led to claims to the effect that 'we developed it first' or 'we demonstrated that property years ago.' This was certainly evident in the debates on recursive partitioning tree classifiers, which were developed in parallel by the machine learning and statistics communities.

Misunderstandings can also arise because different schools place emphasis on different things. Early computer science perspectives on data mining stressed the finding of patterns in databases. This is perfectly natural: it is something often required (e.g. what percentage of my employees earn more than €x p.a.?). However, this is of limited interest to a statistician, who will normally want to make an inference to a wider population or to the future (e.g. what percentage of my employees are likely to earn more than €x p.a. next year?). Much work on association analysis has ignored this inferential aspect. Moreover, much work has also made a false causal assumption:

while it is *interesting* to know that ten times as many people who bought A also bought B, it is *valuable* to know that if people can be induced to buy A they will also buy B, and the two are not the same.

While there have been tensions between the different areas when they develop similar models, each from their own perspective, there is no doubt that these tensions can be immensely beneficial from a scientific perspective. A nice example of this is the work on feedforward neural networks. These originally came from the computer (or, one might argue, the cybernetics, electrical engineering, or even biological) side of things. The perspective of a set of fairly simple interacting processors dominated. Later, however, statisticians became involved and translated the ideas into mathematical terms: such models can be written as nested sequences of nonlinear transformations of linear combinations of variables. Once written in fairly standard terms, one can apply the statistical results of a century of theoretical work. In particular, one could explain that the early neural network claims of very substantial improvement in predictive power were likely to be in large part due to overfitting the design data, and to present ideas and tools for avoiding this problem. Of course, nowadays all these are well understood by the neural network community, but this was certainly not the case in the early days (I can remember papers presenting absurdly overoptimistic claims), even though statisticians had known about the issues for decades.

If the computer is leading to a unification of the data analytic schools, so also are some theoretical developments. The prime examples here, of course, are Bayesian ideas. Bayes's theorem tells us how we should update our knowledge in the light of new information. This is the very essence of learning, so it is not surprising that machine learning uses these ideas. With the advent of practical computational tools for evaluating high dimensional integrals, such as MCMC, statistics has also undergone a dramatic Bayesian revolution, not only in terms of dynamic updating models but also in terms of model averaging. Indeed, model averaging, like the understanding of overfitting (indeed, closely connected to it), has led to deep theoretical advances. Tools such as boosting and bagging are based on these sorts of principles. Boosting, in particular, is interesting from our perspective because it illustrates the potential synergy which can arise from the disparate emphases of the different disciplines. Originally developed by the machine learning community, who proposed it on fairly intuitive grounds and showed that it worked in practical applications, it was then explored theoretically by statisticians, who showed its strong links to generalised additive models, a well-understood class of statistical tools. The most recent tool to experience this initial development, followed by an exposure to the ideas and viewpoints of other data analytic disciplines, is that of support vector machines.

In fact, perceptrons (the progenitor of support vector machines) and logistic discrimination provide a very nice illustration of the difference in emphasis between, in this case, statistical and machine learning models for classification. Logistic discrimination fits a model to the probability that an object with given features $\mathbf{x}$ will belong to class 0 rather than class 1. Typically, the model is fitted by finding the parameters which maximise the design set log likelihood:

$$\log L \propto \sum_{i=1}^{n} \log \hat{p}\left(0 \mid \mathbf{x}_i\right). \tag{1}$$

Classification is then effected by comparing an estimated probability with a threshold. It is immediately clear from (1) that all design set data points contribute - it is really an average of contributions. This is fine if one's model $\hat{p}(0 \mid \mathbf{x})$ has the form of the 'true' function $p(0 \mid \mathbf{x})$. But this is a brave assumption. It is likely that the model is not perfect. If so, one must question the wisdom of letting data points with estimated probability far from the classification threshold contribute the same amount to the fit criterion (1) as do those near to it (see [4]). In contrast, perceptron models focus attention on whether or not the design set points are correctly classified: quality of fit of a model far from the decision surface, which is broadly irrelevant to classification performance, does not come into it.

An example of another area which has been developed in rather different ways by different disciplines is the area I call *pattern discovery*. This is the search for, identification of, and description of anomalously high local densities of data points. The computer science literature has focused on algorithms for finding such configurations. In particular, a great deal of work has occurred when the data are character strings, in, especially text search (e.g. web search engines) and nucleotide sequences. In contrast, the statistical work has concentrated on the inference problem, developing scan statistics for deciding whether a local anomaly represents a real underlying structure is just random variation of a background model. Ideas of this kind have been developed in many application areas, including bioinformatics, technical stock chart analysis, astronomy, market basket analysis, and others, but the realisation that they are all tackling very similar problems appears to be only recent.

Implicit in the last two paragraphs is one of the fundamental differences in emphasis between computational and statistical approaches to data analysis - again an understandable difference in view of their origins. This is the emphasis of the computational approaches on algorithms (e.g. the perceptron error-correcting algorithm) and the emphasis of the statistical approaches on models (e.g. the logistic discrimination model). Both algorithms and models are, of course, important when tackling real problems.

It is my own personal view that one can also characterise the difference between the two perspectives, at least to some extent, in terms of degree of risk. The computational schools seem often prepared to try something without the assurance that it will work, or that it will always work, but in the hope (or knowledge from previous analyses) that it will sometimes work. The statistical schools seem more risk averse, requiring more assurance before carrying out an analysis. Perhaps this is illustrated by the approaches to pattern discovery mentioned above: the data mining community develops algorithms with which to detect possible patterns, while the statistical community develops tools to tell whether they are real or merely chance. Once again, both perspectives are valuable, especially in tandem: adventurous risk-taking offers the possibility of major breakthroughs, while careful analysis shows one that the method gives reliable results.

6 Future Tools and Application Areas?

Of course, the various data analytic disciplines are constantly evolving. We live in very exciting times because of the tools which have been developed over the past few decades, but that development has not stopped. If anything, it has accelerated and will continue to do so as the computational infrastructure continues to develop. This means faster and larger (in terms of all dimensions of datasets). Judging from the past, this will translate into analytic tools about which one previously could only have dreamt, and, further, into tools one could not even have imagined.

If the computer is one force driving the development of new data analytic tools, I can see at least two others.

The first of these are application areas, mentioned above. Certainly, the growth of statistics over the 20th century was strongly directed by the applications. Thus agricultural requirements led to the early development of experimental design, psychology motivated the development of factor analysis and other latent variable models, medicine led to survival analysis, and so on. In other areas, speech recognition stimulated work on hidden Markov models, robotics stimulated work on reinforcement learning, etc. Of course, once developments have been started, and the power of the tools being developed has been recognised, other application areas rapidly adopt the tools.

As with the impact of developing computational infrastructure, I see no reason to expect this influence of application areas to stop. We are currently witnessing the particular requirements of genomic, proteomic, and related data leading to the development of new analytic tools; for example, methods for handling *fat data* - data involving many (perhaps tens of thousands of) variables, but few (perhaps a few tens of) data points. Mathematical finance is likewise an area which is shifting its centre of gravity towards analysis. Until recently characterised by mathematical areas such as stochastic calculus, it is increasingly recognised that data analysis is also needed - the values of the model parameters must come from somewhere. More generally, the area of personal finance is beginning to provide a rich source of novel problems, requiring novel solutions. The world wide web, of course, is another source of new types of data, and new problems. This area, in particular, is a source of data which is characterised by its dynamic properties, and I expect the analysis of dynamic data to play an even more crucial role in future developments. Decisions in telecoms systems, even in day-to-day purchasing transactions, are needed *now*, not after a leisurely three months' analysis of a customer's track record and characteristics. Delay loses business.

The second additional driving force I can see is also not really a new one. It has always been with us, but it will lead to the development of new kinds of tools, in response to new demands and also enabled by the advancing computational infrastructure. This is the need to model finer and finer aspects of the presenting problems. A recent example of this is in the analysis of repeated measures data. The last two decades have witnessed a very exciting efflorescence of ideas for tackling such data. The essential problem is to recognise and take account of the fact that repeated measurements data are likely to be correlated (with the (multiple) series being too short to use time series ideas). Classical assumptions of independence are all very well, but more accurate models and predictions result when the dependence is modelled. Another example of such 'finer aspects' of the presenting problem, which has typically been ignored up until now, is the fact that predictive models are likely to be applied to data drawn from distributions different from that from which the design data were drawn (perhaps a case for dynamic models). There are many other examples.

There is, however, a cautionary comment to be made in connection with this driving force. It is easy to go too far. There is little point is developing a method to cope with some aspect of the data if the inaccuracies induced by that aspect are trivial in comparison with those arising from other causes. Data analysis is not a merely mathematical exercise of data manipulation.

If we data analysts live in exciting times, I think it is clear that the future will be even more exciting. Looking back on the past it is obvious that the tensions between the different data analytic disciplines have, in the end, been beneficial: we can learn from the perspectives and emphases of the other approaches. In particular, we should learn that the other disciplines can almost certainly shed light on and help each of us gain greater understanding of what we are trying to do. We should look for the *synergies*, not the *antagonisms*.

I'd like to conclude with two quotations. The first is from John Chambers, the computational statistician who developed Splus and who won the 1998 ACM Software System Award for that work. He wrote: *'Greater statistics can be defined simply, if loosely, as everything related to learning from data, from the first planning or collection to the last presentation or report. Lesser statistics is the body of specifically statistical methodology that has evolved within the profession - roughly, statistics as defined by texts, journals, and doctoral dissertations. Greater statistics tends to be inclusive, eclectic with respect to methodology, closely associated with other disciplines, and practiced by many outside of academia and often outside of professional statistics. Lesser statistics tends to be exclusive, oriented to mathematical techniques, less frequently collaborative with other disciplines, and primarily practiced by members of university departments of statistics.'* [1]

John has called the discipline of data analysis 'greater statistics', but I am sure we can all recognise what we do in his description. What we call it is not important. As Juliet puts it in Act II, Scene ii of Shakespeare's *Romeo and Juliet*:

> *'What's in a name? that which we call a rose*
> *By any other name would smell as sweet.'*

References

1. Chambers J.M. Greater or lesser statistics: a choice for future research. *Statistics and Computing*, **3**, (1993) 182-184.
2. Giudici P. *Applied Data Mining*. Chichester: Wiley. (2003)
3. Hand D.J., Mannila H., and Smyth P. *Principles of Data Mining*, Cambridge, Massachusetts: MIT Press. (2001)
4. Hand D.J. and Vinciotti V. Local versus global models for classification problems: fitting models where it matters. *The American Statistician*. **57**, (2003) 124-131.

Filtered Reinforcement Learning

Douglas Aberdeen

National ICT Australia, Canberra, Australia
douglas.aberdeen@nicta.com.au
http://csl.anu.edu.au/~daa/

Abstract. Reinforcement learning (RL) algorithms attempt to assign the credit for rewards to the actions that contributed to the reward. Thus far, credit assignment has been done in one of two ways: uniformly, or using a discounting model that assigns exponentially more credit to recent actions. This paper demonstrates an alternative approach to temporal credit assignment, taking advantage of exact or approximate prior information about correct credit assignment. Infinite impulse response (IIR) filters are used to model credit assignment information. IIR filters generalise exponentially discounting eligibility traces to arbitrary credit assignment models. This approach can be applied to *any* RL algorithm that employs an eligibility trace. The use of IIR credit assignment filters is explored using both the GPOMDP policy-gradient algorithm and the Sarsa(λ) temporal-difference algorithm. A drop in bias and variance of value or gradient estimates is demonstrated, resulting in faster convergence to better policies.

1 Introduction

A reinforcement learning (RL) agent performs actions in a world according to a parameterised policy. The agent seeks to adjust the policy in order to maximise a long-term measure of reward. A core difficulty is correctly distinguishing which actions caused high long-term pay offs. This *temporal credit assignment* problem is usually solved in one of two ways: (1) if the task ends in finite time then credit can sometimes be assigned uniformly; (2) if the task has an infinite horizon a discounted model assigns exponentially more credit to recent actions.

This paper shows how to use exact or approximate prior information about reward delays to build a tailored credit assignment model. Taking advantage of such information leads to a reduction in the bias and variance of estimates; either value estimates or gradient estimates depending on the algorithm employed. We demonstrate that the drop in bias and variance can be orders of magnitude given good prior information about the correct way to assign credit to actions.

For example, the action of adding chemicals to a bio-reactor, or the injection of a drug into a patient, will not have an immediate impact. Rather, the response of the system to the input ramps up with time to a maximum, then decays slowly. In this case exponential credit assignment is inappropriate because the majority of the credit goes to the most recent input (or action), rather than the input that is currently dominating the system response.

J.-F. Boulicaut et al. (Eds.): ECML 2004, LNAI 3201, pp. 27–38, 2004.

This paper introduces the use of infinite impulse response (IIR) filters to shape the temporal credit assignment. The IIR filter generalises *eligibility traces* to non-exponential models of credit assignment. IIR models of credit assignment can be applied to any RL algorithm that employs an eligibility trace. This paper uses the GPOMDP policy-gradient algorithm [1], and the Sarsa(λ) algorithm [2].

This rest of this paper is organised as follows. Section 2 describes the algorithms modified in this paper: GPOMDP and Sarsa(λ). Section 3 describes how these algorithms can be extended to arbitrary temporal credit assignment. Section 4 presents experiments that demonstrate the bias and variance improvements that can be gained using IIR filters. Section 5 presents a less trivial example to motivate the use of trace filtering in real world problems.

2 Background

Markov decision processes (MDPs) are a natural framework for RL. Specifically, the GPOMDP and Sarsa(λ) algorithms are described. Both employ exponential credit assignment models that will be generalised to IIR assignment models. The algorithms are described in the fully observable MDP framework for simplicity, but GPOMDP extends to partially observable environments without loss of *local* convergence guarantees [1]. Some experiments in this paper are only partially observable, where an observation replaces the exact state.

2.1 MDPs

A MDP consists of states $\mathcal{S} = \{1, \ldots, |\mathcal{S}|\}$ of the world, actions $\mathcal{A} = \{1, \ldots, |\mathcal{A}|\}$ available to the agent in each state[1], and a (possibly stochastic) reward $r(i)$ for each state $i \in \mathcal{S}$.

Each action $a \in \mathcal{A}$ determines a stochastic matrix $P(a) = [\Pr(j|i, a)]$ where $\Pr(j|i, a)$ denotes the probability of making a transition from state $i \in \mathcal{S}$ to state $j \in \mathcal{S}$ given action $a \in \mathcal{A}$. The GPOMDP and Sarsa(λ) algorithms are *model-free* methods that do not assume explicit knowledge of $P(a)$, however, such knowledge might contribute to the temporal credit assignment modelling.

All policies are stochastic. The probability of choosing action a given state i, and parameters $\theta \in \mathbb{R}^{|\theta|}$ is $\Pr(a|\theta, i)$. The evolution of the world state i is Markov, with an $|\mathcal{S}| \times |\mathcal{S}|$ transition probability matrix $P(\theta) = [\Pr(j|\theta, i)]$ whose entries indexed by i, j are given by

$$\Pr(j|\theta, i) = \sum_{a \in \mathcal{A}} \Pr(a|\theta, i) \Pr(j|i, a). \tag{1}$$

In this paper, the *soft-max* function is used to generate $\Pr(a|\theta, i)$ from the real valued output of a parameterised function. Given a vector $y \in \mathbb{R}^{|\mathcal{A}|}$, the

---

[1] Generally, state spaces may be uncountably infinite. However, the maths becomes more complex without altering the final algorithms.

probability of action $a \in \{1, \ldots, \mathcal{A}\}$ according to the soft-max distribution generated by the vector y is

$$\Pr(a|y) := \frac{\exp(y_a)}{\sum_{m=1}^{|\mathcal{A}|} \exp(y_m)}. \tag{2}$$

The vector y represents the real valued output of a function representing action likelihoods for policy-gradient algorithms, or state/action values for value algorithms. All but the final experiment use parameters $\theta_{a,i}$ representing each likelihood, or value, of action a given state i. I.e., a table lookup representation. Thus, given state i, we have $y = [\theta_{1,i}, \ldots, \theta_{|\mathcal{A}|,i}]$.

2.2 ▫▫▫▫ ▫▫

GPOMDP is an infinite-horizon policy-gradient algorithm [1]. It computes the gradient of the *long-term average reward*

$$\eta(\theta) := \lim_{T \to \infty} \frac{1}{T} \mathbb{E}_\theta \left[\sum_{t=1}^{T} r_t \right], \tag{3}$$

with respect the policy parameters θ. The expectation $\mathbb{E}_\theta$ is over the distribution of states $\{i_0, i_1, \ldots\}$ induced by $P(\theta)$. Updating the policy parameters in the direction of the gradient locally maximises the average reward. Under a standard ergodicity assumption $\eta(\theta)$ is independent of the starting state and is equal to

$$\eta(\theta) = \sum_{i=1}^{|\mathcal{S}|} \pi_i(\theta) r(i) = \pi(\theta)^{\mathsf{T}} r, \tag{4}$$

where $\pi(\theta)$ is the stationary distribution of states induced by the current θ, and $r := [r(1), \ldots, r(|\mathcal{S}|)]^{\mathsf{T}}$.

Theorem 1 (From [1]). *Let I be the identity matrix and let e be a column vector of 1's. Further, drop the explicit dependence of η, P, and π on θ. The true gradient of the long-term average reward with respect to θ is*

$$\nabla \eta = \pi^{\mathsf{T}} (\nabla P) \left[I - P + e\pi^{\mathsf{T}} \right]^{-1} r. \tag{5}$$

This theorem, proved in [1], establishes the true gradient of the long-term average reward with respect to the policy parameters, but requires known $\Pr(j|i, a)$ and also requires inverting a potentially large matrix.

The GPOMDP algorithm computes a Monte-Carlo approximation of (5). The agent interacts with the environment, producing a state, action, reward sequence $\{i_1, a_1, r_1, \ldots, i_T, a_T, r_T\}$. Under mild technical assumptions, including ergodicity and bounding all the terms involved, the approximation is:

$$\widehat{\nabla \eta} = \frac{1}{T} \sum_{t=0}^{T-1} \nabla \log \Pr(a_t|\theta, i_t) \sum_{s=t+1}^{T} \beta^{s-t-1} r_s, \tag{6}$$

where the discount factor $\beta \in [0, 1)$ has been introduced to control the variance of the gradient estimate. The discount factor implicitly assumes that rewards are exponentially more likely to be due to recent actions. Without such an assumption, rewards must be assigned over a potentially infinite horizon, resulting in estimates with infinite variance. As β decreases, the variance decreases, but the bias of the gradient estimate increases [1]. In practice, (6) is implemented efficiently using an exponentially discounted eligibility trace, described in Section 2.4. The algorithmic form of GPOMDP is described in Section 3.1.

2.3 ▫▪▪▪▪(λ)

Sarsa(λ) [2] is introduced only briefly to highlight the general applicability of IIR credit assignment. Sarsa(λ) estimates

$$Q(i, a, \theta) := \lim_{T \to \infty} \mathbb{E}_\theta \left[\sum_{t=1}^{T} \delta^t r_t | i_0 = i, a_0 = a \right],$$

which is the expected discounted sum of rewards over time. Policies in this paper are derived from $Q(i, a, \theta)$ using the soft-max function (2), preferring actions with high value. Updates to θ are driven by temporal differences: the error between the current value estimate and the actual return

$$d(i_t, i_{t+1}) = [r_t + \delta Q(i_{t+1}, a_{t+1}, \theta_t)] - Q(i_t, a_t, \theta_t),$$
$$\theta_{t+1} = \theta_t + \alpha_t d(i_t, i_{t+1}) e_t.$$

The discount factor δ determines the importance of long-term rewards compared to instant rewards, α_t is a possibly variable step size, and e_t is the current eligibility trace that stores how eligible each parameter is for an update in the direction of $d(i_t, i_{t+1})$. Temporal errors can also be computed over multiple time steps, resulting in n-step temporal differences $d(i_t, i_{t+n})$. The Sarsa(λ) algorithm implicitly calculates all such n-step temporal differences to the end of the episode via the use of the eligibility trace. Sarsa(λ) places a weight of λ^{n-1} on the n-step temporal error when updating parameters [2]. Thus, increasing the λ parameter places more weight on temporal differences computed over many steps. As $\lambda \to 1$ we approach a Monte Carlo method that uses the actual sum of returns received from the target state to the terminal state, providing low bias, but high variance. Reducing λ reduces variance at the cost of increased bias [3]. If domain knowledge such as "the rewards received for the first τ steps after actions, are random with mean 0" is available, the exponential weighting model λ^{n-1} is not appropriate. The n-step temporal difference weight should be 0 for the first τ steps, then decay exponentially with $\lambda^{n-\tau}$. For Sarsa(λ), this paper generalises eligibility traces to allow *arbitrary* weights for each n-step temporal difference. Computing the eligibility trace e_t is described in the next section. The algorithmic form of Sarsa(λ) is described in Section 3.2.

2.4   Computing Eligibility Traces

A standard mechanism for implementing temporal credit assignment is the *eligibility trace*. The eligibility trace e is a vector of length $|\theta|$, one element for each parameter $\theta_p \in \theta$. The trace stores how eligible each state/action pair is for receiving the credit for a reward or temporal difference. If function approximation is used the trace stores how eligible each parameter is for being updated.

Eligibility traces work in a similar way for most RL algorithms. After receiving a state i_t and choosing an action a_t, the gradient of the parameterised policy, or Q-function, is computed for action a_t, and added to the trace. At each step the trace is also multiplied by the trace discount. The GPOMDP trace update is

$$e_{t+1} = \beta e_t + \nabla \log \Pr(a_t|\theta, i_t), \tag{7}$$

where $\nabla \log \Pr(a_t|\theta, i_t)$ is the log derivative of the soft-max function (2) for the chosen action. The Sarsa(λ) eligibility trace update is

$$e_{t+1} = \delta \lambda e_t + \nabla Q(i_{t+1}, a_{t+1}, \theta_{t+1}). \tag{8}$$

The use of λ in this equation implements the weighting by λ^{n-1} of the n-step return (see [2] for details). The additional factor of δ in the eligibility trace update is needed to maintain consistency with the discount factor selected for the domain. The value discount factor δ – which changes the quantity being estimated – should not be confused with the GPOMDP discount factor of β, which is introduced to control the variance of estimates of $\nabla \eta$ [2].

The parameterisation of $Q(i, a, \theta)$ in this paper is a lookup table, with one parameter for each combination of state and action. The gradient is 1 for the parameter indexed by the current state and action, and 0 otherwise.

Eligibility traces are used in many RL algorithms including TD(λ), Sarsa(λ), Williams' REINFORCE [4], and GPOMDP. See [2] for a history of eligibility traces.

3   Filtering Traces

Equations (7) and (8) show the usual method of updating the eligibility trace for GPOMDP and Sarsa(λ). Implicit in this update is the idea of assigning exponentially more credit to recent actions. Figure 1 shows how an instantaneous reward of 1 at time t, would be credited to the action chosen τ steps ago with a discount factor of 0.9. Control theorists would view Figure 1 the impulse response of a first order infinite impulse response (IIR) filter.

In this section first order eligibility traces are extended to arbitrary IIR filters, allowing domain specific knowledge about credit assignment to be used. The aim is to subtract a zero-mean, non-zero variance process from the gradient or value estimates, effectively reducing the variance of these estimates. This paper extends the author's early trace filtering work [5] to value-methods, and provides empirical evaluations of the methods. Other relevant work includes

---

[2] However, the two quantities are related to each other [1].

[6], which discusses *replacing* traces, and [1] which mentions the possibility of higher-order trace filters.

IIR filters are a common signal processing tool for producing an output at each time step from a weighted combination of the $|b|$ most recent inputs and the $|a| - 1$ past outputs [7]. The term "infinite" impulse response arises because filters may have an infinitely non-zero response to an impulse input at time 0. IIR filters have uses in many digital signal processing applications. IIR filters allow efficient eligibility traces that can allow arbitrary assignment of credit.

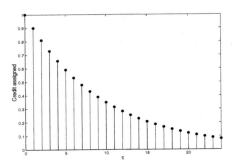

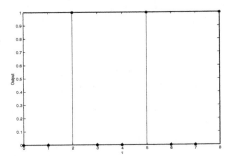

Fig. 1. The first 25 points of the infinite impulse response generated by the $\beta = 0.9$ model.

Fig. 2. The optimal FIR filter for Test I, with parameters $a = [1]$, $b = [0, 0, 1, 0, 0, 1, 0, 0, 1]$.

The general form of an IIR filter is

$$e_{t+1} = - \left(\sum_{n=1}^{|a|-1} a_n e_{t+1-n} \right) + \left(\sum_{n=0}^{|b|-1} b_n x_{t-n} \right), \qquad (9)$$

where $a = [a_0, a_1, \ldots, a_{|a|-1}]$ and $b = [b_0, b_1, \ldots, b_{|b|-1}]$ are vectors of filter coefficients. The x's represent the filter input at each time step. For eligibility traces, the filter input x_t is the gradient of the policy with respect to the chosen action and current parameters. The coefficient a_0 is assumed to be 1. To implement the filter, eligibility traces from the last $|a| - 1$ steps, and gradients x from the last $|b|$ action choices, must be stored, requiring $O(|\theta|(|b| + |a| - 1))$ units of memory.

Let τ denote the delay between an action and a possible reward. Impulse response plots, such as Figure 1, show the filter outputs e_τ after a scalar impulse input of $x_0 = 1$ and $x_\tau = 0$ for all $\tau > 0$. The response at delay τ represents the likelihood of receiving a reward for an action chosen at $\tau = 0$. The filter coefficients determine the poles and zeros of the filter's discrete-time frequency response. Given a desired impulse response, i.e., a desired temporal credit assignment model, filter coefficients can be chosen by a least squares fit of the filter coefficients to the Fourier transform of the impulse response[3]. The complexity of

---

[3] The Matlab function **invfreqz** performs this task.

implementing the filter increases linearly with the number of coefficients. Hence it can be useful to choose a filter that only approximates the desired credit assignment, but has few coefficients. Unsurprisingly, experiments demonstrate it is better to award credit mistakenly than to not award credit where it is due.

A special case of IIR filters are finite impulse response (FIR) filters. FIR filters set $a = [1]$ and the maximum τ for which the impulse response is non-zero is given by $|b|$. FIR filters are useful if actions have short impacts on rewards.

3.1 ▢▢▢▢ ▢▢▣▣▣

Algorithm 3 generalises the original GPOMDP algorithm to arbitrary IIR filters. To recover GPOMDP we use a first order filter which matches standard exponential credit assignment by setting $a = [1.0, -\beta]$, and $b = [1]$.

The gradient estimate returned by GPOMDP(iir) is passed to a Polak-Ribiére conjugate-gradient line-search ascent routine to update the parameters. The whole process repeats until the magnitude of Δ_T drops below 10^{-10}, indicating a local maximum has been reached. Convergence guarantees for GPOMDP [1] tell us that as $\beta \to 1$, and as the number of estimation steps $T \to \infty$, the GPOMDP estimate $\Delta_T = \nabla\eta$ exactly. Here, a similar result is presented for GPOMDP(iir). Without loss of generality the following proposition assumes an FIR filter with an unbounded number of coefficients. This includes all possible IIR filters that. Due to using fewer co-efficients, IIR filters are more efficient.

Proposition 1. *Let the GPOMDP(iir) filter coefficients be $b_n = 1 \; \forall n = 0, \ldots, |b| - 1$. Let Δ_T be the estimate produced by GPOMDP(iir) after T steps. Then under ergodicity assumptions, and if all absolute quantities in Algorithm 3 can be bounded by constants[4], then $\lim_{T \to \infty} \lim_{|b| \to \infty} \Delta_T = \nabla\eta$ w.p.1.*

It states that as the number of estimation steps $T \to \infty$, and as the filter impulse response approaches a step function, the GPOMDP(iir) estimate converges to $\nabla\eta$. The proof can be seen by observing that approaching the step response filter is the same credit assignment model as $\beta \to 1$, then applying the proofs of [1]. If a tailored filter correctly assigns all credit the estimation will be unbiased without needing an infinite step response filter. Compare this with GPOMDP, which cannot produce unbiased estimate unless credit assignment is truly exponential. However, errors in the filter design will introduce bias into gradient estimates.

3.2 ▢▢ ▢▢▢ ▣▣▣

Algorithm 4 shows the SARSA(iir) algorithm for approximating $Q(i,a)$. The IIR filter is implemented by lines 8–11. Lines 8 to 10 pre-discount the currently stored eligibility traces before applying the IIR filter. This is needed to maintain the consistency of value estimates with discount factor δ.

Unlike GPOMDP, SARSA(iir) is an online algorithm that updates parameters at each step. Various termination conditions can be used, including stopping when values change by less than a threshold over a fixed number of iterations.

---

[4] See [1] for the detailed assumptions.

<table>
<tr><td>

1: Set $e_0 = [0]$, and $\Delta_0 = [0]$ ($e_0, \Delta_0 \in \mathbb{R}^{|\theta|}$), T = estimation steps

2: **while** $t < T$ **do**

3:    Observe i_t from the world

4:    Sample $a_t \sim \Pr(\cdot | \theta, i_t)$

5:    $x_t = \nabla \log \Pr(a_t | \theta, i_t)$

6:    $e_{t+1} = -\left(\sum_{n=1}^{|a|-1} a_n e_{t+1-n}\right) + \left(\sum_{n=0}^{|b|-1} b_n x_{t-n}\right)$

7:    $\Delta_{t+1} = \Delta_t + \frac{1}{t+1}[r(i_{t+1})e_{t+1} - \Delta_t]$

8:    Issue action a_t

9:    $t \leftarrow t + 1$

10: **end while**

</td></tr>
</table>

Fig. 3. Algorithm GPOMDP(iir)

<table>
<tr><td>

1: Set $e_0 = 0, \theta_0 = 0$

2: **while** not converged **do**

3:    Sample $a_{t+1} \sim \Pr(\cdot | Q(i_{t+1}, \cdot, \theta_t))$

4:    Observe $i_t, a_t \rightarrow i_{t+1}, a_{t+1}$

5:    Compute $d(i_t, i_{t+1}) = r_t + \delta Q(i_{t+1}, a_{t+1}, \theta_t) - Q(i_t, a_t, \theta_t)$

6:    Set $\theta_{t+1} = \theta_t + \alpha_t d(i_t, i_{t+1})e_t$

7:    Set $x_t = \nabla Q(i_{t+1}, a_{t+1}, \theta_{t+1})$

8:    **for** each $e_{t-n}, n = 0, \ldots, |a|-1$ **do**

9:      $e_{t-n} = \delta e_{t-n}$

10:    **end for**

11:    $e_{t+1} = -\left(\sum_{n=1}^{|a|-1} a_n e_{t+1-n}\right) + \left(\sum_{n=0}^{|b|-1} b_n x_{t-n}\right)$

12: **end while**

</td></tr>
</table>

Fig. 4. Algorithm SARSA(iir)

4   Experimental Bias and Variance

Four simple partially observable (PO)MDPs were contrived as initial test cases: (I) the POMDP of Figure 5 with $p = 0$; (II) the POMDP of Figure 5 with $p = 0.5$; (III) the POMDP of Figure 6 when completely observable; (IV) the POMDP of Figure 6 when only the tree depth is observable.

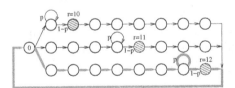

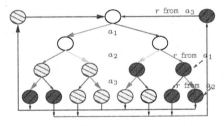

Fig. 5. The completely unobservable MDP used to test IIR trace filtering in Tests I and II. Test I sets $p = 0.0$; Test II sets $p = 0.5$ so that rewards may occur an arbitrarily long time after the action at state 0.

Fig. 6. In tests III and IV rewards have a delay of 1 step. In test IV, only the depth down the tree is observable. In light states $r = 1$, in dark states $r = -1$.

Tests I and II are examples in which normal GPOMDP performs poorly but trace filtering performs well. The optimal policy is to follow the lower path. The 3 actions only have an effect in state 0, deterministically leading to one of the 3 outward transitions. This POMDP is harder than it looks. For GPOMDP with $\beta < 0.97$ the reward discounted back to the action at state 0 appears higher for the upper two paths than for the lower optimal path. Thus for $\beta \leq 0.97$, the gradient will drive parameters away from the optimal policy.

In Tests III and IV the agent must fall down the correct branch of the tree to maximise its reward. The agent can move left or right at each level. The reward is always delayed by 1 step, that is, when the agent makes a decision leaving the top node, level 0, it gets the relevant reward when it reaches level 2. The test is interesting because rewards overlap; the reward received immediately after executing an action is actually due to the previous action.

GPOMDP(iir) was applied to all tests. The number of gradient estimate steps used for each test is shown in Tables 1 and 2. The bias optimal filter for Test I, where $p = 0$ in Figure 5, has a finite response with impulses corresponding to the 3 possible reward delays $\tau = 2, 5$ and 8. This filter is shown in Figure 2. Two filters were applied to Test II. The first is a conservative FIR filter that assumes that rewards must be received between 2–12 steps after the relevant action. It makes no other assumption so all impulses between $\tau = 2$ and $\tau = 12$ have equal value, defining a rectangular filter. A good filter for Test II, where $p = 0.5$, should have an infinite response since rewards can be received an arbitrarily long time into the future. An IIR filter with impulses at the same places as Figure 2 was also tested, but the impulses were allowed to decay exponentially by setting the a_1 weight to -0.75. This filter is shown in Figure 8. It might be suspected that we should decay the impulses by a factor of p, however it was found empirically that this produced a bias and variance worse than the FIR filter. This indicates that it is important to over-estimate credit assignment if bias needs to be minimised. Indeed, it is usually the case that the correct assignment varies with the current state and the current policy. Provided the chosen credit assignment model covers all possible action-reward delays over all states and policies, there is no bias penalty. Even better performance would be obtained if credit assignment dynamically adjusted to state and policy. The optimal filter for Tests III and IV is $a = [1]$ and $b = [0, 1]$, a single impulse for the 1 step delay in rewards. Because the test POMDPs are small, we can compute true gradient by evaluating Equation (5) directly. The true gradient was compared to 50 GPOMDP(iir) gradient estimates for each test and filter. Comparisons were done with GPOMDP discounting at $\beta = 0.9$ and $\beta = 0.99$.

4.1 ▫▫▫▫ ▫▫▭▭ Results

The bias and variance of the estimates are shown in Tables 1 and 2. For Test I, $\beta = 0.9$ produced a gradient pointing in the wrong direction; $\beta = 0.99$ is in the correct direction but the high variance meant a total of around 1,000,000 estimation steps were required to achieve convergence to the correct policy. The simple FIR filter required only around 10,000 total estimation steps. These values are different from T in the first row, which is the steps performed for *single* gradient estimate. In Test II, the FIR filter only marginally improved the bias, however the variance was greatly reduced. The IIR filter improved the bias further because it does not arbitrarily cut off credit after 12 steps, but introducing an infinite response increased the variance. This demonstrates that the bias/variance trade-off in the choice of discount factor is still evident when designing arbitrary filters. Proposition 1 tells us that one choice of unbiased filter for any POMDP is an infinite step response. A large class of POMDPs have unbiased filters that are not infinite step responses. For example, the POMDP of Test I and any POMDP that visits a recurrent state after at most N steps. Tests III and IV also show an order of magnitude improvement in bias (measured in degrees) and variance.

Table 1. Results for Tests I and II.

T	I: 10^6		II: 10^6	
Trace type	*Bias*	*Var.*	*Bias*	*Var.*
$\beta = 0.9$	$176°$	12.3	$176°$	18.4
$\beta = 0.99$	$14.7°$	2090	$14.7°$	2140
FIR	$0.107°$	7.72	$13.9°$	10.71
IIR			$4.35°$	59.5

Table 2. Results of Tests III and IV.

T	III: 1000		IV: 400	
Trace type	*Bias*	*Var.*	*Bias*	*Var.*
$\beta = 0.9$	$0.610°$	0.560	$1.11°$	111
$\beta = 0.99$	$1.15°$	2.88	$2.36°$	655
FIR	$0.0450°$	0.278	$0.394°$	16.7

4.2   ▫▫ ▫▫▫ ▫▪▫▪ Results

The SARSA(iir) algorithm was run on a completely observable version of Test I, comparing it to the performance of Sarsa(λ) with different values of λ. For these experiments, δ was fixed at 0.99 and the parameter step size α was fixed at 0.01. Three filters were used, with 100 training runs of each. The first using the optimal FIR filter of Figure 2, the second using $\lambda = 0.9$, and the third $\lambda = 0.99$. Exploration was encouraged by choosing actions according to a soft-max distribution (2) on the Q-values.

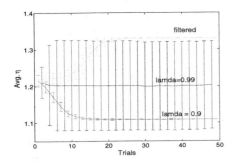

Fig. 7. Results of applying the SARSA(iir) to Test I. The error bars show one standard deviation.

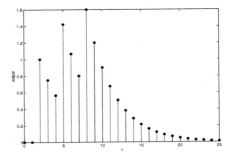

Fig. 8. A good IIR filter for Test II, with parameters $a = [1, -0.75]$, $b = [0, 0, 1, 0, 0, 1, 0, 0, 1]$.

Figure 7 plots the mean reward η received over trials of 1000 steps each, averaged over the 100 optimisation runs. The top line uses the filter of Figure 2, consistently finding the optimal policy in around 25,000 steps. The policy is near random if $\lambda = 0.99$ and the worst policy, with $\eta = 1.11$, coincides with $\lambda = 0.9$.

5   Drug Dosage Control

When drugs are injected into the body they take a few tens of seconds to reach maximum effect. The effect then decreases with time. Figure 9 shows an approximate drug concentration curve for the large class of drugs that follow first order *kinetics of elimination* [8]. The challenge is to choose dosages at each time step to maintain a desired drug concentration. Using Matlab to approximate a filter for Figure 9 results in an IIR filter with coefficients $a = [1.0, -1.30, 0.096, 0.24]$ and $b = [0.0074, 0.039, -0.023, 0.18, 0.092, 0.21]$. These coefficients were used to construct a simulator for the reaction of a person to drug injection actions. The simulator implements (9), allowing an action to be chosen at each discrete time step and outputting the current total concentration from all doses. The state space is a subspace of $\mathbb{R}^{|a|-1+|b|}$, consisting of a vector containing the last 3 total concentrations, and the last 6 actions.

At each time step the agent receives a measurement of the current drug concentration in the patient, i.e., the last output of the simulator's implementation of (9), corrupted by $\mathcal{N}(0, 0.05)$ noise. A neural network is used to parameterise the policy for this continuous state space. The 2 inputs are the desired concentration level and the observed concentration level, normalised to a $[0, 1]$ range. The 3 hidden units are squashed using the tanh function. The agent chooses from 3 actions: 0 dose, 0.5 dose, or 1.0 dose. The 3 network outputs form the y vector, passed to a soft-max function to produce a stochastic policy. The network weights were randomly initialised in $[-0.01, 0.01]$. The desired concentration level was defined as $14.8 \sin(2\pi t/1000)$, forcing the agent to track a moving target.

Five filters were tried over 100 training runs each: standard exponential discounting with $\beta = \{0.8, 0.9, 0.99\}$, a rectangular FIR filter that cuts off credit assignment after $\tau = 40$, and an IIR filter with the same IIR filter coefficients used in the simulator. Each gradient was estimated with $T = 2 \times 10^4$ steps.

5.1   Results

Figure 10 shows the convergence of the two *best* filters. Using the IIR filter instead of discounting with $\beta = 0.9$ improved the average η from 0.621 to 0.675. A single sided t-test indicates this result is significant with 99.9% confidence. The variance of the final IIR solutions was 0.010 compared to 0.014 for $\beta = 0.9$. Random policies achieved $\eta = 0.47$ on average. It took an average of 19.0 seconds to obtain a value of $\eta = 0.8$ (achieved 6/100 times) using a 3GHz Pentium 4, or 1.28 times longer than the exponential discounting took to achieve the same η (which it did 4/100 times). Discounting with $\beta = 0.9$ was the second best filter because of the roughly 0.9 decay rate in Figure 9 after the initial peak. The rectangular filter was the next best with average $\eta = 0.599$, $\beta = 0.8$ returned $\eta = 0.591$, and $\beta = 0.99$ returned $\eta = .520$. Increasing the estimation times for the IIR filter allowed $\eta = 0.812$ to be found consistently.

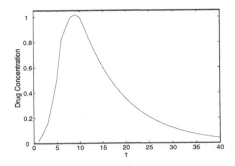
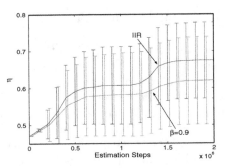

Fig. 9. A first-order kinetics drug-concentration vs. time curve. The drug is injected at $\tau = 0$.

Fig. 10. Drug dosage task results averaged over 100 runs. Error bars indicate one standard deviation.

6 Conclusions and Further Work

Higher-order models of temporal credit assignment can result in greatly reduced bias and variance, both for value estimates and policy-gradient estimates. Trace filtering can be applied to any RL algorithm that uses an eligibility trace. Better theoretical characterisations of the bias-variance trade-offs of IIR filters are needed to aid the choice of robust filters. The preliminary experiments are being extended to problems from non-linear control literature.

Acknowledgements

National ICT Australia is funded by the Australian Government, the Australian Research Council, and the ICT Centre of Excellence program.

References

1. Baxter, J., Bartlett, P.L.: Infinite-horizon policy-gradient estimation. JAIR **15** (2001) 319–350
2. Sutton, R.S., Barto, A.G.: Reinforcement Learning: An Introduction. (1998)
3. Watkins, C.J.C.H.: Learning from Delayed Rewards. PhD thesis, University of Cambridge, England (1989)
4. Williams, R.J.: Simple statistical gradient-following algorithms for connectionist reinforcement learning. Machine Learning **8** (1992) 229–256
5. Aberdeen, D.: Policy-Gradient Algorithms for Partially Observable Markov Decision Processes. PhD thesis, Australian National University (2003)
6. Singh, S.P., Sutton, R.S.: Reinforcement learning with replacing eligibility traces. Machine Learning **22** (1996) 123–158
7. Elliott, S.: Signal Processing for Active Control. Academic Press (2001)
8. Boroujerdi, M.: Pharmacokinetics: Principles and Application. McGraw-Hill, New York, NY (2002)

Applying Support Vector Machines
to Imbalanced Datasets

Rehan Akbani[1], Stephen Kwek[1], and Nathalie Japkowicz[2]

[1] Department of Computer Science, University of Texas at San Antonio
6900 N. Loop 1604 W, San Antonio, Texas, 78249, USA
{rakbani,kwek}@cs.utsa.edu
[2] School of Information Technology & Engineering, University of Ottawa
150 Louis Pasteur, Ottawa, Ontario, K1N 6N5, Canada
nat@site.uottawa.ca

Abstract. Support Vector Machines (SVM) have been extensively studied and have shown remarkable success in many applications. However the success of SVM is very limited when it is applied to the problem of learning from imbalanced datasets in which negative instances heavily outnumber the positive instances (e.g. in gene profiling and detecting credit card fraud). This paper discusses the factors behind this failure and explains why the common strategy of undersampling the training data may not be the best choice for SVM. We then propose an algorithm for overcoming these problems which is based on a variant of the SMOTE algorithm by Chawla et al, combined with Veropoulos et al's different error costs algorithm. We compare the performance of our algorithm against these two algorithms, along with undersampling and regular SVM and show that our algorithm outperforms all of them.

1 Introduction

Support Vector Machines (SVM) were introduced by Vapnik and colleagues [13] and they have been very successful in application areas ranging from image retrieval [12], handwriting recognition [3] to text classification [7]. However, when faced with imbalanced datasets where the number of negative instances far outnumbers the positive instances, the performance of SVM drops significantly [15] (in the remainder of this paper negative is always taken to be the majority class and positive is the minority class). Application areas such as gene profiling, medical diagnosis and credit card fraud detection have highly skewed datasets with a very small number of positive instances which are hard to classify correctly, but important to detect nevertheless [15]. An imbalance of 100 to 1 exists in fraud detection domains, even approaching 100,000 to 1 in other applications [11].

Classifiers generally perform poorly on imbalanced datasets because they are designed to generalize from sample data and output the simplest hypothesis that best fits the data, based on the principle of Occam's razor. This principle is embedded in the inductive bias of many machine learning algorithms including decision trees, which favor shorter trees over longer ones. With imbalanced data, the simplest hypothesis is often the one that classifies almost all instances as negative.

J.-F. Boulicaut et al. (Eds.): ECML 2004, LNAI 3201, pp. 39–50, 2004.

Another factor is that making the classifier too specific may make it too sensitive to noise and more prone to learn an erroneous hypothesis. Certain algorithms specifically modify the behavior of existing algorithms to make them more immune to noisy instances, such as the IB3 algorithm [1] for kNN, or pruning of decision trees, or soft margins in SVM [13]. While these approaches work well for balanced datasets, with highly imbalanced datasets having ratios of 50 to 1 or more the simplest hypothesis is often the one that classifies every instance as negative. Furthermore, the positive instances can be treated as noise and ignored completely by the classifier.

A popular approach towards solving these problems is to bias the classifier so that it pays more attention to the positive instances. This can be done, for instance, by increasing the penalty associated with misclassifying the positive class relative to the negative class. Another approach is to preprocess the data by oversampling the majority class or undersampling the minority class in order to create a balanced dataset.

We combine both of these approaches in our algorithm and show that we can significantly improve the performance of SVM compared to applying any one approach. We also show in this paper that even though undersampling the majority class does improve SVM performance, there is an inherent loss of valuable information in this process. Our goal was to retain and use this valuable information, while simultaneously boosting the efficacy of oversampled data. Combined with this dual approach we also used a bias to make SVM more sensitive to the positive class.

We specifically chose SVM to attack the problem of imbalanced data because SVM is based on strong theoretical foundations [13] and our empirical results show that it performs well with moderately imbalanced data even without any modifications. Its unique learning mechanism makes it an interesting candidate for dealing with imbalanced datasets, since SVM only takes into account those instances that are close to the boundary, i.e. the support vectors, for building its model. This means that SVM is unaffected by non-noisy negative instances far away from the boundary even if they are huge in number.

In Section 2 we outline related work dealing with the problem of imbalanced data. Section 3 investigates the effects of imbalance on SVM, while Section 4 discusses the problems associated with undersampling the majority class. Section 5 presents our approach to the problem and describes our technique (SDC) of combining SMOTE [2] with Different Costs [14]. Finally Section 6 gives the conclusions.

2   Related Work

The problem of imbalanced datasets has been approached from two main directions. The first approach is to preprocess the data by undersampling the majority instances or oversampling the minority instances. Kubat and Matwin [9] proposed a one-sided selection process which undersampled the majority class in order to remove noisy, borderline, and redundant training instances. But for the specific case of SVM, removing redundant (far away) instances has no effect and removing borderline instances may adversely affect the accuracy of the learned hyperplane.

Japkowicz [6] evaluated the oversampling and undersampling techniques for skewed datasets and concluded that both methods were effective. Ling and Li [10] combined oversampling with undersampling, but this combination did not provide significant improvement in the "lift index" metric that they used.

Chawla et al [2] devised a method called Synthetic Minority Oversampling Technique (SMOTE). This technique involved creating new instances through "phantom-transduction." For each positive instance, its nearest positive neighbors were identified and new positive instances were created and placed randomly in between the instance and its neighbors. Since this technique creates new positive instances, we found this technique to be more useful for SVM than simple oversampling.

The other approach to dealing with imbalanced datasets using SVM biases the algorithm so that the learned hyperplane is further away from the positive class. This is done in order to compensate for the skew associated with imbalanced datasets which pushes the hyperplane closer to the positive class. This biasing can be accomplished in various ways. In [15] an algorithm is proposed that changes the kernel function to develop this bias, while in [4] the kernel matrix is adjusted to fit the training data. Veropoulos et al [14] suggested using different penalty constants for different classes of data, making errors on positive instances costlier than errors on negative instances. In this paper we will combine this method together with SMOTE [2] to develop a classifier that performs better than either of these algorithms alone.

3   Effects of Imbalance on SVM

Given a set of labeled instances $X_{train} = \{x_i, \ y_i\}^n_{i=1}$ and a kernel function K, SVM finds the optimal α_i for each x_i to maximize the margin γ between the hyperplane and the closest instances to it. The class prediction for a new test instance x is made through:

$$ sign\left(f(x) = \sum_{i=1}^{n} y_i \alpha_i K(x, x_i) + b \right) \qquad (1) $$

where b is the threshold. 1-norm soft-margin SVMs minimize the primal Lagrangian:

$$ L_p = \frac{\|w\|^2}{2} + C\sum_{i=1}^{n} \xi_i - \sum_{i=1}^{n} \alpha_i \left[y_i (w \cdot x_i + b) - 1 + \xi_i \right] - \sum_{i=1}^{n} r_i \xi_i \qquad (2) $$

where $\alpha_i \geq 0$ and $r_i \geq 0$ [5]. The penalty constant C represents the trade-off between the empirical error ξ and the margin. In order to meet the Karush-Kuhn-Tucker (KKT) conditions, the value of α_i must satisfy:

$$ 0 \leq \alpha_i \leq C \quad \text{and} \quad \sum_{i=1}^{n} \alpha_i y_i = 0 \qquad (3) $$

3.1   Causes of Performance Loss with Imbalanced Data

1. Positive Points Lie Further from the Ideal Boundary. Wu and Chang [15] point out this factor as one source of boundary skew. They mention that the imbalance in the training data ratio means that the positive instances may lie further away from the "ideal" boundary than the negative instances. This is illustrated by way of example that if we were to draw n randomly chosen numbers between 1 to 100 from a uniform distribution, our chances of drawing a number close to 100 would improve with increasing values of n, even though the expected mean of the draws is invariant of n. As a result of this phenomenon, SVM learns a boundary that is too close to and skewed towards the positive instances.

2. Weakness of Soft-Margins. Mathematically, we can see from eq. 2 that minimizing the first term on the right hand side $\|w\|^2/2$, is equivalent to maximizing the margin γ, while minimizing the second term $C\sum\xi$ minimizes the associated error. The constant C specifies what tradeoff we are willing to tolerate between maximizing the margin and minimizing the error. If C is not very large, SVM simply learns to classify everything as negative because that makes the "margin" the largest, with zero cumulative error on the abundant negative examples. The only tradeoff is the small amount of cumulative error on the few positive examples, which does not count for much. This explains why SVM fails completely in situations with a high degree of imbalance. One way to combat this is to increase the tradeoff C^+ associated with the positive examples. This is exactly what Veropoulos et al [14] propose in their paper and this is the strategy we adopt in this paper as well (more about this in Section 5).

3. Imbalanced Support Vector Ratio. Another source of boundary skew according to Wu and Chang [15] is the imbalanced support vector ratio. They found that as the training data gets more imbalanced, the ratio between the positive and negative support vectors also becomes more imbalanced. They hypothesize that as a result of this imbalance, the neighborhood of a test instance close to the boundary is more likely to be dominated by negative support vectors and hence the decision function is more likely to classify a boundary point negative. We would like to point out however, that because of the KKT conditions in eq. 3, the sum of the α's associated with the positive support vectors must be equal to the sum of the α's associated with the negative support vectors. Because there are fewer positive support vectors with correspondingly fewer α's, each positive support vector's α must be larger than the negative support vector's α on average. These α's act as weights in the final decision function (eq. 1) and as a result of larger α's the positive support vectors receive a higher weight than the negative support vectors which offsets the effect of support vector imbalance to some extent. This shows why SVM does not perform too badly compared to other machine learning algorithms for moderately skewed datasets.

4   Problems with Undersampling

Undersampling of the majority class is a popular method for dealing with imbalanced datasets. The rationale behind it is to try to balance out the dataset in an attempt to overcome the idiosyncrasies of the machine learning algorithm. The problem with this approach, however, is that the purpose of machine learning is for the classifier to estimate the probability distribution of the target population. Since that distribution is unknown we try to estimate the population distribution using a sample distribution. Statistics tells us that as long as the sample is drawn randomly, the sample distribution can be used to estimate the population distribution from where it was drawn. Hence, by learning the sample distribution we can learn to approximate the target distribution. Once we perform undersampling of the majority class, however, the sample can no longer be considered random.

A possible defense against this argument is when we assume that in an imbalanced dataset the sample was not drawn randomly to begin with. The assumption is that the sampling mechanism was unfairly biased towards sampling the majority instances. For instance, in detecting credit card fraud, the default assumption is that a transaction is valid unless proven otherwise. As a result, many fraudulent transactions may go undetected by the source labeling the dataset. Similarly, in medical diagnosis, a person with a rare disease may not be properly diagnosed. To counter these inevitable deficiencies, undersampling or oversampling is done to overcome the biases of the sampling mechanism. Even though it is impossible for undersampling or oversampling to make a non-random sample random, in practice these measures have empirically been shown to approximate the target population better than the original, biased sample.

The second problem with undersampling is that we are throwing away valid instances, which contain valuable information. The nature of the information these instances contain can be understood in the following way. The problem with imbalanced datasets is that they skew the boundary towards the positive instances (Figure 1). The classification function for the hard-margin linear SVM [5] is:

$$sign\left(\langle w \, . \, x \rangle + b \right) \tag{4}$$

Where w is a vector that is normal to the separating hyperplane. The norm of w and the variable b decide the distance of the hyperplane from the origin. With non-linear SVMs, the kernel function maps the data into a high-dimensional *feature space* where a hyperplane is used to separate the data. Any hyperplane can be defined by its orientation, given by the direction of w, and its distance from the origin. The task of SVM is to learn the optimal hyperplane in the feature space. In order to do this, it takes cues from the dataset about the orientation and distance of the optimal hyperplane.

We hypothesized that, given a relatively noise-free but imbalanced dataset that is linearly separable in the feature space, SVM will learn to approximate the orientation of the hyperplane better than using the same dataset after it is undersampled. Consider Figure 1. We conducted some experiments with artificial data in which we first defined a boundary and called it the "ideal boundary." We then generated several instances at random above the boundary and labeled them as negative. We also randomly generated a few instances below the boundary and labeled them as positive. The number of negative instances generated far outnumbered the positive instances to simulate imbalanced data. Note that in Figure 1, the negative instances lie much closer to the ideal boundary than the positive instances due to reasons given in Section 2. If, given the dataset, SVM learned the ideal boundary then it would be able to classify all the instances and any test instances perfectly. But as expected, SVM learned a boundary that was midway between the positive and negative support vectors and therefore, much further from the ideal boundary. Such a boundary would not be able to classify test instances very well. Figure 1 and Figure 2 represent some typical results we obtained with our experiments on artificial datasets.

In Figure 1, SVM can obtain reasonable cues about the orientation of the hyperplane from the negative instances that lie close to the boundary. As a result, the learned hyperplane has almost the same orientation as the ideal hyperplane. The only problem is that the distance of the learned hyperplane is too far off to the positive side. In Figure 2, however, the majority instances have been randomly undersampled until their numbers are about equal to the minority instances. In this case, we can see that the negative and positive instances are approximately the same distance away from the ideal hyperplane, making the distance of the learned hyperplane very close to the distance of the ideal hyperplane. But now the problem is that the negative instances can no longer give good cues about the orientation of the hyperplane and there is a greater degree of freedom for the orientation of the hyperplane to vary.

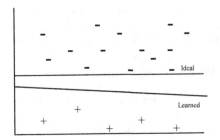
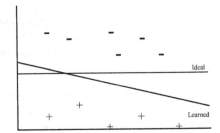

Fig. 1. Positive instances lie further away from the ideal boundary (*horizontal line*) than the negative instances. As a result SVM learns a boundary (*slanted line*) that is too close to the positive support vectors

Fig. 2. After undersampling the minority instances, the learned plane estimates the distance of the ideal plane better than in Figure 1, but the orientation of the learned plane is no longer as accurate

We decided to test this hypothesis on UCI datasets. In order to know what the ideal boundary for these datasets was, it was necessary to start with large, balanced datasets that were relatively noise-free and linearly separable in the feature space. We chose five balanced UCI datasets for this experiment *balance3* (RBF), *chess1*(RBF), *mushroom1* (linear), *ionosphere1* (RBF) and *sonar1* (polynomial). The number in the suffix represents the class we chose to be the positive class while the kernel function is indicated in parenthesis. We trained SVM using three different kernels on these datasets (linear, polynomial with degree 2 and Radial Basis Function with gamma =1), and in each case we obtained nearly 100% accuracy (which is why we chose these datasets). The hyperplane learned was assumed to be the ideal hyperplane i.e. if SVM were to learn this hyperplane then it would be able to classify all instances almost perfectly. We then randomly removed most of the positive instances from each dataset to make them highly imbalanced. We re-trained SVM using these imbalanced datasets to obtain the learned boundary. Next we obtained the dot product of the two vectors w (obtained from the balanced dataset model) and v (the vector obtained from the imbalanced dataset model) and used this dot product to compute θ, the angle between the ideal and the learned hyperplanes. We obtained w from the learned model by applying the following equation for linear SVMs [5]:

$$w = \sum_{i=1}^{n} \alpha_i y_i x_i \tag{5}$$

Each of the three parameters α, y and x (the support vectors) can be obtained directly from the learned model. When using non-linear kernels, calculating w in this way may not represent the absolute angle of the hyperplane in the feature space. However, we are only interested in knowing how different the shape of the boundary is in the balanced vs. the imbalanced case. Computing w in this way and then computing the angle between w and v allows us to estimate this difference in shape.

We repeated this experiment by keeping the positive instances the same as in the imbalanced datasets and reducing the negative instances by gradually randomly undersampling them until eventually the negative instances were equal in number to the positive instances. In each case we measured the angle between the ideal hyperplane and the learned hyperplane. The results are shown below.

Table 1. Angle (in degrees) between the ideal hyperplane and the learned hyperplane as the imbalance ratio (*ratio of negative to positive examples*) is varied

Imbalance	Balance	Chess	Mushroom	Ionosphere	Sonar
15	10.4	24.88	58.1	35.06	65.65
8	10.88	24.87	58.6	36.08	66.32
4	10.57	25.25	58.9	46.77	70.48
2	17.44	28.2	64.58	55.97	79.13
1	26.2	31.92	66.1	65.6	82.76

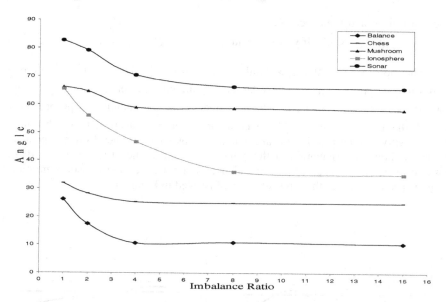

Fig. 3. Graph showing the effect of varying the imbalance ratio (*x*-axis) on angle between the ideal and the learned hyperplane (*y*-axis). The angle is smaller in more imbalanced datasets

The results agree with our hypothesis that undersampling the majority class causes larger angles between the ideal and learned hyperplane due to the reasons given earlier in this section. Undersampling also reduces the total number of training instances which also contributes to increasing angles. Therefore, any benefit from undersampling occurs mainly because of a more accurate estimate of the distance, rather than the orientation, of the hyperplane from the ideal boundary. Oversampling of the minority instances, on the other hand, does not lead to loss of information. Even though it may not make the non-random sample truly random (nothing really can), it has been shown, nevertheless, to make the classifier perform better than with the regular imbalanced sample [6]. As a result we will employ oversampling in our approach.

5 Our Approach – SMOTE with Different Costs (SDC)

As mentioned above, undersampling data has its drawbacks and results in information loss. We would like to devise an approach that keeps the majority instances and yet performs well with imbalanced data. The problem is that with imbalanced datasets, the learned boundary is too close to the positive instances. We need to bias SVM in a way that will push the boundary away from the positive instances. Veropoulos et al [14] suggest using different error costs for the positive (C^+) and negative (C^-) classes. Specifically, they suggest changing the primal Lagrangian (eq. 2) to:

$$L_p = \frac{\|w\|^2}{2} + C^+ \sum_{\{i|yi=+1\}}^{n_+} \xi_i + C^- \sum_{\{j|yj=-1\}}^{n_-} \xi_j \qquad (6)$$

$$- \sum_{i=1}^{n} \alpha_i \left[y_i \left(w \cdot x_i + b \right) - 1 + \xi_i \right] - \sum_{i=1}^{n} r_i \xi_i$$

The constraints on α_i then become:

$$0 \le \alpha_i \le C^+ \text{ if } y_i = +1 \quad \text{and} \quad 0 \le \alpha_i \le C^- \text{ if } y_i = -1 \qquad (7)$$

Furthermore, we note that $\xi_i > 0$ only when $\alpha_i = C$ [5]. Therefore non-zero errors on positive support vectors will have larger α_i while non-zero errors on negative support vectors will have smaller α_i. The net effect is that the boundary is pushed more towards the negative instances. However, a consequence of this is that SVM becomes more sensitive to the positive instances and obtains stronger cues from the positive instances about the orientation of the plane than from the negative instances. If the positive instances are sparse, as in imbalanced datasets, then the boundary may not have the proper shape in the input space as illustrated in Figure 4.

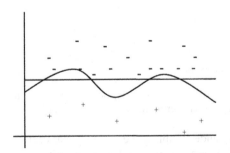 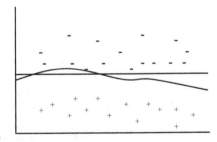

Fig. 4. The learned boundary (*curved line*) in the input space closely follows the distribution of the positive instances. The ideal boundary is denoted by the horizontal line

Fig. 5. After using SMOTE, the positive instances are now more densely distributed and the learned boundary (*curved line*) is more well defined

The solution we adopted to remedy the problem of sparse positive instances is to use Chawla et al's [2] SMOTE algorithm mentioned in Section 2 of this paper. Using the SMOTE technique of oversampling the minority instances, we can make the distribution of positive instances denser. Simply resampling the minority instances merely overlaps the positive instances on top of each other and does not help in "smoothing out" the shape of the boundary. SMOTE synthetically generates new instances between two existing positive instances which helps in making their distribution more well-defined. After using SMOTE, the input space may look like Figure 5.

Therefore, in summary, our strategy consists of:

1. Not undersampling the majority instances since they lead to loss of information.
2. Using different error costs for different classes to push the boundary away from the positive instances.
3. Using SMOTE to make the positive instances more densely distributed in order to make the boundary more well defined.

5.1   Experiments and Results

In order to evaluate classifiers on highly imbalanced datasets, using accuracy as a metric is virtually useless. This is because with an imbalance of 99 to 1, a classifier that classifies everything negative will be 99% accurate, but it will be completely useless as a classifier. The medical community, and increasingly the machine learning community [14, 15], use two metrics, the sensitivity and the specificity, when evaluating the performance of various tests. Sensitivity can be defined as the accuracy on the positive instances (true positives / (true positives + false negatives)), while specificity can be defined as the accuracy on the negative instances (true negatives / (true negatives + false positives)). Kubat et al [9] suggested the g-means metric defined as:

$$g = \sqrt{acc+ \; . \; acc-} \tag{8}$$

Where acc+ = sensitivity and acc- = specificity. This metric has been used by several researchers for evaluating classifiers on imbalanced datasets [8, 9, 15]. We will also use this metric to evaluate our classifier. We also list the sensitivity and specificity separately to give the reader an even better idea of the performance of our classifier.

In our experiments, we compared the performance of our classifier with regular SVM, random undersampling [6], SMOTE [2], and different error costs [14]. We used 10 different UCI datasets with varying degrees of class imbalance (Table 2). Each dataset was randomly split into train and test sets in the ratio 7 to 3, while sampling them in a stratified manner to ensure each of them had the same negative to positive ratio [9, 15]. For the undersampling algorithm, we undersampled the training data until both the classes were equal in number as Japkowicz [6] did in her experiments. For SMOTE [2] we oversampled the data instead of undersampling it. The amount of oversampling is given in Table 2 below. Finally, for the different error costs algorithm, Veropoulos et al [14] have not suggested any guidelines for deciding what the relative ratios of the positive to negative cost factors should be. As a rule of thumb, we empirically found that setting the cost ratio to the inverse of the imbalance ratio gave good results and that is what we have used. The results of our experiments are given below.

Table 2. The table below lists the UCI datasets we used, the kernel function used (based on the best empirical results), the number of positive instances and the number of negative instances in the dataset. It also lists the amount of oversampling of the minority class we did for SMOTE and in our algorithm, SMOTE with Different Costs (SDC), based on the amount of imbalance present in the original dataset. The suffix after each dataset indicates the class we used as the positive class. RBF is the radial basis function with gamma = 1, while the polynomial kernel has degree = 2

Dataset	Kernel	Positive Insts.	Negative Insts.	% Oversampled
Abalone19	Linear	32	4145	1000
Anneal5	Linear	67	831	400
Car3	RBF	69	1659	400
Glass7	RBF	29	185	200
Hepatitis1	Linear	32	123	100
Hypothyroid3	Linear	95	3677	400
Letter26	RBF	734	19266	200
Segment1	RBF	330	1980	100
Sick2	Polynomial	231	3541	100
Soybean12	Linear	44	639	100

Table 3. The table below shows the sensitivity (Se) and Specificity (Sp) of each algorithm. US stands for UnderSampling, DEC stands for Different Error Costs [14], while our algorithm is SDC (SMOTE with Different Costs)

	SVM		US		SMOTE		DEC		SDC	
	Se	Sp	Se	Sp	Se	Sp	Se	Sp	Se	Sp
abalone	0	1	0.778	0.533	0	1	0.889	0.732	0.808	0.687
anneal	1	1	1	1	1	1	1	1	1	1
car	0	1	0.95	0.97	0.97	1	0.1	1	0.97	1
glass	0.75	1	0.875	0.885	0.769	1	0.875	0.967	0.808	1
hepatitis	0.364	0.977	0.727	0.767	0.625	0.881	0.545	0.884	0.708	0.833
hypothy	0.031	1	0.906	0.882	0.646	0.997	0.906	0.972	0.957	0.96
letter	0.67	1	0.996	0.917	0.903	0.995	1	0.975	0.997	0.966
segment	0.99	1	0.99	0.993	0.954	1	0.99	1	0.959	0.998
sick	0	1	0.773	0.756	0.167	0.995	0.864	0.862	0.865	0.874
soybean	0.857	1	1	0.936	1	1	1	1	1	1

Note that SVM has almost perfect specificity, but poor sensitivity because it tends to classify everything as negative. Any algorithm that tries to improve on it inevitably sacrifices some specificity in order to improve the sensitivity. That is why, Kubat and Matwin's [9] g-means metric (Table 4) is the best of the three measures because it combines both the sensitivity and the specificity and takes their geometric mean.

Table 4. The table below shows the performance of the five algorithms using Kubat and Matwin's[9] g-means metric. The last line of the table is the arithmetic mean of each algorithm over all the g-means metrics. This arithmetic mean can be used to quantify the overall performance of each algorithm over all ten datasets

	SVM	US	SMOTE	DEC	SDC
abalone	0	0.6436394	0	0.8064562	0.7449049
anneal	1	1	1	1	1
car	0	0.960104	0.9846381	0.3162278	0.9846381
glass	0.8660254	0.880108	0.877058	0.9199519	0.9405399
hepatitis	0.5959695	0.7470874	0.742021	0.6942835	0.7682954
hypothyroi	0.1767767	0.8938961	0.8025625	0.9384492	0.9581446
letter	0.8182931	0.9555176	0.947737	0.9871834	0.9816909
segment	0.9950372	0.9917748	0.9765287	0.9950372	0.9783467
sick	0	0.7641141	0.4071283	0.8627879	0.8695146
soybean	0.9258201	0.9672867	1	1	1
Mean	**0.537792**	**0.880353**	**0.773767**	**0.852038**	**0.922608**

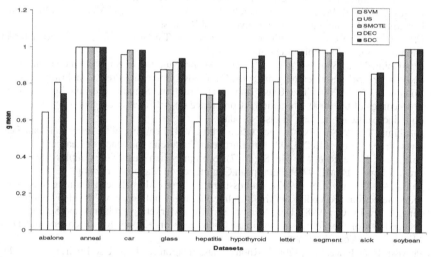

Fig. 6. g-means graphs for the datasets shown in Table 4. The five algorithms, in order, are SVM, Undersampling, SMOTE, Different Error Costs and the last bar is our algorithm SDC

6 Conclusion

The results show that our SDC algorithm outperforms all the other four algorithms. In seven out of the ten datasets our algorithm has the highest g-means metric, and in the remaining three datasets it is not lower by much. It should be noted that our approach never performs worse than SMOTE. In the three cases where our approach performs worse than DEC or other algorithms, it is probably due to the fact that SMOTE itself makes some assumptions about the training set. For instance, it assumes that the space between two positive instances is assumed to be positive and the neighborhood of a positive instance is also assumed to be positive [15], which may not always be true.

Since our algorithm uses SMOTE, it also makes a similar assumption. In datasets where this assumption may not hold, our algorithm will perform slightly worse than the other algorithms.

Undersampling does show significant performance gain, but as noted before the gain is mainly due to accurate estimation of the hyperplane's distance, not its orientation. As a result, it has the highest score in only one dataset where every other algorithm also has a perfect score (anneal). Our algorithm, on the other hand, tries to estimate not only the correct distance but also the correct orientation of the hyperplane and thus performs better than the rest, even in cases where SVM fails completely.

References

1. Aha, D. (1992). Tolerating noisy, irrelevant and novel attributes in instance-based learning algorithms. International Journal Man-Machine Studies, 36, 267-287.
2. Chawla, N., Bowyer, K., Hall, L. & Kegelmeyer, W. (2002). SMOTE: Synthetic Minority Over-sampling Technique. Journal of Artificial Intelligence Research, 16, 321-357.
3. Cortes, C. (1995). Prediction of Generalisation Ability in Learning Machines. PhD thesis, Department of Computer Science, University of Rochester.
4. Cristianini, N., Kandola, J., Elisseeff, A. & Shawe-Taylor, J. (2002). On kernel target alignment. Journal Machine Learning Research, 1.
5. Cristianini, N. & Shawe-Taylor, J. (2000). An Introduction to Support Vector Machines and other kernel-based learning methods. Cambridge University Press, Cambridge, UK.
6. Japkowicz, N. (2000). The Class Imbalance Problem: Significance and Strategies. In Proceedings of the 2000 International Conference on Artificial Intelligence: Special Track on Inductive Learning, Las Vegas, Nevada.
7. Joachims, T. (1998). Text Categorization with SVM: Learning with Many Relevant Features. Proceedings of ECML-98, 10th European Conference on Machine Learning.
8. Kubat, M., Holte, R. & Matwin, S. (1997). Learning when Negative Examples Abound. In Proceedings of ECML-97, 9th European Conference on Machine Learning.
9. Kubat, M. & Matwin, S. (1997). Addressing the Curse of Imbalanced Training Sets: One-Sided Selection. Proceedings of the 14th International Conference on Machine Learning.
10. Ling, C., & Li, C. (1998). Data Mining for Direct Marketing Problems and Solutions. In Proceedings of the Fourth International Conference on Knowledge Discovery and Data Mining, New York, New York.
11. Provost, F. & Fawcett, T. (2001). Robust Classification for Imprecise Environments. Machine Learning, 42/3, 203-231.
12. Tong, S. & Chang, E. (2001). Support Vector Machine Active Learning for Image Retrieval. Proceedings of ACM International Conference on Multimedia, 107-118.
13. Vapnik, V. (1995). The Nature of Statistical Learning Theory. Springer-Verlag, NY.
14. Veropoulos, K., Campbell, C., & Cristianini, N. (1999). Controlling the sensitivity of support vector machines. Proceedings of the International Joint Conference on AI, 55–60.
15. Wu, G. & Chang, E. (2003). Class-Boundary Alignment for Imbalanced Dataset Learning. In ICML 2003 Workshop on Learning from Imbalanced Data Sets II, Washington, DC.

Sensitivity Analysis of the Result in Binary Decision Trees

Isabelle Alvarez[1,2]

[1] LIP6, University of Paris VI, 5 rue Descartes, F-75005 Paris, France
`isabelle.alvarez@lip6.fr`
[2] Cemagref-LISC, BP 50085, F-63172 Aubière Cedex, France

Abstract. This paper proposes a new method to qualify the result given by a decision tree when it is used as a decision aid system. When the data are numerical, we compute the distance of a case from the decision surface. This distance measures the sensitivity of the result to a change in the input data. With a different distance it is also possible to measure the sensitivity of the result to small changes in the tree. The distance from the decision surface can also be combined to the error rate in order to provide a context-dependent information to the end-user.

1 Introduction

Decision trees (DT) are very popular as decision aid systems (see [1] for a short review of real world application), since they are supposed to be easy to build and easy to understand. DT are used for instance in medicine to infer the diagnosis or to establish the prognosis of several diseases (see [2] for references). They are used in credit scoring (see [3] for references) and in other domains to solve classification problems. DT algorithms are also integrated in many software for data mining or decision support purpose. The end-user of a DT submits a new case to the DT which predicts a class. Additional information is generally available to help the end-user to appreciate the result: At least the confusion matrix and some estimate of the error rate (accuracy). Specific rates (like specificity, sensitivity and likelihood ratios which are used in diagnosis) and costs matrix are eventually used to take into account the difference between false positive and false negative [4]. This additional information is essential but generally it focuses exclusively on the result and not on the case itself: This is obvious for global error rates (which are identical for all cases), but it is also true for error rates which are estimated at a leaf. Even if local error rates can estimate the posterior probabilities, they carry much information about the result (the probability of the case to belong to the predicted class), but little about the link between the case and the predicted class. In fact, membership of a particular leaf depends on the path followed in the tree, which is an arbitrary description of the partition of the input space induced by the DT. Therefore its relevance is limited as context-dependent information.

We propose here to provide for the end-user context-dependent information about the result given by the DT for a particular case. This is achieved by a

J.-F. Boulicaut et al. (Eds.): ECML 2004, LNAI 3201, pp. 51–62, 2004.

study of the sensitivity of the result to the change in the input data. Sensitivity analysis consists in the study of the relative position of the input case and the decision surface (the boundary between regions with different class label). It measures the robustness of the result to uncertainty or to small changes in the input data, since it gives the distance of the case from the decision surface. It also exhibit the smallest move to apply to the case to make the decision change. It can also give information about the robustness of the result to small changes in the tree. A simple example[1] shows the interest of sensitivity analysis; Let us consider two different cases from the Pima Indian Diabetes (Pima) database [5], which attributes are shown in Table 1. They are classified by the same leaf. Therefore their error rates are the same. One of the cases is nevertheless very close to the decision surface. A very small change of the value of the attributes can change the decision (moreover it is misclassified). The other case is relatively far from the decision surface. The case can cross the decision boundary only if its attributes values are much modified. Conversely, the decision boundary has to move significantly to make the decision change for the latter case, and it is easy to compute the minimum change of the thresholds of the tests of the DT that is necessary to reach the case. So, in this example, the distance from the decision surface clearly carries interesting information that is not contained in the error rate.

This kind of information is available in geometric classifiers, like support vector machines (SVM). A SVM defines a unique hyperplane in the feature space to classify the data. But in the original input space the corresponding decision surface can be very complex, depending on the kernel that defines the dot product in the feature space [6]. The distance from the decision surface is generally visualized by contour lines, and it can be used to estimate the posterior probabilities [7]. In the case of DT operating on numerical data, the decision surface consists in several pieces of hyperplanes instead of a unique hyperplane. For DT with hyperplanes that are normal to axes (NDT), also called axis-parallel DT, a very simple algorithm can be used to compute the distance of a case from the decision surface, if it is possible to define a metric on the input space. This information can then be used to assess the robustness of the result to changes in the input data and the robustness of the result to changes in the thresholds values of the tests of the tree. It can also be combined with error information to provide case-dependent error rates.

The rest of the paper is organized as follow: Section 2 discusses related work on sensitivity (to change in the input data or in the model) and context-dependent information. Section 3 presents the geometric sensitivity analysis for DT, the algorithm and some properties of the distance from the decision surface: Robustness, influence of the metric and theoretical justification. Section 4 presents our experimental results and possible applications of the sensitivity analysis method. Section 5 presents in a concluding section our remarks and suggestions for further work.

---

[1] The complete example is presented in Sect. 4.1.

2   Related Work

As we have noted in the introduction section, sensitivity analysis gives information on the robustness of the result to changes in the input data and also to changes in the decision surface, that is the model itself. A lot of work has been done to assess the robustness of the classifier, but it is generally considered as a global criteria rather than related to a particular case. The objective is to understand better the learning algorithm (see [8] for references), or to produce a better classifier. For example, methods for model selection (see [9], [10]) try to identify the best model according to a given criteria, generally accuracy or specific error rates. The best model then applies to every new case. Methods based on mixture of expert [11] also aim at producing better model, reducing the variance induced by the partition of the input space. But they cannot easily take into account small changes in the input case, since the predicted class (or predicted probability) is a combination of partial results. Fuzzy DT ([12]) try also to take into account the possible fluctuations of the breakpoint value of the tests, that are calculated on a learning sample. This can be done by defining a fuzzy area around the hyperplane supporting a test with membership functions (see [13] for an example). The uncertainty in the input data is represented by fuzzy data. However, information provided by this method is not easy to use. The computation of the final result is opaque to the end-user, in particular because a point can be close to a hyperplane that has no interest for its classification. For cases outside the fuzzy area, it gives no sensitivity information (for example, how to proceed to significantly change the result).

The main information that is relatively context-dependent is the error rate at the leaf (EL). In most cases it is based on the resubstitution error, with some attempt to correct the overoptimistic bias (see [14], [13], [15], [16]). Cross-validation and resampling techniques are widely used for that purpose. In a similar concern, another approach consists in building DT that estimate directly probability estimators (for example PETs [17] and curtailment [18]). When the EL is correctly estimated, it gives a statistical information on the result obtained at the leaf. In practice, these estimators are not always available, since they are developed and used for the construction of the tree and not for the end-user's need. They are also not necessarily accurate ([9], [19]). Moreover, the leaf is an arbitrary division of the connected component of a case. So the link between the case and the decision surface is not easy to understand.

3   Sensitivity Analysis in DT

3.1   Definitions and Notations

Sensitivity analysis is the study of the relative position of the input case and the decision surface. The result of sensitivity analysis consists in the nearest point of the decision surface to the input case (or, equivalently, in the smallest vector of changes that makes the input data cross the decision boundary). Therefore it assumes that it is possible to define a metric on the input space, eventually with a cost or utility function.

We consider here linear DT (LDT): each test consists in computing the algebraic distance h of a new case x from a hyperplane H. The point x passes the test depending on the sign of $h(x, H)$. When the test involves only one attribute, the hyperplane H is normal to the attribute axis. In NDT, all the hyperplanes defining the tests are normal to an attribute axis.

The DT induces a partition of the input space E. We note Γ the associated decision surface. Γ consists of pieces of hyperplanes, so it is piecewise affine and continuously differentiable almost everywhere. At each point y of Γ, the decision surface is defined by a list $L(y)$ of hyperplanes (often reduced to a unique hyperplane).

Let x be a point of the input space E. The sensitivity at point x is $d(x, \Gamma)$, the distance of x from the decision surface. Actually, any point in the open ball with center at x and radius $d = d(x, \Gamma)$ has the same predicted class as x. There is at least one point in any open Ball with center at x and radius $d + \epsilon$ which predicted class is different from x class. Moreover, if E is a complete metric space, there is at least one point $p(x)$ for which we have $d(x, p(x)) = d(x, \Gamma)$. When E is an Euclidean space, $p(x)$ is the projection of x onto Γ and $\overrightarrow{xp(x)}$ is orthogonal to the vector space associated to $(\bigcap H)_{H \in L(p(x))}$

Definition 1. *The sensitivity at point x is $d(x, \Gamma)$. The sensitive move at point x is the vector $\overrightarrow{xp(x)}$ with $d(x, p(x)) = d(x, \Gamma)$.*

When E is an Euclidean space, there is generally only one sensitive move at point x, since points outside the skeleton[2] of the connected component of their class have a unique projection onto Γ.

3.2   Robustness of the Sensitivity

Sensitivity is not very sensitive to the uncertainty in the new case, and it is relatively robust to the noise in the training data, assuming that only the thresholds of the tests are modified (not the attributes).

Theorem 1. *Close points have similar sensitivity. Let x and y be two input points. We have:*

$$d(x, y) < \epsilon \Rightarrow |d(y, \Gamma) - d(x, \Gamma)| < \epsilon \ . \tag{1}$$

Theorem 2. *Small local deformations of the decision surface lead to small variation of the sensitivity. Let Φ be a small local deformation of the decision surface Γ (such that $\Phi(\Gamma)$ is still a DT surface decision). We have:*

$$\forall z \in \Gamma, d(z, \Phi(z)) < \epsilon \Rightarrow |d(x, \Phi(\Gamma)) - d(x, \Gamma)| < \epsilon \ . \tag{2}$$

---

[2] The skeleton is the locus of the centers of maximal balls. In the case of linear DT, it is complementary to a dense open set, so it is a rather small set.

Proof of Theorems 1 and 2 is straightforward because of triangle inequality.

Theorem 3. *In the NDT case, if E is an Euclidean space, small changes of the thresholds of the tests of the tree lead to relatively small variation of the sensitivity. Let Φ be a deformation of the decision surface such that the thresholds of the tests of the NDT are changed by less than ϵ. We have:*

$$|d(x, \Phi(\Gamma)) - d(x, \Gamma)| < \epsilon\sqrt{dim(E)} \ . \tag{3}$$

Proof. A change of the threshold values implies a translation of the hyperplanes along their normal vector. The points at which Γ is differentiable move from ϵ. The points at which Γ is not differentiable can move from ϵ to $\epsilon\sqrt{dim(E)}$, since $\sqrt{dim(E)}$ is the diagonal of the unit hypercube in the input space E.

Theorem 3 is verified only in the NTD case, since in the general case of oblique linear trees, the decision surface can vary a lot at points where it is not differentiable.

Similar theorems exist for the sensitive move, but the variation ϵ (of the distance of the input point, of the local deformation, of the thresholds) has to be smaller than the distance of x from the skeleton.

3.3   Algorithm in the NDT Case

In the following we shall assume that the input space E is an Euclidean space. Computing the distance from a piecewise linear surface is a very classical problem and many fast converging algorithms are available (see [20] for a review). In the NDT case, however, the set C_f of points classified by a leaf f is an hyperrectangle, and the straightforward projection is easy to compute. Following and idea from [21], we associate to f the list of the tests $(h(x, H_i))_{i \in I}$ that lead to it. f classifies the points that belong to the intersection C_f of the half spaces $E(H_i)$ defined by the tests:

$$C_f = \bigcap_{i \in I} E(H_i) \ . \tag{4}$$

The sensitivity at point x is the smallest distance of x from the leaves which class label $c(f)$ is different from x predicted class $c(x)$. The algorithm sensitivityAt(x,DT) that computes the sensitivity and the sensitive move at point x consists in projecting x onto every leaf f such that $c(f) \neq c(x)$. Then it computes and ranks the distance between x and its projections.

Algorithm 1 *sensitivityAt(x,DT)*
1. *Gather the set F of leaves f of the DT which class $c(f) \neq c(x)$;*
2. *For each $f \in F$ do: {*
3.   *compute $p_f(x) = projectionOntoLeaf(x,f)$;*
4.   *compute and rank $d(x, p_f(x))$ }*
5. *Return $(d(x, p_n(x)), \overrightarrow{xp_n(x)})$ with $n = argmin_{f \in F}(d(x, p_f(x)))$*

The projection onto a leaf f is straightforward since the hyperplanes defining f in Equation 4 are either parallel or orthogonal.

Algorithm 2 *projectionOntoLeaf(x,$(E(H_i))_{i \in I}$)*
1. $y = x$;
2. For $i = 1$ to size(I) do: {
3.   if $y \notin E(H_i)$ then $y_u = b$;
           with u the coordinate corresponding to the attribute defining H_i
              b the threshold value for H_i. }
4. Return y

Remark 1 (invariance of the projection onto a leaf). The projection of a point onto a leaf is invariant under a change of metric (for instance, a dilatation) that conserves the hyperplanes that define the leaf.

The projectionOntoLeaf algorithm doesn't depend on the dimension of the input space. The complexity of the sensitivity algorithm is in $O(Nd)$ where N is the number of tests of the tree and d the dimension of the input space.

4   Experimental Results and Application

Sensitivity information can be used in two ways. First, it gives sensitivity results for individual cases. Second, it measures the sensitivity of the result to uncertainty (in the attributes values), and also the sensitivity to thresholds changes.

4.1   Sensitivity to Input Changes

The first use of the sensitivity information is to measure the possibility of small changes of the input data without changing the class.

The following example come from the Pima Indian Diabetes database (Pima) from the UCI repository [5]. The attributes are female patient information and medical test measurements linked to diabetes. The attributes are meaningful and numerical, and (theoretically) there is no missing value. The database was divided randomly into a training base and a test base (1/3 of the cases), with respect of the prevalence of diabetes in the base (35%). Weka j48 [22], a C4.5-based algorithm [13] was used to grow decision trees on the training database. Then the sensitivity algorithm was applied to the test cases.

We illustrate the first use with two test cases from the Pima database (see Table 1). Both cases are classified by the same leaf.

Two different metrics were used to apply the sensitivity algorithm, the Min-Max (MM) metric and the standard (s) metric. Both metrics are defined with the basic information available on the training data set: An estimate of the range of each attribute i or an estimate of its mean E_i and of its standard deviation s_i. The new coordinate system is defined by Equation 5.

$$y_i^{MM} = \frac{x_i - Min_i}{Max_i - Min_i} \quad \text{or} \quad y_i^s = \frac{x_i - E_i}{s_i} \ . \tag{5}$$

Table 2 shows the sensitivity for both cases. We can see that the sensitivity of Case 188 is very small, since for the Min-Max metric, the maximal size of a

Table 1. Cases of the Pima test database

Attribute	Case 188	Case 63
Glucose concentration in plasma	90	93
Diastolic blood pressure (mmHg)	68	50
Body mass index (kg/m^2)	38.2	28.7
Diabetes pedigree function	0.503	0.356
Age (years)	27	23
Predicted class	0 (not diabetic)	0
Real class	1 (diabetic)	0

vector is $\sqrt{5} \approx 2.24$. It is also very small compared to the norm of the standard error vector. It can also be compared to the maximum possible distance (in the Pima application, one leaf is defined by a single hyperplane, so it gives a base distance). On the contrary, Case 63 is not so close to the decision surface.

The sensitive move of the case 188 is shown in Table 3 (in Table 4 for the case 63). The sensitive move is the smallest change that has to be applied to the case to make the decision change (its norm is the sensitivity). It applies to several attributes that have to be modified together. Its coordinates can be compared to their present value and to several indicators that are generally used to measure uncertainty (percentage of the range, percentage of the standard deviation). We can see that Case 188 is near the decision surface: all the coordinates of its sensitive move are small. Conversely, Case 63 is relatively far from the decision surface: The value of one of its attribute has to increase by more than 50% of its value, which represents also more than 50% of the standard deviation.

The individual sensitivity results can be gathered from a test base, in order to estimate the impact of a variation of the input data on the predicted class. Because of the use of the Euclidean distance, the different attributes can substitute for one another. Table 5 shows the proportion of cases of the test database which class is likely to change for several databases from the UCI repository.

4.2   Sensitivity to Uncertainty and Thresholds Changes

The sensitivity can also be computed, in order to estimate the impact of the uncertainty on the predicted class.

Let x be a point of the input space. When the thresholds of the tests of the tree are modified by ϵ, or when the value of the attributes of x can move at the

Table 2. Sensitivity information for the Pima cases

Metric	Sensitivity Case 188	Sensitivity Case 63	Norm of the SE vector	Max. of the distance
Min-Max	0.038	0.123	0.35	0.7
Standard	0.223	1.474	1	4.3

Table 3. Sensitive move for the Pima case 188

Attribute	Sensitive Move	% of the value	% of the range	% of the standard deviation
Glucose concentration	4.5	5.0	2.3	14.2
Diastolic blood pressure	0	0	0	0
Body mass index	0	0	0	0
Diabetes pedigree function	0.043	8.5	1.8	13.0
Age	1.5	5.6	2.5	12.5

Table 4. Sensitive move for the Pima case 63

Attribute	Sensitive Move	% of the value	% of the range	% of the standard deviation
Glucose concentration	1.5	1.6	0.7	4.7
Diastolic blood pressure	0	0	0	0
Body mass index	0	0	0	0
Diabetes pedigree function	0.19	53.4	8.1	57.6
Age	5.5	23.9	9.2	45.8

most from ϵ, the relative position between x and the decision surface has to be compared not with the Euclidean distance but with the sup-norm distance. The sup-norm of $z = (z_i)_{i \in \{1,\dots,n\}}$ is defined by:

$$\|z\|_\infty = \sup_{i \in \{1,\dots,n\}} |z_i| . \tag{6}$$

Let $p_f(x)$ be the projection of x onto the leaf f, and let $L(p_f(x))$ be the list of the hyperplanes that define Γ at $p_f(x)$ (cf. Section 3.1). We have:

Theorem 4. Let Φ be a deformation of the decision surface such that the thresholds of the tests of the DT are changed by less than ϵ. We note $c_\Phi(x)$ the predicted class of x given by the new DT, $\Phi(DT)$. The class of x remains unchanged if the sup-norm distance $d_\infty(x, \Gamma)$ of x from the decision surface Γ is less than the move of the thresholds.

$$\min_{f \in F} (\max_{H_i \in L(p_f(x))} d(x, H_i)) < \epsilon \Rightarrow c_\Phi(x) = c(x) . \tag{7}$$

Table 5. Proportion of likely class-modified cases in function of the input change

Base	Variation of the distance				
	0.01	0.02	0.05	0.1	0.2
Pima	5.9	10.2	28.1	53.9	90.6
Ionosphere	6.6	12.6	39.1	64.2	81.5
Wine	1.6	1.6	1.6	5.0	6.7

Theorem 5. *Let Φ be a move of the point x such that the coordinates of x are changed by less than ϵ. The class of $\Phi(x)$ is the same as the class of x if the sup-norm distance of x from the decision surface Γ is less than ϵ.*

$$\min_{f \in F}\left(\max_{H_i \in L(p_f(x))} d(x, H_i)\right) < \epsilon \Rightarrow c(\Phi(x)) = c(x) \ . \tag{8}$$

The algorithm sup-sensitivityAt(x,DT) is directly derived from the algorithm sensitivityAt(x,DT). In step 4 and 5 the Euclidean distance is replaced by the sup-norm distance, which is easier to compute.

Algorithm 3 *sup-sensitivityAt(x,DT)*
1. *Gather the set F of leaves f of the DT which class $c(f) \neq c(x)$;*
2. *For each $f \in F$ do: {*
3.   *compute $p_f(x) = projectionOntoLeaf(x,f)$;*
4.   *compute and rank $d_\infty(x, p_f(x))$ }*
5. *Return $(d_\infty(x, p_n(x)), u)$ with $n = argmin_{f \in F}(d_\infty(x, p_f(x)))$*
    and $u = argmax_{i \in (1,\dots,\dim E)} d_\infty(x, p_n(x)) = |x_i - p_n(x)_i|$

The choice of normalization will be guided by the data source. For instance, the accuracy of most sensors is a function of the range, so it suggests to use an adapted version of the Min-Max coordinate system. If a_i is the accuracy of attribute i, the modified coordinate system y_i^{mMM} is defined by Equation 9:

$$y_i^{mMM} = \frac{1}{a_i} \ \frac{x_i - Min_i}{Max_i - Min_i} \ . \tag{9}$$

Remark 2. Since it is a dilatation, if the sensitivity analysis was already done with another coordinate system, it is only necessary to compute and rank again the distance between the test cases and their projections (which are invariant under this change of coordinate system).

Remark 3. In the case of oblique trees also, the sensitivity to attributes changes is the sup-sensitivity, so projection algorithms like in [20] should be modified to use the sup-norm instead of the Euclidean norm. But it is no longer equivalent to the sensitivity to thresholds changes, which has to be computed differently. We suggest to replace Step 3 and 4 of the sensitivity algorithm by the following expression (where $L(f)$ lists the hyperplanes defining f):

    compute and rank $\epsilon_f = |h(x, H_f)|$ with $H_f = argmin_{L(f)} h(x, H)$.

It selects the absolute value of the most negative algebraic distance for each leaf. The minimum ϵ of ϵ_f over F give the sensitivity to threshold changes. If the hyperplanes move along their normal vector from ϵ (in the direction opposite to the interior of the leaf when its class is different than x class), then the decision surface reaches x.

Table 6 shows the proportion of cases of the test database which class is likely to change for several databases from the UCI repository. The proportion of cases can grow quicker than in Table 5 since a move of 1% per attribute leads to a move of total lenght of $\sqrt{\dim E}$.

Table 6. Proportion of likely class-modified cases in function of the input change (in % of the range for each attribute)

Base	Variation of the value of the attributes					
	$\frac{1\%}{\sqrt{\dim E}}$	$\frac{2\%}{\sqrt{\dim E}}$	1%	2%	5%	10%
Pima	3.9	8.2	10.9	25.0	59.8	94.5
Ionosphere	6.6	12.6	24.5	52.3	77.5	90.1
Wine	1.6	1.6	1.6	1.6	1.6	5.0

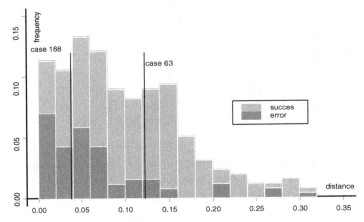

Fig. 1. Frequency histogram of the distance from the decision surface (Pima test base)

4.3   Sensitivity and Error Information

When a sample of labelled test data is available, it could be very interesting to estimate the probability of each class f conditionally to the distance from the decision surface. This is done for other geometric method like SVM (see for references [7]). The posterior probabilities have to be estimated on the test base, not on the training base, since supervised learning algorithms play a part in the localization of errors. Here we just show for the Pima and the Ionosphere databases the frequency histogram of the distribution of the distance from the decision surface, with the proportion of errors and well-classified cases. Better estimates could be obtained with resampling methods. We already see in Figure 1 that it confirms the ordinary hypothesis that errors are mostly located near the decision surface. The end-user can see that for case 188, the proportion of errors at this distance is greater than 40%. For case 63, it is less than 20%. Retrospectively, it also suggests that the distance could be used to rank new and unlabelled cases.

5   Conclusion

In this paper, we have proposed an approach based on geometry, which objective is to provide the end-user with information about the quality of the output of

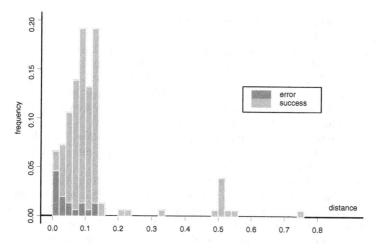

Fig. 2. Frequency histogram of the distance from the decision surface (Ionosphere)

a decision tree used as a prediction tool. Sensitivity analysis gives information that error rates cannot produce. Examples show that it easy to implement in the case of numerical decision trees with linear separators normal to axes. In the case of oblique trees, the main difficulty concerns the algorithm of projection onto a leaf, which is not as simple (but other algorithms could be used, see in [20]). The main limit of the method is that current efficient algorithms need a scalar product. However, the choice of the metric in order to apply sensitivity analysis is not as crucial as it is for other geometric method, where an optimal metric is sought to improve the classification efficiency. For sensitivity analysis the use of the metric is related to a particular point and it has a limited range. All we need is a metric that can be used in a relatively small neighborhood of a particular input case. If it is not possible to define a metric operating everywhere (particularly in the case of non numerical data), it will be necessary to define local metric and scalar product, depending on the domain, for instance by the way of cost or utility functions (or with the help of a domain expert).

The use of geometry was limited here to the definition of a metric for the sensitivity analysis. But it can also be used to describe the relative situation of a case in its own class. Further work is in progress to compute the projection of an input case onto the skeleton of its connected component and see how to use this information to give a global description of the case to the end-user.

References

1. Murthy, S.K.: Automatic Construction of Decision Trees from Data: A Multi-Disciplinary Survey. Data Mining and Knowledge Discovery, **2** 4 (1998) 345-389
2. Nelson L.M., Bloch D.A., Longstreth W. T., Shib H.: Recursive Partitioning for the Identification of Disease Risk Subgroups: A Case-Control Study of Subarachnoid Hemorrhage. Journal of Clinical Epidemiology 51, 3 (1998) 199-209

3. West, D.: Neural network credit scoring models. Computers & Operations Research 27 (2000) 1131-1152

4. Domingos, P.: MetaCost: A General Method for Making Classifiers Cost-Sensitive. Proc. of the Fifth Int. Conf. on K.D. and Data Mining (1999) 155-164

5. Sigillito, V., Blake, C.L., Merz, C.J. : Pima Indian Diabetes. UCI Repository of machine learning databases. University of California, Irvine (1990).

6. Burges, C.: A tutorial on support vector machines for pattern recognition. Data Mining and Knowledge Discovery Vol. 2, 2 (1998) 955-974

7. Platt, J.: Probabilistic outputs for support vector machines. In: Smola, A.J., Bartlett, P., Schoelkopf, B., Schuurmans, D. (eds.): Advances in Large Margin Classifiers. MIT Press (2000) 61-74

8. Domingos, P.: A Unified Bias-Variance Decomposition and its Applications. Proc. of the 17th Int. Conf. on Machine Learning: Morgan Kaufmann (2000) 231-238

9. Kohavi, R.: A study of cross-validation and bootstrap for accuracy estimation and model selection. Proc. Int. Joint Conf. on Artificial Intelligence (1995) 1137-1143

10. Provost, F., Fawcett, T.: Analysis and visualization of classifier performance: Comparison under imprecise class and cost distributions. Proc. Third Int. Conf. on Knowledge Discovery and Data Mining(1997) 43-48.

11. Jordan, M. I., Jacobs, R. A.: Hierarchical mixtures of experts and the EM algorithm. Neural Computation 6 (1994) 181-214

12. Umano, M., Okomato, K., Hatono, I., Tamura, H., Kawachi, F., Umezu, S., Kinoshita, J.: Proc. of the 3rd IEEE Int. Conf. on Fuzzy Systems (1994) 2113–2118

13. Quinlan, J. R.: C4.5: Programs for Machine Learning. Morgan Kaufmann (1993).

14. Breiman, L., Friedman, J. H., Olshen, R. A., Stone, C. J.: Classification and Regression Trees. Belmont: Wadsworth (1984)

15. Esposito, F., Malerba, D., Semeraro G.: A comparative analysis of methods for pruning decision trees. IEEE Trans. on Pattern Analysis and Machine Intelligence 19(5) (1997) 476-491

16. Cestnik, B.: Estimating probabilities: A crucial task in machine learning. In Proceedings of the European Conference on Artificial Intelligence (1990) 147-149

17. Domingos, P., Provost, F.: Well-trained PETs: Improving probability estimation trees. CDER Working Paper #00-04-IS Stern School of Business (2000)

18. Zadrozny, B., Elkan, C.: Obtaining calibrated probability estimates from decision trees and naive bayesian classifiers. Proc. of the 18th Int. Conf. on Machine Learning (2001) 609-616

19. Kearns, M. J., Ron, D.: Algorithmic stability and sanity-check bounds for leave-one-out cross-validation. Proc. of the Tenth Conf. on Computational Learning Theory (1997) 152-162

20. Bauschke, H., Borwein, J.M.: On projection algorithms for solving convex feasibility problems. SIAM Review 38, 3 (1996) 367-426.

21. Bennett, K., Blue, J.: Optimal decision trees. Technical Report 214. R.P.I. Math. Science Dept., Troy, NY 12180(1996).

22. Witten, I., Frank, E.: Data Mining: Practical Machine Learning Tools and Techniques with Java Implementation. Morgan Kaufmann (2000)

A Boosting Approach
to Multiple Instance Learning

Peter Auer and Ronald Ortner

University of Leoben, Franz-Josef-Strasse 18,
8700 Leoben, Austria
{auer,rortner}@unileoben.ac.at

Abstract. In this paper we present a boosting approach to multiple instance learning. As weak hypotheses we use balls (with respect to various metrics) centered at instances of positive bags. For the ∞-norm these hypotheses can be modified into hyper-rectangles by a greedy algorithm. Our approach includes a stopping criterion for the algorithm based on estimates for the generalization error. These estimates can also be used to choose a preferable metric and data normalization. Compared to other approaches our algorithm delivers improved or at least competitive results on several multiple instance benchmark data sets.

1 Introduction

Originally arising from a problem in biochemistry [6] multiple instance learning recently got a lot of attraction (see e.g. [1], [9], [24], [22]). Generally, in a multiple instance learning problem one has to classify sets (so-called *bags*) of instances, where each set is classified positively if it contains at least one instance with a certain property. The difficulty for learning this property is that it is unknown which of the instances is responsible for a positive classification of a bag.

Our motivation to investigate a boosting approach for multiple instance learning comes from object recognition in computer vision. For that we want to learn descriptions of object categories in images from labeled images, where the label indicates whether a relevant object is present in the image or not. Position and pose of the objects in the image are not known. Learning of such object categories by a boosting approach has been demonstrated in [16,10]. In these experiments local feature vectors in $\mathbb{R}^n$ were extracted from the training images, so that each image can be represented by its features. For a a positively classified image it is assumed that this is due to the presence of particular features. According to the training examples weak hypotheses for AdaBoost [7,20] are calculated that indicate if certain features are present in an image or not. This is done by comparing features with a similarity measure. More precisely, the weak hypotheses were chosen as balls around feature vector templates, such that an image is classified positively if it contains a feature vector sufficiently close to that template. Thereby, the templates are chosen from the feature vectors of the training images.

J.-F. Boulicaut et al. (Eds.): ECML 2004, LNAI 3201, pp. 63–74, 2004.

From a more abstract view this learning problem can be seen as multiple instance problem: Many objects – not only relevant ones – may be present in an image, and a feature may come from a relevant or irrelevant object. An image is classified positively if at least one relevant object is present. In fact, in this situation we have a generalized multiple instance problem since a relevant object may be described not necessarily by a single feature but by a combination of features: An image will be classified positively if a certain combination or number of relevant features can be extracted from it. Which of the feature vectors are relevant is initially unknown and has to be learned, what poses a typical (generalized) multiple instance problem.

In this paper we consider this boosting approach to multiple instance learning with balls as weak hypotheses in greater detail, and apply it to some of the multiple instance benchmark problems. We find this approach very competitive and it outperforms several other approaches to multiple instance learning.

Section 2 gives the formal details of the multiple instance setting, an overview of different approaches and a short introduction to AdaBoost, the boosting algorithm we apply. In Section 3 we describe in greater detail how we obtain our weak hypotheses, displaying how to calculate optimal balls, and also showing how suitable hyper-rectangles can be calculated by a greedy algorithm. In Section 4 we explain which experiments were conducted and how our algorithm performed compared to other approaches.

2   Multiple Instance Learning with Boosting

2.1   Multiple Instance Learning

Formally, the multiple instance learning problem we deal with is defined as follows. Let the instance space X be a set and $\mathcal{B}$ a finite collection of finite subsets of X. The elements of $\mathcal{B}$ are called *bags*. An unknown target function $y : \mathcal{B} \to \{+1, -1\}$ indicates whether a bag in $\mathcal{B}$ is classified as positive or negative. Actually, y is supposed to be an extension of a labeling function $y : X \to \{+1, -1\}$ such that a bag $B \in \mathcal{B}$ is classified positively iff it contains a positive element, that is, $y(B) = +1 \iff \exists x \in B : y(x) = +1$. The aim is to learn y from the training examples given in $\mathcal{B}$.

Of course, the considered problem setting is the simplest one can think about. We have already mentioned the possibility of more complex situations when describing applications to vision in the introduction. Thus in a generalized multiple instance setting a bag B is classified positively if e.g. at least a certain number of positive instances are contained in B. Another generalized multiple instance problem is introduced in [19].

Several approaches have been tried to offer solutions to multiple instance learning. Axis-parallel rectangles as hypotheses were used in [3] and [6]. Whereas [3] uses a single rectangle, which works quite well under some assumptions on the distribution of the data, in [6] the authors try to grow axis-parallel rectangles containing at least one instance from each positive bag and no instance from a negative bag. Scott et al. [19] adapt and improve an approach of Goldman et al.

[8] to learn d-dimensional patterns. The latter uses as hypotheses weighted combinations of hyper-rectangles over a discretized feature space, where the weights are learned with Winnow [12]. Scott's modification of the original algorithm allows learning in a generalized multiple instance setting as well. A different approach has been tried in [22]. The k nearest neighbors of a new bag (with respect to a certain distance measure) are taken and a majority vote decides, which label the new bag is assigned. Different variants of the k nearest neighbor concept are considered. The EM-DD algorithm of [24] combines the expected maximization (EM) algorithm with the diverse density (DD) algorithm [13, 14]. The DD algorithm tries to find a single instance that is responsible for the positive classification of a bag. More exactly, the key idea is to identify an instance to which many positive bags have close distances and to which instances of negative bags are far away. The diverse density is a measure that captures this concept and corresponds to the likelihood of the corresponding hypothesis, i.e., a high diverse density indicates a good candidate for a "true" hypothesis. Combining this with the idea of the EM algorithm yields the EM-DD algorithm. There are further approaches using neural networks [17], decision trees [18] and kernel methods [9].

2.2   A Boosting Approach

As already mentioned, our approach is to apply a boosting framework, which means given a set of hypotheses $\mathcal{H}$ we use a suitable subset $\mathcal{H}' \subseteq H$ of weak hypotheses that are combined to give a final hypothesis h_f. The AdaBoost [7, 20] algorithm we are going to use, calculates h_f by assigning weights w_B to the training examples $B \in \mathcal{B}$ and calculates weak hypotheses $h \in \mathcal{H}$ which correctly classify a majority (in respect to their weights) of the training examples. According to the error of such an h a weight α_h is calculated for the weak hypothesis. Furthermore, the weights w_B are recalculated such that more weight is put on the bags that were misclassified. The process of finding a suitable weak hypothesis $h \in \mathcal{H}$ and (re)calculating the weights w_B and α_h is repeated and the final hypothesis h_f is then obtained as weighted majority vote of the weak hypotheses, that is,

$$h_f(B) := sgn(\sum_{h \in \mathcal{H}'} \alpha_h h(B)),$$

where $\mathcal{H}' \subseteq \mathcal{H}$ is the set of used weak hypotheses.

Obviously, the weights of the bags can be normalized to sum up to 1 so that we obtain a distribution $w = (w_{B_1}, \ldots, w_{B_{|\mathcal{B}|}})$ over $\mathcal{B}$. Then given a distribution $w = (w_{B_1}, \ldots, w_{B_{|\mathcal{B}|}})$ one can judge the quality of a weak hypothesis via its *distribution accuracy*, which is defined as

$$D(h, w) := \sum_{\substack{B \in \mathcal{B}: \\ h(B)=y(B)}} w_B.$$

We demand from each weak hypothesis used by AdaBoost that its distribution accuracy is $> \frac{1}{2} + \varepsilon$ for some $\varepsilon > 0$. In this case it can be guarantueed that

AdaBoost's final hypothesis approximates the target function y with arbitrary high accuracy (cf. [7]).

In this paper we consider the instance space $X = \mathbb{R}^n$ and our weak hypotheses are balls of arbitrary center and radius with respect to some metric. Actually, our class $\mathcal{H}$ is a bit more restricted. Let $h(x, r)$ denote the open ball with center x and radius r. Then we choose $\mathcal{H}$ to be the set of all balls $h(x, r)$ whose center is contained in a bag $B \in \mathcal{B}$ with $y(B) = +1$. Furthermore, $\mathcal{H}$ shall contain the empty hypothesis. In Section 3 we describe how we determine for each center x the optimal radius r with respect to the current distribution accuracy. The prediction of a ball $h \in \mathcal{H}$ on a bag B is given by

$$h(B) := \begin{cases} +1 & \text{if } h \cap B \neq \emptyset \\ -1 & \text{otherwise.} \end{cases}$$

The following proposition shows that among these balls there is always a weak hypothesis with distribution accuracy larger than $\frac{1}{2} + \varepsilon$ for some fixed ε.

Proposition 1 *For each weight distribution* $w = (w_{B_1}, \dots, w_{B_{|\mathcal{B}|}})$ *there is a ball* $h = h(x, r)$ *in* $\mathcal{H}$ *such that* $D(h, w) > \frac{1}{2} + \frac{1}{4k+2}$, *where* k *is the number of positive bags in* $\mathcal{B}$.

Proof. Set $\gamma := \frac{1}{4k+2}$ and let W^- and W^+ be the sum of the weights of the negative and the positive bags, respectively. If $W^- > \frac{1}{2} + \gamma$ then it is obviously sufficient to choose the empty hypothesis from $\mathcal{H}$. If $W^+ > \frac{1}{2} + \gamma$ we choose an arbitrary x and a sufficiently large radius r so that $X \subset h(x, r)$.

Thus let us assume that $\frac{1}{2} - \gamma < W^-, W^+ \leq \frac{1}{2} + \gamma$. Clearly, there must be a positive bag B with weight $> \frac{1}{k}(\frac{1}{2} - \gamma)$. Then for a suitable $x \in B$ with $y(x) = +1$ and a sufficiently small radius so that $h(x, r) \cap X = \{x\}$ we have

$$D(h(x, r), w) > W^- + \frac{1}{k}\left(\frac{1}{2} - \gamma\right) > \frac{1}{2} - \gamma + \frac{1}{k}\left(\frac{1}{2} - \gamma\right) = \frac{1}{2} + \gamma$$

by some little calculation. $\qquad\square$

Remark 1. Obviously a weak hypothesis as in the second part of the proof is of little use since it learns a single instance by heart. To achieve reasonable generalization accuracy we need to find weak hypotheses which classify a significant number of training examples correctly.

Remark 2. Complementing Proposition 1 we would like to remind the reader of the following hardness result due to Auer, Long, and Srinivasan [4]. Consider the multiple-instance problem where each bag contains r instances $\in \mathbb{R}^n$ and a bag is classified positively if it contains an instance from an unknown hyper-rectangle. If for this problem there is a polynomial algorithm for learning from arbitrary distributions, then there is a polynomial algorithm for learning r-term DNF formulas over n variables as well. However, whether such an algorithm exists is one of the important unsolved problems of learning theory (see e.g. [11]). This result indicates that even in this rather simple setting multiple instance learning is a hard problem that probably cannot be solved efficiently in full generality.

3   The Algorithm

In this section we explain how to obtain a suitable set of balls, which will serve as weak hypotheses for AdaBoost.

3.1   Calculating the Optimal Ball

We compute for each x in a positive bag $B \in \mathcal{B}$ a ball with center x, such that its radius is optimal with respect to the current distribution w. More exactly, the optimal radius r_0 is defined as

$$r_0 = \max\{r' > 0 \mid D(h(x, r'), w) = \max_r D(h(x, r), w)\}. \qquad (1)$$

Note that we did not make any assumptions concerning the used metric so far. In our experiments we used the metric induced by the 2-norm and the ∞-norm, respectively. In the latter case, our balls are axis-parallel hypercubes.

Computing the optimal radius for each instance is time consuming. To speed up the computation the bags $B \in \mathcal{B}$ can be sorted by their distance to x, which is given by

$$d(x, B) = \min_{x_0 \in B} d(x_0, x)$$

for the chosen metric d. This procedure uses $O(mn + |\mathcal{B}| \log |\mathcal{B}|)$ operations per instance x, where n is the dimension of the instance space X and m is the total number of instances in bags of $\mathcal{B}$, i.e., $m = |\bigcup_{B \in \mathcal{B}} B|$. Taking into account the number of instances in positive bags introduces an additional factor of at most m into the overall complexity, so that the overall time complexity for computing the optimal ball is $O(\ell(mn + |\mathcal{B}| \log |\mathcal{B}|))$, where $\ell = |\bigcup_{B \in \mathcal{B}:y(B)=+1} B|$.

However, since AdaBoost computes a lot of iterations, one may compute the distance from each instance in a positive bag to each bag $B \in \mathcal{B}$ once and keep the corresponding distance matrix in memory. Thus the time complexity for one boosting iteration decreases to $O(\ell|\mathcal{B}| \log |\mathcal{B}|)$, which is much cheaper. Indeed, one may reduce this even to $O(\ell|\mathcal{B}|)$ by saving for each instance x the order of the bags with increasing distance to x.

3.2   Extension of the Optimal Hypercube

When using the metric induced by the ∞-norm we can extend the optimal hypercube computed according to the previous section. Since the radius of this $||\cdot||_\infty$-ball was chosen to be optimal with respect to the distribution accuracy, the latter surely decreases when the radius is increased. Thus each hypercube $h(x, r)$ has a *bad instance* x' on its boundary that is contained in some negative bag B'. Note that B' should be classified negatively according to $h(x, r)$ as well, because otherwise the inclusion of x' wouldn't make any difference to the prediction of B'. Obviously, the bad instance prevents our hypercube from growing, at least in some directions. However, we may grow the hypercube – which now turns into a hyper-rectangle – evenly in all other directions that are not blocked by x'. That way, one determines analogously to (1) above the optimal "radius" for all unblocked directions. Again, some directions are blocked by a bad instance and are accordingly fixed. This process is repeated until each direction is either fixed or the corresponding boundary is set to infinity, because there are no instances left in the respective direction. More formally, the algorithm can be described as follows:

1. Initially the hyper-rectangle $R = \times_{i=1}^{n}(a_i, b_i)$ we consider is the optimal hypercube $h(x, r_0)$. The set F contains the directions which are already fixed, where each direction is represented by the index of the coordinate and a sign indicating whether the positive or the negative direction of the respective coordinate is fixed. Initially, $F := \varnothing$.
2. Determine the bad instance x', that is, the instance on the boundary of R that is contained in some bag B' for which $y(B') = -1$ and $B' \cap R = \varnothing$. If there is more than one instance with that property, choose an arbitrary one.
3. Update F according to the directions blocked by the bad instance x', that is,

$$(i, +) \in F \iff x_i' = b_i,$$
$$(i, -) \in F \iff x_i' = a_i.$$

4. Determine analogously to (1) the optimal "radius" r with respect to distribution accuracy for all directions that are not fixed yet.
5. Update R as follows:

$$a_i := \begin{cases} a_i & \text{if } (i, -) \in F \\ x_i - r & \text{otherwise,} \end{cases} \quad \text{and} \quad b_i := \begin{cases} b_i & \text{if } (i, +) \in F \\ x_i + r & \text{otherwise.} \end{cases}$$

6. Repeat steps 2–5 until each direction is fixed or r was set to infinity.

Obviously, the computation of hyper-rectangles as described above requires multiple passes over the instances and is therefore quite expensive. However, if one sorts the instances within the bags by their distance to the center of the initial optimal hypercube, one can increment the pointers and one pass over all the instances is sufficient. This improvement decreases the running time for the computation of the hyper-rectangle from a hypercube to $O((\ell + n)|\mathcal{B}| \log |\mathcal{B}|)$, where n is the dimension of the instance space X and $\ell = \sum_{B \in \mathcal{B}:y(B)=+1} |B|$ is the number of positive instances.

4   Experiments

4.1   The Data Sets

The musk data set [6,5] originates from the already mentioned problem in biochemistry. One observes different conformations of a molecule and wants to know if a "musk-like" conformation exists for this molecule. For each molecule one is given the set of stable conformations, which constitute a bag as in the definition of the multiple instance problem. A bag is labeled positive, if it contains a musk-like conformation.

The data sets musk1 and musk2 consist of 92 and 102 bags which contain a total of 476 and 6598 instances, respectively, each of which is 168-dimensional.

The robot data set [19] consists of 12 learning problems which are constructed from a basis of 28 bags divided into four categories A,B,C, and D of equal size. Each bag consists of (in average about 34) 2-dimensional instances which represent a 360° light intensity measurement of a robot at a certain position in space. The seven bags in each of the groups A,B,C, and D consist of 'similar' positions.

The learning task is to learn concepts which separate each of the four groups from any two of the others. We label the corresponding learning problems by 'AposBCneg','AposBDneg' etc. corresponding to the choice of groups.

The protein data set [23] consists of 20 positive bags paired with 8 different sets of 20 resp. 28 different negative bags. The data itself is 8-dimensional and consists of 7 characteristics of a protein sequence and information about the position of the window on the whole protein sequence in the remaining coordinate.

4.2   A Stopping Criterion for AdaBoost

For our tests we used the following stopping criterion for the number of boosting iterations. By a leave-one-out cross-validation on the *training examples*[1] we calculated estimates for the generalization error when AdaBoost is run on the *remaining* training examples until the error reached $P\%$, $P = 99, \ldots, 0$. The P^* with the best estimated generalization error was chosen and AdaBoost was run on all training examples until the training error reached $P^*\%$, giving the final hypothesis.

For some data sets it might be advisable to continue boosting even when the training error has reached 0% (cf. [21]). We did not explore this for the data sets we used. However, in this situation a similar approach can be taken to choose the number of boosting iterations: Let M be the number of iterations until training error 0 is reached. Estimate the generalization error when AdaBoost is run for $M \cdot \alpha^k$ iterations, $k = 1, 2, \ldots$, $\alpha > 1$, and choose the best k^*.

4.3   Various Combinations of Metric and Attribute Normalization

We performed experiments with various combinations of metric and attribute normalization. In this respect an interesting question is, if the estimated generalization error from the stopping criterion is a good indicator for which metric and attribute normalization should be chosen. The results seem to answer this question affirmatively. We used the following combinations:

cubes: The weak hypotheses for AdaBoost are balls with respect to the ∞-norm, i.e. axis-parallel hypercubes. No normalization is used.

rectangles: The weak hypotheses for AdaBoost are axis-parallel hyper-rectangles. The hypothesis is grown from the optimal hypercube by the greedy algorithm described in Section 3.2.

---

[1] This is not to be confused with the cross-validation for estimating the test error. No test examples were used by the stopping criterion.

Table 1. Generalization error (GE) and estimated error (EE) for various combinations of metric and normalization for the robot data set.

data set	cubes	rect.	median	minmax	$\|\cdot\|_2$	$\mathcal{N}(0,1)$	$\mathcal{N}(0,I)$
AposBCneg GE	0.1429	0	0.1905	0.0476	0.0952	0.0952	0.0952
AposBCneg EE	0.079	0.0752	0.0833	0.0786	0.0786	0.0781	0.0767
AposBDneg GE	0.1429	0.1429	0.1905	0.0476	0.0952	0.0476	0.0476
AposBDneg EE	0.0438	0.0438	0.0919	0.0381	0.0424	0.0381	0.0381
AposCDneg GE	0.2857	0.0526	0.1429	0.1429	0.0476	0.1905	0.1905
AposCDneg EE	0.0805	0.031	0.0448	0.0448	0.081	0.0348	0.0348
BposACneg GE	0	0	0	0	0	0	0
BposACneg EE	0	0	0	0	0	0	0
BposADneg GE	0	0	0	0	0	0	0
BposADneg EE	0	0	0	0	0	0	0
BposCDneg GE	0	0	0	0	0	0	0
BposCDneg EE	0	0	0	0	0	0	0
CposABneg GE	0	0	0	0	0	0	0
CposABneg EE	0	0	0	0	0	0	0
CposADneg GE	0.2857	0.2857	0	0	0.381	0	0
CposADneg EE	0.0333	0.0333	0	0	0.0295	0	0
CposBDneg GE	0	0	0	0	0	0	0.
CposBDneg EE	0	0	0	0	0	0	0
DposABneg GE	0	0	0	0	0	0	0
DposABneg EE	0	0	0	0	0	0	0
DposACneg GE	0	0	0.1905	0.1905	0	0	0
DposACneg EE	0	0	0.0324	0.0324	0	0	0
DposBCneg GE	0	0	0.381	0	0	0.2381	0.1905
DposBCneg EE	0	0	0.0443	0	0	0.0329	0.0324

median: The data are preprocessed by linearly transforming each coordinate separately, such that the range between the two quartiles is mapped to the interval $[-1,1]$. If the two quartiles are equal, the interval is only centered at the quartiles. Hypercubes are used as weak hypotheses.

minmax: The data are preprocessed by linearly transforming each coordinate, such that the range $[min, max]$ of each coordinate is mapped to the interval $[-1,1]$. Hypercubes are used as weak hypotheses.

$\|\cdot\|_2$: 2-norm balls are used as weak hypotheses. Data are not normalized.

$\mathcal{N}(0,1)$: Each coordinate is linearly transformed for mean 0 and variance 1. 2-norm balls are then used as weak hypotheses.

$\mathcal{N}(0,I)$: A linear transformation of all instances is chosen such that the mean of all attributes is 0 and the covariance matrix is the identity. Then 2-norm balls are used as weak hypotheses.

4.4   The Results

The results for the robot data set are shown in Table 1, which displays the generalization error (GE) calculated by leave-one-out cross-validation, and the best estimated generalization error (EE) calculated by the stopping criterion[2]. For the various combinations of metric and attribute normalization the results show a quite good agreement between the ranking of the generalization error and the ranking of the estimated error.

Table 2. Generalization error of the boosting approach and [19] for the robot data.

data set	Boosting	[19]
AposBCneg	0	0
AposBDneg	0.0476	0.0952
AposCDneg	0.0476	0.0476
BposACneg	0	0.0952
BposADneg	0	0.0952
BposCDneg	0	0
CposABneg	0	0.0952
CposADneg	0	0
CposBDneg	0	0
DposABneg	0	0.0476
DposACneg	0	0
DposBCneg	0	0
Average	0.0079	0.0396

In Table 2 we compare our results with the algorithm by Scott et al. [19] (cf. Section 2.1). For this we have chosen that combination of metric and normalization with the minimal estimated error from the stopping criterion. As can be seen our algorithm outperforms the algorithm of [19].

Table 3. Generalization error (GE) and estimated error (EE) for various combinations of metric and normalization for the musk data sets.

data set	cubes	rect.	median	minmax	$\|\| \cdot \|\|_2$	$\mathcal{N}(0,1)$	$\mathcal{N}(\mathbf{0}, I)$
musk1 GE	0.1511	0.0804	0.2293	0.1554	0.1196	0.088	0.3717
musk1 EE	0.0515	0.0131	0.111	0.058	0.0456	0.0708	0.2469
musk2 GE	0.1402	0.0578	0.1912	0.1431	0.1265	0.1294	0.1902
musk2 EE	0.0824	0.0549	0.0737	0.0515	0.0403	0.0309	0.1215

The results for the musk data as summarized in Table 3 are based on a 10-fold cross-validation, where the values are averaged over ten runs. A comparison of the different approaches was taken from [2] and is reported in Table 4. Again, the numbers for the boosting approach are those that have the minimal estimated error from the stopping criterion. We find that our approach is quite competitive with these other approaches.

To obtain comparable results with [23] for the protein data sets the tests were performed in the following way: For each of the 8 sets of negative bags and each

---

[2] The estimated error (EE) is averaged over all runs of the leave-one-out cross-validation for (GE).

Table 4. Generalization error of the boosting approach and [6, 15] for the musk data.

data set	Boosting	IAPR[6]	DD[15]
musk1	0.08	0.076	0.12
musk2	0.129	0.108	0.16

of the 20 positive bags, a classifier is trained where the set of negative bags and the remaining 19 positive bags are used as training examples, resulting in 160 classifiers. Then each bag is assigned to the majority class among all classifiers for which it was not used as training example. The error of this classification by majority is reported as the generalization error for the positive and negative bags. The results are summarized in Table 5. With the exception of the $\mathcal{N}(\mathbf{0}, I)$-normalization our boosting approach again outperforms the competing approach.

Table 5. Generalization error of the boosting approach and [23] for the protein data.

Protein	cubes	rect.	median	minmax	$\|\cdot\|_2$	$\mathcal{N}(0,1)$	$\mathcal{N}(\mathbf{0}, I)$	[23]
Pos. bags	0	0	0	0	0	0	1	0.25
Neg. bags	0.036	0.095	0.036	0.036	0.036	0.036	0	0.25

5   Conclusion

We presented a boosting approach to multiple instance learning that was inspired by problems stemming from generic object recognition. In this context the application of the AdaBoost algorithm with suitable weak hypotheses worked consistently well. Our approach with balls as weak hypotheses improves over or is at least competitive to other approaches. We think that the results strongly benefit from the introduced stopping criterion. The estimated generalization error used by the stopping criterion also turns out to be a good indicator for choosing a distance metric and an attribute normalization.

Since – as already mentioned in the introduction – computer vision seems to be an obvious area of application for multiple instance learning, and due to the encouraging results so far, we will incorporate our findings in future work on object recognition problems.

Acknowlegements

This work was supported by the European project LAVA (IST-2001-34405). We would like to thank Thomas Korimort for implementing the algorithms and conducting some of the tests.

References

1. Amar, R.A., Dooly, D.R., Goldman, S.A., Zhang, Q.: Multiple-instance learning of real-valued data. In: Proceedings of the Eighteenth International Conference on Machine Learning (ICML 2001), Morgan Kaufmann (2001) 3–10
2. Andrews, S., Tsochantaridis, I., Hofmann T.: Support vector machines for multiple instance learning. In: Advances in Neural Information Processing Systems 15. Papers from Neural Information Processing Systems (NIPS 2002), MIT Press (2002)
3. Auer, P.: On learning from multi-instance examples: Empirical evaluation of a theoretical approach. In: Proceedings of the Fourteenth International Conference on Machine Learning (ICML 1997), Morgan Kaufmann (1997) 21–29
4. Auer, P., Long, P.M., Srinivasan, A.: Approximating hyper-rectangles: Learning and pseudorandom sets, *J. Comput. Syst. Sci.* **57**(3): 376-388 (1998)
5. Blake, C.L., Merz, C.J.: UCI repository of machine learning databases [http://www.ics.uci.edu/~mlearn/MLRepository.html]. Irvine, CA: University of California, Department of Information and Computer Science (1998)
6. Dietterich, T.G., Lathrop, R.H., Lozano-Pérez, T.: Solving the multiple instance problem with axis-parallel rectangles. In: *Artif. Intell.* **89** (1-2): 31–71 (1997)
7. Freund, Y., Schapire, R.E.: A decision-theoretic generalization of on-line learning and an application to boosting. In: *J. Comput. Syst. Sci.* **55**(1): 119–139 (1997)
8. Goldman, S.A., Kwek, S.K., Scott, S.D.: Agnostic learning of geometric patterns. In: *J. Comput. Syst. Sci.* **62**(1): 123–151 (2001)
9. Gärtner, T., Flach, P.A., Kowalczyk, A., Smola, A.J.: Multi-instance kernels. In: Machine Learning. Proceedings of the Nineteenth International Conference (ICML 2002), Morgan Kaufmann (2002) 179-186
10. Fussenegger, M., Opelt, A., Pinz, A., Auer, P.: Object recognition using segmentation for feature detection. Accepted for ICPR 2004 (2004)
11. Klivans, A., Servedio, R.A.: Learning DNF in time $2^{\tilde{O}(n^{1/3})}$ In: Proceedings on 33rd Annual ACM Symposium on Theory of Computing (STOC 2001), ACM (2001) 258-265
12. Littlestone, N.: Learning quickly when irrelevant attributes abound: A new linear threshold algorithm. In: *Machine Learning* **2**(4): 285-318 (1988)
13. Maron, O.: Learning from ambiguity. Technical Report AITR-1639 (1998)
14. Maron, O., Lozano-Pérez, T.: A framework for multiple-instance learning. In: Advances in Neural Information Processing Systems 10 (NIPS 1997), MIT Press (1998)
15. Maron, O., Ratan, A.L.: Multiple-instance learning for natural scene classification. In: Proceedings of the Fifteenth International Conference on Machine Learning (ICML 1998), Morgan Kaufmann (1998) 341-349
16. Opelt, A., Fussenegger, M., Pinz, A., Auer, P.: Weak hypotheses and boosting for generic object detection and recognition. In: Computer Vision - ECCV 2004. 8th European Conference on Computer Vision. Proceedings, Part II. Lecture Notes in Computer Science 3022, Springer (2004) 71-84
17. Ramon, J., Raedt, L.D.: Multi instance neural networks. In: Proceedings of IMCL-2000 workshop on Attribute-Value and Relational Learning (2000)
18. Ruffo, G.: Learning single and multiple instance decision trees for computer security applications. Doctoral dissertation. Department of Computer Science, University of Turin, Torino, Italy (2000)

19. Scott, S.D., Zhang, J., Brown, J.: On generalized multiple-instance learning. Technical report UNL-CSE-2003-5, University of Nebraska (2003)
20. Schapire, R.: The boosting approach to machine learning: An overview. In: MSRI Workshop on Nonlinear Estimation and Classification, Berkeley, CA, Mar. (2001)
21. Schapire, R.E., Freund, Y., Bartlett, P., Lee, W.S.: Boosting the margin: A new explanation for the effectiveness of voting methods. In: *Ann. Statist.* **25**(5): 1651–1686 (1998)
22. Wang, J., Zucker, J.D.: Solving the multiple-instance problem: A lazy learning approach. In: Proceedings of the Seventeenth International Conference on Machine Learning (ICML 2000), Morgan Kaufmann, San Francisco, CA (2000) 1119–1126
23. Wang, C., Scott, S.D., Zhang, J., Tao, Q., Fomenko, D.E., Gladyshev, V.N. : A study in modeling low-conservation protein superfamilies. Technical report UNL-CSE-2004-0003, University of Nebraska (2004)
24. Zhang, Q., Goldman, S.: EM-DD: An improved multiple-instance learning technique. In: Advances in Neural Information Processing Systems 14 (NIPS 2001), MIT Press (2001) 1073–1080

An Experimental Study of Different Approaches to Reinforcement Learning in Common Interest Stochastic Games

Avi Bab and Ronen Brafman

Ben-Gurion University, Beer-Sheva 84105, Israel

Abstract. Stochastic (a.k.a. Markov) Games pose many unsolved problems in Game Theory. One class of stochastic games that is better understood is that of Common Interest Stochastic Games (CISG). CISGs form an interesting class of multi-agent settings where the distributed nature of the systems, rather than adverserial behavior, is the main challenge to efficient learning. In this paper we examine three different approaches to RL in CISGs, embedded in the FriendQ, OAL, and Rmax algorithms. We show the performance of the above algorithms on some non-trivial games that illustrate the advantages and disadvantages of the different approaches.

1 Introduction

Learning in Common Interest Stochastic Games (CISGs) provides an interesting intermediate ground between single-agent reinforcement learning (RL) [1] and general multi-agent RL (MARL). CISGs pose all the standard challenges of single-agent RL, in particular the need to balance exploration and exploitation [2] and to exhaust information (i.e propagate new experience) [1,3]. In addition, they challenge the agents to coordinate behavior, without confronting the more difficult task of optimizing behavior against an adversary [4].

CISGs require inter-agent coordination at two levels: (i) selecting whether to explore or exploit in unison; (ii) coordinating the exploration and exploitation moves. This requirement stems from the dependence of the team's next state on the actions of *all* its members. Hence, it is impossible for the team to explore (or exploit) unless all agents explore/exploit together. Moreover, even when the model is known, multiple Nash equilibria are likely to exist, and the agents still face the task of reaching consensus on which specific Nash equilibrium to play.

We compare three algorithms for learning in CISGs: OAL [5], FriendQ [6], and Rmax [7]. They were selected because each embodies a different approach to these learning tasks, while guaranteeing convergence to optimal behavior in CISGs. We examine diverse variants of these algorithms with the aim of gaining better understanding of their performance w.r.t. their approach to exploration-exploitation, information exhaustion, and coordination tasks.

The main phenomenon demonstrated by our experiments is the high sensitivity of FriendQ and OAL to the topology and dynamics of the environment vs. Rmax's stability. Even moderate-sized physical domains lead to numerous

J.-F. Boulicaut et al. (Eds.): ECML 2004, LNAI 3201, pp. 75–86, 2004.

Nash-equilibria, where Rmax's exploration bias, efficient implicit model-based coordination and information exhaustion lead to superior performance.

The paper is structured as follows: Section 2 provides the necessary background on multi-agent reinforcement learning. Section 3 describes the algorithms involved. Section 4 describes our experiments, and Section 5 concludes the paper.

2   Multi-agent Reinforcement Learning

In MARL, the environment is modeled as a Stochastic Game(SG). An SG is a tuple $\langle P, S, A, R, T \rangle$ where: P is a set of n agents; S, a state space; $A = \times A_{i=1...n}$, a set of joint-actions, where A_i is the set of private-actions available to agent i; $R = \{R_1, R_2, \ldots, R_n\}$ is a set of reward functions for the agents where $R_i : S \times A \to \mathbb{R}$ is the reward function for agent i and $R_i(s, a)$ is the expected reward for agent i when joint action $a \in A$ is performed in state $s \in S$; and $T : S \times A \times S \to [0, 1]$ is a stochastic transition function where $T(s, a, s')$ is the probability of reaching state s' when joint action a is played in state s. In CISGs, all agents have identical interests, i.e., $R_i = R_j \ \forall i, j \in P$.

Each agent in an SG attempts to maximize its expected value, i.e., its expected sum of discounted rewards: $E[\sum_{t=0}^{\infty} \gamma^t (r_{i,t})]$ where $r_{i,t}$ is agent i's reward at time t, and $\gamma \in (0, 1)$ is a discount factor. In CISGs, this means that agents attempt to maximize their common expected value. Thus, CISGs can model RL by a distributed team of agents.

A deterministic *joint policy* $\pi = \{\pi_1 \ldots \pi_n\}$ is a mapping from states to joint actions where $\pi_i(s)$ is agent i's part of the joint action $\pi(s) = (\pi_1(s), \ldots, \pi_n(s))$. Every CISG has at least one deterministic policy π^* that achieves optimal value. Any such policy π^* satisfies $\pi^*(s) = argmax_a Q^*(s, a)$. $Q^*(s, a)$ is called the Q value of s and a. It is the expected sum of rewards received for taking action a in state s and behaving optimally thereafter, i.e.,: $Q^*(s, a) = R(s, a) + \gamma \sum_{s' \in S} T(s, a, s') \max_{a' \in A} Q^*(s', a')$.

A joint policy $\{\pi_1 ... \pi_n\}$ is a *Nash equilibrium* if each individual policy π_i is a best response to the others. That is $V(s, \{\pi_1 ... \pi_i ... \pi_n\}) \geq V(s, \{\pi_1 ... \pi_i' ... \pi_n\})$ for all $i \in P$, $s \in S$, and individual policy $\pi_i' \neq \pi_i$, and where $V(s, \pi)$ is the expected return when joint policy π is played starting from state s. An *optimal Nash equilibrium* is a Nash equilibrium that maximizes the expected return.

We shall concentrate on CISG learning under *perfect monitoring*, where each agent sees the actions of all agents. OAL and FriendQ rely on this assumption. Rmax can handle scenarios in which each agent sees its own private action only.

3   The Learning Algorithms

Next we describe the three different reinforcement learning algorithms we studied.

3.1   FriendQ

FriendQ [6] extends basic Q-learning into CISGs. It attempts to learn Q-values without maintaining a model of the environment. After taking a joint action

$a = (a_1, ..., a_n)$ in state s at time t and reaching state s' with reward r_{imm} the agents update the Q-value of $\langle s, a \rangle$ as follows:

$$Q_t(s, a_1, \ldots, a_n) \leftarrow (1 - \alpha_t)Q_{t-1}(s, a_1, \ldots, a_n) +$$
$$+ \alpha_t(r_{imm} + \gamma \max_{b_1, \ldots, b_n} Q(s', b_1, \ldots, b_n))$$

where $\alpha_t \in (0, 1]$ is a learning rate parameter and γ the discount factor. Given that $\sum_{t=0}^{\infty} \alpha_t = \infty$, $\sum_{t=0}^{\infty} \alpha_t^2 < \infty$ and that every joint action is performed infinitely often in every state, the Q-values are guaranteed to converge asymptotically to Q^* [8]. In online learning, convergence to optimal behavior is considered. This is achieved using "Greedy in the Limit with Infinite Exploration"(GLIE) learning policies. In GLIE every state-action pair is visited infinitely often, and in the limit, the action selection is greedy w.r.t. the Q-values w.p.1. Two common GLIE policies are Boltzman distributed action selection and ϵ-greedy action selection. FriendQ lacks a measure for private actions, required for Boltzman exploration, so we use it with ϵ-greedy exploration only. In ϵ-greedy exploration, each agent randomly picks an exploratory private-action with probability ϵ, and with probability $1 - \epsilon$ takes it's part of an optimal (greedy) joint-action w.r.t. the current Q-value. ϵ is asymptotically decreased to zero over time.

All agents make the same observations, so they maintain identical Q-values. But two problems arise: (i) Because randomization is used to select exploration *or* exploitation, the agents cannot coordinate their choice of when and what to explore. (ii) In case of multiple optimal policies, i.e., several joint actions with maximal Q values in a certain state, the agents must agree on one such action. The original FriendQ algorithm has no explicit mechanism for handling these issues. Here, we examined some enhanced versions of FriendQ: We begin with Uncoordinated FriendQ (UFQ), the simple version described above. We then examine the effect of adding coordination of greedy joint actions by utilizing techniques introduced in [9], basically, a shared order over joint actions is used for selecting among equivalent Nash equilibria. If such an order is not built into the agents, it is established during a preliminary phase (see [9] for more details). This version is referred to as Coordinated FriendQ (CFQ). For comparison we also combine this equilibrium selection technique with the model based Q-learning algorithm used by OAL. We call this combination ModelQ (MQ). We continue with Deterministic FriendQ (DFQ) in which the agents explore and exploit in unison, always exploring the least tried joint action. An exploratory action is taken each $\lfloor 1/\epsilon \rfloor'th$ move. Finally we add Eligibility Traces [1] to DFQ (ETDFQ).

3.2 OAL

OAL [5] combines classic model-based Q-learning with a new fictitious play algorithm for action and equilibrium selection named BAP (Biased Adaptive Play). The Q-value update rule is:

$$Q_{t+1}(s, a) = R_t(s, a) + \gamma \sum_{s'} T_t(s, a, s') \max_{a'} Q_t(s', a')$$

where R_t, the approximated mean reward, and T_t, the approximated transition probability are estimated using the statistics gathered up to time t. Using GLIE policy, OAL converges in the limit to optimal behavior.

An OAL agent records the last m joint-actions taken at each state. Each round, the agent randomly samples k joint-actions from the last m joint-actions ($k < m$) taken at the current state. Greedy private-action selection is done using BAP. BAP treats the stage-games in the CISG (the single-state games induced by the Q-values at each state). At each round BAP builds and plays a Virtual Game (VG) for the current stage-game. The VG has reward 1 for any optimal equilibrium and reward 0 for all other joint actions. Unless equilibrium-selection conditions are met, BAP chooses the best response private-action according to the current model and w.r.t. the current history sample, i.e., private-action that maximizes expected payoff assuming the history sample represents the other agents strategies[1]. If equilibrium selection conditions are met – i.e., if in all k current samples the other agents chose the same part of some optimal equilibrium (w.r.t. the current VG) and if, in at least one of the k samples, a complete optimal joint action was played – the agent plays its part of the last such action in the sample. (Recall that different agents may sample different past plays).

OAL can use Boltzman distributed exploration. In Boltzman exploration a private action $a_i \in A_i$ is taken with probability $\frac{e^{ER(a_i)/\tau}}{\sum_{a' \in A_i} e^{ER(a')/\tau}}$ where $ER(a_i)$ is the expected payoff of private-action a_i. τ, the temperature, is a positive parameter decreased over time asymptotically to zero. High temperatures cause the actions to be all nearly equi-probable and when $\tau \to 0$ action selection becomes completely greedy. We also examine OAL with an addition of Prioritized Sweeping [3] to the underlying Q-learning algorithm (PSOAL).

3.3   Rmax

Rmax [7] is a model-based algorithm designed to handle learning in MDPs and in zero-sum stochastic games. The agent maintains a model of the environment, initialized in a particular optimistic manner. It always behaves optimally w.r.t. its current model, while updating this model (and hence its behavior) when new observations are made. Because the initialization and model-update steps are deterministic, so is the whole algorithm. Recall that a CISG can be viewed as an MDP controlled by a distributed team. [9] observes that such a team can coordinate its behavior given a deterministic algorithm such as Rmax. At each point in time, all agents have an identical model of the environment and know what joint-action needs to be executed next[2]. Thus, each agent plays its part of this action. When a number of actions are optimal w.r.t. the current state, the agents utilize a shared order over joint-actions to select among these actions. [9] shows how such an order can be set-up, how even weaker coordination devices that do not require such an order can be used, and how these ideas can be employed even under imperfect monitoring.

The model M' used by Rmax consists of $n + 1$ states $S' = \{s_0, ..., s_n\}$ where $s_1, ..., s_n$ correspond to the real states and s_0 is a fictitious state[3]. The transition

---

[1] This is known as fictitious play [10].

[2] Knowledge of fellow agents (private) action sets can be acquired online.

[3] The model may be constructed online as states are discovered.

probabilities in M' are initialized to $T_{M'}(s, a, s_0) = 1 \; \forall \langle s, a \rangle \in S' \times A$. The reward function is initialized to $R_{M'}(s, a) = R_{max} \; \forall \langle s, a \rangle \in S' \times A$, where R_{max} is an upper bound on $max_{s \in S, a \in A} R(s, a)$. Each state/joint-action pair in M' is classified either as *known* or as *unknown*. Initially, all entries are unknown.

Rmax computes an optimal policy with respect to M' and follows this policy until some entry becomes known. It keeps the following records: (i) number of times each action was taken at each state and the resulting state. (ii) the actual rewards r_{ac} received at each entry. An entry (s, a) becomes known after it has been sampled $K1$ times, such that with high probability $T_M(s, a, s') - \rho \leq PE(s, a, s'|K1) \leq T_M(s, a, s') + \rho$ where T_M is the transition function in M, $PE(s, a, \cdot |K1)$ the empirical transition probability according to the $K1$ samples, and ρ the accuracy required from M'. When (s, a) becomes known the following updates are made: $T_{M'}(s, a, \cdot) \leftarrow PE(s, a, \cdot |K1)$ and $R_{M'}(s, a) \leftarrow r_{ac}(s, a)$. Once a new entry becomes known, Rmax computes the new deterministic optimal policy w.r.t. the updated model M' and follows it.

The known (worst-case) polynomial bounds on $K1$ are impractical. In the experiments we violated these bounds. This enables to eliminate knowledge of the state space size. We also do not assume R_{max} is known, instead we initialize R_{max} to some positive value and update it online to be twice the highest reward encountered so far.

3.4   Discussion of Algorithms

Efficiency of GLIE learning policies depends on the topology and dynamics of the environment. If the probability to explore falls low before "profitable" parts of the environment are sufficiently sampled, the increasing bias to exploit may keep the agents in sub-optimal states. This means that GLIE policies can exhibit significant differences depending on the particular schedule of exploration. GLIE policies also suffer from their inability to completely stop exploration at some point. Thus, even when greedy behavior is optimal, the agent is unable to attain optimal return. The exploration method of Rmax is less susceptive to the structure of the environment. As long as Rmax cannot achieve actual reward ϵ-close to optimal it will have a strong bias for exploration since unknown entries seem very attractive. This strategy is profitable when the model can be learned in a short time. However, the theoretical worst-case bounds for convergence in Rmax [7] are impractical. In practice, much lower values of $K1$ suffice. Bayesian exploration [11,12] and locality considerations might help to obtain better adaptive bounds, but we did not pursue these approaches here.

GLIE makes learning "slower" as the agents get "older". To accelerate learning one must use new experience in an exhaustive manner (i.e, use current experience to improve behavior in previously visited states). Eligibility traces are used to propagate information in model-free algorithms. In model-based algorithms an exhaustive computation per new experience is too expensive (in cpu time) and Prioritized Sweeping [3] is a well known solution, yet not exhaustive. Rmax makes one exhaustive computation each time a new entry becomes known (and does no further computation).

Exploration in FriendQ and OAL algorithms is not coordinated. Each of the agents independently chooses an exploratory action with some diminishing probability. Thus, joint-actions that have no element (private-action) of some optimal joint-action have a lower chance of being explored. Hence, some popular techniques for decreasing exploration in the single agent case lead to finite exploration in the multi agent case. For example taking $\epsilon = 1/time$ for ϵ-greedy policies will make the chance of exploring such joint actions $1/time^n$, where n is the number of agents.

Equilibrium selection in Rmax and CFQ comes with no cost. In OAL it is essentially a random protocol for achieving consensus. This protocol may take long to reach consensus w.r.t. the current Q-values, but provides for another exploration mechanism at early stages, when Q-values are frequently updated.

Parameter tuning is task specific and based more on intuition and trial and error than on theoretical results. FriendQ has a range of parameters for decaying the learning rate, the exploration probability and the eligibility traces which also pose inter-parameter dependencies. For decreasing the learning rate parameter we used the results presented in [13]. OAL takes parameters for history sample size and for exploration. In this respect, we found Rmax superior. It has a single and very intuitive parameter - number of visits to declare an entry *known*.

4   Experimental Results and Analysis

We exhibit results on two 2-agent grid games. The games were designed to evaluate the effects of exploration, coordination and information exhaustion methods on performance in different environments. The game environments are grids in which the agents can move using the actions *up, down, left, right, stand*. Agent position pairs constitute the state space of the underlying stochastic game.

The games were played under deterministic and stochastic transition probabilities. In stochastic mode, each action (excluding *stand*) succeeds with probability 0.6. With probability 0.1 the agent is moved to an adjacent cell or stays in place. *stand* succeeds w.p.1.

We tested the algorithms on the first set of experimental conditions (see below Game1 with deterministic setup) with a range of different parameters. The parameters that achieved best results were then used throughout:

FriendQ
Exploration: ϵ-greedy with – (i) $\epsilon_t \leftarrow 1/count_t^{0.5000001}$ where $count_t$ is the number of exploratory steps taken by time t. (ii) $\epsilon_t \leftarrow 0.99998^{count_t}$. (unless specified otherwise, (i) is used)[4]. **Learning rate:** $\alpha_{s,a} \leftarrow 1/n(s,a)^{0.5000001}$ where $n(s,a)$ is the number of times action a was taken in state s.

OAL
Exploration: For ϵ-greedy, $\epsilon_t \leftarrow 1/count_t^{0.5000001}$, as in FriendQ. For Boltzman exploration the temperature parameter was decreased by $\tau \leftarrow 100/count^{0.7}$ **History:** Random history sample size = 5. History memory size $m = 20$ (m must

---

[4] Exponential decay of ϵ violates the "infinite exploration" condition for convergence.

satisfy $m \geq k \times (number\ of\ agents + 2)$.) We refer to OAL with ϵ-greedy exploration as ϵ-OAL, and to OAL with Boltzman exploration as B-OAL.

Rmax

Sampling: values of 50, 100, 200 for K1 (visits to mark an entry known) were tested. **Accuracy of policy iteration:** Offline policy iterations was halted when the difference between two successive approximations was less than 0.001

Each set of experimental conditions, other than those related to Rmax, was subjected to 100 repeated trials. For Rmax, 20 trials were done using K1=50, 40 with K1=100 and 40 with K1=200. The discount factor was 0.98 in all trials.

Fig. 1. Game 1 - Initial and Goal states.

4.1   Game 1

This game was devised to emphasize the effects of equilibrium selection methods. It has a single goal state (the only reward yielding state) and several optimal ways of reaching it. The game is depicted in Figure 1. $S(X)$ and $T(X)$ are the respective initial and goal positions of agent X. The underlying SG has 71 states. The goal state T (both agents in goal positions) generates a reward of 48. Upon reaching the goal the agents are reset to their initial position. The optimal behavior is to reach T in four steps. Under deterministic setup, this yields an average reward per step of 12. There are 11 optimal different equilibria. The optimal policies are the same under the stochastic setting, with ~6.14 average reward per step. Algorithms were executed for 10^7 rounds on both settings. For the deterministic setup Table 1 classifies the number of trials (of 100 in total) according to the algorithms and learned policies. Here xFQ is a variant of FriendQ in which the agents explore in unison but do not coordinate exploratory actions. The suffix "ϵed" of DFQϵed denotes exponential decay of ϵ. In the present context, the agents' learning of an optimal policy means that their greedy choice of actions is optimal. Because of continued exploration, this does not

Table 1. Game1 – Number of Trials Per Learned Policies under Deterministic Setup.

steps to goal	UFQ	CFQ	xFQ	DFQ	DFQϵed	ϵ-OAL	B-OAL	B-OALPS	MQ	Rmax
4	62	49	47	100	100	26	49	41/60	1	100
5	38	49	46			62	51	19/60	49	
6+		2	7			12			29	
∞									21	

necessarily yield optimal behavior. Figure 2 presents the average reward obtained by the agents over time under deterministic setup.

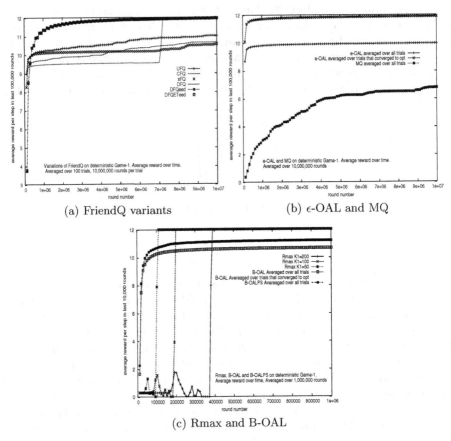

(a) FriendQ variants   (b) ε-OAL and MQ

(c) Rmax and B-OAL

Fig. 2. Game 1 – Avg. Reward under Deterministic Setup. Graphs for Rmax and B-OAL are over 10^6 Rounds Only.

FriendQ converges quickly to second-best behavior (Fig. 2a). From that point on, the average learning curve of UFQ, CFQ and xFQ increases stepwise rather than continuously. This results from a sudden switch of the FriendQ agents from sub-optimal to optimal behavior upon restructuring of the Q-values series. We would expect ε-OAL to present a similar trend but when OAL converges to the second-best behavior in the first 5×10^5 rounds, it fails to order the Q-values properly even after 10^7 rounds. In DFQ since exploration is deterministic this switch is always after 7×10^6 rounds(Fig. 2a).

Surprisingly, UFQ fares better than CFQ (Fig. 2a). At an early learning stage dis-coordination leads to exploration. We discovered that, later on, the estimated Q-values of optimal actions are rarely equal, and thus, coordinating exploitation does not pose a problem (at the examined time interval). Exponential decay of ϵ supplies more exploration at an early period then polynomial decay leading to faster convergence of DFQϵed(Fig. 2a). The eligibility traces do not contribute much in this example. We found the parameters of eligibility traces very hard to tune and very sensitive to change in other parameters or environment dynamics.

OAL agents converge relatively quickly to optimal or second-best behavior, and from that time onwards stick to their behavior (Figs 2b,c). B-OAL converges faster and more often to optimal than ϵ-OAL. This stems from more exploration supplied by the Boltzman method than by the ϵ-greedy method in early period of learning. Later on, ϵ-greedy maintains a low exploration probability that decays very slowly while Boltzman exploration drops faster to zero. Thus, when ϵ-OAL learns optimal behavior it keeps achieving only near-optimal average-reward. As expected Prioritized Sweeping improves the performance of B-OALPS.

The performance of ModelQ is inferior to that of OAL (Fig. 2b) presumably because ModelQ does not explore as much as OAL: at early stages of learning fictitious play provides OAL with other means of exploration. When the agents make many stochastic action choices in early stages of learning, fictitious play amplifies the random behavior. However, at later stages of learning, deviation from constant action choice is rare and will probably not affect fictitious play.

The results on the stochastic setup are presented in Figure 3. By contrast to the deterministic case, MQ performs better than ϵ-OAL. This improvement is attributable to additional exploration stemming from the stochastic nature of the environment. For the same reason CFQ performs the same as UFQ. The slower climb of DFQϵed in relation to U/CFQ at first 10^6 rounds is because the additional early exploration supplied by ϵed is redundant in the stochastic case. The slightly higher return gained by DFQϵed later on is due to the faster decay of ϵ. Rmax behaves similarly in the stochastic and deterministic setups. While the other algorithms achieve only near-optimal return Rmax spends the same amount of time to discover all entries and then attains optimal return.

Rmax's strong exploration bias results in low return until model entries are known (Fig. 3c). From that point on, Rmax attains an optimal return. Very low K1 values, which mean rough transition probability estimates, are enough for computing optimal behavior.

The phenomena observed in Game 1 repeated in Game 2. Therefore, in the following we discuss only phenomena not observed in Game 1.

4.2   Game 2

This game was designed to minimize the effects of equilibrium selection and to show how GLIE policies may keep agents exploiting suboptimal possibilities and the importance of coordinated exploration. The game has four goal states and one optimal equilibrium. The game is depicted in Figure 4(a). It consists of an additional element, an object that can be moved by the agents. Agents can push the object by standing to its right(left) and moving left(right) and pull the object by standing to its right(left) and moving right(left). However, the object is too

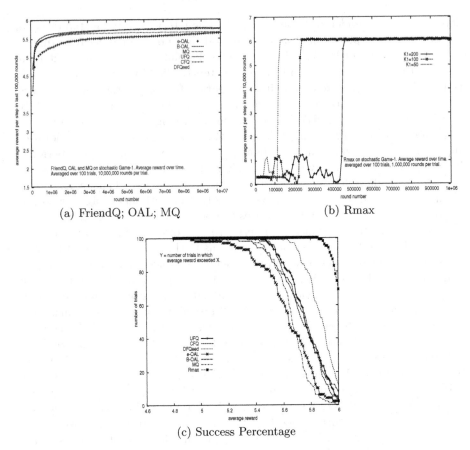

(a) FriendQ; OAL; MQ

(b) Rmax

(c) Success Percentage

Fig. 3. Game1 – Avg. Reward and Success Percentage under Stochastic Setup.

heavy for one agent and requires cooperation of the two agents to be moved. The manner by which the object is moved is depicted in figure 4(b).

The agents' goal is to move the object into one of the upper corners of the grid, at which point the game is reset to its initial state. Moving the object to the upper right (G_1) or left (G_2) corner yields a reward of 80 and 27, respectively. The optimal behavior is to move the object to G_1 in 8 steps. The average reward per step of an optimal strategy under deterministic setup is 10, and the discounted return is ~ 465. The "second best" strategy is moving the object to G_2 in 3 steps, with an average reward per step of 9 and discounted return of ~ 440. The optimal and second best strategies are the same under stochastic setup. The average reward per step of the optimal policy is ~ 4.8. The underlying CISG contains 164 states. Algorithms were executed for 3×10^7 rounds.

Table 2 classifies the number of trials (of 100 in total) according to the algorithms and learned policies under the deterministic setup.

Figure 5 shows the average reward over time obtained by the different algorithms under the deterministic setup. The results are averaged over all trials.

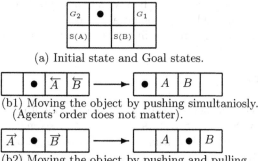

(a) Initial state and Goal states.

(b1) Moving the object by pushing simultaniosly.
(Agents' order does not matter).

(b2) Moving the object by pushing and pulling
simultaniosly. (Agents' order does not matter).

Fig. 4. Game 2.

Table 2. Game2 – Number of Trials Per Learned Policies under Deterministic Setup.

Goal steps to goal	CFQ	CFQεed	DFQεed	ε-OAL	B-OAL	Rmax
G_1 8			100		1	100
G_2 3	99	39/60		54	91	
G_2 4	1	21/60		46	8	

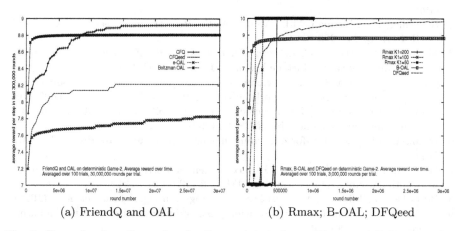

(a) FriendQ and OAL   (b) Rmax; B-OAL; DFQeed

Fig. 5. Game 2 – Avg. Reward under Deterministic Setup. Rmax and Boltzman OAL
are presented on a scale of 3×10^6 rounds.

The main reasons for the poor performance of OAL and CFQ in this game are
(i) random exploration has a greater chance of reaching G_2 than G_1. Discovering
G_2 before G_1 further reduces the chance of visiting G_1 because of the increasing
bias towards exploitation. (ii) exploration of the CFQ and OAL agents is not
coordinated. If reaching G_2 is the current greedy policy then G_1 will not be
visited unless both agents explore simultaneously. Fig. 5a shows that CFQ does

better with polynomial decay of ϵ then with exponential decay. This stems from finite exploration supplied by exponential decay. However, this finite amount of exploration is sufficient given coordinated exploration as shown by Fig. 5b.

5   Summary

We presented an experimental study of three fundamentally different algorithms for learning in CISGs. Our results illustrate the strength and weaknesses of different aspects of these algorithms in different settings, highlighting the accentuated importance of effective exploration in this class of games, the importance of coordinated exploration, the confidence gained by deterministic behavior and the benefits of exhaustion of information. For lack of space we did not exhibit or discuss situations in which it is impractical or inefficient to explore the whole state space. Such situations may occur when optimum can be gained in any local subset of states or when the state space is large in relation to agents lifetime.

A longer version of this paper containing additional results and analysis is available from the authors.

References

1. Sutton, R.S., Barto, A.G.: Reinforcement Learning: An Introduction. MIT Press (1998)
2. Kaelbling, L.P., Littman, M.L., Moore, A.W.: Reinforcement learning: A survey. JAIR **4** (1996) 237–285
3. Moore, A.W., Atkeson, C.G.: Prioritized sweeping: Reinforcement learning with less data and less time. Machine Learning **13** (1993) 103–130
4. Claus, C., Boutilier, C.: The dynamics of reinforcement learning in cooperative multi-agent systems. In: Proc. Workshop on Multi-Agent Learning. (1997) 602–608
5. Wang, X., Sandholm, T.: Reinforcement learning to play an optimal nash equilibrium in team markov games. In: NIPS'02. (2002)
6. Littman, M.L.: Friend-or-foe q-learning in general-sum games. In: Proc. ICML'01. (2001)
7. Brafman, R.I., Tennenholtz, M.: R-max – a general polynomial time algorithm for near-optimal reinforcement learning. JMLR **3** (2002) 213–231
8. Bertsekas, D., Tsitsiklis, J.: Neuri-Dynamic Programming. Athena Scientific (1996)
9. Brafman, R.I., Tennenholtz, M.: Learning to coordinate efficiently: A model based approach. JAIR **19** (2003) 11–23
10. Fudenberg, D., Levine, D.: The theory of learning in games. MIT Press (1998)
11. Dearden, R., Friedman, N., Andre, D.: Model based bayesian exploration. In: UAI'99. (1999)
12. Chalkiadakis, G., Boutilier, C.: Coordination in multiagent reinforcement learning: A bayesian approach. In: AAMAS'03. (2003)
13. Even-Dar, E., Mansour, Y.: Learning rates for Q-learning. In: COLT'01. (2001)

Learning from Message Pairs
for Automatic Email Answering

Steffen Bickel and Tobias Scheffer

Humboldt-Universität zu Berlin, School of Computer Science
Unter den Linden 6, 10099 Berlin, Germany
{bickel,scheffer}@informatik.hu-berlin.de

Abstract. We consider the problem of learning a mapping from question to answer messages. The training data for this problem consist of pairs of messages that have been received and sent in the past. We formulate the problem setting, discuss appropriate performance metrics, develop a solution and describe two baseline methods for comparison. We present a case study based on emails received and answered by the service center of a large online store.

1 Introduction

The email domain is an interesting, commercially relevant, and therefore very popular field of machine learning applications. Several different problem settings with distinct levels of user benefit and required user interaction have been identified. Recognition of spam emails has been studied intensely (*e.g.,* [4, 16, 6]). Similarly frequently, the problem of sorting emails into folders, prioritizing and forwarding emails has been investigated (*e.g.,* [2, 7]). All of these problems fit into the supervised learning paradigm; class labels are obtained from the folder in which the emails are found or, in case of personalized spam filtering, from additional user interaction.

By contrast, the problem of *answering* emails is not well subsumed by the classification framework. The available training data consist of pairs of inbound and corresponding outbound emails – typically, very large amounts are stored on corporate servers. In its full generality, the problem is clearly AI-complete. However, in specific environments – such as call centers – we may expect to find sufficiently strong regularities for machine learning algorithms to be applicable.

Our paper makes several contributions. We motivate and formulate the message answering problem setting. We discuss two baseline solutions: an instance-based method which retrieves the answer to the most similar inbound training message and a classification-based solution. The latter requires a user to additionally label messages; while this approach is less practical, it provides us with an approximate upper bound of how accurate we can possibly learn from just the message pairs. We then develop a solution to the message answering problem that does not require additional user interaction. Finally, we present a case-study and evaluate the discussed methods using emails that have been received and answered in the service center of a large online store.

J.-F. Boulicaut et al. (Eds.): ECML 2004, LNAI 3201, pp. 87–98, 2004.
© Springer-Verlag Berlin Heidelberg 2004

The rest of our paper is organized as follows. We review related work in Section 2. We formulate the problem setting and appropriate performance metrics in Section 3. In Section 4, we discuss "baseline" methods; in Section 5, we develop our solution that learns from message pairs and present a case study on these methods in Section 6. Section 7 concludes.

2   Related Work

The problem of filtering spam emails has been studied frequently. Methods based on the naive Bayes algorithm have been explored [12, 16, 10] and compared to keyword based approaches [1], rule induction [4, 14] and Support Vector Machines [6]. Machine learning of personalized spam classifiers requires the user to manually label emails as spam; for instance, the Netscape email client has been equipped with "this is spam" and "this is not spam" buttons.

Furthermore, the problem of filing emails into a list of folders has been studied. Filtering rules [11] that can be defined in email clients such as Outlook have been found to be unpopular [7]. On the other hand, training data for the email filing problem (previously filed emails) can be obtained without additional user interaction. Several methods and email assistance systems have been presented, including Re:agent [2], MailCat [18], iFile which is based on naive Bayes [15], Support Vector Machines and unigram language models [3], filtering rules [13], co-trained Support Vector Machines [9], and systems which use first-order representations and methods of inductive logic programming [19, 5].

The benefit of automatic email filing is large for users who spend substantial time sorting their emails. Addressing the problem of *email answering* is clearly more difficult, but promises a potentially much greater benefit. A system and a case study has been discussed [17], in which a classifier is used to map inbound emails to a set of manually defined standard answers. In order to train the system, standard answers have to be defined, and example inbound emails which can be answered by each of the standard answers have to be selected as training instances for the classifier. This rather high level of additional user interaction reduces the user benefit and possibly the acceptance of the system.

Our problem setting differs substantially from the *question answering* problem (*e.g.,* [8]). In our setting, many message pairs are available for training, and a large fraction of all inbound messages can be answered with a modest number of distinct answers.

3   Problem Setting

A *message answering problem* is constituted by a distribution $p(x, y)$ over *inbound messages* $x \in X$ and *outbound messages* $y \in Y$, and a binary *acceptance function*, *accept* : $(x, y) \mapsto \{0, 1\}$, that decides whether an answer is acceptable. Neither $p(x, y)$ nor *accept* are known or available to the learning algorithm. X and Y are typically the set of all strings.

The *training data* are a sequence $M = \langle (x_1, y_1), \ldots, (x_m, y_m) \rangle$ of message pairs, governed by $p(x, y)$. The data contain some information about *accept*: for each message pair $(x_j, y_j) \in M$, $accept(x_j, y_j) = 1$. A *message answering hypothesis* is a mapping f that accepts an inbound message x and produces either an outbound message y, or the special symbol $\perp$, indicating that f is unable to answer x.

What is the appropriate performance measure for this problem? For an inbound message x, an acceptable answer $accept(x, f(x)) = 1$ is the most desirable, a wrong answer $accept(x, f(x)) = 0$ the least desirable outcome; rejection of a message $f(x) = \perp$ denotes that the message has to be answered manually.

Among the answers that are sent, we would like to have a large fraction of acceptable answers. At the same time, we desire a large percentage of the incoming emails answered automatically. We can estimate the *precision* by counting, for a given test collection, the number of acceptable answers over all answered messages (Equation 1); we estimate the *recall* as the number of acceptably answered messages over all messages (Equation 2).

$$\widehat{Precision}(f) = \frac{\text{acceptably answered messages}}{\text{answered messages } (f(x) \neq \perp)} \tag{1}$$

$$\widehat{Recall}(f) = \frac{\text{acceptably answered messages}}{\text{all messages}} \tag{2}$$

Message answering methods – such as the algorithm presented in Section 5 – will typically determine a value that quantifies their confidence. By thresholding this confidence measure, we obtain a *precision-recall curve* that characterizes a message answering method.

The *accept* function models a user's decision about whether $f(x)$ is an appropriate answer to x. How can we estimate the performance of a message answering system without having a human "in the loop"? We manually divide a test collection into partitions $\mathbb{S} = \{S_1, S_2, \ldots, S_n\}$, such that each partition $S_i = \langle (x_1, y_1), \ldots, (x_{m_i}, y_{m_i}) \rangle$ contains only semantically equivalent answers. Answers that cannot be grouped into sufficiently large equivalence classes are collected in S_n, a special partition for "miscellaneous" answers. In order to evaluate the message answering methods described in this paper we define *accept* as follows. Given an example $(x_j, y_j) \in M$, the conjectured answer $f(x_j)$ is accepted – $accept(x_j, f(x_j)) = 1$ – if both y_j and $f(x_j)$ occur in the same partition S_i, and S_i is not the "miscellaneous" group S_n. Otherwise, $accept(x_j, f(x_j)) = 0$.

4   Baseline Methods

In this section we describe two baseline methods: an instance-based method that serves as a lower bound and a supervised classification method that receives additional information and can serve as an approximation to an upper bound for the performance achievable for the answering approach presented in Sec. 5.

4.1   Instance-Based Method

The learning phase of the instance-based answering method consists of just storing all training message pairs in M. Finding the appropriate answer to a new question x means finding the most similar question x_j in the training data. The corresponding answer y_j is the answer for x. According to this procedure, $f(x)$ is defined in Equation 3.

$$f_\theta(x) = \begin{cases} y_j | \ \underset{(x_j,y_j)\in M}{\text{argmax}} \ \text{sim}(x,x_j) & \text{if } \text{sim}(x,x_j) > \theta \\ \bot & \text{otherwise} \end{cases} \quad (3)$$

The parameter θ is a measure for the desired level of confidence. We use a tfidf vector space representation for the messages. The similarity measure can be defined as $\text{sim}(x_1, x_2) = \cos(x_1, x_2) = \frac{x_1 \cdot x_2}{\|x_1\| \cdot \|x_2\|}$.

After retrieving the answer y_j to the most similar training message x_j, an adaptation step that mainly involves generating a proper salutation line has to be executed. We exclude this rather technical issue from our discussion.

4.2   Supervised Classification Method

In order to find an approximation to an upper bound for the answering performance that we can achieve by an answer clustering approach as described in Section 5, we extend our training data by additional information. We group all answers into semantically equivalent classes. Mapping inbound messages to one of several equivalence classes is then essentially a classification problem. Note, however, that in an application scenario the definition of equivalence classes and partitioning of answers into those classes requires unacceptably high user effort.

The collection of training message pairs is manually partitioned into $\mathbb{S} = \{S_1, S_2, ..., S_n\}$, where each $S_i = \langle (x_1,y_1), \ldots, (x_{m_i}, y_{m_i}) \rangle$ contains only pairs such that there is a single outbound message y_i^* that is acceptable for all inbound messages in S_i: $(x_j, y_j) \in S_i \Rightarrow accept(x_j, y_i^*) = 1$. Besides partitioning the messages, we require the user to formulate these answer templates y_i^*. S_n contains miscellaneous pairs that do not form sufficiently large groups of equivalent answers. We would now like to find a classifier which maps a message x to an equivalence class of answers $f(x) = y_i^*$.

We transform $\mathbb{S}$ into a training set for the corresponding classification problem. The positive examples for class i consist of the sequence of inbound messages in $S_i = \langle (x_1,y_1) \ldots, (x_{m_i}, y_{m_i}) \rangle$: $Pos_i = \langle x_1, \ldots, x_{m_i} \rangle$. Since no two distinct equivalence classes are equivalent, the messages in Pos_i are negative examples for all other classes $Pos_{j \neq i}$.

We have now transformed the message answering problem into a classification problem. Now, we will describe how we solve this classification problem using Support Vector Machines. We first have to reduce the multi-class learning problem to a set of binary learning problems. In our application, the classes are very unevenly distributed. Therefore, we found both, the one-against-all and one-against-one approach to perform unsatisfactorily. We use a probabilistic one-against-all approach that explicitly considers the prior probabilities.

For each equivalence class i, we learn a decision function $g_i(x)$ using the inbound messages Pos_i as positive, and all $Pos_{j \neq i}$ as negative examples. Now we assume that the decision function values are governed by normal distributions: $P(g_i(x)|i) = N[\mu_i, \sigma_i^2]$. We estimate μ_i, σ_i, $\bar{\mu}_i$, and $\bar{\sigma}_i^2$ from the training data: we learn a decision function $g_i(x)$ and estimate mean value μ and variance σ_i^2 of the positive and $\bar{\mu}_i^2$ and $\bar{\sigma}_i^2$ of the negative examples. The prior probabilities $P(i)$ are estimated by counting the relative size of the partitions S_i. In the next step we calculate the posteriors $P_i(i|g_i(x))$ by applying Bayes' equation as shown in Equation 4.

$$P_i(i|g_i(x)) = \frac{N[\mu_i, \sigma_i^2](g_i(x))P(i)}{N[\mu_i, \sigma_i^2](g_i(x))P(i) + N[\bar{\mu}_i, \bar{\sigma}_i^2](g_i(x))P(\bar{i})} \tag{4}$$

We have several one-against-all classifiers that independently estimate $P_i(i|g_i(x))$. Variance of these estimators can lead to posteriors which do not exactly sum up to 1; we therefore normalize the posterior estimates in Equation 5.

$$P(i|x) = \frac{P_i(i|g_i(x))}{\sum_j P_j(j|g_j(x))} \tag{5}$$

A new question x is answered as follows. The collection of decision functions is evaluated, Equations 4 and 5 yield an estimate of the posterior $P(i|x)$. We select $f(x)$ to be the manually selected template for class i, y_i^*, where $i = \mathrm{argmax}_i P(i|x)$. Once again, the answer has to be adapted by formulating an appropriate salutation line. This leads to the definition of $f(x)$ in Equation 6. The found answer template y_i^* is returned as $f_\theta(x)$, if $P(i|x)$ exceeds a given threshold θ and if the equivalence class S_i is not the "miscellaneous" class S_n; otherwise, $f_\theta(x) = \bot$.

$$f_\theta(x) = \begin{cases} y_i^*|\mathrm{argmax}_i P(i|x) & \text{if } P(i|x) > \theta, i \neq n \\ \bot & \text{otherwise} \end{cases} \tag{6}$$

5 Learning from Message Pairs

The answering method described in Section 4.2 is not suited for real applications because a user is forced to manually partition hundreds of messages into equivalence classes before an answering system can start to support the task of answering emails. This is prohibitive in practice. The method described in Section 4.1 does not need this preparatory work but uses only a limited amount of the available information; each conjectured answer is only based on one single training instance (one message pair).

To overcome these limitations, we will now discuss a method that generates a message answering hypothesis from pairs of training messages. The key idea is that we replace the manual partitioning of answer messages by a clustering step. On the answers of the training message pairs, a clustering algorithm creates a partitioning $\mathbb{C} = \{C_1, C_2, \ldots, C_r\}$, where the $C_i = \langle (x_1, y_1), \ldots, (x_{m_i}, y_{m_i}) \rangle$ are message pairs whose answers y_j lie in the same cluster i.

Table 1. Algorithms for learning from message pairs and answering new questions.

Learning from message pairs.

Input: A sequence $M = \langle (x_1, y_1), \ldots, (x_m, y_m) \rangle$ of message pairs, variance threshold σ_τ^2, pruning parameter π.

1. Recursively cluster answers y_j for all $(x_j, y_j) \in M$ into clusters $C_1, C_2, \ldots, C_{r-1}$. End the recursion when cluster variance lies below σ_τ^2.
2. Prune all clusters with less than π elements. C_r is the sequence of pairs whose clusters have been pruned.
3. For each cluster $C_i \in \{C_1, C_2, \ldots, C_{r-1}\}$, find the answer template y_i^* which is closest to the centroid according to Equation 7.
4. For all clusters $C_i = \langle (x_1, y_1) \ldots, (x_{m_i}, y_{m_i}) \rangle$, let $Pos_i = \langle x_1, \ldots, x_{m_i} \rangle$ be the positive examples.
5. For all clusters C_i, $1 \leq i \leq r$:
   (a) Train a Support Vector Machine with resulting decision function g_i using Pos_i as positive, and all other $Pos_{j \neq i}$ as negative examples.
   (b) Estimate mean value and variance μ_i, σ_i^2, $\bar{\mu}_i$, $\bar{\sigma}_i^2$ of the decision function values of positive and negative examples.
6. Return answering hypothesis f according to Equation 8.

Answering new questions.

Input: New inbound message $x \in X$, message answering hypothesis f, confidence threshold θ.

1. Calculate SVM-decision function values $g_i(x)$ for $i = 1, \ldots, r$.
2. Assume Gaussian likelihoods and estimate $P(i|x)$ according to Equations 4 and 5. Parameters μ_i, σ_i^2, $\bar{\mu}_i$, and $\bar{\sigma}_i^2$ are part of the answering hypothesis f.
3. If $\text{argmax}_i P(i|x) = r$ (the "miscellaneous" cluster is most likely) or $\max_i P(i|x) \leq \theta$, then return $\perp$.
4. Otherwise, return y_i^* with $i = \text{argmax}_i P(i|x)$ (according to Equation 8).

For each cluster i, we construct an answer template y_i^*. Because we do not want to require a user to manually define a template as in Section 4.2, we select y_i^* to be the closest answer to the centroid of the cluster C_i (Equation 7).

$$y_i^* = \underset{y:(x,y)\in C_i}{\text{argmax}} \ \text{sim} \left(y, \frac{1}{|C_i|} \sum_{(x_j, y_j) \in C_i} y_j \right) \qquad (7)$$

As clustering algorithm, we use EM with mixtures of two Gaussian models recursively. In each recursive step the data are split into two clusters until a predefined cluster variance threshold is reached or a cluster with one element remains. We now prune all clusters which do not have sufficiently many examples; C_r collects message pairs of pruned clusters. In the next step we train r binary linear SVM classifiers on the question messages according to the procedure described in Section 4.2.

A new inbound message x is answered as follows. After classifying x into a partition $C_i \in \mathbb{C}$ analogously to Section 4.2, we return the corresponding answer template y_i^*, where i maximizes the posterior estimate $P(i|x)$. Equation 8 shows the resulting definition of $f_\theta(x)$ which is analogous to Equation 6. $P(i|x)$ is computed analogously to Equations 4 and 5. The resulting algorithm is shown in Table 1.

$$f_\theta(x) = \begin{cases} y_i^*|\mathrm{argmax}_i P(i|x) & \text{if } P(i|x) > \theta, i \neq r \\ \bot & \text{otherwise} \end{cases} \tag{8}$$

6 Case Study

The study is divided into three subsections. We first examine properties of the used data set. Secondly, we compare our method for learning from message pairs with the baseline methods; and finally, we analyze the dependency between answering performance and the parameters of the clustering algorithm.

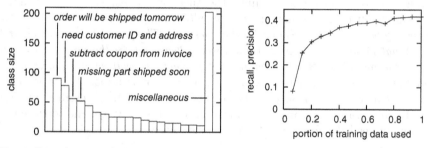

Fig. 1. Distribution of class sizes with descriptions for largest classes (left); learning curve for precision/recall of the supervised classification problem (right).

6.1 Data Set Properties

The data set used in the study was provided by a large online store. A total of 805 question-answer pairs represent the emails answered by one customer service employee within one month. The questions mostly deal with problems regarding late delivery, incomplete shipment, and defective products. In order to evaluate the performance of the message answering methods via the *accept* function, and to obtain the required partitioning for the supervised classification method, we manually group the answers into 19 semantically equivalent classes.

Figure 1 (left) shows the distribution of class sizes for the data set. We choose ten as the minimum size of a class. All messages in smaller groups fall into the "miscellaneous" group that contains 203 messages and is shown as the rightmost bar. In order to examine whether the size of the data set is sufficient, or whether additional training data would improve the answering performance, we provide a learning curve in Figure 1 (right). We use a confidence threshold of $\theta = 0$; since every question is answered, precision equals recall. We display the precision/recall of the answering performance for the supervised classification method described in Section 4.2. We can see that the curve approaches saturation for the available 805 training instances. This curve, as well as all succeeding diagrams, are based on 10-fold cross validation.

Figure 1 (right) shows a maximum recall of 42%. In order to judge whether this is a "good" or a "poor" result, let us take a closer look at our data set. We study which of all $\frac{19 \cdot 18}{2} = 171$ pairwise combinations of $S_1, S_2 \ldots, S_{n-1}$ are separable. We learn a binary SVM decision function for each pair of classes (using 10-fold cross validation) and measure the separability of each pair in terms of its *AUC performance*. The area under the *receiver operating characteristic (ROC) curve* of a binary decision function is just the probability that, when we draw one positive and one negative example at random, the decision function assigns a higher value to the positive than to the negative example.

Figure 2 shows a graph in which each class is a node, and each inseparable pair (indicated by a low AUC value) is an edge. The different line styles represent different AUC value ranges. We notice that there are several AUC values below 60%. These critical pairs are cases in which distinct answers are sent in response to equivalent questions. For example, the question *"When can I expect delivery?"* can result either in answer *"Order will be shipped tomorrow."* or *"Order has already been shipped."* Similarly, the question *"The product you sent doesn't work. What now?"* can result in the answer *"Please return the product, we will send replacement"* or *"Please discard the product, we will send replacement"*, depending on the value of the item. In these cases, it is impossible to identify the correct answer based on just the text of the question. A possible solution would be to extract a customer identification from the message, and retrieve the additionally needed information by a database query.

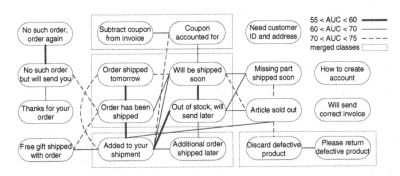

Fig. 2. Inseparability graph: Nodes represent answer classes, edges represent inseparability relations (low AUC values); dashed line boxes show merged classes.

In order to simulate the performance that we would obtain if we had additional information from the order processing database, we merge some answer classes that are based on identical questions but could be distinguished with information from the database. The merged classes are shown in Figure 2 by dashed line boxes. We look at the *precision-recall curves* in Figure 3 (left), where curves are displayed for the merged and original answer classes using the supervised classification method described in Section 4.2. Over the recall levels, this improves the precision by 10-20%. Figure 2 shows that we still have indistinguishable pairs in distinct sections of the graph. This is the reason why we still do not exceed 50% recall.

We notice that 35% of the inbound messages contain quotes of old messages in addition to the actual question. How do these quotes affect the answering performance? We automatically remove the quotes and compare the performance in Figure 3. We see that removing quotes is slightly detrimental, the quotes seem to contain additional useful information.

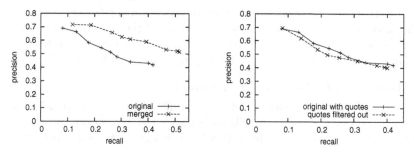

Fig. 3. Precision-recall curves for merged/original answer classes and for question messages with/without quotes.

6.2 Comparison of the Different Answering Methods

We compare the *precision-recall curves* of the two baseline methods of Section 4 to the method for learning from message pairs discussed in Section 5. All presented results for learning from message pairs are based on the averaged precision and recall values over ten different clustering runs to compensate for the randomized cluster initialization. The 10-fold cross validation is nested into ten clustering runs so each value is based on 100 learning cycles.

Figure 4 (left) shows the curves for the data set with *excluded* "miscellaneous" class. Our motivation for excluding the miscellaneous class is that our evaluation metric considers all miscellaneous messages to be answered wrongly which might

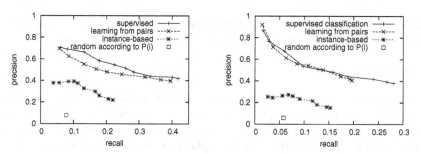

Fig. 4. Precision-recall curves for learning from message pairs and the two baseline methods; message pairs of "miscellaneous" class *excluded* (left)/*included* (right) from training set.

impose a pessimistic bias. Figure 4 (right) shows the same methods and curves with *included* "miscellaneous" class. In both settings, the learning from message pairs method is by far better than the instance-based method and, needless to say, better than random assignment according to $P(i)$. We notice also that the difference between supervised learning and learning from message pairs is only small. Especially in Figure 4 (right), where "miscellaneous" messages are included, the difference is marginal. This is surprising because for the supervised learning method a user has manually labeled all training messages with one of 19 answer templates. By contrast, our algorithm for learning from message pairs has achieved nearly the same result without any manual labeling.

Additionally, we are interested in the variance of the performance of learning from message pairs as a result of the random influence in the EM-clustering. The standard deviations are rather low, 1.7% (precision) and 1.6% (recall) for $\theta = 0$.

6.3 Influence of Clustering Parameters

We want to find out to what extent the results depend on optimally chosen clustering parameters σ_τ^2 and π. Figure 5 shows the *precision-recall curves* for different values of σ_τ^2 (right) and π (left). We notice that the performance differences are marginal. Over the range of settings for σ_τ^2 and π, we observe quite diverse clusterings with between 12 and 30 clusters. However, the clustering has only a small influence on the answering performance of the resulting classifier. When a class is split up into two clusters and two distinct classifiers are learned for these clusters, this has only a marginal influence on the resulting performance because confusions between these two do not result in wrong answers.

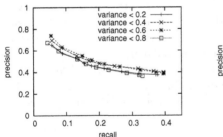 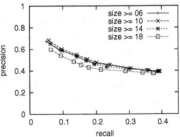

Fig. 5. Precision-recall curves for different variance threshold (left)/pruning (right) parameter values of the clustering algorithm ($\sigma_\tau^2 = 0.4$, left, and $\pi = 10$, right).

7 Conclusion

We identified *message answering* as a new problem setting. The message answering task is to learn a mapping from inbound to outbound messages; the training data consist of message pairs recorded from past communication. This setting is motivated by a practically relevant application that is not appropriately subsumed under the classification framework: email communication in service centers. Rather than a concluding solution, this paper provides a starting point for discussion of the message answering problem.

We first used a supervised classification approach which requires a user to label all message pairs with a small set of answer templates. An instance based approach that retrieves the answer to the most similar question served as lower baseline. Our solution clusters the answer messages, and then uses the inbound messages associated to each cluster of outbound messages as positive examples for a support vector classifier. Our case study showed that the classification based approach achieves only marginally higher precision and recall values (but a higher maximum recall) than our solution for learning from message pairs. The instance-based method, by comparison, performs substantially worse.

Precision and recall were only marginally influenced by the choice of clustering parameters, even though the clusterings obtained for distinct parameters were diverse. A small but significant additional result is that removing quotes from inbound messages deteriorates the answering performance.

We see two options for integrating the presented method into an actual answering system. One is to automatically answer high confidence messages and route low confidence messages to a human agent. A second option is to integrate the predictor into an email client which would then propose answers for incoming emails; these answers can be manually accepted, rejected or modified.

Whether the precision/recall values that we observed are sufficient for practical applications depends on several factors – such as whether the goal is to interactively generate a proposal or whether the emails are actually answered automatically, as well as the volume of emails received. In order to quantify the actual user benefit and economic impact, we will conduct an additional field study.

In the service center setting of our data set, answers do not need to incorporate specific details of the question; *e.g.,* the question "What should I do with the defective *screwdriver set?*" results in the general answer "Please return defective *product.*" There might be settings in which an answer needs to repeat specific information of a question. This case is not covered by our current solution; here, an analysis of repeated phrases in question and answers during training and an additional information extraction step for answering a new question are needed.

The data set that we studied contains no questions with multiple topics; but for other settings, this might be different. An additional challenge is to interpret the question and answer messages as a mixture of multiple question and answer topics and allow the answering hypothesis to identify different question topics and generate a mixed answer.

One might argue that, if answer topics are stable over time and their number is small, a manual labeling of training messages is manageable. But first of all the answer topics might not be stable in practice and secondly, even if a manual labeling of several hundreds of emails sounds easy to us, it would prevent many users from using such a system. A "plug & play" approach like our learning from message pairs seems much more promising for fast acceptance in practical settings.

Acknowledgment

This work has been supported by the German Science Foundation DFG under grant SCHE540/10-1.

References

1. I. Androutsopoulos, J. Koutsias, K. Chandrinos, and C. Spyropoulos. An experimental comparison of naive Bayesian and keyword based anti-spam filtering with personal email messages. In *Proceedings of the International ACM SIGIR Conference*, 2000.
2. T. Boone. Concept features in Re:Agent, an intelligent email agent. *Autonomous Agents*, 1998.
3. J. Brutlag and C. Meek. Challenges of the email domain for text classification. In *Proceedings of the International Conference on Machine Learning*, 2000.
4. W. Cohen. Learning rules that classify email. In *Proceedings of the IEEE Spring Symposium on Machine Learning for Information Access*, 1996.
5. E. Crawford, J. Kay, and E. McCreath. IEMS - the intelligent email sorter. In *Proceedings of the International Conference on Machine Learning*, 2002.
6. H. Drucker, D. Wu, and V. Vapnik. Support vector machines for spam categorization. *IEEE Transactions on Neural Networks*, 10(5), 1999.
7. N. Ducheneaut and V. Belotti. Email as habitat: an exploration of embedded personal information management. *Interactions*, 8:30–38, 2001.
8. B. Galitsky. *Natural Language Question Answering Systems*. Advanced Knowledge International, 2003.
9. S. Kiritchenko and S. Matwin. Email classification with co-training. Technical report, University of Ottawa, 2002.
10. A. Kolcz and J. Alspector. SVM-based filtering of e-mail spam with content-specific misclassification costs. In *Proceedings of the ICDM Workshop on Text Mining*, 2001.
11. W. Mackay. Triggers and barriers to customizing software. In *Proceedings of the International Conference on Human Factors in Computing Systems*, 1991.
12. P. Pantel and D. Lin. Spamcop: a spam classification and organization program. In *Proceedings of the AAAI Workshop on Learning for Text Categorization*, 1998.
13. M. Pazzani. Representation of electronic mail filtering profiles: a user study. In *Proceedings of the ACM Conference on Intelligent User Interfaces*, 2000.
14. J. Provost. Naive Bayes vs. rule-learning in classification of email. Technical Report AI-TR-99-284, University of Texas at Austin, 1999.
15. J. Rennie. iFILE: an application of machine learning to email filtering. In *Proceedings of the SIGKDD Text Mining Workshop*, 2000.
16. M. Sahami, S. Dumais, D. Heckerman, and E. Horvitz. A Bayesian approach to filtering junk email. In *Proceedings of the AAAI Workshop on Learning for Text Categorization*, 1998.
17. T. Scheffer. Email answering assistance by semi-supervised text classification. *Intelligent Data Analysis*, 8(5), 2004.
18. R. Segal and J. Kephart. Mailcat: An intelligent assistant for organizing mail. In *Autonomous Agents*, 1999.
19. K. Shimazu and K. Furukawa. Knowledge discovery in databases by Progol – design, implementation, and its application to expert system building. In *Proceedings of the ACM Symposium on Applied Computing*, 1997.

Concept Formation
in Expressive Description Logics

Nicola Fanizzi, Luigi Iannone, Ignazio Palmisano, and Giovanni Semeraro

Dipartimento di Informatica, Università degli Studi di Bari
Via Orabona 4, 70125 Bari, Italy
surname@di.uniba.it

Abstract. We investigate on the automated construction of terminologies from assertions in an expressive Description Logics representation like $\mathcal{ALC}$. The overall unsupervised learning problem is decomposed into smaller supervised learning problems once clusters of disjoint concepts are detected. In turn, these problems are solved by means of refinement operators[1].

1 Motivation

In the perspective of the Semantic Web [1], an effort is required for supporting interoperability at a semantic level. Ontological knowledge is to be employed for organizing and classifying resources on the ground of their meaning. Such knowledge bases can be a powerful tool for supporting many other services, such as reasoning and retrieval. In the proposed frameworks, an ontology is cast as a concept graph, accounting for concepts and relationships, in specific or larger contexts, intended for being used by machines. Each class of resources is defined extensionally by the set of the resources it represents, and intensionally by descriptions which account for them and possibly also for instances that may be available in the future. Annotating resources after semantic criteria is not a trivial and inexpensive task. Thus, the problem is how to support the construction of such ontological knowledge. In this context, we focus on the induction of definitions for classes of resources from their available assertions. Indeed, supervised maintenance tools can be an important factor to boost the realization of the Semantic Web. In a learning service for the Semantic Web, representation languages that are typical in this context have to be considered. Such languages are closely related to the family of languages known as *Description Logics* (henceforth DL), which are endowed with well founded semantics and reasoning procedures [2]. In DL knowledge bases, the *world state* (extension) is given by an *A-box* to be regarded as a collection of assertions about the resources, while the structural descriptions of their classes (intension) are maintained in a *T-box*. The induction of structural knowledge, like the T-box taxonomies, is not new in machine

---

[1] This research was partially funded by the European Commission under the IST Integrated Project VIKEF - Virtual Information and Knowledge Environment Framework (Contract no. 507173); more information at http://www.vikef.net.

learning, especially in the context of *concept formation* where clusters of similar objects are aggregated in hierarchies according to heuristic criteria or similarity measures. Most of the methods apply to simple (propositional or equivalent) representations, whereas ontologies require richer structural languages. Yet, the induction of structural knowledge turns out to be a hard problem in first-order logic representations or fragments therein [3]. In *Inductive Logic Programming* (ILP), attempts have been made to extend relational learning techniques towards more expressive languages [4] or hybrid representations [5]. In the DL literature, often inductive methods are based on a heuristic search to cope with the problem complexity. They generally implement bottom-up operators, such as the *least common subsumer* defined for various DL languages [6], that tend to induce correct yet overly specific concept definitions that may have poor predictive capabilities. Moreover, for the sake of efficiency, simple DLs have been taken into account which are less expressive than the current standards for ontology markup languages. In the proposed methodology, an expressive language like $\mathcal{ALC}$ [2] is adopted. As in previous work [7], though on different representations, the overall unsupervised learning problem is decomposed into smaller supervised learning problems. Initially, a basic taxonomic structure of the search space is induced from the A-box. This phase elicits clusters of mutually disjoint concepts that require a discriminant definition. Thus, several smaller supervised learning problems are issued. This task is cast as a search for correct definitions for a concept in the context of its cluster(s). Therefore, investigating the properties of the search space and the related operators, we also define a method for induction and refinement in $\mathcal{ALC}$. This method, relying on the notion of counterfactuals [8], can exploit more intensively the knowledge provided by the available assertions. The paper is organized as follows. In Sec. 2 the search space and its properties are presented. The method for knowledge base induction is illustrated and discussed in Sect. 3. Sect. 4 concludes examining possible extensions.

2   Preliminaries on the Search Space

The theoretical setting of learning in DL spaces requires the definition of syntax and semantics for the proposed representation. The data model should be expressed by means of DL concept languages for which reasoning tools are already available. Furthermore, the learning problem is cast as a search in the space of candidate definitions induced by the reference representation.

2.1   Knowledge Bases in Description Logics

In a DL language [2], primitive *concepts* $N_C = \{C, D, \ldots\}$ are interpreted as subsets of a certain domain of objects and primitive *roles* $N_R = \{R, S, \ldots\}$ are interpreted as binary relations. In $\mathcal{ALC}$ [2] complex descriptions can be built from primitive concepts and roles by means of the constructors given in Tab. 1. In an *interpretation* $\mathcal{I} = (\Delta^{\mathcal{I}}, \cdot^{\mathcal{I}})$, $\Delta^{\mathcal{I}}$ is the domain of the interpretation and the functor $\cdot^{\mathcal{I}}$ maps the concepts to their extensions (subsets of the domain $\Delta^{\mathcal{I}}$).

Table 1. $\mathcal{ALC}$ constructors and related interpretation.

CONSTRUCTOR	SYNTAX	SEMANTICS $\mathcal{I}$
top concept	$\top$	$\Delta^{\mathcal{I}}$
bottom concept	$\bot$	$\emptyset$
concept negation	$\neg C$	$\Delta^{\mathcal{I}} \setminus C^{\mathcal{I}}$
concept conjunction	$C_1 \sqcap C_2$	$C_1^{\mathcal{I}} \cap C_2^{\mathcal{I}}$
concept disjunction	$C_1 \sqcup C_2$	$C_1^{\mathcal{I}} \cup C_2^{\mathcal{I}}$
value restriction	$\forall R.C$	$\{x \in \Delta^{\mathcal{I}} \mid \forall y \ (x,y) \in R^{\mathcal{I}} \rightarrow y \in C^{\mathcal{I}}\}$
existential restriction	$\exists R.C$	$\{x \in \Delta^{\mathcal{I}} \mid \exists y \ (x,y) \in R^{\mathcal{I}} \wedge y \in C^{\mathcal{I}}\}$

A *knowledge base* $\mathcal{K} = \langle \mathcal{T}, \mathcal{A} \rangle$ contains a T-box $\mathcal{T}$ and an A-box $\mathcal{A}$. $\mathcal{T}$ is a set of (acyclic) concept definitions $C \doteq D$, meaning $C^{\mathcal{I}} = D^{\mathcal{I}}$, where C is the concept name and D is a DL description given in terms of the language constructors. $\mathcal{A}$ contains extensional assertions on concepts and roles, e.g. $C(a)$ and $R(a,b)$, meaning respectively that $a^{\mathcal{I}} \in C^{\mathcal{I}}$ and $(a^{\mathcal{I}}, b^{\mathcal{I}}) \in R^{\mathcal{I}}$. A notion of *subsumption* between concepts (or roles) is given in terms of their interpretations:

Definition 2.1 (subsumption). *Given two concept (role) definitions D_1 and D_2 in a T-box $\mathcal{T}$, D_1 subsumes D_2 iff $D_1^{\mathcal{I}} \supseteq D_2^{\mathcal{I}}$ holds for every interpretation $\mathcal{I}$ of $\mathcal{T}$. This is denoted by $D_1 \sqsupseteq_{\mathcal{T}} D_2$, or simply $D_1 \sqsupseteq D_2$ when $\mathcal{T}$ is obvious.*

Example 2.1. An example of concept definition in the proposed language:
Father $\doteq$ Male $\sqcap$ $\forall$hasChild.Being $\sqcap$ $\exists$hasChild.Being
which translates the sentence *"fathers are male that have beings as their children, and precisely at least one child"*. A specialized concept definition is:
FatherWithoutSons $\doteq$ Male $\sqcap$ $\exists$hasChild.Being $\sqcap$ $\forall$hasChild.(Being $\sqcap$ ¬Male)
It holds that: Father $\sqsupseteq$ FatherWithoutSons.
Examples of A-box assertions are the following:
Father(zeus), Male(zeus), God(zeus), ¬Father(era), hasChild(zeus, apollo),
hasChild(zeus, hercules), ¬$\forall$hasChild.God(zeus)

A concept may have many semantically equivalent, yet syntactically different, descriptions that can be reduced to a normal form by means of equivalence-preserving rewriting rules (see [2]). Preliminarily, the different parts of a description are to be designated: $\mathsf{prim}(C)$ is the set of the concepts at the top-level conjunction of C; if there exists a universal restriction $\forall R.C'$ at the top-level of C then $\mathsf{val}_R(C) = C'$ otherwise $\mathsf{val}_R(C) = \top$; $\mathsf{ex}_R(C)$ is the set of the descriptions C' in existential restrictions $\exists R.C'$ at the top-level conjunction of C.

Definition 2.2 (normal form). *An $\mathcal{ALC}$ concept description D is in* normal form *iff $D \equiv \bot$ or $D \equiv \top$ or if $D = D_1 \sqcup \cdots \sqcup D_n$ $(\forall i \in \{1, \ldots, n\} \ D_i \not\equiv \bot)$ with*

$$D_i = \bigsqcap_{A \in \mathsf{prim}(D_i)} A \ \sqcap \bigsqcap_{R \in N_R} \left[\bigsqcap_{V \in \mathsf{val}_R(D_i)} \forall R.V \ \sqcap \bigsqcap_{E \in \mathsf{ex}_R(D_i)} \exists R.E \right]$$

where and $\forall R \in N_R$ every description in $\mathsf{ex}_R(D_i) \cup \mathsf{val}_R(D_i)$ is in normal form.

2.2   Induction as Search

Provided that an order is imposed on the concept descriptions, the induction of the definitions for undefined concepts in the A-box can be cast as a search process. The *search space* depends on the order adopted that induces a generalization model. This provides a criterion for traversing the space of solutions by means of suitable operators [9]. They allow for the treatment of induction as a search process that is decoupled from the specific heuristics to be employed.

Definition 2.3 (refinement operators). *Given a quasi-ordered set $(S, \succeq)$, a downward (resp. upward) refinement operator ρ (resp. δ) is a mapping from S to 2^S, such that $D' \in \rho(D)$ implies $D \succeq D'$ (resp. $D' \in \delta(D)$ implies $D' \succeq D$). The closure of the operator τ for $C \in S$ is defined: $\tau^*(C) = \bigcup_{n \geq 0} \tau^n(C)$, where $\tau^0(C) = \{C\}$ and $\tau^n(C) = \{D \in S \mid \exists E \in \tau^{n-1}(C): D \in \tau(E)\}$.*

The properties of the operators depend on the order adopted.

Definition 2.4 (properties). *In a quasi-ordered set $(S, \succeq)$, a refinement operator τ is locally finite iff $\forall C \in S : \tau(C)$ is finite and computable. A downward (resp. upward) refinement operator ρ (resp. δ) is proper iff $\forall C \in S: D \in \rho(C)$ implies $C \succ D$ (resp. $D \in \delta(C)$ implies $D \succ C$). A downward (resp. upward) refinement operator ρ (resp. δ) is complete iff $\forall C, D \in S, D \succ C$ implies $\exists E \in \rho^*(D)$ such that $E \equiv C$ (resp. $C \succ D$ implies $\exists E \in \delta^*(D)$ such $E \equiv C$). A locally finite, proper and complete operator is defined as ideal.*

In inductive reasoning, it is necessary to test the coverage of candidate hypotheses with respect to the examples. Coverage also determines the decisions on the possible refinement of such hypotheses. However, it should be noted that in the DL settings the *Open World Assumption* (OWA) is adopted, differently from the context of learning or query answering where the *Closed World Assumption* (CWA) is commonly made. It is supposed that preliminarily a representative at the concept language level is derived in the form of *most specific concept (msc)* [6, 2]. The *msc* required by the following algorithms is a concept description, entailing the given assertion, that it is bound to be among the most specific ones. Hence, the examples will be represented with very specific conjunctive descriptions obtained by means of the *realization* [2] of the assertions. Since an *msc* need not to exist in $\mathcal{ALC}$, for each individual, we consider an approximation of its *msc* with respect to $\mathcal{A}$, up to a certain depth k [2]:

Definition 2.5 (coverage). *Given the knowledge base $\langle \mathcal{T}, \mathcal{A} \rangle$, the definition of a concept $C \doteq D$ covers an assertion $C(e)$ iff $\exists k: D \sqsupseteq_{\mathcal{T}} msc_{k,\mathcal{A}}(e)$*

The unsupervised learning problem can be formally stated as follows:

Definition 2.6 (DL learning problem). *In a search space $(S, \sqsupseteq)$*
Given *a knowledge base $\mathcal{K} = \langle \mathcal{T}, \mathcal{A} \rangle$, supposed that $\mathcal{T}$ does not contain definitions for all the concepts with assertions in $\mathcal{A}$*
Induce *a set of concept definitions, by means of refinement operators, $\mathcal{T}_C = \{C_1 \doteq D_1, C_2 \doteq D_2, \ldots\}$ such that $\forall i \forall C_i(e) \in \mathcal{A}: \mathcal{T} \cup \mathcal{T}_C$ covers $C_i(e)$*

The problem requires to find definitions $\mathcal{T}_C$ for undefined concepts concerning assertions in the A-box. $\mathcal{T}$ can be regarded as a sort of background knowledge (possibly imported from higher level ontologies), which is supposed to be correct but also incapable to account for all of the assertions in the A-box.

3   Induction of $\mathcal{ALC}$ Concept Descriptions

A method for concept formation in the referred representation is presented[2]. After inferring the basic structure of the search space, the concept characterization requires the solution of supervised learning problems. Albeit these can be solved by means of refinement operators and heuristics, a more knowledge-intensive method based on counterfactuals is used to increase the process efficiency.

3.1   A Concept Formation Algorithm

The main concept formation algorithm applied in our method is presented in Fig. 1. As mentioned, it consists of two phases: construction of the basic taxonomy and solution of the induced learning problems.

The basic taxonomy of primitive concepts is built from the knowledge available in the starting A-box $\mathcal{A}$: if also $\mathcal{T}$ is non-empty, then $\mathcal{A}$ is augmented with assertions obtained by saturation with respect to $\mathcal{T}$. This phase also singles out domains and ranges of the roles as the starting superconcepts SCs (step 5). Direct subsumption relationships between the concept extensions are detected (*level-wise*) so to build up a hierarchy based on them. Meanwhile, the relationships of pairwise disjointness among the subconcepts Cs_j that can induced from the A-box are exploited to infer the candidate clusters of concepts $MDCs$ (steps 6–12). A MDC stands for the maximal set of *mutually disjoint concepts*, i.e. a cluster of disjoint subconcepts of the same concept. $MDCs$ are built by iteratively splitting by disjointness the sets of (direct) subconcepts of a superconcept SC_j. At each iteration, the set of the subconcepts replaces the current set of superconcepts SCs for the next level (until a base level is reached). However, finding the $MDCs$ has a superpolynomial worst case complexity [7].

Mutually disjoint concepts within an MDC require non-overlapping definitions. This is aimed at during the supervised phase (steps 13–25). Each non-primitive subconcept C_i in the selected MDC needs a discriminating definition that is induced as the result of a separate supervised learning problem, where the instances of disjoint subconcepts in the MDC act as negative examples. Thus, a loop is repeated looking for a candidate definition D_i for each concept in the selected MDC using an upward operator δ. A disjoint per loop is calculated covering (part of) the positive instances $\mathcal{A}_i$ related to concept C_i. When a definition D_i covers negative examples represented by the instances of other concepts in the context of the MDC, it has to be specialized by a downward operator. A given threshold $\min_q$ states the minimum quality for a candidate definition D_i.

---

[2] It was inspired by KLUSTER [7] where the BACK language [2] is adopted.

Tbox-induction$(\mathcal{A}, \mathcal{T}, \mathcal{T}_C)$
input $\mathcal{A}$: A-box; $\mathcal{T}$: T-box
output $\mathcal{T}_C$: T-box
1. **if** $\mathcal{T} \neq \emptyset$ **then** $\mathcal{A} \leftarrow \mathcal{A} \cup$ saturate$(\mathcal{A}, \mathcal{T})$
2. **for each** primitive concept C_i with assertions in $\mathcal{A}$ **do**
3. $D_i \leftarrow \bot$
4. $\mathcal{A}_i \leftarrow \{C_i(e) \in \mathcal{A}\}$
5. $SCs \leftarrow \{domain(R) \mid R \in N_R(\mathcal{A})\} \cup \{range(R) \mid R \in N_R(\mathcal{A})\}$
6. **repeat** (* find the MDCs *)
7.   **for each** $SC_j \in SCs$ **do**
8. $Cs_j \leftarrow \{C \sqsubseteq SC_j \mid \nexists C': C \sqsubseteq C' \sqsubseteq SC_j\}$
9. $MDCs_j \leftarrow$ split_disjoint(Cs_j)
10. $MDCs \leftarrow MDCs \cup MDCs_j$
11. $SCs \leftarrow \bigcup_j Cs_j$
12. **until** $SCs = \emptyset$ (* no direct subconcepts *)
13. **repeat** (* supervised phase *)
14. $MDC \leftarrow$ select$(MDCs)$
15.   **repeat** (* solve next supervised learning problem *)
16.   choose $C_i \in MDC$ such that $\mathcal{A}_i \neq \emptyset$
17. $D_i \leftarrow D_i \sqcup$ generalize$(D_i, \mathcal{A}_i, \delta)$
18. $q \leftarrow$ eval(D_i, MDC)
19.   **while** $q < min_q$ **and** refinable(C_i) **do**
20. $D_i \leftarrow$ specialize(D_i, MDC, ρ)
21. $q \leftarrow$ eval(D_i, MDC)
22. $\mathcal{A}_i \leftarrow \mathcal{A}_i \setminus \{C_i(e) \in \mathcal{A}_i \mid D_i$ covers $C_i(e)\}$
23.   **until** $\forall C_i \in MDC: \mathcal{A}_i = \emptyset$
24. $MDCs \leftarrow MDCs \setminus MDC$
25. **until** $MDCs = \emptyset$
26. $\mathcal{T}_C \leftarrow \{C_i \doteq D_i \mid for\ each\ concept\}$
27. **return** $\mathcal{T}_C$

Fig. 1. The main T-box induction algorithm.

Like in the *lcs*-based approach [6], the initial characterization of a concept is modeled like a bottom-up search for generalizations. In [9] a different strategy is proposed. The search should start from the most general definition $\top$, and then it would repeatedly apply a downward refinement operator ρ up to finding discriminating generalizations for the target concepts. The method described in [7] employs incomplete specialization and generalization operators. It is not guaranteed to find a correct definition, since the search space is limited in order to preserve efficiency. For example, the generalization algorithm follows a predefined schema that forces an order in the refinement graph which may not lead to the correct definitions.

3.2   Refinement Operators for $\mathcal{ALC}$ and Heuristics

Given the ordering relationship induced by subsumption for the space of hypotheses $(\mathcal{ALC}, \sqsupseteq)$, it is possible to specify how to traverse this space by means of refinement operators. Preliminarily, the definition of a difference operator is needed for both conjunctive and disjunctive descriptions. In the former case, $C = C_1 \sqcap \cdots \sqcap C_n$, the difference is the generalized conjunct resulting from removing one conjunct: $C - C_i = \sqcap_{k \neq i} C_k$. In latter case, $D = D_1 \sqcup \cdots \sqcup D_m$, the difference is the specialized disjunct $D - D_j = \sqcup_{k \neq j} D_k$. Considered the $\mathcal{ALC}$ normal form, each level of a concept description interleaves disjunctive or conjunctive descriptions. Thus, the operators should accommodate either case.

Definition 3.1 (downward operator). *In the search space* $(\mathcal{ALC}, \sqsupseteq)$, *the* downward refinement operator $\rho_\sqcup$ *for disjunctive concept descriptions (in* $\mathcal{ALC}$ *normal form)* $D = D_1 \sqcup \cdots \sqcup D_n$ *is defined as follows:*

- $D' \in \rho_\sqcup(D)$ *if* $D' = D - D_i$ *for some* $1 \leq i \leq n$
- $D' \in \rho_\sqcup(D)$ *if* $D' = (D - D_i) \sqcup D'_i$ *for some* $D'_i \in \rho_\sqcap(D_i)$, $1 \leq i \leq n$

The downward refinement operator $\rho_\sqcap$, *given a conjunctive concept description* $C = C_1 \sqcap \cdots \sqcap C_m$, *is defined as follows:*

- $C' \in \rho_\sqcap(C)$ *if* $C' = C \sqcap C_{j+1}$ *for some* $C_{j+1} \not\sqsupseteq C$
- $C' \in \rho_\sqcap(C)$ *if* $C' = (C - C_j) \sqcap C'_j$ *for some* $1 \leq j \leq m$, *where:*
  - $C'_j = \exists R.D'_j$, $C_j = \exists R.D_j$ *and* $D'_j \in \rho_\sqcup(D_j)$ *or*
  - $C'_j = \forall R.D'_j$, $C_j = \forall R.D_j$ *and* $D'_j \in \rho_\sqcup(D_j)$

It is straightforward to define the dual upward operator that seeks for more general hypotheses by adding disjuncts or refining them.

Definition 3.2 (upward operator). *In the search space* $(\mathcal{ALC}, \sqsupseteq)$, *the* upward refinement operator $\delta_\sqcup$ *for disjunctive concept descriptions (in* $\mathcal{ALC}$ *normal form)* $D = D_1 \sqcup \cdots \sqcup D_n$ *is defined as follows:*

- $D' \in \delta_\sqcup(D)$ *if* $D' = D \sqcup D_{n+1}$ *for some* D_{n+1} *such that* $D_{n+1} \not\sqsubseteq D$
- $D' \in \delta_\sqcup(D)$ *if* $D' = (D - D_i) \sqcup D'_i$ *for some* $D'_i \in \delta_\sqcap(D_i)$, $1 \leq i \leq n$

The upward refinement operator $\delta_\sqcap$, *given a conjunctive concept description* $C = C_1 \sqcap \cdots \sqcap C_m$, *is defined:*

- $C' \in \delta_\sqcap(C)$ *if* $C' = C - C_j$ *for some* $1 \leq j \leq m$
- $C' \in \delta_\sqcap(C)$ *if* $C' = (C - C_j) \sqcap C'_j$ *for some* $1 \leq j \leq m$, *where:*
  - $C'_j = \exists R.D'_j$, $C_j = \exists R.D_j$ *and* $D'_j \in \delta_\sqcup(D_j)$ *or*
  - $C'_j = \forall R.D'_j$, $C_j = \forall R.D_j$ *and* $D'_j \in \delta_\sqcup(D_j)$

It can be shown that these operators are complete although highly redundant and therefore non ideal. Ideal refinement operators have been proven not to exists in spaces where infinite chains of descriptions occur [10]. In our case, one can consider the infinite chain $\exists R.\top \sqsupseteq \exists R.\exists R.\top \sqsupseteq \exists R.\exists R.\exists R.\top$, etc... Owing to the large extent of the search space, heuristics should be used together with refinement operators in order to focus their search. Defining suitable heuristics based on the available assertions can address a refinement operator to promising regions of the search space. The candidate hypotheses evaluation should take into account the coverage of positive and negative examples in the learning problem. Intuitively, a good hypothesis should cover as many positive examples as possible and reject the negative ones. Moreover, other limitations are typically made upon the size of the hypotheses, in favor of the simpler ones (those containing less restrictions and with the lowest nesting factor, in the adopted language). In the algorithm presented, a possible form for the evaluation function of the i-th concept definition with respect to the j-th MDC may be:

$$\text{eval}(D_i, MDC_j) = w_p \cdot pos_{ij} - w_n \cdot neg_{ij} - w_s \cdot size_i$$

here pos_{ij} and neg_{ij} are determined by the rate of examples covered by the candidate hypothesis over the examples in the MDC, while $size_i$ should be calculated on the ground of its syntactic complexity (each term adds 1 to the size plus the size of the nested concept description, if any). Although this approach may seem quite simplistic, it has proven effective in an ILP context. It should be noted that subsumption in $\mathcal{ALC}$ is computationally expensive and it is known to be hardly reducible to structural operations [2]. Therefore, pursuing a mere *generate and test* strategy for solving supervised learning problems, even investigating better operators, is bound to be inefficient. Better methods should be devised for solving supervised learning problems. The information conveyed by the assertions is to be exploited in the refinement process rather than being tested afterwards.

3.3 Solving Supervised Learning Problems

A learning methodology is proposed based on the notion of counterfactuals built on the ground of residual learning problems [8]. The learning algorithm relies on two interleaving routines performing, respectively, generalization and specialization, that call each other for converging toward a correct concept definition.

The generalization algorithm (Fig. 2) is a greedy covering one: it tries to define positive examples by constructing disjunctive definitions. At each outer iteration, the msc of an example is selected as a starting seed for a new partial generalization; then, iteratively, the hypothesis is generalized by means of the operator δ (with a heuristic that privileges the refinements that cover the most of positives) until all positive concept representatives are covered or some negative representatives are explained. In such a case, the current concept definition $ParGen$ has to be specialized by some counterfactuals. The co-routine, which receives the covered examples as its input, finds a sub-description K that is capable of ruling out the negative examples previously covered.

In the specializing routine (Fig. 3), given a previously computed hypothesis $ParGen$, which is supposed to be complete yet inconsistent with respect to some negative assertions, it must find counterfactuals that, conjuncted to the incorrect definition, can restore its correctness by ruling out the covered negative instances. The algorithm is based on the construction of residual learning problems based on the sub-descriptions that caused the subsumption of the negative examples, represented by their msc's. In this case, a residual is derived by considering that part of the incorrect definition $ParGen$ that did not play a role in the

generalize(*Positives, Negatives, Generalization*)
input   *Positives, Negatives*: positive and negative instances at concept level;
output   *Generalization*: generalized concept definition
1.   *ResPositives* ← *Positives*
2.   *Generalization* ← ⊥
3.   **while** *ResPositives* ≠ ∅ **do**
4.   *ParGen* ← select_seed(*ResPositives*)
5.   *CoveredPos* ← {*Pos* ∈ *ResPositives* | *ParGen* ⊒ *Pos*}
6.   *CoveredNeg* ← {*Neg* ∈ *Negatives* | *ParGen* ⊒ *Neg*}
7.   **while** *CoveredPos* ≠ *ResPositives* **and** *CoveredNeg* = ∅ **do**
8.   *ParGen* ← select(δ(*ParGen*), *ResPositives*)
9.   *CoveredPos* ← {*Pos* ∈ *ResPositives* | *ParGen* ⊒ *Pos*}
10.   *CoveredNeg* ← {*Neg* ∈ *Negatives* | *ParGen* ⊒ *Neg*}
11.   **if** *CoveredNeg* ≠ ∅ **then**
12.   *K* ← **specialize**(*ParGen, CoveredPos, CoveredNeg*)
13.   *ParGen* ← *ParGen* ⊓ ¬*K*
14.   *Generalization* ← *Generalization* ⊔ *ParGen*
15.   *ResPositives* ← *ResPositives* \ *CoveredPos*
16. **return** *Generalization*

Fig. 2. The generalizing routine.

subsumption. The residual will be successively employed as a positive instance of that part of description that should be ruled out of the definition (through negation). Analogously, the msc's derived from positive assertions plays the opposite role of negative instances for the residual learning problem under construction. Finally, this problem is solved by conjoining the negation of the generalization returned by the co-routine, applying it to these example descriptions.

The refinement method is somehow *specialization-oriented* being the generalization mechanism weaker than the one used for specializing the concept definitions. Thus, for the algorithm to work it is required that the starting approximations calculated on the ground of the negative examples be not greater than those relative to the positive ones. The function for calculating residuals is essentially a difference function. In the case of the $\mathcal{ALC}$ language, it is easy to define it as $C - D \equiv C \sqcup \neg D$.

Example 3.1. Suppose that the starting A-box is[3] $\mathcal{A} = \{M(d), r(d, l), r(j, s),$ $\neg M(m), r(m, l), \neg M(a), w(a, j), r(a, s), F(d), F(j), \neg F(m) \neg F(a)\}$.

Let F be the target concept, thus the examples and counterexamples are: *Positives* = $\{d, j\}$ and *Negatives* = $\{m, a\}$. The approximated msc's are:
$$msc(j) = \exists r.\top \qquad\qquad msc(d) = M \sqcap \exists r.\top$$
$$msc(m) = \neg M \sqcap \exists r.\top \qquad msc(a) = \neg M \sqcap \exists r.\top \sqcap \exists w.\top$$
In Fig. 4 learning process step-wise run is reported. The result is $F = M \sqcap \exists r.\top$.

It can be proven that, provided that the adopted language bias is appropriate, the method actually converges to a solution of the learning problem [11]:

---

[3] F stands for **Father**, M for **Man**, r for the **parentOf** role while w represents **wifeOf**.

specialize(*ParGen, CoveredPos, CoveredNeg, K*)
input   *ParGen*: inconsistent concept definition
                CoveredPos, CoveredNeg: covered positive and negative descriptions
output   *K*: counterfactual
1. *NewPositives* ← ∅
2. *NewNegatives* ← ∅
3. **for each** $N_i \in CoveredNeg$ **do**
4. $NewP_i$ ← residual(N_i, *ParGen*)
5.   *NewPositives* ← *NewPositives* ∪ {$NewP_i$}
6. **for each** $P_j \in CoveredPos$ **do**
7. $NewN_j$ ← residual(P_j, *ParGen*)
8.   *NewNegatives* ← *NewNegatives* ∪ {$NewN_j$}
9. K ← **generalize**(*NewPositives, NewNegatives*)
10. **return** K

Fig. 3. The specializing routine.

Theorem 3.1 (correctness). *The algorithm eventually terminates computing a correct concept definition when this exists.*

The process terminates because the *generalize* routine produces one disjunct at each outer iteration, accommodating at least one positive example which is successively removed. Then the termination of the routine is guaranteed, provided that the inner loop terminates. This loop generalizes the seed-definition by applying δ. Eventually, it terminates either because the generalization is correct or it covers some negative example. This is the case when the *specialize* co-routine is invoked. This routine contains two initial loops that are controlled by the sizes of the input example sets. Each loop produces a residual concept definition to be used for the successive generalization. Provided that the other routine produces a correct generalization of the residual concept then also the specializing routine terminates. As regards the correctness, it is to be proven that, on return from the routine, the following relations hold: 1. $\forall Pos \in CoveredPos$: $(ParGen \sqcap \neg K) \sqsupseteq Pos$ and 2. $\forall Neg \in Negatives$: $(ParGen \sqcap \neg K) \not\sqsupseteq Neg$. If the call to *generalize* succeeds then for all $NewN_j \in NewNegatives$: $K \not\sqsupseteq NewN_j$. By definition, $P_j \in Positives$ implies that residual(P_j, *ParGen*) ∈ *NewNegatives*. Hence $K \not\sqsupseteq$ residual(P_j, *ParGen*). Since $\forall Pos \in Positives = CoveredPos$: $ParGen \sqsupseteq Pos$ condition 1. holds. For condition 2., recall that $(ParGen \sqcap \neg K) \not\sqsupseteq Neg$ iff $ParGen \not\sqsupseteq Neg$ or $ParGen \sqsupseteq Neg$ and $K \sqsupseteq$ residual(Neg, *ParGen*). Considering all $Neg \in Negatives$, if $ParGen \not\sqsupseteq Neg$ then the condition holds. Otherwise, if $ParGen \sqsupseteq Neg$ then the routine builds a residual element residual(Neg, *ParGen*) for *NewPositives*. Thus, on return from *generalize*, K is a generalization of every description in *NewPositives*, and hence $K \sqsupseteq$ residual(Neg, *ParGen*). Here, it is assumed that the language bias is adequate for the target problem otherwise the algorithm would fail to discriminate between identical descriptions. In this case, new concepts or roles may be introduced (*constructive induction*) for building discriminating definitions [7]. This goes beyond the scope of our present work. The specialization routine is linear in the number of examples except for the

generalize:
ResidualPositives $\leftarrow$ {msc(d), msc(j)}
Generalization $\leftarrow \perp$
    /* Outer while loop */
    ParGen $\leftarrow msc(d) = M \sqcap \exists r.\top$
    CoveredPos $\leftarrow \{msc(d)\}$ and CoveredNeg $\leftarrow \{\}$
    ParGen $\leftarrow \exists r.\top$ /* M dropped in the inner loop step 8.*/
    CoveredPos $\leftarrow \{msc(d), msc(j)\}$ and CoveredNeg $\leftarrow \{msc(m), msc(a)\}$
    Call **specialize**$(\exists r.\top, \{msc(d), msc(j)\}, \{msc(m), msc(a)\})$
    specialize:
        NewP$_1 \leftarrow \neg M \sqcap \exists r.\top \sqcup \neg \exists r.\top = \neg M$
        NewPositives $\leftarrow \{\neg M\}$
        NewP$_2 \leftarrow \neg M \sqcap \exists r.\top \sqcap \exists w.\top \sqcup \neg(\exists r.\top) = \neg M \sqcap \exists w.\top$
        NewPositives $\leftarrow \{\neg M, \neg M \sqcap \exists w.\top\}$
        NewN$_1 \leftarrow M \sqcap \exists r.\top \sqcup \neg \exists r.\top = M$
        NewNegatives $\leftarrow \{M\}$
        NewN$_2 \leftarrow \top$
        NewNegatives $\leftarrow \{M, \top\}$
        Call **generalize**$(\{\neg M, \neg M \sqcap \exists w.\top\}, \{M, \top\})$
        generalize:
            ResidualPositives $\leftarrow \{\neg M, \neg M \sqcap \exists w.\top\}$
            Generalization $\leftarrow \perp$
            /* Outer while loop */
            ParGen $\leftarrow \neg M \sqcap \exists w.\top$
            CoveredPos $\leftarrow \{\neg M \sqcap \exists w.\top\}$ and CoveredNeg $\leftarrow \{\}$
            /* Second while loop*/
                ParGen $\leftarrow \neg(M \sqcup \neg(M \sqcap \exists w.\top) = \neg M$
                CoveredPos $\leftarrow \{\neg M, \neg M \sqcap \exists w.\top\}$ and CoveredNeg $\leftarrow \{\}$
                Generalization $\leftarrow \neg M$
          Return $\neg M$
        Return $\neg M$ /* back to first call to Generalization */
    ParGen $\leftarrow \exists r.\top \sqcap \neg(\neg M)$
    Generalization $\leftarrow \exists r.\top \sqcap \neg(\neg M)$
    ResidualPositives $\leftarrow \{\}$
Return $\exists r.\top \sqcap M$
$F = M \sqcap \exists r.\top$

Fig. 4. The learning process for the A-Box in Ex. 3.1.

dependency on the generalization algorithm. Then it suffices here to discuss the complexity of such an algorithm. The generalization proposed here is a generic divide and conquer algorithm which performs a greedy search using the refinement operator δ. The number of iterations is linear in the number of instances. The actual source of complexity are the subsumption tests which are known to be PSpace-complete in $\mathcal{ALC}$ [2].

4   Conclusions and Future Work

While deductive reasoning and querying for knowledge bases in DL representation are well assessed, their construction can be a complex task for knowledge engineers which calls for semi-automatic tools. A method for concept formation in the $\mathcal{ALC}$ description logic has been presented. We applied a two-step algorithm where the first step induces level-wise supervised learning problems solved in the second step. The learning process can be performed by using the proposed refinement operators and heuristics. Besides, we have developed a more efficient method based on counterfactuals learning from the available assertions. The proposed framework could be extended along three directions. First, a more expressive language bias could be chosen: e.g. the transitivity of relations would allow to learn recursive concepts. Secondly, inductive construction should be employed to introduce new concept and roles that help the definition and organization of the knowledge bases. Finally, we want to investigate learning with hybrid representations, where clausal logic descriptions are mixed with description logics, the latter accounting for the available ontological knowledge.

References

1. Berners-Lee, T.: Design Issues: Technical and philosophical notes on web architecture (1990-2002) http://www.w3.org/DesignIssues.
2. Baader, F., Calvanese, D., McGuinness, D., Nardi, D., Patel-Schneider, P., eds.: The Description Logic Handbook. Cambridge University Press (2003)
3. Haussler, D.: Learning conjuntive concepts in structural domains. Machine Learning **4** (1989) 7–40
4. Nienhuys-Cheng, S., Laer, W.V., Ramon, J., Raedt, L.D.: Generalizing refinement operators to learn prenex conjunctive normal forms. In: Proceedings of the International Conference on Inductive Logic Programming. Volume 1631 of LNAI., Springer (1999) 245–256
5. Rouveirol, C., Ventos, V.: Towards learning in CARIN-$\mathcal{ALN}$. In Cussens, J., Frisch, A., eds.: Proceedings of the 10th International Conference on Inductive Logic Programming. Volume 1866 of LNAI., Springer (2000) 191–208
6. Cohen, W., Hirsh, H.: Learning the CLASSIC description logic. In Torasso, P., Doyle, J., Sandewall, E., eds.: Proceedings of the 4th International Conference on the Principles of Knowledge Representation and Reasoning, Morgan Kaufmann (1994) 121–133
7. Kietz, J.U., Morik, K.: A polynomial approach to the constructive induction of structural knowledge. Machine Learning **14** (1994) 193–218
8. Vere, S.: Multilevel counterfactuals for generalizations of relational concepts and productions. Artificial Intelligence **14** (1980) 139–164
9. Badea, L., Nienhuys-Cheng, S.H.: A refinement operator for description logics. In Cussens, J., Frisch, A., eds.: Proceedings of the 10th International Conference on Inductive Logic Programming. Volume 1866 of LNAI., Springer (2000) 40–59
10. Nienhuys-Cheng, S., de Wolf, R.: Foundations of Inductive Logic Programming. Volume 1228 of LNAI. Springer (1997)
11. Esposito, F., Fanizzi, N., Iannone, L., Semeraro, G.: Refinement of conceptual descriptions in $\mathcal{ALC}$ knowledge bases. Technical Report DL-2004-01, LACAM, Dipartimento di Informatica, Università degli Studi di Bari (2004)

Multi-level Boundary Classification
for Information Extraction

Aidan Finn and Nicholas Kushmerick

Smart Media Institute, Computer Science Department, University College Dublin, Ireland
{aidan.finn,nick}@ucd.ie

Abstract. We investigate the application of classification techniques to the problem of information extraction (IE). In particular we use support vector machines and several different feature-sets to build a set of classifiers for IE. We show that this approach is competitive with current state-of-the-art IE algorithms based on specialized learning algorithms. We also introduce a new technique for improving the recall of our IE algorithm. This approach uses a two-level ensemble of classifiers to improve the recall of the extracted fragments while maintaining high precision. We show that this approach outperforms current state-of-the-art IE algorithms on several benchmark IE tasks.

1 Introduction

Information extraction (IE) is the process of identifying a set of pre-defined relevant items in text documents. Numerous IE algorithms based on machine learning techniques have been proposed recently. Many of these algorithms are "monolithic" in the sense that there is no clean separation between the learning algorithm and the features used for learning. Furthermore, many of the proposed algorithms effectively reinvent some aspects of machine learning, using their own specialized learning algorithms, rather than exploit existing machine learning algorithms.

In this paper, we investigate how relatively "standard" machine learning techniques can be applied to information extraction. We adopt the standard "IE as classification" formalization [6, 3], in which IE becomes the task of classifying every document position as either the start of a field to extract, the end of a field, or neither. We investigate how different feature-sets contribute to the performance of our algorithm. We show that this approach with support vector machine classification is competitive and in many cases superior to current state of the art approaches based on algorithms crafted specifically for IE.

Based on these initial results, we then describe improvements on this basic approach that give superior performance on a variety of benchmark IE tasks. Our enhancements – which we call multi-level boundary classification – consist of combining the predictions of two sets of classifiers, one set with high precision and one with high recall.

The intuition behind this approach is as follows. Our system consists of two sets of classifiers (L1 and L2). The L1 classifiers adopt the the standard "IE as classification" approach. L2 uses a second level of "biased" classifiers. To extract a fragment we need to identify both its start and end. If the L1 classifier predicts one end of the fragment (ei-

J.-F. Boulicaut et al. (Eds.): ECML 2004, LNAI 3201, pp. 111–122, 2004.
© Springer-Verlag Berlin Heidelberg 2004

ther the start or the end, but not both) we assume that it is correct. We use this prediction as a guide to the L2 classifier to identify the complete fragment (see Fig. 1).

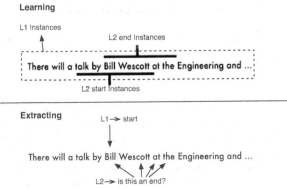

Fig. 1. L1 and L2: An example

We make two contributions. First, we show that the use of an off-the-shelf support vector machine implementation is competitive with current IE algorithms based on specialized learning algorithms. Second, and more significant, we introduce a novel multi-level boundary classification approach, and demonstrate that this new approach outperforms current IE algorithms on a variety of benchmark tasks.

2   Prior Research

We begin with a discussion and comparison of some of the more prominent adaptive IE algorithms.

RAPIER [2] uses inductive logic programming techniques to discover rules for extracting fields from documents. It does not try to identify start and end tags separately, but learns to identify relevant strings in their entirety. RAPIER performs specific-to-general bottom-up search by starting with the most specific rule for each positive training example and repeatedly trying to generalize these rules to cover more positive examples. RAPIER uses as its features the tokens, part-of-speech information and some semantic class information.

BWI [6] learns a large number of simple wrapper patterns, and combines them using boosting. BWI learns separate models for identifying start and end tags and then uses a histogram of training fragment lengths to estimate the accuracy of pairing a given start and end tag. BWI learns to identify start and end tags using a form of specific-to-general search. BWI's features consist of the actual tokens, supplemented by a number of orthographic generalizations (alphabetic, capitalized, alphanumeric, lower-case, numeric, punctuation), as well as a modest amount of lexical knowledge (a list of first and last names).

LP^2 [3] learns symbolic rules for identifying start and end tags. Like BWI, it identifies the starts and ends of fields separately. In addition to token and orthographic features, LP^2 uses some shallow linguistic information such as morphological and part-of-speech information. It also uses a user-defined dictionary or gazetteer. Its learning algorithm is a covering algorithm which starts with specific rules and tries to generalize them to cover as many positive examples as possible. This process is supplemented by learning correction rules that shift predicted tags in order to correct some errors that the learner makes.

SNoW-IE [13]: SNoW [12] is a relational learning algorithm that is specifically tailored towards large scale learning tasks such as IE. SNoW-IE identifies fragments to be extracted rather than separately identifying start and end tags. It uses token, orthographic, POS and semantic features. It learns in two stages. The first stage involves filtering all the candidate fragments while the second involves picking the correct fragments from those remaining.

BWI uses the fewest features: it uses just the tokens and some orthographic information. LP^2 ,RAPIER and SNoW-IE supplement these features with part-of-speech and semantic information.

3   The ELIE Algorithm

Information Extraction as Classification. We treat tasks with multiple fields as multiple independent single-field extraction tasks i.e. we only extract one field at a time. Following [6, 3], we treat the identification of field start and end positions as distinct token classification tasks. All tokens that begin a labeled field are positive instances for the start classifier, while all the other tokens become negative instances for this classifier. Similarly, the positive examples for the end classifier are the last tokens of each labeled field, and the other instances are negative examples.

Features and Encoding. Each instance has a set of features that describe the given token. The features include the specific token, as well as part-of-speech (POS), chunking, orthographic and gazetteer information.

Token. The actual token.

POS. The part-of-speech of the token. Each token is tagged with its corresponding POS using Brill's POS tagger [1]. We also represent chunking information about the tokens. The POS tags are grouped into noun-phrases and verb-phrases.

Gaz. The values associated with the token in a gazetteer. The gazetteer is a user-defined dictionary. It contains lists of first-names and last-names taken from the U.S. census bureau, a list of countries and cities, time identifiers (am, pm), titles (Jr., Mr), and a list of location identifiers used by the U.S. postal service (street, boulevard).

Orthographic. These features give various orthographic information about the token. Examples of these features include whether the token is upper-case, lower-case, capitalized, alphabetic, numeric or punctuation.

Encoding all tokens in the dataset in this manner gives a very large number of attributes. We therefore filter the attributes according to information gain [11] in order to discard irrelevant features and reduce learning time.

Relational information is encoded using additional features. To represent an instance, we encode all these features for that particular token. In addition, for a fixed window size of w, we add the same features for the previous w tokens and the next w tokens. For example, if we use a window size of 1, then each instance has a feature to represent the token for that instance, the token of the preceding instance and the token of the next instance. Similarly, there are features to represent the POS, gaz and orthographic information of the current instance and the previous and next instances.

Learning with ELIE. The ELIE algorithm has two distinct phases. In the first phase, ELIE simply learns to detect the start and end of fragments to be extracted. Our experiments demonstrate that this first phase generally has high precision but low recall. The second phase is designed to increase recall. We find that very often false negatives are "almost" extracted (the start but not the end is correctly identified, or the end but not the start). In the second phase ELIE is trained to detect either the end of a fragment given its beginning, or the beginning of a fragment given its end.

Level One (L1) learning. The L1 learner treats IE as a standard classification task, augmented with a simple mechanism to attach predicted start and end tags.

Fig. 2 shows the learning process. The set of training examples are converted to a set of instances for the start and end tags as described above. Each token in each training document becomes a single instance, and is either a positive or negative example of a start or end tag. Each of these instances is encoded according to several features for the particular token in question and the tokens surrounding it. Then the attributes are filtered according to information gain. These instances are passed to a learning algorithm[1] which uses them to learn a model. At the end of the L1 training phase we have models for start and end tags and all the start-end pairs.

The start-end pairs are passed to the tag-matcher which is charged with matching start and end tags. Our experiments involve a tag-matcher which derives a histogram based on the number of tokens between each start and end tag in the training data. When matching predictions, the probability of a start-tag being paired with an end-tag is estimated as the proportion with which a field of that length occurred in the training data. This approach performs adequately and we don't focus on the tag-matching further in this paper. A more intelligent tag-matcher may improve performance in the future. For example, the tag-matcher might incorporate a learning component that learns to shift tags and correct errors in the output predictions.

Level Two (L2) Learning. The L1 learner builds its model based on a very large number of negative instances and a small number of positive instances. Therefore the prior probability that an arbitrary instance is a boundary is very small. This very low prior probability means that the L1 model is much more likely to produce false negatives than false positives.

The L2 learner is learned from training data in which the prior probability that a given instance is a boundary is much higher than for the L1 learner and the number of irrelevant instances is vastly reduced. This "focused" training data is constructed as follows. When building the L2 start model, we take only the instances that occur a fixed

---

[1] Our current experiments are based on Weka [14]. We used Weka's SMO [10] algorithm for the learner, but other algorithms could be substituted.

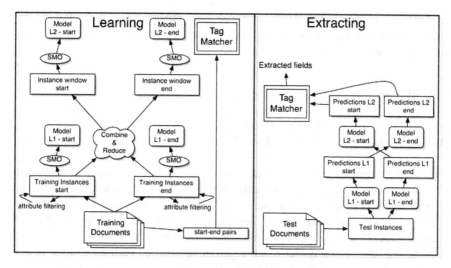

Fig. 2. ELIE architecture

distance before an end tag. Similarly, for the L2 end model, we use only instances that occur a fixed distance after a start tag.

Fig. 1 shows an example of the the instances used by L1 and L2 with a lookahead/lookback of 3. In this example the token "Bill" is the start of a field and the token "Wescott" is the end of a field. When building the L1 classifiers we use all the available instances. When building the L2 start model we use the end token and the 3 tokens preceding it. When building the end model we use the start token and the three tokens following it. Note that these L2 instances are encoded in the same way as for L1; the difference is simply that the L2 learner is only allowed to look at a small subset of the available training data. When extracting, the L2 end classifier is only applied to the three tokens following the token which L1 tagged as a start and the token itself. Similarly the L2 start classifier is only applied to instances tagged as an end by L1 and the three preceding tokens.

This technique for selecting training data means that the L2 models are likely to have much higher recall but lower precision than L1 models. If we were to blindly apply the L2 model to the entire document, it would generate a lot of false positives. Therefore, as shown in Fig. 2 and Fig. 1, the reason we can use the L2 model to improve performance is that we only apply it to regions of documents where the L1 model has made a prediction. Specifically, during extraction, the L2 classifiers use the predictions of the L1 models to identify parts of the document that are predicted to contain fields. Since the L1 classifiers generally have high precision but low recall, the intent is that this procedure will enable ELIE to converge to the correct boundary classifications.

The two level approach takes advantage of the fact that at L1 we have two highly dependent learners, each with very high precision. Thus a prediction by one of them indicates with very high probability that the second should make a prediction. When training the L2 classifier, we drastically alter the prior probabilities of the training data by using only the instances within a fixed distance before or after an annotated start or end. This L2 classifier is much more likely to make predictions as it was trained on a much smaller set of negative instances. Thus it is more likely to identify starts or ends that the L1 classifier missed.

4 Experiments

We evaluated our ELIE algorithm on three benchmark datasets and compared the results to those achieved by other IE algorithms.

Evaluation Method. A truly comprehensive comparison would compare each algorithm on the same dataset, using the same splits, and the exact same scoring method. Unfortunately, a conclusive comparison of the different IE algorithms is impossible using the published results. The other algorithms are evaluated using slightly different methodologies [7] or simply do not report results for every corpus.

There are several orthogonal issues regarding evaluation such as whether to give credit for partial matches and whether all occurrences of the field must be extracted. Our evaluation is conservative and so it is likely that our results are understated in comparison to competitors which have adopted a more liberal evaluation strategy.

Experimental Setup. We evaluate our algorithm on three standard benchmark datasets, the seminar announcements ("SA") dataset [5], the job postings ("Jobs") dataset [2], and the Reuters corporate acquisitions ("Reuters") dataset [5], using 31 fields (see Fig 3). SA consists of 485 seminar announcements annotated for 4 fields detailing upcoming seminars. Jobs consists of 300 newsgroup messages detailing jobs available in the Austin area. The dataset has been annotated for 17 fields. Reuters consists of 600 Reuters articles describing corporate acquisitions. This dataset has been annotated for 10 fields. It is a more difficult task than the other two because some of the fields are related. For example, there are separate annotations for the name of a company and abbreviated versions of the company name.

We used a 50:50 split of the dataset repeated 10 times. All experiments use a window of length 3 tokens, and L2 lookahead/lookback of 10 tokens. On the SA dataset, this typically gives a set of approximately 80 thousand training instances (a few hundred of which are positive) and approximately 50 thousand attributes. These experiments have all features enabled initially, and then the top 5000 features ranked by information gain are used for learning the model.

We compare our system against BWI, RAPIER, LP^2 and SNoW-IE using the available published results for each system. Many of the systems have not published results for all the fields.

Experimental Results. Fig. 3 compares the performance of L1 and L2. The L1 results are measured by passing the predictions of the L1 classifiers directly to the Tag-Matcher, bypassing the L2 classifiers (see Fig. 2). All fields are shown together. The first 4 are from SA, the next 17 from Jobs and the last 10 from Reuters. On every field L1 has equal or higher precision than L2. On every field, L2 has higher recall than L1. On several fields, especially those with lower performance, the increase in recall is large.

There are only three fields where L1 has higher f-measure than L2. Thus L2 causes precision to drop and recall to rise. But in most cases the increase in recall is greater than the drop in precision giving a corresponding increase in f-measure.

Fig. 4 compares the precision, recall and f-measure of ELIE_{L2} with BWI, RAPIER, LP^2 and SNoW-IE. For each graph the horizontal axis shows the performance of ELIE_{L2} while the vertical axis shows the performance of the other IE systems. Points below the diagonal indicate that ELIE_{L2} outperformed the particular IE system on a particular field. Points above the diagonal indicate that the competitor IE system outperformed ELIE_{L2}.

On recall and f-measure ELIE_{L2} outperforms the other algorithms on most of the fields. Some of the other systems perform better than ELIE_{L2} when precision is considered. However ELIE_{L2} improved recall at the expense of precision and if the task requires high precision then ELIE_{L1} can be used instead.

Learning Algorithms and Features. To test how the learning algorithm and the different feature-sets contribute to performance, we evaluated ELIE with various learning algorithms and reduced sets of features on the SA dataset.

We compared SMO with several well-known learning algorithms: naive Bayes, Winnow [8] and Ripper [4]. For SA, naive Bayes performs quite poorly on all fields. Winnow performs well on the etime field, but poorly on the other fields. Ripper performs well on all fields and is competitive with SMO.

Experiments using different feature-sets showed that for the location, stime and etime fields most of the performance comes using the token features alone. For each of these fields adding the POS, GAZ or orthographic features only gives a small increase in performance.

For the speaker field, we get F1=65.0% using only the token features, compared to 88.5% using all features. Using either the POS or orthographic features in addition to the token features gives an 7% increase in performance, while using the token and GAZ features gives a 16% increase over using token features alone. This indicates that the use of a gazetteer significantly enhances performance on this field. This is unsurprising as the gazetteer contains a list of first and last names. However the addition of POS and orthographic also provide significant benefit. On most fields the gazetteer provides little benefit. However for most fields our gazetteer did not contain information relevant to that field. An appropriate gazetteer list could improve performance on several fields but in general this may involve significant additional effort.

ELIE Error Analysis. Table 5 shows details of the errors made by ELIE. For all fields in the three benchmark datasets we show the ratio of false positives to false negatives (FP:FN). It also shows the percentage of false positives that were partially correct and the percentage of false negatives that were partially predicted.

For a false positive to be partially correct means ELIE extracted a fragment, but that it was correct at only one end (either the start or end was not predicted exactly). These kinds of predictions are still useful in a practical setting and a less conservative method of evaluation might give some credit for these kinds of errors. On several fields, a large proportions of the errors are of this form.

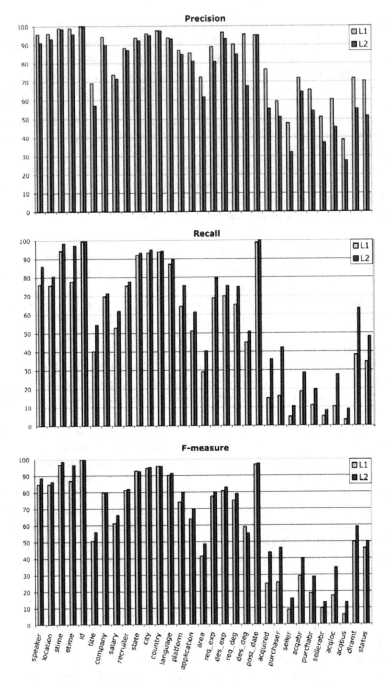

Fig. 3. Comparison of performance of L1 versus that of L2

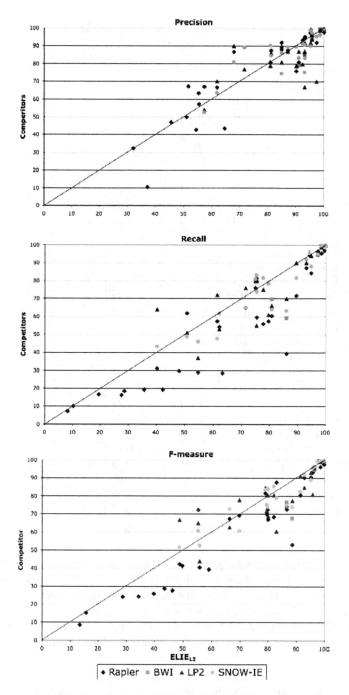

Fig. 4. Comparison of Elie$_{L2}$ with other IE systems

		L1			L2		
Dataset	Field	FP:FN	%FP$_{ptl}$	%FN$_{ptl}$	FP:FN	%FP$_{ptl}$	%FN$_{ptl}$
SA	speaker	0.17	22	62	1.05	17	8
SA	location	0.19	76	67	0.51	75	20
SA	stime	0.2	27	86	4.72	9	36
SA	etime	0.05	64	92	0.93	36	18
Jobs	id	0	0	100	0	0	100
Jobs	title	0.29	71	58	0.9	56	23
Jobs	company	0.14	9	10	0.27	14	2
Jobs	salary	0.4	76	68	0.66	68	43
Jobs	recruiter	0.41	22	22	0.52	21	11
Jobs	state	0.79	9	24	1.11	9	6
Jobs	city	0.56	1	28	0.95	1	1
Jobs	country	0.36	0	6	0.44	0	3
Jobs	language	0.25	41	45	0.52	30	10
Jobs	platform	0.27	43	43	0.54	37	10
Jobs	application	0.18	23	27	0.38	14	3
Jobs	area	0.15	34	25	0.41	25	6
Jobs	req_exp	0.28	8	41	0.92	6	9
Jobs	des_exp	0.09	100	10	0.23	54	12
Jobs	req_degree	0.21	0	34	0.53	2	1
Jobs	des_degree	0.04	0	10	0.51	5	0
Jobs	post_date	4.8	0	100	∞	0	0
Reuters	acquired	0.05	32	32	0.45	18	3
Reuters	purchaser	0.13	10	35	0.7	8	3
Reuters	seller	0.06	1	6	0.24	2	0
Reuters	acqabr	0.09	9	14	0.22	8	1
Reuters	purchabr	0.07	5	11	0.20	8	1
Reuters	sellerabr	0.05	1	4	0.15	2	0
Reuters	acqloc	0.07	16	27	0.46	16	3
Reuters	acqbus	0.05	29	14	0.26	25	4
Reuters	dlramt	0.24	27	53	1.39	15	14
Reuters	status	0.22	23	35	0.87	21	8

Fig. 5. ELIE error analysis

For a false negative to be partially predicted means that for a fragment that we failed to extract, we predicted either the start or the end correctly, but may not have predicted the other. These are the kinds of errors that facilitate the improvement shown by L2 over L1. In general L2 gives a large reduction in these partial errors.

The ratio FP:FN shows that at L1, most of the errors are false negatives, while at L2 we generally see an increase in false positives and a reduction in false negatives.

Discussion and Summary. Our system outperformed those compared against on most fields in terms of recall or f-measure. If high precision is required then ELIE$_{L1}$ can be used. We evaluated our system conservatively so its performance may be understated in relation to competitors.

The L2 learner consistently improves recall while keeping precision high. On more difficult fields the improvements are generally larger. The L2 classifier always improves recall and usually keeps precision high enough to improve F1.

An investigation of the errors that ELIE produces reveals that most errors are false negatives. Those that are false positives are mostly of two kinds. The first are as a result of using exact matching for evaluation, where we have tagged one end of the field correctly but not the other. The second occur as a result of labeling errors on the data where we extract something that should have been labeled but was not.

It is likely that the accuracy of ELIE has two main sources. Firstly, since the L1 classifier alone often gives better performance than other IE algorithms, we conclude that the use of support vector machines as the learning algorithm gives rise to substantial improvement compared to the specialized learning algorithms used by most IE algorithms. Secondly the two-level classification that we have described can give significant increases in performance. It increases recall while maintaining good precision. In many cases, L2 improves ELIE's L1 performance substantially.

5   Conclusion

We have described an approach that treats Information Extraction as a token classification task. Using SMO, a fast support vector machine implementation, our ELIE algorithm learns a set of classifiers for information extraction that are competitive with, and in many cases outperform, current IE algorithms based on specialized learning algorithms.

We also described multi-level boundary classification, a new way of combining classifiers for Information Extraction that yields significant performance improvements. This approach exploits the high precision of token classifiers to increase the recall of the IE algorithm. Our algorithm outperformed current IE algorithms on three benchmark datasets. On several fields, especially those that are more difficult, it gave large improvements in performance.

There is scope for improvement in ELIE. We plan to analyze in detail why the L2 approach can give such dramatic improvements in recall, and specify precisely what properties of the algorithm and/or documents facilitate this.

Other learning components may improve ELIE's performance further, e.g. a component that learns to recognize and correct prediction errors similar to LP^2's correction rules. Another modification might add a third level classifier that takes the predictions of L1 and L2 and classifies the extracted fragment as being correct or not.

Performance may be improved by changing how ELIE combines L1 and L2 predictions. Currently ELIE uses all the L1 and L2 predictions. However it might be feasible to use the L2 predictions to identify incorrect predictions from L1 and remove them. Finally, a more sophisticated tag-matcher could improve overall performance.

Acknowledgments

This research was funded by Science Foundation Ireland and the US Office of Naval Research. Thanks to Fabio Ciravegna for access to LP^2.

References

1. Eric Brill. Some advances in transformation-based parts of speech tagging. In *AAAI*, 1994.
2. Mary Elaine Califf and Raymond J. Mooney. Relational learning of pattern-match rules for information extraction. In *Proc. 16th Nat. Conf. Artifical Intelligence*, 1999.
3. Fabio Ciravegna. Adaptive information extraction from text by rule induction and generalisation. In *Proc. 17th Int. Joint Conf. Artificial Intelligence*, 2001.
4. William Cohen. Fast effective rule induction. In *ICML*, 1995.
5. Dayne Freitag. *Machine Learning for Information Extraction in Informal Domains*. PhD thesis, Carnegie Mellon University, 1998.
6. Dayne Freitag and Nicholas Kushmerick. Boosted wrapper induction. In *Proc. 17th Nat. Conf. Artificial Intelligence*, 2000.
7. Alberto Lavelli, Mary Elaine Califf, Fabio Ciravegna, Dayne Freitag, Claudio Giuliano, Nick Kushmerick, and Lorenza Romano. A critical survey of the methodology for IE evaluation. In *4th International Conference on Language Resources and Evaluation*, 2004.
8. Nick Littlestone. Learning quickly when irrelevant attributes abound: A new linear-threshold algorithm. *Machine Learning*, 2(4):285–318, 1988.
9. Leonid Peshkin and Avi Pfeffer. Bayesian information extraction network. In *Proc.18th Int. Joint Conf. Artifical Intelligence*, 2003.
10. John C. Platt. Fast training of support vector machines using sequential minimal optimization. In B. Schölkopf, C. Burges, and A. Smola, editors, *Advances in Kernel Methods - Support Vector Learning*. MIT Press, 1998.
11. Ross Quinlan. *C4.5: Programs for Machine Learning*. Morgan Kaufman, 1993.
12. Dan Roth. Learning to resolve natural language ambiguities: A unified approach. In *National Conference on Artificial Intelligence*, 1998.
13. Dan Roth and Wen-Tau Yih. Relational learning via propositional algorithms: An information extraction case study. In *17th International Joint Conference on Artificial Intelligence*, 2001.
14. Ian H. Witten and Eibe Frank. *Data Mining: Practical Machine Learning Tools and Techniques with Java Implementations*. Morgan Kaufmann, 2000.

An Analysis of Stopping
and Filtering Criteria for Rule Learning

Johannes Fürnkranz[1] and Peter Flach[2]

[1] TU Darmstadt, Knowledge Engineering Group
Hochschulstraße 10, D-64289 Darmstadt, Germany
fuernkranz@informatik.tu-darmstadt.de
[2] Department of Computer Science, University of Bristol
Merchant Venturers Building, Woodland Road, Bristol BS8 1UB, UK
Peter.Flach@bristol.ac.uk

Abstract. In this paper, we investigate the properties of commonly used pre-pruning heuristics for rule learning by visualizing them in PN-space. PN-space is a variant of ROC-space, which is particularly suited for visualizing the behavior of rule learning and its heuristics. On the one hand, we think that our results lead to a better understanding of the effects of stopping and filtering criteria, and hence to a better understanding of rule learning algorithms in general. On the other hand, we uncover a few shortcomings of commonly used heuristics, thereby hopefully motivating additional work in this area.

1 Introduction

Noisy data and the problem of overfitting theories is typically addressed by biasing the learner towards simpler concepts. In the area of inductive rule learning, there are two fundamental approaches for achieving this goal: *pre-pruning* in the form of stopping and filtering criteria that decide when a rule should no longer be specialized, and *post-pruning*, which simplifies overfitting rules by generalizing them as long as their performance on an independent part of the training set increases [6]. The predominant strategy is pruning, which is mostly due to the success of Ripper [3], arguably the most powerful rule learning algorithm available today. Pre-pruning approaches, such as those used in CN2 [2, 1] or Foil [14], turn out to be inferior in practice.

In this paper, we analyze commonly used pre-pruning heuristics. Our main analytical tool is visualization in PN-space, a variant of ROC-space that is particularly suited for rule learning. We will briefly review PN-spaces in Section 2. There are two slightly different approaches to pre-pruning in rule learning, namely filtering of irrelevant candidate rules and early stopping of the refinement process. We will discuss their differences on the examples of Foil [14] and CN2 [2] in Section 3 before we turn to the main part of our analysis in Section 4. Parts of this paper also appear in [9].

2 PN-Space

Our main tool of analysis will be PN-spaces as introduced in [8]. In brief, *PN-space* is quite similar to ROC-space, the main differences being that PN-spaces work with absolute numbers of covered positive and negative examples, whereas ROC-spaces work

J.-F. Boulicaut et al. (Eds.): ECML 2004, LNAI 3201, pp. 123–133, 2004.

with true positive and false positive rates. A rule that covers p out of a total of P positive examples and n out of N negative examples is represented as a point in PN-space with the co-ordinates (n, p).

The covering or separate-and-conquer strategy for rule learning [7] proceeds by learning one rule at a time. Adding a rule to a rule set means that more examples are classified as positive, i.e., it increases the coverage of the rule set. All positive examples that are uniquely covered by the newly added rule contribute to an increase of the true positive rate on the training data. Conversely, covering additional negative examples may be viewed as increasing the false positive rate on the training data. Therefore, adding rule r_{i+1} to rule set R_i effectively moves from point $R_i = (n_i, p_i)$ (corresponding to the number of negative and positive examples that are covered by previous rules), to a new point $R_{i+1} = (n_{i+1}, p_{i+1})$ (corresponding to the examples covered by the new rule set). Moreover, R_{i+1} will typically be closer to (N, P) and farther away from $(0, 0)$ than R_i.

Consequently, learning a rule set one rule at a time may be viewed as a path through PN-space, where each point on the path corresponds to the addition of a rule to the theory. Such a *PN-path* starts at $(0, 0)$, which corresponds to the empty theory that does not cover any examples. Figure 1 shows the PN-path for a theory with three rules. Each point R_i represents the rule set consisting of the first i rules. Adding a rule moves to a new point in PN-space, corresponding to a theory consisting of all rules that have been learned so far. Removing the covered examples has the effect of moving to a subspace of the original PN-space, using the last rule as the new origin. Thus the path may also be viewed as a sequence of nested PN-spaces PN_i. After the final rule has been learned, one can imagine adding yet another rule with a body that is always true. Adding such a rule has the effect that the theory now classifies *all* examples as positive, i.e., it will take us to the point $\tilde{R} = (N, P)$. Even this theory might be optimal under some cost assumptions.

For finding individual rules, the vast majority of algorithms use a heuristic top-down hill-climbing[1] or beam search strategy, i.e., they search the space of possible rules by successively specializing the current best rule [7]. Rules are specialized by greedily adding the condition which promises the highest gain according to some *evaluation metric*. Like with adding rules to a rule set, this successive refinement describes a path trough PN-space (Figure 1, right). However, in this case, the path starts at the upper right corner (covering all positive and negative examples), and successively proceeds towards the origin (which would be a rule that is too specific to cover any example).

PN-spaces are also well-suited for visualizing the behavior of evaluation metrics. For this purpose, we look at their *isometrics*, i.e., the lines that connect the points that are evaluated equal by the used heuristic [8]. In this paper, we employ this methodology for visualizing stopping and filtering criteria of rule learning algorithms.

---

[1] The term "top-down hill-climbing" may seem somewhat contradictory: hill-climbing refers to the process of greedily moving towards a (local) optimum of the evaluation function, whereas top-down refers to the fact that the search space is searched by successively specializing the candidate rules, thereby moving downards in the generalization hierarchy induced by the rules.

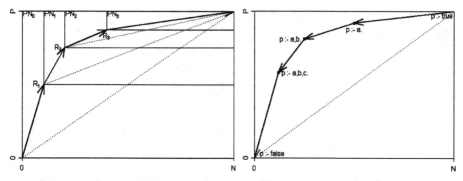

Fig. 1. Schematic depiction of the PN-paths for (left) the covering strategy of learning a theory by adding one rule at a time and (right) greedy specialization of a single rule.

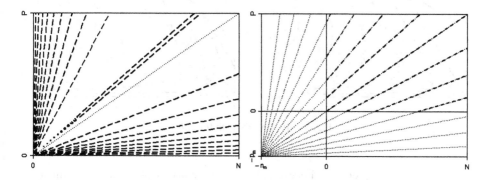

Fig. 2. Isometrics for entropy (left) and the m-estimate (right).

3   Stopping vs. Filtering

In addition to their regular evaluation metric, many rule learning algorithms employ separate criteria to filter out uninteresting candidates and/or to fight overfitting. There are two slightly different approaches: *stopping criteria* determine when the refinement process should stop whereas *filtering criteria* determine regions of acceptable performance.

As an illustration, let us compare the strategies used by Foil and CN2. CN2 evaluates rules on an absolute scale, using either entropy or the m-estimate. Figure 2 shows their isometrics. For 2-class problems, entropy is more or less equivalent to precision, i.e., its isometrics rotate around the origin $(0, 0)$. The only difference is that entropy is symmetric around the 45 degree line ($p = n$). The reason is that early versions of CN2 assigned the class label after the rule has been learned. If a rule is in the area above this line, it will be assigned the positive label, below this line the negative class.

The basic idea of the m-estimate is to assume that each rule covers a certain number of examples *a priori*. It computes a precision estimate, but assumes that it has already observed a total of m examples distributed according to the prior probabilities ($N/(P+$

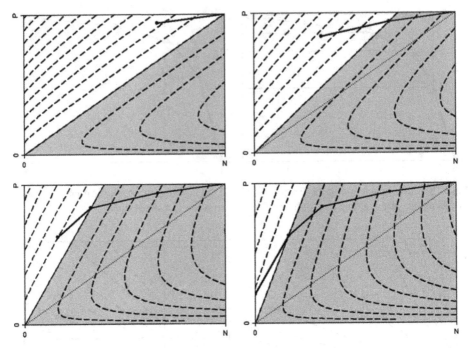

Fig. 3. A typical PN-path for *Foil*.

N), $P/(P+N)$) of the domain. For example, in the special case of the Laplace estimate, both the positive and negative coverage of a rule are initialized with 1 (thus assuming an equal prior distribution). This has the effect that the rotation point of the precision estimate is moved to a point $(-n_m, -p_m)$, where $n_m = p_m = 1$ in the case of the Laplace heuristic, and $p_m = m * P/(P + N)$ and $n_m = m - p_m = m * N/(P + N)$ for the m-estimate. Note that for $m \to \infty$, the isometrics of the m-estimate become increasingly parallel to the diagonal of the PN-space. This is the defining characteristic of weighted relative accuracy [11], which has also been tested in a CN2-like algorithm [16]. Thus, the m-estimate may be considered as a means for trading off precision and WRA.

CN2 evaluates all possible candidate refinements of a rule according to one of these measures. As the evaluation function does not change during the search, the evaluations of all searched rules are comparable. As a consequence, CN2 continues to search until no further refinements are possible, and the *best* rule (the one with the highest evaluation) encountered during this search is returned.

On the other hand, Foil, which forms the basis of many rule learning algorithms, most notably Ripper [3], does not evaluate rules on an absolute scale but relative to their respective predecessors. Hence, the evaluation of two rules with different predecessors are not directly comparable. For this reason, Foil-like algorithms always return the last rule searched. This process is illustrated in Figure 3. In the upper left graph, we see the initial situation: the starting rule covers all examples, i.e., it lies on the upper right corner of PN-space. Foil evaluates its rules using a heuristic based on information gain.

This heuristic has value 0 when a refinement has no gain over its predecessor rule. In the beginning, all such rules lie on the the diagonal. In the area above the 0-gain line, the isometrics are almost parallel to this line, i.e., in this region the heuristic behaves almost like a cost-weighted version of accuracy [8]. The area below the 0-gain area (the gray area in the graphs of Figure 3) is not interesting because these are rules that have an information loss, i.e., their quality is worse than the quality of their predecessor.

When Foil adds a condition to a rule, the resulting rule becomes the new starting point for the next refinement step. Consequently, the 0-gain line is rotated until it goes through the point corresponding to this rule. The isometrics of the heuristic rotate with this line and become steeper and steeper the closer the rule moves towards the upper left corner of PN-space. This rotation of the 0-gain line around the origin has an interesting parallel to the use of precision as a search heuristic. The main difference is that, due to the (almost) parallel lines above the 0-gain line, information gain has a tendency to prefer more general refinements, thus trying to stay in the upper regions of PN-space. This may also be interpreted as a method for implementing "patient" rule induction, as advocated in [4].

Because of this cost rotation, Foil will (almost) always find an improvement over its predecessor, because the point (0.1), covering no negative examples and a single positive example, is an improvement over all predecessor rules that cover at least 1 negative example. Therefore, Foil's refinement process will usually continue until a pure rule is found. As this typically leads to overfitting, it is crucial to have a good *stopping* criterion, which determines when the refinement process should terminate. For CN2-type algorithms this is not so crucial, because the rule returned is not necessarily the last rule searched, but the rule with the highest evaluation encountered during the search. In this case, the role of a stopping criterion is replaced with a *filtering* criterion that filters out unpromising candidates, but does not directly influence the choice of the best rule. This observation was already made in [1]. As we will see in the next session, filtering criteria typically define an area of PN-space that is ignored by the search space.

Filtering and stopping criteria are closely related. In particular, filtering criteria can also be used as stopping criteria: If no further rule can be found within the acceptable region of a filtering criterion, the learned theory is considered to be complete. Basically the same technique is also used for refining single rules: if no refinement is in the acceptable region, the rule is considered to be complete, and the specialization process stops. For this reason, we will often use the term stopping criterion instead of filtering criterion because this is the more established terminology.

4   Analysis of Common Criteria

In the following, we illustrate prominent filtering and stopping criteria for greedy specialization: minimum coverage constraints, support and confidence, significance tests, encoding length restrictions, and correlation cutoff. We use PN-space to analyze stopping criteria, by visualizing regions of acceptable hypotheses.

4.1   Minimum Coverage Constraints

The simplest form of overfitting avoidance is to disregard rules with low coverage. For example, one could require that a rule covers a certain minimum number of examples

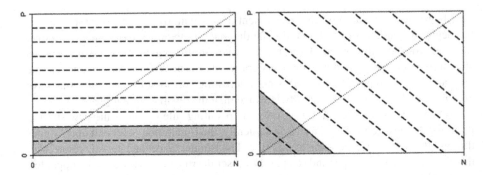

Fig. 4. Thresholds on minimum coverage of positive examples (left) and total number of examples (right).

or a minimum number of positive examples. These two cases are illustrated in Figure 4. The graph on the left shows the requirement that a minimum fraction (here 20%) of the positive examples in the training set are covered by the rule. All rules in the gray area are thus excluded from consideration. The right graph illustrates the case where a minimum fraction (here 20%) of examples needs to be covered by the rule, regardless of whether they are positive or negative. Changing the size of the fraction will cut out different slices of the PN-space, each delimited with a coverage isometric (-45 degrees lines). Clearly, in both cases the goal is to fight overfitting by filtering out rules whose quality cannot be reliably estimated because of the small number of training examples they cover. Notice that different misclassification costs can be modeled in this framework by changing the slope of the coverage isometrics.

4.2   Support and Confidence

There is no reason why a single measure should be used for filtering out unpromising rules. The most prominent example for combining multiple estimates are the thresholds on support and confidence that are used mostly in association rule mining algorithms, but also in classification algorithms that obtain the candidate rules for the covering loop in an association rule learning framework [12, 13, 10].

Figure 5 illustrates the effect of thresholds on support and confidence in PN-space. Together, they specify an area for valid rules around the $(0, P)$-point in ROC-space. Rules in the gray areas will be filtered out. The dark gray region shows a less restrictive combination of the two thresholds, the light gray region a more restrictive setting. In effect, confidence constrains the quality of the rules, whereas support aims at ensuring a minimum reliability by filtering out rules whose confidence estimate originates from too few positive examples.

4.3   Foil's Encoding Length Restriction

Foil uses a criterion based on the minimum description length (MDL) principle [15] for deciding when to stop refining the current rule. For explicitly indicating the p positive examples covered by the rule, one needs h_{MDL} bits:

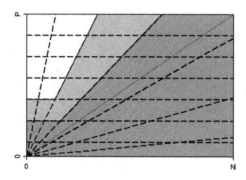

Fig. 5. Filtering rules with minimum support and minimum confidence.

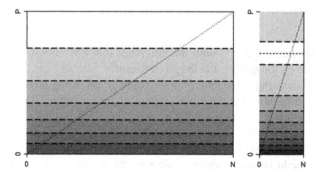

Fig. 6. Illustration of Foil's encoding length restriction for domains with $P < N$ (left) and $P > N$ (right). Lighter shades of gray correspond to larger encoding lengths for the rule.

$$h_{MDL} = \log_2 (P + N) + \log_2 \binom{P + N}{p}$$

For the purposes of our analysis, we interpret h_{MDL} as a heuristic that is compared to a variable threshold the size of which depends on the length of the rule $l(r)$. If $h_{MDL}(r) < l(r)$, i.e., if the encoding of the rule is longer than the encoding of the examples themselves, the rule is rejected. As $l(r)$ depends solely on the encoding length (in bits) of the current rule, Foil's stopping criterion depends on the size of the training set: the same rule that is too long for a smaller training set might be good enough for a larger training set, in which it covers more examples.

Figure 6 shows the behavior of h_{MDL} in PN-space. The isometric landscape is equivalent to the minimum support criterion, namely parallel lines to the N-axis. This is not surprising, considering that h_{MDL} is independent of n, the number of covered negative examples.

For $P < N$, h_{MDL} is monotonically increasing with p. If we see this in connection with Foil's search heuristic (Figure 3), we note that while the rule refinement process rotates the 0-gain line towards the right, the MDL metric steadily increases a minimum support constraint. Thus, the combined effect is the same as the effect of support and

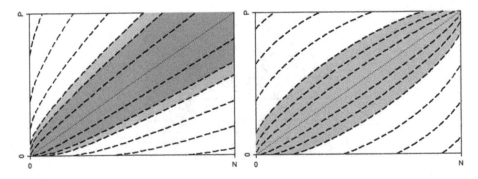

Fig. 7. Left: CN2's significance test, with the regions that would not pass a 95% (dark gray) and a 99% (light gray) significant test. Right: Fossil's cutoff criterion. The gray region corresponds to the cutoff threshold 0.3.

confidence constraints (Figure 5) with the difference that Foil chooses the thresholds dynamically based on the quality and length of the rules.

Particularly interesting is the case $P > N$ (right graph of Figure 6): the isometric landscape is still the same, but the labels are no longer monotonically increasing. In fact, h_{MDL} has a maximum at the point $p = (P + N)/2$. Below this line (shown dashed in Figure 6), the function is monotonically increasing (as above), but above this line it starts to decrease again. Thus, for skewed class distributions with many positive examples, there might be cases where a rule r is acceptable, while a rule r' that has the same encoding length ($l(r') = l(r)$), covers the same number or fewer negative examples ($n(r') \leq n(r)$), but more positive examples ($p(r') > p(r)$) is *not* acceptable. For example, in the example shown on the right of Figure 6, for a certain rule length l, only rules that cover between 65% and 80% of the positive examples are acceptable. A rule of the same length that covers all positive and no negative examples would not be acceptable. This is very counter-intuitive and sheds some doubts upon the suitability of Foil's encoding length restriction for such domains.

4.4   CN2's Significance Test

CN2 filters rules for which there is no statistically significant difference between distribution of the covered examples and the distribution of examples in the full data set. To this end, it computes the *likelihood ratio statistic*:

$$h_{lrs} = 2(p \log \frac{p}{e_p} + n \log \frac{n}{e_n})$$

where $e_p = (p + n)\frac{P}{P+N}$ and $e_n = (p + n)\frac{N}{P+N} = (p + n) - e_p$ are the number of positive and negative examples one could expect the rule to cover if the $p + n$ examples covered by the rule were distributed in the same way as the $P + N$ examples in the full data set.

The left graph of Figure 7 illustrates CN2's filtering criterion. The dark gray area shows the location of the rules that will be filtered out because it can not be established with 95% confidence that their distribution is different from the distribution in the full dataset. The light gray area shows the set of rules that will be filtered out if 99% confidence in the difference is required. The area is symmetric around the diagonal, which represents all rules that have the same distribution as the full example set.

Note that the likelihood ratio isometrics do not depend on the size of the training set. Any graph corresponding to a bigger training set with the same class distribution will contain this graph in its lower left corner. In other words, whether a rule covering p positive and n negative examples is significant according to h_{lrs} depends on the class distribution of the examples it covers, and on the absolute number of positive and negative examples covered by a rule. Thus, similar to Foil's case the same rule that is not significant for one dataset, might be good enough for a larger training set, in which it has a larger empirical support.

The isometric structure of this heuristic is quite similar to those of precision or the m-heuristic, with the difference that the isometrics are not linear but tilted towards the origin. Thus, the significance test has a tendency to prefer purer rules. As small pure rules are often the result of overfitting, it is questionable whether this strategy is reasonable if the primary goal of the significance test is to counter overfitting. The main purpose is to filter out uninteresting rules, i.e., rules for which the class distribution of the covered examples does not differ significantly from the *a priori* distribution.

This similarity between search and stopping heuristic also throws up the question why different heuristics are used. It seems to be unlikely that CN2's behavior would be much different if the likelihood statistics is directly used as a search heuristic. Conversely, thresholds upon the m-heuristic would have a similar effect than CN2's significant test (although the semantics of the associated significance levels would be lost).

4.5 Fossil's Correlation Cutoff

Fossil [5] imposes a threshold upon the correlation heuristic h_{corr}.

$$h_{corr} = \frac{p(N-n) - (P-p)n}{\sqrt{PN(p+n)(P-p+N-n)}} = \frac{pN - Pn}{\sqrt{PN(p+n)(P-p+N-n)}}$$

Only rules that evaluate above this threshold are admitted. The left graph of Figure 7 shows the isometric landscape of the correlation heuristic and the effect of a cutoff of 0.3, which appears to perform fairly well over a variety of domains [6]. Fossil uses this criterion as a stopping criterion. Like Foil, it does not return the rule with the highest evaluation, but it continues to add conditions until the stopping criterion fires. Thus, the cutoff line shown in Figure 7 may be viewed as a minimum quality line: learning stops as soon as the path of the learner crosses this line (from the acceptable region to the non-acceptable region), and the last rule above this line is returned[2].

It can be clearly seen that, like CN2, Fossil focuses upon filtering out uninteresting rules, i.e., rules whose example distribution does not deviate much from the example

---

[2] The reason for this is that as in Foil, the heuristic is only used for determining the best refinement of the currently searched rule, and not for finding an optimum among all candidate rules. For this type of algorithms, the stopping criterion is particularly crucial. Later versions of Fossil switched to a global evaluation, but no strict empirical comparison of the approaches was performed.

distribution in the full training set. Similar to CN2, rules that cover few negative examples are preferred by the bended shape of the isometric lines. A major difference between these two approaches is that h_{corr} is independent of the size of the training set, i.e., it always fits the same isometric landscape into PN-space. As a result, the evaluation of a point (n, p) depends on its relative location $(n/N, p/P)$. In this case, the same rule will always be evaluated in the same way, as long as it covers the same fraction of the training data. This differs from the behavior of CN2 and Foil, where the filtering of a rule depends on its absolute location (n, p). It is still an open question which approach is preferable in practice, but there is considerable evidence that Foil's and CN2's pre-pruning heuristic are inefficient in preventing overfitting in the presence of noisy data [5, 16].

5   Conclusions

In this paper we continued our analysis of rule learning heuristics. While previous work [8] concentrated on learning heuristics, this work focused on pre-pruning heuristics, in particular those that are used in the Foil and CN2 rule learning algorithms. Our main results are

- Foil's MDL-based filtering is quite similar to support/confidence filtering with a dynamic adjustment of the thresholds.
- Foil's criterion has an erratic behavior for class distributions with a majority of positive examples. In these cases, rules that cover more positive and fewer negative examples than the current, acceptable rule may be rejected.
- Fossil's cutoff criterion and CN2's significance test aim at filtering out uninteresting rules (rules for which the distribution of the covered examples does not deviate much from the *a priori* distribution), but do not explicitly address overfitting.
- Whether a rule is filtered by Foil's or CN2's filtering criterion depends on the *absolute* number of covered examples, whereas Fossil filters based on their *relative* number. This may explain the ineffectiveness of Foil's and CN2's pre-pruning heuristics, which is known from several independent studies.

Overall, we believe that our analysis has shown that we are still far from a systematic understanding of pre-pruning heuristics. The fact that, unlike decision-tree algorithms, most state-of-the-art rule learning algorithms use post-pruning for noise-handling may not necessarily be a strong indicator for the superiority of this approach, but may also be interpreted as an indicator of the inadequacy of currently used stopping and filtering criteria.

For this reason, we hope that our work will also support future efforts on designing novel stopping and filtering criteria. Working in PN-space allows one to simply draw the region of PN-space that is intended to be filtered out and find a function that approximates this decision boundary. For stopping criteria, more dynamic criteria can be imagined. For example, a simple criterion would be to stop the generation process whenever the PN-path of the rule set crosses the line that starts in the upper left corner $(0, P)$ and decreases with an angle of -45 degrees. This line represents the points where $p + n = P$, i.e., where the number of examples that are predicted positive equals the number of examples that are actually positive. Thus, a theory that is near this line will adhere to the prior probability of the positive class. Eventually, our work should lead to a broad empirical comparison of different stopping criteria, both new and old, which is currently in preparation.

References

[1] Peter Clark and Robin Boswell. Rule induction with CN2: Some recent improvements. In *Proceedings of the 5th European Working Session on Learning (EWSL-91)*, pages 151–163, Porto, Portugal, 1991. Springer-Verlag.

[2] Peter Clark and Tim Niblett. The CN2 induction algorithm. *Machine Learning*, 3(4):261–283, 1989.

[3] William W. Cohen. Fast effective rule induction. In A. Prieditis and S. Russell, editors, *Proceedings of the 12th International Conference on Machine Learning (ML-95)*, pages 115–123, Lake Tahoe, CA, 1995. Morgan Kaufmann.

[4] Jerome H. Friedman and Nicholas I. Fisher. Bump hunting in high-dimensional data. *Statistics and Computing*, 9(2):1–20, 1999.

[5] Johannes Fürnkranz. FOSSIL: A robust relational learner. In F. Bergadano and L. De Raedt, editors, *Proceedings of the 7th European Conference on Machine Learning (ECML-94)*, volume 784 of *Lecture Notes in Artificial Intelligence*, pages 122–137, Catania, Italy, 1994. Springer-Verlag.

[6] Johannes Fürnkranz. Pruning algorithms for rule learning. *Machine Learning*, 27(2):139–171, 1997.

[7] Johannes Fürnkranz. Separate-and-conquer rule learning. *Artificial Intelligence Review*, 13(1):3–54, February 1999.

[8] Johannes Fürnkranz and Peter Flach. An analysis of rule evaluation metrics. In T. Fawcett and N. Mishra, editors, *Proceedings of the 20th International Conference on Machine Learning (ICML-03)*, pages 202–209, Washington, DC, 2003. AAAI Press.

[9] Johannes Fürnkranz and Peter Flach. Roc 'n' rule learning - towards a better understanding of covering algorithms. *Machine Learning*, To appear.

[10] Viktor Jovanoski and Nada Lavrač. Classification rule learning with APRIORI-C. In P. Brazdil and A. Jorge, editors, *Proceedings of the 10th Portuguese Conference on Artificial Intelligence (EPIA 2001)*, pages 44–51, Porto, Portugal, 2001. Springer-Verlag.

[11] Nada Lavrač, Peter Flach, and Blaz Zupan. Rule evaluation measures: A unifying view. In S. Džeroski and P. Flach, editors, *Proceedings of the 9th International Workshop on Inductive Logic Programming (ILP-99)*, volume 1634 of *Lecture Notes in Artificial Intelligence*, pages 174–185. Springer-Verlag, 1999.

[12] Bing Liu, Wynne Hsu, and Yiming Ma. Integrating classification and association rule mining. In R. Agrawal, P. Stolorz, and G. Piatetsky-Shapiro, editors, *Proceedings of the 4th International Conference on Knowledge Discovery and Data Mining (KDD-98)*, 1998.

[13] Bing Liu, Yiming Ma, and Ching-Kian Wong. Improving an exhaustive search based rule learner. In D. A. Zighed, H. J. Komorowski, and J. M. Zytkow, editors, *Proceedings of the 4th European Conference on Principles and Practice of Knowledge Discovery in Databases (PKDD-2000)*, pages 504–509, Lyon, France, 2000.

[14] J. Ross Quinlan. Learning logical definitions from relations. *Machine Learning*, 5:239–266, 1990.

[15] J. Rissanen. Modeling by shortest data description. *Automatica*, 14:465–471, 1978.

[16] Ljupčo Todorovski, Peter Flach, and Nada Lavrač. Predictive performance of weighted relative accuracy. In D.A. Zighed, J. Komorowski, and J. Zytkow, editors, *Proceedings of the 4th European Conference on Principles of Data Mining and Knowledge Discovery (PKDD-2000)*, pages 255–264, Lyon, France, 2000. Springer-Verlag.

Adaptive Online Time Allocation to Search Algorithms

Matteo Gagliolo, Viktor Zhumatiy, and Jürgen Schmidhuber

IDSIA, Galleria 2, 6928 Manno-Lugano, Switzerland
{matteo,viktor,juergen}@idsia.ch

Abstract. Given is a search problem or a sequence of search problems, as well as a set of potentially useful search algorithms. We propose a general framework for online allocation of computation time to search algorithms based on experience with their performance so far. In an example instantiation, we use simple linear extrapolation of performance for allocating time to various simultaneously running genetic algorithms characterized by different parameter values. Despite the large number of searchers tested in parallel, on various tasks this rather general approach compares favorably to a more specialized state-of-the-art heuristic; in one case it is nearly two orders of magnitude faster.

1 Introduction

Suppose we have a finite or infinite set A of search algorithms $a_1, a_2, \ldots$. For example, A could be the infinite set of all programs of a particular programming language, or a finite set of genetic algorithms (GAs) [6] that differ only by certain parameters such as mutation rate and population size.

Given some problem or problem sequence, we would like to *automatically* – not manually as in much traditional work! – collect experience with various elements of A, in order to allocate more time to more "promising" $a_i \in A$, such that the total computational effort is small. Towards this end we introduce the following general framework.

The life of our Adaptive Online Time Allocator (AOTA) consists of steps $1, 2, \ldots$. At step k it tries to solve current problem $r(k)$ by allocating discrete computation time $t(k)$ to algorithm $a(k) \in A$. After its time has expired, $a(k)$ will pause and output a D-dimensional data vector $d(k) \in \mathbb{R}^D$ conveying information such as: did $a(k)$ converge on $r(k)$? How much did $a(k)$ improve some $r(k)$-specific fitness function? For all k, the pair

$$(a(k), t(k)) = f(r(k), H(k), P) \tag{1}$$

is a function of the historic experience set $H(k) = \{(i, r(i), a(i), t(i), d(i)) : 0 < i < k\}$ and the initial bias P, typically a probability distribution over A.

If the problems $r(k)$ change over time we may speak of *inter-problem* adaptation, or *inductive transfer* from one problem to the next. Otherwise we speak of *intra-problem* adaptation[1].

---

[1] Note that we always refer to the adaption of the time allocation schedule, not of the parameters themselves. The parameters of each a stay fixed. A broader class of AI algorithms, which we do not consider here, deals with the adaption of parameter values themselves, e.g. by decreasing a learning rate according to the current convergence, etc.

J.-F. Boulicaut et al. (Eds.): ECML 2004, LNAI 3201, pp. 134–143, 2004.

In the following we briefly present a few existent (sect. 1.1) and possible (sect. 1.2) examples of both kinds of adaptation, then we introduce our intra-problem approach applied to GA parameter selection (sect. 1.3), and give experimental results for it (sect. 2).

1.1 Previous Work

Certain previous methods may be viewed as instances of this framework. For example, the A of the Optimal Ordered Problem Solver (OOPS) [12] may include all programs of a universal programming language. The initial bias P is a probability distribution on A. As OOPS is solving more and more problems, it may reuse programs computing solutions to previous problems, increasing the probabilities of formerly unlikely programs in bias-optimal fashion [12], and with an optimal order of computational complexity. However, the feedback data $d(k)$ used by OOPS is quite limited: it just says whether $a(k)$ has halted or not, and whether it has solved the current problem. That is, OOPS performs inter-problem adaptation and does not exploit intra-problem information.

A theoretical description of a similar inter-problem adaption scheme, with some form of intra-problem adaption, is given in [14], where a system solves function inversion and time-limited optimization problems by searching in a space of problem solving techniques described in a Lisp-like language, allocating time to them according to their probabilities, and updating the probabilities according to positive and negative results on a sequence of problems.

Examples of simple intra-problem AOTAs are racing algorithms [10, 1]. Their finite A contains different parameterizations of a given supervised algorithm. Each is repeatedly run on a sequence of leave-one-out training sets; the $d(k)$ provide current mean errors and relative confidence intervals of each $a \in A$; badly performing $a \in A$ are progressively discarded as statistically sufficient evidence is gathered against them. This straight-forward approach, however, cannot be immediately extended to algorithms with unknown convergence time, e.g. GAs.

The "parameterless GA" [5] also may be viewed as a specialized intra-problem AOTA. Its A contains generational GAs a_i with population size 2^i (without mutation), which are generated and executed according to a fixed interleaving schedule that assigns runtime to $a_i \in A$ in proportion to a variable bias p_i, initialized by 2^{-i}. Once the population of a_i converges, or some a_j $(j > i)$ achieves higher average fitness, p_i becomes 0 and all $p_j(j > i)$ are doubled. This simple heuristic is motivated by the fact that, in the absence of mutation, convergence of a population is irreversible, and once the population of a_{i+1} reaches the average fitness of the population of a_i while being run half the time of a_i, then the population of a_i is probably drifting too slowly, so one may safely stop executing it, as it is unlikely that a smaller population will eventually produce a better solution than a larger one.

1.2   Choices for Learning Procedure f

Generally speaking, we might use all kinds of well-known learning algorithms to implement f. For example, we could use all or recent parts of the history $H(k)$ to train a neural network or a support vector machine to predict $d(k + 1)$ from inputs representing possible combinations of $a(k + 1)$ and $t(k + 1)$. The predictive model could then be used to find a pair $(a(k+1), t(k+1))$ that maximizes predicted success. Or, in a Reinforcement Learning (RL) setting [8], we may view each sequence $H(k)$ as a point in a huge, possibly continuous *state space*. The *action* at step k is the selection of pair $(a(k), t(k))$; the *reward* for solving a problem is inversely proportional to the total search time. Meta-learning techniques for algorithm recommendation [13, 9, 3], in which the relative performances of different $a \in A$ are predicted based on results on previous problems, could in principle be used as a base for inter-problem adaption.

Next we will present first results with a novel AOTA system that allocates time to GAs differing in more than just one parameter, and that implements f in a simple yet non-trivial way by extrapolating a linear best fit model of previous observations of performance improvements.

1.3   Intra-problem AOTA for Genetic Algorithms

The probability update scheme of the parameterless GA discussed above relies on specific issues related to population size. It cannot be extended to the choice of other parameters such as mutation rate. The AOTA system below is more general, but we will see that it does not suffer much from its increased generality, matching or even greatly exceeding the performance of the parameterless GA on several test problems.

We consider a single problem $r(k) = r$ for all k, a finite set of GAs $A = \{a_i, i = 1..n\}$ generated by combining different parameter settings, a bias $P(k) = \{p_i(k) = \Pr\{a_i\}$ at step $k, i = 1..n\}$ defined as a probability distribution over it, obtained by applying a function f_P to a set of values $U(k) = \{u_i(k), i = 1..n\}$ that we will relate to each algorithm's performance through a function f_u. Our $d(k)$ contains only the current average fitness of the individuals in the population of GA $a(k)$, that is, the history $H_i(k)$ of each a_i, $H_i(k) = \{(t(k), d(k))|a(k) = a_i\}$, is simply a table of time versus average fitness values. Machine time is subdivided in small slots of duration ΔT, and a sequence of pairs $(a(k), t(k)) = (a_i, p_i \Delta T)$ is generated, allocating the slot to the various algorithms proportionally to this bias, as follows:

Method 1 (Bias based AOTA) *Initialize ΔT and $u_i(0)$, $i = 1..n$, and set $k = 1$.*

> *While (r not solved)*
>> *Update $P_A(k) = f_P(U_A(k))$*
>> *For each $i = 1..n$*
>>> *Generate and execute pair $(a(k), t(k)) = (a_i, p_i \Delta T)$*
>>> *Update $u_i(k+1) = f_u(H_i(k))$.*
>>> *$k = k+1$*
>> *End*
> *End*

As for the choice of f_u: from H_i, we try to give an estimate of the time $T_{i,sol}$ at which a_i would reach the target fitness value, and set $u_i(k) = 1/(T_{i,sol} - T_i(k))$, where $T_i(k) = \sum_{a(k)=a_i} t(k)$ is the time spent on a_i up to step k. In this way a suboptimal searcher on which we already have spent a lot of time can receive more credit than a faster searcher whose execution just started. With a linear regression based on a shifting window of the most recent c values in $H_i(k)$ (see Fig. 1), we estimate $T_{i,sol}$ as the time at which the resulting linear model predicts the target fitness value[2], rounded up to the nearest multiple of the time taken to run one generation of GA a_i, which is equivalent to population size z_i if we measure time in fitness function evaluations.

The size c of the shifting window used for the regression should be small enough, such that the linear model quickly reacts to changes in trend of the average fitness (e.g. when a population converges), but large enough to compensate for noise on the average fitness values. For example, different window sizes should be used for a_i's with different mutation rates, and preliminary experiments with a fixed window size gave best results for different values of c on different problems. For such reasons we plug *adaptive window sizing* into our AOTA framework, drawing inspiration from a financial forecasting method developed by Chow [4]. We set $c_i = 2$ and keep updating three linear models, one using window size c_i, the others $2 * c_i$, and $\max(2, c_i/2)$, respectively. At each step k we compare the new $d(k)$ with the values predicted by the three linear models. The window size for which the smallest error is achieved becomes the current c_i.

For all $a_i \in A$ the initial bias $p_i(0)$ is inversely proportional to population size z_i, as in parameterless GA. We initialize $u_i(0) = \text{const}/z_i$; each time an a_i is run for the first time, the estimated u_i is used to initialize $u_j = u_i z_i / z_j$ for all a_j's that have not started yet. Subsequent updates are only due to f_u, such that this initial bias can be quickly modified by experience.

For f_P we use plain normalization $p_i = u_i / \sum_{j \in I} u_j$; and compare to a greedy normalization, in which half of the current time slot is allocated to the current best a_i, the other half according to normalized u_i values.

Our method strives to be *algorithm independent*, i.e. we view our a_i's as black box searchers with unknown inner structure and properties. For example, we do not exploit the fact that in absence of mutation convergence is irreversible; neither do we try to infer relationships between the various a_i, e.g. by interpolating their performances across parameter space. Each u_i is updated independently; the only interaction between the a_i is due to their competition for runtime, mediated by the normalization process f_P. The need of algorithm specific knowledge is limited to the choice of the algorithm set A, the state information d, and the initial bias P.

2 Experiments

We tested our method on the following set of problems:

CNF3 SAT $m\ n$ is a conjunctive normal form (CNF) satisfiability problem, with n clauses, each being a logical OR of three variables chosen from a set of m boolean variables and their negations. The problem consists in finding an instantiation of the variables that verifies all clauses, and is termed *satisfiable* if it can be solved.

---

[2] The algorithm already solves the problem when the best fitness value reaches the target, but this value is usually noisier than the average fitness, and leads to less reliable predictions. Some upper limit can be used if no target value is known: with a higher target y^*, more credit is given to the slope α_i of the linear model, and less to the current average fitness y_i obtained by a_i, as it can be shown that $p_i \propto \frac{\tan \alpha_i}{y^* - y_i}$.

It can be expressed as a fitness maximization problem and addressed by a GA with bitstrings of length m as genomes, each representing an instantiation of the variables, with fitness equal to the number of satisfied clauses, between 0 and n.

We chose three satisfiable instances from SATLIB [7], namely CNF3 SAT 20 91 (20 variables, 91 clauses, file uf20-91/uf20-01.cnf); CNF3 SAT 50 218 (50 variables, 218 clauses, file uf50-218/uf50-01.cnf); CNF3 SAT 75 325 (75 variables, 325 clauses, file uf75-325/uf75-01.cnf).

ONEMAX a simple toy problem, also reported in [5], that consists in maximizing the number of ones in a bitstring of length 100.

TRAP a deceptive artificial problem from [5], consisting in 10 copies of a 4-bit trap function. Each 4-bit block of a bitstring of length 40 gives a fitness contribution of 4 if all four bits are 1, and of $3 - q$ if $q < 4$ bits are 1.

TSP The Traveling Salesman Problem (TSP) requires to find the shortest path through a fully connected graph, without revisiting nodes. It can be solved by a GA with node lists as genomes. We expressed it as a fitness maximization problem, in which a path of length l is given fitness $1/l$. We considered two real instances from TSPLIB [11], with known best path: TSP burma 14 (14 nodes, file burma14.tsp) and TSP gr 17 (17 nodes, file gr17.tsp).

In all cases fitness values were normalized between 0 and 1. Machine time was always realistically measured in number of fitness evaluations, such that a GA with population size z takes z time steps to run for one generation.

In a first group of experiments we used the exact settings of the parameterless GA in [5]: a set A_1 of 19 simple generational GAs, with no mutation, uniform crossover with probability 0.5, tournament selection without replacement, tournament size 4, and population sizes $2^i, i = 1..19$. We then repeated the experiments with a set A_2 of twice the size (this implies double-sized search space), obtained by instantiating each algorithm in A_1 with mutation probabilities 0 and $0.7/L$, where L is the genome length, for a total of $19 \times 2 = 38$ competing algorithms. The search space was made again twice as large in set A_3 by adding a binary parameter representing a choice between uniform and one-point crossover ($19 \times 2 \times 2 = 76$ competing search algorithms).

Distance Preserving Crossover (DPX [2]) was used for TSP problems, along with swap mutation; Partial Match Crossover, as implemented in GALib [15], was added in A_3.

In table 1 we give results for four variations of our method, obtained by combining plain (p) and greedy (g) probability update with fixed (f) and adaptive (a) window size. We label these methods AOTA$_{pf}$, AOTA$_{pa}$, AOTA$_{gf}$, AOTA$_{ga}$.

For comparison, we also give results for a parameterless GA over set A_1 only, labeled PLESS[3]; and of the *a priori unknown* fastest (on average) element of the three sets, labeled bestGA. The latter provoked counter-intuitive results, especially on set A_1, where bestGA is much slower than the time allocation procedures. This is because GAs in set A_1 do not use mutation, so a very large population is required to avoid premature convergence on all 40 runs executed, even if in most cases a smaller population

---

[3] Since the set A of this algorithm is in principle unbounded, we applied a variation of the algorithm with limited maximal population size: to avoid penalizing PLESS, we ran the limit population whenever a larger population was requested.

Table 1. Mean time (upper part), expressed in fitness function evaluations, and overhead (lower part) for each problem (columns), with 0.95 confidence intervals. Rows correspond to different algorithms: four variations of our AOTA on three different algorithms sets; the Parameterless Genetic Algorithm PLESS [5]; the fastest (on average) element of the three sets, labeled BestGA. See Sect. 2 for details.

	CNF3 SAT 20 91	CNF3 SAT 50 218	CNF3 SAT 75 325	ONEMAX	TRAP	TSP burma14	TSP gr17
$AOTA_{pf}(A_1)$	6945 ± 2357	303060 ± 62335	399775 ± 172026	11755 ± 946	3963348 ± 874795	13486 ± 4258	28064 ± 7973
$AOTA_{pa}(A_1)$	6466 ± 2434	296863 ± 62227	413921 ± 191802	11013 ± 917	4020018 ± 900687	15360 ± 5288	28342 ± 7259
$AOTA_{gf}(A_1)$	6194 ± 1864	252444 ± 53584	363694 ± 161169	10216 ± 849	3376378 ± 790406	13131 ± 4129	27602 ± 7117
$AOTA_{ga}(A_1)$	6179 ± 2396	251212 ± 51853	361868 ± 175230	9443 ± 810	3426109 ± 744091	15333 ± 5176	27940 ± 7346
$PLESS(A_1)$	6632 ± 2644	340789 ± 81220	603822 ± 334786	10407 ± 849	3047100 ± 681355	27578 ± 9579	42335 ± 10787
$best\ GA(A_1)$	14029 ± 1450	251904 ± 11788	1305805 ± 52936	8320 ± 122	3135898 ± 138343	32768 ± 4110	39946 ± 4001
$AOTA_{pf}(A_2)$	3552 ± 986	193704 ± 52459	297488 ± 99135	7184 ± 659	5429640 ± 1396380	12027 ± 3963	26603 ± 7942
$AOTA_{pa}(A_2)$	5114 ± 1857	201848 ± 51284	334076 ± 94351	7809 ± 837	4883354 ± 1258636	11902 ± 4404	28001 ± 8389
$AOTA_{gf}(A_2)$	3210 ± 996	158633 ± 42683	245983 ± 90511	5509 ± 547	4913763 ± 1263639	11021 ± 3707	24263 ± 8781
$AOTA_{ga}(A_2)$	4998 ± 1370	165137 ± 39958	277641 ± 86052	5552 ± 584	4602811 ± 1163608	11974 ± 4333	21557 ± 5548
$best\ GA(A_2)$	901 ± 334	32043 ± 10656	23236 ± 5582	1317 ± 91	2385510 ± 259136	20275 ± 2219	28431 ± 3056
$AOTA_{pf}(A_3)$	4164 ± 1336	310671 ± 76962	407563 ± 110573	11754 ± 1020	88051 ± 12688	20624 ± 6940	77288 ± 24584
$AOTA_{pa}(A_3)$	5939 ± 1634	357713 ± 87217	499665 ± 118741	12203 ± 1340	78981 ± 11555	18628 ± 6657	46806 ± 16950
$AOTA_{gf}(A_3)$	4282 ± 1178	262784 ± 66468	331002 ± 84824	8502 ± 738	69698 ± 9628	20004 ± 7350	76455 ± 25324
$AOTA_{ga}(A_3)$	6133 ± 1574	273006 ± 71425	382091 ± 99094	8223 ± 932	61481 ± 9802	17697 ± 6216	40562 ± 11598
$best\ GA(A_3)$	901 ± 334	32043 ± 10656	23236 ± 5582	1317 ± 91	20480 ± 1139	20275 ± 2219	28431 ± 3056
$AOTA_{pf}(A_1)$	4.27 ± 0.50	3.57 ± 0.13	3.11 ± 0.09	2.93 ± 0.07	3.64 ± 0.15	3.90 ± 0.46	3.37 ± 0.44
$AOTA_{pa}(A_1)$	3.64 ± 0.26	3.48 ± 0.12	3.04 ± 0.10	2.73 ± 0.05	3.42 ± 0.15	3.92 ± 0.36	4.11 ± 0.46
$AOTA_{gf}(A_1)$	3.97 ± 0.61	2.97 ± 0.13	2.72 ± 0.09	2.54 ± 0.06	2.99 ± 0.17	3.67 ± 0.44	3.22 ± 0.38
$AOTA_{ga}(A_1)$	3.39 ± 0.37	2.97 ± 0.13	2.62 ± 0.10	2.34 ± 0.05	3.05 ± 0.17	3.81 ± 0.46	4.03 ± 0.58
$PLESS(A_1)$	3.47 ± 0.62	3.79 ± 0.27	3.74 ± 0.30	2.59 ± 0.04	2.79 ± 0.11	6.42 ± 0.67	6.00 ± 1.08
$AOTA_{pf}(A_2)$	8.36 ± 0.96	7.34 ± 0.44	6.36 ± 0.27	6.01 ± 0.25	8.32 ± 0.66	8.84 ± 0.90	6.91 ± 1.02
$AOTA_{pa}(A_2)$	6.85 ± 0.46	6.64 ± 0.29	6.06 ± 0.21	5.29 ± 0.26	7.49 ± 0.58	7.50 ± 0.47	8.02 ± 0.86
$AOTA_{gf}(A_2)$	7.33 ± 1.35	5.94 ± 0.43	5.24 ± 0.33	4.48 ± 0.30	7.43 ± 1.29	7.51 ± 0.86	6.18 ± 0.75
$AOTA_{ga}(A_2)$	7.67 ± 2.27	5.57 ± 0.42	4.99 ± 0.37	3.70 ± 0.20	6.55 ± 0.79	7.28 ± 0.61	7.06 ± 0.77
$AOTA_{pf}(A_3)$	13.15 ± 1.34	14.26 ± 0.81	12.34 ± 0.47	10.52 ± 0.44	12.02 ± 0.47	14.72 ± 1.36	13.92 ± 1.37
$AOTA_{pa}(A_3)$	12.99 ± 0.88	13.23 ± 0.59	11.66 ± 0.41	9.20 ± 0.36	10.88 ± 0.44	11.98 ± 0.72	13.26 ± 1.48
$AOTA_{gf}(A_3)$	12.39 ± 2.05	12.14 ± 1.05	10.48 ± 1.17	7.13 ± 0.49	9.31 ± 0.45	12.06 ± 1.01	13.63 ± 1.21
$AOTA_{ga}(A_3)$	12.38 ± 1.30	10.57 ± 0.82	9.20 ± 0.58	5.85 ± 0.43	8.37 ± 0.60	10.93 ± 1.12	12.86 ± 1.42

would suffice. For PLESS and AOTA, many GAs are available at each run: if one a_i reaches the solution on all but a few unlucky runs, in which a_{i+1} wins, the resulting average performance will be largely determined by the faster a_i.

A better performance indicator are *overhead values*: the ratios between total search time and time spent on the a_i that first solves the problem.

In most cases, our method performs at least as well as PLESS. It is remarkable that despite its large search space of parameter combinations and simultaneously running search algorithms, our rather generic algorithm achieves results comparable to those of a highly specific algorithm incorporating detailed knowledge of GAs.

As expected, moving from set A_1 to set A_2 generally improved the performance, as it added faster solvers to the set[4], except for the deceptive problem TRAP, in which mutation is actually a slight disadvantage. Here the size of A was doubled through adding a_i's with performances very similar to those of A_1; hence the total search time increased. Use of the largest (least biased) A_3 led to slightly worse but still comparatively good performances on TSP and the two more difficult SAT problems, while the improvement on TRAP was dramatic, corresponding to a speed-up factor of roughly 30: this problem can in fact be solved much faster using one-point mutation, as it tends to preserve its building blocks.

Concerning f_P, the greedy approach performs almost always better than plain normalization, but the latter might generally be less risky. Fixed and adaptive window size led to similar results, with a slight advantage for the first. But since the adaptive scheme relieves the user from setting one parameter, it is preferable.

Figure 1 displays snapshots from three instants in the solution of the ONEMAX problem on set A_3. A value τ_{22} is obtained as current time-to-goal estimate, subtracting the time already spent (T_{22}) from the time $T_{22,sol}$ at which the resulting linear model reaches the target fitness value (Fig. 1 a); u_{22} is then set to $1/\tau_{22}$, and a portion $p_{22} \propto u_{22}$ of next time slot ΔT is allocated to a_{22}. (Fig. 1 b) displays bar graphs relative to the state of the $a \in A_3$: probability values (P), total time spent (T), average (avg) and best fitness. The arrows point to data relative to a_{22}, whose parameters are: pop size 2^3, mutation rate 0.007, uniform crossover, and which will eventually be the first to solve the problem, reaching the target fitness value 1 at $T_{22} = 1072$, after a total time of 7268 fitness function evaluations.

3   Conclusion and Outlook

The literature on search and optimization algorithms includes many papers on methods whose performance depends on numerous parameters. Typically, these parameters are adjusted by hand. The time that went into fine-tuning them is usually not reported.

Here we made first steps towards establishing a general framework for *automatically* adjusting such parameters. We let numerous search algorithms with alternative parameter settings compete against each other, allocating more computation time to the "more promising" ones in online fashion, where the notion of "more promising" is derived from an adaptive model of the experience so far.

---

[4] Smaller populations, and shorter execution times, are typically needed in presence of mutation, at least when the fitness landscape is not deceptive.

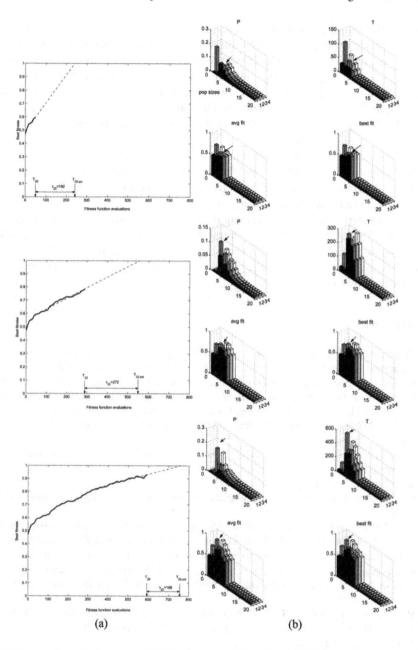

Fig. 1. Three snapshots from our AOTA at work, solving the ONEMAX problem on set A_3. (a) The learning curve for algorithm a_{22} (thick line), with its linear regression (thin dashed line). (b) Bar graphs relative to the state of the $a \in A_3$: probability values (P), total time spent (T), average (avg) and best fitness. The bars are lined according to population size z, from 1 ($z_1 = 2$) to 19 ($z_{19} = 2^{19}$): for each size there are four a differing in mutation rate (rows 1,3: 0; rows 2,4: 0.007) and crossover operator used (rows 1,2: uniform; rows 3,4: one-point). The arrows point to data relative to a_{22}, which will eventually be the first to solve the problem.

In a particular instantiation of this framework, we used a simple linear best fit model that maps online experience with algorithm-specific time allocation to expected performance improvements. The model is used to predict useful pairs of particular genetic algorithms and corresponding time allocations. Despite the relative generality of the approach and its comparatively large search space, its performance in terms of total computation time sometimes not only matches but greatly exceeds the one of a well-known but less general approach, although the latter has a much smaller search space motivated by human insight.

Future research will follow different directions, including the design of alternative adaptive performance models f_u, and their application to search spaces including algorithms other than GAs. The obtained techniques could then be used as plugins for inter-problem search, which is our longer-term goal.

A further step could be made leaving the framework presented in 1, in favour of a more general intra/inter-problem search in spaces of programs that can combine other algorithms as primitive actions, modifying their parameters online, possibly also performing conditional jumps to earlier parts of the code, in the style of the universal language used by OOPS [12].

References

1. M. Birattari, T. Stützle, L. Paquete, and K. Varrentrapp. A racing algorithm for configuring metaheuristics. In W. Langdon et al., editor, *GECCO 2002: Proceedings of the Genetic and Evolutionary Computation Conference*, pages 11–18. Morgan Kaufmann Publishers, 2002.
2. B. Freisleben and P. Merz. New Genetic Local Search Operators for the Traveling Salesman Problem. In H.-M. Voigt, W. Ebeling, I. Rechenberg, and H.-P. Schwefel, editors, *Parallel Problem Solving from Nature IV*, volume 1141 of *Lecture Notes in Computer Science*, pages 890–900. Springer, 1996.
3. J. Fürnkranz, J. Petrak, P. Brazdil, and C. Soares. On the use of fast subsampling estimates for algorithm recommendation. Technical Report TR-2002-36, Österreichisches Forschungsinstitut für Artificial Intelligence, Wien, 2002.
4. E. S. Gardner Jr. Exponential smoothing: the state of the art. *Journal of Forecasting*, 4:1–28, 1985.
5. G. R. Harick and F. G. Lobo. A parameter-less genetic algorithm. In Wolfgang Banzhaf, Jason Daida, Agoston E. Eiben, Max H. Garzon, Vasant Honavar, Mark Jakiela, and Robert E. Smith, editors, *Proceedings of the Genetic and Evolutionary Computation Conference*, volume 2, page 1867, Orlando, Florida, USA, 13-17 July 1999. Morgan Kaufmann.
6. J. H. Holland. *Adaptation in Natural and Artificial Systems*. University of Michigan Press, Ann Arbor, 1975.
7. H. H. Hoos and T. Stützle. SATLIB: An Online Resource for Research on SAT. In T. Walsh I.P.Gent, H.v.Maaren, editor, *SAT 2000*, pages 283–292. IOS press, 2000. http://www.satlib.org.
8. L.P. Kaelbling, M.L. Littman, and A.W. Moore. Reinforcement learning: a survey. *Journal of AI research*, 4:237–285, 1996.
9. Alexandros Kalousis, Jo ao Gama, and Melanie Hilario. On data and algorithms: Understanding inductive performance. *Mach. Learn.*, 54(3):275–312, 2004.
10. A. W. Moore and M. S. Lee. Efficient algorithms for minimizing cross validation error. In *Proceedings of the 11th International Conference on Machine Learning*, pages 190–198. Morgan Kaufmann, 1994.

11. G. Reinelt. Tsplib 95. `http://www.iwr.uni-heidelberg.de/groups/comopt/software/TSPLIB95`.
12. J. Schmidhuber. Optimal ordered problem solver. *Machine Learning*, 54:211–254, 2004. Short version in *NIPS 15*, p. 1571–1578, 2003.
13. Carlos Soares, Pavel B. Brazdil, and Petr Kuba. A meta-learning method to select the kernel width in support vector regression. *Mach. Learn.*, 54(3):195–209, 2004.
14. Ray J. Solomonoff. Progress in incremental machine learning. Technical Report IDSIA-16-03, IDSIA, 2003.
15. M. Wall. GAlib, A C++ Genetic Algorithms Library. `http://lancet.mit.edu/ga`.

Model Approximation
for HEXQ Hierarchical Reinforcement Learning

Bernhard Hengst

National ICT Australia, University of New South Wales, Sydney NSW 2052, Australia
bernhard.hengst@nicta.com.au

Abstract. HEXQ is a reinforcement learning algorithm that discovers hierarchical structure automatically. The generated task hierarchy represents the problem at different levels of abstraction. In this paper we extend HEXQ with heuristics that automatically approximate the structure of the task hierarchy. Construction, learning and execution time, as well as storage requirements of a task hierarchy may be significantly reduced and traded off against solution quality.

1   Introduction

Not only do humans have the ability to form abstractions, but we control the amount of detail required to represent complex situations for decision making.

Take the familiar problem of deciding the best way to travel to a business conference or holiday destination. We first choose the mode of transport and best route between major cities. To make this decision we may even take into consideration potential connections and delays at either end for each mode of primary transport. However, the side we get out of bed on the morning of departure or the way we leave our home (front door, back door or garage door) is unlikely to be an influencing factor in our decision, although in the final execution of the plan will need to decide to get out of the bed on one side and use one of the doors to exit the home. How can a reinforcement learner model these pragmatics?

Interestingly, hierarchical reinforcement learning (HRL) can provide a natural solution. In hierarchical reinforcement learning the overall problem may be broken down into smaller subtasks and represented as a task hierarchy. Subtasks at the top or the root of the task hierarchy tend to model the more global aspects of the problem at a coarser level. Subtasks near the bottom or the leaves of the task hierarchy tend to model the more local aspects of the problem in finer detail. Hierarchical reinforcement learners generally search for an optimal solution[1] to the overall problem by considering the subtasks at all levels in the task hierarchy. It can be expensive to search a subtask hierarchy, particularly when there are several levels with a high branching factor. In practice, for many problems, it may be possible to find good solutions by ignoring details at the lower levels when deciding the subtask policies at higher levels.

---

[1] Optimal in some sense, e.g. hierarchical or recursively.

J.-F. Boulicaut et al. (Eds.): ECML 2004, LNAI 3201, pp. 144–155, 2004.

The contribution of this paper is to present several model approximations by setting the degree of coarseness that is used in the construction, learning and execution of a task hierarchy for hierarchical reinforcement learning. We will consider approximations to the decomposed value function by limiting the hierarchical depth of evaluation. We will also look at the degree of coarseness at which subtask termination conditions are modelled with two different heuristics. The main benefit is to speed up the learning and execution of the hierarchical policy, and to reduce the total number of subtasks required to represent the problem.

Different approaches to hierarchical reinforcement learning include Options [7], HAMQ [6] and MAXQ [2], and more recently ALisp [1] and HEXQ [4]. Each approach can be interpreted in terms of a task hierarchy in which a higher level parent subtask may invoke the policy of its child subtask as an abstract action over several time steps. Parent subtasks are represented using a semi Markov decision problem formalism (e.g. [8]). This formalism extends Markov decision problems by allowing actions to be temporally extended. We will use the abbreviation, MDP, to refer to both Markov and semi-Markov decision problems.

HEXQ in particular, is designed to automatically construct a task hierarchy based on a search for invariant subtasks. It performs automatic safe state abstraction during the construction process, not only finding reusable subtasks, but abstracting subtasks at the next level. The approximations work automatically during HEXQ hierarchy construction. The degree of coarseness is set manually and trades off efficiency against solution quality.

We will start with a simple illustrative example where a robot must learn to navigate through a multi-storey building. We review the automatic problem decomposition by HEXQ, noting in particular the hierarchy of abstract models generated. Three approximation heuristics are then introduced and results presented showing the computational saving.

2   Simple Grid-World Maze

This example is based on similar grid-world room problems found elsewhere in the literature (eg [7]), except here we add another dimension to allow us to illustrate the generality over multiple levels of hierarchy. In this problem a robot must find its way to a goal location in middle of the ground floor of a 10 storey building after starting anywhere at random. The lower two floors of the building are shown in figure 1 (a). The floors are interconnected by four lifts. Each floor has nine identical interconnected rooms as shown in (c). Each room is discretised into a nine by nine array of locations. The position of the robot in the building is described by three variables, the floor-number (0-9), the room-number on each floor (0-8) and the location-in-room (0-80). The encoding of room numbers is the same on each floor. The encoding of room locations is the same for each room.

The robot has six primitive actions to move one cell North, South, East, West or pressing Up or Down. The first four actions are used to navigate on each floor

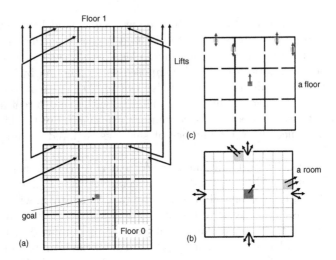

Fig. 1. (a) Two floors of a ten storey building showing an identical room layout for each floor and four lifts interconnecting the floors. (b) a typical room showing door exits and possible location of the lifts and destination. (c) a typical floor plan showing the location of the lift wells and possible destination location.

and are stochastic in the sense that the robot moves in the intended direction 80% of the time and 20% of the time slips to either the left or right with equal likelihood. The Up and Down actions are deterministic and work only in the four elevators cells on each floor by moving the robot one floor up or down. A move into a barrier leaves the robot where it is. Each primitive action costs one unit and the robot is rewarded with 100 units when it signals arrival at the goal position by pressing Up.

The flat reinforcement learning[2] problem defines the state space as the Cartesian product of the three variables, uses the six primitive actions above and minimises the number of steps to reach the goal.

3   HEXQ Hierarchical Decomposition

The hierarchical reinforcement learner HEXQ, using the same information as the flat learner, solves the problem by first constructing a task hierarchy. The decomposition process is briefly described next. A more detailed account can be found in [4].

HEXQ is designed to tackle any finite episodic multivariate MDP. The algorithm is not given the underlying model beforehand, but must discover it for itself, as well as automatically constructing the task hierarchy. It first orders the variables by their frequency of change as the robot takes exploratory random actions. Clearly the location-in-room will change most frequently followed

---

[2] It is assumed the reader has at least an introductory knowledge of reinforcement learning. Introductory material can be found in [5] and [10].

by room-number. The floor-number will change rarely. HEXQ constructs a three level task hierarchy with one level for each variable. It begins construction of leaf node subtasks based on the most frequently changing variable, location-in-room.

HEXQ tests individual location-in-room state transitions and the rewards received to see if they are invariant in all contexts defined by the value of the other variables. Because we are dealing with stochastic problems we need to test the invariance of the probability distribution of possible next states and rewards. This is achieved using a Chi squared test on samples from different contexts or time periods. Invariance is also violated if any of the other variables changes value or the problem terminates. Any state-action pair causing a transition that is not invariant is designated an *exit*. HEXQ partitions the state space into blocks where each block has the property that it is possible to find a policy to reach and take any block exit with certainty. Reusable subtasks are constructed to be the different ways of exiting each block of the partition.

For the multi-storey maze, there is only one block (a room) that includes all location-in-room states. Exits are at the doorways, the lifts and the goal location. The room block is illustrated in figure 1 (b). For example, pressing up in an elevator location may change the floor-number. Therefore, (location-in-room=at-elevator, action=up) is an example of an exit. Other intra-room transitions are invariant throughout the building with the same probability of transitioning to the next state and with the same probability of receiving the reward. The subtasks are the 17 ways to exit a room and require 7 smaller MDPs to find the different policies to reach each of the 7 exit states (4 doorways, two lifts and 1 goal)[3].

In constructing the second level of subtasks, HEXQ uses the Cartesian product of the block identifier from the level below and the next variable in the frequency ordering, the room-number, to define an abstract projected state space. In this case, as there is only one block at the bottom level, the state space is simply described by the nine states of the room-number variable. The state space is abstracted because the detail of intra-room locations has been factored out. It is projected because we are ignoring the floor-number variable. The procedure of finding invariant transitions is repeated at this level, except that this time the actions are the room exiting policies from the level below and referred to using the exit notation from level 1[4]. Exits at the second level are declared when the remaining variable, the floor-number, changes or the problem terminates.

Again, the second level partition only contains one block, a whole floor, as illustrated in figure 1 (c). There are 9 exit state-action pairs at this level. For example, (state=north-west-room,action=(navigate-to-lift1,press-up)). Note

---

[3] A subtask is a policy to reach an exit state <u>and</u> take the exit action. Note that at each doorway state there are three actions that can result in an exit because of the stochastic slip. At each elevator, actions Up and Down are both exit actions. Hence there are 17 possible exit state-action pairs in total.

[4] Exits at level 2 and above use a nested notation, $(s^2, (s^1, a))$, where (s^1, a) is an abstract action at level 2 that has the task of reaching and executing the exit (s^1, a) at level 1. s^e is a level e state, a is a primitive action.

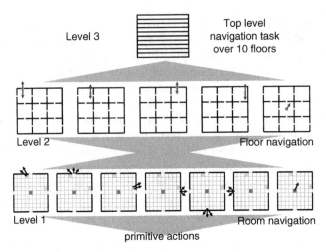

Fig. 2. The HEXQ generated task hierarchy.

that this time the exit action is temporally extended or abstract, as are all actions at this level. Because the policy to navigate to a lift can be shared between the two tasks to catch a lift up or down, only five smaller MDPs are required to find policies for the 9 subtasks. Nevertheless, even though only 5 MDPs are required, why do we need two separate ones for the robot to find its way to the north-west room and also two for the north-east room when the state space is at the granularity of rooms? The reason is that the best way to navigate between rooms may be influenced by where exactly in the destination room the elevators are located. By ignoring this detail we will later see how to save two MDPs and possibly four subtasks at this level.

The top level of the task hierarchy is a single MDP with only 10 abstracted floor states. The total task hierarchy constructed by HEXQ for the multi-storey building problem is shown in figure 2. There are 9 subtasks in the middle level implemented using 5 MDPs and 17 subtasks at the bottom level using 7 MDPs.

The value function, given a policy for each subtask, is found by simply summing the value of a state in each of the invoked subtasks on a path through the hierarchy[5]. To find the best action in any subtask state it is necessary to perform a depth first search in the task hierarchy using the recursive equation:

$$V_m^*(s) = \max_a[V_{m-1}^*(s) + E_m^*(g, a)] \tag{1}$$

where $V_m^*(s)$ is the optimum value function for state s in subtask m. Abstract action a invokes child subtask $m - 1$. Block g contains state s. For leaf subtasks $V_{m-1}^* = 0$ as all primitive actions are considered exit actions and do not invoke lower level routines.

---

[5] The decomposition of the HEXQ value function was inspired by MAXQ but differs in its formulation in that the reward on subtask exit is not included in the internal value of a subtask state.

The *HEXQ action-value function E* for all states s in block g is the expected value of future rewards *after completing* the execution of the (abstract) action a and following the hierarchical policy, in this case the optimal policy, $*$, thereafter. Function E plays the same role in a hierarchic fashion as the action-value function Q in flat reinforcement learning. It is the action-value function E that is learnt by HEXQ for each subtask.

$$E_m^*(g, a) = \sum_{s'} P^\pi(s'|g, a)[R_{exit} + V_m^*(s')] \tag{2}$$

$P^\pi(s'|g, a)$ is the probability of transition to a next state s' after (abstract) action a terminates from any state $s \in g$ and R_{exit} is the expected final primitive reward on transition to state s'.

HEXQ employs two forms of safe state abstraction, subtask reusability and subtask abstraction. Subtask reusability means multiple instances of the same subtask are only represented once. Subtask abstraction means that the states of each subtask block are aggregated at the next level in the hierarchy. Safe state abstraction means that for the task hierarchy generated by HEXQ the value function calculated using the above recursion is identical to the value function for the flat learner executing the same policy.

For this problem HEXQ saves over an order of magnitude in value function storage space and converges an order of magnitude faster than flat Q-learning. It is desirable to reduce the space and time requirements even further and still find good solutions within the resources available. We will now describe three heuristics that allow HEXQ to automatically construct a more compact task hierarchy.

4   Varying the Coarseness of the Value Function

HEXQ uses a best first search[6] as a result of the recursion present in equation 1 to decide the best next action. This search is necessary even after learning has completed as the compacted value function needs to be reconstituted to execute the optimal policy.

Limiting the depth of the search will approximate the hierarchial optimal policy if the expected internal reward inside each subtask at the depth limit is a near constant multiple, say k, of the primitive reward on exit of the subtasks. The full depth search value function is then a multiple, $k + 1$, of the limited depth search value function. This follows as the value function is defined as the expected sum of future rewards and each reward is effectively increased by k times its value. Changing a value function by a constant factor does not change the optimal policy.

Special cases of this condition include subtasks where internal rewards offer a substantially diminished contribution to the value function, i.e. k is close to zero, and cases where the internal rewards are the same and the exit rewards are the same for all subtasks at the specified search depth.

---

[6] As does MAXQ [2].

Recall that in Q learning the optimal value of a state $V^*(s) = \max_a Q^*(s, a)$. In the extreme case in which we limit the depth of search to zero for HEXQ, the value contribution of the child subtask is ignored, that is, $V^*_{m-1} = 0$. Equation 1 simplifies to $V^*_m(g) = \max_a E^*_m(g, a)$ for every subtask m in the task hierarchy, reducing nicely to the usual "flat" Q learning representation for the most abstract approximation of the problem.

It is important to note that limiting the search to a particular depth does not effect the ability to operate at more detailed levels[7]. For example, at level 3 a depth limit of 1, searches to level 2, and at level 2 the search extends to level 1. Also, an overall solution to the original problem is always guaranteed as all subtasks terminate by construction. The degradation of the solution quality with a reduced search depth will depend on the how closely we can match the above criteria.

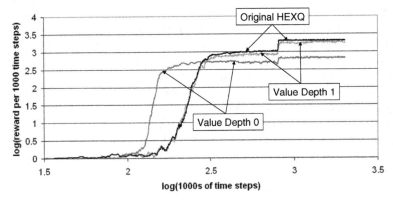

Fig. 3. Performance comparison for value function evaluations depth limited to zero and one against the original HEXQ results.

In the multi-storey building example, limiting the value function to a depth of zero at the top level would result in choosing an arbitrary (e.g. the first) elevator from the abstract action list to reach the next floor. In this case the robot may lengthen its journey considerably by travelling to a non-optimal elevator. At the room level a depth zero value function search would ignore the robot's location in a room to decide how best to reach the room containing the elevators or goal. Again this may increase the journey time. Increasing the depth of search to 1 results in a much better solution as the distance to each elevator room is included in the decision at the top level and location in room is included for navigating about a floor.

The results for limiting the depth of value function search to zero and one are illustrated in figure 3. A depth zero search improves the learning time of HEXQ but performance suffers significantly. The deterioration is explained by the depth zero search not considering distance to elevators when deciding how

---

[7] Levels are numbered from the leaf to root nodes.

Table 1. HEXQ performance for various depth limited searches of the value function. A depth limit of 2 is equivalent to the original HEXQ solution and is taken as the 100% baseline.

Depth	Storage		Execution		Performance	
		%		%		%
2	4257	100	918	100	3.31	100.0
1	4257	100	216	28	3.26	98.5
0	4257	100	32	3	2.82	85.3

to travel between floors. With the value function search depth limited to one, the learning time shows no improvement, but the performance is close to that of the original HEXQ result.

The major benefit, however, from limiting the depth of search is the significant and noticeable improvement in the time it takes to make the next decision to act. In table 1 the column headed *Execution* gives the number of E values that need to be looked up to evaluate equation 1. It is a direct measure of the time complexity to decide on the next primitive action when executing the task hierarchy from its root task. With a search depth limited to zero the execution time reduces to only 3% of that required for the original HEXQ solution. At a depth limit of one, the execution time is reduced to 28% and achieves 98.5% of the optimal performance.

For the Tower of Hanoi puzzle, decomposed by HEXQ in [4], inherent constraints in the puzzle ensure that the cost of an abstract action is constant at each level. This satisfies the criteria above and means that a depth zero search is sufficient to ensure an optimal policy. It reduces the time complexity of the search from exponential to linear in the number of discs. For the 7 disk version this means a reduction in E table lookups from $6^7 = 279,936$ to only 42, a more than 3 orders of magnitude saving per search!

While for hierarchical execution most searches do not need to start at the top level, in many problems hierarchically greedy execution leads to a better policy [2], and this means a new search is initiated from the root node after every primitive action step.

In applications where actions need to be taken in real time, the available computing resources may limit the amount of processing that can be devoted to deciding the next best action. Employing iterative deepening [9] of the value function search will provide these reinforcement learners with an anytime solution to maximise their performance.

Limiting the depth of the value function search does not reduce the storage requirements to represent the value function as show in table 1. The next two approximations save on storage as well, by constructing more approximate task hierarchies.

5 Varying the Coarseness of Exit States

Recall from section 3 that when constructing level 2 of the task hierarchy, the learner is working with the room-number abstract states to learn how to navigate on a floor. To reach the North-West room HEXQ constructs two MDPs. This is necessary because the optimal policy to navigate from room to room may depend on which of the two elevators in the North-West room is the desired destination.

This suggests another approximation. The robot's task can be simplified by navigating to the North-West room without resolving the location of its two elevators. Having entered the room, the robot can focus on reaching its desired elevator.

A multi-dimensional state in an original problem is represented as a sequence of abstract states at each level of the task hierarchy. We will refer to this sequence description of a state as the *hierarchical state*. A *hierarchical exit state* at any level is the hierarchical state associated with an exit. It is the sequence of states in an exit. The hierarchical exit state for the exit $(s^e, (s^{e-1}, (\ldots (s^1, a^1) \ldots)))$ at level e is $(s^1, s^2, \ldots, s^e)$. When hierarchical exit states are the same for different exits, HEXQ only constructs one MDP for these exits. When they differ, separate MDPs are required to ensure safe state abstraction.

The hierarchical lift exit states for the North-West room clearly differ as the lifts are at different locations. HEXQ therefore constructs separate MDPs.

One way to approximate, is to only generate different MDPs if the most abstract states in the hierarchical state sequence differ. We refer to this as a depth zero exit state coarseness.

The exit value function, E at level 2 in the building example stores values using abstract room states. When there is only one MDP for both elevator exits in the North-East room, function E cannot learn to distinguish between them. It will store a value that is in the range between the distances to the two elevators.

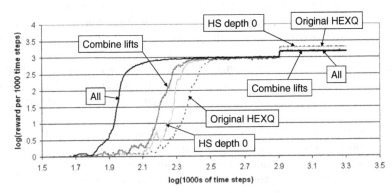

Fig. 4. Performance comparison for approximations combining exit states, exits and for all approximations against the original HEXQ.

The results for a depth zero exit state coarseness are shown in figure 4 as "HS depth 0" and in table 2 as row "HS-0". This approximation does not effect the execution efficiency as all subtasks are retained and hence the branching is unaltered in the task hierarchy for the value function search. It does improve the learning time and the storage requirements as a direct result of the reduction in the number of MDPs from 5 to 3 at level 2 in the task hierarchy.

Table 2. Performance characteristics for approximations combining exit states (HS-0), combining exits (C.Lifts) and for all approximations, tabled against the original HEXQ taken as the 100% baseline.

Approx.	Storage		Exec.		Perform.	
	%		%		%	
HEXQ	4257	100	918	100	3.31	100.0
HS-0	3951	93	918	100	3.30	97.7
C.Lifts	3351	79	270	29	3.18	92.2
All	3108	73	15	2	3.17	95.9

It is easy to imagine, matching the hierarchical exits states to any depth to reduce the coarseness, thereby creating a similar trade-off in resource requirements and performance to the variable depth value function search.

6   Varying the Coarseness of Exits

The final approximation we will consider is to combine exits. In flat reinforcement learning if two actions have the same transition and reward function for all states then one of them can be eliminated without effecting the optimal policy. This leads to the intuition in hierarchical reinforcement learning that abstract actions that have the same transition and reward function in the same context at an abstract state level may be replaced by just one abstract action to a first approximation.

Take our multi-storey building example. The two room leaving exits that involve taking each lift up to another floor always end up in the same room-number and are therefore combined. Similarly, the two elevator-down room exits are combined. In this case, combining exits at level 1 reduces the number of abstract actions and the number of exits at level 2. Now there is only one exit at level 2 to move up and one to move down in the North-West room. Similarly the number of exits for the North-East room has been reduce from 4 to 2.

The precise lift to use is now no longer resolved and HEXQ can reduce the number of MDPs required. When the robot enters the lift room it will travel to the nearest lift, as there is no longer an abstract action allowing it to choose between them.

Moving up a level in the task hierarchy, we can also combine the exits to move up a floor, and those for moving down a floor, for similar reasons.

Combining exits makes it easier for MDPs to exit and this will in general increase the internal value function of a subtask. On the other hand there is an increased loss of control as exits cannot be discriminated at the next level. The net effect on the value function and resultant policy will depend on each specific problem instance.

HEXQ relies on the exit values E to be independent of how a subtasks is entered to allow subtasks abstraction. When exits are combined, the exit value will now depend on how the MDP was entered. Nevertheless, combining exits will provide an approximation to the safe state abstracted case because of the criteria that the combined states have the same transition and reward function at the abstract level. The criteria can be made more stringent by only combining exits with equal transition and reward functions down to a specified level of coarseness, making this approximation variable as well.

The graph labelled "Combined lifts" in figure 4 and row "C.Lifts" in table 2 show the effect of combining the lift exits discussed above. Storage requirements are reduced to 79% because one MDP can be saved at the bottom level of the task hierarchy by combining the lifts, two MDPs are saved at the room level by combining the inter-floor actions and the number of abstract actions is reduced.

Even with the value function being evaluated to its maximum depth the execution time drops to 29% as the branching is reduced. Combining lift exits reduces the performance to 92.6%

It is possible to combine each of the three room leaving actions for the same exit state. The issue here is that the while the next abstract room states are always the same, the probability distribution varies for each exit action due to varying directional stochasticity of the actions. Nevertheless, combining door exits achieves a performance of 99.7% of the original HEXQ solution.

If all the approximations discussed above (zero depth search, combining exit states and exits) are activated concurrently we save 27% in storage requirements, learning is 250% faster and execution speeds up by a factor of 50. All these saving are achieved with only a 4.1% drop in performance as shown in figure 4 and table 2. How the approximations interact is not easy to predict. Indeed, computational complexity and performance may improve simultaneously.

7   Discussion and Future Work

When introducing heuristic approximations we admit the possibility of suboptimal results and aim to find trade-offs with computational complexity.

The variable coarseness heuristics discussed in this paper cannot give any optimality guarantees, but they contribute to simpler solutions. It is of course easy to find examples where these approximations show poor performance. Future work on defining more precisely the conditions under which the approximations are particulary appropriate is suggested. Estimation of solution quality in relation to a hierarchical optimal solution would also be useful, for example, by measuring the limits on abstract transition probabilities and task rewards and employing bounded parameter MDPs [3].

These approximations are invoked automatically during the discovery of the task hierarchy and the coarseness depth is set manually. It is conceivable that the appropriate level of coarseness of each approximation may itself be able to be learnt at different levels in the task hierarchy to achieve good performance.

For future practical applications of hierarchical reinforcement learning it is important to find ways to scale up to more complex problems and to do so without a designer having to manually construct a good and efficient task hierarchy. The approximation techniques in this paper can of course be used to assist manual problem decomposition for other approaches to hierarchical reinforcement learning.

We have presented and demonstrated rational approximations that significantly improve the learning time, reduce the storage requirements and deliver any-time performance during the automatic construction of a task hierarchy over and above that achieved with HEXQ.

Acknowledgements

National ICT Australia is funded through the Australian Government's *Backing Australia's Ability* initiative, in part through the Australian Research Council.

References

1. David Andre and Stuart J. Russell. State abstraction for programmable reinforcement learning agents. In Rina Dechter, Michael Kearns, and Rich Sutton, editors, *Proceedings of the Eighteenth National Conference on Artificial Intelligence*, pages 119–125. AAAI Press, 2002.
2. Thomas G. Dietterich. Hierarchical reinforcement learning with the MAXQ value function decomposition. *Journal of Artificial Intelligence Research*, 13:227–303, 2000.
3. Robert Givan, Sonia M. Leach, and Thomas Dean. Bounded-parameter markov decision processes. *Artificial Intelligence*, 122(1-2):71–109, 2000.
4. Bernhard Hengst. Discovering hierarchy in reinforcement learning with HEXQ. In Claude Sammut and Achim Hoffmann, editors, *Proceedings of the Nineteenth International Conference on Machine Learning*, pages 243–250. Morgan-Kaufman, 2002.
5. Tom M. Mitchell. *Machine Learning*. McGraw-Hill, Singapore, 1997.
6. Ronald E. Parr. *Hierarchical Control and learning for Markov decision processes*. PhD thesis, University of California at Berkeley, 1998.
7. Doina Precup. *Temporal Abstraction in Reinforcement Learning*. PhD thesis, Univeristy of Massachusetts, Amherst, 2000.
8. Martin L. Puterman. *Markov Decision Processes: Discrete Stochastic Dynamic Programming*. John Whiley & Sons, Inc, New York, NY, 1994.
9. Stuart Russell and Peter Norvig. *Artificial Intelligence: A Modern Approach*. Prentice Hall, Upper Saddle River, NJ, 1995.
10. Richard S. Sutton and Andrew G. Barto. *Reinforcement Learning: An Introduction*. MIT Press, Cambridge, Massachusetts, 1998.

Iterative Ensemble Classification for Relational Data: A Case Study of Semantic Web Services

Andreas Heß and Nicholas Kushmerick

Computer Science Department, University College Dublin, Ireland
{andreas.hess,nick}@ucd.ie

Abstract. For the classification of relational data, iterative algorithms that feed back predicted labels of associated objects have been used. In this paper we show two extensions to existing approaches. First, we propose to use two separate classifiers for the intrinsic and the relational (extrinsic) attributes and vote their predictions. Second, we introduce a new way of exploiting the relational structure. When the extrinsic attributes alone are not sufficient to make a prediction, we train specialised classifiers on the intrinsic features and use the extrinsic features as a selector. We apply these techniques to the task of semi-automated Web Service annotation, a task with a rich relational structure.

1 Introduction

In a variety of learning tasks, a number of related views on a problem exist. Several approaches have been suggested for how to make use of these different views for improving accuracy by using more than one classifier. These approaches include ensemble learning, co-training, and link-based classification for relational data. For the latter, the second view for a given object is derived from the objects with which it is related. This view is also known as the *extrinsic* view (as opposed to the *intrinsic* view). The intuition is that an object's class can be predicted from information about related objects.

Iterative classification algorithms for relational data have been proposed to address this setting (e.g. [10]). These algorithms are based on the assumption that, as we classify objects, these predictions have an influence on related objects. Initially, a preliminary set of predictions is made based only on the intrinsic features. Then, predicted labels are fed back to the classifier. Classification accuracy is expected to improve over time, as the labels of related objects become known with more certainty.

In this paper, we present a generic framework for iterative classification of relational data. We combine the intrinsic and the extrinsic view using an ensemble of two classifiers. The first classifier is based on a set of static features: the intrinsic features associated with the object or related objects. We denote the static classifier as A.

The second classifier B is derived from the labels of related objects. In some classification tasks, the dynamic view may be sufficient to classify an object, so

J.-F. Boulicaut et al. (Eds.): ECML 2004, LNAI 3201, pp. 156–167, 2004.

we train B on all the objects and combine the results of the A and B classifier by voting. In more challenging tasks, the dynamic view alone may be insufficient, so we use the extrinsic features to select a specialised intrinsic classifier C trained only on the subset of training instances with the same extrinsic features. This is a novel approach, and we will explain it in detail in the next section.

The task of semi-automatically generating semantic annotation for Web Services serves as a motivating example and case study. The basic idea behind our approach is that Web Service descriptions are structured objects, and that there are dependencies between the components of these objects that we can exploit. In previous work [8], we used a Bayesian setting and evaluated it on Web forms. In this paper, we present an iterative classification algorithm similar to the one introduced by Neville and Jensen in [10].

2   Semantic Web Services

We have built a tool that learns from Web Services with existing semantic annotation and provides the user with annotation recommendations in an interactive fashion. We present this application called ASSAM[1] in greater detail in [7].

The predictions made by an algorithm that classifies parts of Web Services do not have to be perfectly accurate to be helpful. In fact, the classification task is quite hard, because the domain ontologies can be very large. But for that reason it is very helpful for a human annotator if he or she could choose only between a small number of ontological concepts rather than from the full domain ontology. In previous work [8] we have shown that the category of a service can be reliably predicted, if we stipulate merely that the correct concept be one of the top few (e.g., three) suggestions.

Before describing our approach in detail, we begin with some terminology. Our terminology is a bit different from the terminology used in Web Services and Semantic Web description languages, but by introducing this terminology we do not intend to advocate a new standard. Instead we believe that our approach is generic and independent of the actual format used for the semantic Web Service description. However, in the application that we have built the input consists of Web Services in the Web Service Description Language (WSDL [3]) format, and the final annotations can be exported as OWL-S [12].

A WSDL Web Service corresponds in many ways to a set of methods in any programming language. The equivalent of a method is called an *operation*. Operations can have input, output and fault *messages*. This corresponds to a method's parameters, return values and possible exceptions. A single parameter in WSDL is called a *part* in a message. It is also possible to make use of *complex types* defined in XML Schema. This corresponds to a structure in a typical programming language.

We use the word *category* to denote the semantic meaning of the service as a whole. For example, the Amazon Web Service belongs to the "book selling" category. The category ontology corresponds to a *profile hierarchy* in OWL-S.

---

[1] Automated Semantic Service Annotation with Machine learning

We use the word *domain* to denote the semantic meaning of an operation. For example, a particular operation in the Amazon Web Service called "QueryAuthor" would belong to the "Query books by author name" domain. An operation in WSDL usually maps to an *atomic process* in OWL-S, but there is no direct relation between the domain of an operation and OWL-S, as atomic processes are only characterised through their inputs, outputs, preconditions and effects. One could think of the *domain* as describing the semantics of the preconditions and effects, but we currently do not use the domain annotation for our OWL-S export.

We use the word *datatype* to denote the semantic type of a single variable. This applies to message parts as well as complex types. This usage of the word datatype is consistent with how the word is used when describing a property in an ontology, but should not be confused with low-level syntactic datatypes such as "integer" or "string". For example, the input parameter for the "QueryAuthor" operation mentioned above would be of the datatype "author".

For information retrieval or classification tasks the objects that are classified or searched are also referred to as documents. When we use the word *document*, we mean the Web Service as whole as represented by its WSDL. We use *document part* to denote an object within the Web Service that we want to classify: Operations, input and output messages, XML schema types etc. are document parts or *object components*.

3   Iterative Ensemble Classification

Following [10], we distinguish between *intrinsic, static extrinsic* and *dynamic extrinsic* features. In contrast to [10], we assume that the object graph has more than one connected component. In our example, we have one connected component for each Web Service.

Static intrinsic features are attributes that are inherent to the component that is to be classified. We denote the static intrinsic features for a component j as a_j. Dynamic extrinsic features derive from the relationship between different components. We denote dynamic extrinsic features as b_j. In our Web Services dataset, we use the class labels of linked components as dynamic extrinsic features. Static extrinsic features are based on other components, but do not change when more classifications are made. Static extrinsic features are static intrinsic features of linked components. When we speak of extrinsic features in the remaining sections, we usually mean dynamic extrinsic features if not otherwise stated.

Initially, when the adjacent objects are unlabeled, the dynamic extrinsic features are unknown. In the first pass classifications are made based on the intrinsic features only. In subsequent iterations we include extrinsic features that are based on the class labels predicted in the previous round. The classification process is repeated until a certain termination criterion (e.g. either convergence or a fixed number of iterations) is met.

Our iterative algorithm differs in some points from Neville and Jensen's algorithm. In their approach, one single classifier is trained on all (intrinsic and extrinsic) features. In a variety of tasks, ensembles of several classifiers have been shown to be more effective (e.g., [4]). For this reason, we train two separate classifiers, one on the intrinsic features ("A") and one on the extrinsic features ("B"), and vote together their predictions. Another advantage of combining the evidence in that way is that the classifier cannot be mislead by missing features in the beginning when the extrinsic features are yet unknown, because the classifier trained on the extrinsic features is simply not used for the first pass.

Specialised Classifiers. This split approach, where the A and B classifiers are combined using voting, works best, when both views would by themselves be sufficient to make a prediction. This intuition is the same as behind Co-Training [1]. However, in more challenging prediction tasks, the extrinsic view alone gives additional evidence, but is not sufficient to make a prediction. In our Web Services dataset, this is the case on the datatype level. The fact that a Web Service belongs to the "book selling" category is by itself not sufficient to classify its input parameters, but the information is still useful. We therefore introduce a second mode for incorporating the extrinsic features: We train a set of classifiers on the intrinsic features of the components, but each of them is only trained on the subset of the instances that belong to one specific class. In our setting, we train specialised classifiers on the datatypes level on all instances that belong to the same category[2].

To formally specify these specialised classifiers, we first define what we mean by a specialisation. We take a very generic view: the k'th specialisation for component j is formally just a set Φ_j^k of instances of component j that satisfy the specialisation.

In our example, if component j represents a parameter, then one Φ_j^k might be "all parameters of services that are in the 'book selling' category."

We require that all specialisations for j be mutually exclusive and exhaustive. Let $\phi_j^k(b_j) = 1$ if there exists an instance in Φ_j^k with extrinsic features b_j, and 0 otherwise. Mutually exclusiveness and exhaustivity means simply that $\forall_j : \sum_k \phi_j^k(b_j) = 1$.

The specialisation Φ_j^k is used to define a set of training data for learning a specialised classifier C_j^k. Specifically, C_j^k is trained on the a_j features for every training instance of component j in Φ_j^k.

To avoid biasing the algorithm too strongly, we still combine the results of the C classifier with the A classifier in each iteration. For each level we use either the B or C classifier, but not both. We chose the C method for the datatypes and the B method for the category and the domain.

Algorithm 1 explains our iterative classification ensemble, and Fig. 1 illustrates its classification phase. In Fig. 1 and algorithm 1, let n denote the number

---

[2] To avoid over-specialisation, these classifiers are actually not trained on instances from a single category, but rather on instances from a complete top-level branch of the hierarchically organised category ontology. Note that this is the only place where we make use of the fact that the class labels are organised as an ontology, and we do not do any further inference

---

Algorithm 1 Iterative Ensemble Classification

---

for $j \leftarrow 1 \ldots n$ **do**
  $\alpha_j \leftarrow$ predictions made by A_j with features a_j
end for
$(b_1, \ldots, b_n) \leftarrow (\alpha_1, \ldots, \alpha_n)$
for a fixed number of iterations **do**
  for $j \leftarrow 1 \ldots n$ **do**
    $\beta_j \leftarrow$ predictions made by B_j or C_j with features b_j
    $\pi_j \leftarrow \alpha_j * \beta_j$
  end for
  $(b_1, \ldots, b_n) \leftarrow (\pi_1, \ldots, \pi_n)$
end for
return $(\pi_1, \ldots, \pi_n)$

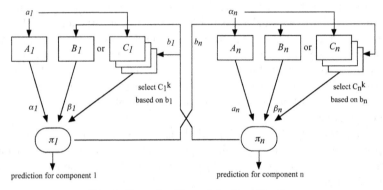

Fig. 1. Iterative Ensemble Classification

of object components; a_j the static and b_j the dynamic features; A_j and B_j the intrinsic and extrinsic classifiers, and C_j^k denotes a specialised classifier as discussed above. α_j denotes the predictions made by A_j and β_j the predictions made by the extrinsic classifier B_j resp. C_j^k.

4   Related Work

Several variations of link-based text classification have been proposed. The classical task here is to classify web pages connected by hyperlinks. Lu and Getoor address this task in [9]. They cast the problem as predicting the classes of objects or nodes in a graph considering links between objects or edges in the graph. However, in their model only one flavour of objects exists: the classes for all objects are drawn from only one ontology. Iterative classification algorithms were also used by Chakrabarti [2] before. We already mentioned the approach by Neville and Jensen [10].

    Although not mentioned explicitly, our C approach is used by Finn and Kushmerick [6] for information extraction. They use a two-level learning approach.

At the first level (L1), each token in a document is predicted either as the start of a text fragment to extract, or not. L1 is trained on all available data. A second classifier (L2) is then used to identify the end of a fragment, given that its start was predicted by L1. L2 is trained on just the subset of the training data, namely a window of tokens near field starting positions. In our terminology, the L2 classifier is a specialised classifier C, and the L1 predictions are used to decide when to invoke L2, just as we use extrinsic features to select the appropriate C.

Clearly, our approach is related to ensemble learning (e.g. [4]). We have used ensemble learning in a non-iterative fashion for classifying the category of a web service in our earlier paper [8]. Another well-known way to combine the output of multiple classifiers is stacked generalization [14]. We already mentioned Co-Training [1] shortly; however, note that our data is fully labeled.

Related Work in the Web Services Area. As far as we are aware, we were the first to propose the use of machine learning for the task of semi-automatically annotating Semantic Web Services. However, this task could also be viewed as a schema matching problem. Patil et al [11] are working on matching XML schemas to ontologies. They use a combination of lexical and structural similarity measures. They assume that the user's intention is not to annotate similar services with one common ontology, rather they also address the problem of choosing the right domain ontology among a set of ontologies. The Web Service search engine Woogle [5] allows not only for keyword queries, but also for searching structurally similar operations.

5   Parameters

In an iterative feed-back setting such as ours, a sensible choice of all parameters is both crucial and rewarding: An improvement in one of the classifiers can lead to an improvement in other classifiers as well. In some respects the parameters we discuss here are relevant not only to our specific setting, but are common to all iterative classification algorithms. The important parameters are:

1. Structure: Which layers of the model are used for feedback and how?
2. Voting: How are the results of the different views combined?
3. Termination criterion: What number of iterations is optimal?
4. Inference, Constraints: Use information from the class ontologies?
5. Features: Use binary or continuous features?
6. Classification algorithms: Which one to use?

Structure. One might expect that this structure is inherent to the problem, but this is only partly true. In our Web Services dataset, we have identified three layers of semantic metadata, as described in section 1: the category of the service as a whole, the domain of the service's operations and the datatypes of its input and output parameters. This leaves a variety of possible choices how the feed-back is actually performed. One might say that the category of a service is determined by the domain of its operations, and the domain of the operations is determined by the datatypes of its input and output parameters. But it is also possible to see it the other way around: The datatypes of an operation's parameters are dependent on the operation's domain, which is dependent on the service's category. Instead of choosing either a top-down or bottom-up approach, our framework also allows for modeling both dependencies at the same time.

Preliminary tests showed that it is not guaranteed that using as many extrinsic features as possible automatically yields the best results. It is best to choose between either the B or C classifier based on the nature of the extrinsic view: If the extrinsic view alone provides enough information to make a reliable prediction, it is best to combine the extrinsic and intrinsic view in an ensemble way. If the extrinsic view alone is not sufficient for a reliable classification, it is better to use the C classifier. There are, however, two points that are important when considering the C classifier: Using a set of specialised classifiers means that there are as many classifiers as there are distinct class labels in the extrinsic view and each classifier is only trained on a subset of the available training data. To have a set of many classifiers can not only be computationally expensive, it also means that the number of training instances for each classifier is only a fraction of the total number of training instances.

We used *static* extrinsic features on the domain and datatype level by incorporating text from children nodes: Text associated with messages was added to the text used by the operations classifier, and text associated with elements of complex types were added to the text used by the datatype classifier classifying the complex type itself. Note that this appears to contradict our earlier results [8], where we claimed that simply adding text from child nodes does not help. In [8], we where classifying the category level only, and the bag of words for the domain and datatype classifiers consisted of text for all operations/datatypes in that

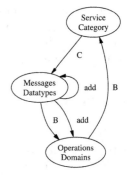

Fig. 2. Feedback structure

service. In our present experiment, the classifier for the operations and datatypes classify one single operation or parameter only, and in this case it apparently helps to add more text.

Given these arguments for and against the different modes of incorporating the extrinsic evidence and some empirical preliminary tests, we eventually decided to use the setup shown in Fig. 2, where "add" denotes the use of static extrinsic features by incorporating text.

Combining Static and Dynamic Features. One of the fundamental differences between our approach and the original algorithm by Neville and Jensen is the way the different views – i.e., the intrinsic and extrinsic features – are combined. Neville and Jensen's approach is to add the extrinsic features as additional attributes in a stacking-like fashion and train a single classifier on all features. Neville and Jensen tested their algorithm on a low-dimensional dataset. On our dataset, however, this way of combining the evidence of the static and dynamic features did not work. In section 6 we also report results for a setup that combines static and dynamic features in this "non-ensemble" way. We conclude that this is due to fact that both the static and the dynamic features are quite high-dimensional, and that the initial noise in the dynamic features strongly affects the overall performance of the classifier.

Number of Iterations. The iterative classification is not guaranteed to converge, and it is also not guaranteed that more iterations always produce better results, as the predictions might get stuck in a local maximum. We tried several fixed numbers of iterations in preliminary experiments, and eventually decided to terminate the classification process after five iterations.

Inference and Constraints. In our Web Services dataset as well as in many other relational learning tasks, the class labels are not arbitrary but rather they are organised as an ontology. This ontology could be a simple hierarchical structure, but it could also convey more complex constraints. In our datatypes ontology, it would be possible to model restrictions on the relations between complex types and their elements. For example, a complex type that represents a book in the datatypes ontology can only have elements that are assigned a class label that represents a property of book in the ontology.

In the present setting we do not make use of constraints that can be inferred from the ontology, with one exception. As mentioned in section 3, we use the hierarchy in the services ontology to prevent over-specialisation of the C classifiers. However, we believe that the use of inference that can be derived from the ontologies where the class labels are drawn from could greatly increase classification accuracy. We will investigate this in future work.

Features. The well-known range of choices for representing words in a bag-of-words model as features in a classifier includes binary features, term frequency and TFIDF. In our case, we also have to choose a suitable representation for the extrinsic features. We can choose between a single feature denoting the most common linked class or use a feature vector with one element per possible class. When using the latter, the feature vector can be binary or frequency based. It is also possible to use the complete ranked distribution or the top n of classes as output by the classifiers instead of just the absolute predictions.

In our experiments, using a single feature for the extrinsic view does not make much sense, as we are using a separate classifier for the dynamic view. In preliminary experiments, using the complete ranked distributions did not work. We believe that this is due to the fact that in conjunction with the base classification algorithm we used and the one-vs-all setting, the absolute confidence values in the ranked distribution are too close together, and that then combining the distributions for all linked objects introduces too much noise.

We decided to use a binary feature vector with one attribute per possible linked class for the dynamic features. For the static features, we decided to use binary features as well. In section 3, we already described another method of incorporating dynamic extrinsic features, the specialised classifiers, and the possibility to add terms from linked document parts as a way to use static extrinsic features.

Classification Algorithms. Due to the large number of classifiers and evaluations in our iterative framework, it is desirable to use a fast classification algorithm, especially if the intended application requires user interaction and low response-times are necessary.

In our implementation we are using the Weka library of classifiers [13] off the shelf. For our experiments we chose the HyperPipes algorithm in a one-against-all configuration, as it offered a good tradeoff between speed and accuracy. We did not use the SMO algorithm because it turned out to be computationally much more expensive.

6   Evaluation

We evaluated our algorithm using a leave-one-service-out methodology. We compared it against a baseline classifier with the same setup for the static features, but without using the dynamic extrinsic features.

To determine the upper bound of improvement that can be achieved using the extrinsic features, we tested our algorithm with the correct class labels given as the extrinsic features. This tests the performance of predicting a class label for a document part when not only the intrinsic features but also the dynamic features (the labels for all other document parts) are known. Following [10], we refer to this upper bound as the "ceiling".

We also compared it against a non-ensemble setup, where the extrinsic features are not added using a separate classifier but rather are just appended to the static features. Classification is then done with a single classifier. This setup closely resembles the original algorithm proposed by Neville and Jensen. Again, the same set of static features was used.

In the evaluation we ignored all classes with one or two instances, such as occurred quite frequently on the datatype level. The distributions are still quite skewed and there is a large number of classes. There are 22 classes on the category level, 136 classes on the domain level and 312 classes on the datatype level. Our corpus consists of 164 services with a total of 1138 annotated operations and 5452 annotated parameters.

Fig. 3 shows the accuracy for categories, domains and datatypes. As mentioned earlier, in mixed-initiative scenario such as our semi-automated ASSAM tool, it is not necessary to be be perfectly accurate. Rather, we strive only to ensure that that the correct ontology class is in the top few suggestions. We therefore show how the accuracy increases when we allow a certain tolerance. For example, if the accuracy for tolerance 9 is 0.9, then 90% of the time, the correct prediction is within the top 10 of the ranked predictions. Note that on the datatypes level, macroaveraged F1 (as shown in Fig. 3) for the iterative ensemble is worse than for the baseline while accuracy is still above the baseline. This is

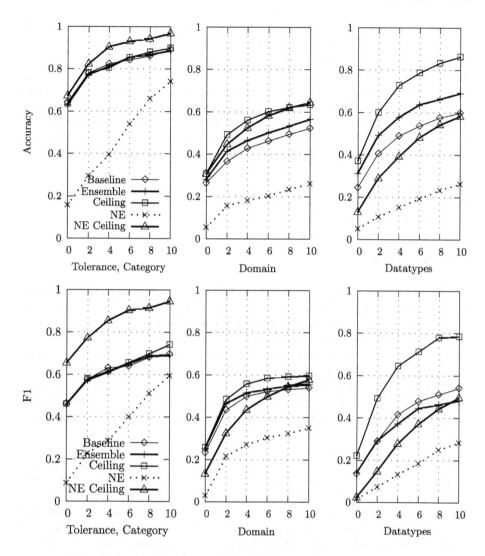

Fig. 3. Accuracy and macroaveraged F1 on the three ontologies

due to the fact that at this level of tolerance the baseline has a higher recall for many small classes. Macroaveraged precision is still higher for the iterative ensemble.

Note that on the category level incorporating the additional evidence from the extrinsic features does not help. In fact, for some tolerance values the ceiling accuracy is even worse than the baseline.

Also, we could not achieve good results with the non-ensemble setup (denoted as "NE"). This setup scored worse than the baseline. For the datatypes, even the ceiling accuracy (denoted as "NE Ceiling") was below the baseline.

On the datatype level, our algorithm achieves 31.2% accuracy, where as the baseline scores only at 24.5%. Thus, our algorithm improves performance by almost one third. The overall performance might be considered quite low, but due to the high number of classes it is a very hard classification problem. Given that in two of three cases the user has to choose only between 10 class labels rather than between all 312 labels in the datatype ontology we are still convinced that this could save a considerable amount of workload. We evaluated the statistical significance of the accuracy improvement of our algorithm with a Wilcoxon Matched-Pairs Signed-Ranks Test. Our algorithm performs significantly better $(p < 0.001)$.

On the domain level, our approach increases the accuracy for exact matches from 26.3% to 28%. This is statistically significant $(p < 0.05)$ according to a Wilcoxon Test. For both significance tests we performed a 20-fold random split.

7   Conclusion

We have demonstrated two extensions to prior research on iterative classification algorithms for relational tasks. First, we have shown that in a high-dimensional environment such as text classification it is better to use separate classifiers for the intrinsic and extrinsic features and vote their predictions rather than to use one classifier trained on both types of features. Second, we have introduced a new mode for relational classification where the extrinsic features serve as a selector for a specialised intrinsic classifier trained on a subset of the training instances. We have applied these techniques to the domain of semi-automatically annotating Semantic Web Services, and shown that it outperforms conventional approaches.

Future Work. As mentioned, we believe that incorporating domain knowledge in the classification process can increase the overall performance. In future work we will investigate the use of inference over the ontology and how it can help the machine learning algorithm. In particular, currently we ignore the hierarchical structure of the class labels, but we will explore whether this structure can be exploited to improve prediction accuracy. On the application side, we will continue to improve our WSDL annotator tool. We believe that tools such as ours are needed to bootstrap the Semantic Web and Semantic Web Services, and that machine learning is a very helpful technique that should be applied here.

Acknowledgments

This research was supported by grants SFI/01/F.1/C015 from Science Foundation Ireland, and N00014-03-1-0274 from the US Office of Naval Research. We thank Martina Naughton, Jessica Kenny, Wendy McNulty and Andrea Rizzini for helping us manually annotating the corpus of Semantic Web Services used in our evaluation. Thanks to Rinat Khoussainov and Thomas Gottron for helpful discussions.

References

1. Avrim Blum and Tom Mitchell. Combining labeled and unlabeled data with co-training. In *COLT: Proceedings of the Workshop on Computational Learning Theory*, San Francisco, 1998. Morgan Kaufmann.
2. Soumen Chakrabarti, Byron E. Dom, and Piotr Indyk. Enhanced hypertext categorization using hyperlinks. In Laura M. Haas and Ashutosh Tiwary, editors, *Proceedings of SIGMOD-98, ACM International Conference on Management of Data*, pages 307–318, Seattle, US, 1998. ACM Press, New York, US.
3. Erik Christensen, Francisco Curbera, Greg Meredtih, and Sanjiva Weerawarana. *Web Services Description Language (WSDL) 1.1*. World Wide Web Consortium, 2001.
4. T. G. Dietterich. Ensemble methods in machine learning. In *Lecture Notes in Computer Science*, volume 1857.
5. Xin Dong, Alon Havey, Jayant Madhavan, Ema Nemes, and Jun Zhang. Similarity search for web services. In *Proceedings of the 30th VLDB Conference*, Toronto, Canada, 2004.
6. Aidan Finn and Nicholas Kushmerick. Multi-level boundary classification for information extraction. In *Proceedings of the European Conference on Machine Learning*, Pisa, 2004.
7. Andreas Heß, Eddie Johnston, and Nicholas Kushmerick. ASSAM: A tool for semi-automatically annotating semantic web services. Submitted to the 3rd International Semantic Web Conference, 2004.
8. Andreas Heß and Nicholas Kushmerick. Learning to attach semantic metadata to web services. In *Proceedings of the 2nd International Semantic Web Conference*, 2003.
9. Qing Lu and Lise Getoor. Link-based classification. In *Int. Conf. on Machine Learning*, Washington, D.C., August 2003.
10. Jennifer Neville and David Jensen. Iterative classification in relational data. In *Proceedings of the AAAI 2000 Workshop Learning Statistical Models from Relational Data*, pages 42–49. AAAI Press, 2000.
11. Abhijit Patil, Swapna Oundhakar, Amit Sheth, and Kunal Verma. Meteor-s web service annotation framework. In *Proceedings of the 13th International World Wide Web Conference*, New York, USA, May 2004.
12. The DAML services coalition. Owl-s 1.0. White Paper, 2003.
13. I. H. Witten and Eibe Frank. *Data Mining: Practical Machine Learning Tools with Java Implementations*. Morgan Kaufmann, San Francisco, 1999.
14. David H. Wolpert. Stacked generalization, 1990.

Analyzing Multi-agent Reinforcement Learning Using Evolutionary Dynamics

Pieter Jan 't Hoen[1] and Karl Tuyls[2,*]

[1] Center for Mathematics and Computer Science (CWI)
P.O. Box 94079, 1090 GB Amsterdam, The Netherlands
[2] Computational Modeling Lab, Department of Computer Science
Vrije Universiteit Brussel, Belgium
hoen@cwi.nl, ktuyls@vub.ac.be

Abstract. In this paper, we show how the dynamics of Q-learning can be visualized and analyzed from a perspective of Evolutionary Dynamics (ED). More specifically, we show how ED can be used as a model for Q-learning in stochastic games. Analysis of the evolutionary stable strategies and attractors of the derived ED from the Reinforcement Learning (RL) application then predict the desired parameters for RL in Multi-Agent Systems (MASs) to achieve Nash equilibriums with high utility. Secondly, we show how the derived fine tuning of parameter settings from the ED can support application of the COllective INtelligence (COIN) framework. COIN is a proved engineering approach for learning of cooperative tasks in MASs. We show that the derived link between ED and RL predicts performance of the COIN framework and visualizes the incentives provided in COIN toward cooperative behavior.

1 Introduction

In this work, we present a novel approach to study Reinforcement Learning (RL) applied to Multi-Agent Systems (MASs), a growing area of research [3, 10, 7, 1, 9]. The challenge for a MAS is to achieve a high degree of performance as the agents learn in parallel. In this work, the dynamics of the RL process are visualized and analyzed from a perspective of Evolutionary Dynamics. More specifically, we show how ED from Evolutionary Game Theory (EGT) can be used as a model for Q-learning in stochastic games. We show a one-to-one connection between RL and the ED from evolutionary game theory. More precisely, we connect the Replicator Dynamics (RD) and a mutation term mathematically with Q-learning. Analysis of the evolutionary stable strategies and attractors of the ED aid in setting the parameters for the RL algorithms to achieve desired Nash equilibriums with high utility. This is a step forward from the classic approach of trial and error when deciding upon what parameters to use in MAS RL. The link between RL and ED can help in understanding the development

---

* Author funded by a doctoral grant of the institute for advancement of scientific technological research in Flanders (IWT)

J.-F. Boulicaut et al. (Eds.): ECML 2004, LNAI 3201, pp. 168–179, 2004.
© Springer-Verlag Berlin Heidelberg 2004

of the MAS during learning. We show how the ED can visualize some of the phenomena troubling MAS learning and assist in analysis of the performance and convergence properties of the MAS.

We illustrate our contributions using Dispersion Games [6]. In this cooperative game, n agents each have to decide which of the k tasks they are to undertake. Agents acting in parallel and using local feedback with no central control must learn to arrive at an optimal distribution over the available tasks. Such problems are typical for a growing class of large-scale distributed applications such as load balancing, niche selection, division of roles within robotics, or application in logistics. We investigate the case for when $n = k$ which we call *full Dispersion Games*. Full utility is achieved only when every one of the n tasks is chosen by exactly one of the n agents. The joint action state space is n^n while there are only $n!$ desirable Nash Equilibriums with full utility. This makes the full Dispersion Game a challenging task for growing n and a possible benchmark for MAS applications.

We present the ED of this full dispersion game for n≥2 agents and show the match between the predicted behavior from EGT perspective and the observed behavior in the MAS using RL. Strong attractors in the ED become strategies to which agents will converge with high probability if seen from a RL (Q-learner) perspective. Furthermore, the settings in the ED for desirable attractors indicate the correct choice for parameters in the used RL algorithms.

As the second part of our contribution, we present work on the Replicator Dynamics applied to the COllective INtelligence (COIN) framework. COIN is used in cooperative MASs to induce incentives for actions by agents that promote the global utility of the system. This is in line with a growing collection of work where the goal is to establish conditions for MASs such that they are most likely to exhibit good emergent behavior [2, 11, 3]. The effectiveness of the COIN top-down approach has been demonstrated by applying the COIN framework to a number of example problems: network routing [25], increasingly difficult versions of the El Farol Bar problem [18], Braess' paradox [19], and complex token retrieval tasks [17]. Analyzing the COIN approach from the ED perspective is shown to give an indication through the attractors for ED as to what parameters to apply for COIN. Furthermore, the ED visualize the incentives in COIN for agents to strive for a high global utility using local learning. The ED hence offer the possibility to Analise advanced MAS design methodologies.

The rest of this document is structured as follows. Section 2 introduces the ED and the link with RL. Section 3 shows the analysis of the full Dispersion Games. Section 4 presents the COIN framework and Section 5 presents the use of the ED in COIN. Section 6 discusses and concludes.

2   Replicator Dynamics and RL

This section provides some background in learning in games, RL, and the replicator dynamics. Game theory [12, 13, 8, 5, 23], offers the mathematical foundation for the analysis and synthesis of problems in decentralized control. A game consists of more than one player and results in an outcome for every player depending on the overall behavior of all the players. Formally it can be described by a tuple $(n, A_1 \ldots A_n, R_1 \ldots R_n)$ where n is the number of players, A_i the set of actions available to player i and $R_i : A_1 \times \ldots \times A_n \to \Re$ is the payoff function for player i. When games are played repeatedly a sequential decision problem arises. In this paper players are modeled as Q-learners [22], which are described in the following subsection.

2.1   Q-Learning in Games

A model of Reinforcement Learning consists of: a discrete set of environment states, a discrete set of agent actions and a set of scalar reward signals. On each step of interaction the agent receives a reward and some indication of the current state of the environment, and chooses an action. The agent's job is to find a policy, i.e. a mapping from states to actions, that maximizes some long-term measure of reward.

Common Reinforcement Learning methods, which can be found in [16] are structured around estimating value functions. A value of a state or state-action pair, is the total amount of reward an agent can expect to accumulate over the future, starting from that state. Q-learning, investigated here, is an adaptive value iteration method (see [16, 22]), which bootstraps its estimate for the state-action value $Q_{t+1}(s, a)$ at time $t + 1$ upon its estimate for $Q_t(s', a')$ with s' the state where the learner arrives after taking action a in state s:

$$Q_{t+1}(s, a) \leftarrow (1 - \alpha)Q_t(s, a) + \alpha(r + \gamma\, max_{a'}Q_t(s', a')) \tag{1}$$

with α the usual step size parameter, γ a discount factor, and r the immediate reinforcement.

2.2   The Replicator Equations

The basic concepts and techniques developed in EGT were initially formulated in the context of evolutionary biology [23, 13]. One way in which EGT proceeds is by constructing a dynamic process in which the proportions of various strategies in a population evolve. Examining the expected value of this process gives an approximation which is called the Replicator Dynamics (RD). RD highlights the role of selection; it describes how systems consisting of different strategies change over time. They are formalized as a system of differential equations. Each replicator (or genotype) represents one (pure) strategy. This strategy is inherited by all the offspring of the replicator. The general form of a replicator dynamic is the following:

$$\frac{dx_i}{dt} = [(A\mathbf{x})_i - \mathbf{x} \cdot A\mathbf{x}]x_i \tag{2}$$

In equation (2), x_i represents the density of strategy i in the population, A is the payoff matrix which describes the different payoff values each individual replicator receives when interacting with other replicators in the population.

The state of the population ($\mathbf{x}$) can be described as a probability vector $\mathbf{x} = (x_1, x_2, ..., x_J)$ which expresses the different densities of all the different types of replicators in the population. Hence $(A\mathbf{x})_i$ is the payoff which replicator i receives in a population with state x and $\mathbf{x} \cdot A\mathbf{x}$ describes the average payoff in the population. The growth rate $\frac{\frac{dx_i}{dt}}{x_i}$ of the population share using strategy i equals the difference between the strategy's current payoff and the average payoff in the population. For further information we refer the reader to [23, 8].

For the case of 2 agents p and q, we need two systems of differential equations: one for the player (p) and one for the player (q). In this case p_j represents the density of strategy j in the strategy population of the row player and q_i the density of strategy i in the strategy population of the column player. This setup corresponds to a RD for asymmetric games. If $A = B^t$, equation (2) would again emerge. This translates into the following replicator equations for the two populations:

$$\frac{dp_i}{dt} = [(A\mathbf{q})_i - \mathbf{p} \cdot A\mathbf{q}]p_i, \frac{dq_i}{dt} = [(B\mathbf{p})_i - \mathbf{q} \cdot B\mathbf{p}]q_i \tag{3}$$

As can be seen in equations 3, the growth rate of the types in each population is now determined by the composition of the other population. Note that, when calculating the rate of change using these systems of differential equations, two different payoff matrices (A and B) are used for the two different players.

2.3   The Q-Learning Dynamics

In this section we briefly repeat the main results of [21]. In this paper however, we will extend the results of that previous work. More precisely, we will apply these results to stochastic Dispersion Games. The experiments of [21] were conducted in one-stage games. In this paper we will extend this approach to multi-state one-stage games, i.e. stochastic Dispersion Games. Moreover, we will show that this evolutionary game theoretic approach enhances the COIN framework of Wolpert et al. and we will show that this approach is scalable to Dispersion Games with many agents.

We now first present the relation between Q-learning and the RD (see sections 2.1 and 2.2)[1]. More precisely we present a continuous time limit of the Q-learning model, where Q-values are interpreted as Boltzmann probabilities for the action selection.

For simplicity we discuss results as games between 2 players, and hence also two tasks. Note that this scenario is also interpreted as a game of one agent versus the rest of the MAS. Scenarios (not shown here) of the row player opposing a column player representing one or more agents in the MAS targeting the same tasks as the row agent were illustrative of behavior of the row and the collective of the column agent in such settings. A good understanding of the MAS was found by analyzing the behavior of one row player and his preference for one

---

[1] The reader who is interested in the complete derivation and discussion is referred to [21, 20].

task compared to the other tasks while playing versus respectively one, two, or more opposing agents playing the role of the column player.

Each agent(or player(s)) has a probability vector over his action set, more precisely $x_1, ..., x_n$ over action set $a_1, ..., a_n$ for the first player and $y_1, ..., y_m$ over $b_1, ..., b_m$ for the second player. Formally the Boltzmann distribution is described by,

$$x_i(k) = \frac{e^{\tau Q_{a_i}(k)}}{\sum_{j=1}^{n} e^{\tau Q_{a_j}(k)}} \tag{4}$$

where $x_i(k)$ is the probability of playing strategy i at time step k and τ is the temperature[2]. The temperature determines the degree of exploring different strategies. As the trade-off between exploration-exploitation is very important in RL, it is important to set this parameter correctly. Now suppose that we have payoff matrices A and B for the 2 players. Calculating the time limit, as established in [20], results in,

$$\frac{dx_i}{dt} = x_i \alpha \tau((A\mathbf{y})_i - \mathbf{x} \cdot A\mathbf{y}) + x_i \alpha \sum_j x_j ln(\frac{x_j}{x_i}) \tag{5}$$

for the first player and analogously for the second player in,

$$\frac{dy_i}{dt} = y_i \alpha \tau((B\mathbf{x})_i - \mathbf{y} \cdot B\mathbf{x}) + y_i \alpha \sum_j y_j ln(\frac{y_j}{y_i}) \tag{6}$$

Comparing (5) or (6) with the RD in (2), we see that the first term of (5) or (6) is exactly the RD and thus takes care of the selection mechanism, see [23]. The mutation mechanism for Q-learning is therefore left in the second term, and can be rewritten as:

$$x_i \alpha \sum_j x_j ln(x_j) - ln(x_i) \tag{7}$$

In equation (7) we recognize 2 entropy terms, one over the entire probability distribution x, and one over strategy x_i.

Relating entropy and mutation is not new. It is a well known fact [14, 15] that mutation increases entropy. In [15], it is stated that the concepts are familiar with thermodynamics in the following sense: the selection mechanism is analogous to *energy* and mutation to *entropy*. So generally speaking, mutations tend to increase entropy. Exploration can be considered as the mutation concept, as both concepts take care of providing variety.

Equations 5 and 6 now express the dynamics of both Q-learners in terms of Boltzmann probabilities, from which the RD emerge. In the next section we apply the equations to Dispersion Games.

---

[2] Used in the literature either in the numerator or in the denominator in Equation 4.

3   Applying the Q-Learning Dynamics to Stochastic Games

In this section we apply the Q-learning dynamics to multi-state stochastic games. In table 1a, a stochastic game is defined. The payoffs are listed as tuples for agents one and two respectively. This is the Dispersion Game for two agents where one agent is called the row player and the other the column player. The $i-th$ row for a row player represents the choice for execution of task t_i, and similarly the $i-th$ column for the column player . The highest possible global utility is achieved by the two players if (and only if) different tasks are chosen. Otherwise, the overly chosen task is randomly assigned (with 50% (0.5) probability) with reward 1 to either the row or column player and 0 for the other player. In this case, only half of the full global utility is achieved in the Dispersion Game.

Table 1. Example of a stochastic (multi-state) game

(a)	(b)	(c)

(a)

0.5 | 1,0 0.5 | 0,1	1,1	
1,1	0.5 | 1,0 0.5 | 0,1	

(b)

state 1	state 2	state 3	state 4
1,0 | 1,1 1,1 | 1,0	0,1 | 1,1 1,1 | 1,0	0,1 | 1,1 1,1 | 0,1	1,0 | 1,1 1,1 | 0,1

(c)

0.5,0.5	1,1
1,1	0.5,0.5

The stochastic payoff table 1a has four possible states that each represent one of the possible outcomes. These are expanded in payoff Table 1b.

For each of these different states we can now apply the ED equations 5 and 6 by filling in the payoff tables for A and B for the row and column player. Doing this allows us to plot the direction field for each state. This is a general approach to reduce stochastic payoffs to ED we can plot as in [21].

We show two direction plots in Figures 1 for a temperatures of $\tau = 2$ ((a) and (b)), and for $\tau = 10$ ((c) and (d)). The plots show the preferences of the choice of strategies for the row and column players for the representative states one and two of Table 1b respectively. The direction fields of the other two states (not shown) are the complement of the fields for state 1 and 2. The preference the row player has for choosing task t_1 is shown along the x axis and the preference the column player has for the same task is shown along the y axis. A point (p_1, p_2) in a graph is hence the joint (but independent) probability for choosing task t_1 and it also determines the complement for choosing task t_2 $(1 - p_1, 1 - p_2)$. The ED predict the changes in behavior of both players.

In Figure 1a, for state 1, the row player receives a reward of 1 independently of the choice of task of the column player. There is hence no incentive for the row player to focus on one of the tasks. The resulting attractor in the ED is a mixed strategy $(0.5, 0.5)$ where the choice of task execution is entirely random as the column player likewise follows suit. If however there is a bias in payoff like in Figure 1b for state 2, there is a shift in preference of the row player. In the second case, task t_2 gives an average higher reward and the row player will converge to this task and the column player converges to task t_1. Mirrored results hold for the mirrored scenarios of states 3 and 4 from table 1b (not shown) for the column player.

These phenomena are more strongly pronounced if the temperature is increased as can be seen in Figure 1c and d for a temperature τ of 10 instead of 2. The ED hence give an indication of the strength of the attractors for the possible states and show what parameter setting to use to produce strong, desired attractors. In this case, a temperature of $\tau = 2$ is too low as neither the row or column player when seen as a Q-learner is then expected to converge to a strategy where deterministically a unique task per agent is chosen. Both players are expected to converge to a mixed strategy of $\approx (0.83, 0.17)$ (or $(0.17, 0.83)$) and full utility will not be achieved by the MAS on average.

(a)   (b)   (c)   (d)

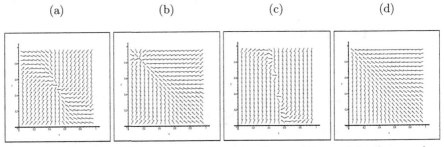

Fig. 1. The direction field plots of the Dispersion Game with $\tau = 2$ for the row player states 1 and 2 ((a) and (b)), and for $\tau = 10$ ((c) and (d))

Table 1c gives the average expected payoff for the joint actions of the row and column agent. Figure 2 shows the ED of this averaged payoff for $\tau = 10$. This figure is equivalent to the ED of Table 1a for equiprobable choice of states from Table 1b . The row player, and conversely also the column player, initially play an equilibrium strategy where both tasks are equally likely if the system is started with all preferences of all agents for all tasks identical, i.e. point $(0.5, 0.5)$ in figure 2a. A slight bias in preference by one of the agents for either task will however likely push the system away from this weak equilibrium as one of the agents, say the row player, chooses more than average one of the tasks in exploration, say t_1. This means that for the column player, any shift towards a preference for task t_2 will result in a strengthening of this shift. As the row player moves along one of the diagonals away from the mixed equilibrium strategy of $(0.5, 0.5)$, towards 0 or 1 along the x-axis, the column player will have an incentive to move towards 1 or 0 along the y-axis respectively. More precisely, if the row player gets a bias towards task t_1, and thus towards a preference of a 100% chance of choice of task t_1, the column player will develop a bias towards task t_2, and thus towards a preference of 0 for task t_1 (or a preference of a 100% of chance of choosing task t_2) and the dynamics end in point $(1, 0)$ of Figure 2a.

There are now three Nash Equilibriums: $\{(1, 0), (0, 1)\}, \{(0, 1), (1, 0)\}$, and $\{(0.5, 0.5), (0.5, 0.5)\}$. However, only the first two are stable as can be seen from the plot in Figure 2a. The mixed equilibrium is very unstable as any small perturbation away from this equilibrium will typically lead the dynamics to one of the 2 pure equilibriums. Note that this Dispersion Game is similar to the battle of the sexes game [5, 23].

In Figure 2b we plot a typical Q-learning process using Equation 1 for the above game with the same settings as for the system of differential equations with the sufficiently high temperature of $\tau = 10$ as predicted by the ED. For **only** the row player, the x-axis represents the chance of choosing task t_1 while the y-axis represents the (complementary) chance of choosing task t_2 as defined by the Q-values for these two tasks and the Boltzmann distribution of Equation 4.

As starting points for the Q-learning process we chose a grid of 25 representative points that are chosen so as to keep the plots clear and well-organized. In every point a learning path starts and converges to a particular point where the MAS achieves full utility as the column player develops mirrored preferences. The direction field plots for the value of $\tau = 10$ of Figure 2a predict the expected sample paths of the learning process in the RL domain. The instability of the mixed equilibrium is the reason why this equilibrium does not emerge from the sampled learning process. Of interest for future work is to examine how well the ED can be used to predict the learning trajectories of the Q-learners when an adaptive temperature τ is used in the course of learning as in [4], or how well the ED can predict the impact of learning parameters other than the temperature.

(a)   (b)

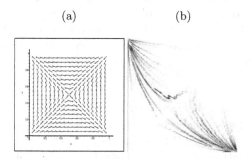

Fig. 2. The Evolutionary Dynamics and Q-learner with $\tau = 10$

4   COllective INtelligence

In this Section, we briefly outline the theory of COllective INtelligence (COIN) as developed by Wolpert et al., e.g. [26, 24]. Broadly speaking, COIN defines the conditions that an agent's private utility function has to meet to increase the probability that learning to optimize this function leads to increased performance of the collective of agents. Thus, the challenge is to define suitable private utilities function for the individual agents, given the performance of the collective.

Formally, let ζ be the joint moves of all agents. A function $G(\zeta)$ provides the utility of the collective system, the *world utility*, for a given ζ. The goal is to find a ζ that maximizes $G(\zeta)$. Each individual agent η has a private utility function g_η that relates the reward obtained by the collective to the reward that the individual agent collects.

Following a mathematical description of this issue, Wolpert et al. propose the **Wonderful Life Utility** (WLU) as a private utility function that is both *learnable* and *aligned* with G, and that can also be easily calculated.

$$WLU_\eta(\zeta) = G(\zeta) - G(CL_{S_\eta^{eff}}(\zeta)) \qquad (8)$$

The function $CL_{S_\eta^{eff}}(\zeta)$ as classically applied "clamps" or suspends the choice of task by agent η and returns the utility of the system without the effect of agent η on the remaining agents $\hat{\eta}$ with which it possibly interacts. For our problem domain, the clamped effect set are those agents $\hat{\eta}$ that are influenced in their utility by the choice of task of agent η.

For example, if agent η picks a task τ which is not chosen by the other agents, the first term of Equation 8 increases appropriately while the second term remains unchanged. Agent η hence receives a reward of $V(\tau)$, where V assigns a value to a task τ. Here, this reward is equal to 1. If the task chosen and executed by η is however also chosen by any of the other agents, the first term $G(\zeta)$ of Equation 8 is unchanged (at least one of the agents executes this task). However, the second term can increase with the value of $V(\tau)$ as agent η "no longer" competes for completion of the task when it is clamped. Agent η then, according to the WLU utility, receives a penalty $-V(\tau)$ for competing for a task targeted by one of the other agents $\hat{\eta}$. The WLU hence has a built in incentive for agents to find an unfulfilled task and hence for each agent to strive for a high global utility in its search for maximizing its own rewards.

The mathematical analysis of the WLU is calculated for the 2 agent full Dispersion Game in payoff Table 3a. Payoffs for the choice of an identical task by the agents in the system are no longer stochastic but are interpreted as a penalty. Behaviors where agents do not interfere in the pursuit of global utility, for example the row agent chooses task t_1 and the column agent chooses task t_2, however receive the original full payoff. Note that the Q-learner update rules of Section 2 are not changed and the agents still act as if they optimize their immediate (discounted) reward. An implementation of a distributed RL system can hence be reused.

5   Evolutionary Dynamics for COIN

The full Dispersion Game has $n!$ stable equilibriums where each of the n agents each fulfills one unique task. These equilibriums coincide with the states of the system that provide full utility. These states are unfortunately increasingly difficult to find in the RL exploration phase as the full joint action state space of the agents is of size n^n. Straightforward use of RL for 100 or more agents (not shown) leads to a maximum performance of ≈ 0.8 as agents prematurely converge to a subset of the tasks [18]. As can be seen in Figure 3b, the COIN framework with the WLU is however able to efficiently solve the assignment problem as the system is scaled whereas classical RL fails. The y-axis shows the utility of the system (1 represents execution of all tasks, utility averaged over 30

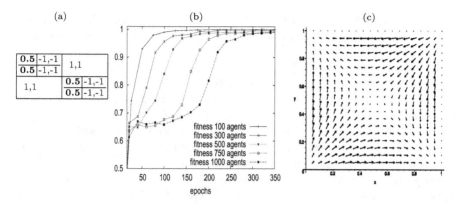

Fig. 3. Details WLU

runs) and the x-axis shows the number of required epochs for the Q-learners of Section 2.

The added value of the COIN framework can be explained by a closer study of the the ED for 2 agents. In Figure 3c we show the differences in the ED with respect to the original ED of the stochastic payoff of Figure 2a for a temperature of $\tau = 10$. This vector field shows where the increased dynamics lead to and the size of the individual vectors show how large the differences are. The differences for just 2 agents are slight, but indicative of the increasing added value as the MAS is scaled. The penalties imposed by the WLU strongly push the MAS away from states where agents choose to execute the same tasks. Aggregations of agents converging on the same task are quickly dispersed in the COIN framework. The ED then indicate that then the agents are on route to desired, optimal and stable Nash equilibriums. Straightforward RL however misses this built in incentive and only improves marginally on the initial random behavior of the system as the number of considered agents is increased. ED plots (not shown) for classical RL where the column agent plays the role of the other agents in the MAS, show that the agents in the MAS on average orbit around the homogeneous preference for all tasks and hence suffer from policy oscillations or converge to a task that is already targeted by another agent.

In further favor of COIN, the added value of the WLU as observed in the ED plots as compared to the standard RL was found to increase as the temperature of the system was increased. This sensitivity analysis, along with the found ED and corresponding attractors give an indication of what settings for the Q-learners will lead to a MAS with a high global utility. As such, the ED are a possible venue to investigate to acquire an indication of viable parameters for COIN and RL, in this case Q-learners.

6   Conclusion

In this work, we presented a novel approach to analyze Reinforcement Learning (RL) for Multi-Agent Systems (MASs). Learning in MASs is a growing area of research. How to achieve a high global utility on a cooperative task is however still an open question. This work shows a step forward by linking the field of Evolutionary Game Theory (EGT) and engineering approaches for Reinforcement Learning for MASs.

The dynamics of the RL learning process are visualized and analyzed from a perspective of Evolutionary Dynamics. We show how the ED from EGT can be used as a model for Q-learning in stochastic games. We show a one-to-one connection between the behavior of the RL and the ED from evolutionary game theory. Analysis of the evolutionary stable strategies and attractors of the derived ED from the RL application predict the parameters for the RL algorithms to achieve desired Nash equilibriums with high utility.

Secondly, we show how the derived parameter settings from the ED can support application of the COllective INtelligence (COIN) framework. COIN is a proved engineering approach for successful learning of cooperative tasks in MASs. The utilities of the agents are re-engineered to contribute to the global utility. We show that the derived link between ED and RL predicts performance of the COIN framework and visualizes the incentives provided in COIN toward cooperative behavior.

The above approach is potentially viable to apply to other MAS learning methodologies, not just COIN. The one-to-one mapping between the predicted behavior from RD and the observed behavior of the RL'ers is a guide in the design of a MAS.

References

1. B. Banerjee and J. Peng. Adaptive policy gradient in multiagent learning. In *AAMAS*, 2003.
2. A. Barto and S. Mahadevan. Recent advances in hierarchical reinforcement learning. *Discrete-Event Systems journal, Special issue on Reinforcement Learning*, 13:41–77, 2003.
3. R. Becker, S. Zilberstein, V. Lesser, and C. V. Goldman. Transition-independent decentralized Markov decision problems. In *AAMAS*, 2003.
4. C. Claus and C. Boutilier. The dynamics of reinforcement learning in cooperative multiagent systems. In *AAAI/IAAI*, pages 746–752, 1998.
5. C. Gintis. *Game Theory Evolving*. Princeton University Press, 2000.
6. T. Grenager, R. Powers, and Y. Shoham. Dispersion games: general definitions and some specific learning results. In *AAAI 2002*, 2002.
7. C. Guestrin, D. Koller, C. Gearhart, and N. Kanodia. Generalizing plans to new environments in relational MDPs. In *International Joint Conference on Artificial Intelligence (IJCAI-03)*, 2003.
8. J. Hofbauer and K. Sigmund. *Evolutionary Games and Population Dynamics*. Cambridge University Press, 1998.
9. P. Huang and K. Sycara. Multi-agent learning in extensive games with complete information. In *AAMAS*, 2003.
10. H. Jung and M. Tambe. Performance model for large scale multiagent systems. In *AAMAS*, 2003.
11. M. Lauer and M. Riedmiller. An algorithm for distributed reinforcement learning in cooperative multi-agent systems. In *Proc. 17th International Conf. on Machine Learning*, pages 535–542. Morgan Kaufmann, San Francisco, CA, 2000.

12. M. Osborne and A. Rubinstein. *A Course in Game Theory*. The MIT Press, Cambridge, MA, 1994.
13. L. Samuelson. *Evolutionary Games and Equilibrium Selection*. MIT Press, Cambridge, MA, 1997.
14. T. Schneider. Evolution of biological information. journal of NAR, volume 28, pages 2794 - 2799., 2000.
15. D. Stauffer. Life, love and death: Models of biological reproduction and aging. Institute for Theoretical physics, Köln, Euroland, 1999.
16. R. Sutton and A. Barto. *Reinforcement learning: An introduction*. MIT-press, Cambridge, MA, 1998.
17. P. 't Hoen and S. Bohte. COllective INtelligence with sequences of actions. In *14th European Conference on Machine Learning*, Lecture Notes in Artificial Intelligence, LNAI 2837. Springer, 2003.
18. P. 't Hoen and S. Bohte. COllective INtelligence with task assignment. In *Proceedings of CDOCS03, fortcoming. Also available as TR*, Lecture Notes in Artificial Intelligence. Springer, 2003.
19. K. Tumer and D. Wolpert. COllective INtelligence and Braess' paradox. In *Proceedings of the Sixteenth National Conference on Artificial Intelligence*, pages 104–109, Austin, Aug. 2000.
20. K. Tuyls, D. Heytens, A. Nowe, and B. Manderick. Extended replicator dynamics as a key to reinforcement learning in multi-agent systems. In *ECML*, Lecture Notes in Artificial Intelligence, LNAI 2837, 2003.
21. K. Tuyls, K. Verbeeck, and T. Lenaerts. A selection-mutation model for Q-learning in multi-agent systems. In *AAMAS*, The ACM International Conference Proceedings Series, 2003.
22. Watkins and Dayan. Q-learning. *Machine Learning*, 8:279–292, 1992.
23. J. Weibull. *Evolutionary Game Theory*. The MIT Press, Cambridge, 1995.
24. D. Wolpert and K. Tumer. Optimal payoff functions for members of collectives. *Advances in Complex Systems*, 4(2/3):265–279, 2001.
25. D. H. Wolpert, K. Tumer, and J. Frank. Using collective intelligence to route internet traffic. In *Advances in Neural Information Processing Systems-11*, pages 952–958, Denver, 1998.
26. D. H. Wolpert, K. R. Wheeler, and K. Tumer. General principles of learning-based multi-agent systems. In O. Etzioni, J. P. Müller, and J. M. Bradshaw, editors, *Proceedings of the Third Annual Conference on Autonomous Agents (AGENTS-99)*, pages 77–83, New York, May 1–5 1999. ACM Press.

Experiments in Value Function Approximation with Sparse Support Vector Regression

Tobias Jung and Thomas Uthmann

Institut für Informatik
Johannes Gutenberg-Universität
55099 Mainz, Germany
{tjung,uthmann}@informatik.uni-mainz.de

Abstract. We present first experiments using Support Vector Regression as function approximator for an on-line, *sarsa*-like reinforcement learner. To overcome the batch nature of SVR two ideas are employed. The first is sparse greedy approximation: the data is projected onto the subspace spanned by only a small subset of the original data (in feature space). This subset can be built up in an on-line fashion. Second, we use the sparsified data to solve a reduced quadratic problem, where the number of variables is independent of the total number of training samples seen. The feasability of this approach is demonstrated on two common toy-problems.

1 Introduction

One central approach to solve reinforcement learning (RL) problems relies on estimating value functions either from simulation-based experience or model-based search (e.g. [10]). For problems with large or continuous state spaces it becomes necessary to represent the value function by some form of function approximator in order to generalize estimated values from previously visited states to similar but never seen before ones. Although many different approximation architectures are possible – both parametric (e.g. Neural Networks, RBF-Networks, tile coding) and non-parametric (e.g. locally weighted regression) have been tried to a varying degree of success – value function approximation remains one of the key obstacles in scaling RL to high-dimensional control tasks.

Support Vector Machines (SVM) could represent a powerful alternative: in principle unharmed by the dimensionality, trained by solving a well defined optimization problem, and with generalization capabilities presumably superior to local instance-based methods. The goal of our ongoing work reported herein is to utilize SV-Regression to approximate the value function in common RL algorithms. Related results are limited to off-line learning: in [3] SVR has been applied along the lines of approximate value iteration. Inputs to the SVR were the real targets, solved by value iteration on a subset of states, and presented in batches to the approximator. However, for the on-line case this has not been attempted before, as far as we are aware.

J.-F. Boulicaut et al. (Eds.): ECML 2004, LNAI 3201, pp. 180–191, 2004.
© Springer-Verlag Berlin Heidelberg 2004

A reason could be that value function approximation is plagued by some peculiar characteristics that do not agree very well with the instance-based nature of SVR. We are facing the following two problems: First, RL proceeds iteratively. Thus training samples arrive one at a time from an endless stream which is generated while the learning agent interacts with its environment. Second, many RL algorithms usually rely on bootstrapped samples that are continually updated with new estimates. Therefore we have to track a highly non-stationary target function and need to access and modify the stored training samples. Both of these points pose no problems for parametric function approximators, since their gradient based training deals naturally with incremental learning. Non-parametric function approximators, however, are memory-based and must explicitly remember all training data. Either adding a new example or updating an old one both amount to a change to the stored training samples. In this case, however, learning cannot be done incrementally so that we have to re-train the SVR every time-step anew. Moreover, a SVR is usually solved by a constrained quadratic optimization problem where the number of variables equals the number of training examples. Clearly, a constantly increasing number would sooner or later render the computational cost completely prohibitive. In order to keep this problem tractable it is necessary to keep this number from growing linearly in time.

Fortunately, we do not have to remember every training sample. As was pointed out in [4] one can eliminate those from the final expansion that are linear dependant (in feature space) without changing the obtained solution. Thus, it is reasonable to store only a few selected examples in a reduced dictionary. Examples of how to arrive at sparse dictionaries can be found in [9, 12, 7], along with applications of how to benefit from it. In particular, in [6, 5] a sparse algorithm is presented that greedily adds examples to the reduced dictionary and is especially suited to on-line applications. Together with this sparsification procedure the authors propose in [6] an incremental SVR-algorithm where the solution is obtained by only considering the samples in the reduced dictionary. This way, the per-time-step complexity is limited by the intrinsic dimensionality of the data in the feature space instead of the ever increasing number of arriving training examples.

Here we will pursue a similar approach and apply their greedy sparsification method to obtain a function approximator suitable for RL. The remainder of the paper is structured as follows: Sect. 2 briefly reviews RL, Sect. 3 and Sect. 4 describe the modified sparsification method. In Sect. 5 everything is wrapped up in some experiments that demonstrate the feasability of this approach, and Sect. 6 concludes.

2   A Brief Reminder of Reinforcement Learning

Reinforcement learning belongs to a class of optimal control methods that are based on estimating value functions either from simulation-based experiences (Monte-Carlo or Temporal Difference branch) or model-based search (Dynamic

Programming branch), e.g. see [1, 10]. In this work we make the following assumptions: we consider the case of time-discrete control tasks with continuous states and discrete action set. Once the value function is known we assume that the learner has access to a model to derive the best course of actions.

The goal is to (approximately) compute the value function which is here defined to be the infinite horizon, discounted sum of rewards

$$V^\pi(s) = E^\pi \left(\sum_{t=0}^{\infty} \gamma^t r_t \;\middle|\; s_0 = s \right) \tag{1}$$

when starting in state s and choosing actions according to policy π. Here $\gamma \in [0, 1)$ denotes the discount factor and r_i the reward obtained while traversing from s_i to s_{i+1}. For a given policy π we can compute V^π by iteratively applying the TD(0) rule

$$V(s) \leftarrow V(s) + \alpha[r + \gamma V(s') - V(s)] \tag{2}$$

where s' and r is the state and reward following s while executing π, and $\alpha \in [0, 1]$ is the step size. Applying (2) infinitely often to every state (assuming a finite state set) in arbitrary order is guaranteed to yield (1). Once the value function V^{π_k} is known for a fixed policy π_k (policy evaluation step) we can derive the greedy policy w.r.t. V^{π_k} to otain a new policy π_{k+1}

$$\pi_{k+1}(s) = \operatorname*{argmax}_a \sum_{s'} P^a(s, s')[R^a(s, s') + \gamma V^{\pi_k}(s')] \tag{3}$$

in the so called policy improvement step. Many popular RL algorithms adhere to the framework of alternately carrying out policy evaluation and policy improvement. Roughly speaking, they only vary the extent to which policy evaluation is executed before improving the current policy. Throughout this paper we will use an on-line variant thereof, see algorithm 1 below.

Parameter: ϵ, α, γ
Initialize: function approximator F
loop
    $s \leftarrow$ start state
    while s is not terminal **do**
        $v \leftarrow \operatorname{predict}(F, s)$
        $a \leftarrow \operatorname{policy-action}(F, s)$ from (3) {ϵ-greedy}
        execute a, observe r, and s'
        if s' is terminal **then**
            $v \leftarrow v + \alpha[r - v]$
        else
            $v \leftarrow v + \alpha[r + \gamma \operatorname{predict}(F, s') - v]$
        $\operatorname{learn}(F, s, v)$
        $s \leftarrow s'$

Algorithm 1. Model-based *sarsa* with instance-based function approximator

3   Sparse Support Vector Regression

3.1   The SVR Problem

We start by restating the standard formulation[1] of the SVR problem with ε-insensitive cost function [8]. Consider some training data $\{(\mathbf{x}_1, y_1), \ldots, (\mathbf{x}_\ell, y_\ell)\}$, where $\mathbf{x}_i \in \mathbb{R}^n$ are the input-patterns and $y_i \in \mathbb{R}$ are the target outputs. The overall idea is to map the input-patterns into some high-dimensional feature space, and to perform linear regression in that feature space. Let Φ be the non-linear function that maps the input-patterns to this feature space. Considering functions $f(\cdot) = \langle \mathbf{w}, \Phi(\cdot) \rangle + b$ that are linearly parametrized in the feature space the objective is to find one that minimizes the regularized risk

$$R_{reg}(\mathbf{w}) = C \frac{1}{\ell} \sum_{i=1}^{\ell} |y_i - (\langle \mathbf{w}, \Phi(\mathbf{x}_i) \rangle + b)|_\varepsilon + \frac{1}{2} \|\mathbf{w}\|^2 \tag{4}$$

where C is a constant penalizing complexity. The ε-insensitive cost function $| \cdot |_\varepsilon \overset{\text{def}}{=} \max(0, | \cdot | - \varepsilon)$ only takes into account deviations larger than ε and enforces sparsity in the final regressor. It is known that the function minimizing (4) can be expressed solely in terms of the input-patterns (Representer Theorem) and has the form $f(\cdot) = \sum_{i=1}^{\ell} (\alpha_i^* - \alpha_i) \langle \Phi(\mathbf{x}_i), \Phi(\cdot) \rangle + b$. The coefficients α_i^*, α_i of the solution satisfy $\alpha_i^*, \alpha_i \geq 0$ and $\alpha_i^* \alpha_i = 0$. They are obtained by solving the constrained quadratic optimization problem (dual)

$$\max_{\boldsymbol{\alpha}^*, \boldsymbol{\alpha} \in \mathbb{R}^\ell} \quad -\frac{1}{2} \sum_{i,j=1}^{\ell} (\alpha_i^* - \alpha_i)(\alpha_j^* - \alpha_j) \langle \Phi(\mathbf{x}_i), \Phi(\mathbf{x}_j) \rangle$$

$$-\varepsilon \sum_{i=1}^{\ell} (\alpha_i^* + \alpha_i) + \sum_{i=1}^{\ell} y_i (\alpha_i^* - \alpha_i) \tag{5}$$

$$\text{s.t.} \qquad 0 \leq \alpha_i^*, \alpha_i \leq C \quad i = 1 \ldots \ell$$

$$\sum_{i=1}^{\ell} (\alpha_i^* - \alpha_i) = 0$$

What is commonly referred to as 'kernel-trick' allows us to replace the inner product in feature space $\langle \Phi(\mathbf{x}_i), \Phi(\mathbf{x}_j) \rangle$ by a Mercer kernel function $k(\mathbf{x}_i, \mathbf{x}_j)$. Thus once the solution to (5) has been worked out we obtain the final regressor

$$f(\mathbf{x}) = \sum_{i=1}^{\ell} (\alpha_i^* - \alpha_i) k(\mathbf{x}_i, \mathbf{x})$$

where usually many of the coefficients α_i^*, α_i vanish.

---

[1] Note that we stick to the standard notation of denoting the input with $\mathbf{x}_i$ and the output with y_i. Since SVR is used to approximate the value function, we are actually dealing with input-output pairs of the form $(\mathbf{s}, \tilde{V}(\mathbf{s}))$, with $\tilde{V}(\mathbf{s})$ being the new estimated target for the (vector-valued) state $\mathbf{s}$

3.2   Sparse Greedy Matrix Approximation

Unfortunately SVM methods were developed primarily with batch function approximation in mind. The setting of on-line learning differs considerable: here we assume that we have a (possible infinite) stream of incoming data. Recall that we wish to apply SVR as function approximator for *sarsa*-like on-line reinforcement learning (cf. Algorithm 1). At every step t we add the current state and its (re-) estimated value to the stored instances and thus end up with a training set consisting of *all* updates made to this point. At every time step we also need to make a new prediction that incorporates the previous changes. Hence we need to re-train the SVR once every single step. As there is generally no efficient way to get this done incrementally this task would be computationally completely infeasable: it would require that we solve the ever-increasing optimization problem (5) in t variables once every step[2]. Likewise the time to perform the prediction would also increase linearly in t.

Clearly the per-time-step complexity should not depend on the iteration count t. One way to deal with this problem are sparse greedy approximation techniques [6, 9]. The underlying idea is based on the observation that usually the mapped data $\Phi(\mathbf{x}_i)$ spans a subspace whose effective dimension is surprisingly low when compared to the dimension of the feature space. Therefore we can easily remove many of the input-patterns with negligible impact in the precision. This can be done by picking a subset (called 'dictionary' in [6]) of the input-patterns and representing the remaining patterns as linear combination in feature space. Thus after having chosen a dictionary of m inputs $\{\tilde{\mathbf{x}}_1, \dots, \tilde{\mathbf{x}}_m\}$ we can approximate the remaining features $\{\Phi(\mathbf{x}_1), \dots, \Phi(\mathbf{x}_\ell)\} \setminus \{\Phi(\tilde{\mathbf{x}}_1), \dots, \Phi(\tilde{\mathbf{x}}_m)\}$ by

$$\Phi(\mathbf{x}_i) \approx \tilde{\Phi}(\mathbf{x}_i) := \sum_{j=1}^{m} a_{ij} \Phi(\tilde{\mathbf{x}}_j)$$

Since the approximation is carried out in feature space, we need to find coefficients a_{ij} such that the distance $d_i := \|\Phi(\mathbf{x}_i) - \tilde{\Phi}(\mathbf{x}_i)\|^2$ is minimized. Remembering to replace the inner products with kernels, this is equivalent to

$$\min_{\mathbf{a}_i \in \mathbf{R}^m} k(\mathbf{x}_i, \mathbf{x}_i) - 2 \sum_{j=1}^{m} a_{ij} k(\tilde{\mathbf{x}}_j, \mathbf{x}_i) + \sum_{j,l=1}^{m} a_{ij} a_{il} k(\tilde{\mathbf{x}}_j, \tilde{\mathbf{x}}_l) \tag{6}$$

or written in more convenient matrix notation $\min_{\mathbf{a}_i} \{k_{ii} - 2\mathbf{a}_i^T \tilde{\mathbf{k}}_i + \mathbf{a}_i^T \tilde{K} \mathbf{a}_i\}$ where $[\tilde{K}]_{ij} = k(\tilde{\mathbf{x}}_i, \tilde{\mathbf{x}}_j)$, $k_{ii} = k(\mathbf{x}_i, \mathbf{x}_i)$, and $\tilde{\mathbf{k}}_i = (k(\tilde{\mathbf{x}}_1, \mathbf{x}_i), \dots, k(\tilde{\mathbf{x}}_m, \mathbf{x}_i))^T$. Setting the derivates to zero we find that the minimizer of (6) is given by

$$\mathbf{a}_i = \tilde{K}^{-1} \tilde{\mathbf{k}}_i \tag{7}$$

Once we have determined $\mathbf{a}_i$ for input-pattern $\mathbf{x}_i$ we simultaneously obtain

$$d_i = k_{ii} - \tilde{\mathbf{k}}_i^T \mathbf{a}_i \tag{8}$$

---

[2] In everything but the most trivial problem the step count easily ranges in the 100,000s and more

as the distance to the span of the dictionary. Using this byproduct as a criterion to judge whether or not the current dictionary approximates a given input well enough, the authors in [6] turn this procedure into an on-line algorithm. Imagine running sequentially through the full training set, one can add the current $\mathbf{x}_i$ to the dictionary whenever the corresponding d_i is worse than some tolerance TOL2.

3.3   Solving a Reduced Problem

Let $[A]_{ij} \in \mathbb{R}^{\ell \times m}$ be the matrix consisting of rows $\mathbf{a}_i$ from (7) for the full training set $\{(\mathbf{x}_1, y_1), \ldots, (\mathbf{x}_\ell, y_\ell)\}$ and the fixed dictionary $\{\tilde{\mathbf{x}}_1, \ldots, \tilde{\mathbf{x}}_m\}$. Note that if $\mathbf{x_k}$ belongs to the dictionary then $\mathbf{a}_k$ is the kth unit vector $(0, \ldots, 1, 0 \ldots)^T$ since $\Phi(\mathbf{x}_k)$ is exactly representable by itself. This way we can use the reduced kernel matrix $\tilde{K} \in \mathbb{R}^{m \times m}$ and the transformation A to obtain a (low-rank) approximation to the full kernel matrix $K \in \mathbb{R}^{\ell \times \ell}$ with $K \approx A\tilde{K}A^T$.

Now we come to the all-decisive step: this approximation can be used to derive a new reduced QP in $m \ll \ell$ variables, which can be solved instead of the original problem to yield approximately the same regressor but requring only a fraction of the time. First, writing the objective function of our constrained QP (5) in matrix notation

$$\min_{\boldsymbol{\alpha}, \boldsymbol{\alpha}^* \in \mathbb{R}^\ell} -\frac{1}{2}(\boldsymbol{\alpha}^* - \boldsymbol{\alpha})^T K (\boldsymbol{\alpha}^* - \boldsymbol{\alpha}) - \varepsilon(\boldsymbol{\alpha}^* + \boldsymbol{\alpha})^T \mathbf{e} + (\boldsymbol{\alpha}^* - \boldsymbol{\alpha})^T \mathbf{y} \qquad (9)$$

we can replace in (9) kernel matrix K with its approximation $A\tilde{K}A^T$. Next, we define the $2m$ new variables $\tilde{\boldsymbol{\alpha}} = (\tilde{\alpha}_1, \ldots, \tilde{\alpha}_m)^T$ through $\tilde{\boldsymbol{\alpha}} = A^T \boldsymbol{\alpha}$, and similarly $\tilde{\boldsymbol{\alpha}}^* = A^T \boldsymbol{\alpha}^*$. Before we can complete the change of variables we must compensate the transformation for the remaining summands in (9) using the (pseudo-)inverse $A^\dagger = (A^T A)^{-1} A^T$. Thus define the new targets $\tilde{\mathbf{y}} = A^\dagger \mathbf{y}$. Now we arrive at a reduced QP with objective function

$$\min_{\tilde{\boldsymbol{\alpha}}, \tilde{\boldsymbol{\alpha}}^* \in \mathbb{R}^m} -\frac{1}{2}(\tilde{\boldsymbol{\alpha}}^* - \tilde{\boldsymbol{\alpha}})^T \tilde{K} (\tilde{\boldsymbol{\alpha}}^* - \tilde{\boldsymbol{\alpha}}) - \varepsilon(\tilde{\boldsymbol{\alpha}}^* + \tilde{\boldsymbol{\alpha}})^T A^\dagger \mathbf{e} + (\tilde{\boldsymbol{\alpha}}^* - \tilde{\boldsymbol{\alpha}})^T \tilde{\mathbf{y}} \qquad (10)$$

in the $2m$ variables $\tilde{\boldsymbol{\alpha}}, \tilde{\boldsymbol{\alpha}}^*$ instead of (9). Solving the reduced problem (10) we obtain the regressor $\tilde{f}(\cdot) = \sum_{j=1}^{m}(\tilde{\alpha}_j^* - \tilde{\alpha}_j)k(\tilde{\mathbf{x}}_j, \cdot)$ which is approximately the one we would have obtained solving the full problem:

$$\tilde{f}(\cdot) = \sum_{j=1}^{\ell}(\alpha_j^* - \alpha_j) \sum_{l=1}^{m} a_{jl} k(\tilde{\mathbf{x}}_l, \cdot)$$

$$\approx \sum_{j=1}^{\ell}(\alpha_j^* - \alpha_j)k(\mathbf{x}_j, \cdot) = f(\cdot)$$

To illustrate the approximation quality we ran some tests on the synthetic problem $\sin\|\mathbf{x}\|/\|\mathbf{x}\|$ where $\mathbf{x} \in [10, 10]^2$ was scaled to lie inside the unit cube. Table 1 shows that for various different settings the final test-error from the regressor obtained by solving (10) closely resembles that of the full problem, at significantly lower training costs.

Table 1. Performance of sparse greedy approximation. Results for solving the 2-dimensional *sinc* function are shown for the full problem (9) and the reduced problem (10) for Gaussian kernels $k(x,y) = \exp(-\|x-y\|^2/\sigma)$. The training set consisted of 500 randomly drawn examples. Each regressor was tested on a 40×40 grid. With $\|\mathbf{y} - AA^\dagger\mathbf{y}\|^2$ we measure the error induced by projecting the data. All error-terms are given as sum of squared errors

Kernel width σ	Test-error full	TOL2	m	$\|\mathbf{y} - AA^\dagger\mathbf{y}\|^2$	Test Error Reduced
$\sigma = 0.2$		10^{-1}	15 (03.0%)	9.9087	42.6080
$C_{\text{full}} = 2500$	8.4440	10^{-3}	36 (07.2%)	7.2672	31.2892
$C_{\text{red}} = 5000$		10^{-6}	73 (14.6%)	0.2134	20.2643
$\sigma = 0.1$		10^{-1}	25 (05.0%)	8.4494	35.7908
$C_{\text{full}} = 50$	0.3589	10^{-3}	60 (12.0%)	0.5141	3.4052
$C_{\text{red}} = 5000$		10^{-6}	117 (23.4%)	$< 10^{-4}$	0.0049
$\sigma = 0.04$		10^{-1}	58 (11.6%)	0.4152	1.1733
$C_{\text{full}} = 1$	0.0037	10^{-3}	125 (25.0%)	0.0002	0.0043
$C_{\text{red}} = 500$		10^{-6}	220 (44.0%)	$< 10^{-7}$	0.0028

4 The Complete Algorithm

Let us now walk through a complete iteration of our SVR-RL approximator. Let t be the current iteration count and $(\mathbf{x}_t, y_t)$ the current sample from algorithm 1. Assume we have assembled the following

- $X_{\text{old}} \in \mathbb{R}^{\ell \times m}$ and $\mathbf{y}_{\text{old}} \in \mathbb{R}^\ell$ the training set of all ℓ sufficiently 'different' instances (see Step 1 below) seen up to time t where usually $\ell < t$.
- $D_{\text{dict}} = \{\tilde{\mathbf{x}}_1, \ldots, \tilde{\mathbf{x}}_m\}$ the dictionary consisting of m linear independent inputs where $m \ll t$.
- $\tilde{K}_{\text{old}}^{-1} \in \mathbb{R}^{m \times m}$ the inverse of $[\tilde{K}]_{ij} = k(\tilde{\mathbf{x}}_i, \tilde{\mathbf{x}}_j)$ (which is not stored).
- $A_{\text{old}} \in \mathbb{R}^{\ell \times m}$ consisting of rows $\mathbf{a}_i$ from (7).
- $(A^T\mathbf{y})_{\text{old}} \in \mathbb{R}^m$
- $(A^T A)_{\text{old}}^{-1} \in \mathbb{R}^{m \times m}$
- $\tilde{\mathbf{y}}_{\text{old}} \in \mathbb{R}^m$ the targets $\tilde{\mathbf{y}}_{\text{old}} := A_{\text{old}}^\dagger \mathbf{y}_{\text{old}} = (A^T A)_{\text{old}}^{-1}(A^T\mathbf{y})_{\text{old}}$ for the reduced problem (10).

Step 1: Tribute to the non-stationarity of RL. First we need to check whether $\mathbf{x}_t$ is a state for which we already have stored a value. In that case we will interpret y_t as an update (a new estimated value). Otherwise we need to add it to the training set, GOTO STEP 2. The criterion we use is proximity in feature space, that is if

$$\min_{i=1\ldots\ell} \|\Phi(\mathbf{x}_t) - \Phi(X_{\text{old}}[i,:])\|^2 < \text{TOL1} \tag{11}$$

is below some chosen tolerance TOL1 we update that component from $\mathbf{y}_{\text{old}}$ for which the index in (11) attains its minimum, i.e. the 'nearest' state. Once $\mathbf{y}_{\text{old}}$ is modified to yield $\mathbf{y}_{\text{new}}$ we need to compute $\tilde{\mathbf{y}}_{\text{new}}$ which, unfortunately, cannot be done incrementally in this case. Thus we first need to re-compute $(A^T\mathbf{y})_{\text{new}} = A_{\text{old}}^T\mathbf{y}_{\text{new}}$ and then $\tilde{\mathbf{y}}_{\text{new}} = (A^T A)_{\text{old}}^{-1}(A^T\mathbf{y})_{\text{new}}$. Finally we need to re-train the regressor, proceed with STEP 3.

Step 2: Sparse Approximation. The current state is sufficiently new and thus added to the full training set: append a row in $X_{\text{new}} = \begin{bmatrix} X_{\text{old}}^T & \mathbf{x}_t \end{bmatrix}^T$ and $\mathbf{y}_{\text{new}} = \begin{pmatrix} \mathbf{y}_{\text{old}}^T & y_t \end{pmatrix}^T$. Increment the number of training samples ℓ. Now we test if $\mathbf{x}_t$ can be approximated by D_{dict}: compute $\mathbf{a}_t$ from (7) using $\tilde{K}_{\text{old}}^{-1}$ and obtain d_t from (8). If d_t is below some chosen tolerance TOL2 then $\mathbf{x}_t$ is approximately linearly dependent on the dictionary and thus does not contribute to the number of variables in the reduced problem, GOTO CASE 2.2. Otherwise, we need to add $\mathbf{x}_t$ to the dictionary, GOTO CASE 2.1.

Case 2.1: Add $\mathbf{x}_t$ to the dictionary and increment its size m. Since $\mathbf{x}_t$ was linearly independent the approximation coefficient $\mathbf{a}_t$ becomes $(0, \ldots, 0, 1)^T$ and so every expression involving A_{old} is very cheaply updated:

$$A_{\text{new}} = \begin{bmatrix} A_{\text{old}} & \mathbf{0} \\ \mathbf{0}^T & 1 \end{bmatrix}, \qquad (A^T A)_{\text{new}}^{-1} = \begin{bmatrix} (A^T A)_{\text{old}}^{-1} & \mathbf{0} \\ \mathbf{0}^T & 1 \end{bmatrix} \qquad (12)$$

$$(A^T \mathbf{y})_{\text{new}} = \begin{bmatrix} (A^T \mathbf{y})_{\text{old}} \\ y_t \end{bmatrix}, \tilde{\mathbf{y}}_{\text{new}} = \begin{bmatrix} (A^T A)_{\text{old}}^{-1} & \mathbf{0} \\ \mathbf{0}^T & 1 \end{bmatrix} \begin{bmatrix} (A^T \mathbf{y})_{\text{old}} \\ y_t \end{bmatrix} = \begin{bmatrix} \tilde{\mathbf{y}}_{\text{old}} \\ y_t \end{bmatrix} \qquad (13)$$

However, augmenting the dictionary means updating $\tilde{K}_{\text{old}}^{-1}$. Fortunately, this can be done efficiently since $\tilde{K}_{\text{new}}$ and $\tilde{K}_{\text{old}}$ differ only by a rank-1 update. Again denote by $\tilde{\mathbf{k}}_t = \big(k(\tilde{\mathbf{x}}_1, \mathbf{x}_t), \ldots, k(\tilde{\mathbf{x}}_m, \mathbf{x}_t)\big)^T$ and $k_{tt} = k(\mathbf{x}_t, \mathbf{x}_t)$. Then [8]

$$\tilde{K}_{\text{new}}^{-1} = \begin{bmatrix} \tilde{K}_{\text{old}} & \tilde{\mathbf{k}}_t \\ \tilde{\mathbf{k}}_t^T & k_{tt} \end{bmatrix} = \begin{bmatrix} \tilde{K}_{\text{old}}^{-1} + \eta^{-1} \mathbf{a}_t \mathbf{a}_t^T & -\eta^{-1} \mathbf{a}_t \\ -\eta^{-1} \mathbf{a}_t^T & \eta^{-1} \end{bmatrix} \qquad (14)$$

where $\eta = (k_{tt} - \tilde{\mathbf{k}}_t^T \tilde{K}_{\text{old}}^{-1} \tilde{\mathbf{k}}_t)$ and $\mathbf{a}_t$ from (7). GOTO STEP 3.

Case 2.2 The current input $\mathbf{x}_t$ is linearly dependent on the dictionary, thus D_{dict}, its size m, and $\tilde{K}_{\text{new}}^{-1} = \tilde{K}_{\text{old}}^{-1}$ remain unchanged. Append the approximation coefficients $\mathbf{a}_t$ from (7) as row in $A_{\text{new}} = \begin{bmatrix} A_{\text{old}}^T & \mathbf{a}_t \end{bmatrix}^T$. To update $(A^T A)_{\text{old}}^{-1}$ note that $(A^T A)_{\text{new}} = (A^T A)_{\text{old}} + \mathbf{a}_t \mathbf{a}_t^T$ and so, using the matrix inversion lemma, we obtain the recursive update formula

$$(A^T A)_{\text{new}}^{-1} = (A^T A)_{\text{old}}^{-1} - \frac{(A^T A)_{\text{old}}^{-1} \mathbf{a}_t \mathbf{a}_t^T (A^T A)_{\text{old}}^{-1}}{1 + \mathbf{a}_t^T (A^T A)_{\text{old}}^{-1} \mathbf{a}_t} \qquad (15)$$

Now we take care of $(A^T \mathbf{y})_{\text{new}}$, and $\tilde{\mathbf{y}}_{\text{new}}$. While the first part is obtained easily, the second part has no recursive update and must be computed anew

$$(A^T \mathbf{y})_{\text{new}} = (A^T \mathbf{y})_{\text{old}} + y_t \mathbf{a}_t, \qquad \tilde{\mathbf{y}}_{\text{new}} = (A^T A)_{\text{new}}^{-1} (A^T \mathbf{y})_{\text{new}} \qquad (16)$$

Again, GOTO STEP 3.

Step 3: Solve the reduced problem. Finally, we use the sparsified training set $\{(\tilde{\mathbf{x}}_1, \tilde{y}_1), \ldots, (\tilde{\mathbf{x}}_m, \tilde{y}_m)\}$ with $\tilde{\mathbf{y}}_{\text{old}} = (\tilde{y}_1, \ldots, \tilde{y}_m)^T$ to solve the reduced QP (10).

Paramater: TOL1, TOL2, C, ε and kernel
Initialize: $X_{\text{old}} = [\mathbf{x}_1], \mathbf{y}_{\text{old}} = (y_1), \tilde{\mathbf{y}}_{\text{old}} = (y_1), D_{\text{dict}} = \{\mathbf{x}_1\}, \tilde{K}_{\text{old}}^{-1} = [k_{tt}^{-1}], A_{\text{old}} = [1], (A^T\mathbf{y})_{\text{old}} = [y_1], (A^TA)_{\text{old}}^{-1} = [1], m = 1, \ell = 1$
for $t = 1, 2, \ldots$ **do**
    Get new sample $(\mathbf{x}_t, y_t)$ from algorithm 1
    if $\min_{i=1\ldots\ell} \|\Phi(\mathbf{x}_t) - \Phi(X_{\text{old}}[i,:])\|^2 <$ TOL1 **then**
        $\mathbf{y}_{\text{old}}[k] \leftarrow y_t$ where k is argmin from (11)
        Compute $(A^T\mathbf{y})_{\text{new}}$ and $\tilde{\mathbf{y}}_{\text{new}} = (A^TA)_{\text{old}}^{-1}(A^T\mathbf{y})_{\text{new}}$
    else
        $X_{\text{new}} = [X_{\text{old}}^T \quad \mathbf{x}_t]^T, \mathbf{y}_{\text{new}} = (\mathbf{y}_{\text{old}}^T \quad y_t)^T, \ell = \ell + 1$
        Compute $\tilde{\mathbf{k}}_t$
        Compute $\mathbf{a}_t$ from (7) and d_t from (8)
        if $d_t >$ TOL2 **then**
            Add $\mathbf{x}_t$ to $D_{\text{dict}}, m = m + 1$
            Compute $\tilde{K}_{\text{new}}^{-1}$ from (14)
            Compute A_{new} and $(A^TA)_{\text{new}}^{-1}$ from (12)
            Compute $(A^T\mathbf{y})_{\text{new}}$ and $\tilde{\mathbf{y}}_{\text{new}}$ from (13)
        else
            $A_{\text{new}} = [A_{\text{old}}^T \quad a_t]^T$
            Compute $(A^TA)_{\text{new}}^{-1}$ from (15)
            Compute $(A^T\mathbf{y})_{\text{new}}$ and $\tilde{\mathbf{y}}_{\text{new}}$ from (16)
    Solve the reduced QP (10) for $\{(\tilde{\mathbf{x}}_1, \tilde{y}_1), \ldots, (\tilde{\mathbf{x}}_m, \tilde{y}_m)\}$

Algorithm 2. Sparse on-line SVR for *sarsa* function approximation

5   Experiments

We applied the *sarsa* and SVR combination to two control tasks with continuous states. The training procedure consisted of a series of trials each starting in a state chosen randomly and proceeding thereafter until the goal was reached.

The first domain is a 21×21 gridworld embedded inside the unit cube. Starting in the bottom row the goal was to get to the upper right corner $(1, 1)$ in minimum time. Reaching the goal ends the episode, every other step entails a cost of -1. Actions were the four compass directions. The corresponding value function is made discontinuous by introducing a vertical barrier. Parameters for the *sarsa* component were $\gamma = 1, \alpha = 0.7$, and $\epsilon = 0.1$, the last choice has been made as to ensure sufficient exploration. For the SVR component we chose $C = 10, \varepsilon = 0.1$, TOL1 $= 0.005$, and TOL2 $= 0.1$. Kernels were the Gaussian $k(x, y) = \exp(-\|x - y\|^2/\sigma)$. The QP was solved using the C++ package *libSVM* [2]. Figure 1 shows the resulting approximation for various kernel widths σ after 5000 trials. As could be expected, wide kernels entail a large approximation error near the barrier. Yet in all cases a nearly optimal path to the goal was learned.

As second task we tried the well-known mountain car problem. The objective is trying to drive a car to the top of a steep hill. However, the car is not powerful enough to directly drive to the goal. Instead it must first go up the opposite direction to build up enough momentum. The two dimensional state space consists of the position and speed, and again was scaled to lie inside the

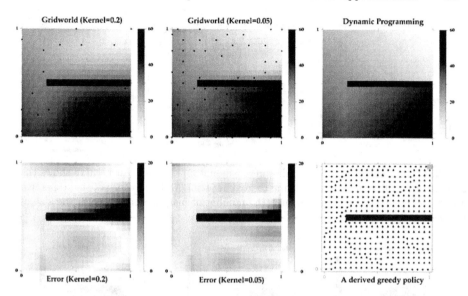

Fig. 1. Approximated value function for the gridworld task after 5000 trials for wide and narrow kernels. Black dots mark the states that were admitted to the dictionary. From left to right: $\sigma = 0.2$ with $m = 21$, $\sigma = 0.05$ with $m = 63$, and the optimal value function. The bottom row shows the corresponding approximation error and a derived greedy policy

unit cube. Three actions are possible: forward, backward, and coast. Failing to reach the goal within 500 steps terminates the trial, but no additional penalty is incurred. The remaining setup and simulated dynamics are identical to those used in [10]. The parameters for SVR and *sarsa* were the same as before.

First, we were interested in the on-line performance. In Fig. 2 we compare the results of our SVR method with the very popular tile coding function approximator [11]. We used 10 overlapping tilings, each consisting of 10×10 grids. As baseline we also included the optimal number of steps computed on a 200×200 grid. To make the results more comparable, each trial started at the bottom of the valley with zero velocity. The performance measure we considered were the steps-to-goal during a trial and the return of the corresponding greedy policy, which was evaluated independently. Each curve shows the average of 10 completely different runs. As can be seen from the plots the overall performance of SVR is roughly on par with tile coding, and even exceeds it later on. The total number of parameters (i.e. weights) that have to be adjusted in the SVR expansion ($m = 37$ for $\sigma = 0.05$) is only a fraction of the number of weights in tile coding ($10 \times 10 \times 10$). However, we should also mention that in return the overall computional costs are considerably higher for SVR.

Second, we plotted the approximation quality for various kernel widths after 10000 trials, where as before each trial started in a randomly chosen state, see Fig. 3. Although we could evidently derive a fairly optimal policy previously,

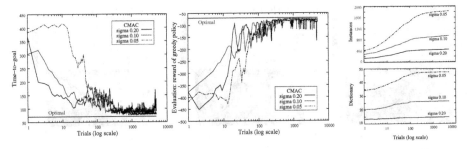

Fig. 2. Comparing SVR to tile coding in the mountain car task. Each curve shows the average of 10 different runs. Left: time-to-goal per trial. Middle: return of the respective greedy policy. The last plot compares the number of instances stored with the size of the dictionary

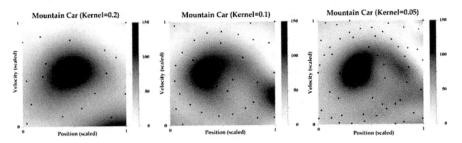

Fig. 3. Approximated value function for the mountain car task after 10000 trials for various kernel widths σ. Black dots mark the states that were admitted to the dictionary. From left to right: $\sigma = 0.2$ with $m = 19$, $\sigma = 0.1$ with $m = 33$, and $\sigma = 0.05$ with $m = 57$. For wide kernels the discontinuities are smeared out. With narrow kernels the boundaries are sharpened and more pronounced

the quality of the approximation near the discontinuities (in particular for wide kernels) is far from good. Note the way in which the states in the dictionary are distributed. The circular, spiraling pattern corresponds to the initial trajectories of the learner, oscillating back and forth between the two hill tops.

6   Conclusion and Future Research

We demonstrated experimentally that on-line RL in conjunction with SVR function approximation is possible. The SVR method described in this paper relied on solving a reduced QP obtained from projecting the data on a small subset of the original training samples. This way the main workload during training only depends on the effective dimensionality of the data which can be considered as being asymptotically independent of the total number of training pairs encountered in the RL algorithm. Another consequence is that one obtains a very sparse regressor which, when used as predictor in subsequent operations such as the policy improvement step, again helps to reduce the computational complexity. The resulting SVR-RL framework was shown to solve two common toy-problems and to approximate the optimal value function.

The algorithm and simulations that were presented can only be considered as a first step to demonstrate the overall feasability of this approach. Additional conceptual and algorithmic refinements and more experimentation are needed. The framework very naturally carries over to other RL methods: currently we are extending it to include the model-free case and to perform TD(λ) policy-evaluation. In particular, we expect it to work well when coupled with off-line control methods like partially optimistic policy-iteration, since here the updates to the value function can be carried out in a batch manner.

References

1. D. Bertsekas and J. Tsitsiklis. *Neuro-dynamic programming*. Athena Scientific, 1996.
2. Chih-Chung Chang and Chih-Jen Lin. *LIBSVM: a library for support vector machines*, 2001. Software available at http://www.csie.ntu.edu.tw/~cjlin/libsvm.
3. T. Dietterich and X. Wang. Batch value function approximation via support vectors. In *NIPS 14*, pages 1491–1498, 2002.
4. T. Downs, K. E. Gates, and A. Masters. Exact simplification of support vector solutions. *Journal of Machine Learning Research*, 2:293–297, 2001.
5. Y. Engel, S. Mannor, and R. Meir. Kernel recursive least squares. In *Proc. of 13th European Conference on Machine Learning*. Springer, 2002.
6. Y. Engel, S. Mannor, and R. Meir. Sparse online greedy support vector regression. In *Proc. of 13th European Conference on Machine Learning*. Springer, 2002.
7. S. Fine and K. Scheinberg. Efficient SVM training using low-rank kernel representation. *Journal of Machine Learning Research*, 2:243–264, 2001.
8. B. Schölkopf and A. Smola. *Learning with Kernels*. Cambridge, MA: MIT Press, 2002.
9. A. J. Smola and B. Schölkopf. Sparse greedy matrix approximation for machine learning. In *Proc. of 17th ICML*, 2000.
10. R. Sutton and A. Barto. *Reinforcement Learning: An Introduction*. MIT Press, 1998.
11. R. S. Sutton. Generalization in reinforcement learning: successful examples using sparse coarse coding. In *NIPS 7.*, pages 1038–1044, 1996.
12. C. Williams and M. Seeger. Using the nyström method to speed up kernel machines. In *NIPS 13*, pages 682–688, 2001.

Constructive Induction
for Classifying Time Series

Mohammed Waleed Kadous and Claude Sammut

University of New South Wales, Sydney, Australia
{waleed,claude}@cse.unsw.edu.au

Abstract. We present a method of constructive induction aimed at learning tasks involving multivariate time series data. Using metafeatures, the scope of attribute-value learning is expanded to domains that contain instances that have some kind of recurring substructure, such as strokes in handwriting recognition, or local maxima in time series data. These substructures are used to construct attributes. Metafeatures are applied to two real-world domains: sign language recognition and ECG classification. Using a very generic set of metafeatures we are able to generate classifiers that are either comprehensible or accurate, producing results that are comparable to hand-crafted preprocessing and comparable to human experts.

Keywords: machine learning, constructive induction, time series

1 Introduction

There are many domains that do not easily fit into the static attribute-value model so common in machine learning. These include multivariate time series, optical character recognition, sequence recognition, basket analysis and web logs. Consequently, researchers hoping to use attribute-value learners on these domains have few choices: apply hand-crafted preprocessing, write a learner specifically designed for the domain, or use a learner with a more powerful representation, such as relational learning or graph-based induction.

Each of these has problems. Hand-crafted preprocessing is frequently used, but requires extensive domain knowledge and concept descriptions are sometimes unnatural. Writing a custom learner is possible, but is labour-intensive. Relational learning techniques tend to be very sensitive to noise and to the particular clausal representation selected. They are typically unable to process large data sets in a reasonable time frame, and/or require the user to set limits on the search such as refinement rules [3]. Furthermore, their most powerful feature – the use of relations – is sometimes not used.

In this paper, we use a generic constructive induction technique to allow for domains where instances exhibit recurring substructures. The user defines the recurring substructures, but subsequent steps are automated. Further, the substructures are reusable across domains. These substructures are extracted, and a novel clustering algorithm is used to construct synthetic attributes based on the presence or absence of certain substructures. Standard learners can then be applied.

J.-F. Boulicaut et al. (Eds.): ECML 2004, LNAI 3201, pp. 192–204, 2004.

Learnt concepts are expressed using the same substructures identified by the user. Since these substructures are frequently the same concepts humans use themselves in classifying instances, this results in very readable descriptions.

We begin with an overview of applying metafeatures. Experimental results are presented, and we review related work. Finally, we conclude and make some suggestions for future work.

2   Overview

To explain the application of metafeatures, we present a simple pedagogical domain. SoftCorp develops and supports software. Help desk calls are recorded for later analysis. SoftCorp wants to find the critical difference between happy and angry customers.

An engineer suggests that the volume level indicates frustration. Each call is therefore divided into 30-second segments; and the average volume in each segment is calculated. If it is high volume, it is marked as "H", while if it is at a reasonable volume, it is labelled as "L". On a subset of their data, they determine the outcome by independent means. These are shown in Table 1.

Table 1. The training set for the Tech Support domain, showing observed LoudRun events.

Call	Loudness (over time)		Observed events	Class
	0 1			
	0 1 2 3 4 5 6 7 8 9 0 1 2 3 4			
1	L L L H H H L L L L L L		$\{(3,3)\}$	Happy
2	L L L H L L L H L L H H H H		$\{(3,1),(6,1),(9,4)\}$	Angry
3	L L H L L H L L L L L L H H H		$\{(2,1),(5,1),(12,3)\}$	Angry
4	L L L L H H H H L L L L L		$\{(4,4)\}$	Happy
5	L L L H H H L L L L		$\{(3,3)\}$	Happy
6	L L H H L L H L L H H		$\{(2,2),(6,1),(9,3)\}$	Angry

One expert advises that "runs" of high volume conversation – continuous periods where the conversation runs at a high volume level – are important for classification. Runs of loud volume could be represented as a tuple (t, d) where t is the time at which the conversation becomes loud and d and how long it remains loud. This is an example of a **metafeature**, called LoudRun.

Each instance can now be characterised as having a set of LoudRun events – the LoudRun events are the recurrent substructures appropriate for this domain. These can be extracted by looking for sequences of high-volume conversation. For example, call 2 has one run of highs starting at time 3 lasting for 1 timestep, a high run starting at time 6 lasting for one timestep and a high run starting at time 9 for 4 timesteps. Hence the set of LoudRuns produced from call 2 is $\{(3,1),(6,1),(9,4)\}$.

To take advantage of attribute-value learners, these sets must be converted into propositional form. A good hypothesis language for such domains consists of rules that check for combinations of particular kinds of events that are critical for classification. For example, in the sign language domain, an upwards motion early in the sign *and* a movement of the hand forward later in the sign *without* a closed hand means `thank`. Thus we break the learning into two stages: the first to pick out the prototypical instances of an event – in this case: the upwards motion, the movement of the hand forward and the closed hand; and the second to create rules using the prototypical instances. To accomplish the first task, we use a clustering technique similar to instance-based learning, and for the second we use an attribute-value learner.

To complete the first stage, the events extracted above can be plotted in the two-dimensional space shown in Figure 1. This is the **parameter space**. This two-dimensional space consists of one axis for the start time and another for the duration.

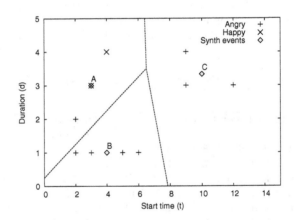

Fig. 1. Paramater space and synthetic events around them for LoudRuns in the Tech Support domain.

Once the points are in parameter space, "typical examples" of LoudRuns can be selected. In this case, the points labelled A, B and C have been selected, as shown in Figure 1. These are termed **synthetic events**. They may or may not be the same as an observed event – so for example, point A actually corresponds to a real event (the event (3,3) was observed in the data), whereas B and C do not.

These synthetic events can be used to segment the parameter space into different regions by computing the Voronoi tiling: for each point in the parameter space, the nearest synthetic event is found. The set of points associated with each synthetic event form a region and the boundaries of each region are calculated. These are shown as dotted lines in Figure 1.

To accomplish the second stage, each region constructed in the first stage is used as a test: if a training instance has an event in a region, it "passes" the test. Each training instance is labelled with the test results, each test result effectively becomes an attribute. In this case, three tests A, B and C are constructed and the results shown in Table 2. To construct this table, the "observed events" in Table 2 are examined, and for each region if there is an event that lies within it, a **synthetic attribute** corresponding to the point is marked as a "yes".

Table 2. Attribution of synthetic attributes for the Tech Support domain.

Stream	Class	Synth Attrib		
		A	**B**	**C**
1	Happy	Yes	Yes	No
2	Angry	No	Yes	Yes
3	Angry	No	Yes	Yes
4	Happy	Yes	Yes	No
5	Happy	Yes	Yes	No
6	Angry	Yes	Yes	Yes

As a result of the clustering stages above, the initial time series has been converted into a table suitable for learning. In fact, if C4.5 is run on it, the simple tree in Figure 2 results.

```
rgnC = yes: Angry (3.0)
rgnC = no: Happy (3.0)
```

Fig. 2. Rule for telling happy and angry customers apart.

This tree says that if the training instance has an event that lies within in region C (i.e. a run of high values that starts around time t=10 and goes for approximately 3.33 timesteps), then its class is Angry. In other words, as long as there is not a long high-volume run towards the end of the conversation, the customer is likely to be happy.

3   Detailed Description

While the idea of metafeatures is simple, there are several possible enhancements and features that need to be considered when implementing a practical system. The *TClass* algorithm is shown in Table 3. Explanation of each of the components follows.

3.1   Inputs

The input is specified as a set of streams S_{train}. Each stream represents a single training instance; for example, a single sign. We are also given class labels.

The temporal characteristics are represented by a list of time series. Each time series is called a *channel*. While the Tech Support domain has a single

Table 3. *TClass* training algorithm.

Inputs:
$S_{train} = [\mathbf{s_1}, ..., \mathbf{s_n}]$ /* Training streams */
$G_{train} = [\mathbf{g_1}, ..., \mathbf{g_n}]$ /* Specified global attributes */
$L_{train} = [l_1, ..., l_n]$ /* Class labels of training streams */
$\mathbf{f} = [f_1, ..., f_m]$ /* Metafeature extraction functions */
$\mathbf{w} = [w_1, ..., w_p]$ /* Global attribute calculators */

Outputs:
$E = [\mathbf{e_1}, \mathbf{e_2}, ..., \mathbf{e_m}]$ /* Synthetic events (each is a set) */
d_P /* Learnt classifier */
h /* Human-readable description of learnt concept */

Temporary:
$O_{train} = [\mathbf{o_{11}}, ..., \mathbf{o_{nm}}]$ /* Observed events*/
$A_{train} = [\mathbf{a_1}, ..., \mathbf{a_n}]$ /* Global attribute calculator results */
$I_{train} = [\mathbf{i_1}, ..., \mathbf{i_n}]$ /* Synthetic attributes */
$B_{train} = [\mathbf{b_1}, ..., \mathbf{b_n}]$ /* All attributes combined */

procedure **Train**
$O_{train} := \text{ExtractObservedEvents}(S_{train}, \mathbf{f})$
$E := \text{SelectSyntheticEvents}(O_{train}, L_{train})$
$I := \text{EvaluateSyntheticAttributes}(O_{train}, E)$
$A := \text{CalculateGlobalAttributes}(S_{train}, \mathbf{w})$
$B_{train} := \text{CombineAttributes}(I_{train}, A_{train}, G_{train})$
$d_P := \text{Learn}(B_{train}, L)$
$h := \text{ProduceComprehensibleDescription}(d_P, E, O_{train})$
End

channel (the volume level); the Auslan domain, for example has 22 channels representing various hand position and orientation measures.

In addition to temporal characteristics, many domains have non-temporal attributes that are important for classification. For example, when diagnosing ECGs, age, height, weight and gender are important. *TClass* allows the integration of these conventional features.

It is also useful in temporal classification tasks to examine aggregate values of signals and use them as propositional attributes. For example, for continuous channels, the global maximum and minimum value of a channel, or the mean of each channel may be important attributes. These are termed **aggregate global attributes** – they measure some property of each training instance as a whole, rather than looking at the temporal structure. To support the use of such aggregate features, *TClass* supports the use of global attribute calculators. In *TClass* the global attribute calculators are provided a vector of functions, each function acting on each training stream.

Metafeatures form the most critical component of *TClass*. The formal definition of a metafeature is very simple. It consists of:

- A tuple of parameters $p = (p_1, ..., p_k)$, which represents a particular **event**. Let P_i represent the set of possible values of the parameter p_i. Let P be the space of possible parameter values, i.e. $P = P_1 \times P_2 \times ... \times P_k$. P is termed the **parameter space**.
- An **extraction function** $f : S \to \mathbb{P}(P)$ which takes a stream **s** and returns a set of observed events from P.

Metafeatures capture a type of recurring temporal substructure, which can then be used as the basis of constructing a propositional feature learner. This work uses a generic set of metafeatures, that are hopefully useful in diverse temporal domains. The metafeatures used are Increasing and Decreasing with the parameter space (`time, average, gradient, duration`); Plateau with the parameter space (`time, average, duration`); and LocalMax and LocalMin which detect local maxima and minima on a single channel (`time, value`). Additional metafeatures can be easily implemented.

3.2 Processing

Once the metafeatures have been selected, the extraction of observed events is accomplished by applying each metafeature to each training instance. For each metafeature and training instance, a list of the observed events is stored for the the later synthetic event selection. It is also retained for use in attribution.

Now that a list of all observed events has been constructed, the synthetic events must be selected. The key insight to selecting these synthetic events is that the distribution of observed events in the parameter space is probably not uniform.

An initial approach might be to use standard clustering algorithms, such as K-Means, in the parameter space, i.e., clustering that groups points in such a way that the distance between points within the same cluster is small, and distances between points in different clusters is large. However, this is merely one approach to answering the real question: "Which are the observed events whose presence or absence indicate that the instances belong to a particular class?" The clustering approach can certainly be used to answer this question – the theory being that the different clusters represent different types of observed events. This is an example of **unsupervised segmentation.**

Another approach is to re-pose the question as: "Are there regions in the parameter space where the class distribution is significantly different to what is statistically expected?" This question is very similar to typical problems of supervised classification. This is an example of **supervised segmentation**: segmentation directed towards creating good features for learning by explicitly considering the class from which an observed event originated.

This suggests a more refined approach. Let the set of all observed events be O. Let the set of points we select be $E = \{e_1, e_2, ..., e_k\}$, where there are k points selected. Define the set of regions $R = \{R_1, ..., R_k\}$ as:

$$R_i = \{x \in P | closest(x, E) = e_i\}$$

and

$$\text{closest}(x, E) = \underset{e \in E}{\text{argmin}} \; dist(x, e)$$

where $dist$ is the distance metric we are using for the parameter space.

In other words, each region R_i is defined as the set of points in the parameter space P for which e_i is the closest point (using the distance metric $dist$) in the set E. This is the definition of a Voronoi diagram.

If the distribution of observed events in a region differs significantly from the global class distribution, then this would be a good feature for classification. Asking whether a training stream has an observed event within a region would be informative of the class of the training stream that the observed event came from.

Measuring the disparity between global and local distributions is well studied in both machine learning and statistics [19]. We will term this measure the **disparity measure**. Typical disparity measures include χ^2 tests, information gain, gain ratio and Gini coefficients. Our objective is to find E such that:

$$R = \underset{E \in \mathbb{P}(O)}{\text{argmax}} \; DispMeas(E)$$

In other words, we are looking to find the subset of O (the set of all observed events), E, for which the disparity measure is the greatest.

The search, however, is difficult. Hence a "random search" can be employed to solve the problem. While it may first seem that using a random search algorithm is not productive, work by Ho [6] in the field of ordinal optimisation shows that random search is an effective means of finding near-optimal solution. This was also used by Srinivasan [18] in his *Aleph* ILP system where it was shown to perform well even compared to complex search methods.

The random search algorithm is incredibly simple; it picks random subsets of O with an upper bound on the size (in this work we allow subsets with up to ten elements), evaluates the disparity measure on this subset, and if it is the greatest disparity seen so far, it saves the subset. This is repeated for a fixed number of iterations (in this paper, 10,000 iterations are made). The best subset is returned as the set E.

We now have a set of synthetic events for each metafeature. Each synthetic event from each metafeature is converted into a synthetic attribute. Each attribute is a test based on whether a given training instance has an observed event that lies within the region around that particular synthetic event.

In Table 2, the attributes generated are binary – i.e., we are checking for the presence of particular events. However, this allows only simple decision boundaries. By using the measure $D = log_2(\frac{d_2}{d_1})$, where d_1 is the distance to the nearest centroid and d_2 is the distance to the second nearest centroid, the backend learner itself can choose the cutpoint and hence decision boundaries can have a more complex shape. This measure has useful properties; for instance, a point on the boundary between two regions has $D = 0$, whereas the centroid has a measure of $D = \infty$. This expands the hypothesis language significantly and makes the classification more robust.

Attributes are then combined for each instance from the three sources: synthetic attributes, specified global attributes, and calculated global attributes.

With this in place, an attribute-value learner can be applied. *TClass* can use any learner provided by Weka [21]. Both bagging [2] and boosting [16] can also be used.

There is a further possibility resulting from the random nature of the synthetic event selection algorithm. Each time the synthetic event selection algorithm runs, it results in a different set of synthetic attributes. Multiple runs of synthetic event selection and the subsequent evaluation and learning stages can be used to create a stochastic ensemble, resulting in improved accuracy, but at the cost of reduced incomprehensibility.

```
Does have a Loud run
    starting between time 9 and 12 AND
    lasting between 3 and 4 timesteps: Angry (3.0)
Otherwise: Happy (3.0)
```

Fig. 3. Comprehensible description generated from learnt concept.

Finally, if the learner used at the backend produces descriptions of the form `rgnC = yes`, then these can be used to create comprehensible descriptions by substituting the synthetic event in place of the attribute name. Hence Figure 2 can be converted into Figure 3. The bounds on these values are obtained by drawing a bounding box in the original parameter space of all the instances belonging to region C. Looking at Figure 1, we see that all the points in region C lie within the bounding box $d = [3, 4], t = [9, 12]$.

Note that this is not the same concept that the classifier uses on unseen instances, but it is still useful as an approximation. An obvious modification of this approach allows it to be used with relative membership.

3.3   Testing

The testing algorithm employed by *TClass* is shown in Table 4. As can be seen it reuses many of the same components used from training. Note that the global attribute calculators and metafeature extraction functions must be the same for both training and testing.

As before, the observed events are extracted, but the synthetic events selected in the training stage are used to create the synthetic attributes. Once the attributes are combined, the classifier built in the training stage can be employed to give a classification.

4   Experiments

We tested *TClass* on a number of domains. Only brief descriptions are included here; more information can be found in [8].

Table 4. *TClass* testing algorithm.

```
Inputs:
    S_test = [s_1, ..., s_n] /* Test streams */
    G_test = [g_1, ..., g_n] /* Specified global attributes */
    f = [f_1, ..., f_m] /* Metafeature extraction functions */
    w = [w_1, ..., w_p] /* Global attribute calculators */
    E = [e_1, e_2, ..., e_k] /* Synthetic events from training */
    d_P /* Learnt classifier from training */

Outputs:
    L_test = [l_1, ..., l_n] /* Test set labels */

Temporary:
    O_test = [o_11, ..., o_nm] /* Observed events */
    A_test = [a_1, ..., a_n] /* Global attribute calculated */
    I_test = [i_1, ..., i_n] /* Synthetic attributes */
    B_test = [b_1, ..., b_n] /* Combination of all attributes from all sources */

procedure Test
    O_test := ExtractObservedEvents(S_test, f)
    I := EvaluateSyntheticAttributes(O_test, E)
    A := ExtractGlobalAttributes(S_test, w)
    B_test := CombineAttributes(I_test, A_test, G_test)
    L_test := Classify(B_test, d_P)
End
```

- The cylinder-bell-funnel (CBF) domain. This domain, proposed by [15], has a single channel and three classes.
- A new artificial domain, called *TTest*, which we created to overcome the limitations of the CBF domain.
- Auslan sign recognition: Auslan is the language of the Australian Deaf community. 95 signs were selected and recorded from a native Auslan signer using instrumented gloves. This data has a total of 22 channels covering both hands' position, orientation and finger bends.
- ECG classification: Electrocardigraphs of patients who were healthy or suffered from one of six ailments such as acute myocardial infarctions were recorded. The data has 15 channels in all. The data has a skewed class distribution; with the most common class having approximately 8 times as many examples as the least common class.

For comparison, we also applied two baseline learners:

- A "naive segmentation" approach, where each channel was subdivided into a certain number of intervals and the mean for each interval computed. This was then fed to a learner. The number of intervals tested were 3, 5, 10, 20. The best results are shown in the table.

– Hidden Markov models were applied using Entropic's HTK [22]. A number of different transition models were considered, such as ergodic, left-right, left-right with one skip. 3,4 and 5-state HMMs were tested. The best results are shown in the table.

For the back-end learning, the following learners were used from the Weka package [21]: J48, PART, and bagging and boosting using J48 as the base learner. Also, voting of the boosted learner was performed, using 11 runs of synthetic event construction. The error rates are shown in Table 5. It shows the mean error (percentage) for ten-fold[1] cross-validation and the standard error of the mean. The first five use metafeatures, and the last two are baseline learners. The stochastic ensemble employed AdaBoost as the base learner. The χ^2 disparity measure was used for supervised segmentation.

Table 5. Error rates on *TClass* domain.

Alg	CBF	*TTest*	Auslan	ECG
J48	2.3 ± 0.7	3.3 ± 0.9	14.5 ± 0.4	45.5 ± 1.7
PART	4.6 ± 0.8	2.3 ± 0.3	16.7 ± 0.9	41.9 ± 2.1
Bag	1.9 ± 0.5	2.5 ± 0.4	9.4 ± 0.8	35.1 ± 2.6
AB	1.4 ± 0.3	1.0 ± 0.3	6.4 ± 0.4	32.9 ± 2.4
Stochastic Ensemble	$\mathbf{0 \pm 0}$	$\mathbf{0.5 \pm 0.2}$	$\mathbf{2.1 \pm 0.2}$	$\mathbf{28.2 \pm 1.8}$
Naive	0 ± 0	7.2 ± 0.7	5.5 ± 0.5	28.5 ± 2.6
HMM	0 ± 0	4.4 ± 0.5	12.9 ± 0.6	33.5 ± 1.7

The results in Table 5 are very promising, although there are some qualifications. Firstly, in every domain, *TClass* performs as well or better than other learners and the baseline learners – the Auslan and *TTest* domains are significantly better at the 99.5 per cent level[2].

The stochastic ensemble is significantly better than any other *TClass* method in two of the domains. However, such solutions are less readable, hence forcing a tradeoff between readability and accuracy. The results for Auslan converge with 9 voters, and 11 voters for *TTest*.

The results on the ECG data are worthy of particular note, since de Chazal [4] obtained an error of $28.6\% \pm 2.4$ by hand-crafting an attribute set for a neural network. Given that we were using generic metafeatures and not making use domain knowledge, this result is surprising and promising – since we obtained similar accuracy results ($28.2\% \pm 1.8$). Furthermore, in a survey completed by Willems [20], he found that on the same dataset a median human cardiologist obtained an error of 29.7% – less accurate than our system. We were also surprised by the success of the naive approach – almost as accurate as *TClass* on

---

[1] For consistency with previous results, 5-fold cross validation was used for the Auslan domain.

[2] All significance statements are made using a paired t-test.

this domain. We do not understand why it performs so well, and we plan to explore this in future work.

As for comprehensibility, for the Auslan domain, definitions generated by *TClass* compared favourably to the definitions found in the Auslan dictionary [7]. Furthermore, ruleset sizes were reasonable for the Auslan domain of 1.14 rules per class using PART. In the ECG domain, a simple set of 24 rules was found that obtained 40.5 per cent error. Some of these rules showed close correlations with the rules used by existing expert systems [17]. With the *TTest* domain, it was able to reconstruct the generating concept exactly at low to medium noise levels. In general, in domains with many classes (such as Auslan), it was found that binarizing the learning problem led to more comprehensible definitions than trying to understand complex rules that cover all 95 possible classes.

5   Related Work

This work closely relates to the areas of feature extraction and construction [11], although the formal definitions of extraction and construction assume attribute-vector representation [11, p. 4]. Liu and Motoda do point to automated pre-processing (or data categorization) as future work [11, p. 9]. They also point to the importance of comprehensibility. It also closely relates to Michalski's work [12] on constructive induction, but again the work assumes that examples are described in attribute-value format.

There are some general techniques that can be applied to temporal and structured domains. The best developed technique for temporal classification is the hidden Markov model [13]. However, they do suffer some serious drawbacks for general use. Firstly, the structure of the HMM – similar to that of a finite state machine – needs to be specified *a priori*. Secondly, extracting comprehensible rules from HMMs is not at all easy. Thirdly, there are frequently hundreds or thousands of parameters per HMM. As a result, many training instances are required to learn effectively. Recurrent neural networks and Kohonen maps have also been used to solve temporal and sequence domains [1], but suffer similar problems.

Keogh and Pazzani [9] have worked on improving and extending dynamic time warping to temporal domains by representing the time series hierarchically. Lee and Kim [10] take a syntactic approach to time series recognition. Based on knowledge of the financial markets, they develop a grammar for events. Recent interest has also arisen in applying ILP to temporal classification problems. [14] is an interesting example of this, using a tailored search algorithm designed to cope with temporal constraints, although the scalability of this approach is an issue. [5] also presents a system that uses ILP for temporal classification.

6   Conclusions and Future Work

Metafeatures have been applied to diverse domains that exhibit difficult properties: it has been tested on domains with up to 22 channels, 110 metafeatures,

200 megabytes of data, 95 classes, and highly skewed class distributions. They have been shown capable of producing high-accuracy classifiers; in fact, classifiers that match hand-crafted preprocessing techniques. Although the user must define the metafeatures, we have shown that a generic family of metafeatures work for temporal domains. Furthermore, they produce comprehensible descriptions. However, results show that the best accuracy results are achieved using techniques that produce less comprehensible descriptions.

This suggests one avenue for future work. The marked difference between the stochastic ensemble and other results points to the weakness of the random search for a good segmentation. For those interested in *TClass*, it is available at: http://www.cse.unsw.edu.au/~waleed/tclass/

References

1. Yoshua Bengio. *Neural Networks for Speech and Sequence Recognition*. International Thomson Publishing Inc., 1996.
2. Leo Breiman. Bagging predictors. *Machine Learning*, 24:123–140, 1996.
3. W. W. Cohen. Learning to classify English text with ILP methods. In L. De Raedt, editor, *Proceedings of the 5th International Workshop on Inductive Logic Programming*, pages 3–24. Department of Computer Science, Katholieke Universiteit Leuven, 1995.
4. Philip de Chazal. *Automatic Classification of the Frank Lead Electrocardiogram*. PhD thesis, University of New South Wales, 1998.
5. Pierre Geurts. Pattern extraction for time series classification. In Luc de Raadt and Arno Sieves, editors, *Principles of Data Mining and Knowledge Discovery, 5th European Conference, PKDD 2001, Freiburg, Germany, September 3-5, 2001, Proceedings*, Lecture Notes in Computer Science. Springer-Verlag, 2001.
6. Y. C. Ho, R. S. Sreenivas, and P. Vakili. Ordinal optimization of DEDS. *Discrete Event Dynamic Systems: Theory and Applications*, 2(1):61–88, 1992.
7. Trevor Johnston. *Auslan Dictionary: a Dictionary of the Sign Language of the Australian Deaf Community*. Deafness Resources Australia Ltd, 1989.
8. Mohammed Waleed Kadous. *Temporal Classification: Extending the Classification Paradigm to Multivariate Time Series*. PhD thesis, School of Computer Science and Engineering, University of New South Wales, 2002. Awaiting review.
9. Eamonn Keogh and Michael Pazzani. Dynamic time warping with higher order features. In *SIAM International Conference on Data Mining, SDM 2001*. SIAM, 2001.
10. Jae Kyu Lee and Hyun Soon Kim. *Intelligent Systems for Finance and Business*, chapter 13. John Wiley and Sons Ltd, 1995.
11. Huan Liu and Hiroshi Motoda, editors. *Feature Extraction, Construction and Selection: A Data Mining Perspective*. Kluwer Academic Publishers, 1998.
12. R. S. Michalski. *Machine Learning: An Artificial Intelligence Approach*, chapter A Theory and Methodology of Inductive Learning. Tioga Publishers, 1983.
13. Lawrence R. Rabiner. A tutorial on hidden markov models and selected applications in speech recognition. *Proceedings of the IEEE*, 77(2):257–286, February 1989.
14. Juan J. Rodríguez, Carlos J. Alonso, and Henrik Boström. Learning first order logic time series classifiers. In J. Cussens and A. Frisch, editors, *Proceedings of ILP2000*, pages 260–275, 2000.

15. Naoki Saito. *Local feature extraction and its application using a library of bases.* PhD thesis, Yale University, December 1994.
16. Robert E. Schapire. A brief introduction to boosting. In *Proceedings of the Sixteenth International Joint Conference on Artificial Intelligence*, 1999.
17. Schiller Medical. *The Schiller ECG Measurement and Interpretation Programs Physicians Guide*, 1997.
18. Ashwin Srinivarsan. The Aleph manual. Technical report, Oxford University, 2000.
19. Allan P. White and Wei Zhong Liu. Bias in information-based measures in decision tree induction. *Machine Learning*, 15:321–329, 1994.
20. J. L. Willems, C. Abreu-Lima, P. Arnaud, C.R. Brohet, and B. Denic. Evaluation of ECG interpretation results obtained by computer and cardiologists. *Methods of Information in Medicine*, 29(4):pp. 308–316, 1990.
21. Ian H. Witten and Eibe Frank. *Data Mining: Practical Machine Learning Tools and Techniques with Java Implementations*. Morgan Kaufmann, 1999.
22. Steve Young, Dan Kershaw, Julian Odell, Dave Ollason, Valtcho Valtchev, and Phil Woodland. *The HTK Book*. Microsoft Corporation, 1998.

Fisher Kernels for Logical Sequences

Kristian Kersting[1] and Thomas Gärtner[2]

[1] University of Freiburg, Institute for Computer Science, Machine Learning Lab,
Georges-Koehler-Allee 079, 79110 Freiburg, Germany
kersting@informatik.uni-freiburg.de
[2] Fraunhofer Institut Autonome Intelligente Systeme, Knowledge Discovery Team,
Schloß Birlinghoven, 53754 Sankt Augustin, Germany
thomas.gaertner@ais.fraunhofer.de

Abstract. One approach to improve the accuracy of classifications based on generative models is to combine them with successful discriminative algorithms. *Fisher kernels* were developed to combine generative models with a currently very popular class of learning algorithms, kernel methods. Empirically, the combination of hidden Markov models with support vector machines has shown promising results. So far, however, Fisher kernels have only been considered for sequences over flat alphabets. This is mostly due to the lack of a method for computing the gradient of a generative model over structured sequences. In this paper, we show how to compute the gradient of *logical hidden Markov models*, which allow for the modelling of logical sequences, i.e., sequences over an alphabet of logical atoms. Experiments show a considerable improvement over results achieved without Fisher kernels for logical sequences.

Keywords: Hidden Markov Models, Fisher Kernels, Logical Sequences

1 Introduction

Generative models in general and hidden Markov models (HMMs) [17] in particular are widely used in computational biology. One of their application areas there is protein fold recognition where one tries to understand how proteins fold up in nature. Usually, for every protein with unknown structure one aims at finding the most similar protein with known structure (or fold) in a database.

From a machine learning perspective, fold recognition can be regarded as a classification problem: One tries to estimate the dependence of a target variable y on some observation x, based on a finite set of observations for which the value of the target variable is known. More technically, given a finite set of training examples $\{(x_i, y_i)\}_{i=1}^{m} \subseteq \mathcal{X} \times \{-1, +1\}$, one tries to find a function $f : \mathcal{X} \to \{-1, +1\}$ with low approximation error on the training data as well as on unseen examples. For HMMs it is common to use the *plug-in estimate*

$$f(x) = \text{sign}[P(y = +1 \mid x, \theta^*) - 0.5]$$

The maximum likelihood parameters θ^* of the given HMM are usually estimated using the EM algorithm, for example by the Baum-Welch procedure. Despite of their success, HMMs have two major weaknesses:

J.-F. Boulicaut et al. (Eds.): ECML 2004, LNAI 3201, pp. 205–216, 2004.

(A) they are able to only handle sequences over flat alphabets, and
(B) the predictive performance of the plug-in estimate is often lower than that
of discriminative classifiers.

To overcome **(A)**, *logical hidden Markov models* (LOHMMs) [14] have recently been introduced as an extension of HMMs. They allow for *logical sequences*, i.e., sequences of atoms in a first order logic. In [14], LOHMMs have been applied to the problem of discovering structural signatures of protein folds and led to more compact models. The trained LOHMM consisted of 120 parameters corresponding to an HMM with more than 62000 parameters.

To overcome **(B)**, i.e., to improve the classification accuracy of generative models — usually HMMs — different kernel functions have been proposed in order to make use of the good predictive performance of kernel methods such as the support vector machine (SVM) [19]. The most prominent of these kernel functions is the *Fisher kernel* [11]. The key idea there is to use the gradient of the log likelihood of the generative model with respect to its parameters as feature vector. The motivation to use this feature space is that the gradient of the log-likelihood with respect to the parameters of a generative model captures the generative process of a sequence better than just the posterior probabilities.

Fisher kernels have successfully been applied in many learning problems where the instances are sequences over a flat alphabet. Many sequences occurring in real-world problems, however, exhibit internal structure. The elements of such sequences can be seen as atoms in a first order logic (see e.g. [16] for an introduction to first order logic). For example, the secondary structure of the Ribosomal protein L4 can be represented as

$$
\text{st}(\text{null}, 2), \text{he}(\text{h}(\text{right}, \text{alpha}), 6), \text{st}(\text{plus}, 2), \text{he}(\text{h}(\text{right}, \text{alpha}), 4),
$$
$$
\text{st}(\text{plus}, 2), \text{he}(\text{h}(\text{right}, \text{alpha}), 4), \text{st}(\text{plus}, 3), \text{he}(\text{h}(\text{right}, \text{alpha}), 4), \quad (1)
$$
$$
\text{st}(\text{plus}, 1), \text{he}(\text{h}(\text{right}, \text{alpha}), 6)
$$

Here, helices of a certain type and length he(*HelixType,Length*), and strands of a certain orientation and length st(*Orientation,Length*) are structured symbols, i.e., atoms over logical predicates. It has been argued that using secondary structure information is likely to improve fold recognition results, see e.g. [7]. The application of HMMs to such sequences requires one to either ignore the structure of helices and strands, which results in a loss of information, or to take all possible combinations (of arguments such as orientation and length) into account, which leads to a combinatorial explosion in the number of parameters.

The main contribution of this paper is a method to compute the gradient of the log likelihood with respect to the parameters of a LOHMM. Though we focus on classification using Fisher kernels and SVMs, in general, such a method can also be used to devise fast gradient-based methods [18] and accelerated EM algorithms [4] for parameter estimation. We empirically compare the accuracy achieved in [14] with the accuracy achieved by Fisher kernels and SVMs using the same LOHMMs and datasets as in [14]. Furthermore, we conduct experiments on tree structured data in a mRNA signal structure detection task. Both results show that the predictive accuracy of LOHMMs can considerably be improved using Fisher kernels and SVMs.

The outline of the paper is as follows. In Sections 2 and 3 we briefly review Fisher kernels and LOHMMs. Then, in Section 4, we devise a method to compute the gradient of the log likelihood of LOHMMs which is essential to define Fisher kernels for logical sequences. In Section 5, we experimentally evaluate Fisher kernels for logical sequence. Before concluding, we discuss related work.

2   Kernels Methods and Probabilistic Models

Support vector machines [19] are a kernel method that can be applied to binary supervised classification problems. Being on one hand theoretically well founded in statistical learning theory, they have on the other hand shown good empirical results in many applications.

The characteristic aspect of this class of learning algorithms is the formation of hypotheses by linear combination of positive-definite kernel functions 'centred' at individual training examples. It is known that such functions can be interpret as the inner product in a Hilbert Space. The solution of the support vector machine is then the hyperplane in this Hilbert space that separates positive and negative labelled examples, and is at the same time maximally distant from the convex hulls of the positive and the negative examples. Conversely, every inner product in a linear space is a positive-definite kernel function.

Approaches for defining valid kernel functions for a given type of data can be distinguished as *syntax-driven* or *model-driven* [5]. We summarise some syntax-driven kernels in Section 6. The most prominent model-driven approach is the *Fisher kernel*. There, a kernel function is derived from a generative probability model of the domain. More precisely, every learning example is mapped to the gradient of the log likelihood of the generative model with respect to its parameters. The kernel is then the inner product of the examples' images under this map. The motivation to use this feature space is that the gradient of the log-likelihood with respect to the parameters of a generative model captures the generative process of a sequence better than just the posterior probabilities.

Given a parametric probability model M with parameters $\theta = (\theta_1, \ldots, \theta_n)^\top$, maximum likelihood parameters θ^*, and output probability $P(x \mid \theta, M)$, the Fisher score mapping U_x is defined as

$$U_x = \nabla_\theta \log P(x \mid \theta^*, M) = \left(\frac{\partial \log P(x \mid \theta^*, M)}{\partial \theta_1}, \ldots, \frac{\partial \log P(x \mid \theta^*, M)}{\partial \theta_n} \right)^\top .$$

The Fisher information matrix is the expectation of the outer product of the Fisher scores over $P(x \mid \theta, M)$, more precisely,

$$J_\theta = E_x \left[\nabla_\theta \log P(x \mid \theta, M) \right] \left[\nabla_\theta \log P(x \mid \theta, M) \right]^\top .$$

Given these definitions, the Fisher kernel is defined as

$$k(x, x') = U_x^\top J_{\theta^*}^{-1} U_{x'} = \left[\nabla_\theta \log P(x \mid \theta^*, M) \right]^\top J_{\theta^*}^{-1} \left[\nabla_\theta \log P(x' \mid \theta^*, M) \right] . \quad (2)$$

In practice often the role of the Fisher information matrix J_θ is ignored, yielding the kernel $k(x, x') = U_x^\top U_{x'}$. In the remainder of this paper we will follow this habit mainly to reduce the complexity of computation.

3   Probabilistic Models for Logical Sequences

The logical component of HMMs corresponds to a *Mealy machine*, i.e., to a finite state machine where output symbols are associated with transitions. This is essentially a propositional representation because the symbols used to represent states and outputs are flat, i.e., not structured. The key idea to develop a probabilistic model for structured sequences is to replace these flat symbols by abstract symbols. *Logical hidden Markov models* (LOHMMs) replace them by logical atoms. In this section, we will briefly review LOHMMs [15, 13].

First-Order Predicate Logic: Based on the representation of the Ribsomal protein $L4$ given in (1) we describe the necessary concepts of first-oder predicate logic. The symbols st, null, 2, he, h, ... are distinguished into predicate and function symbols. Associated with every symbol is the *arity*, i.e., number of arguments. In the example, st/2 and he/2 are predicates of arity 2, h/2 is a function of arity 2, and plus/0, 1/0, ... are functions of arity 0, i.e., constants. The *first-order logic alphabet* Σ consists of predicates, functions, and variables (e.g., X). A *term* is a variable or a function symbol followed by its arguments in brackets such as h(right, X) or 4; an *atom* is a predicate symbol followed by its arguments in brackets such as he(h(right, X), 4). Valid arguments of functions and predicates are terms. That one atom is a logical consequence of another is denoted by an *iterative clause*, such as st(X, 12) ← st(X, 10). A *ground term, atom,* or *clause* is one that does not contain any variables. In the protein example st(null, 2), he(h(right, alpha), 6), ... are ground atoms and null, 2, h(right, alpha), right, alpha, ... are ground terms. A substitution $\sigma = \{X/plus\}$ is an assignment of terms plus to variables X. Applying a substitution σ to a term, atom or clause e yields the instantiated term, atom, or clause $e\sigma$ where all occurrences of the variables X are simultaneously replaced by the term plus, e.g., (st(X, 12) ← st(X, 10))\{X/plus\} yields st(plus, 12) ← st(plus, 10). The set of all ground atoms constructed from an alphabet Σ is the Herbrand base hb$_\Sigma$. For every atom A we define $G_\Sigma(A) = \{A\sigma \in hb_\Sigma : \text{substitution } \sigma\}$. A substitution σ is a *unifier* of a finite set of atoms S if $S\sigma$ is singleton; if furthermore for every unifier σ' of S there is a substitution σ'' such that $\sigma = \sigma'\sigma''$ then σ is the *most general unifier* (MGU) of S.

Logical Hidden Markov Models (LOHMMs): The sequences generated by LOHMMs are sequences of ground atoms rather than flat symbols. Within LOHMMs, the flat symbols employed in traditional HMMs are replaced by logical atoms such as st(X, 10). Each atom st(X, 10) there represents the set of ground atoms $G_\Sigma(st(X, 10))$.

Additionally, we assume that the alphabet is typed which in our case means that there is a function mapping every predicate r/m and number $1 \le i \le m$ to

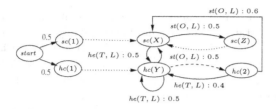

Fig. 1. A logical hidden Markov model. The vertices denote abstract (hidden) states where `hc(ID)` (resp. `sc(ID)`) represents a block `ID` of consecutive helices (resp. strands). Solid edges encode abstract transitions. Dotted edges indicate that two abstract states behave in exactly the same way. Dashed edges represent a *more general than* relation.

the set of ground terms allowed as the i-th argument of predicate r/m. This set is called the domain of the i-th argument of predicate r/m.

Figure 1 shows a LOHMM graphically. The states, observations, and transitions of LOHMMs are **abstract** in the sense that every abstract state or observation A represents all possible concrete states in $G_\Sigma(A)$. In Figure 1 *solid edges* encode **abstract transitions**. Let H and B be logical atoms representing abstract states, let O be a logical atom representing an abstract output symbol. An abstract transition from state B with probability p to state H and omitting O is denoted by $p : H \xleftarrow{0} B$. If H, B, and O are all ground, there is no difference to 'normal' transitions. Otherwise, if H, B, and O have no variables in common, the only difference to 'normal' transitions is that for each abstract state (resp. observation) we have to sample which concrete state (resp. observation) we are in. Otherwise, we have to remember the variable bindings. More formally, let $B\sigma_B \in G_\Sigma(B)$, $H\sigma_B\sigma_H \in G_\Sigma(H\sigma_B)$, $O\sigma_B\sigma_H\sigma_0 \in G_\Sigma(O\sigma_B\sigma_H)$, and let μ be a **selection distribution**. Then with probability $p \cdot \mu(H\sigma_B\sigma_H \mid H\sigma_B) \cdot \mu(O\sigma_B\sigma_H\sigma_0 \mid O\sigma_B\sigma_H)$, the model makes a transition from state $B\sigma_B$ to $H\sigma_B\sigma_H$ and emits symbol $O\sigma_B\sigma_H\sigma_0$.

A selection distribution specifies for each abstract state (respectively observation) A over the alphabet Σ a distribution $\mu(\cdot \mid A)$ over $G_\Sigma(A)$. Consider, for example, the abstract transition $0.5 : s(Z) \xleftarrow{o(X,Y,Z)} s(X)$. Suppose, $B\sigma_B = s(1)$, $\mu(s(3) \mid s(Z)) = 0.2$, and $\mu(o(1,2,3) \mid o(1,Y,3)) = 0.05$. Then, from state $s(1)$ with probability $0.5 \times 0.2 \times 0.05 = 0.005$ the output symbol is $o(1,2,3)$ and the next state is $s(3)$. To reduce the model complexity, we employ a naïve Bayes approach. For each domain D_i there is a probability distribution P_{D_i}. Let $vars(A) = \{V_1, \ldots, V_l\}$ be the variables occurring in A, and let $\sigma = \{s_1/V_1, \ldots s_l/V_l\}$ be a substitution grounding A. Each V_j is then considered a random variable over the domain of the first argument of r/m it appears in, denoted by D_{V_j}. Then,

$$\mu(A\sigma \mid A) = \prod_{j=1}^{l} P_{D_{V_j}}(V_j = s_j).$$

Indeed, multiple abstract transitions can match a given ground state. Consider $hc(Y)$ and $hc(2)$ in Figure 1. For the state $hc(2)$ the matching abstract transitions do not sum to 1.0. To resolve this, we only consider the maximally specific transitions (with respect to the body parts B) that apply to a state in order to determine the successor states. This **conflict resolution strategy** is encoded in Figure 1 by *dashed edges* which represent the *more-general-than* relation among abstract states. It ensures that for $hc(2)$ only the outgoing transitions of $hc(2)$ fire whereas for $hc(3)$ only the outgoing transitions of $hc(Y)$ fire. The rational behind this is that if there exists a substitution σ such that $B_2\sigma = B_1$, i.e., B_2 subsumes B_1, then the first transition can therefore be regarded as more informative than the second one because $G_\Sigma(B_1) \subseteq G_\Sigma(B_2)$.

Finally, *dotted edges* indicate that two abstract states behave in exactly the same way. If we follow a transition to an abstract state with an outgoing dotted edge, we will automatically follow that edge making appropriate unifications.

Definition 1 *A logical hidden Markov model (LOHMM) is a tuple $M = (\Sigma, \mu, \Delta)$ where Σ is a first-order logical alphabet, μ a selection probability over Σ, and Δ is a set of abstract transitions. Let* $\mathbf{B}$ *be the set of all atoms that occur as the body part of transitions in Δ. We require $\forall B \in \mathbf{B} : \sum_{p:H \xleftarrow{\,0\,} B \in \Delta} p = 1$.*

In [13] it is proven that LOHMMs specify a unique probability measure over hb_Σ. Here, we would like to exemplify that LOHMMs are generative models. Consider the model in Figure 1. Starting from $start$, it chooses an initial abstract state, say $hc(1)$. Forced to follow the dotted edge, it enters the abstract state $hc(Y)$. In each abstract state, the model samples values for all variables that are not instantiated yet according to the *selection distribution* μ. Since the value of Y was already instantiated in the previous abstract state $hc(1)$, it does not sample a value for Y. Now, it selects a transition, say to $hc(Y)$, observing $he(T, L)$. Since Y is shared among the head and the body, the state $hc(1)$ is selected with probability 1.0. The observation $he(h(right, 3to10), 10)$ is sampled from $he(T, L)$ using μ. Now, the model goes over to $sc(X)$, emitting $st(plus, 10)$ which in turn was sampled from $st(0, L)$. Variable X in $sc(X)$ is not yet bound; so, a value, say 2, is sampled using μ. Next, we move on to abstract state $sc(Z)$, emitting $st(plus, 15)$. The variable Z is sampled to be 3. The dotted edge brings us back to $sc(X)$ and automatically unifies X with Z, which is bound to 3. Emitting $he(h(right, alpha), 9)$, the model returns to abstract state $hc(Y)$. Assume that it samples 2 for variable Y, it has to follow the dashed outgoing edge to $hc(2)$.

4   Fisher Kernels for Logical Sequences

In Equation (2), we gave the definition of the Fisher kernel based on the gradient of the log likelihood of a set of observations with respect to the parameters θ of a generative Model M. In this section we derive a Fisher Kernel for logical sequences by employing LOHMMs. Let $O = \{0_1, \ldots, 0_m\}$ be a set of ground observation sequences. A single ground observation sequence 0_i consists of a sequence $o_{i1}, o_{i2}, \ldots, o_{iT_i}$ of ground atoms. We assume that $T_1 = T_2 = \ldots = T_m$ and that the 0_i are independently identically distributed (iid). Thus,

$$\frac{\partial \log P(O \mid \theta, M)}{\partial \theta} = \sum_{k=1}^{m} \frac{\partial \log P(0_k \mid \theta, M)}{\partial \theta} = \sum_{k=1}^{m} \frac{1}{P(0_k \mid \theta, M)} \cdot \underbrace{\frac{\partial P(0_k \mid \theta, M)}{\partial \theta}}_{(*)}$$

The key step to derive the gradient formula is to rewrite:

$$P(\mathsf{O}_k \mid \theta, M) = \sum_{\mathsf{s} \in S_t} P(\mathsf{o}_{k1}, \ldots, \mathsf{o}_{kt}, s_t = \mathsf{s} \mid \theta, M)$$

$$\cdot P(\mathsf{o}_{kt+1}, \ldots, \mathsf{o}_{kT_k} \mid s_t = \mathsf{s}, \theta, M)$$

$$= \sum_{\mathsf{s} \in S_t} \alpha_t(\mathsf{s}) \cdot \beta_t(\mathsf{s}) \tag{3}$$

where $\alpha_t(\mathsf{s})$ is the forward probability of state s and $\beta_t(\mathsf{s})$ is the backward probability of state s for O_k. The term S_t denotes the set of hidden states the system can be in at time t.

The parameter vector θ defines the set of parameters for all abstract transitions and for all selection distributions in the LOHMM. We will now show how to compute the partial derivatives $(*)$ for transition probabilities and for selection probabilities μ separately.

Abstract Transitions: Let θ_{ij} be an abstract transition probability, i.e., a probability value associated to the jth abstract transition $\mathsf{T} \equiv \theta_{ij} : \mathsf{H} \overset{0}{\leftarrow} \mathsf{B}$ of the ith abstract body B in $\mathbf{B}$. Due to the chain rule it holds

$$\frac{\partial P(\mathsf{O}_k \mid \theta, M)}{\partial \theta_{ij}} = \sum_{t=0}^{T+1} \sum_{\mathsf{s}_\mathsf{H} \in S_t} \frac{\partial P(\mathsf{O}_k \mid \theta, M)}{\partial \alpha_t(\mathsf{s}_\mathsf{H})} \times \frac{\partial \alpha_t(\mathsf{s}_\mathsf{H})}{\partial \theta_{ij}}. \tag{4}$$

By independence of $\alpha_t(\mathsf{s}_\mathsf{H})$ and $\beta_t(\mathsf{s}_\mathsf{H})$ in Equation (3):

$$\frac{\partial P(\mathsf{O}_k \mid \theta, M)}{\partial \alpha_t(\mathsf{s}_\mathsf{H})} = \beta_t(\mathsf{s}_\mathsf{H}) \tag{5}$$

The partial derivative of $\alpha_t(\mathsf{s}_\mathsf{H})$ w.r.t. θ_{ij} in Equation (4) can then be deduced from the *forward procedure*, see e.g. [15]:

$$\frac{\partial \alpha_t(\mathsf{s}_\mathsf{H})}{\partial \theta_{ij}} = \sum_{\mathsf{s}_\mathsf{B} \in S_{t-1}} \xi(\mathsf{T}, \mathsf{s}_\mathsf{B}, \mathsf{s}_\mathsf{H}, \mathsf{o}_{kt-1}) \cdot \alpha_{t-1}(\mathsf{s}_\mathsf{B}) \cdot \mu(\mathsf{s}_\mathsf{H} \mid \mathsf{H}\sigma_{\mathsf{s}_\mathsf{B}}) \cdot \mu(\mathsf{o}_{kt-1} \mid \mathsf{O}\sigma_{\mathsf{s}_\mathsf{B}}\sigma_{\mathsf{s}_\mathsf{H}}) ,$$

where $\xi(\mathsf{T}, \mathsf{s}_\mathsf{B}, \mathsf{s}_\mathsf{H}, \mathsf{o}_{kt-1})$ indicates that 1) B is maximally specific for s_B, 2) s_H unifies with H, and 3) o_{kt-1} unifies with O, and σ_- are the corresponding MGUs.

Selection Distribution: Now, let θ_{ij} be a selection probability value. Let r/n be a predicate with domains $D_1, \ldots, D_n$, where $D_i = \{d_{i1}, \ldots, d_{im_i}\}$. Furthermore, assume that the the selection distribution for r is specified by $\theta_{ij} = P(D_i = d_{ij})$. Equations (4) and (5) remain the same. The term $\partial \alpha_t(\mathsf{s})/\partial \theta_{ij}$ is zero whenever d_{ij} was not *selected* to "ground" $\mathsf{H}\sigma_\mathsf{b}$ or $\mathsf{O}\sigma_\mathsf{b}\sigma_\mathsf{h}$. Because, the selection distribution follows a naïve Bayes scheme and $\frac{\partial x^m}{\partial x} = m \cdot x^{m-1} = m \cdot \frac{x^m}{x}$, this yields:

$$\frac{\partial \alpha_t(\mathsf{s}_\mathsf{H})}{\partial \theta_{ij}} = \sum_{\mathsf{s}_\mathsf{B} \in S_{t-1}} \sum_{\mathsf{T} \equiv p : \mathsf{H} \overset{0}{\leftarrow} \mathsf{B} \in \Delta} \xi(\mathsf{T}, \mathsf{s}_\mathsf{B}, \mathsf{s}_\mathsf{H}, \mathsf{o}_{kt-1}) \cdot c_{ij}(\mathsf{s}_\mathsf{B}, \mathsf{s}_\mathsf{H}, \mathsf{o}_{kt-1}) \cdot$$

$$\cdot \frac{\alpha_{t-1}(\mathsf{s}_\mathsf{B}) \cdot p \cdot \mu(\mathsf{s}_\mathsf{H} \mid \mathsf{H}\sigma_{\mathsf{s}_\mathsf{B}}) \cdot \mu(\mathsf{o}_{kt-1} \mid \mathsf{O}\sigma_{\mathsf{s}_\mathsf{B}}\sigma_{\mathsf{s}_\mathsf{H}})}{\theta_{ij}} , \tag{6}$$

where $c_{ij}(\mathsf{T}, \mathsf{s_B}, \mathsf{s}, \mathsf{o}_{kt-1})$ denotes the number of times, the domain element d_{ij} has been selected in order to ground $\mathsf{s_B}$, s, and o_{kt-1} when following abstract transition T.

Constraint Satisfaction: So far, we have not taken the constraint into account that the parameter vector consists of probability values, i.e. $\theta_{ij} \in [0,1]$ and $\sum_j \theta_{ij} = 1$. A general solution, which we used in our experiments, is to reparameterise the problem so that the new parameters automatically respect the constraints on θ_{ij} no matter what their values are. To do so, we define the parameters $\bar{\theta}_{ij} \in \mathbb{R}$ such that $\theta_{ij} = exp(\bar{\theta}_{ij})/(\sum_l exp(\bar{\theta}_{il}))$. This enforces the constraints given above, and a local maximum w.r.t. $\bar{\theta}$ is also a local maximum w.r.t. θ, and vice versa. The gradient w.r.t the $\bar{\theta}$ can be found by computing the gradient w.r.t the θ and then deriving the gradient w.r.t. $\bar{\theta}$ using the chain rule.

5   Experiments

Having described how to compute the gradient of the log likelihood of LOHMMs with respect to its parameters, we are now ready to experimentally evaluate Fisher Kernels of LOHMMs. In this section we thus compare results achieved by LOHMMs alone with results achieved by LOHMMs combined with Fisher kernels. The experiments put the following hypothesis to test:

H The predictive accuracy of LOHMMs can be improved considerably using Fisher kernels and SVMs.

The experiments took place in two different bioinformatical domains: Protein fold recognition and mRNA signal structure detection. Both problems are multiclass problems with 5 different classes each. In order to tackle the multiclass problem with SVMs, we create for each class a binary classification problem, treating instances of this class as positive and all other instances as negative (one-against-all). As all binary classification problems consist of the same instances and the SVMs on each classification problem were trained with the same parameters, the resulting models are comparable. That is, to create a multiclass classification we compare the numerical output of the binary support vector machines on each test instance, and assign the class corresponding to the maximal numerical output. Finally, to overcome the problem that the number of instances per class strongly varies between classes, we set the misclassification cost in each binary problem to the fraction of positive instances in that dataset. The SVM implementation used in our experiments was SVM-light [12].

mRNA Signal Structure Detection: This experiment is concerned with identifying subsequences in mRNA that are responsible for biological functions[1]. In contrast to the secondary structure of proteins that form chains (see next experiment), the secondary structure of mRNAs form trees. As trees can not easily

---

[1] The *Science Magazine* listed RNA as one of the runner-up breakthroughs of the year 2003.

be handled using HMMs, mRNA secondary structure data is more interesting than that of proteins.

The first application of machine learning to recognise the signal structure class of mRNA molecules was described in [9]. The dataset we used[2] is the one used in [13], where LOHMMs were applied with the plug-in estimate. In total, there are 93 logical sequences (in total 3122 ground atoms) composed of 15 and 5 SECIS (Selenocysteine Insertion Sequence), 27 IRE (Iron Responsive Element), 36 TAR (Trans Activating Region) and 10 histone stemloops.

As the dataset is rather small, we used leave-one-out error estimation and did not further optimise the SVM parameters. That is, we used a linear kernel and let SVM-light choose the default complexity constant. The error rate of LOHMMs with the plugin estimate of 4.3% could be reduced to 2.2% by using Fisher kernels. More precisely, the Fisher kernels managed to resolve two misclassifications, one of IRE and one of SECIS. The result improves the error rate of 4.6% reported in [9]. This suggests that hypothesis **H** holds.

Protein Fold Recognition: This experiment is concerned with how proteins fold up in nature. This is an important problem, as the biological functions of proteins depend on the way they fold up. A common approach to protein fold recognition is to start from a protein with unknown structure and search for the most similar protein with known structure (or protein fold) in the database. This approach has been followed in [14] where LOHMMs with the plugin estimate were able to considerably improve over these results. Notice that the number of parameters of the LOHMMs used were by an order of magnitude smaller than the number of an equivalent HMM (120 vs. approx. 62000).

The data consists of logical sequences of the secondary structure of protein domains[3]. The task is to predict one of five SCOP [10] folds for 2187 test sequences given a LOHMM trained on 200 training sequences per fold. As this dataset is bigger than the previous, we were able to perform a proper parameter selection. We first performed a leave-one-out error estimation in the training set to choose the parameter of the Gaussian kernel function. Of the tested parameters ($\gamma \in \{10^{-1}, 10^{-2}, 10^{-3}, 10^{-4}, 10^{-5}\}$), $\gamma = 10^{-3}$ clearly performed best over all binary problems. We then fixed this parameter and optimised the complexity constant. Of the tested parameters ($C \in \{10^{-1}, 10^0, 10^1, 10^2\}$), $C = 100$ clearly performed best over all binary problems (testing bigger values was not necessary, as we already achieved 0 unbounded support vectors).

Using Fisher kernels with the same LOHMMs as in [14] and the above described SVM parameters, we were able to reduce the error rate of the plugin

---

[2] The dataset is not the same as described in [9] due to problems in obtaining the original dataset. We will compare to the smaller data set used in [9] which consisted of 66 signal structures and is very close to our data set. On a larger data set (with 400 structures) [9] report an error rate of 3.8% .

[3] A domain can be viewed as a sub-section of a protein which appears in a number of distantly related proteins and which can fold independently of the rest of the protein.

Table 1. Precision and recall values (precision/recall) for the protein fold experiment. The first row shows the values for LOHMMs alone. The second row shows the values for Fisher kernels of LOHMMs and SVMs.

	fold1	fold2	fold23	fold37	fold55
LOHMMs	0.86/0.78	0.69/0.67	0.56/0.71	0.72/0.66	0.86/0.96
Fisher Kernels	0.87/0.90	0.80/0.86	0.84/0.77	0.71/0.71	0.88/0.74

estimate of 26% to an error rate of 17.4%. As Table 1 shows, the precision and recall values were well balanced within each class. This suggest that $\mathbf{H}$ holds.

6   Related Work

The past few years have witnessed a significant interest in *kernels* and *probabilistic models for structured data*. Despite this interest in both fields, to the best of our knowledge, the work of Taskar et al. [20] is the only work which aims at the same goal, namely discriminative models for structured data. However, Taskar et al. do not consider sequential but relational data and they do not explore kernel functions but discriminative learning of relational probabilistic models. Discriminative learning here means that instead of maximising the joint probability $P(y_i, x_i)$, the conditional probability $P(y_i \mid x_i)$ is maximised.

Support Vector Machines for Structured Data: In principle, there are two ways to apply support vector machines to structured data: Using *syntax-driven* and *model-driven* kernel functions. For an overview, we refer to [5].

An integral part of many *syntax-driven* kernels for structured data is the *decomposition* of an object into a set of its parts and the *intersection* of two sets of parts. The kernel on two objects is then defined as a measure of the intersection of the two corresponding sets of parts. In the case that the sets are finite or countable sets of vectors it is often beneficial to sum over all pairwise kernels on the elements. This idea of intersection and crossproduct kernels is reflected in most work on kernels for structured data, from the early and influential technical reports [8, 23] through work on string kernels, kernels for higher order terms and trees, to more recent work on graph kernels.

An alternative to syntax-driven kernel functions are *model-driven kernel* functions like the Fisher kernel introduced above. Based on the idea of maximising the the posterior probability estimated by the optimal logistic regressor in the extracted feature space, [21] introduced the so-called TOP kernel function. The TOP kernel function is the scalar product between the posterior log-odds of the model and the gradient thereof. The posterior log-odds is defined as the difference in the logarithm of the probability of each class given the instance. Marginalised kernels [22] have later been introduces as a generalisation of Fisher kernels. Here, a kernel over both the hidden and the observed data is assumed to be given. Then, the marginalised kernel for the visible data is obtained by taking the expectation with respect to hidden variables.

Probabilistic Models for Structured Data: LOHMMs combine two different research directions. On the one hand, they are related to several extensions of HMMs, such as hierarchical HMMs [3] or factorial HMMs [6]. Here, the underlying idea is to decompose the state variables into smaller units. For instance, to derive factorial HMMs, one factors the hidden state variable into k state variables which depend on one another only through the observation The key difference with LOHMMs is that these approaches do not employ the logical concept of unification. Unification is essential because it allows us to introduce abstract transitions, which do not consist of more detailed states.

On the other hand, they are also related to the recent interest in combining inductive logic programming principles with probability theory, see [2] for an overview. Most attention has been devoted to developing highly expressive formalisms. LOHMMs can be seen as an attempt towards *downgrading* such highly expressive frameworks. As a consequence, LOHMMs represent an interesting position on the expressiveness scale. Whereas they retain most of the essential logical features of the more expressive formalisms, they seem easier to understand, adapt and learn.

Most closely related to LOHMMs are *relational Markov models* [1]. Here, states can be of different types, with each type described by a different set of variables. The domain of each variable is hierarchically structured. The main difference is that variable bindings, unification, and hidden states are not used.

7 Conclusions

So far, Fisher kernels have only been considered for sequences of flat symbols. In this paper, Fisher kernels for logical sequences, i.e., sequences over an alphabet of logical atoms have been introduced and experimentally investigated. The experimental results show that Fisher kernels can handle logical sequences and that they can improve considerably the predictive performance of plug-in estimates of probabilistic models for logical sequences.

We are confident that Fisher kernels can be used to also improve the discriminative power of other approaches combining inductive logic programming principles with probability theory. Exploring this family of *logical Fisher kernels* is a promising future research direction.

Acknowledgements. The research was supported in part by the European Union under contract number FP6-508861, *Application of Probabilistic Inductive Logic Programming II*, and in part by the DFG project (WR 40/2-1) *Hybride Methoden und Systemarchitekturen für heterogene Informationsräume*.

References

1. C. R. Anderson, P. Domingos, and D. S. Weld. Relational Markov Models and their Application to Adaptive Web Navigation. In *Proceedings of the Eighth International Conference on Knowledge Discovery and Data Mining (KDD)*, 2002.

2. L. De Raedt and K. Kersting. Probabilistic Logic Learning. *ACM-SIGKDD Explorations*, 5(1):31–48, 2003.
3. S. Fine, Y. Singer, and N. Tishby. The hierarchical hidden markov model: analysis and applications. *Machine Learning*, 32:41–62, 1998.
4. J. Fischer and K. Kersting. Scaled CGEM: A Fast Accelerated EM. In N. Lavrac, D. Gamberger, H. BLockeel, and L. Todorovski, editors, *Proceedings of the Fourteenth European Conference on Machine Learning (ECML-03)*, pages 133–144, Cavtat, Croatia, September 22–26 2003.
5. T. Gärtner. Kernel-based Learning in Multi-Relational Data Mining. *ACM-SIGKDD Explorations*, 5(1):49–58, 2003.
6. Z. Ghahramani and M. Jordan. Factorial hidden Markov models. *Machine Learning*, 29:245–273, 1997.
7. J. Hargbo and A. Elofsson. Hidden markov models that use predictied secondary structure for fold recognition. *Proteins: Structure, Function, and Genetics*, 36:68–76, 1999.
8. D. Haussler. Convolution kernels on discrete structures. Technical report, Department of Computer Science, University of California at Santa Cruz, 1999.
9. T. Horváth, S. Wrobel, and U. Bohnebeck. Relational Instance-Based learning with Lists and Terms. *Machine Learning*, 43(1/2):53–80, 2001.
10. T. Hubbard, A. Murzin, S. Brenner, and C. Chotia. *SCOP*: a structural classification of proteins database. *NAR*, 27(1):236–239, 1997.
11. T.S. Jaakkola and D. Haussler. Exploiting generative models in discriminative classifiers. In *Adv. in Neural Information Processing Systems 11*. MIT Press, 1999.
12. T. Joachims. *Learning to Classify Text Using Support Vector Machines: Methods, Theory and Algorithms*. Kluwer, 2002.
13. K. Kersting, L. De Raedt, and T. Raiko. Logical hidden markov models. 2004. (submitted).
14. K. Kersting, T. Raiko, S. Kramer, and L. De Raedt. Towards discovering structural signatures of protein folds based on logical hidden markov models. In *Proceedings of the Pacific Symposium on Biocomputing (PSB-03)*, 2003.
15. K. Kersting, T. Raiko, and L. De Raedt. A Structural GEM for Learning Logical Hidden Markov Models. In *Working Notes of the Second KDD-Workshop on Multi-Relational Data Mining (MRDM-03)*, 2003.
16. J. W. Lloyd. *Foundations of Logic Programming*. Springer, 2. edition, 1989.
17. L. R. Rabiner. A Tutorial on Hidden Markov Models and Selected Applications in Speech Recognition. *Proceedings of the IEEE*, 77(2):257–286, 1989.
18. R. Salakhutdimov, S. Roweis, and Z. Ghahramani. Optimization with EM and Expectation-Conjugate-Gradient. In *Proceedings of the Twentieth International Conference on Machine Learning (ICML03)*, 2003.
19. B. Schölkopf and A.J. Smola. *Learning with Kernels*. MIT Press, 2002.
20. B. Taskar, P. Abbeel, and D. Koller. Discriminative Probabilistic Models for Relational Data. In *Proceedings of the Eighteenth Conference on Uncertainty in Artificial Intelligence (UAI-02)*, 2002.
21. K. Tsuda, M. Kawanabe, G. Rätsch, S. Sonnenburg, and K.-R. Müller. A new discriminative kernel from probabilistic models. In *Adv. in Neural Information Processing Systems*. MIT Press, 2002.
22. K. Tsuda, T. Kin, and K. Asai. Marginalized kernels for biological sequences. *Bioinformatics*, 2002.
23. C. Watkins. Kernels from matching operations. Technical report, Department of Computer Science, Royal Holloway, University of London, 1999.

The Enron Corpus:
A New Dataset for Email Classification Research

Bryan Klimt and Yiming Yang

Language Technologies Institute
Carnegie Mellon University
Pittsburgh, PA 15213-8213, USA
{bklimt,yiming}@cs.cmu.edu

Abstract. Automated classification of email messages into user-specific folders and information extraction from chronologically ordered email streams have become interesting areas in text learning research. However, the lack of large benchmark collections has been an obstacle for studying the problems and evaluating the solutions. In this paper, we introduce the Enron corpus as a new test bed. We analyze its suitability with respect to email folder prediction, and provide the baseline results of a state-of-the-art classifier (Support Vector Machines) under various conditions, including the cases of using individual sections (From, To, Subject and body) alone as the input to the classifier, and using all the sections in combination with regression weights.

1 Previous Work on Email Classification

Email classification can be applied to several different applications, including filtering messages based on priority, assigning messages to user-created folders, or identifying SPAM. We will focus on the problem of assigning messages to a user's folders based on that user's foldering strategy. One major consideration in the classification is that of how to represent the messages. Specifically, one must decide which features to use, and how to apply those features to the classification. Manco, et al. [8] defined three types of features to consider in email: unstructured text, categorical text, and numeric data. Relationship data is another type of information that could be useful for classification.

Unstructured text in email consists of fields like the subject and body, which allow for natural language text of any kind. Generally, these fields have been used in classification using a bag-of-words approach, the same as with other kinds of text classification [2,8,10]. Stemming and stop word removal are often used, as they are useful in general text classification, although their usefulness in email in particular has not yet been studied thoroughly. It has been found that some of these fields are more important that others in classifying email [4,8].

Categorical text includes fields such as "to" and "from" [8]. These differ from unstructured text fields in that the type of data which can be used in them is very well defined. However, these fields have typically been treated the same as the unstructured text fields, with the components added to the bag of words [2,8].

J.-F. Boulicaut et al. (Eds.): ECML 2004, LNAI 3201, pp. 217–226, 2004.

These fields have been found to be very useful in automatic email classification, although not as useful as the unstructured data [4,8].

Numeric Data in email includes such features as the message size, number of recipients [8], and counts of particular characters [4]. So far, every test has found that these features can contribute little towards email classification.

Studies on the use of relationship data in email foldering have not yet been published to our knowledge. Relationship data consists of the connections between an email message and other types of objects, such as users, folders, or other emails. One such relationship between emails is that of *thread membership* [7,9]. A thread is a set of email messages sent among a set of users discussing a particular topic. We believe that use of thread information could improve the results of email classification. The reasoning behind this is that often, in a message that is part of a long discussion, not everything from the earlier parts of the discussion is repeated. This missing information could provide important clues about how to classify a message.

The difference between thread information and the other kinds of email data is that thread data is not provided explicitly. It must be deduced from other data fields. There has not been much work in how to detect thread information automatically. One study by Murakoshi, et al. looked at finding thread structure using linguistic analysis, which is a difficult natural language problem, and is difficult to evaluate [9]. Another approach, introduced by Lewis and Knowles, was to use the hierarchy of message replies as an approximation of the thread structure, although it is obvious that it will not be perfect [7]. They examined how to find this structure automatically. Their best results were from using quoted text in a message as a query and ranking the other emails in the corpus by their cosine similarity to the query. They reported about .71 accuracy in determining the parent message of messages known to be in threads. The retrieval algorithm in their study did not take advantage of word order. It also did not address how to determine whether or not a particular email was a member of a thread to begin with.

It is not yet known which classification algorithms will work best for automatic folder classification. In fact, the literature suggests that the variation in performance between different users varies much more than the variation between different classification algorithms [1]. Kiritchenko and Matwin found that SVM worked better than Naïve Bayes, with 75-87% accuracy, depending on user [6]. Brutlag and Meek also found SVM to perform best, but only for dense folders, i.e. folders with at least twenty messages [1]. They found that for sparse folders, on the other hand, TF-IDF similarity worked best for most users, with 67-95% accuracy. TF-IDF has been tested by others [3,11], with accuracies in a similar range, as has Naïve Bayes [4,10]. Several studies have tried approaches based on automatic learning of rules for classification, with accuracies similar to those of the other methods [2,3,5]. None of these studies, however, has shown that any particular method outperforms the others for a large variety of data sets.

There has not yet emerged a common data set for use in evaluating email folder classification, so it is hard to compare the results of different researchers.

Most studies so far have used personal collections of the people working on the experiments [1,2,3,4,6]. These sets have been incredibly small, on the order of one to five users. Since email organization strategies vary from user to user, it will be necessary to perform studies with larger data sets before conclusions can be made about which algorithms work best for email classification.

2   Enron Dataset

A large set of email messages, the Enron corpus, was made public during the legal investigation concerning the Enron corporation. The raw corpus is currently available on the web at `http://www-2.cs.cmu.edu/~enron/`. The current version contains 619,446 messages belonging to 158 users. We cleaned the corpus for use in these experiments by removing certain folders from each user, such as "discussion_threads" and "notes_inbox". These folders were present for most users, and did not appear to be used directly by the users, but rather were computer generated. Many, such as "all_documents", also contained large numbers of duplicate email messages, which were already present in the users' other folders. Since our goal in this paper is to explore how to classify messages as organized by a human, these folders would have likely been misleading.

In our cleaned Enron corpus, there are a total of 200,399 messages belonging to 158 users with an average of 757 messages per user. This is approximately one third the size of the original corpus. Figure 1 shows the distribution of emails per user. The users in the corpus are sorted by ascending number of messages along the x-axis. The number of messages is represented in log scale on the y-axis. The horizontal line represents the average number of messages per user (757).

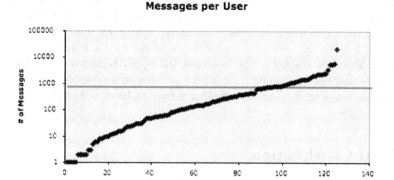

Fig. 1.

As can be seen from the graph, the messages are distributed basically exponentially, with a small number of users having a large number of messages. However, there are users distributed along the entire graph from one message to

100,000 messages, which shows that the Enron dataset provides data for users with all amounts of email. More important in folder classification, though, is the number of folders each user has. The distribution of folders for each user is shown in figure 2. Each point is a user, and shows the number of folders and messages the user has.

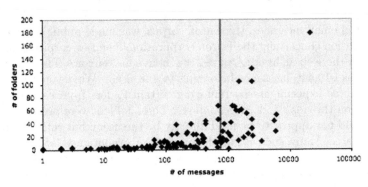

Fig. 2.

Figure 2 illustrates that the Enron dataset is consistent with many of the assumptions made about email folder classification. Most importantly, it shows that most users do use folders to organize their email. If users did not categorize their email into folders, then automatic classification would not be useful for them. Secondly, it shows that the number of messages a user has does not necessarily provide a lower bound for the number of folders that person uses. Some users with many messages have a relatively small number of folders. The number of messages does, however, obviously provide an upper bound for the number of folders the user has. Unsurprisingly, no user has more folders than messages. More interesting is the fact that the upper bound for the number of folders of a user appears to be a log of the number of messages of that user. In other words, users with more total messages tend to have more messages in each individual folder.

3   SVM Classification

The dataset was evaluated using a state-of-the-art text classifier on various representations of each email. SVM was used first to classify the folder of each email based solely on a particular field of data from the email. The fields used were "From", "Subject", "Body", and "To, CC". The date field was not used, as it is not text information, and the problem of how to apply date information to email classification has not been fully explored. Next, SVM was used on each email treated as a single bag-of-words. This approach is labeled "All" in the analysis below. For this representation, the fields used in the previous experiments were concatenated and used in the classification. Thus, if the same term appears in both the subject and body of a message, it is considered to be multiple occurrences of the same feature. For the final approach, labeled "linear combination" below, the SVM scores from the "From", "Subject", "Body", and "To, CC" classifiers were combined linearly. The weights for each section were learned for each folder of a particular user, using ridge regression on the training data.

To create training and testing sets, the data for each user was sorted chronologically, and then split in half. The earlier half of the messages was used for training, while the later half was used for testing. Standard text parsing routines were applied to each of the fields in the email to produce the list of terms. Stemming was also performed on the body of the message. The terms were then given weights using the standard "ltc" formula, and given to SVM, using the one-vs-rest method for multi-class classification.

For binary decisions, optimal thresholds were found for each folder (category). In many previous experiments, binary decisions were based on choosing only the highest ranked folder for each message, making precision the only relevant evaluation metric. However, it has been suggested [11] that it can be beneficial to the user to present multiple possible assignments for each email. Therefore, we obtained thresholds using score-based local optimization, known as SCut [12], and evaluated using F1 scores, which measure both precision and recall. The folder hierarchy was flattened for these experiments. In other words, the "correct" folder for a given message was considered to be the lowest level folder containing the email. The reason for this is so that a correct classification is only given credit once. Otherwise, scores would be inflated significantly by large root folders, such as "Inbox", which contain many other folders. The results for the evaluation are given in Figure 3.

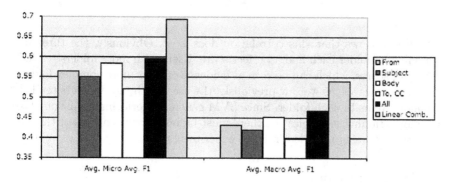

Fig. 3.

Each bar in the figure represents the average score of all of the users for a particular test. The most useful feature on average is the body of the email, although it was not significantly better than the From field. The least useful feature is clearly the To and CC fields of the email. This is understandable, as most of the messages going to a user have the same address in the To field, so that address is not a very discriminative feature. As for the methods that used multiple fields of the emails' data, using ridge regression to combine the individual scores linearly proved significantly more effective than treating the fields as a single bag of words. The fact that one feature does not dominate the other features here shows that the users in the Enron corpus do not use a single field in determining email organization, but rather use of combination of the data in their organizational scheme.

Figure 4 shows the correlation between the number of messages a user has and the linearly combined F1 score for that user. The number of messages a user has is clearly not strongly correlated with the performance of the text classifier on his or her email. This result is reasonable, though. If a user has many messages, but they are all in the same folder, classification is trivial. If however, they are spread out, the performance of the classifier depends on the foldering strategy of the user. In other words, the number of folders a user has should be a much bigger predictor of the ease of automatic classification for a user.

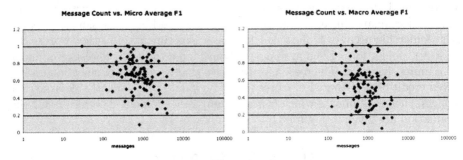

Fig. 4.

Figure 5 shows that this correlation does exist. Obviously, the three users with only one folder each had a perfect score. Users with more folders tended to have lower scores, which can be seen as evidence of their more complex foldering strategies. However, as we saw previously, the users with more folders tended to have more items in each folder. Since SVM generally performs better on classes with more training examples [1], there must be important features of the email which are not being modeled in these experiments.

4   CMU Dataset

To determine if the classification results for the Enron dataset were reasonable, a second data set was used for the experiments. The CMU dataset was collected over several months from several students and a faculty member at the Language Technology Institute of CMU.

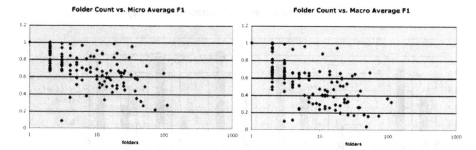

Fig. 5.

	number of messages
user 1	1338
user 2	1438
user 3	403
user 4	703
user 5	4381

The results with this test set are similar to the results with the Enron dataset, with a micro average F1 score near .7 and a macro average score near .55. Micro averages are generally higher than their corresponding macro averages, which may reflect the previous observation that SVM tends to work much better on folders with more messages [1], as macro-averages are dominated by small categories. We see that From and Body are the best performing representations for email classification, while To and CC are less useful. The linear combination of scores again outperformed the bag of words representation on average, although not by as large a margin as with the Enron dataset. This shows that, in total, the users in the Enron dataset most likely use more diverse foldering strategies than the users in the CMU dataset, as combining evidence from different sections better improves results relative to the individual sections used seperately. The overall similarity of these results, however, reinforces the idea that the Enron dataset is a useful dataset representative of common users.

5   Threads

We have also briefly analyzed the nature of email "threads" in this corpus. For this analysis, membership in a thread was determined by two factors. Emails were considered to be in the same thread if they contained the same words in their subjects and they were among the same users (addresses). Messages with empty subjects were not considered to be a thread. No evaluations were conducted to test the quality of the thread detection algorithm. The main reason for this is that threads are rather subjective, and user judgments are difficult to obtain. Lewis [7] had used the "in-reply-to" headers in email messages as the truth about thread membership to test his thread detection algorithm. Unfortunately,

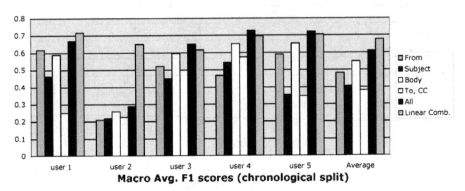

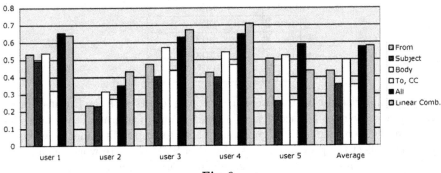

Fig. 6.

it appears that some current email clients do not use this header, as the Enron corpus has very few messages with it. Also, the algorithm could not be evaluated against the results from the previous paper, as the corpus used in that paper is no longer available. The algorithm used in that paper also does not provide a mechanism for determining whether a message is in a thread at all, as only messages known to be in threads were used in the experiments.

Investigation of the use of threads to improve email classification would provide an indirect evaluation of our detection algorithm, and would be an interesting topic for future research. We will now, however, only provide some statistics of the threads present in the Enron dataset as determined by our algorithm. Hopefully, our analysis will be useful for future research on thread detection and use.

Out of the total 200,399 messages in the Enron corpus, we detected 101,786 threads. 71,695 of these threads were *trivial* threads, consisting of only one message. These threads would clearly not be useful for classification, so there are 30,091 remaining useful threads in the corpus, consisting of 123,501 of the 200,399 total messages. In other words, a full 61.63% of messages in the corpus is in a thread. This makes the average thread size 4.10 messages. The median useful thread size, however, is only 2.00. So, there are a few large threads in the corpus, and many small threads. In fact, the distribution of thread sizes is as follows:

thread size:	2	3	4	5	6	7	8	9	10	(10-20]	(20-30]	(30-40]	(40-50]	51+
# of threads	16736	4782	3049	1282	879	903	378	214	178	1260	209	79	54	88

The larger threads should be more useful, since they provide more information about the relationships of a message, but they are less common. However, more important than the size of the thread is the information the thread can provide. The average number of folders containing the messages of a thread is 1.37. This means, given an average thread, the messages in that thread are distributed among only 1.37 folders. This information could be very useful in email classification.

The major drawback of this thread information is that it may be redundant when used with the other kinds of evidence discussed in this paper. Since subject words are used to detect threads, a thread based classifier may not provide any information not already available, if it is used as just another feature. One example of a redundancy problem is with the largest thread in the Enron corpus, messages with the subject "Demand Ken Lay Donate Proceeds from Enron Stock Sales" belonging to user "lay-k". There are 1124 messages in this thread and they are all in the same folder (Deleted Items)! This would be incredible evidence for classification by itself. However, all of the messages in the thread are virtually identical; they appear to be SPAM. Since the messages are identical, there is already incredibly strong evidence from other features, without even detecting the thread.

Thread information may be useful in conjunction with other fields, but one must use a method that can infer more from thread membership than the redundant information provided by other fields. The Enron corpus has a large number of threads and would be useful as a test set for these methods.

6   Conclusions and Future Work

There are many more ways to model email than the methods attempted in this paper. More research needs to be done into using the relationships between emails to reinforce knowledge about a particular message. One of these relationships is thread membership. While a small amount of research has been done into how to detect threads, no one has studied how to use the threads for the task of email classification. Time information was also left out of these experiments, while it seems clear that it could be useful. Time cannot be used in the same way as other fields though, obviously, so work must be done to determine how time affects the foldering strategies of a user.

In order to compare new techniques for email classification, a large standard test dataset, such as the newly available Enron corpus, could be very valuable. It can be used both as a large sample of real life email users and as a standard corpus for comparison of results using different methods. We have provided evaluations of baseline experiments on the dataset. We have also provided a brief analysis of the dataset itself.

Acknowledgements

The authors would like to thank Fan Li for providing original experiment designs and baseline results for the CMU dataset using SVM with ridge regression. We would also like to thank William Cohen for promoting the Enron dataset, by providing it to us, and by giving it a home on the web.

References

1. J. D. Brutlag, C. Meek: Challenges of the Email Domain for Text Classification. ICML 2000: 103-110
2. W. W. Cohen: Learning Rules that classify E-mail. In Proc. of the 1996 AAAI Spring Symposium in Information Access, 1996.
3. E. Crawford, J. Kay, and E. McCreath: Automatic Induction of Rules for e-mail Classification. In ADCS2001 Proceedings of the Sixth Australasian Document Computing Symposium, pages 13-20, Coffs Harbour, NSW Australia, 2001.
4. Y. Diao, H. Lu, and D. Wu: A comparative study of classification-based personal e-mail filtering. In Proc. 4th Pacific-Asia Conf. Knowledge Discovery and Data Mining (PAKDD'00), pages 408-419, Kyoto, JP, 2000.
5. E. Hung: Deduction of Procmail Recipes from Classified Emails. CMSC724 Database Management Systems, individual research project report. May, 2001
6. S. Kiritchenko, S. Matwin: Email classification with co-training. In Proc. of the 2001 Conference of the Centre for Advanced Studies on Collaborative Research, page 8, Toronto, Ontario, Canada, 2001
7. D. D. Lewis, K. A. Knowles: Threading Electronic Mail: A Preliminary Study. In Information Processing and Management, 33(2): 209-217, 1997
8. G. Manco, E. Masciari, M. Ruffolo, and A. Tagarelli: Towards an Adaptive Mail Classifier. AIIA 2002, Sep. 2002.
9. H. Murakoshi, A. Shimazu, and K. Ochimizu: Construction of Deliberation Structure in Email Communication In Pacific Association for Computational Linguistics (PACLING'99), pages 16-28, Aug. 1999.
10. J. Rennie: ifile: An Application of Machine Learning to E-Mail Filtering. In Proc. KDD00 Workshop on Text Mining, Boston, 2000.
11. R. B. Segal and J. O. Kephart. MailCat: An Intelligent Assistant for Organizing E-Mail. In Proc. of the 3rd International Conference on Autonomous Agents, 1999.
12. Y. Yang: A Study of Thresholding Strategies for Text Categorization. In Proc. of the 24th Annual International ACM SIGIR Conference on Research and Development in Information Retrieval, pages 137-145, New Orleans, LA, 2001.

Margin Maximizing Discriminant Analysis

András Kocsor[1], Kornél Kovács[1], and Csaba Szepesvári[2]

[1] Research Group on Artificial Intelligence of the Hungarian Academy of Sciences,
University of Szeged, Aradi vértanúk tere 1., 6720 Szeged, Hungary
{kocsor,kkornel}@inf.u-szeged.hu
[2] Computer and Automation Research Institute of the
Hungarian Academy of Sciences, Kende u. 13-17, 1111 Budapest, Hungary
szcsaba@sztaki.hu

Abstract. We propose a new feature extraction method called Margin Maximizing Discriminant Analysis (MMDA) which seeks to extract features suitable for classification tasks. MMDA is based on the principle that an ideal feature should convey the maximum information about the class labels and it should depend only on the geometry of the optimal decision boundary and not on those parts of the distribution of the input data that do not participate in shaping this boundary. Further, distinct feature components should convey unrelated information about the data. Two feature extraction methods are proposed for calculating the parameters of such a projection that are shown to yield equivalent results. The kernel mapping idea is used to derive non-linear versions. Experiments with several real-world, publicly available data sets demonstrate that the new method yields competitive results.

1 Introduction

In this paper we consider feature extraction in a classification context. Feature extraction can be used for data visualization, e.g. plotting data in the coordinate system defined by the principal components of the data covariance matrix. Visualization may help us to find outliers, or meaningful clusters. Another good use of feature extraction is noise reduction. In classification the goal is to suppress irrelevant information in order to make the classification task using the transformed data easier and simpler.

Feature extraction is the process of transforming the input patterns either by means of a linear or a non-linear transformation. Linear transformations are more amenable to mathematical analysis, while non-linear transformations are more powerful. When linear methods are applied to non-linearly transformed data, the full method becomes non-linear. One important case is when the linear method uses only dot-products of the data. In this case the kernel mapping idea [1, 15, 19] can be used to obtain an efficient implementation whose run time does not depend on the dimensionality of the non-linear map's image space. This 'kernel mapping' idea applies to many well-known feature extraction methods like principal component analysis and linear discriminant analysis. In classification, the best known example utilizing this idea is the support vector machine (SVM) [19].

J.-F. Boulicaut et al. (Eds.): ECML 2004, LNAI 3201, pp. 227–238, 2004.

Principal component analysis (PCA) [9] is one of the most widely-known linear feature extraction methods used. It is an unsupervised method that seeks to represent the input patterns in a lower dimensional subspace such that the expected squared reconstruction error is minimized. By its very nature PCA is not meant for classification tasks. So, in the worst case, the Bayes error rate may become arbitrarily bad after the data is projected onto the first few principal components even if the untransformed data was perfectly classifiable. We shall call this phenomenon a *filtering disaster*. PCA can still be very useful e.g. for suppressing "small noise" which corrupts the input patterns regardless of the class labels. PCA has been generalized to KPCA [18] by using the kernel mapping idea.

Classical linear discriminant analysis (LDA) [7] searches for directions that allow optimal discrimination between the classes provided that the input patterns are normally distributed for all classes $j = 1, \ldots, m$ and share the same covariance matrix. If these assumptions are violated LDA becomes suboptimal and a filtering disaster may occur. Recently, LDA has been generalized using the kernel mapping technique [2, 14, 17] as well.

Discriminant analysis as a broader subject addresses the problem of finding a transformation of the input patterns such that classification using the transformed data set becomes easier (e.g. by suppressing irrelevant components, or noise). More recent methods in discriminant analysis include the "Springy Discriminant Analysis" (SDA) (and its non-linear kernelized counterpart, KSDA), which was derived using a mechanical analogy [10, 11] or, in a special case, as a method for maximizing the between-class average margin itself averaged for all pairs of distinct classes [12]. The goal of the algorithm proposed in [6] is to find a linear transformation of the input patterns such that the statistical relationship between the input and output variables is preserved. The authors of this article use reproducing kernel Hilbert spaces (RKHS) to derive an appropriate contrast function. One distinctive feature of their approach is that the method is completely distribution free. There are many other methods available but we will not discuss them here due to lack of space.

In this paper we propose a new linear feature extraction method that we will call Margin Maximizing Discriminant Analysis (MMDA). MMDA projects input patterns onto the subspace spanned by the normals of a set of pairwise orthogonal margin maximizing hyperplanes. The method can be regarded as a non-parametric extension of LDA which makes no normality assumptions on the data but, instead, uses the principle that the separating hyperplane employed should depend on the decision boundary only. A deflation technique is proposed to complement this principle to extract a sequence of orthogonal projection directions. A corresponding non-linear feature extraction method is derived using the kernel mapping technique. The performance of the proposed methods is examined on several real-world datasets. Our findings show that the new method performs quite well and, depending on the dataset may sometimes perform better than any of the other methods tested, resulting in an increase in classification accuracy.

2 Principles of MMDA

MMDA makes use of the principal idea underlying LDA: projecting the input data onto the normal of a given hyperplane which separates the two classes best and provides all the information a decision maker needs to classify the input patterns. However, at this point LDA places normality assumptions on the data, whereas we make no such assumptions, but propose to employ margin maximizing hyperplanes instead.

This choice was motivated by the following desirable properties of such hyperplanes [5, 3, 8]: (i) without any additional information they are likely to provide good generalization on future data; (ii) these hyperplanes are insensitive to small perturbations of correctly classified patterns lying further away from the separating hyperplane; moreover, (iii) they are insensitive to small variations in their parameters. In addition to these properties, margin maximizing hyperplanes are insensitive to the actual *probability distribution* of patterns lying further away from the decision boundary. Hence when a large mass of the data lies far away from the ideal decision boundary we can expect the new method to win against those methods that minimize some form of average loss/cost since those methods necessarily take into account the full distribution of the input patterns. An example of such a situation is depicted in Figure 1. Note that such situations are expected to be quite common in practical applications like character recognition and text categorization. Actually, the original motivation of MMDA stems from a character recognition problem. Suppose that there are two character classes. Suppose also that the input space is the space of character images. Then, let us concentrate only on two pixels. Specifically, let us assume that pixel 1 is such that for characters in class 1, it can be 'on' or 'off', but in the majority of cases it is 'on'. Further, let us assume that pixel 1 is never 'on' for characters in class 2. Suppose too that pixel 2 is such that it is always 'off' for characters in class 1 and it is always 'on' for characters in class 2. Admittedly, these are strong simplifying assumptions, but similar cases do occur in real-world character recognition tasks. In this simplified case, the ideal feature extractor should actually work like a feature selection method: since the two classes are well separated by using pixel 2, it should project the 2D space of the two pixels onto the second coordinate. Now notice that this is the situation depicted in Figure 1. LDA and PCA fail to find such a projection, but MMDA succeeds in doing so.

We supplement the idea of projecting onto the space spanned by the normal of a margin maximizing hyperplane by a deflation technique which guarantees that all subsequent hyperplanes (and all subsequent normals) are orthogonal to each other. As a result each successive feature extraction step extracts "new" information unrelated to information extracted in the previous steps.

Deflation can be incorporated as a step to transform the data covariance matrix. However, we can also incorporate a suitable orthogonality criterion in the equations defining the margin maximizing hyperplane. We will show the equivalence of these two approaches in the next section and discuss their relative merits.

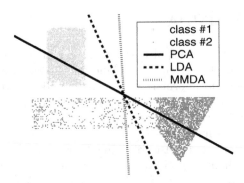

Fig. 1. An illustration of the behavior of PCA, LDA and MMDA for a binary classification problem. The figure shows the one-dimensional subspace represented by a hyperplane that PCA, LDA and MMDA project the data onto. Although the data is linearly separable, PCA and LDA fail to find a subspace such that the data when projected onto the subspace remains linearly separable. MMDA avoids this problem by projecting onto the normal of a separating hyperplane when such a hyperplane exists.

3   Linear Feature Extraction

3.1   The Deflation Approach

Let X, y be the training data, where $X = (x_1, \ldots, x_n)$ are the input patterns $(x_j \in \mathbb{R}^d)$ and $y \in \{-1, +1\}^n$ are the corresponding target labels. We will assume that (x_i, y_i), $i = 1, \ldots, n$ are independent, identically distributed random variables.

Assuming that the data (X, y) is separable, the maximum margin separating hyperplane can be found as a solution of a quadratic programming problem [5]. When the data is not separable the maximum margin separation problem is modified to simultaneously maximize the margin and minimize the error [19]. This still results in a quadratic programming problem. In order to introduce the corresponding equations formally, let us fix a positive real number C that we will use to weight the misclassification cost. Then the maximum margin separation (MMS) problem is defined as follows: Given (X, y, C) find $w \in \mathbb{R}^d$, $b \in \mathbb{R}$ and $\xi = (\xi_1, \ldots, \xi_n)^T \in \mathbb{R}^n$ such that[1]

$$\frac{1}{2}\|w\|_2^2 + C \sum_{i=1}^{n} \xi_i \to \min \text{ s.t.}$$
$$y_i(w^T x_i + b) \geq 1 - \xi_i, \tag{1}$$
$$\xi_i \geq 0, \quad i = 1, \ldots, n.$$

MMDA now proceeds as follows: Given (X, y, C), find the solution of the MMS problem (X, y, C). Let this solution be (w_1, b_1). The first extracted feature component is $f_1(x) = w_1^T x$. Now transform the data by projecting it onto a space

---

[1] Here $\|w\|_2$ denotes the ℓ^2 norm of w.

orthogonal to w_1. For simplicity, assume that w_1 is normalized so $\|w_1\|_2 = 1$. Then the projected data is given by

$$x_i' = x_i - (w_1^T x_i)w_1. \tag{2}$$

Let X' denote the matrix $(x_1', \ldots, x_n')$ and let (w_2, b_2) be the solution of the MMS problem (X', y, C). Then the second extracted feature component is $f_2(x) = w_2^T x'$, where $x' = x - (w_1^T x)w_1$. This procedure can be repeated as many times as desired. The following proposition shows that w_1 and w_2 are orthogonal.

Proposition 1 *Let (w_1, b_1) be the solution of the MMS problem (X, y, C) and (w_2, b_2) be the solution of the MMS problem (X', y, C), where $X' = (x_1', \ldots, x_n')$ with x_i' defined by (2). Then the vectors w_1 and w_2 are orthogonal[2].*

A corollary of this proposition is that $f_2(x) = w_2^T(x - (w_1^T x)w_1) = w_2^T x$. Similarly, if $w_3, \ldots, w_r$ $(r \leq d)$ are the normals extracted up to step r then $w_1, \ldots, w_r$ are pairwise orthogonal and the ith feature value $f_i(x)$ can be computed via:

$$f_i(x) = w_i^T x. \tag{3}$$

In order to derive our first practical algorithm let us note that the solution of the MMS problem is typically obtained via the Langrangian dual of (1):

$$-\frac{1}{2}\alpha^T R\alpha + \alpha^T 1 \to \max$$
$$\text{such that} \quad y^T \alpha = 0, \quad 0 \leq \alpha \leq C1, \tag{4}$$

where the matrix R is defined by $R = YX^T XY$ and $Y = \text{diag}(y_1, \ldots, y_n)$ and $\alpha \in \mathbb{R}^n$ [19]. Here $C1 = (C, \ldots, C)^T \in \mathbb{R}^d$ and the comparison of vectors is made one component at a time. Given α, the solution of (4), the solution of the MMS problem (X, y, C) is recovered through $w = X\alpha$ and $b = 1^T \alpha$. We shall call (4) the dual MMS problem parameterized by (R, y, C).

Let X' be defined as before. Notice that (4) depends on the data vector X only through the matrix R. Hence, the Langrangian dual defined for the transformed data X' takes the form in (4), but R needs to be recalculated. The next proposition shows how to do this in the general case when the data is projected onto a subspace spanned by an orthonormal system:

Proposition 2 *Let X' be the data X projected onto a space orthogonal to the orthonormal system $W = (w_1, \ldots, w_r)$. Then*

$$R' = Y(X')^T X'Y = Y\left(X^T X - V^T V\right)Y, \tag{5}$$

where we define V by $V = W^T X$. In particular, if $W = XA$ for some matrix A then R' can be calculated by $R' = Y\left(K - (KA)(KA)^T\right)Y$, where $K = X^T X$.

The significance of this result is that it shows it is possible to use existing SVM code to extract a sequence of orthogonal margin maximizing hyperplanes just by transforming the matrix R. This proposition is given extra weights as it shows that it is possible to apply the kernel mapping idea to MMDA. This will be considered in more detail in Section 4.

---

[2] We omit the proofs where needed throughout the paper due to a lack of space.

3.2 The Direct Method

The deflation approach requires $O(n^2)$ calculations when calculating the transformed matrix R'. The method we consider in this section avoids this at the price of slightly increasing the dimensionality of the quadratic programming problem.

Let us define the maximum margin separation problem with orthogonality constraint (MMSO problem) as follows: Let u be a d-dimensional vector: $u \in \mathbb{R}^d$. The MMSO problem parameterized by (X, y, C, u) is to find $w \in \mathbb{R}^d$, $b \in \mathbb{R}$ and $\xi = (\xi_1, \ldots, \xi_n) \in \mathbb{R}^n$ such that

$$\frac{1}{2}\|w\|_2^2 + C \sum_{i=1}^{n} \xi_i \rightarrow \min \text{ s.t.}$$

$$y_i(w^T x_i + b) \geq 1 - \xi_i, \tag{6}$$

$$\xi_i \geq 0, \quad i = 1, \ldots, n,$$

$$u^T w = 0.$$

Let $H = H_{(u,0)}$ be a hyperplane with normal $u \in \mathbb{R}^d$ (we assume $\|u\|_2 = 1$ as before) and bias 0. Let $X' = (x'_1, \ldots, x'_n)$ be the matrix whose columns are composed of the x_i vectors projected onto H: $x'_i = x_i - (u^T x_i)u$ as before. The following proposition shows the equivalence of the solutions of MMSO problem and the solutions obtained using the deflation approach:

Proposition 3 *Let C have a fixed positive value. Given the data (X, y) and the hyperplane H with normal u satisfying $\|u\|_2 = 1$ and bias 0, the following holds: Let X' denote the data projected onto the hyperplane H. Then the solutions of the MMS problem (X', y, C) and the MMSO problem (X, y, C, u) coincide.*

According to this last proposition, we obtain equivalent solutions to those gotten using the deflation approach when orthogonality constraints are added to the MMS problem. It is readily seen that the proposition remains true when the number of orthogonality constraints – r, say – is bigger than one. The corresponding MMSO problem will be denoted by (X, y, C, U), where $U = (u_1, \ldots, u_r)$ is the matrix of vectors that are used to define the orthogonality constraints.

It is not difficult to prove that the solution of an MMSO problem (X, y, C, U) may be obtained by solving the following dual quadratic programming problem:

$$-\frac{1}{2}\left(\alpha^\top Y K Y \alpha + \gamma^\top U^T U \gamma\right) + \alpha^\top 1 + \gamma^\top U^T X Y \alpha \rightarrow \max \tag{7}$$

$$\text{such that} \quad y^T \alpha = 0, \quad 0 \leq \alpha \leq C1.$$

Since the number of columns of U is r, the dimensionality of γ will also be r, and hence the number of variables in the above quadratic programming problem will be $n + r$.

The direct method works as follows: Given the data (X, y, C), let (w_1, b_1) be the solution of the MMS problem (X, y, C). Assuming that the solution vectors $(w_1, b_1), \ldots, (w_{r-1}, b_{r-1})$ have already been computed, (w_r, b_r) is obtained as the solution of the MMSO problem (X, y, C, W_{r-1}), where $W_{r-1} = (w_1, \ldots, w_{r-1})$.

Now we will show (i) that the dual MMSO optimization problem (X, y, C, W_r) can be put into a form where the dependence on X is only through the dot product matrix $K = X^T X$ and (ii) that the matrices involved in the dual MMSO optimization problem can be computed in an incremental manner in time $O(mn)$, where m is the number of non-zero elements of $\alpha^{(r)}$. We know that the vectors in W_r lie in the span of X: $w_i = X\alpha^{(i)}$. Therefore $W_r = XA_r$ where $A_r = (\alpha^{(1)}, \ldots, \alpha^{(r)})$. Hence, $W_r^T W_r = A_r^T K A_r$ and $W_r^T XY = A_r^T KY$. So $W_r^T W_r = [A_{r-1}, \alpha^{(r)}]^T K[A_{r-1}, \alpha^{(r)}]$, where the subblocks can be computed by $A_{r-1}^T K A_{r-1}$, $A_{r-1}^T \alpha^{(r)}$, $(\alpha^{(r)})^T A_{r-1}$ and $(\alpha^{(r)})^T K\alpha^{(r)}$, respectively. Further, $W_r^T XY = A_r^T KY$ and hence $(W_r^T XY)^T = (YKA_{r-1}, YK\alpha^{(r)})$. Thus the direct method may be computationally cheaper than the deflation approach when the value of m (the number of support vectors) obtained in step r is much smaller than the number of data points.

4 Non-linear Feature Extraction

It is often the case that the problem of extracting relevant features can be made substantially easier when the data is mapped into an appropriate high dimensional space by some non-linear mapping ϕ and linear methods are applied to the transformed data. If the algorithm is expressible in terms of dot products and if the non-linear mapping $\phi : \mathbb{R}^d \to \mathcal{H}$ is such that the dot products of the images of any two points x and y under ϕ can be computed as a function of x and y only and in poly(d)-time without explicitly calculating $\phi(x)$ or $\phi(y)$ then the algorithm remains tractable, regardless of the dimensionality of $\mathcal{H}$. This allows us to consider very high or even infinite dimensional image spaces $\mathcal{H}$. We may as well start by choosing a symmetric positive definite function $k : \mathbb{R}^d \times \mathbb{R}^d \to \mathbb{R}$, called the kernel function (see e.g. [5]). Then the closure of the linear span of the set $\{ k(x, \cdot) \mid x \in \mathbb{R}^d \}$ gives rise to a Hilbert space $\mathcal{H}$ where the inner product is defined such that it satisfies $\langle k(x_1, \cdot), k(x_2, \cdot) \rangle = k(x_1, x_2)$ for all points $x_1, x_2 \in \mathbb{R}^d$ [13]. The choice of k automatically gives rise to the mapping $\phi : \mathbb{R}^d \to \mathcal{H}$ defined by $\phi(x) = k(x, \cdot)$. This is called the kernel mapping idea [1, 15, 19].

It is clear that the kernel mapping idea can be used to obtain an efficient non-linear version of MMDA too: Firstly, the MMS problem at the heart of MMDA is actually the problem solved by SVMs, which itself builds on the kernel mapping idea [5]. It is well known that the MMS problem can be efficiently solved in the $\mathcal{H}$ feature space. However, for the sake of completeness, we shall briefly describe how to 'kernelize' the MMS problem. The input patterns X appear in Equation (4) only through the dot product matrix $X^T X$. Hence, defining the matrix K by

$$K_{ij} = k(x_i, x_j), \quad 1 \leq i, j \leq n \tag{8}$$

and replacing $X^T X$ in Equation (4) by K, we obtain a quadratic programming problem such that (if α denotes its solution) $w(\cdot) = \sum_{i=1}^n \alpha_i k(x_i, \cdot)$ and $b = \alpha^T 1$ is the solution of the MMS problem (Φ, y, C), where $\Phi = (\phi(x_1), \ldots, \phi(x_n))$.

Now assuming that r directions $W = (w_1, \ldots, w_r)$ have already been determined, the $(r+1)$th direction can be computed as the solution of the dual

Table 1. The characteristics of datasets used in the experiments. In the cases marked by * 10-fold class-balanced cross-validation was used to measure performances.

Dataset	# classes	# attribs	# train	# test
Bupa	2	7	699	*
Pima	2	8	768	*
Iono	2	34	351	*
Heart	2	13	303	*
DNA	3	181	2000	1186
Satimage	6	36	4435	2000
Optdigits	10	64	3823	1797

MMS problem with R replaced by R', where R' is defined in Proposition 2. Since $W = \Phi A$ for an appropriate matrix A (the jth column of A is the solution of the jth dual subproblem) and $\Phi = (\phi(x_1), \dots, \phi(x_n))$, R' can be computed by Proposition 2, where K is now defined by (8). It was also found that the dual of the MMSO problem can be expressed in terms of $X^T X$ when W lies in the span of X. Hence the dual of the MMSO problem can also be expressed using K only, and thus it can be solved efficiently, regardless of the dimensionality of $\mathcal{H}$.

Finally, rewriting (3) in terms of the kernel function we find that the ith component of the feature extraction mapping can be evaluated using

$$f_i(x) = \sum_{j=1}^{n} \alpha_j^{(i)} k(x_i, x), \qquad (9)$$

where $\alpha^{(i)}$ is the solution of the ith dual subproblem. Eq. (9) follows directly from $w_i(\cdot) = \sum_{j=1}^{n} \alpha_j^{(i)} k(x_i, \cdot)$ and the fact that

$$f_i(x) = \langle w_i, \phi(x) \rangle = \sum_{j=1}^{n} \alpha_j^{(i)} \langle \phi(x_i), \phi(x) \rangle.$$

5   Experimental Results

In the first experiment we sought to demonstrate the visualization capability of MMDA. We used the *Wine* dataset from the UCI machine learning repository [4] which has 13 continuous attributes, 3 classes and 178 instances. We applied PCA, LDA and MMDA to these data sets. Two dimensional projections of the data are shown in Figure 2. In the case of PCA and LDA, the data is projected onto the eigenvectors corresponding to the two largest eigenvalues. Since MMDA is defined for binary classification problems, with multi-class problems we need to group certain classes together. In this example the first direction is obtained by grouping classes 2 and 3 together into a single class, while the second direction is obtained by grouping classes 1 and 3 together. It can be seen that for both LDA and MMDA the data became separable in the projection space. It was also noticed that the margin of separation is larger for the case of MMDA, as

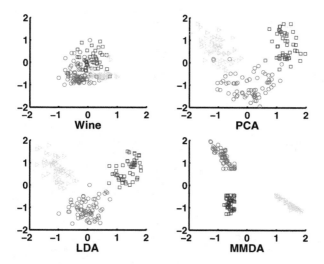

Fig. 2. Scatter plot of wine data projected onto a two-dimensional subspace. The upper left subfigure shows the projection onto the first two attributes, while the other three show the results of a PCA, LDA and MMDA transformation, respectively.

expected. Note that the size of the margin can be controlled to some extent by the parameter C. For this figure we used $C = 1$ and the data was centered and scaled to have unit variance (this transformation was applied in all of our other experiments as well). Actually, the data is not linearly separable in the case of the PCA projection.

Next we investigate whether MMDA can estimate useful subspaces that preserve information necessary for the classification task. For this we ran MMDA on a number of binary classification problems. We changed the number of dimensions of the estimated subspace and measured the classification accuracy that could be achieved by projecting data on the extracted subspace. This experiment was run with both the linear and kernelized versions of MMDA. Since there is obviously no optimal classifier we decided to estimate the quality of the extracted subspace by training an artificial neural network (ANN) classifier on the projected data. The ANN was trained for a fixed number of iterations using batch gradient descent with a constant learning rate. There is one hidden layer and the number of hidden nodes is three times the number of inputs. Our experiments showed that, on the datasets used, this method is competitive with the results of SVMs. We chose to combine ANNs with linear feature extraction since (i) we wanted to keep the algorithms simple and since (ii) the test speed of the resulting composite classifier was then usually very high. High classification speed is important for some applications like OCR. SVMs need special postprocessing to achieve comparably high speeds, therefore we decided to use ANNs.

The characteristics of the datasets used in this experiment are shown in Table 1, while the results are presented in Figure 3. The results labeled 'original' were obtained using an ANN trained on the original, untransformed data. It may be seen that for a number of datasets very good classification rates are achieved

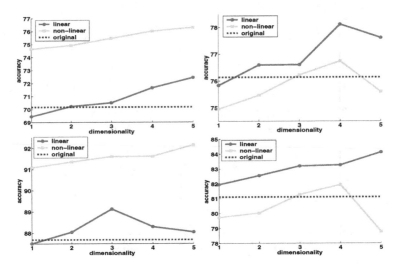

Fig. 3. Accuracies achieved by training a neural network on the subspace extracted by (K-)MMDA shown for 4 dataset. The figures in the top-to-down and left-to-right order are results obtained for the datasets called Bupa, Pima, Ionosphere and Heart Disease.

with only a few features. Also, in certain cases performance drops when the dimensionality of the subspace is increased.

Next, we tested the performance of the method on a number of larger multi-class problems. For multi-class problems we used the "one vs. all" approach: basically when the number of classes wa m we ran (K-)MMDA m times with one class against all the others. We chose this approach for its simplicity. This is probably a suboptimal approach, though our initial experiments with output-coding suggests that accuracies obtained this way are quite good[3]. In this case we tested the interaction of MMDA with several classifiers. These were the ANN introduced earlier, support vector machines with the linear kernel and C4.5 [16]. The results for the three datasets are shown in Figure 4. For comparision we also included the results obtained with 'no feature extraction', PCA and LDA. For the datasets DNA and Optdigits we got competitive results, but for Satimage the result for the tested cases were worse than those obtained with the other methods tested. In particular, in the case of Satimage all feature extractors yielded worse results than those using *no* feature extractor. We conjecture that the optimal subspace for Satimage might be just the (untransformed) space of input patterns[4].

---

[3] Note that we lose pairwise orthogonality (directions extracted for different subproblems are not necessarily orthogonal). In the future we plan to investigate the case when pairwise orthogonality is enforced. Note here that as a kernel for K-MMDA fourth order cosine kernels were used.

[4] In these experiments K-MMDA was implemented using a Gauss-Seidel iteration (or the Adatron) and (without loss of generality) we set $b = 0$.

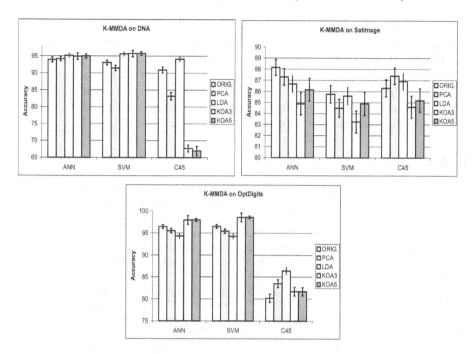

Fig. 4. The interaction of classifiers and feature extractors. The results for K-MMDA are shown. The label KOA$< i >$ means that K-MMDA was run in a one-vs-all manner, and for each subproblem where i is the number of directions extracted per subproblem.

6   Discussion and Conclusions

One common feature of PCA, LDA and SDA is that they require finding a number of principal eigenvectors of a matrix whose dimension scales with the dimensionality of the input space in the linear case, and scales with the number of input patterns in the non-linear case. Our method requires the solution of constrained quadratic optimization problems. As a result, in the case of non-linear feature extraction our method extracts sparse solutions, whilst the kernelized versions of PCA, LDA and SDA extract dense solutions (when no additional 'tricks' are used). The maximum number of features derived using LDA is actually the minimum of the dimensionality of the space and the number of classes minus one. For high dimensional spaces with a few classes this limits the use of LDA [12]. Unlike the standard LDA with (linear) MMDA we can extract as many features as the dimensionality of the pattern space (feature space) allows.

Non-linear MMDA should benefit more from the margin maximizing idea than the linear version as the non-linear version typically works in very high dimensional (sometimes infinite dimensional) feature spaces. This was partially confirmed by our experiments where, for certain datasets, K-MMDA was shown to give excellent results.

In summary, our experiments so far have shown that MMDA can indeed compete with other alternative feature extraction methods. One nice aspect of MMDA is that it can be implemented on top of existing SVM software. Therefore we believe that the proposed method will be a useful tool for researchers using machine learning. In the future we plan to investigate the properties of MMDA more thoroughly (e.g. in multi-class problems). Extensions that make use of different norms penalizing w may also be of interest.

References

1. M. Aizerman, E. Braverman, and L. Rozonoer. Theoretical foundations of the potential function method in pattern recognition learning. *Automation and Remote Control*, 25:821–837, 1964.
2. G. Baudat and F. Anouar. Generalized discriminant analysis using a kernel approach. *Neural Computation*, 12(10):2385–2404, 2000.
3. K. P. Bennett and C. Campbell. Support vector machines: Hype or hallelujah? *SIGKDD Explorations*, 2(2):1–13, 2000.
4. C.L. Blake and C.J. Merz. UCI repository of machine learning databases, 1998.
5. B.E. Boser, I. Guyon, and V. Vapnik. A training algorithm for optimal margin classifiers. In *Computational Learing Theory*, pp. 144–152, 1992.
6. K. Fukumizu, F.R. Bach, and M.I. Jordan. Dimensionality reduction for supervised learning with reproducing kernel Hilbert spaces. *Journal of Machine Learning Research*, 5:73–99, 2004.
7. K. Fukunaga *Statistical Pattern Recognition*. Acad. Press, NY, 1989.
8. R. Herbrich and T. Graepel. A PAC-bayesian margin bound for linear classifiers: Why SVMs work. In *Advances in Neural Information Processing Systems 13*, pp. 224–230, Cambridge, MA, 2000. MIT Press.
9. I.J. Jolliffe. *Principal Component Analysis*. Springer-Verlag, NY, 1986.
10. A. Kocsor, K. Kovács. Kernel Springy Discriminant Analysis and Its Application to a Phonological Awareness Teaching System, in: P. Sojka, I. Kopecek, K. Pala (Eds.): *Proc. of TSD 2002*, LNAI 2448, pp. 325-328, Springer Verlag, 2002.
11. A. Kocsor, L. Tóth. Kernel-Based Feature Extraction with a Speech Technology Application. *IEEE Trans. Signal Processing*. 52(8), 2004.
12. H. Li, T. Jiang, and K. Zhang. Efficient and robust feature extraction by maximum margin criterion. In *Advances in Neural Information Processing Systems 16*, pp. 97 - 104, Vancouver, Canada, 2003.
13. J. Mercer. Functions of positive and negative type and their connection with the theory of integral equations. *Phil. Trans. Roy. Soc. London, A*, 209:415–446, 1909.
14. S. Mika, G. Rätsch, J. Weston, B. Schölkopf, and K.-R. Müller. Fisher discriminant analysis with kernels. In Y.-H. Hu, J. Larsen, E. Wilson, and S. Douglas, editors, *Neural Networks for Signal Processing IX*, pp. 41–48. IEEE, 1999.
15. T. Poggio. On optimal nonlinear associative recall. *Biol. Cyber.*, 19:201–209, 1975.
16. J.R. Quinlan. C4.5: Programs for Machine Learning, Morgan Kaufmann, San Mateo, CA, 1993.
17. V. Roth and V. Steinhage. Nonlinear discriminant analysis using kernel functions. In *Adv. in Neural Information Processing Systems NIPS 12*, pp. 568–574, 1999.
18. B. Schölkopf, A. Smola, and K. Müller. Kernel principal component analysis. In *Adv. in Kernel Methods - SV Learning*, pp. 327–352. MIT Press, Cambr., MA, 1999.
19. V. Vapnik. *The Nature of Statistical Learning Theory*. Spr.-Verl., NY, USA, 1995.

Multi-objective Classification with Info-Fuzzy Networks

Mark Last

Department of Information Systems Engineering
Ben-Gurion University of the Negev
Beer-Sheva 84105, Israel
Telephone: +972-8-6461397, Fax: +972-8-6477527
mlast@bgumail.bgu.ac.il

Abstract. The supervised learning algorithms assume that the training data has a fixed set of predicting attributes and a single-dimensional class which contains the class label of each training example. However, many real-world domains may contain several objectives each characterized by its own set of labels. Though one may induce a separate model for each objective, there are several reasons to prefer a shared multi-objective model over a collection of single-objective models. We present a novel, greedy algorithm, which builds a shared classification model in the form of an ordered (oblivious) decision tree called Multi-Objective Info-Fuzzy Network (M-IFN). We compare the M-IFN structure to Shared Binary Decision Diagrams and bloomy decision trees and study the information-theoretic properties of the proposed algorithm. These properties are further supported by the results of empirical experiments, where we evaluate M-IFN performance in terms of accuracy and readability on real-world multi-objective tasks from several domains.

Keywords: Multi-objective classification, info-fuzzy networks, information theory, decision graphs, multiple output function.

1 Introduction

Mitchell [25] defines the *classification* task as "to classify examples into one of a discrete set of possible categories" (p. 54). This definition is very similar to the one provided by Fayyad et al. [12]. Such formulation of the classification problem subsumes that the class labels (categories) in question are mutually exclusive, i.e. an object cannot belong to more than one class at the same time. In the training set, the class of each instance is given by one of its attributes, called the *class label attribute* [15]. Over the years, a wide range of *supervised learning* algorithms have been developed for inducing classification models from "labeled" training examples, i.e. data items with non-empty values of the class label attribute. Examples include the Back-propagation algorithm [25], Naïve Bayes Classifier [25], C4.5 [27], IFN [23], and many others.

As indicated in [7] and [29], the assumption that a learning task has only one objective is very restrictive. Data objects in many real-world databases may be simultaneously assigned multiple class labels related to multiple tasks. These objectives (dimensions) may be strongly related to each other, completely unrelated, or just weakly related. Examples include student's grades in several courses, symptoms and diagnoses of a given patient, phonemes and stresses associated with a given word [10], etc.

J.-F. Boulicaut et al. (Eds.): ECML 2004, LNAI 3201, pp. 239–249, 2004.

Time series prediction (see [19]) is another learning task, where each sequential observation (e.g., daily stock price) is an objective in its own right. More examples of concurrent learning tasks are described in [6].

The most straightforward approach to the problem of multi-objective classification is to induce a separate model for each objective using any single-objective classification algorithm. Though the resulting models may be the best (e.g., the most accurate) ones for every individual objective, the user may find a single multi-objective model much more comprehensible than a collection of single-objective models. In nonstationary processes (see [20]), storage and maintenance of multiple models may become a tedious task. Moreover, as demonstrated by Caruana [6], the combination of several classification tasks in a single model may even increase the overall predictive accuracy.

To provide a unified framework for single-objective and multi-objective classification, we study here an *extended classification task* which includes the following components (based on [23] and [29]):

- $R = (A_1,..., A_n)$ - a set of *n candidate input features* ($n \geq 1$), where A_i is an attribute *i*. The values of these attributes (features) can be used to predict the values of *class dimensions* (see next).
- $O = (C_1,..., C_m)$ - a non-empty subset of *m class dimensions* ($m \geq 1$). This is a subset of tasks (objectives) to predict. The *extended classification task* is to build an accurate model (or models) for predicting the values of *all* class dimensions, based on the corresponding *dependency subset* (or subsets) $I \subseteq R$ of *input features*.

Section 2 of this paper discusses the related work. The methodology for inducing Multi-Objective Info-Fuzzy Networks is presented in Section 3. We are also trying to answer the following critical questions: *why* multi-objective models should work better than single-objective models and *when* the proposed algorithm is expected to maximize the predictive accuracy of the induced model. To show the practical significance of our theoretical findings, Section 4 compares the performance of single-objective and multi-objective models in terms of predictive accuracy and model simplicity. The empirical comparison is based on three multi-objective classification tasks from the areas of web mining, meteorology, and microbiology. Finally, in Section 5, we sum-up the presented methodology and discuss open problems in multi-objective classification.

2 Related Work

Based on the framework in Section 1 above, the Single-Objective Classification task can be extended to the Multi-Objective Classification task of simultaneously predicting the values of several class dimensions for a given object. The Multi-Objective Classification task is different from *Multitask Learning* described by Caruana in [6]. The explicit goal of Multitask Learning is to improve the accuracy of predicting the values of a *single-dimensional class* (defined as the *main* learning task) by training the classification model, such as a neural network or a decision tree, on several *related* tasks (additional class dimensions). This is called *inductive transfer* between learning tasks. As emphasized by [6], the only concern of Multitask Learning is the generalization accuracy of the model, not its intelligibility. "The reason for training multiple tasks on one learner is so one task can benefit from the information contained in the training signals of other tasks, *not to reduce the number of models that must be learned*" ([6], p. 68). In contrast to [6], this paper focuses on multi-objective classification rather than on multi-task learning, since it proposes a model for simultaneous prediction of *equally important* class dimensions.

A multi-objective classifier called a *bloomy decision tree* is presented in [29]. Like ID3 and C4.5, it employs a "divide and conquer" strategy by recursively partitioning the training set. However its leaf nodes (called *flower nodes*) may predict only a subset of class dimensions. Recursive partitioning along a given path continues as long as there are unpredicted class dimensions left. Consequently, the same path may include a "sandwich" of several flower and split nodes, which need to be traversed in order to predict the values of all class dimensions. This approach significantly increases the total number of internal nodes in a tree (each path may have a flower node for every dimension), while reducing the number of dimensions predicted by smaller partitions of the training set (known as the fragmentation problem).

Representation of multiple-output functions, where all outputs are equally important, is a well-known problem in VLSI design, system testing, and other areas of computer science. *Binary Decision Diagrams* [5][24] are commonly used for representing single-output and multiple-output Boolean functions due to their time and space efficiency. A Binary Decision Diagram is a rooted acyclic graph containing two types of vertices: *non-terminal* vertices related to input variables and *terminal* vertices representing the possible output values of a Boolean function. A *Function Graph* [5] is an *ordered* Binary Decision Diagram, where the input variables appear in the same order on every path of the graph. As shown by Bryant in [5], each Boolean function has a unique (up to isomorphism) reduced function graph representation, while any other function graph denoting the same function contains more vertices.

Function graphs can be easily enhanced for representation of multi-input multi-output functions (see [24]). The idea is to construct a *Shared Binary Decision Diagram* with multiple roots (one for each output variable) [1]. The number of terminal nodes in a typical *Shared Binary Decision Diagram* is two as long as all functions are assumed to have binary outputs only. Such a diagram can be easily converted into a decision tree, where the top level(s) are used for output selection [2].

Kohavi ([17] and [18]) has extended the internal structure of non-shared (i.e. single-objective) Multi-Terminal Binary Decision Diagrams by allowing any number of outgoing edges at non-terminal nodes. Kohavi has called his model an *Oblivious Read-Once Decision Graph (OODG)*. As explained in [18], "read-once" means that each nominal feature is tested at most once along any path, which is a common property of most decision-tree algorithms such as C4.5 [27]. The name "oblivious" indicates the fact that all nodes at a given level are labeled by the same feature. As indicated above, the same ordering restriction is imposed by Bryant [5] on *Function Graphs*. An entropy-based algorithm for inducing oblivious read-once decision trees and decision graphs from data is described and evaluated in [18]. The extensive experiments performed on benchmark datasets have revealed no consistent difference between the accuracy of Kohavi's algorithm and C4.5: on average, both methods perform the same. However, in terms of *representation*, the experiments have clearly shown the capability of the OODG algorithm to produce smaller models than C4.5 for most datasets. This empirical result supports the theorem proven by Bryant in [5] that each Boolean function has a unique function graph representation having a minimal number of vertices.

A single-objective *Info-Fuzzy Network* (see [21] and [23]) has nearly the same structure as an oblivious read-once decision graph with two important differences: it extends the "read-once" restriction of [18] to continuous features by allowing *multi-way splits* of a continuous domain at the same level and it associates *probability estimates* rather than categorical predictions with each leaf node. The *predicted value* of a categorical class dimension at a terminal node is found by the popular *maximum a posteriori* rule: the predicted class is the one with the highest probability [21]. In case of a continuous class dimension, its predicted value is calculated as the mean value of all training cases associated with the particular terminal node. As demonstrated in [21], the single-objective Info-Fuzzy Network induction algorithm produces much more compact models than C4.5, while preserving nearly the same level of classification accuracy. The rest of this paper is dedicated to adaptation of info-fuzzy networks to the task of multi-objective classification. The "fuzzy" aspect of info-fuzzy networks is related to evaluation of data reliability and it is beyond the scope of this paper. An interested reader is referred to [23] for details.

3   Multi-objective Info-Fuzzy Networks

3.1   Definition of Network Structure

We assume that a multi-objective info-fuzzy network (M-IFN) has a single *root node* and its internal "read-once" structure is identical for all class dimensions. This means that every internal node is shared among *all* objectives, which makes M-IFN an extreme case of a Shared Binary Decision Diagram, where only some nodes are shared among several output functions (see [5] and [24]). This also means that each terminal (leaf) node is connected to at least one *target node* associated with a value of every class dimension. "Flower nodes" connected to only a subset of class dimensions are not allowed in M-IFNs.

M-IFNs are different from multitask decision trees [6] and bloomy decision trees [29] in two additional aspects: they are *function graphs*, since they have an oblivious read-once structure and they are also *probability estimation trees* [26], since the same terminal node may be related to several values of the same class dimension. Based on the properties of shared binary decision diagrams and function graphs (see [5]), we believe that the proposed structure should produce compact multi-objective models. Our hypothesis is tested empirically in Section 4 of this paper.

The algorithms for inducing single-objective networks from training data have been thoroughly described in previous works (see [21] and [23]). A novel algorithm for constructing a multi-objective network is presented in the next sub-section.

3.2   The M-IFN Construction Algorithm

The M-IFN induction procedure starts with defining the target layer, which has a node for each category, or value, of every class dimension and the "root" node representing an empty set of input attributes. The direct connections between the root node and the target nodes represent unconditional (prior) probabilities of the target values. Unlike CART [4], C4.5 [27], and EODG [18], the M-IFN construction algorithm has only the growing (top-down) phase. The top-down construction is terminated (pre-pruned) by a statistical significance test (see below), and, consequently, there is no need in bottom-up post-pruning of the network branches. The detailed process of building the network is explained below.

M-IFN construction is an *iterative* rather than a *recursive* process. At every iteration, the algorithm utilizes the entire set of training instances to choose an input (predicting) feature (from the set of unused "candidate input" features), which maximizes the decrease in the total conditional entropy of *all* class dimensions. The conditional entropy decrease, also called *conditional mutual information* [9] or *information gain* [25], is a very common feature selection criterion in single-objective and multi-objective decision-tree algorithms (see [4] [6] [18] [27] [29], etc.).

In information theory (see [9]), conditional entropy measures the degree of uncertainty of a random variable Y given the values of other random variables $X_1, ..., X_n$ and it is calculated as $H(Y / X_1, ..., X_n) = -\Sigma p(x_1, ..., x_n, y) \log p(y / x_1, ..., x_n)$. If a given function is deterministic (noiseless) the conditional entropy of every output is zero.

The conditional mutual information of the class dimension Y_i and the input feature X_n given the features $X_1, ..., X_{n-1}$ is calculated by [9]:

$$MI(Y_i; X_n / X_1, ..., X_{n-1}) = H(Y_i / X_1, ..., X_{n-1}) - H(Y_i / X_1, ..., X_n) =$$
$$\sum_{x_1 \in X_1, ..., x_n \in X_n, y_i \in Y_i} p(x_1, ..., x_n, y_i) \log \frac{p(y_i, x_n / x_1, ..., x_{n-1})}{p(y_i / x_1, ..., x_{n-1}) p(x_n / x_1, ..., x_{n-1})} \tag{1}$$

At *n-th* iteration, the M-IFN algorithm chooses the input feature X_{j*}, which maximizes the sum of information gains over all class dimensions by finding

$$j^* = \arg\max_j \sum_{i=1}^{m} MI(Y_i; X_j / X_1, ..., X_{n-1}) \tag{2}$$

In a multi-objective info-fuzzy network having $n-1$ layers, each internal node in the last layer represents a conjunction of values of $n-1$ input features $X_1, ..., X_{n-1}$. Consequently, the conditional mutual information of a class dimension Y_i and an input feature X_n given the features $X_1, ..., X_{n-1}$ can be calculated as a sum of information gains of Y_i and X_n over all terminal nodes z in the last layer L_{n-1}:

$$MI(Y_i; X_n / X_1, ..., X_{n-1}) = \sum_{z \in L_{n-1}} MI(Y_i; X_n / z) \tag{3}$$

The algorithm evaluates nominal and continuous features in a different way. Thus, the conditional mutual information of each nominal input feature X_j and the class dimension Y_i given a terminal node z is calculated by the following formula:

$$MI(Y_i; X_j / z) = \sum_{x_j \in X_j, y_i \in Y_i} p(z, x_j, y_i) \log \frac{p(y_i, x_j / z)}{p(y_i / z) p(x_j / z)} \tag{4}$$

Where x_j and y_i are distinct values of variables X_j and Y_i respectively.

In the M-IFN algorithm, we use the *Likelihood-Ratio Test* to evaluate the actual capability of an internal node to decrease the conditional entropy of an output by splitting it on the values of a particular input feature. The likelihood-ratio statistic of a nominal input feature X_j and the class dimension Y_i given a terminal node z is measured by the following expression (based on [28]):

$$G^2(Y_i; X_j / z) = 2 \sum_{x_j \in X_j, y_i \in Y_i} N_z(x_j, y_i) \ln \frac{N_z(x_j, y_i)}{p(y_i / z) E_z(x_j)} \qquad (5)$$

where $N_z(x_j, y_i)$ is the number of instances taking an input value x_j and an output value y_i at the node z and $E_z(x_j)$ is the total number of instances taking an input value x_j at the same node.

The Likelihood-Ratio Test is a general-purpose method for testing the null hypothesis H_0 that two random variables are statistically independent. Following our previous experience with single-objective IFN [23], the default significance level (*p-value*) for rejecting the null hypothesis by the M-IFN algorithm is set to 0.1%. If the likelihood-ratio statistic is significant *for at least one class dimension*, the algorithm marks the node z as "split" on the values of an input feature X_j. However, the conditional mutual information of Y_i and X_j (see Eq. (3) above) is incremented by the result of Eq. (4) only if splitting z on X_j proved to be statistically significant with respect to the class dimension Y_i. In other words, the algorithm treats statistically insignificant values of information gain as zeros. As mentioned above, M-IFN is based on the pre-pruning approach: when no input feature causes a statistically significant decrease in the conditional entropy of *any* class dimension, the top-down network construction is terminated.

Unlike EODG [19], the M-IFN induction algorithm uses *multi-way splits* on continuous input features. The threshold splits are identical for all nodes of a given layer and they are determined by a procedure similar to the information-theoretic heuristic of Fayyad and Irani [11]: recursively find a binary partition of an input feature that minimizes the total conditional entropy of all class dimensions. However, the stopping criterion we are using is different the minimum description length principle of [11]. Like in the case of nominal features (see above), we make use of the likelihood-ratio test [28] with respect to the conditional entropy of every class dimension. The search for the best partition of a continuous attribute is dynamic: it is performed each time a candidate input attribute is considered for inclusion in the network. After discretization, each hidden node in the new layer of the network is associated with an interval of the selected feature.

In Table 1 below, we show the main steps for constructing a multi-objective info-fuzzy network from a set of candidate input features.

As indicated above, the *multi-objective classification task* is to find an accurate model (or models) for predicting the values of m equally important class dimensions. The M-IFN induction procedure shown in Table 1 is a greedy algorithm that builds a *single model* aimed at minimizing the *sum of conditional entropies* of all dimensions. In [30], we show the M-IFN algorithm to have the following information-theoretic properties:

- The average conditional entropy of m class dimensions in an n-input m-dimensional model M is not greater than the average conditional entropy over m single-objective models S_i $(i=1, ..., m)$ based on the same n input features. This inequality is strengthened if the multi-objective model M is trained on more features than the single-objective models. Consequently, we may expect that the *aver-*

Table 1. Multi-objective Network Construction Algorithm

Input:	The set D of training examples; the set R of candidate input features; the set O of class dimensions; the minimum significance level $sign$ for splitting a network node (default: $sign = 0.1\%$).
Output:	A dependency subset I of input features and an info-fuzzy network. Each input feature has a corresponding hidden layer in the network.
Step 1	Initialize the info-fuzzy network (single root node representing all examples, no hidden layers, and a target layer for all values of the class dimensions). Initialize the set I of selected inputs as an empty set: $I = \varnothing$.
Step 2	While the number of layers $|I| < n$ (total number of candidate input features) **do**

Step 2.1	**For each** candidate input X_j / $X_j \in R$; $X_j \notin I$ **do**
	 If X_j is continuous **then**
	 find the best threshold splits of X_j over all class dimensions O
	 Calculate the total conditional mutual information between X_j and the class dimensions O: $cond\_MI_j = \sum_{Y_i \in O} MI(Y_i; X_j / I)$
	 End Do

Step 2.2	Find the candidate input X_{j*} maximizing $cond\_MI_j$

Step 2.3	**If** $cond\_MI_{j*} = 0$, **then**
	 End Do.
	 Else
	 Expand the network by a new hidden layer associated with the feature X_{j*}, and add X_{j*} to the set I of input features $I = I \cap X_{j*}$.

Step 2.4	End Do
Step 3	Return the set of input features I and the network structure

age accuracy of a multi-objective model in predicting the values of m class dimensions will not be worse, or even will be better, than the average accuracy of m single-objective models that use the same set of input features.

- If all class dimensions are either mutually independent or totally dependent on each other, the input feature selected by the algorithm will minimize the joint conditional entropy of all class dimensions. The first case extends the scope of multitask learning [7], where "extra" tasks are assumed to be related to the main task.

4 Case Studies

Most datasets stored in the UCI Machine Learning Repository [3], UCI KDD Archive [16], and other collections of benchmark data have only one class dimension, which makes them inappropriate for the multi-objective classification task. After a careful search, we have located at [16] three datasets, which apparently have more than one class dimension. These datasets belong to three distinct domains: analysis of WWW user surveys (web mining), prediction of weather conditions (meteorology), and the impact of water quality on algae concentration (microbiology). For each data set, we run the single-objective IFN algorithm against each class dimension and compare the average classification accuracy of the single-objective models to the accuracy of the M-IFN model. For benchmark purposes, we also present the results of additional classification / prediction algorithms that were applied in literature to these tasks. Finally, we compare the size of the multi-objective model, in terms of nodes and prediction rules, to the overall size of the single-objective models.

The *Internet Usage* dataset contains selected results of the 8th WWW User Survey conducted by the Graphics and Visualization Unit (GVU) at Georgia Tech in 1997 [13]. More than 10,000 respondents could check any number of answers out of a list of 19 not-purchasing reasons. This is a typical multi-objective classification task, where we have 19 binary-valued class dimensions. Table 2 shows the overall misclassification rates of three algorithms: C4.5 [27], single-objective IFN, and M-IFN. All three algorithms were used with their default settings. One can see that the average performance of IFN appears to be slightly better than C4.5, while there is no overall difference between IFN and M-IFN. We may conclude that the Internet Usage task agrees with the M-IFN information-theoretic properties: the multi-objective model does not decrease the average predictive accuracy, which compares fairly with the accuracy of a state-of-the-art classification algorithm (C4.5). At the same time, M-IFN has reduced the total number of nodes by 70% and the number of rules by nearly 68%.

Table 2. Internet Usage Data:Summary of Results

	C4.5	IFN	M-IFN	Change vs. IFN
Average Error Rate	0.1580	0.1524	0.1524	0.0%
Internal Nodes		342	102	-70.2%
Prediction Rules		268	86	-67.9%

The *El Nino Data Set* includes 533 meteorological measurements taken between May 23 and June 5, 1998. To find potential relationships between the measured variables, we have identified three class dimensions. Since IFN and M-IFN algorithms can handle discrete class dimensions only, the values of every continuous output have been discretized to ten intervals of equal frequency. Multiple linear regression, which was used as a benchmark method, can directly handle the continuous dependent variables. Table 3 shows the Root Mean Square Error (RMSE) of multiple linear regression, single-objective IFN, and M-IFN on the three class dimensions of El Nino dataset. Despite discretization, the single-objective IFN was superior to regression on all three class dimensions. M-IFN has further improved the average predictive performance of the single-objective IFN algorithm. Thus, the results of the El Nino task support M-IFN information-theoretic properties by showing an improvement in the average predictive accuracy of M-IFN vs. the single-objective models.

Table 3. El Nino Data: Summary of Results

	Regression	IFN	M-IFN	Change vs. IFN
RMSE	2.860	2.520	2.107	-16.4%
Internal Nodes		82	41	-50.0%
Prediction Rules		63	33	-47.6%

The data used in 1999 Computational Intelligence and Learning (*COIL*) competition comes from a microbiological study. The collected data included 340 water quality samples each containing 18 values. The seven class dimensions of each observation are the distribution of different kinds of algae. Since info-fuzzy networks can handle discrete class dimensions only, the continuous values of every output have been discretized to ten intervals of equal frequency. The results of a multi-objective artificial neural network (ANN) [8] were used as a benchmark. These results have been awarded the runner-up prize at the COIL competition. Table 4 shows the Root Mean Square Error (RMSE) of artificial neural network, single-objective IFN, and M-IFN on the seven class dimensions (algae kinds) of COIL 1999 dataset. Apparently, the performance of info-fuzzy models was slightly worse than the performance of the neural network. However this gap may be explained by the power transformations applied to the original variables before training the ANN algorithm [8]. The results of IFN algorithms presented here are based on the raw, untransformed values of all features. In any case, these results confirm again the information-theoretic properties of M-IFN by showing a slight decrease in the average error of M-IFN vs. the overall error of the seven single-objective models. We also observe a 54% decrease in the number of hidden nodes and a 50% decrease in the number of rules as a result of using a multi-objective info-fuzzy model, which on average provides us with more accurate predictions than the single-objective info-fuzzy models.

Table 4. COIL 1999 Data: Summary of Results

	Neural Network	IFN	M-IFN	Change vs. IFN
RMSE	9.069	9.841	9.657	-1.9%
Internal Nodes		37	17	-54.1%
Prediction Rules		24	12	-50.0%

5 Conclusions

In this paper, we have introduced a novel classification algorithm called M-IFN (Multi-objective Info-Fuzzy Network) for inducing an oblivious decision graph from a multi-objective data set. Using theoretical analysis and empirical evaluation, we have shown that multi-objective algorithms in general and the M-IFN algorithm in particular have a sound potential for producing compact and accurate classification models in a complex and multi-faceted learning environment.

Adaptation of other classification algorithms, such as C4.5, for the multi-objective classification task has yet to be explored. In addition, it would be interesting to see applications of M-IFN and other multi-objective classification algorithms to real-world learning tasks in health care, time series analysis, and other areas. Multi-objective models can also contribute to design of black-box test cases for multi-output software systems [22]. The information-theoretic properties of M-IFN suggest that multi-objective classification can be enhanced by analyzing dependency relations between class dimensions. This is another important direction for future research.

Acknowledgement. This work was partially supported by the National Institute for Systems Test and Productivity at University of South Florida under the USA Space and Naval Warfare Systems Command Grant No. N00039-01-1-2248.

References

1. Babu H. & Sasao T. (1998). Shared Multi-Terminal Binary Decision Diagrams for Multi-ple-Output Functions. *IEICE Trans. Fundamentals of Electronics, Communications and Computer Sciences*, Vol. E81-A, No.12, pp. 2545-2553.
2. Babu, H. & Sasao T. (1999). Representations of Multiple-Output Functions Using Binary Decision Diagrams for Characteristic Functions. *IEICE Trans. Fundamentals*, Vol. E82-A, No. 11, pp. 2398 – 2406.
3. Blake, C. & Merz C. J. (2000). UCI Repository of Machine Learning Databases. Machine-readable data repository, Department of Information and Computer Science, University of California at Irvine, Irvine, CA. Available at
  [http://www.ics.uci.edu/~mlearn/MLRepository.html]
4. Breiman, L., Friedman, J.H., Olshen, R.A., & Stone, P.J. (1984). Classification and Re-gression Trees, Wadsworth.
5. Bryant, R. E. (1986). Graph-Based Algorithms for Boolean Function Manipulation. *IEEE Transactions on Computers*, C-35-8, 677-691.
6. Caruana, R. (1993). Multitask Learning: A Knowledge-Based Source of Inductive Bias. Proceedings of the 10th International Conference on Machine Learning, ML-93, Univer-sity of Massachusetts, Amherst, pp. 41-48.
7. Caruana, R. (1997). Multitask Learning. *Machine Learning*, 28, pp. 41–75.
8. Chan, R. (1999). Protecting Rivers & Streams by Monitoring Chemical Concentrations and Algae Communities. In: The 3rd International Competition of Data Analysis by Intel-ligent Techniques [http://www.erudit.de/erudit/competitions/ic-99/]
9. Cover T. M. & Thomas, J.A. (1991). *Elements of Information Theory*, Wiley.
10. Dietterich, T. G., Hild, H., & Bakiri, G. (1995). A Comparison of ID3 and Backpropaga-tion for English Text-to speech Mapping. Machine Learning, 18 (1), pp. 51-80.
11. Fayyad U. & Irani, K. (1993). Multi-Interval Discretization of Continuous-Valued Attrib-utes for Classification Learning. Proc. Thirteenth Int'l Joint Conference on Artificial Intel-ligence, pp. 1022-1027, San Mateo, CA.
12. Fayyad, U., Piatetsky-Shapiro, G., & Smyth, P. (1996). From Data Mining to Knowledge Discovery: An Overview. In U., Piatetsky-Shapiro, G., Smyth, P. & Uthurusamy, R. (Eds.), *Advances in Knowledge Discovery and Data Mining*, Fayyad, AAAI/MIT Press.
13. GVU's WWW User Survey (1998). Georgia Tech Research Corporation.
  [www.gvu.gatech.edu/user_surveys].
14. Han, T.S. (1978). Nonnegative Entropy Measures of Multivariate Symmetric Correlations, *Information and Control*, 36 (2):133-156.
15. Han J. & Kamber, M. (2001). *Data Mining: Concepts and Techniques*, Morgan Kauf-mann.
16. Hettich, S. & Bay, S. D. (1999). The UCI KDD Archive [http://kdd.ics.uci.edu]. Irvine, CA: University of California, Department of Information and Computer Science.
17. Kohavi, R. (1994). Bottom-Up Induction of Oblivious Read-Once Decision Graphs, Pro-ceedings of the European Conference on Machine Learning.
18. Kohavi R. & Li, C-H. (1995). Oblivious Decision Trees, Graphs, and Top-Down Pruning, Proc. of International Joint Conference on Artificial Intelligence (IJCAI), pages 1071-1077.
19. M. Last, Y. Klein, A. Kandel (2001). Knowledge Discovery in Time Series Databases. *IEEE Transactions on Systems, Man, and Cybernetics*, Volume 31: Part B, No. 1, pp. 160-169.
20. Last, M. (2002). Online Classification of Nonstationary Data Streams", *Intelligent Data Analysis*, Vol. 6, No. 2, pp. 129-147.
21. Last M. & Maimon, O. (2004). A Compact and Accurate Model for Classification. *IEEE Transactions on Knowledge and Data Engineering*, Vol. 16, No. 2, pp. 203-215.

22. Last, M., Friedman, M. & Kandel, A. (2003). The Data Mining Approach to Automated Software Testing. *Proceedings of the Ninth ACM SIGKDD International Conference on Knowledge Discovery and Data Mining (KDD-2003)*. pp. 388 - 396.
23. Maimon O. & Last, M. (2000). *Knowledge Discovery and Data Mining – The Info-Fuzzy Network (IFN) Methodology*. Kluwer Academic Publishers, Massive Computing, Boston.
24. Minato, S. (1996). Graph-Based Representations of Discrete Functions. In Sasao T. & Fujita M. (Eds.), *Representations of Discrete Functions*. Kluwer Academic Publishers, pp. 1 – 28,
25. Mitchell, T.M. (1997). *Machine Learning*, McGraw-Hill.
26. Provost, F. & Domingos P. (2003). Tree Induction for Probability-Based Ranking. Machine Learning, 52, pp. 199–215.
27. Quinlan, J. R. (1993). *C4.5: Programs for Machine Learning*. Morgan Kaufmann.
28. Rao C.R. & Toutenburg, H. (1995). Linear Models: Least Squares and Alternatives. Springer-Verlag.
29. E. Suzuki, M. Gotoh, and Y. Choki (2001). Bloomy Decision Tree for Multi-objective Classification. L. De Raedt and A. Siebes (Eds.): *PKDD 2001*, LNAI 2168, pp.436 –447.
30. Last M. & Friedman M. (2004). Black-Box Testing with Info-Fuzzy Networks. In Last, M., Kandel, A., and Bunke H. (Eds.), *Artificial Intelligence Methods in Software Testing*, World Scientific, pp. 21-50.

Improving Progressive Sampling
via Meta-learning on Learning Curves

Rui Leite and Pavel Brazdil

LIACC/FEP, University of Porto
Rua do Campo Alegre, 823, 4150-180 Porto
{rleite,pbrazdil}@liacc.up.pt

Abstract. This paper describes a method that can be seen as an improvement of the standard progressive sampling. The standard method uses samples of data of increasing size until accuracy of the learned concept cannot be further improved. The issue we have addressed here is how to avoid using some of the samples in this progression. The paper presents a method for predicting the stopping point using a meta-learning approach. The method requires just four iterations of the progressive sampling. The information gathered is used to identify the nearest learning curves, for which the sampling procedure was carried out fully. This in turn permits to generate the prediction regards the stopping point. Experimental evaluation shows that the method can lead to significant savings of time without significant losses of accuracy.

1 Introduction

The existence of large datasets creates problems for many data mining algorithms that are readily available. Memory requirements and processing times are often rather excessive. Besides, using all the data does not always lead to marked improvements. The models generated on the basis of a part of the data (sample) are often precise enough for the given aim, while the computational cost involved is incomparably lower.

These problems have motivated research in different data reduction methods. In this paper we are concerned with one particular data reduction method, which is oriented towards reducing the number of examples to be used, and is often referred to as sampling.

The aim of the sampling methods is, in general, to determine which proportion of the data should be used to generate the given model type (e.g. a decision tree). At the same time, we want the model to be comparable to the model that would be generated using all the available data. The existing methods can be divided into two groups: Static sampling methods and dynamic sampling methods [3]. As for the first group, the aim is generate a sample by examining the data, but without considering the particular machine learning algorithm to be used afterwards. Some researchers refer to this method as a *filter approach*.

In contrast to this the *dynamic sampling methods* take the machine learning algorithm into account. The final sample is determined by searching though the space of alternatives. The system explores the alternatives in a systematic

J.-F. Boulicaut et al. (Eds.): ECML 2004, LNAI 3201, pp. 250–261, 2004.

manner and the performance of the machine learning algorithm is used to guide the future search. Some researchers refer to this method as a *wrapper approach*. It was shown that the dynamic (wrapper) methods obtain in general better results than the static (filter) methods, although they tend to be slower [3].

One particular dynamic method that can be used in conjunction with large datasets is called *efficient progressive sampling* [2]. The method starts with a small data sample and in each subsequent step uses progressively larger sample to generate a model and to check its performance. This continues until no significant increase in accuracy is observed. One important characteristic is the size of the samples used in each subsequent step. The sizes follow a geometric progression. Another important aspect is how convergence is detected. The authors use a method referred to as LRLS (linear regression with local sampling). This method works as follows. Supposing the algorithm is examining sample n_i, LRLS uses 10 samples of similar size to generate models and estimate their accuracies. These estimates are supplied to linear regression algorithm and the inclination of the resulting line is examined. If it is about horizontal (i.e. the inclination is sufficiently near to zero), the process of sampling is terminated. As it was shown by the authors, this method worked well with the large datasets considered. However, a question arises when exactly this method is useful.

We have re-implemented a similar method and used it on a conjunction of both large and medium size datasets. We have verified that in many medium size datasets the method required more time than a simple scheme that would learn from all the data. This is easy to explain. The method constructs a succession of models using progressively increasing samples. However, in many cases the accuracy will simply keep increasing and hence the stopping condition will not be satisfied. This means that the algorithm will process all the data, but with an additional overhead of using a succession of increasing samples beforehand.

Our aim was to improve the method so that it could be applied to any dataset, no matter what its size is. The basis strategy relies on eliminating some samples from consideration. We use previous knowledge about the algorithm itself, that is, meta-learning on past results. This is justified by quite good previous results with this technique [6].

The rest of the paper is organized as follows. Section 2 describes the proposed method in detail. Section 3 describes the evaluation method and experimental results obtained. Finally, we present the conclusions.

2   Predicting the Stopping Point in Sampling

Dynamic sampling methods use a succession of models generated by a given learning algorithm on the basis of a sequence of progressively increasing samples. The aim is to determine the point in which the accuracy does not increase any more. We call this point a stopping point. Fig. 1 shows a typical learning curve and the stopping point is represented by p^*. Our aim is to predict the point p^* using an initial segment consisting of #p points. Let us examine again the learning curve represented in Fig. 1. Suppose the points p_1, p_2, p_3 and p_4

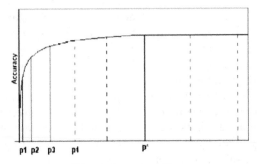

Fig. 1. Learning Curve

constitute the initial segment. So, our aim is to estimate the stopping point using these four points, without considering the points further on.

The prediction of p^* is done on the basis of previous knowledge about the algorithm in question. The knowledge used is in the form of learning curves obtained before on other (similar) datasets. The aim is to use these curves to predict the stopping point on a curve that is only partly known (we have information about the initial segment only).

The details of this method are described in the following. First, we will discuss how the learning curves are represented. Then, we will show how certain learning curves are identified on the basis of existing information for the purpose of prediction. Finally, we show how the prediction of the stopping point is generated. The reader can consult Fig. 2. for an overview of the method.

2.1 Representation of Learning Curves and Identifying the Stopping Point

Suppose we have datasets $\{D_1, D_2, ..., D_n\}$ and for each one we have a learning curve available (later we will discuss a variant of this basic method which uses N learning curves per dataset). Each learning curve is represented by a vector

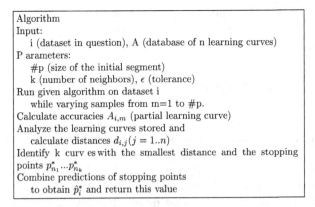

Algorithm
Input:
    i (dataset in question), A (database of n learning curves)
P arameters:
    #p (size of the initial segment)
    k (number of neighbors), ϵ (tolerance)
Run given algorithm on dataset i
    while varying samples from m=1 to #p.
Calculate accuracies $A_{i,m}$ (partial learning curve)
Analyze the learning curves stored and
    calculate distances $d_{i,j}(j = 1..n)$
Identify k curv es with the smallest distance and the stopping points $p^*_{n_1} ... p^*_{n_k}$
Combine predictions of stopping points
    to obtain $\hat{p}^*_i$ and return this value

Fig. 2. The basic algorithm for predicting stopping points

$< A_{i,1}, A_{i,2}, .., A_{i,z} >$, where $A_{i,m}$ represents the accuracy of the given algorithm on dataset D_i on m-th sample in the sequence. Following Provost et al. [2] the sizes follow a geometric progression. The sequence spans across the whole dataset.

The particular stopping point p_i^* for dataset i can be readily identified. This is done as follows. First, we identify the global maximum using $A_{i,pmax} = max(A_{i,j})$. Then, given a tolerance ϵ, we identify the earliest point in the sequence whose accuracy is within the tolerance limit of the global maximum. This can be formulated as follows:

$$p_i^* = min\{n : |A_{i,pmax} - A_{i,n}| < \epsilon\} \tag{1}$$

2.2 Identification of Appropriate Learning Curves for the Purpose of Prediction

Suppose we are interested in dataset D and we have information about the initial segment of the learning curve (e.g. the first #p=4 points). We employ a nearest neighbor algorithm (k-NN) to identify similar datasets (as in [6]) and retrieve the appropriate learning curves. Here the k-NN algorithm represents a meta-learner that helps us to resolve the issue of predicting the stopping point. As k-NN uses a distance measure to identify k similar cases, we need to adapt the method to our problem. Here we just use the information concerning the initial segment. The distance function between datasets D_i and D_j is defined by

$$d(i,j) = \sum_{m=1}^{\#p} (A_{i,m} - A_{j,m})^2 \tag{2}$$

where m spans across the initial segment.

2.3 Generating the Prediction Concerning the Stopping Point

Once k learning curves have been identified, we can generate the prediction regards the stopping point on a new curve. This is done by retrieving the stopping points associated with k learning curves and generating a prediction using this information. Let us see how this is done in detail.

Let the associated indeces of the k most similar learning curves be n_1, $n_2, ..., n_k$. Then let the stopping points of each curve be $p_{n_1}^*, p_{n_2}^*, ..., p_{n_k}^*$. In general, the values can differ. One obvious way to estimate the stopping point p_i on the basis of this information is by using the *median* (or the *mean*) value[1].

2.4 Using Aggregated Learning Curves

It is a well known fact that the performance of many algorithms may vary substantially, as data is drawn from a given source. This phenomenon is usually

---

[1] In all experiments reported here we have used the *median*, as it is less sensitive to outliers.

referred to as variance [4]. The problem is even more apparent if we use small samples. As a consequence, the learning curves do not always look like the one shown in Fig. 1 which is monotonically increasing. The curves obtained from real data often include points that appear to jump up and down. This has an adverse effect on the method described earlier.

To minimize this problem we have decided to generate a smoothed-out curve on the basis of N learning curves per dataset. Each individual learning curve is obtained using a different portion of the data, using a method similar to N cross-validation. Each point $A_{i,m}$, the m-th point of smoothed curve for dataset i, represents the mean of the corresponding points of the individual learning curves.

In the following the method described in this section is referred to shortly as MPS (meta-learning + progressive sampling).

3   Empirical Evaluation

To evaluate the method MPS proposed above we have used the leave-one-out evaluation strategy. We identify a dataset, say D_i, and the aim is to predict the stopping point for this dataset. All other datasets except D_i (and with the associated initial segments) are used to generate the prediction $\hat{p}_i^*$, in the way described earlier. The predicted stopping point is compared to the true stopping point (retrieved from our database). Besides, we also compare the errors associated with the two stopping points and the times used to obtain each solution.

We have used 60 datasets in the evaluation. Some come from UCI [1], others were used within project METAL [5]. All datasets used are shown in Table 2 in the Appendix.

The samples are generated using a geometric progression as follows. The size of m_i-th sample is set to the rounded value of $2^{6+0.5 \times m_i}$. Thus the size of the first sample is $2^{6.5}$, giving 91 after rounding, and the second sample is 2^7, giving 128 etc. Table 1 shows the relationship between the sample number and the actual sample size.

Table 1. Relationship between the sample number and the actual sample size

m	1	2	3	4	5 ...	10	15	20	25
size	91	128	181	256	362 ...	2048	11585	65536	370728

We have used C5.0 [8] as the base algorithm. That is, our aim was to predict the stopping point of C5.0 on the basis of the initial segment. In the experiments reported here the initial segment included 4 points (#p=4). The tolerance limit ϵ was set to 0.001. In the experiments presented here we also used the dataset size as a predictive attribute. For each dataset we have retrieved a smoothed-out curve.

Regards the meta-learning method, we have used k-NN. In the experiments reported here k was set to 3^2.

3.1   Results Concerning Savings and Losses

The results obtained are shown in Fig. 3. As we can see, there is on the whole quite good agreement between the predicted stopping point and the true value. Here we use the re-scaled values shown in Table 1. The points can be divided into three groups. The first one includes perfect predictions ($\hat{p}_i = p_i^*$). The second group includes all cases for which $\hat{p}_i < p_i^*$. That is, if we followed the prediction, the sampling process would terminate somewhat prematurely. In general, one would expect that this would affect the error of the base algorithm (in general the error will be a bit larger than it would be, if it terminated at the right point). The third group includes all cases for which $\hat{p}_i > p_i^*$. In general, this will not affect the error, unless of course, the base algorithm suffers from overfitting.

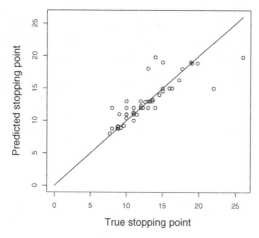

Fig. 3. Comparison between predicted and true stopping points

We can analyse the situation in Fig. 3 more closely and examine the differences between the predicted and the true value and calculate The Mean Absolute Error (MAE). This calculation gives the value 1.04. In other words, our predictions are about 1.04 steps off the ideal value.

Let us now see what would happen if we used a fixed prediction throughout. The best fixed prediction is the mean of the true stopping points (12.59). If we used this, the Mean Absolute Error (MAE) would be 2.67. This value is substantially larger than the value obtained using the method MPS.

We can analyse the computational savings achieved. We compare two situations. One involves using the traditional progressive sampling method while

---

[2] This value lead to the best results. Later on we discuss this issue further.

trying to identify the true stopping point. In general we need to run through at least p_i^* points.

The second situation involves our method, that is training the base algorithm on #p=4 points to be able to obtain the predicted stopping point. In addition, we need to train the base algorithm on the corresponding sample. So we can compare how many points we effectively skip and this gives an indication of the computational savings. If we carry out the calculations, we see that on average the savings is 7.6 points (varying between 2 and 20). That is, our method avoids constructing and evaluating at least 7x10 classifiers on average when compared to the progressive sampling method.

3.2   Results Concerning Actual Times and Accuracies

The analysis presented so far was oriented towards comparing the predicted stopping point with the actual one. In this section we will provide figures concerning actual times, and also, analyse the impact of being off target on accuracy of the base algorithm.

In Fig. 4 we compare the times of two approaches. The first one is our method (MPS), which requires training #p+1 classifiers (vertical axis). The second one is the baseline method representing a simplified version of the progressive sampling method [2] (horizontal axis). As can be seen in practically all datasets the method leads to time significant savings. Our method is 12.25 faster on average.

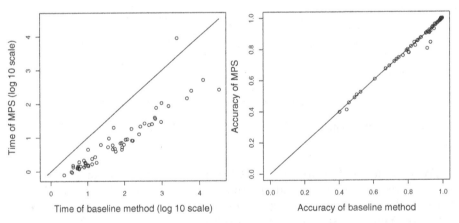

Fig. 4. Comparison of total training times   **Fig. 5.** Comparison of accuracies

The comparison of accuracies of the two methods for various datasets is shown in Fig. 5. The differences in accuracies for the two methods are relatively small. However, as could be expected, the accuracy of our method is a bit lower than the accuracy of the baseline method. On average the difference is 0.51%. This could be considered as the price to pay for the speed-up.

Closer analysis shows that for 32 datasets the difference is zero. On the other hand, in few datasets there is a noticeable difference. This is due to the fact that the method has identified a stopping point which is in fact premature.

4 Parameters of Our Method: The Values Used and Future Work

The method described involves various parameters. Our aim here is to briefly review the set of parameters involved and justify why certain choices were made and discuss futher work.

As has been pointed out earlier, the method requires that experiments be conducted on different datasets. The aim of these is to obtain learning curves that are stored for future use together with the true stopping point. As each learning curve is represented by a sequence of points, we need to determine how the learning curves are represented, how many learning curves are constructed per dataset and how the true stopping point is identified.

Given a new dataset, the method uses a k-NN to identify the most similar cases. In this step we need to determine the size of the initial segment of the learning curve in the matching procedure and which characteristics of the dataset should be taken into account. Finally we need to set the value of k in the k-NN procedure.

All these parameters can be varied and we could study what the effects of these variations on the overall result. We have done some studies to this effect, but obviously an exhaustive study is not practicable. In the following we give a short overview of our position on these issues and point out to further work that could be carried out.

Choice of Datasets: The study carried out by Provost et al [2] was limited to relatively few large datasets. We have used many more datasets (60) here, but we did not follow any particular strategy when selecting these. Further work could be carried out to see what the results would be if we focused the study on certain datasets only (e.g. datasets above certain size or satisfying some other criterion).

Representation of the Learning Curve: Each learning curve is represented by a sequence of points. The sample sizes follow a geometric progression. Both the initial size (91 cases) and the increment represent parameters of the method are considered fixed. Other settings could be tried in future, although we do not think the results could be improved dramatically this way. Besides, instead of saving point-to-point information about learning curves, one could take a model-based approach. In principle it would be possible to fit a predefined type of curve through the points and save the curve parameters. The distance measure could then be redefined accordingly. As the curve fitting is subject to errors, it remains to be seen, whether this approach would lead to better results.

Number of Curves Constructed per Dataset: We have used both a single curve and N=10 curves per dataset. As has been pointed out earlier, the N curves were compacted into a single aggregated smoothed-out curve. The results with this curve (representing 10 individual curves) were much better than the results with a single curve. The number of curves (10 in our case) is a parameter of the method. Further work could be done to determine the advantages / disadvantages of using other values. In one earlier study [7] we have used also 10 curves per dataset, without generating a smoothed-out curve. The k-NN matching procedure was more complex. The initial segment obtained on a new dataset was then matched against all the individual curves and average distance calculated. The overall results were comparable to the results presented here. The advantage of using smoothed-out curves is that the matching procedure is much simpler. A more comprehensive comparison could be carried out in future. Besides, we could try to establish whether one method is significantly better than another.

Detection of the True Stopping Point: As has been described earlier the detection of the true stopping point involves constant ϵ, which was set to 0.001 (the differences of accuracy less than this value are considered insignificant). The choice of this value affects both the position of the stopping point on a curve and the overall precision of the method. If a larger value were chosen (e.g. 0.01), the stopping point would, in general, appear earlier. More work could be done to characterize the effect of these choices quantitatively.

Size of the Initial Segment of the Learning Curve Used in Matching: As has been pointed out earlier, the size of the initial segment was set to 4 points. We have experimented with other different values. Reducing the number (e.g. to 1,2 or 3) led, on the whole, to comparable or inferior performance. Increasing the number did not seem to bring further benefits and this is why we have settled for the value of 4.

Using Data Characteristics: In this work we have used not only the learning curves, but in addition, used one particular characteristic of the dataset, which is dataset size (i.e. number of cases). Dropping this attribute led to marked decrease of performance (MAD would rise from 1.04 to 1.89).In future we intend to investigate whether some other characteristics could be useful (e.g. number or entropy of classes etc.).

Weights of the Initial Segment and the Dataset Characteristics: As the k-NN matching procedure uses both the initial segment consisting of N points and one characteristic - the dataset size - it is important to determine the weights that should be attributed to each of these items in the k-NN matching procedure.

We have begun by using equal weights for all parts, but then found that this was not the best setting. To our surprise the best results were obtained when relatively large weight was attributed to dataset size (94%), and relatively little weight to the initial segment (6%). Despite its rather small weight, the initial segment was important. If it were dropped all together (corresponding to giving it weight 0), the overall MAD value would rise from 1.04 to 1.2.

An interesting question arises why the dataset size appears to be so important. We have carried out a study to clarify this. The results are shown in Fig. 6, showing where the stopping points lie for different datasets. Each dataset is represented by a point positioned at a particular coordinate X,Y. The X coordinate (horizontal axis) corresponds to the dataset size and Y coordinate (the vertical axis) to the stopping point. Both values are rescaled values, expressed in terms of the points in the geometrical progression adopted (see Table 1 for details on re-scaling). As can be seen many points lie on the diagonal. These are the datasets for which the stopping point lies exactly at the end. In all these cases the best thing to do is to use all the data. The finding above suggests that

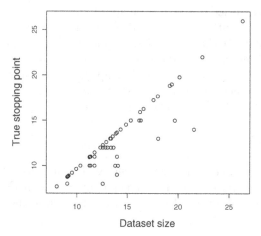

Fig. 6. Dataset sizes vs stopping points (both expressed in terms of the number of the sample)

we could use a simplified method probably without deterioration of performance. If we can confidently classify a case using a k-NN on the basis of the dataset size only, we could skip construction of the initial segment. Future work could be carried out, to evaluate how this would work in practice. Another interesting issue is how well the method would work if we focussed the attention on large datasets only, where presumably the stopping point does not coincide with the full data. This will be investigated in future.

Value of k in the k-NN Procedure: In our experiments we have used the value k=3. We have experimented with other different values (both lower and higher than 3), but the results were on the whole comparable or inferior to the ones obtained with the setting used. These results could be validated further by conducting further experiments.

5   Conclusions

We have described a method that can be seen as an improvement of the standard progressive sampling. We have been concerned with the issue of how to avoid using some of the samples in this progression. We have employed a meta-learning approach that enables us to predict the position of the stopping point. The method requires just four iterations of the progressive sampling and the information gathered is used to identify the nearest learning curves. This in turn permits to generate the prediction regards the stopping point.

We have carried out experimental evaluation of the method using 60 datasets. We have shown that the method can lead to significant savings of time. The experimental results indicate that it is possible to skip 7 or 8 samples on average, leading to significant savings of time. On average our method is 12.25 faster than the standard method. The accuracy of the method presented is a bit lower, but this is an acceptable price to pay for the speed-up.

The work carried out led to some unexpected surprises, however. We have found that some dataset characteristics, such as dataset size, are quite informative and help to improve the results. We have carried out a study that helps to explain why the dataset size appears to be important. An interesting issue arises whether there are other characteristics that could be used, which would work even better, this should be investigated in future.

Acknowledgments

The authors wish to thank anonymous referees for their useful comments. The authors gratefully acknowledge the financial support from FCT within multi-annual funding (Financiamento Pluriannual) attributed to the Portuguese R&D Units.

References

1. Blake C.L. and Merz C.J. UCI repository of machine learning databases, 1998.
2. Provost Foster J., Jensen David, and Oates Tim. Efficient progressive sampling. In *Knowledge Discovery and Data Mining*, pages 23–32, 1999.
3. John George H. and Langley Pat. Static versus dynamic sampling for data mining. In Evangelos Simoudis, Jiawei Han, and Usama M. Fayyad, editors, *Proc. 2nd Int. Conf. Knowledge Discovery and Data Mining, KDD*, pages 367–370. AAAI Press, 2–4 1996.
4. Breiman L. Bias, variance, and arcing classifiers. Technical Report 460, Statistics Department, University of California, 1996.
5. Metal project site. http://www.metal-kdd.org/.
6. Brazdil P., Soares C., and Costa J. Ranking learning algorithms: Using IBL and meta-learning on accuracy and time results. *Machine Learning*, 50:251–277, 2003.
7. Leite R. and Brazdil P. Improving progressive sampling via meta-learning. In *Progress in Artificial Intelligence, 11th Portuguese AI Conference (EPIA03)*. Springer-Verlag, 2003.
8. Quinlan R. C5.0 "an informal tutorial". RuleQuest, http://www.rulequest.com/see5-info.html, 1998.

Appendix

Table 2. Datasets used

dataset	n cases	dataset	n cases	dataset	n cases
acetylation	1511	connect.4	67557	Adult	32560
covtype	581012	Byzantine	17750	dis	3772
contraceptive	1473	heart.disease.clev.	1541	dna.splice	3186
hypothyroid	3163	ibm.stock.val	8087	isolet	7797
injury.severity	7636	krkopt	28056	internetad	3279
kr.vs.kp	3196	led24	3200	letter.recognition	20000
led7	3200	mfeat	2000	mushrooms	8124
musk.clean2	6598	mushrooms.exp	8416	nettalk	146934
musk	6598	nursery	12960	parity	1024
optdigits	5620	quisclas	5891	page.blocks	5473
recljan2jun97	33170	pendigits	10992	task1	111077
pyrimidines	6996	taska.part.hhold	17267	quadrupeds	5000
taska.part.related	18254	sat	6435	taskb.hhold	12934
segmentation	2310	ad	3279	shuttle	58000
adult	48842	sick	3772	agaricus.lepiota	8124
sick.euthyroid	3163	allbp	3772	spambase	4601
allhyper	3772	splice	3190	allhypo	3772
thyroid0387	9172	allrep	3772	triazines	52264
ann	7200	waveform21	5000	car	1728
waveform40	5000	cmc	1473	yeast	1484

Methods for Rule Conflict Resolution

Tony Lindgren

Department of Computer and Systems Sciences,
Stockholm University and Royal Institute of Technology,
Forum 100,
164 40 Kista, Sweden
tony@dsv.su.se

Abstract. When using unordered rule sets, conflicts can arise between the rules, i.e., two or more rules cover the same example but predict different classes. This paper gives a survey of methods used to solve this type of conflict and introduces a novel method called Recursive Induction. In total nine methods for resolving rule conflicts are scrutinised. The methods are explained in detail, compared and evaluated empirically on an number of domains. The results show that Recursive Induction outperforms all previously used methods.

1 Introduction

Two major strategies are used to induce rules in machine learning systems: Divide-And-Conquer (DAC) [9] and Separate-And-Conquer (SAC) [4]. These two strategies induce rules with different characteristics. The main difference is that rules generated by DAC cannot overlap while rules generated by SAC can. Below follows an informal description of DAC and SAC that explains this difference.

DAC divides an overly general rule on an attribute, creating as many new specialised rules (nodes) as there are values for the attribute (in the discrete case). Learning stops when a specific stopping criterion is met (e.g., class purity). A node that has met the stopping criterion is said to be a leaf node. When all nodes have met the stopping criterion the algorithm is finished. The product of DAC induction can be visualised as an upside down tree (hence its other common name, decision tree induction) with the class labels on the end of the branches (the leaf nodes). Each possible path from the root to a leaf can be transformed into a rule or be directly used for classification.

SAC does not divide an attribute on its values exhaustively but rather separates the rule by specialising/generalising the rule with one attribute-value pair at a time (depending if it starts with a overly general rule or an overly specific rule). The stopping criterion is then checked, if it is met, the examples covered by the rule are separated out of the training set. The algorithm then starts over again with an overly general/specific rule to cover the examples left in the training set. This continues until the training set is empty, i.e., all examples have been covered. The induction strategy that SAC uses can lead to rules that cover

J.-F. Boulicaut et al. (Eds.): ECML 2004, LNAI 3201, pp. 262–273, 2004.

the same examples. The rules can be ordered in a hierarchy to avoid conflicts (which results in so called decision lists [12]) or they may be used without any ordering [2, 3].

After inducing rules using SAC, when using these rules for classification, the algorithm may be faced with the problem of having two (or more) rules covering the same example while having different majority classes. This type of conflict must be handled by the classification algorithm. How this type of conflict can be handled is the focus of this work. The problem of solving rule conflicts has not attracted much interest even though there can be significant gains in accuracy made from choosing the right method for solving rule conflicts.

This paper gives a survey of different methods that have been used to solve the problem of rule conflicts in the past, and also introduces a novel method for solving rule conflicts called Recursive Induction. The different methods are compared empirically on a number of domains. It is shown that Recursive Induction outperforms the previously used methods.

The paper is organised as follows. In section 2, a review of the different methods is given, including the novel method Recursive Induction. In section 3, the different methods are compared empirically and the results are presented and discussed. Finally, in section 4, conclusions are made and possible future work is outlined.

2 Different Ways of Resolving Classification Conflicts

In this section, different methods to solve rule conflicts are described. The workings of each method will be illustrated on a hypothetical scenario presented in Figure 1.

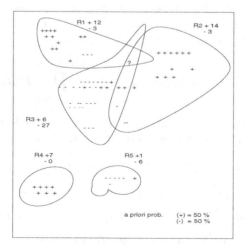

Fig. 1. Three rules covering an example to be classified (marked with '?'). The training examples are labelled with their respective classes (+ and −).

2.1   CN2

The system CN2 [2] resolves classification conflicts between rules in the following way. Given the examples in Figure 1, the class frequencies of the rules that cover the example to be classified (marked with '?') are calculated:

$$C(+) = covers(R_1, +) + covers(R_2, +) + covers(R_3, +) = 32$$
$$C(-) = covers(R_1, -) + covers(R_2, -) + covers(R_3, -) = 33$$

where $covers(R, C)$ gives the number of examples of class C that are covered by Rule R. This means that CN2 would classify the example as belonging to the negative class $(-)$. More generally:

$$CN2 = argmax_{C_i \in Classes} \sum_{j=1}^{|CovRules|} covers(R_j, C_i)$$

where $CovRules$ is the set of rules that cover the example to be classified, and $covers$ is the function defined above.

2.2   Naive Bayes Classification

In the machine learning system of Rule Discovery System (RDS) [10], naive Bayes is used to resolve rule conflicts. Bayes theorem is as follows:

$$P(C|R_1 \wedge \ldots \wedge R_n) = P(C) \frac{P(R_1 \wedge \ldots \wedge R_n|C)}{P(R_1 \wedge \ldots \wedge R_n)}$$

where C is a class label for the example to be classified and $R_1 \ldots R_n$ are the rules that cover the example. As usual, since $P(R_1 \wedge \ldots \wedge R_n)$ does not affect the relative order of different hypotheses according to probability, it is ignored. Assuming (naively) that $P(R_1 \wedge \ldots \wedge R_n|C) = P(R_1|C) \ldots P(R_n|C)$, the maximum a posteriori probable hypothesis (MAP) is:

$$h_{MAP} = argmax_{C_i \in Classes} P(C_i) \prod_{R_j \in Rules}^{|CovRules|} P(R_j|C_i)$$

where $CovRules$ is the set of rules that covers the example to be classified. If we again consider the example shown in Figure 1, we get:

$$P(+|R_1 \wedge R_2 \wedge R_3) = P(+) * P(R_1|+) * P(R_2|+) * P(R_3|+) =$$

$$40/80 * 12/40 * 14/40 * 6/40 = 0.0079$$

$$P(-|R_1 \wedge R_2 \wedge R_3) = P(-) * P(R_1|-) * P(R_2|-) * P(R_3|-) =$$

$$40/80 * 3/40 * 3/40 * 27/40 = 0.0019$$

This means that the naive Bayes classification results in that the example with the unknown class label is classified as positive $(+)$.

Note that if a rule involved in a conflict does not cover any examples of a particular class, this would eliminate the chances for that class to be selected, even if there are several other rules that cover the example with a high probability for that class. To overcome this problem, Laplace-1 correction (described in [6]) is used in the experiments.

2.3   C5.0/See5

The machine learning system C5.0/See5 produced by RuleQuest Research [11] uses a voting method to solve rule conflicts. Each applicable rule votes for its predicted class with a weight equal to the probability of the given class, the votes are summed up, and the class with the highest probability is chosen as the final prediction.

$$See5(voting) = argmax_{C_i \in Classes} \sum_{j=1}^{|CovRules|} \begin{cases} P(C_i|R_j) \ if \ P = max \ P \ for \ R_j \\ 0 \qquad\qquad otherwise \end{cases}$$

Here $CovRules$ is the set of rules that covers the example to be classified. In the tutorial of See5 [11] another method for resolving rule conflicts is mentioned, and that uses the rule with the highest probability (confidence) of all the rules in conflict.

$$See5(max\,prob) = argmax_{C_i \in Classes} P(C_i|R_j \in CovRules)$$

Both these methods are used in our experiments. Applying these methods to the situation in Figure 1 leads to the following:

$$See5(voting) = P(+|R_1) + P(+|R_2) + P(+|R_3)$$
$$= 12/40 + 14/40 + 0 = 26/40$$
$$See5(voting) = P(-|R_1) + P(-|R_2) + P(-|R_3) = 0 + 0 + 27/40 = 27/40$$
$$See5(max\,prob) = P(+|R_1) = 12/40, \ See5(max\,prob) = P(-|R_1) = 3/40$$
$$See5(max\,prob) = P(+|R_2) = 14/40, \ See5(max\,prob) = P(-|R_2) = 3/40$$
$$See5(max\,prob) = P(+|R_3) = 6/40, \ See5(max\,prob) = P(-|R_3) = 27/40$$

Here we see that both methods would assign the negative $(-)$ class to the example.

2.4   Intersecting Rules

The idea behind Intersecting Rules [7] is that one should use the information in the intersection of the conflicting rules. If there are not any training examples in the intersection of the examples in conflict, Intersecting rules partition these rules in as few non-empty partitions as possible and uses these partitions to find the most probable class.

If we would use Intersecting Rules on the example scenario in Figure 1 where no training example is present in the intersection of these three rules, the partitions would be: R_2, R_3 and R_1 as the intersection between R_2 and R_3 is non-empty. This gives the following probabilities:

$$P(+|R_1 \wedge R_2 \wedge R_3) = P(+) * P(R_2 \wedge R_3|+) * P(R_1|+) =$$
$$40/80 * 2/40 * 12/39 = 0.00769$$
$$P(-|R_1 \wedge R_2 \wedge R_3) = P(-) * P(R_2 \wedge R_3|-) * P(R_1|-) =$$
$$40/80 * 1/40 * 3/39 = 0.000962$$

Here Intersecting Rules would assign the positive (+) class to the example. Consider again the scenario in the Figure 1 with the exception that training examples do reside in the intersection between R_1 and R_3. In this case two possible partitions are possible. The previously used partition and R_1, R_3 and R_2. In this paper two different methods are used to handle the problem of multiple partitions. The first method computes the joint class-probability of the partitions and selects the class with the highest probability. The second method computes the maximum class-probability for each partition and selects the class with the highest probability, and hence selects one partition (dependency model). The latter method was used in [7], while the former is new.

It is worth noting two things about Intersecting Rules. First, if indeed there are examples in the intersection, Intersecting Rules is really just using Bayes rule to compute the most probable class. If it is necessary to partition the rules, Intersecting Rules is essentially moving from an assumption of dependence between the rules towards independence. Hence if no non-empty partitions are found at all, the method degenerates to the naive Bayes classifier.

2.5   Double Induction

The idea of Double Induction [8] is to induce new rules based on the examples that are covered by the rules in conflict. By doing so, a completely fresh set of rules is obtained, tailor-made to separate the examples in this subset of the whole domain. By concentrating on a small subspace of the example space there is a higher chance to find rules that separate the classes better. These new rules are then used to classify the unlabelled example, either with naive Bayes (if there is a conflict) or directly. The Double Induction algorithm is given in Table 1.

2.6   Recursive Induction

Recursive Induction extends Double Induction in the following way: When inducing new rules from the examples covered by the conflicting rules, if these newly induced rules have rule conflicts between them Recursive Induction does yet another induction, using the examples covered by the rules of this "new" rule conflict. Two different stopping conditions are used by Recursive Induction. The first stops learning if the induction algorithm cannot find rules that differ from the rules that were previously induced. The second stopping condition uses the naive Bayes most probable class value as a quality measure of the rules induced. If the value for the most probable class decreases from one induction round to the next, the learning is stopped. In our experiments, we use two different versions of Recursive Induction, one which only uses the first stopping

Table 1. The Double Induction algorithm.

Input: R_1 = rules from the first induction round, e = example to be
classified, E_1 = training examples
Output: C = a class assigned to e

```
collect all rules R₁,ₑ ⊆ R₁ that cover e
if conflictingRules(R₁,ₑ) then
    collect all training examples E₂ ⊆ E₁ covered by R₁,ₑ
    induce new rules R₂ from E₂
    collect all rules R₂,ₑ ⊆ R₂ that cover e
    if conflictingRules(R₂,ₑ) then
        let C = naiveBayes(R₂,ₑ,E₂)
    else let C = majorityClass(R₂,ₑ)
else let C = majorityClass(R₁,ₑ)
```

condition and another version which utilises both stopping conditions. If any of
theses conditions hold, then the algorithm stops and naive Bayes is used to solve
the conflict (using the previous set of rules). Otherwise new rules are induced
recursively until no conflict is present in the rule set. The Recursive Induction
algorithm is given in Table 2.

Table 2. The Recursive Induction algorithm.

Input: R_n = rules from the n:th induction round, e = example to be
classified, E_n = training examples
Output: C = a class assigned to e

```
collect all rules Rₙ,ₑ ⊆ Rₙ that cover e
  if conflictingRules(Rₙ,ₑ) then
    collect all training examples Eₙ' ⊆ Eₙ covered by Rₙ,ₑ
    induce new rules Rₙ' from Eₙ'
    collect all rules Rₙ',ₑ ⊆ Rₙ' that cover e
    if Rₙ,ₑ same Rₙ',ₑ (or nBquality(Rₙ,ₑ,Eₙ) > nBquality(Rₙ',ₑ,Eₙ')) then
      let C = naiveBayes(Rₙ,ₑ,Eₙ)
    else call Recursive Induction with Rₙ', e and Eₙ'
  else let C = majorityClass(Rₙ,ₑ)
```

A few things are worth noting: The number of examples used to induce new
rules is always decreasing or constant but is never increasing. So iteratively the
example-space that the induction algorithm has to cope with shrinks. When
inducing rules, the examples are randomly divided into two halves in order to
create a grow set (to induce rules) and a prune set (to prune rules). In Recursive
Induction and Double Induction this stochastic selection of examples helps the
induction algorithm to avoid getting stuck, i.e., inducing exactly the same set of
rules as before.

In [7] it is empirically shown that it is worthwhile to weight the examples in the intersection as more important than examples outside the intersection, for a correct classification (after all, Bayes theorem only considers the evidence in the intersection). This can be done by a concatenation of all the covered examples of every rule, in which some examples may be present more than once (i.e., a multi-set). An example is present in the multi-set as many times as it is covered by different rules and hence weighted as so many times more important than those examples covered by only one rule. When using this weighting scheme, the induction algorithm focuses on separating the examples located around the example that is to be classified. This weighting scheme is also used in Double Induction.

If the Recursive Induction gets stuck, naive Bayes is used to solve the conflict. The a priori probability is then computed from the examples covered by the previously conflicting rules. This means that the a priori probability reflects the probability distribution of this example-space (contained by the rules in conflict), rather than the a priori probability of the whole domain. This is also the case for Double Induction when using naive Bayes.

Consider again the scenario shown in Figure 1. Given the examples covered by R_1, R_2 and R_3, Separate-and-Conquer may come up with the three new rules shown in Figure 2. The unlabelled example is then classified using these newly induced rules. In our hypothetical scenario, the example is covered by R_6 resulting in that the positive class (+) is assigned to the example.

3   Empirical Evaluation

3.1   Experimental Setting

The search strategy employed in the experiments is Separate-and-Conquer together with information gain to greedily choose what condition to add when

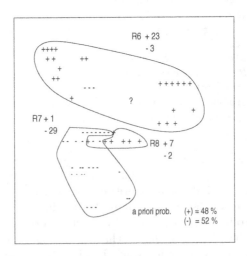

Fig. 2. Three new induced rules.

refining a rule. One half of the training set was used as grow set and the second half was used as pruning set. The rules were pruned using Incremental Reduced Error Pruning (IREP) [5]. These settings were used in all inductions of rules, i.e., both when inducing the initial set of rules and when resolving rule conflicts with Recursive Induction and Double Induction.

The experimental results were obtained by ten-fold cross-validation, with exactly the same rule conflicts to solve for the different methods. All datasets used were taken from the UCI Machine Learning Repository except the King-Rook-King-Illegal (KRKI) database which comes from the Machine Learning group at the University of York, and Titanic dataset which comes from the Delve datasets at the University of Toronto. The datasets used in the experiments are all the possible datasets (in total forty domains) that we could get hold of and run (in reasonable time), and hence use in the experiment. There is quite a diversity of characteristics in the datasets used; from 2 class problems to problems with 24 classes, from datasets with 32 examples to 12960 examples. This diversity will hopefully reveal the behaviour of the different rule conflict resolving methods.

To minimise the amount of work within Recursive Induction, Double Induction and Intersecting Rules, the conflicts already seen (for a particular fold) are saved to allow reuse of the generated rules in the second round whenever the same conflict is observed again (within the same fold).

3.2   Experimental Results

All rule conflict resolution methods were tested on forty domains. In nine of these domains there was no conflict between the rules. The domains without conflict were: Bupa liver-disorders, Ionosphere, Sonar, Pima indians diabetes, Glass, Spambase, SPECTF heart, Post operation patients and Haberman's survival data. The accuracies for the different methods are shown in Table 3. In the first column the domain is denoted, then follows the accuracies for the different methods. The methods are (from left to right): Recursive Induction using naive Bayes as stopping criterion (RI-s), Recursive Induction (RI), Double Induction (DI), Intersecting Rules using highest class-probability (IR), Intersecting Rules using joint highest class-probability (IR-j), naive Bayes (Bayes), Frequency-based classification (CN2), See5 using voting (See5-v) and See5 using highest probability (See5-hp). If there exists a single method that achieves higher accuracy than all other methods for a domain, then this method's accuracy is denoted by bold typesetting in Table 3.

Table 4 shows the significant differences for each method compared with the other methods. Each line in the table shows the number of wins and losses for the method compared to other methods (the methods' names in top of the column). An asterix (*) denotes that the amount of wins and losses is statically significant. The p-value of significance is set to 0.05, the p-value computed with an exact version of McNemar's test. This test was also originally used to compute the statistical significance of the accuracies.

The methods in Table 4 can be divided into three sets with roughly equal performance. The first group contains Recursive Induction, Double Induction

Table 3. Accuracies of the different rule conflict resolving methods.

Domain	RI-s	RI	DI	IR	IR-j	Bayes	CN2	See5-v	See5-hp
Balance scale	82.07	**83.13**	82.43	82.95	79.96	81.90	82.25	81.55	77.15
Car evaluation	82.75	**84.47**	83.70	80.84	80.84	79.69	78.23	82.62	81.67
TicTacToe	98.28	98.39	98.39	98.39	98.28	97.93	85.65	94.49	98.28
Breast cancer	70.38	70.00	70.77	72.69	72.69	72.31	73.46	71.92	69.62
Dermatology	**88.59**	88.29	87.99	85.29	84.98	85.59	83.48	86.49	86.49
C. Voting	94.19	**95.20**	94.95	94.95	94.70	94.44	94.70	94.95	94.95
KRKI	99.34	99.34	99.23	98.68	98.68	98.02	94.84	98.24	99.12
New thyroid	89.29	89.29	89.29	88.78	88.78	88.78	88.78	88.78	88.78
Lymphograpy	81.48	82.22	82.22	79.26	79.26	80.00	77.78	79.26	80.74
Primary tumor	39.48	**42.72**	42.39	40.13	39.81	37.22	35.60	40.78	41.42
Shuttle	98.02	98.02	98.02	96.05	96.05	93.68	93.68	94.47	94.47
Credit	83.92	**85.98**	85.19	83.12	83.60	83.44	82.96	80.89	85.03
Ecoli	80.39	**81.70**	80.72	80.39	80.39	80.07	77.45	80.39	80.39
Hepatitis	80.85	80.85	79.43	79.43	79.43	79.43	79.43	80.85	80.85
Iris	90.51	90.51	90.51	90.51	90.51	90.51	88.32	88.32	90.51
Nursery	80.31	**81.09**	80.65	79.96	79.88	79.87	75.59	79.61	80.49
C. bands	76.78	**77.80**	76.99	73.12	73.52	73.93	69.45	72.10	72.51
Cl. heart	59.06	**59.42**	59.06	57.61	57.61	57.25	57.25	57.97	58.33
Image segmentation	71.73	71.73	71.73	69.11	69.11	69.11	69.11	68.59	67.54
Wine	86.42	86.42	86.42	87.04	87.04	87.04	86.42	86.42	86.42
Audiology	66.48	67.58	67.58	65.38	65.38	59.89	59.89	65.38	65.38
B. c. Wisconsin	93.43	93.43	93.30	93.03	93.03	93.30	92.90	93.16	92.76
KR vs KP	99.24	**99.35**	99.21	99.24	99.24	98.49	95.83	98.69	98.83
Lung cancer	55.17	55.17	**58.62**	51.72	51.72	51.72	51.72	51.72	55.17
Mushroom	100.00	100.00	100.00	100.00	100.00	100.00	98.46	100.00	100.00
Promoters	79.80	78.79	78.79	74.75	73.74	78.79	75.76	79.80	79.80
Sick euthyroid	95.34	**96.42**	95.48	94.37	94.47	92.11	91.90	94.02	92.84
Soybean large	76.07	**78.21**	74.29	63.21	63.21	61.79	60.00	61.43	60.36
Tae	49.64	**56.20**	51.20	44.53	45.26	43.80	43.80	41.61	40.88
Zoo	91.30	91.30	91.30	91.30	91.30	91.30	91.30	89.13	89.13
Titanic	78.81	78.91	78.86	79.11	79.11	78.61	68.32	78.91	78.86

and Recursive Induction using naive Bayes. The second group is Intersecting Rules, Intersecting Rules using joint probability, naive Bayes, See5-voting and See5 using highest probability. In the last group CN2 resides.

The first group includes methods which all outperform the rest of the methods. They all win significantly more times than they loose. Within this group RI is best, beating RI-s with 4–0 and DI with 4–0. Second in the group is DI which beats RI-s with 2–0. All methods in the second group beat CN2 significantly. But internally no significant differences are present in the group. The methods in the second group could be ranked in the following way according to their performance. Best is both Intersecting Rules methods, then comes both See5 methods followed by naive Bayes. CN2 shows to perform significantly worse than all other methods and is in a group of its own.

Table 4. Result of McNemar's test comparing wins and losses for all domains with a significant difference.

	RI-s	RI	DI	IR	IR-j	Bayes	CN2	See5-v	See5-hp
RI-s	-	0,4	0,2	7,0*	7,0*	9,0*	14,0*	10,0*	7,0*
RI	4,0	-	4,0	10,0*	10,0*	12,0*	16,0*	12,0*	10,0*
DI	2,0	0,4	-	6,0*	7,0*	10,0*	14,0*	10,0*	9,0*
IR	0,7*	0,10*	0,6*	-	2,0	5,0	9,0*	3,1	4,1
IR-j	0,7*	0,10*	0,7*	0,2	-	4,0	9,0*	4,1	4,1
Bayes	0,9*	0,12*	0,10*	0,5	0,4	-	11,0*	3,3	2,6
CN2	0,14*	0,16*	0,14*	0,9*	0,9*	0,11*	-	1,11*	2,11*
See5-v	0,10*	0,12*	0,10*	1,3	1,4	3,3	11,1*	-	4,4
See5-hp	0,7*	0,10*	0,9*	1,4	1,4	6,2	11,2*	4,4	-

Table 5 compares all wins and losses, not just the significant wins and losses as Table 4. Otherwise the table has a similar structure. An asterix (*) denotes that the amount of wins and losses is statically significant. The p-value of significance is set to 0.05, the p-value computed with an exact version of McNemar's test. The results from Table 4 are amplified in Table 5.

Recursive Induction is significantly better than any other method. Then comes Double Induction and Recursive Induction with stop, between them their is no significant difference, even tough DI wins with 16–7. Both methods are significantly better than all other methods except RI. Intersecting Rules is significantly better than naive Bayes, See5 and CN2. Intersecting Rules using joint probability comes next followed by See5-highest probability, See5-voting, naive Bayes and CN2. All methods are significantly better than CN2.

Table 5. Result of McNemar's test comparing wins and losses for all domains.

	RI-s	RI	DI	IR	IR-j	Bayes	CN2	See5-v	See5-hp
RI-s	-	4,15*	7,16	18,7*	21,7*	25,3*	26,3*	20,5*	18,5*
RI	15,4*	-	18,2*	24,4*	26,3*	26,1*	28,1*	24,3*	25,1*
DI	16,7	2,18*	-	19,5*	24,3*	22,3*	26,1*	23,4*	26,2*
IR	7,18*	4,24*	5,19*	-	6,4	17,6*	24,2*	17,6*	15,11
IR-j	7,21*	3,26*	3,24*	4,6	-	16,7	21,3*	16,8	13,12
Bayes	3,25*	1,26*	3,22*	6,17*	7,16	-	18,3*	13,15	9,18
CN2	3,26*	1,28*	1,26*	2,24*	3,21*	3,18*	-	6,21*	5,24*
See5-v	5,20*	3,24*	4,23*	6,17*	8,16	15,13	21,6*	-	10,10
See5-hp	5,18*	1,25*	2,26*	11,15	12,13	18,9	24,5*	10,10	-

3.3 Discussion About the Results

One conclusion that can be drawn from the experiments is that the computationally expensive methods obtain higher accuracy than methods that are less computationally expensive. Both RI methods have a very high computional cost but also perform very well. The worst-case time complexity for SAC is quadratic [1] in the number of examples, and since DI uses SAC to induce new rules this holds for DI as well. This figure for RI depends on the number of recursive steps it takes and is even worse. For IR this figure is even worse in theory as the computational cost grows exponentially with the number of rules in conflict. In reality though it is faster than RI as the number of rules in conflict is often not so high compared to the number of examples covered by the rules in conflict. In fact most of the time there is no need to partition the rules at all. The rest of the methods have the same computional cost. This is also reflected in their performance with the exception of CN2, which for some reason fails miserably.

One of the reasons why DI performs better than RI-s is because the stopping criterion hinders RI-s to do any new inductions at all. This is the case when the naive Bayes value decreases compared to the originally induced rules. When this happens RI-s behaves just like naive Bayes. Still this does not happen that often as it does perform better than naive Bayes.

4   Conclusions

In this paper a survey of different rule resolving methods have been presented and compared. A novel method called Recursive Induction based on Double Induction was also presented. Recursive Induction proved to solve rule conflicts so good that it with statistical significance achieved higher accuracy than all other methods except for Double Induction. On the other side of the scale is CN2, as this method was beaten significantly by all other methods. Double Induction and Recursive Induction using naive Bayes as stopping criterion were both shown to significantly outperform all other methods except Recursive Induction. Intersection rules was shown to significantly outperform naive Bayes and See5-voting. Between the rest of the methods no significant differences were found. One of the major drawbacks of using Recursive Induction is the computional cost. However, if accuracy is of uttermost importance and quick response time is not, then it is a useful technique.

One issue that needs further investigation when it comes to Recursive Induction and Double Induction is the use of other weighting schemes than the one used in our experiments, which is quite conservative. Another issue to address is to find a more suitable stopping criterion than to use naive Bayes as a quality measure together with Recursive Induction.

References

1. H. Boström and P. Idestam-Almquist. Induction of logic programs by example-guided unfolding. *Journal of Logic Programming, Vol. 40 (2-3)*, pages 226–237, 1999.
2. P. Clark and R. Boswell. Rule induction with CN2: some recent improvements. In *Proceedings of the Fifth European Working Session on Learning*, pages 151–163, Berlin, 1991. Springer-Verlag.

3. P. Clark and T. Niblett. The CN2 induction algorithm. *Machine Learning, 3, 261-283*, 1989.
4. J. Fürnkranz. Separate-and-conquer rule learning. *Artificial Intelligence Review*, 1999.
5. J. Fürnkranz and G. Widmer. Incremental reduced error pruning. In W.W. Cohen and H. Hirsh, editors, *Proceedings of the 11th International Conference on Machine Learning*, pages 70–77. Morgan Kaufmann, 1994.
6. R. Kohavi, B. Becker, and D. Sommerfield. Improving simple bayes. In *Proceedings of the European Conference on Machine Learning*, 1997.
7. T. Lindgren and H. Boström. Classification with intersecting rules. In *Proceedings of the 13th International Conference on Algorithmic Learning Theory (ALT'02)*, pages 395–402. Springer-Verlag, 2002.
8. T. Lindgren and H. Boström. Resolving rule conflicts with double induction. In *Proceedings of the 5th International Symposium on Intelligent Data Analysis*. Springer-Verlag, 2003.
9. J. R. Quinlan. Induction of decision trees. *Machine Learning*, 1:81–106, 1986.
10. RDS. Rule discovery system (RDS) – 1.0, Compumine AB, 2003. www.compumine.com.
11. RuleQuest Research. See 5: an informal tutorial, 2003. www.rulequest.com/see5-win.html.
12. R. Rivest. Learning decision lists. *Machine Learning, 2(3), 229-246*, 1987.

An Efficient Method to Estimate Labelled Sample Size for Transductive LDA(QDA/MDA) Based on Bayes Risk

Han Liu[1], Xiaobin Yuan[2], Qianying Tang[3], and Rafal Kustra[2]

[1] Department of Computer Science, University of Toronto
M5S 3G4 Toronto, Canada
hanliu@cs.toronto.edu
[2] Department of Statistics, University of Toronto, M5S 3G3 Toronto, Canada
{yuanx,r.kustra}@utoronto.ca
[3] Department of Electronics and Computer Engineering, University of Toronto
tangq@eecg.utoronto.ca

Abstract. As semi-supervised classification drawing more attention, many practical semi-supervised learning methods have been proposed. However,one important issue was ignored by current literature–how to estimate the exact size of labelled samples given many unlabelled samples. Such an estimation method is important because of the rareness and expensiveness of labelled examples and is also crucial in exploring the relative value of labelled and unlabelled samples given a specific model. Based on the assumption of a latent gaussian-distribution to the domain, we described a method to estimate the number of labels required in a dataset for semi-supervised linear discriminant classifiers (Transductive LDA) to reach an desired accuracy. Our technique extends naturally to handle two difficult problems: learning from gaussian distributions with different covariances, and learning for multiple classes. This method is evaluated on two datasets, one toy dataset and one real-world wine dataset. The result of this research can be used in areas such text mining, information retrieval or bioinformatics.

1 Introduction

Machine learning falls into two broad categories: supervised learning and unsupervised learning, primarily distinguished by the use of labelled and unlabelled data. Semi-supervised learning has received considerable attention in the literature due to its potential in reducing the need for expensive labelled data [1]. A general strategy is to assume that the distribution of unlabelled data is linked to their labels. In fact, this is a necessary condition for semi-supervised learning to work. Existing approaches make different assumptions within this common framework. Generative mixture model method[2] assumes that data comes from some identifiable mixture distribution, with unlabelled data, the mixture components can be identified independently. Transductive Support Vector Machines[3] take the metrics space to be a high-dimensional feature space defined by the

J.-F. Boulicaut et al. (Eds.): ECML 2004, LNAI 3201, pp. 274–285, 2004.

kernel, and by maximizing the margin based on the unlabelled data, effectively assume that the model is maximally smooth with respect to the density of unlabelled data in feature space. Co-training[4] assumes that data attributes can be partitioned into groups that individually sufficient for learning but conditionally independent given the class, and working by feeding classifications made by one learner as examples for the other and vice versa. Graph methods[5] assume a graph structure underlying the data and the graph structure coincide with classification goal. The nodes of the graph are data from the dataset, and edges reflect the proximity of examples. The intuition is that close examples tend to have similar labels, and labels can propagate along dense unlabelled data regions.

While many practical semi-supervised classification algorithms have been proposed, an important issue is ignored: Given many unlabelled samples, what is the minimum labelled samples we need while achieving a desired classification performance? Given labels to more training samples lowered the classification errors, but increased the cost when obtaining those labels. Thus, a method to estimation the minimum labelled sample size becomes a necessity. Moreover, a detailed analysis of labelled sample size under specific model assumption can improve our understanding of the relative values of labelled and unlabelled samples.

In this paper, our labelled sample size estimation method was derived by computing the bays error for a binary semi-supervised linear classifier(i.e. transductive LDA), and estimating the appropriate number of labels necessary for the a certain classification accuracy . We chose transductive LDA in our setting since as a generalization of regular LDA and based on the assumption of a latent gaussian-distribution to the domain,it has a relatively large bias but little variance, and avoid overfitting effectively when sample size is small. Besides a theoretical underpinning, we also developed a computationally tractable implementation based on simple parameter vector space transformation for our estimation method. Detailed discussion and analysis are presented to show that the technique could extend naturally to quadratic classifiers and to multi-class classifiers. The next section provided background information on transductive LDA as discussed in the literature of semi-supervised learning. Section 3 detailed a mathematical derivation of the labelled sample size estimation method for transductive LDA classifiers. Section 4 discussed the extension of our estimation method to the case of quadratic discriminant analysis and multi-class classification. Experimental results on both toy data and real world dataset were shown in Section 5. Summarization and future work were discussed in section 6. the last part was the acknowledge.

2   Transductive Linear Discriminant Analysis

2.1   Formalization of Labelled Sample Size Estimation Problem

We begin with a domain of objects $X = \{x_1, ..., x_n\}$. Each object x_i is associated with a vector of observable features(also denoted x_i). We are given labels $Y_l = \{y_1, ..., y_l\}$ for the first l objects($l << n$), and our goal is to infer the labels

$Y_u = \{y_{l+1}, ..., y_n\}$ of the $n-l$ unlabelled data. We refer to $X_l = \{x_1, ...x_l\}$ as the "labelled sample", and the complement $X_u = X - X_l$ as the "unlabelled sample". For now we assume a binary classification problem, with $Y = Y_l \cup Y_u \in \{1, 0\}^{|X|}$, The labels y_i are independent random variables satisfying $Pr\{y_i = 1\} = \pi_1$, $Pr\{y_i = 0\} = 1 - \pi_1$; generalization to the multi-class is straightforward. We use $R(l, u)$ to denote the classification error with l labelled data and u unlabelled data while R^* denotes bayes risk.

$$R^* = \int min\{\pi_1 f_1(x), (1 - \pi_1)f_2(x)\}dx$$

The labelled sample size estimation problem is formulated as given an acceptable additional probability of error $\triangle_{err}$ of any Bayesian solution to a classification problem with a smooth prior, $0 < \triangle_{err} < 1$, from current X and Y_l, how many more x_k should be given labels, so that the difference between real classification error and bayes error $R(l, u) - R^*$ will be less then $\triangle_{err}$.

We also assume that the underlying distributions of the samples are mixture of gaussian with identical covariance matrix, i.e., each class conditional distribution has the form $p_{y_i}(\cdot) \sim N(\mu_i, \Sigma)$, where $p_{y_i}(\cdot)$ denotes the distribution of samples for class i. Given a large number of unlabelled samples, this assumption is reasonable because of central limited theorem as a theoretical foundation. The assumption of identical covariance is crucial for LDA to work. Even though such an assumption is very strong, LDA is shown to work well in many applications in real-word datasets. In addition, we can extend LDA to Quadratic Discriminant Analysis(QDA) naturally to relax this assumption.

2.2   Transductive LDA

Transductive LDA is a semi-supervised version of common LDA. Expectation-Maximization(EM) approach can be applied to this learning problem, since the labels of unlabelled data can be treated as missing values. Let the entire training dataset D be a union of labelled dataset L and unlabelled dataset U, and assume each sample is independent, the joint probability density of the hybrid dataset can be written as:

$$p(x|\theta) = \prod_{x_i \in X_u} \sum_{k=1}^{K} p(y_i = k|\theta)p(x_i|y_i = k; \theta) \cdot \prod_{x_i \in X_l} p(y_i = k)p(x_i|y_i = k; \theta)$$

where $k = 1$ or $k = 2$, representing the categories. The first part of this equation is for the unlabelled dataset, and the second part is for the labelled data.

The parameters $\theta = (\pi_1, \mu_k, \Sigma)^T$ can be estimated by maximizing *a posteriori* probability $p(\theta|D)$. Equivalently,this can be done by maximizing the log likelihood $\log p(D|\theta)$ when the prior probability is uniform. The likelihood is given as:

$$L(\pi_1, \mu_k, \Sigma) = (2\pi)^{-\frac{np}{2}} |\Sigma|^{-\frac{n}{2}} \cdot \prod_{x_i \in Y_u} (\pi_1 e_{1i} + \pi_2 e_{2i})$$

$$\prod_{x_i \in Y_l} \{(\pi_1 \cdot e_{1i})^{y_i} \cdot [(1 - \pi_1)e_{2i}]^{1-y_i}\}$$

where $e_{ki} = \exp\{-\frac{1}{2}(x_i - \mu_k)^T \Sigma^{-1}(x_i - \mu_k)\}$. Thus the log likelihood is $l(\theta; D) = \log L(\pi_1, \mu_k, \Sigma)$. Assume that $l_{uk} = \log p(x^u, y = k|\mu_k, \Sigma)$ and $l_u = \log p(x^u) = \log \sum_k p(x^u, y = k|\mu_k, \Sigma)$, where x^u denotes all the $x \in X_u$. When using EM algorithm to estimate the probability parameters π_1, μ_k, Σ by an iterative hill climbing procedure, the E-step and M-step are designed as follows, for the E-step:

$$r_{uk} = p(y = k|x^u) = \frac{p(x^u, y = k)}{p(x^u)} = \exp\{l_{uk} - l_u\}$$

For the M-step: $\pi_1 = \frac{\sum_u r_{uk} + l_1}{u + l}$, $\pi_2 = 1 - \pi_1$, $\mu_k = \frac{\sum_u r_{uk} x^u + \sum x_k^l}{\sum_u r_{uk} + l_k}$, and

$\mu_k' = \frac{\sum_u r_{uk} x^u}{\sum_u r_{uk}}$. Σ is computed as:

$$\Sigma = \frac{\sum_k (\sum_u r_{uk}(x^u - \mu_k')(x^u - \mu_k')^T + \sum_l (x_k^l - \bar{x}_k^l)(x_k^l - \bar{x}_k^l)^T)}{\sum_u \sum_k r_{uk} + l}$$

where l_k denotes the number of labelled data in class k, x_k^l denotes the number of x^l in class k, $\bar{x}_k^l$ is the mean of all the x^l in class k. When the size of the labelled dataset is small, EM basically performs an unsupervised learning, except that the labelled data are used to identify the components. Detailed analysis for this issue could be found in [2]. After the EM progress, all the parameters needed for linear discriminant analysis are tuned, and discriminant functions for conducting classification can be obtained based on this parameters(as described in the next section).

3 Labelled Sample Size Estimation Technique

3.1 Bayes Risk for LDA Rule Classifier

In this section we present the equation for calculating bayes risk R^* of a LDA classifier $\hat{G}$. For all feature vectors X and a class membership G, we let $L(G, \hat{G}(X))$ be the loss function of a misclassification, and furthermore assume it only has 0-1 values, meaning all misclassification are charged a single unit, as in the case of many discriminant analysis. Next, we model each class conditional density as multivariate Gaussian, i.e. $X|G = g_k \sim N(\mu_k, \Sigma)$, where g_k is the class label, and the discriminant functions are therefore given by $\delta_k(x) = x^T \Sigma^{-1} \mu_k - \frac{1}{2}\mu_k^T \Sigma^{-1} \mu_k + \log \pi_k$ and $G(x) = \arg\max_k \delta_k(x)$. For two classes, the LDA rule classifies to class 2 if $\delta_2(x) > \delta_1(x)$ and class 1 otherwise. With $\pi_2 = 1 - \pi_1$, the Bayes risk R^* is given by

$$R^* = \pi_1 P_1(X^T \Sigma^{-1}(\mu_2 - \mu_1) > \frac{1}{2}\mu_2^T \Sigma^{-1} \mu_2 - \frac{1}{2}\mu_1^T \Sigma^{-1} \mu_1 + \log \frac{\pi_1}{\pi_2})$$

$$+ \pi_2 P_2(X^T \Sigma^{-1}(\mu_2 - \mu_1) < \frac{1}{2}\mu_2^T \Sigma^{-1} \mu_2 - \frac{1}{2}\mu_1^T \Sigma^{-1} \mu_1 + \log \frac{\pi_1}{\pi_2})$$

In class g_1, $X \sim N(\mu_1, \Sigma)$, and $Z_1 = X^T \Sigma^{-1}(\mu_2 - \mu_1)$ is transformation of X and is a univariate Gaussian random variable with mean $(\mu_2 - \mu_1)^T \Sigma^{-1} \mu_1$, and variance $\sigma^2 = (\mu_2 - \mu_1)^T \Sigma^{-1}(\mu_2 - \mu_1))$. Z can be transformed to a standard Gaussian random variable $\frac{Z-(\mu_2-\mu_1)^T \Sigma^{-1}\mu_1}{\sigma} \sim N(0,1)$. In class g_2, Z has similar distribution except for its mean and $\frac{Z-(\mu_2-\mu_1)^T \Sigma^{-1}\mu_2}{\sigma} \sim N(0,1)$. Thus, the Bayes risk can be calculated as

$$\pi_1 P_1 \left(\frac{Z - (\mu_2 - \mu_1)^T \Sigma^{-1}\mu_1}{\sigma} > a_1 \right) + \pi_2 P_2 \left(\frac{Z - (\mu_2 - \mu_1)^T \Sigma^{-1}\mu_2}{\sigma} > a_2 \right)$$

where

$$a_1 = \frac{\frac{1}{2}\mu_2^T \Sigma^{-1}\mu_2 - \frac{1}{2}\mu_1^T \Sigma^{-1}\mu_1 + \log \frac{\pi_1}{\pi_2} - (\mu_2 - \mu_1)^T \Sigma^{-1}\mu_1}{\sigma}$$

$$a_2 = \frac{\frac{1}{2}\mu_2^T \Sigma^{-1}\mu_2 - \frac{1}{2}\mu_1^T \Sigma^{-1}\mu_1 + \log \frac{\pi_1}{\pi_2} - (\mu_2 - \mu_1)^T \Sigma^{-1}\mu_2}{\sigma}$$

Let Φ denote the cumulative distribution function for a standard Gaussian model. R^* can be written as $\pi_1(1 - \Phi(\frac{\frac{1}{2}\sigma^2 + \log \frac{\pi_1}{\pi_2}}{\sigma})) + \pi_2 \Phi(\frac{-\frac{1}{2}\sigma^2 + \log \frac{\pi_1}{\pi_2}}{\sigma})$.

3.2   Labelled Sample Size Estimation Method

The estimation of an appropriate size of the labelled samples is determined by the required reduction in $R(l,u) - R^*$, which is affected by the current size of unlabelled data, dimensionality of the sample space and the separability of the two classes. We first derive a way to calculate $R(l,u) - R^*$. $R(l,u)$ is a function of θ, where $\theta = (\pi_1, \mu_1, \mu_2, \Sigma^{-1})^T$. We let θ^* denotes the true value of θ and $\hat{\theta}$ denotes the estimated value, and using Taylor series expansion of $R(\hat{\theta})$ up to second term, we obtain

$$R(\hat{\theta}) = R(\theta^*) + \frac{\partial R(\theta)^T}{\partial \theta}|_{\theta=\theta^*}(\hat{\theta} - \theta^*) + \frac{1}{2}tr\{\frac{\partial^2 R(\theta)^T}{\partial \theta^2}|_{\theta=\theta^*}(\hat{\theta} - \theta^*)(\hat{\theta} - \theta^*)^T\}$$

where $tr(A)$ denotes the trace of a matrix A. The term $\frac{\partial R(\theta)}{\partial \theta}|_{\theta=\theta^*}$ is zero since θ^* is an extreme point of $R(\theta)$. Assuming the bias of $\hat{\theta}$ is negligible, i.e. $(E\{\hat{\theta}\} = \theta^*)$, $R(l,u) - R^*$ can be approximated as $\frac{1}{2}tr\{\frac{\partial^2 R(\theta)}{\partial \theta^2}|_{\theta=\theta^*}cov(\hat{\theta})\}$. By asymptotic theory, as the sample size approaches infinity, $\hat{\theta} \sim N(\theta^*, J^{-1}(\theta))$, where $J(\theta) = -\frac{\partial^2 l(\theta)}{\partial \theta \partial \theta^T}$, with $l(\theta)$ representing the log likelihood of θ, is the observed fisher information matrix of θ, and an approximation of the covariance matrix $cov(\hat{\theta})$. $J(\theta)$ is calculated by the summation of two parts: $J_l(\theta)$ from the labelled data, and $J_u(\theta)$ from the unlabelled data. Let n be the total sample size; $\overline{J_l}(\theta)$ and $\overline{J_u}(\theta)$ be the observed information of a single observation for labelled and unlabelled data respectively. If given an required reduction in classification error $\triangle_{err}$, we can find the labelled sample size l needed from

$$tr\{\frac{\partial^2 R(\theta)}{\partial \theta^2}|_{\theta=\hat{\theta}}(l\overline{J_l}(\hat{\theta}) + (n-l)\overline{J_u}(\hat{\theta}))^{-1}\} < 2 \cdot \triangle_{err} \qquad (*)$$

Since $\overline{J_l}(\theta) = J_l(\theta)/l'$ and $\overline{J_u}(\theta) = J_u(\theta)/(n-l')$, where l' is current labelled sample size, and since $n - l \approx n - l'$ ($n >> l'$ and $n >> l$), formula (*) can be simplified as follows,

$$tr\{\frac{\partial^2 R(\theta)}{\partial \theta^2}|_{\theta=\hat{\theta}}(l\overline{J_1}(\hat{\theta}) + J_2(\hat{\theta}))^{-1}\} < 2 \cdot \triangle_{err} \qquad (**)$$

3.3   Computational Consideration

According to formula (*), quantities $\frac{\partial^2 R(\theta)}{\partial \theta^2}|_{\theta=\hat{\theta}}$, $\overline{J_l}(\hat{\theta})$ and $\overline{J_u}(\hat{\theta})$ need to be computed first when estimating the desired labelled sample size l. However, when the dimensionality p of the feature space is very large, the computation is very intensive. To illustrate, if $R(\theta)$ is a continuous function, the $\frac{\partial^2 R(\theta)}{\partial \theta^2}|_{\theta=\hat{\theta}}$ is a $(p^2+5p+2)/2 \times (p^2+5p+4)/2$ dimensional matrix, not mentioning the product of two such high-scale matrix! Finding a computationally tractable method to compute formula (**) is therefore of great practical benefit. In this section, we develop a method to reduce the computational load of $\frac{\partial^2 R(\theta)}{\partial \theta^2}|_{\theta=\hat{\theta}}$ to a 2×2 matrix calculation based on simple vector space transformation, while at the same time reduce the matrix production calculation of two $(p^2+5p+2)/2 \times (p^2+5p+4)/2$ dimensional matrix production to two 2×2 matrix production. According to the proof in [7], in the case of LDA, $R(l, u)$ only depends on π_1 and $\sigma^2(\sigma^2 = (\mu_2 - \mu_1)^T \Sigma^{-1}(\mu_2 - \mu_1))$ instead of the full parameter set. Let $\varphi = (\sigma^2, \pi_1)$, and let φ^* denotes the true value of φ and $\hat{\varphi}$ denotes the estimation, by Taylor series expansion of $R(\hat{\varphi})$ up to second order, we obtain

$$R(\hat{\varphi}) = R(\varphi^*) + \frac{\partial R(\varphi)^T}{\partial \varphi}|_{\varphi=\varphi^*}(\hat{\varphi} - \varphi^*) + \frac{1}{2}tr\{\frac{\partial^2 R(\varphi)^T}{\partial \varphi^2}|_{\varphi=\varphi^*}(\hat{\varphi} - \varphi^*)(\hat{\varphi} - \varphi^*)^T\}$$

Again, the term $\frac{\partial R(\varphi)}{\partial \varphi}|_{\varphi=\varphi^*}$ is zero since φ^* is an extreme point of $R(\varphi)$. If the bias of $\hat{\varphi}$ is negligible, i.e., $(E\{\hat{\varphi}\} = \varphi^*)$, $R(l, u) - R^*$ can be approximated as,

$$R(l, u) - R^* = \frac{1}{2}tr\{\frac{\partial^2 R(\varphi)}{\partial \varphi^2}|_{\varphi=\varphi^*}cov(\hat{\varphi})\}$$

The approximated covariance matrix of $\hat{\varphi}$ can be obtained from the inverse of observed fisher information matrix $J(\tilde{\theta}) = -\frac{\partial^2 l(\tilde{\theta})}{\partial \tilde{\theta}\partial \tilde{\theta}^T}|_{\tilde{\theta}=\tilde{\theta}^*}$, where $l(\tilde{\theta})$ is the log likelihood of $\tilde{\theta}$ based on the ladled and unlabel samples. $\tilde{\theta}$ is reparameterized from the old parameter $\theta = (\pi_1, \mu_{12}, ...\mu_{1p}, \mu_{22}, ..., \mu_{2p}, a_{ij})^T$, where a_{ij} is the elements of the matrix Σ^{-1}, $i = 1, ..., p, j = 1, ..., p$.

We map the elements in the original parameter space of θ to the new parameter space $\tilde{\theta}$ by letting $\tilde{\theta} = (\pi_1, \sigma^2, \mu_{12}, ...\mu_{1p}, \mu_{22}, ..., \mu_{2p}, a_{ij}|_{i,j \neq 1})^T$, i.e., removing the term a_{11} from θ and adding the term σ^2. The vector space of φ is a subspace of vector space $\tilde{\theta}$. Since θ and $\tilde{\theta}$ have the same dimensionality, the mapping is guaranteed to be one to one transformation, with a_{11} expressed by the elements of $\tilde{\theta}$ as

$$a_{11} = \frac{\sigma^2 - \sum_{i,j \neq 1} a_{ij}(\mu_{1i} - \mu_{2i})(\mu_{1j} - \mu_{2j})}{(\mu_{11} - \mu_{21})^2}$$

Again a_{ij} is the element of Σ^{-1}. The new log likelihood $l(\tilde{\theta})$ can be easily obtained from the original $l(\theta)$ and can be differentiated with respect to $\tilde{\theta}$. The information $J(\tilde{\theta})$ is also the summation of two parts: $J_l(\tilde{\theta})$ from the labelled data and $J_u(\tilde{\theta})$ from the unlabelled data. We let n be the total sample size, $\overline{J_l}(\tilde{\theta})$ and $\overline{J_u}(\tilde{\theta})$ be the observed information of a single observation for labelled and unlabelled data respectively. Similar to the derivation above, $J(\tilde{\theta}) \approx l\overline{J_l}(\tilde{\theta}) + J_u(\tilde{\theta})$ and thus $J^{-1}(\tilde{\theta}) \approx (l\overline{J_l}(\tilde{\theta}) + J_u(\tilde{\theta}))^{-1}$. Let $I(l)$ denotes the matrix made of the first two columns and first two rows, under our differentiation order of $\tilde{\theta}$, we can prove that $I(l) \approx cov(\hat{\varphi})$. The detailed proof is omitted here. After the vector space transformation, given $\triangle_{err}$, formula (**) is equivalent to

$$tr\{\frac{\partial^2 R(\varphi)}{\partial \varphi^2}|_{\varphi=\hat{\varphi}}(I(l)\} < 2 \cdot \triangle_{err} \qquad (***)$$

which is computationally tractable.

From the mathematical derivation above, we can see that the labelled sample size l is determined by several factors. Because the log likelihood is the likelihood for both labelled and unlabelled data, the final l is affected by the number of unlabelled data and also the dimensionality of the sample space. Furthermore, σ^2 and μ_k determines whether the two classes are easily classifiable, and it is an important factor in our estimation equation.

4   Relax the Strong Assumptions to Transductive QDA and Transductive MDA

4.1   From Transductive LDA to Transductive QDA

In this section, we discuss how to relax the strong assumption of identical covariance in gaussian mixtures by extending Transductive LDA to Transductive QDA. The modification of EM algorithm is trivial, requiring changes only in the M-step, i.e, $\Sigma_k^{new} = \frac{(\sum_u r_{uk}(x^u-\mu_k')(x^u-\mu_k')^T + \sum_l(x_k^l-\bar{x}_k^l)(x_k^l-\bar{x}_k^l)^T)}{\sum_u r_{uk}+l_k}$. We also need modifications to the estimation method when relaxing the identical covariance assumption. For quadratic discriminant analysis, each class conditional density is modelled as $X|G = g_k \sim N(\mu_k, \Sigma_k)$, and the discriminant functions are given as $\delta_k(x) = x^T \Sigma_k^{-1} \mu_k - \frac{1}{2}\mu_k^T \Sigma_k^{-1} \mu_k + \log \pi_k$ and $G(x) = arg \max_k \delta_k(x)$. In the case of two classes, the corresponding Bayes risk R^* is $\pi_1 P_1(X^T(\Sigma_2^{-1}\mu_2 - \Sigma_1^{-1}\mu_1) > \frac{1}{2}\mu_2^T \Sigma_2^{-1}\mu_2 - \frac{1}{2}\mu_1^T \Sigma_1^{-1}\mu_1 + \log \frac{\pi_1}{\pi_2}) + \pi_2 P_2(X^T(\Sigma_2^{-1}\mu_2 - \Sigma_1^{-1}\mu_1) < \frac{1}{2}(\mu_2^T \Sigma_2^{-1}\mu_2 - \mu_1^T \Sigma_1^{-1}\mu_1) + \log \frac{\pi_1}{\pi_2})$. In class g_1, $X \sim N(\mu_1, \Sigma_1)$, $Z = X^T(\Sigma_2^{-1}\mu_2 - \Sigma_1^{-1}\mu_1)$ is a univariate gaussian random variable, which is a transformation of X, with the distribution, $Z \sim N((\mu_2^T \Sigma_2^{-1} - \mu_1^T \Sigma_1^{-1})\mu_1, \sigma_1)$ where $\sigma_1 = (\mu_2^T \Sigma_2^{-1} - \mu_1^T \Sigma_1^{-1})\Sigma_1(\Sigma_2^{-1}\mu_2 - \Sigma_1^{-1}\mu_1)$. By defining $mean_1 = (\mu_2^T \Sigma_2^{-1} - \mu_1^T \Sigma_1^{-1})\mu_1$ and $mean_2 = (\mu_2^T \Sigma_2^{-1} - \mu_1^T \Sigma_1^{-1})\mu_2$, $\sigma_2 = (\mu_2^T \Sigma_2^{-1} - \mu_1^T \Sigma_1^{-1})\Sigma_2(\Sigma_2^{-1}\mu_2 - \Sigma_1^{-1}\mu_1)$ We have $\frac{Z-mean_1}{\sigma_1} \sim N(0,1)$. In class g_2, Z has similar distribution such that $\frac{Z-mean_2}{\sigma_2} \sim N(0,1)$. Thus, the Bayes risk for QDA can be calculated as

$$R^* = \pi_1 P_1(\frac{Z - mean_1}{\sigma_1} > a_1) + \pi_2 P_2(\frac{Z - mean_2}{\sigma_2} > a_2)$$

where $a_1 = \frac{\frac{1}{2}\mu_2^T \Sigma_2^{-1} \mu_2 - \frac{1}{2}\mu_1^T \Sigma_1^{-1} \mu_1 + \log \frac{\pi_1}{\pi_2} - mean_k}{\sigma_k}$, $k = 1, 2$. Let Φ denote the cumulative distribution function for a standard Gaussian model. R^* can then be calculated by $\pi_1(1 - \Phi(a_1)) + \pi_2 \Phi(a_2)$. The above method is a theoretical analysis, in fact, after tuning out the covariance matrix Σ_1 and Σ_2, we can simply use a very naive method to merge these two different matrices into one single matrix $\Sigma_{common} = (\pi_1^2 \cdot \Sigma_1 + \pi_2^2 \cdot \Sigma_2)/(\pi_1^2 + \pi_2^2)$, which is still a semi-positive definite and can be used instead to apply the estimation technique for Semi-supervised LDA directly. Another important point to note is that without the assumption of identical covariance matrix, $R(l, u)$ does not depend on (σ^2, π_1) only. Consequently, our computational tractable approach dose not hold. Yet, one can still use formula (**) to estimate the appropriate size of labelled samples. For a domain with a very flexible distribution but relatively small dimensionality, applying Semi-Supervised QDA would be more suitable.

4.2   From Two-Class Classification to Multi-class Classification

Some limitations exist when applying transductive LDA to multi-class classification problems, especially when the size of the labelled set is small. In such situation, the EM algorithm may fail if the distribution structure of the data set is unknown. A natural solution in dealing with multi-class classification is to map the original data samples into a new data space such that they are well clustered in the new space, in which case the distributions of the dataset can be captured by simple gaussian mixtures and LDA can be applied in the new space.

Transductive Multiple Discriminant Analysis(MDA)[8] used this idea and defined a linear transformation W of the original p_1-dimension data space to a new p_2-dimension space such that the ratio of between-class scatter S_b to within-class scatter S_w is maximized in the new space, mathematically, $W = \arg max_W \frac{|W^T S_b W|}{|W^T S_w W|}$. suppose x is an p-dimensional random vector drawn from C classes in the original data space. The kth class has a probability P_k and a mean vector μ_k. thus $S_w = \sum_{k=1}^{C} P_i E[(x - \mu_k)(x - \mu_k)^T | c_i]$ and $S_b = \sum_{k=1}^{C} P_i(\mu_k - \sum_{i=1}^{C} P_i \mu_i)(\mu_k - \sum_{i=1}^{C} P_i \mu_i)^T$. The main advantage of transductive MDA is that the data are clustered to some extent in the projected space, which simplifies the selection of the structure of Gaussian mixture models. The EM algorithm for semi-supervised MDA can be found in [9]. Because semi-supervised MDA is just another perspective of semi-supervised LDA, our labelled sample size estimation method also applies well in this setting. Assuming there are k classes altogether, the bayes risk is calculated as follows,

$$R^* = \pi_1 P_1(\delta_1 < \max(\delta_2, ..., \delta_k)) + \pi_2 P_2(\delta_1 < \max(\delta_1, \delta_3, ..., \delta_k)) + \cdots \cdots +$$

$$\pi_i P_i(\delta_1 < \max(\delta_1, ..., \delta_i, \delta_{i+1}, ..., \delta_k)) + \pi_k P_k(\delta_1 < \max(\delta_2, ..., \delta_{k-1}))$$

which can be computed quite efficiently.

5   Experiments and Results

5.1   Toy Data of Mixture of Gaussian with Six Components

To illustrate the performance of our estimation method, first we show an example of no obvious practical significance. Consider Gaussian observation (X, Y) taken from six classes $g_1, g_2, ..., g_6$. We know that X and Y are Gaussian variables, and we know exactly the means of $(X, Y$ is (μ_{ix}, μ_{iy}) and variance-covariance matrices is $|Sigma_i$ given that the class $G = g_i$. We need to estimate the mixing parameter $p_i = p(G = g_i)$. The data is sampled from a distribution with mixing parameter α_i. The total number of our data is 900, with dimensionality equals to two, and are divided into 6 classes: 100 data for class g_1, 100 for class g_2,150 for class g_3,150 for class g_4,200 for class g_5 and 200 for class g_6. The means and covariance matrices are shown as follows: $\mu_1 = (-\frac{3}{2}, 1/2)^T$, $\mu_2 = (2, 2)^T$, $\mu_3 = (-\frac{1}{2}, \frac{5}{2})^T$, $\mu_4 = (\frac{1}{2}, 0)$, $\mu_5 = (\frac{1}{3}, -2)^T$ and $\mu_6 = (\frac{7}{2}, -\frac{1}{2})^T$. For their covariance matrices:

$$\Sigma_1 : \begin{pmatrix} 3 & \frac{1}{2} \\ \frac{1}{2} & 1 \end{pmatrix} \Sigma_2 : \begin{pmatrix} 3 & \frac{1}{2} \\ \frac{1}{5} & 1 \end{pmatrix} \Sigma_3 : \begin{pmatrix} 3 & 1 \\ \frac{1}{5} & \frac{1}{2} \end{pmatrix} \Sigma_4 : \begin{pmatrix} \frac{5}{2} & \frac{1}{2} \\ \frac{2}{3} & \frac{3}{2} \end{pmatrix} \Sigma_5 : \begin{pmatrix} 3 & 1 \\ \frac{1}{5} & 1 \end{pmatrix} \Sigma_6 : \begin{pmatrix} \frac{1}{3} & \frac{1}{10} \\ \frac{1}{2} & \frac{1}{2} \end{pmatrix}$$

and their mixing parameters $\pi_1 = \frac{1}{9}$,$\pi_2 = \frac{1}{9}$, $\pi_3 = \frac{1}{6}$, $\pi_4 = \frac{1}{6}$,$\pi_5 = \frac{2}{9}$, $\pi_6 = \frac{1}{9}$. Based on these information, 900 data were randomly generated. For our experiment, the initial number of the labelled data is 4 for each class. Applying semi-supervised QDA on the data, we obtained a classification result shown in the first plot of figure 1. Given the desired $\triangle_{err} = 0.05$, by our algorithm, the estimated labelled data number is 90, thus at least 15 labels are needed for each class.

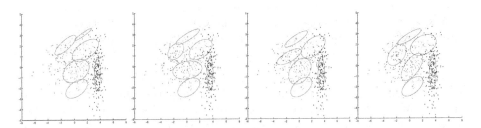

Fig. 1. Illustration of the fitting with 4 labels, 7 labels, 15 labels and 22 labels for each class respectively, in this first 2 cases, the number of labelled data is not large enough, thus can not give out enough information for fitting, while in the latter 2 cases,the number of labelled data is enough,the fitting is good, but given more data can not improve the fitting significantly

From the first plot in figure 1, it is easy to see that the fitting is not quite good. the shape of the gaussian and the position is quite different from the original figure. plot 2 was generated from 7 labels per class, the fitting is still not good enough. While plot 3 represents the fitting condition with 15 labels for each class, the fitting result is satisfiable; plot 4 is generated with 22 labels for each classes, we can see that the fitting performance does not improve much from the 15 labels case. The classification error for each class is shown in table 1 below: Running for every label size 10 times. The box plot for these 4 conditions are shown in figure 2, From the box plot above, we can see that with the increase number of the labelled data, the overall error rate was reduced significantly at first, but slightly after it exceeds a threshold. Normally, we use 5% as this threshold.

Table 1. Classification error for each classes of toy data

label number	4/class	7/class	15/class	22/class
error for g_1	0.70515	0.47788	0.54221	0.55176
error for g_2	0.77217	0.73579	0.65222	0.55411
error for g_3	0.18903	0.10350	0.14149	0.04770
error for g_4	0.53220	0.60979	0.60518	0.57308
error for g_5	0.17077	0.10841	0.10666	0.10176
error for g_6	0.16513	0.13630	0.10500	0.12819
overall error	0.35856	0.31040	0.29419	0.28778

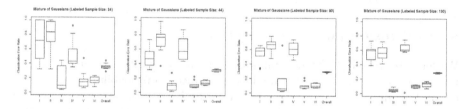

Fig. 2. Illustration of the box plot for 4 labels, 7 labels 15 labels and 22 labels per class respectively

5.2 Real World Dataset: Wine Recognition Data

In order to test the idea of our estimation method, we applied it to the problem of wine recognition. These data are the results of a chemical analysis of wines grown in the same region in Italy but derived from three different cultivars. The analysis determined the quantities of 13 constituents found in each of the three types of wines[11]. There are 59 data in the class g_1, 71 data in the class g_2 and 48 data in the class g_3, with 13 predictors, i.e., the dimensionality is 13. After randomly choosing 16 labelled data for every class, and requiring $\triangle_{err} = 0.05$, our estimated number of the labels needed is $l = 60$, meaning at least 20 labels are need for each class. the classification errors for each class were shown in table 2 above.

From which, we can see the data is easily to be fitted by QDA− thus it satisfies the gaussian assumptions well. The computed bayes risk for this data set is about 0.06948-0.05=0.01948. From the original data set, compute pairwise about the bayes risk R^*, it's 0.01966. the result is very close. The box plot for the classification of each class is shown below:

Table 2. Classification error for each classes of wine data

label number	16/class	20/class	22/class	24/class
error for g_1	0.08093	0.01281	0.00000	0.01143
error for g_2	0.13134	0.04256	0.04887	0.01190
error for g_3	0.37941	0.20619	0.08066	0.04138
overall error	0.13646	0.06948	0.04191	0.01980

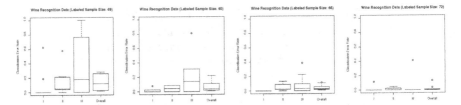

Fig. 3. Illustration of the box plot for 16 labels, 20 labels, 22 labels and 24 labels per class respectively

6   Conclusion and Future Extension

We have examined a labelled sample size estimation problem under a specific model, i.e., semi-supervised LDA. Given an additional probability of error $\triangle_{err}$ of any Bayesian solution to the classification problem with respect to a smooth prior, $\triangle_{err} = R(l, u) - R^*$, under the gaussian-distribution domain assumption, we presented a practical labelled sample size estimation method and a computationally tractable approach. Possible extensions and future work are discussed below. This research result could be applied in different semi-supervised learning domain with probability model type 1 [10].

Linear discriminant analysis and logistic regression are two main representatives of these two classes. Our labelled sample size estimation method applies on semi-supervised LDA well, but not on logistic regression. We believe that similar research on logistic regression model would be very meaningful. Based on the detailed analysis for these two types of models, a common labelled sample size estimation framework maybe built and based on this architecture, interesting research topic can be found.

Acknowledgment

The authors would like to thank Dr Sam Roweis's comment and Kannan Achahan's suggestions. This work is also supported by scholarship from University of Toronto.

References

1. M. Seeger *Learning with labeled and unlabeled data*, (Technical Report), Institute for Adaptive and Neural Computation, University of Edinburgh, Edinburgh, United Kingdom, pp. 609-616, 2001

2. Kamal Nigam, Andrew Kachites McCallum, Sebastian Thrun, and Tom Mitchell *Text classification from labeled and unlabeled documents using EM*, Machine Learning, 39(2/3): pp.103-134, 2000

3. Kristin Bennett and A.Demiriz *Semi-supervised support vector machines*,Advances in Neural Information Processing Systems (NIPS) [NIPS99] pp1-7. 1999.

4. Avrim Blum and Tom Mitchell *Combing labeled and unlabeled data with co-training*,Proc. Of the 1998 Conference on Computational Learning Theory, pp.1-10, 1998

5. A.Blum and S.Chawla *Learning from labeled and unlabeled data using graph mincut*,In proc. 17th Intl Conf. on Machine Learning (ICML) ,pp.1181-1188, 2001

6. Mardia,K., Kent, J. and Bibby,J. *Multivariate Analysis*, Academic Press. 1979

7. T.O'Neil. *Normal discrimination with unclassified observations*, Journal of American Statistical Association, Volume 73, no. 364, pp 821-826, Dec. 1978

8. R.Duda and P.Hart. *Pattern Classification and Scene Analysis*, New York: Wiley, 1973

9. Ying Wu, Qi Tian, Thomas S. Huang. *Discriminant-EM Algorithm with Application to Image Retrieval*, Technical Report,UIUC,USA 1999

10. T.Zhang and F.Oles. *A probability Analysis on the value of unlabeled data for classification problem.*, ICML pp.1191-1198 2000

11. Forina, M.et al, PARVUS. *An Extensdible Package for Data Exploration, Classification and Correlation.*,Institute of Pharmaceutical and Food Analysis and Technologies, Via Brigata Salerno, Italy.

Analyzing Sensory Data Using Non-linear Preference Learning with Feature Subset Selection*

Oscar Luaces, Gustavo F. Bayón, José R. Quevedo, Jorge Díez,
Juan José del Coz, and Antonio Bahamonde

Artificial Intelligence Center
University of Oviedo at Gijón
Campus de Viesques, s/n
E-33271 Gijón, Spain
{oluaces,gbayon,quevedo,jdiez,juanjo,antonio}@aic.uniovi.es

Abstract. The quality of food can be assessed from different points of view. In this paper, we deal with those aspects that can be appreciated through sensory impressions. When we are aiming to induce a function that maps object descriptions into ratings, we must consider that consumers' ratings are just a way to express their preferences about the products presented in the same testing session. Therefore, we postulate to learn from consumers' preference judgments instead of using an approach based on regression. This requires the use of special purpose kernels and feature subset selection methods. We illustrate the benefits of our approach in two families of real-world data bases.

1 Introduction

The quality of food can be assessed from different points of view. In this paper we are concerned with sensory quality from the perspective of consumers. This is a very important issue for food industries since they are aiming to adapt their production processes to improve the acceptability of their specialties. Thus, they need to discover the relationship between product descriptions and consumers' sensory degree of satisfaction. An excellent survey of the use of sensory data analysis in the food industry can be found in [1]; for a Machine Learning perspective, see [2, 3].

From a conceptual point of view, sensory data can include the assessment of food products provided by two different kinds of groups of people usually called *panels*. The first one is made up of a small selected group of expert, trained judges; they will rate different aspects of products related to their taste, odor, color, etc... The most essential property of expert panelists, in addition to their discriminatory capacity, is their own coherence, not the uniformity of the group. We must assume that a given rating means the same for a given expert in every

---

* The research reported in this paper has been supported in part under Spanish Ministerio de Ciencia y Tecnología (MCyT) and Feder grant TIC2001-3579.

J.-F. Boulicaut et al. (Eds.): ECML 2004, LNAI 3201, pp. 286–297, 2004.

product; though not necessarily for every expert. Experts' panel will play the role of a bundle of sophisticated sensors; their ratings are used to describe each product, probably in addition to some chemical or physical devices.

The second kind of panel is made up of a group of untrained consumers (C); they are asked to rate their degree of acceptance or satisfaction about the tested products on a scale. Usually, this panel is organized in a set of *testing sessions*, where a group of potential consumers assess some instances from a sample E of the tested product. In general, each consumer only participates in a small number (sometimes only one) of testing sessions, usually in the same day.

In this paper we propose to tackle sensory data analysis by learning *consumers' preferences*, see [4–6] where training examples will be represented by *preference judgments*: pairs of vectors (v, u) where someone expresses that prefers the object represented by v to the object represented by u. We will show that this approach can induce more useful knowledge than other approaches, like regression based methods. The main reason is due to the fact that preference judgments sets can represent more relevant information to discover consumers' preferences.

At the end of the paper we show experimental results of preference learning in two real-world data bases taken from sensory data analysis of beef meat and traditional Asturian cider. In both cases, non-linear preference functions can explain consumers' preferences better than other methods. Additionally, as happens with any other machine learning application, feature subset selection (FSS) plays a very important role. In fact, sometimes FSS marks the difference between useful tools and merely academic developments [3]. In this paper we show how it is possible to adapt to preference learning some state of the art FSS methods designed for SVM (Support Vector Machines) [7] with non-linear kernels.

2   Why Using Preference Learning?

Initially, sensory data can be viewed as in regression problems: the sensory descriptions (human and mechanical) of each object $x \in E$ are endowed with a rating $r(x)$ that represents the degree of satisfaction for each consumer or the average value for a group of them. So, a straightforward approach to handle sensory data can be based on regression. However, this is not a faithful capturing of people's preferences [8, 9]. The main reason is due to the fact that sensory data, expressed as a regression problem, do not represent all available knowledge. In particular, we would like to remark that consumers' ratings are just a way for expressing a relative ordering. There is a kind of *batch effect* that often biases the ratings so that a product will obtain a higher/lower rating when it is assessed together with other products that are clearly worse/better. Therefore, we must consider as a very important issue the information about the batches tested by consumers in each rating session.

Traditionally the process given to these data sets includes testing some statistical hypothesis [10, 1]. On the other hand, the approach followed in [2] is based

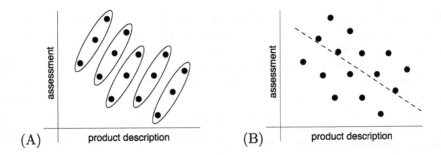

Fig. 1. Each ellipse in (A) represents the assessments for a given session, where the assessment function is clearly different than the one obtained in (B) by a regression method applied to the whole set of assessments without information about sessions.

on the use of Bayesian belief networks. In both cases, these approaches demand that all available food products (the objects x) must be rated by all consumers; in practice, this is an impossible assumption most of the times. In general, each consumer will only assess a small number of products. Thus, we will have sets of ratings $(r_i(\boldsymbol{x}) : \boldsymbol{x} \in E_i)$ for each consumer or group of consumers $i \in C$, where $\cup(E_i : i \in C) = E$. In addition to this fact, let us emphasize some important peculiarities of the whole data collected in a sensory study that we have to take into account: i) we have different scales in the ratings, given that the assessments come from different sets of consumers; additionally, ii) these ratings suffer the batch effect alluded to previously.

The importance of these factors is graphically depicted in Figure 1. Here there is a collection of consumers' assessments (represented in the vertical axis) about some products whose descriptions are given by a single number x represented in the horizontal axis. If we observe Figure 1A, where the assessments of the same session are drawn inside ellipses, we can say that in each session the message of the consumers is the same: the more x the better. However, there are discrepancies about how this knowledge is expressed in different sessions. Probably because there are different consumers in each session; or perhaps because the same consumer forgets the exact number used to assess a given degree of satisfaction; or the sensory reactions were forgotten from one session to another.

If we do not consider sessions, the data collected become the cloud of points represented in Figure 1B. Then, it will be difficult for a regression method to discover the unanimous opinion of consumers. In fact, in this case, regression methods will conclude that the more x the worse, since that seems to be the general orientation of those points in the space. Therefore, the information about the sessions must be integrated in the data to be processed with the rest of sensory opinions and descriptions of the products tested by consumers. In the next section we will present our approach to deal with sessions explicitly. The overall idea is to avoid trying to predict the exact value of consumer ratings; instead we will look for a function that returns higher values to those products with higher ratings.

3   Learning Preferences: An SVM Approach

Although there are other approaches to learn preferences, following [4–6] we will try to induce a real *preference* or *ranking function* f from the space of objects considered, say $\mathbb{R}^d$, in such a way that it maximizes the probability of having $f(v) > f(u)$ whenever v is preferable to u. This functional approach can start from a set of objects endowed with a (usually ordinal) rating, as in regression, but essentially, we need a collection of preference judgments

$$PJ = \{v_j > u_j : j = 1, \ldots, n\} \qquad (1)$$

When we have a family of ratings $(r_i(x) : x \in E_i)$ for $i \in C$, we transform them into a preference judgments set PJ considering all pairs (v, u) such that objects v and u were presented in the same session to a given consumer i, and $r_i(v) > r_i(u)$. Hence, without any lost of generality, we can assume a set PJ as in formula (1).

In order to induce the ranking function, we can use the approach presented by Herbrich et al. in [4]. So, we look for a function $F : \mathbb{R}^d \times \mathbb{R}^d \to \mathbb{R}$ such that

$$\forall x, y \in \mathbb{R}^d, F(x, y) > 0 \Leftrightarrow F(x, 0) > F(y, 0) \qquad (2)$$

Then, the ranking function $f : \mathbb{R}^d \to \mathbb{R}$ can be simply defined by

$$\forall x \in \mathbb{R}^d, f(x) = F(x, 0) \qquad (3)$$

Given the set of preference judgments PJ (1), we can specify F by means of the constraints

$$F(v_j, u_j) > 0 \text{ and } F(u_j, v_j) < 0, \quad \forall j = 1, \ldots, n \qquad (4)$$

Therefore, we have a binary classification problem that can be solved using SVM. If we represent preference judgments pairs (v, u) in a higher dimensional feature space by means of $(\phi(v), \phi(u))$, we will obtain a function of the form:

$$F(x, y) = \sum_{i=1}^{n} \alpha_i z_i \mathcal{K}(x_i^{(1)}, x_i^{(2)}, x, y) = \langle w, (\phi(x), \phi(y)) \rangle \qquad (5)$$

where the pairs $x_i^{(1)}, x_i^{(2)}$ are the support vectors; w is the vector of weights in the higher dimensional feature space; and $\mathcal{K}$ is the kernel used by SVM. The key idea of this approach is the definition of the kernel $\mathcal{K}$ as follows

$$\mathcal{K}(x_1, x_2, x_3, x_4) = k(x_1, x_3) - k(x_1, x_4) - k(x_2, x_3) + k(x_2, x_4) \qquad (6)$$

where k is a kernel function defined as the inner product of two objects represented in the feature space, that is, $k(x, y) = \langle \phi(x), \phi(y) \rangle$. In this case, it is easy to proof that F fulfills the conditions expressed in equation (2). In the experiments reported in Section 5, we will employ a polynomial kernel, defining

$k(\boldsymbol{x}, \boldsymbol{y}) = (\langle \boldsymbol{x}, \boldsymbol{y} \rangle + c)^g$, with $c = 1$ and $g = 2$. Notice that, in general, according to the previous definitions,

$$f(\boldsymbol{x}) = \sum_{i=1}^{n} \alpha_i z_i (k(\boldsymbol{x}_i^{(1)}, \boldsymbol{x}) - k(\boldsymbol{x}_i^{(2)}, \boldsymbol{x})) \tag{7}$$

Hence, for the polynomial kernel we will obtain a non-linear function that assesses the ranking for each object $\boldsymbol{x}$.

4   FSS in Non-linear Preference Learning

A major issue when dealing with real-world problems involving sensory data is to find out those features which have more influence on the tastes of consumers; thus, the production process can focus on them to improve the acceptability of the final product. Additionally, reducing the number of features describing objects decreases the cost of data acquisition, which in many cases can make these machine learning techniques applicable in industrial processes [3].

In recent years several methods related to feature selection when using SVM have been developed. One of the most remarkable is RFE (Recursive Feature Elimination) [11]. Given a data set with objects described by a set of d features, $\mathcal{F}_d$, the method considers that i is the less useful feature if $|\boldsymbol{w}_i|$ is the smallest weight (see eq. 5). Then this feature is removed, giving rise to a subset $\mathcal{F}_{d-1}$ with $d - 1$ features. The process is successively repeated until no more features are left. Notice that in this way, we obtain a ranking of the original d features, and a sequence of models, each one obtained using the corresponding subset of i features, $\mathcal{F}_i$. A chunk of features can also be removed instead of only one at each iteration, as suggested in [11].

However, RFE's criterion is not directly applicable for non-linear kernels, so we have used two state of the art methods to achieve ordered lists of features in non-linear scenarios. Moreover, we must take into account an important peculiarity of preference learning data sets. In this case, the examples are formed by pairs of objects $(\boldsymbol{v}, \boldsymbol{u})$, and both objects are described by the same set of d features. Therefore, somehow we must consider twice the merits of each feature to be removed and, in each iteration, we have to get rid of the two copies of the selected feature.

4.1   Feature Ranking Methods for Non-linear Preference Kernels

Method 1.- The first method that we have applied to obtain a ranking of features with non-linear kernels was proposed by Rakotomamonjy [12]; its ranking criterion orders the list of features according to their influence in the variations of feature's weight; in fact, it is an extension of RFE to the non-linear case. In symbols, the method removes in each iteration the feature with the lowest ranking value:

$$R_1(i) = |\nabla_i \| \boldsymbol{w} \|^2| = \left| \sum_{k,j} \alpha_k \alpha_j z_k z_j \frac{\partial K(\boldsymbol{s} \cdot \boldsymbol{x}_k, \boldsymbol{s} \cdot \boldsymbol{x}_j)}{\partial s_i} \right|, \quad i = 1, \ldots, d \quad (8)$$

where $\boldsymbol{s}$ is a scaling factor used to simplify the computation of partial derivatives. Given that we are facing a preference learning problem, where every example is a preference judgment like in (1), then we must modify the use of $\boldsymbol{s}$: we need 4 copies, one for each object involved in the definition of the kernel. Thus, according to (6), we compute

$$\frac{\partial K(\boldsymbol{s} \cdot \boldsymbol{x}_1, \boldsymbol{s} \cdot \boldsymbol{x}_2, \boldsymbol{s} \cdot \boldsymbol{x}_3, \boldsymbol{s} \cdot \boldsymbol{x}_4)}{\partial s_i} = \frac{\partial k(\boldsymbol{s} \cdot \boldsymbol{x}_1, \boldsymbol{s} \cdot \boldsymbol{x}_3)}{\partial s_i} -$$
$$- \frac{\partial k(\boldsymbol{s} \cdot \boldsymbol{x}_1, \boldsymbol{s} \cdot \boldsymbol{x}_4)}{\partial s_i} - \frac{\partial k(\boldsymbol{s} \cdot \boldsymbol{x}_2, \boldsymbol{s} \cdot \boldsymbol{x}_3)}{\partial s_i} + \frac{\partial k(\boldsymbol{s} \cdot \boldsymbol{x}_2, \boldsymbol{s} \cdot \boldsymbol{x}_4)}{\partial s_i} \quad (9)$$

In this formula, for a polynomial kernel $k(\boldsymbol{x}, \boldsymbol{y}) = (\langle \boldsymbol{x}, \boldsymbol{y} \rangle + c)^g$ and a vector $\boldsymbol{s}$ such that $\forall i, s_i = 1$ we have that

$$\frac{\partial k(\boldsymbol{s} \cdot \boldsymbol{x}, \boldsymbol{s} \cdot \boldsymbol{y})}{\partial s_i} = 2g(x_i y_i)(c + \langle \boldsymbol{x}, \boldsymbol{y} \rangle)^{g-1} \quad (10)$$

Method 2.- The second method was developed by Degroeve et al. [13] for splice site prediction of DNA sequences. This method uses a ranking criterion such that features are ordered with respect to the loss in predictive performance when they are removed. In [13] the authors approximate the generalization performance when removing the i-th feature by the accuracy on the training set while setting the value of that feature, in every instance, to its mean value. When using this method for preference learning with the kernel of equation (6) the ranking criterion can be expressed as

$$R_2(i) = \left(\sum_k z_k \cdot \sum_j \alpha_j z_j K(\boldsymbol{x}_j^{(1),i}, \boldsymbol{x}_j^{(2),i}, \boldsymbol{x}_k^{(1),i}, \boldsymbol{x}_k^{(2),i}) \right) \quad (11)$$

where $\boldsymbol{x}^i$ denotes a vector describing an object where the value for the i-th feature was replaced by its mean value. Notice that a higher value of $R_2(i)$, that is, a higher accuracy on the training set when removing feature i-th, means a lower relevance of that feature. Therefore, we will remove the feature yielding the highest ranking value, as opposite to the ranking method described previously.

4.2   Model Selection

Once obtained the ranked list of feature subsets, the next step shall be to select one of them. In general, we will be interested in a subset $\mathcal{F}_i$ which lets the learner yield the best performance, in terms of accuracy; so we need to estimate the performance for every feature subset.

Following the same approach as in [6], we will not use cross-validation for this purpose; its main disadvantages are its computational cost as well as its high variance, so we will use an alternative model selection: ADJ, a metric-based method [14] devised to choose the appropriate level of complexity required to fit to data. In our case, given the nested sequence of feature sets provided by any of the ranking methods described previously, $\mathcal{F}_1 \subset \mathcal{F}_2 \subset \ldots \subset \mathcal{F}_d$, ADJ would provide a procedure to select one of the models f_i induced by SVM from the corresponding $\mathcal{F}_i$.

The key idea is the definition of a metric on the space of hypothesis. Thus, given two different hypothesis f and g, their distance is calculated as the expected disagreement in their predictions

$$d(f,g) \stackrel{\text{def}}{=} \varphi \left(\int err(f(\boldsymbol{x}), g(\boldsymbol{x})) d\text{P}_X \right) \tag{12}$$

where $err(f(\boldsymbol{x}), g(\boldsymbol{x}))$ is the measure of disagreement on a generic point $\boldsymbol{x}$ in the input space X. Given that these distances can only be approximated, ADJ establishes a method to compute $\hat{d}(g,t)$, an *ADJusted distance estimate* between any hypothesis f and the *true* target classification function t. Therefore, the selected hypothesis is

$$f_k = \arg\min_{f_l} \hat{d}(f_l, t) \tag{13}$$

The estimation of distance, $\hat{d}$, is computed by means of the expected disagreement in the predictions in a couple of sets: the training set T, and a set U of unlabeled examples, that is, a set of cases sampled from P_X but for which the pretended *correct* output is not given. The ADJ estimation is given by

$$ADJ(f_l, t) \stackrel{\text{def}}{=} d_T(f_l, t) \cdot \max_{k<l} \frac{d_U(f_k, f_l)}{d_T(f_k, f_l)} \tag{14}$$

where, for a given subset of examples S, $d_S(f,g)$ is the expected disagreement of hypothesis f and g in S. To avoid the impossibility of using the previous equation when there are zero disagreements in T for two hypotheses we propose to use the Laplace correction to the probability estimation; thus,

$$d_S(f,g) \stackrel{\text{def}}{=} \frac{1}{|S|+2} \left(1 + \sum_{x \in S} 1_{f(x) \neq g(x)} \right) \tag{15}$$

In general, it is not straightforward to obtain a set of unlabeled examples, so [15] proposed a sampling method over the available training set. However, for learning preferences, we can easily build the set of unlabeled examples: new preference judgment pairs can be formed by arranging real objects randomly selected from the original data.

4.3   Dealing with Redundant Features

As we have previously pointed out, sensory data include ratings of experts for different characteristics of the assessed products; it is not rare that several experts have similar opinions about a given characteristic. Some physical and chemical features can also present this kind of similarities. Therefore, these data sets may frequently present a certain degree of redundancy to describe an object more precisely. Trying to take advantage of these redundancies, we have developed a simple but quite effective filtering process, RF, to be applied to sensory data sets before any other feature subset selection process. On the other hand, this filter provides an additional benefit for feature selection algorithms, since the number of features to deal with is reduced.

RF is an iterative process where in each step the two most *similar* features are replaced by a new one whose values are computed as the average of them. Considering two features represented by a_i and a_j as (column) vectors whose dimension is the number of examples in the data set, the similarity can be estimated by means of their cosine; that is,

$$\text{similarity}(a_i, a_j) = \frac{\langle a_i, a_j \rangle}{\|a_i\| \cdot \|a_j\|} \tag{16}$$

Applying this method, we obtain a sequence of different descriptions of the original data set, each one with one feature less than the previous. To select an adequate description in terms of prediction accuracy, we use again ADJ. The selected description can be considered a summarized version of the original data set to be processed by the feature subset selection methods previously described.

5   Experimental Results

To illustrate the benefits of our approach, we have conducted some experiments with a couple of sensory data bases. The first one comes from a study carried out to determine the features that entail consumer acceptance of beef meat from seven Spanish breeds [16]. Each piece of meat was described by: weight of the animal, aging time, breed, 6 physical features describing its texture and 12 sensory characteristics rated by 11 different experts (132 ratings). Given that breed was represented by 7 boolean features, the whole description of each piece of meat uses 147 features. In each testing session, 4 or 5 pieces of meat were tested and a group of consumers were asked to rate only three different qualities: tenderness, flavor and acceptance. These three data sets have over 2420 preference judgments.

The second data base deals with sensory data about traditional Asturian cider [17]. In this case, the description of each cider was given just by 64 chemical and physical features, without any expert rating. In fact, the consumers here were a set of 14 candidates to become experts, and the rating sessions (of 3, 4 or 5 ciders) were taken during the training and selection stage. These potential experts were asked to rate a high number of qualities of ciders: bouquet, color, acidity, bitterness, 4 additional visual aspects and 3 more flavor related aspects. Thus, we have 12 qualities of cider, that is, 12 different data sets of over 225 preference judgments.

5.1   Preference Learning vs. Regression

First, we performed a comparison between the scores achieved by preference approaches and those obtained by regression methods. As was explained in Section 2, the core point of preference learning approach is the concept of testing session. Thus, for each session, to summarize the opinions of consumers, we computed the mean of the ratings obtained by each food product, which was endowed to the objects' descriptions to conform the regression training sets. These sets can be used to induce a function that predicts numerical ratings of consumers. We have experimented with a simple linear regression and with a well reputed regression algorithm: Cubist, a commercial product from RuleQuest Research.

To interpret regression results we used the relative mean absolute deviation ($rmad$), which is computed from the mean absolute distance or deviation, mad, of the function f learned by the regression method:

$$\mathrm{rmad}(f) = 100 \cdot \frac{\mathrm{mad}(f)}{\mathrm{mad}(mean)} \tag{17}$$

where $mean$ is the constant predictor that returns the mean value in all cases.

On the other hand, we can obtain some preference judgments from the ratings of the sessions comparing the rating of each product with the rest, one by one, and constructing the corresponding pair. To learn from preference judgment data sets, we used SVM[light] [18] with linear and polynomial kernels. In this case, the errors have a straightforward meaning as misclassifications; so in order to allow a fair comparison between regression and preference learning approaches, we also tested regression models on preference judgments test sets, calculating their misclassifications.

Table 1 reports the 10-fold cross validation scores achieved with the real-world data sets described, both with regression and preference learning methods. The scores show that regression methods are unable to learn any useful knowledge: their relative mean absolute deviation ($rmad$) is above 100% in almost all cases, that is, usually the mean predictor performs better. Even when these regression models are tested on preference judgment sets, the percentage of misclassifications is over 40%, clearly higher than those obtained when using the preference learning approach. SVM-based methods can reduce these errors up to an average near 30% with a linear kernel (SVM_l with $k(\boldsymbol{x}, \boldsymbol{y}) = \langle \boldsymbol{x}, \boldsymbol{y} \rangle$), and near 20% if the kernel is a polynomial of degree 2 (SVM_p with $k(\boldsymbol{x}, \boldsymbol{y}) = (\langle \boldsymbol{x}, \boldsymbol{y} \rangle + 1)^2$). The rationale behind the improvement, when using non-linear kernels, can be explained taking into account that the positive appreciation of food products usually requires an equilibrium of its components, and the increase or decrease of any value from that point is frequently rejected.

5.2   FSS in Non-linear Preference Learning

In order to find out those features which have more influence on the tastes of consumers, we have applied the feature subset selection methods described in Section 4. For the sake of simplicity, in what follows FSS_1 and FSS_2 will denote

Table 1. Results on cider and beef meat data sets. For regression methods we report the relative mean absolute deviation; for preference learning, the percentage of preference judgments pairs misclassified is shown. The number of selected features is also shown for the FSS algorithms. Let us recall that original cider and meat data sets have 64 and 147 features, respectively. All these results have been obtained by a 10-fold cross-validation.

	Regression		Preferences				Preferences (SVM_p+FSS)									
	Linear	Cubist	Linear	Cubist	SVM_l	SVM_p	FSS_1		FSS_2		RF		RF+FSS_1		RF+FSS_2	
	Rmad	Rmad	Error	Error	Error	Error	Error	#Att.	Error	#Att.	Error	#Att.	Error	#Att.	Error	#Att.
acidity	103.0%	109.4%	40.0%	42.4%	29.9%	18.0%	17.2%	18.2	17.6%	16.9	16.4%	47.5	14.7%	19.3	19.3%	18.5
bitterness	105.8%	111.9%	56.0%	47.4%	30.5%	23.1%	25.1%	29.4	21.2%	22.0	20.8%	39.0	18.2%	23.9	22.9%	27.6
flavor-1	105.3%	111.7%	42.4%	44.3%	27.2%	17.1%	18.5%	30.0	21.4%	26.2	20.6%	36.0	20.1%	24.1	19.7%	22.2
flavor-2	107.2%	116.0%	45.6%	45.0%	28.6%	17.9%	19.1%	27.0	15.6%	26.3	17.8%	40.5	17.8%	22.9	16.5%	18.1
flavor-3	110.3%	107.7%	43.8%	41.8%	33.6%	17.7%	22.7%	28.8	21.8%	19.8	19.3%	30.0	20.1%	17.6	18.4%	18.3
bouquet	104.0%	110.2%	43.5%	42.7%	26.4%	21.0%	16.7%	30.0	18.9%	28.1	19.8%	45.0	18.8%	24.1	18.0%	23.1
color	98.4%	109.9%	41.3%	43.4%	26.1%	17.8%	19.5%	32.0	22.0%	22.6	19.5%	41.5	21.6%	24.3	24.9%	21.0
visual-1	103.2%	113.0%	41.7%	43.1%	25.9%	13.4%	11.5%	30.4	13.8%	24.5	12.0%	34.5	14.7%	24.5	13.8%	18.1
visual-2	102.3%	112.0%	43.8%	45.7%	34.0%	20.0%	21.1%	30.5	18.9%	23.8	19.9%	35.5	21.2%	27.1	19.4%	23.2
visual-3	107.2%	120.5%	45.6%	49.3%	25.3%	20.6%	16.1%	18.4	15.6%	18.0	13.8%	32.5	13.4%	24.6	13.4%	25.3
visual-4	98.7%	97.2%	36.5%	38.2%	23.0%	14.0%	14.1%	25.5	15.0%	19.4	14.1%	38.5	14.7%	22.4	12.1%	19.2
Average cider	104.1%	110.9%	43.7%	43.9%	28.2%	18.2%	18.3%	27.3	18.3%	22.5	17.6%	38.2	17.7%	23.2	18.0%	21.3
tenderness	96.3%	97.8%	41.5%	43.1%	29.6%	19.4%	-	-	-	-	20.0%	50.0	21.8%	27.0	21.3%	37.5
flavor	99.3%	103.4%	43.8%	46.5%	32.7%	23.8%	-	-	-	-	25.0%	65.0	26.5%	33.5	26.1%	29.0
acceptance	94.0%	97.2%	38.4%	40.2%	31.9%	22.1%	-	-	-	-	24.7%	39.5	24.8%	30.0	25.3%	26.7
Average meat	96.5%	99.5%	41.2%	43.3%	31.4%	21.8%	-	-	-	-	23.2%	51.5	24.4%	30.2	24.2%	31.1
Total average	102.5%	108.4%	43.1%	43.8%	28.9%	19.0%	18.3%	27.3	18.3%	22.5	18.8%	41.1	19.2%	24.7	19.4%	23.4

the selectors that use ranking *Method 1* and *Method 2* respectively. Additionally, we used RF in two senses: as a feature subset selector, and as a filter to be applied before FSS_1 and FSS_2. In all cases we used ADJ to choose among the subsets of features. The learner used was SVM_p, given that it was the most accurate in our tests. On the beef meat data sets it is almost impractical to use FSS_1 and FSS_2 due to its computational cost, unless a previous reduction in the number of features can be achieved; therefore we only have results for this data sets when RF is used as a previous filter. Moreover, features were processed in chunks of five for the meat data sets, while they were removed one by one for the cider data sets.

We can see (Table 1) that FSS_1, FSS_2, and RF considerably reduce the number of features without (in general) loss of accuracy. In the cider data sets, all methods obtain similar accuracy scores (non-significant differences), but FSS_2 is significantly better than FSS_1 reducing the number of features, while RF achieves the poorest scores in this task. For the cider data sets, accuracy scores obtained by FSS_1 and FSS_2 are slightly improved when RF is previously used. However, for the meat data sets, accuracy decreases slightly when we use the RF filter with respect to the accuracy obtained on the original data set by SVM_p; it also decreases when using FSS_1 and FSS_2 after RF. We think that this behavior is due to the the fact that we are removing chunks of five features in each iteration.

6   Conclusions

The analysis of sensory data is a very useful tool for food industries because it provides the knowledge to satisfy the tastes of consumers. These data sets present some peculiarities that make difficult the use of regression based algorithms: each consumer does not rate all available products; and they give numerical assessments only as a way to express a relative preference in a rating or testing session (batch effect).

Preference learning does not try to learn the exact rating; however, it finds out models able to explain consumer preferences. We have observed that the accuracy increases significantly with non-linear functional models in the two real-world data bases analyzed. In general, the usefulness of these models can be improved with the use of specially fitted FSS methods.

Another interesting peculiarity of sensory data sets is that, frequently, there are blocks of features describing the same aspect. To take advantage of these redundancies we have developed a filtering process that can be applied to improve the performance of the learner.

Acknowledgements

We would like to thank Carlos Sañudo (Animal Production at the University of Zaragoza) for providing us with the beef meat data sets [16]; we also thank Anna Picinelli (Cider group at SERIDA, Asturias) for allowing us to use cider data sets [17].

References

1. Murray, J., Delahunty, C., Baxter, I.: Descriptive sensory analysis: past, present and future. Food Research International **36** (2001) 461–471
2. Corney, D.: Designing food with bayesian belief networks. In: Proceedings of the International Conference on Adaptive Computing in engineering Design and Manufacture. (2002) 83–94
3. Goyache, F., Bahamonde, A., Alonso, J., López, S., del Coz J.J., Quevedo, J., Ranilla, J., Luaces, O., Alvarez, I., Royo, L., Díez, J.: The usefulness of artificial intelligence techniques to assess subjective quality of products in the food industry. Trends in Food Science and Technology **12** (2001) 370–381
4. Herbrich, R., Graepel, T., Obermayer, K.: Support vector learning for ordinal regression. In: Proceedings of the Ninth International Conference on Artificial Neural Networks, Edinburgh, UK (1999) 97–102
5. Joachims, T.: Optimizing search engines using clickthrough data. In: Proceedings of the ACM Conference on Knowledge Discovery and Data Mining (KDD). (2002)
6. Bahamonde, A., Bayón, G.F., Díez, J., Quevedo, J.R., Luaces, O., del Coz, J.J., Alonso, J., Goyache, F.: Feature subset selection for learning preferences: A case study. In: Proceedings of the International Conference on Machine Learning (ICML '04), Banff, Alberta (Canada). (2004)
7. Vapnik, V.: Statistical Learning Theory. John Wiley, New York, NY (1998)
8. Cohen, W., Shapire, R., Singer, Y.: Learning to order things. Journal of Artificial Intelligence Research **10** (1999) 243–270
9. Dumais, S., Bharat, K., Joachims, T., Weigend, A., eds.: Workshop on implicit measures of user interests and preferences. In ACM SIGIR Conference, Toronto, Canada (2003)
10. Næs, T., Risvik, E.: Multivariate analysis of data in sensory science. Elsevier (1996)
11. Guyon, I., Weston, J., Barnhill, S., Vapnik, V.: Gene selection for cancer classification using support vector machines. Machine Learning **46** (2002) 389–422
12. Rakotomamonjy, A.: Variable selection using SVM-based criteria. Journal of Machine Learning Research **3** (2003) 1357–1370
13. Degroeve, S., De Baets, B., Van de Peer, Y., Rouzé, P.: Feature subset selection for splice site prediction. Bioinformatics **18** (2002) 75–83
14. Schuurmans, D., Southey, F.: Metric-based methods for adaptive model selection and regularization. Machine Learning **48** (2002) 51–84
15. Bengio, Y., Chapados, N.: Extensions to metric-based model selection. Journal of Machine Learning Research **3** (2003) 1209–1227
16. Gil, M., Serra, X., Gispert, M., Oliver, M., Sañudo, C., Panea, B., Olleta, J., Campo, M., Oliván, M., Osoro, K., Garcia-Cachan, M., Cruz-Sagredo, R., Izquierdo, M., Espejo, M., Martín, M., Piedrafita, J.: The effect of breed-production systems on the myosin heavy chain 1, the biochemical characteristics and the colour variables of longissimus thoracis from seven spanish beef cattle breeds. Meat Science **58** (2001) 181–188
17. Picinelli, A., Suárez, B., Moreno, J., Rodríguez, R., Caso-García, L., Mangas, J.: Chemical characterization of Asturian cider. Journal of Agricultural and Food Chemistry **48** (2000) 3997–4002
18. Joachims, T.: Making large-scale support vector machines learning practical. In B. Schölkopf, C. Burges, A.S., ed.: Advances in Kernel Methods: Support Vector Machines. MIT Press, Cambridge, MA (1998)

Dynamic Asset Allocation Exploiting Predictors in Reinforcement Learning Framework

Jangmin O[1], Jae Won Lee[2], Jongwoo Lee[3], and Byoung-Tak Zhang[1]

[1] School of Computer Science and Engineering, Seoul National University, San 56-1,
Shillim-dong, Kwanak-gu, Seoul, Korea 151-742
{jmoh,btzhang}@bi.snu.ac.kr
[2] School of Computer Science and Engineering, Sungshin Women's University,
Dongsun-dong, Sungbuk-gu, Seoul, Korea 136-742
jwlee@cs.sungshin.ac.kr
[3] Department of Multimedia Science, Sookmyung Women's University,
53-12 Chongpa-dong 2-ga, Yongsan-gu, Seoul, Korea 140-742
jwlee44@naturesol.co.kr

Abstract. Given the pattern-based multi-predictors of the stock price, we study a method of dynamic asset allocation to maximize the trading performance. To optimize the proportion of asset to be allocated to each recommendations of the predictors, we design an asset allocator called meta policy in the Q-learning framework. We utilize both the information of each predictor's recommendations and the ratio of the stock fund over the asset to efficiently describe the state space. The experimental results on Korean stock market show that the trading system with the proposed asset allocator outperforms other systems with fixed asset allocation methods. This means that reinforcement learning can bring synergy effects to the decision making problem through exploiting supervised-learned predictors.

1 Introduction

During the last a few decades, several algorithms have been applied to the stock market problems [4]. But attempts on modeling or predicting the stock market have not been successful in *consistently* beating the market. This is the famous EMH (Efficient Market Hypothesis) saying that the future prices are unpredictable since all the information available is already reflected on the history of past prices [7]. However, if we step back from *consistently*, then we can find several empirical results saying that the market might be somewhat predictable [1]. Especially, the newest algorithms in artificial intelligence, equipped with powerful representational and modeling power, have been applied to the problems of the stock market, such as price prediction, risk management and portfolio optimization.

Many works have been applied to the price prediction. Supervised learning such as neural networks, decision trees, and SVMs (Support Vector Machines) are intrinsically well suited to the problem [5, 11]. The risk management and

J.-F. Boulicaut et al. (Eds.): ECML 2004, LNAI 3201, pp. 298–309, 2004.

portfolio optimization have been intensively studied in reinforcement learning [6, 8–10].

In this paper, we confine our main interest on trading the individual stocks in the market. The works with the stock price prediction based on supervised learning [5, 11] lack in considering the risk management and portfolio optimization.

The mechanism of the time delayed learning with the cumulative rewards in reinforcement learning makes it natural to consider the risk management and portfolio optimization. But the researches [9] put simple assumptions on the market to make the problem manageable in the reinforcement learning framework. Also the portfolios of the researches [8] are simple because they focus on switching just between two price series. The works [6, 10] treat trading individual stocks in reinforcement learning but lack in asset allocation.

In order to handle both stock price prediction and trading with efficient asset allocation, we dive the problem into two separate parts. For the price prediction, we adopt neural networks approach. But rather than an all-purpose predictor, we build a multi-predictors approach based on several meaningful patterns. For the asset allocation, we want the asset to be dynamically distributed on each predictor's recommendation. To achieve this aim we design a Q-learning framework of the dynamic asset allocator called *meta policy* which makes a decision on the asset allocation exploiting the information of recommendations of the multi-predictors and the stock fund ratio over the total asset.

The resulting trading performance is compared with the performances of other fixed asset allocation techniques through a simulation on Korean stock market.

2   Summary of Predictors

We have constructed the pattern based predictors. Rather than only one predictor to cover the whole stock price patterns, we focus only on several typical patterns. Table 1 represents the price patterns our predictors treat[1]. The patterns cover roughly 80% of stock price series in Korean stock market. The predictors, *engine_bear*, *engine_bull*, *engine_GC* and *engine_TU* are developed from these datasets using artificial neural networks.

Table 1. Patterns of predictors used in this paper

Pattern	Description
D_{bull}	Moving average lines are arranged in order.
D_{bear}	Moving average lines are arranged in reversed order.
D_{GC}	Golden cross between moving average lines occurs.
D_{TU}	Sign of gradient of moving average line is changed.

---

[1] For more detailed description about the meaning of Table 1, see [3].

After each prediction engine was trained, its performance might be evaluated using several criteria. Many evaluation criteria are summarized in [2] but we have adopted a simulation-based evaluation using, $\mathcal{LP}$, called *local policy*.

Definition 1. *Given a space* $\Omega = (B\_THRES, A\_THRES, H\_DURATION)$, *a local policy* $\mathcal{LP}$ *is a set of optimized parameters for each predictor.*

$$\mathcal{LP}(predictor) = (b\_thres, a\_thres, h\_duration).$$

Table 2 shows the meaning of each parameter. We regard the prediction values of a predictor larger than b_thres as bid signals. a_thres is the threshold for ask signals and $h\_duration$ is the maximal duration of holding a stock. Using an $\mathcal{LP}$, the trading based on each predictor is simulated as follows. The stocks of which predicted values are larger than b_thres are retrieved and each purchased stock is sold when its predicted value becomes lower than a_thres or its number of holding days expires. For each predictor, its $\mathcal{LP}$ is greedily optimized over the parameter space. For comparison, two metrics, PPT and accuracy, are used. PPT means average profit rate of the trades and accuracy is defined as;

$$accuracy = \frac{\#\text{of successful trades}}{\#\text{of recommendations}}, \tag{1}$$

where successful trade means the trade achieving positive profit after subtracting the transaction cost.

Table 3 summarizes the results. The *engine_normal* corresponds to all-purpose predictor. The accuracy of each predictor is improved 12% compared with *engine_normal*. The predictors are remarkably superior to *engine_normal*. Although our multi-predictors approach can not cover whole patterns of stock prices, this result is very promising.

3   Need for Meta-policy

Here we analyze the tendencies of our predictors. Figure 1 is the bar graph of the successful or failed recommendations of *engine_bear* with its $\mathcal{LP}$. This figure shows that the profitable recommendations are not equally distributed over the trading period. They are concentrated on some specific days. It means that profits induced from the trades of a few days dominate others.

Table 2. Parameters of the local policy of an predictor

Name	Meaning
b_thres	threshold of bid signal
a_thres	threshold of ask signal
h_duration	period of holding a stock

Table 3. Performances of the predictors

Engine	Accuracy(%)	PPT(%)
engine_normal	57.10	0.79
engine_bear	69.42	1.41
engine_bull	73.37	1.99
engine_GC	71.10	1.72
engine_TU	70.97	1.63

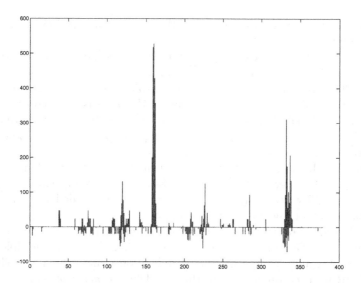

Fig. 1. The tendency of recommendations of *engine_bear*: x-axis represents trading days. y-axis represents the total profits induced by recommendations of a day. Up-headed bar means the trades of the day result in positive profit, and vice versa

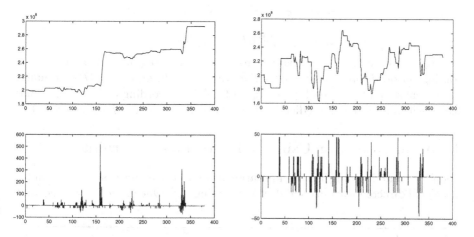

Fig. 2. Funding log and traded recommendations when the purchase money per recommendation is 0.4 million Won

Fig. 3. Funding log and traded recommendations when the purchase money per recommendation is 40 million Won

To explore this, we simulate the tradings with two different purchase money per recommendation (PMR), 0.4 and 40 million Won, given initial asset 200 million Won[2]. Figure 2 is for the former and Fig. 3 is for the latter. The upper

---

[2] Won is a monetary unit of Korea.

part of each figure shows the history of the asset change and the lower part is the bar graph.

With a small PMR we can trade most of the recommended stocks even when a number of recommendations are made on a specific day, such as around the 160-th or 340-th trading day. These many profitable trades increase the asset volume. But in this case, too small portion of the asset is invested to the stocks in usual days with small number of recommendations. In those days, though the trades of the recommended stocks induce high profits, the total asset is little influenced by those trades.

Whereas with a large PMR, the asset is heavily affected by individual trades. The history of the asset in Fig. 3 says the asset is fluctuated by trades. Moreover, with a large PMR we can trade just a few stocks recommended at the peak days. So the bar graph of Fig. 3 looks less profitable.

Therefore, it is desirable to adapt the amount of PMR in order to achieve more effective trading performance. Furthermore since we have multiple predictors, we need a more complicated asset allocation policy which can effectively adjust PMR for each predictor. For this, we define a *meta policy*:

Definition 2. *Let the number of recommendations of multi-predictors be* $\mathcal{N} = (N_{bear}, N_{bull}, N_{GC}, N_{TU})$ *and the ratio of stock fund over the total asset be* $\mathcal{SF}$. *A meta policy* $\mathcal{MP}$ *is defined as a function over* $\mathcal{N}$ *and* $\mathcal{SF}$,

$$\mathcal{MP}(\mathcal{N}, \mathcal{SF}) := (P_{bear}, P_{bull}, P_{GC}, P_{TU}),$$

where P_{engine} *is the proportion of PMR for engine.*

Figure 4 summarizes the trading process with a meta policy. At t-th day of T trading period, E predictors retrieve their recommendations and $\mathcal{MP}$ determines the purchase money for each predictor of that day according to $N_1, \ldots, N_E$ and $\mathcal{SF}$. Each candidate of a predictor is traded according to the $\mathcal{LP}$ of the predictor.

4   Asset Allocator Using Reinforcement Learning

Reinforcement learning is a computational approach to understand and automate goal directed learning and decision making [12]. One of the most important

```
for t = 1 to T
    for e = 1 to E
        S_e = retrieve(D_e, b_thres)
        N_e = numberof(S_e)
    end for
    (P_1, ··· , P_E) = MP(N_1, ··· , N_E, SF)
    for e = 1 to E
        local_trade(P_e, S_e, LP(P_e))
    end for
end for
```

Fig. 4. Trading process with a meta policy

keys to achieve reasonable performance in machine learning is the representation of the input space. Specially reinforcement learning is an art of the design of state and reward [10]. Here, we describe how we formulate a meta policy in the Q-learning framework.

The state s_t is a state vector at time t that the environment gives to the agent. We define s_t as;

$$s_t = (N_1^{bits}(t), N_2^{bits}(t), N_3^{bits}(t), N_4^{bits}(t), F^{bits}(t)).$$

The state is divided into two parts one about the predictors and the other part about the stock fund ratio. Each $N_i^{bits}(t)$ is the bit vector which represents the number of recommendations of predictor i at time t. Since the number of recommendations is unbounded integer valued, we use an orthogonal vector representation with its length restricted to 10 as in Table 4.

Table 4. Bit vector of a predictor's recommendations

# of recommendations	bit vector
0	0000000000
1	0000000001
...	...
8	0100000000
9~	1000000000

Table 5. Bit vector of the stock fund ratio

ratio of the stock fund	bit vector
$[0, 5)$	00000000000000000001
$[5, 10)$	00000000000000000010
...	...
$[90, 95)$	01000000000000000000
$[95, 100)$	10000000000000000000

$F^{bits}(t)$ is a bit vector representing the ratio of the stock fund[3] over the asset. Since the ratio can range between 0% to 100%, we discretize it into 20 intervals and express it with 20 bit orthogonal vector as in Table 5.

The action a_t at s_t is a PMR of each predictor over the asset. Although it is natural to use real valued ratio, it is hard to consider the real valued action under Q-learning . We have to properly discretize to reduce the cardinality of the candidate actions. If we restrict the ratio to take one of four values, $(0.5, 1.0, 3.0, 5.0)$, the action can be written as

$$a_t = (P_1^{bits}(t), P_2^{bits}(t), P_3^{bits}(t), P_4^{bits}(t)),$$

where $P_i^{bits}(t)$ is four bit vector to pick up one of the four values. After all, the number of possible actions is 256.

If we use a table representation as the conventional Q-learning does, we might need $10^4 \times 20 \times 4^4 = 51.2$ million entries. The table size is pretty big, but not unmanageable in the present computing power. Here we do not adopt any function approximators for Q-value but use only the table representation.

---

[3] Stock fund is the estimated money of stocks the investor is holding. Ready fund if the difference between total asset and stock fund.

```
Initialize Q(s, a) as zero.
Repeat (for specified number of episodes):
    Make an episode by sampling T₁ and Tₙ.
    Environment initializes asset_{T₁} and s_{T₁}.
    for t = T₁ to T_{n-1}
        a_t ⟵ Action(s_t)
        asset_{t+1} ⟵ Trade(asset_t, a_t)
        if t < T_{n-1} then
            r_t ⟵ 0
        else
            r_t ⟵ profit ratio
        end if
        Environment produces s_{t+1}
        δ_t ⟵ r_t + γ max_{a'} Q(s_{t+1}, a') − Q(s_t, a_t)
        Q(s_t, a_t) ⟵ Q(s_t, a_t) + α × δ_t
    end for
```

Fig. 5. Q-learning algorithm for meta policy

Figure 5 describes our Q-learning framework with a meta policy. To produce episodes as many as over the training period, both the start and the end day of an episode are uniformly sampled over the total training period. While an episode is lasting, the agent chooses an action from the function $Action$, trades stocks with chosen action, is given reward, and updates the table of Q-value. The function $Trade(asset_t, a_t)$ simulates one-day trading process according to a_t with initial asset $asset_t$. The output of $Trade$ is the initial asset of the next day.

As the reward function, we choose the profit ratio on the trading period which is defined as

$$\text{profit ratio} = 100 \times \frac{\text{asset}_{T_n} - \text{asset}_{T_1}}{\text{asset}_{T_1}}. \tag{2}$$

The reward of each action is zero during the inside of the trading period and is given only when the final day of the episode.

5   Experiments

In this section, we experimented the performance of the trading system with meta policy optimized by Q-learning, named MPG. Two other trading systems, named trader1 and trader2 as shown in table 6, were used for the performance comparison. Each trading system shares the predictors, which were constructed on the stock price data of Korean Stock Exchange market[4] from January 1998 to March 2000, but trades on its own asset allocation policy.

---

[4] Korean Composite Stock Price Index (KOSPI) is widely used as an abbreviated word for Korean Stock Exchange Market.

Table 6. Policies of the Trading Systems

name	description
trader1	Fixed policy, initially partitioned asset
trader2	Fixed policy, united asset
MPG	Adaptive policy, united asset

5.1   Asset Allocation Policy and Performance of Each System

In case of trader1, as if we had a sub-trading systems per predictor, an initial asset was equally divided into parts, totally the number of predictors. The stocks recommended by a predictor were traded with the exclusive asset for that predictor. The exclusive asset can not be utilized to trade the recommended stocks from other predictors. The asset allocation policy of trader1 consists of four constants,

$$\mu_{bear}, \mu_{bull}, \mu_{GC}, \mu_{TU},$$

where μ_e is the proportion of the asset as purchase money of predictor e . For each predictor the constants were calculated so that it could achieve maximal profit on the period between April 2000 to December 2001.

In trader2, the initial asset was not divided but was managed as united form. Whenever there are any recommendations from predictors, trader2 allocates $1/k_0$ times of asset to purchase, where k_0 was tuned on the same period as trader1.

5.2   Training MPG

MPG was constructed by Q-learning as described in Sect. 4. It was trained on the period from April 2000 to December 2001, the same period as the tuning period of trader1 and trader2. To optimize MPG, we specified the parameters for Q-learning as follows. γ was set to 0.9, α was set to 0.02 and ϵ was set to 0.2. High uncertainty of the stock market makes the overfitting on the training period inevitable. Therefore, for the training set of MPG, we excluded the last six months of the training set as the validation set.

Figure 6 shows the training tendency of MPG. Whenever 1,000 episodes were experienced, we plotted the trading performances both on the entire training period and the validation period. Horizontal axis is each measuring point and vertical axis is the trading performance, the profit ratio. Solid line is the profit ratio on the training period and dotted line is on the validation period. On the validation period, after the best performance reaches about 210% with 500,000 episodes experienced, the performance is declined, which means the more updating Q-values leads overfitting on the training set. So we stop further training and produce the final MPG at that step.

5.3   Trading Performances

Figure 7 shows the comparison of three trading systems on the test period from January 2002 to May 2003. Horizontal axis is the trading day and vertical axis

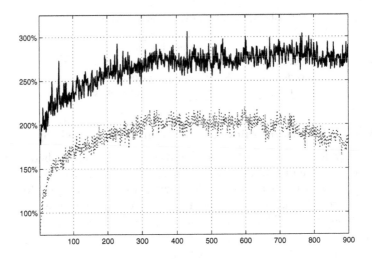

Fig. 6. Training tendency of MPG

Table 7. Profit induced by each trading system

trading systems	profit ratios	relative profit ratios
trader1	76.92%	102.49%
trader2	115.74%	146.92%
MPG	257.76%	309.46%

is the total asset. Each trading system started with its trading money 25 million Won. The KOSPI values were scaled up so that it looks as if it were 25 million Won at January 2, 2002. Solid line is the history of asset of MPG, dashed-dotted is of trader1, dashed line is of trader2, and dotted line is of composite index.

Table 7 summarizes the performance induced by each trading system. Profit ratio is calculated as Eq. (2) and the relative profit ratio is the relative profit compared with composite index at the end of trading period. Clearly, MPG outperforms other two trading systems. After 17 months' trading, its asset rose by nearly 65 million Won, or 257.76%, to about 90 million Won. trader1 shows the worst among three trading systems. There may be some situations where one predictor meets too many recommendations to manage only using its ready fund, while there are much of ready funds for other predictors.

trader2 also shows limited performance. Since it tries to buy stocks whenever any predictor recommends, it might avoid the ill conditions of trader1. Although it outperforms trader1 over most of periods, trader2 does not consider the relationship between predictors or the ratio of stock fund. During the hard time of August and September 2002, trader1 and trader2 suffer the decline of asset, but MPG endures this hard period. It shows somewhat avoiding the risky declination and getting more chance of level up of the total asset using adaptive asset allocation.

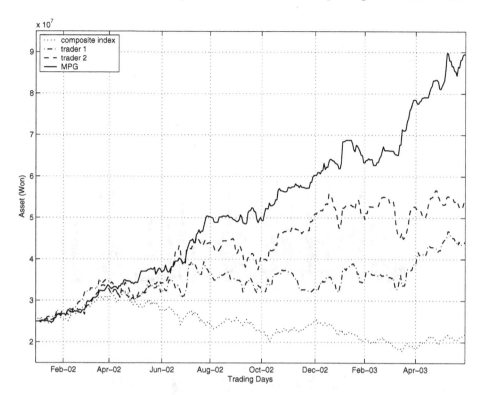

Fig. 7. A comparison of the performances of the trading systems

6   Discussion

Figure 8 shows a synthetic analysis of MPG including the proportion of stock fund and the information of recommendations. Upper part of the figure is about asset history, middle part is about the proportion of stock fund to total asset, and lower part is about the sums of positive or negative profits of each day under the assumption that every recommendation might be purchased. After April 2002, KOSPI is in bear market. From late June 2002 to mid July 2003, there is a sharp rally in KOSPI. *engine_bear* meets its explosive recommending day at June 27, 2002. The asset allocation rule of that day is $(5.0, 0.5, 0.5, 1.0)$, where 5.0 is for *engine_bear*. Stock fund is 5% at June 27, 2002, so we can purchase most of the recommendations. As the result, stock fund of June 28, 2002 increases to 98%.

While KOSPI is in its declining bear at late December 2002, the number of recommendations leading to loss increases. At December 20, 2002 *engine_bear* and *engine_bull* recommend 4 and 6 stocks respectively. But their allocation ratios are 0.5 and 0.5. During a few consecutive dangerous days, the small allocation ratios for corresponding predictors prevent the stock fund from being dangerously increased. Although some amount of loss is inevitable, it is more stable than other traders. This situation is more vivid in early March 2003 when **trader2** suffers severe loss of the asset while MPG can minimize the fatality.

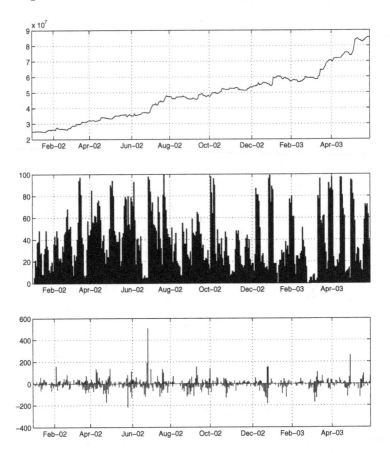

Fig. 8. Synthetic Analysis of MPG

However MPG is not always winning. For example, during late January 2003, the stock fund increases with wrong recommendations purchased by somewhat large amount money. Since the four predictors are not perfect, it is not possible to induce constantly winning trades. But, the higher level consideration of several predictors and stock fund ratio in MPG makes trading more profitable and unrisky.

7   Conclusion

In this paper, the multi-predictor approach is further utilized by reinforcement learning to adaptively allocate the asset over the recommendations from each predictor. We make an adaptive asset allocator, meta policy, incorporating the information of recommendations of predictors and the stock fund ratios as the part of the state representation of Q-learning.

Using meta policy induces more profits than the trading based on other fixed asset allocation methods in the simulation on Korean stock market over specified test period. This results show that using reinforcement learning to utilize supervised learning can makes the complex problems manageable such as the stock trading as well as synergetic effect of both algorithms in decision making.

Acknowledgement

This research was supported in part by the Ministry of Education and Human Resources Development under the BK21-IT Program. The RIACT at Seoul National University provides research facilities for this study. The Nature Solutions Corp. provides the stock data and simulation tools.

References

1. E. F. Fama and K. R. French, Dividend Yields and Expected Stock Returns, *Journal of Financial Economics*, 22, pp. 3-26, 1988.
2. T. Hellström, *A Random Walk through the Stock Market*, ph.D. Thesis, Department of Computing Science, Umeå University, 1998.
3. P. J. Kaufman, *The New Commodity Trading Systems and Methods*, Wiley, NewYork, 1987.
4. S. M. Kendall and K. Ord, *Time Series*, Oxford, New York, 1997.
5. S. D. Kim, J. W. Lee, J. Lee, and J.-S. Chae, A Two-Phase Stock Trading System Using Distributional Differences, *In Proceedings of International Conference on Database and Expert Systems Applications*, pp. 143-152, 2002.
6. J. W. Lee and J. O, A Multi-agent Q-learning Framework for Optimizing Stock Trading Systems, *In Proceedings of International Conference on Database and Expert Systems Applications*, pp. 153-162, 2002.
7. B. G. Malkiel, *A Random Walk Down Wall Street*, Norton, New York, 1996.
8. J. Moody and M. Saffell, Learning to Trade via Direct Reinforcement, *IEEE Transactions on Neural Networks*, 12(4), pp. 875-889, 2001.
9. R. Neuneier, Risk Sensitive Reinforcement Learning, *Advances in Neural Information Processing Systems*, pp. 1031-1037, MIT Press, Cambridge, 1999.
10. J. O, J. W. Lee, and B.-T. Zhang, Stock Trading System Using Reinforcement Learning with Cooperative Agents, *In Proceedings of International Conference on Machine Learning*, pp. 451-458, Morgan Kaufmann, 2002.
11. E. W. Saad, D. V. Prokhorov, D. C. Wunsch II, Comparative Study of Stock Trend Prediction Using Time Delay, Recurrent and Probabilistic Neural Networks, *IEEE Transactions on Neural Networks*, 9(6), pp. 1456-1470, 1998.
12. R. S. Sutton and A. G. Barto, *Reinforcement Learning : An Introduction*. MIT Press, Cambridge, 1998.

Justification-Based Selection
of Training Examples for Case Base Reduction

Santiago Ontañón and Enric Plaza

IIIA, Artificial Intelligence Research Institute
CSIC, Spanish Council for Scientific Research
Campus UAB, 08193 Bellaterra, Catalonia, Spain
{santi,enric}@iiia.csic.es, http://www.iiia.csic.es

Abstract. Maintaining compact and competent case bases has become a main topic of Case Based Reasoning (CBR) research. The main goal is to obtain a compact case base (with a reduced number of cases) without losing accuracy. In this work we present JUST, a technique to reduce the size of a case base while maintaining the classification accuracy of the CBR system. JUST uses *justifications* in order to select a subset of cases from the original case base that will form the new reduced case base. A justification is an explanation that the CBR system generates to justify the solution found for a given problem. Moreover, we present empirical evaluation in various data sets showing that JUST is an effective case base reduction technique that maintains the classification accuracy of the case base.

Keywords: CBR, Case Base Management, Case Base Reduction.

1 Introduction

Maintaining compact and competent case bases has become a main topic of Case Based Reasoning (CBR) research. The main goal is to obtain a compact case base (with a reduced number of cases) without losing problem solving accuracy. In modern CBR systems, with large case bases, it has been found that adding new cases into the case base is not always beneficial. Smyth and Cunningham [7] analyze this problem and find that although similarity-based methods (such as the ones typically used in CBR) do not usually suffer from overfitting when adding new cases into the case base, the efficiency of the system can degrade. The efficiency of the system can be divided in two factors: the retrieval time and the reuse time. While reuse time diminishes as the case base grows, retrieval time increases. Therefore, by adding new cases into an already saturated cases base, the same problem solving performance is achieved, but with a reduced efficiency.

There has been significant research in case base maintenance recently. Aha et al. [2, 1] propose several algorithms for reducing case bases (CBL2, CBL3 and CBL4) based on the rule "if I can correctly solve a P with a case base C, then it is not interesting to add P to C". Related to CBL2 is also the Condensed Nearest Neighbor algorithms [4, 9, 5].

J.-F. Boulicaut et al. (Eds.): ECML 2004, LNAI 3201, pp. 310–321, 2004.

Another line of case base maintenance policies are those of Smyth and Keane [8]. They define several competence metrics based on finding "competence groups" inside a case base that they later use to define case base maintenance policies by deleting from the case base those cases with minimum competence. Later, Zhu and Yang [10] propose an alternative version of the Smyth and Keane strategy based on case addition instead of case deletion.

Salamó and Golobardes [6] propose two deletion policies for CBR systems based on the rough set theory: *Accuracy-Classification Case Memory* ACCM and *Negative Accuracy-Classification Case Memory* NACCM. Both ACCM and NACCM are able to keep classification accuracy at a very high level (sometimes even improving the accuracy of the complete case base), but the reduction of cases obtained is not as large as algorithms such as CBL2.

In this paper we present a novel approach to case base maintenance based on the concept of *justifications*. A justification is an explanation that the CBR system generates to justify the solution found for a given problem. The analysis of justifications is able to find the weak points (or the "competence holes") of a case base. We will present a technique called JUST (JUstification-based Selection of Training examples) to reduce the size of a case base while maintaining the classification accuracy of the CBR system. Suppose that we have a CBR system with a case base C consisting of n cases. JUST will construct a reduced case base C^r by selecting cases from C. JUST follows the case addition strategy presented by Zhu and Yang [10] (in the sense that it also constructs a new case base by selecting cases from C) but using justifications in order to select which cases to select from C instead of a competence measure.

The structure of the paper is as follows. First, in Section 2, we formally present the idea of justifications. Then, Section 3 presents the JUST technique. After that, we present an empirical evaluation of JUST and the paper closes with the conclusions section.

2   Justifications

Let $C = \{c_1, \ldots, c_n\}$ be the case base of a CBR system, composed of n cases. Each case $c_i = \langle P, S \rangle$ is a tuple containing a problem P and a solution S. We will use the dot notation to refer to the elements inside a tuple, i.e. we will note $c_i.S$ to make reference to the solution in case c_i. Usually, when a classifier solves a problem P, the output is only a solution class (or at most a ranked list of solution classes with an associated probability). However, some machine learning methods can provide more information than just the solution class. Specifically, some methods can output a *justification*.

Definition: A *justification* J built by a CBR method to solve a problem P that has been classified into a solution class S_k is a description containing the relevant information of P for having predicted S_k as the solution for P.

In our work, we use LID [3], a lazy learning method for CBR systems capable of building symbolic justifications. LID uses the feature term formalism to represent cases. *Feature Terms* (or ψ-terms) are a generalization of the first order

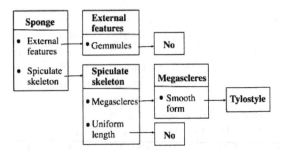

Fig. 1. Simbolic justification returned by LID.

terms. The main difference is that in first order terms (e.g. $person(x_1, x_2, x_3)$) the parameters of the terms are identified by position, while in a feature term the parameters (called *features*) are identified by name (e.g. $person[name \doteq x_1, father \doteq x_2, mother \doteq x_3]$). Another difference is that feature terms have a *sort*, for instance, the previous example belongs to the sort *person*. These sorts can have subsorts (e.g. *man* and *woman* are subsorts of *person*). Feature terms have an informational order relation ($\sqsubseteq$) among them called subsumption, where $\psi \sqsubseteq \psi'$ means all the information contained in ψ is also contained in ψ'. We say that ψ subsumes ψ' (or that ψ' satisfies ψ); we can also say that ψ is a generalization of ψ'. When a feature term has only a sort and no features, it is called a *leaf*.

Figure 1 shows a symbolic justification J returned by LID, represented as a feature term. Each box in the figure represents a node. On the top of a box the sort of the node is shown, and on the lower part, the features with a known value are shown. The arrows mean that the feature on the left part of the arrow takes the node at the right as value; nodes *No* and *Tylostile* are leaf nodes. LID has returned the justification J for classifying a problem P in a specific solution class S_k such that $J \sqsubseteq P$. In addition, there is a subset of cases $c_1, \ldots c_r$ retrieved from the case base such that $\forall c_i \in \{c_1, \ldots c_r\}, J \sqsubseteq c_i.P$. These are the cases that *endorse* S_k as a solution for P, since all (or the majority) of them have solution S_k. Moreover, J is a symbolic similarity description since it contains what is shared between P and $c_1, \ldots, c_r$ and that is relevant (not all that is shared). Notice that albeit J is a generalization of all the cases $c_1, \ldots, c_r$ and of the problem P LID is still a lazy learning method. The difference between induction and lazy learning is that induction builds a global approximation of the concept to be learnt, while lazy learning builds local approximations around the problem P to be solved. From this viewpoint, a justification J for a problem P is the local approximation built by LID, and the form of J is a symbolic description that generalizes $c_1, \ldots, c_r$ and P.

3   Justification-Based Selection of Training Examples

This section presents the JUST (Justification-based Selection of Training examples) technique. JUST is a case base reduction technique whose goal is to reduce the number of cases in a given case base without reducing the classification accuracy obtained with that case base.

JUST is an iterative technique that selects cases from case base C and adds them to another (reduced) case base C^r, until certain termination criterion is met. The termination criterion could be any property of the new case base C^r, but we will focus on these two: finding a case base C^r with at most M cases, finding a case base C^r with a certain accuracy level α. Before explaining JUST, we need to introduce some concepts:

Definition: An *exam* $E = \{P_1, ..., P_m\}$ is a set of problems (i.e. unlabeled examples) for which the system knows the solution and that JUST has still not added into C^r, i.e. $E \subseteq \{c_i.P | c_i \in C \land c_i \notin C^r\}$

The way JUST builds exams is by maintaining a set C^u of cases that are present in C and that are not in C^r. The problems in any subset of cases from C^u are a valid exam. The idea of the exams is to build a set of problems with which to evaluate the performance of the new case base C^r. Moreoever, when the system solves a problem, a *Justified Endorsing Record* is built:

Definition: A Justified Endorsing Record (JER) $\mathbf{J}^k = \langle P_k, S, J \rangle$ is a tuple containing the problem P_k, the solution class S predicted for the problem P_k, and the justification J for S being a solution for P_k.

We will note $\mathbf{J}_E = \{\mathbf{J}^k | \mathbf{J}^k.P = P_k \in E\}$ the set of JERs build by the system using the reduced case base C^r for each problem $P_k \in E$. Moreover, since we know that the correct solution for P_k is S_k, we can define the set of incorrect JERs $\mathbf{J}_E^- = \{\mathbf{J}^k | \mathbf{J}^k \in \mathbf{J}_E \land \mathbf{J}^k.S \neq S_k\}$ (i.e. the JERs for the problems in E for which the system has predicted an incorrect solution using the case base C^r.

A case c_i is a *counterexample* of an incorrect JER ($\mathbf{J}^k \in \mathbf{J}_E^-$) if $c_i.P$ is subsumed by the incorrect justification $\mathbf{J}^k.J$ and $c_i.S$ is a different solution class than the predicted one, i.e. $\mathbf{J}^k.J \sqsubseteq c_i.P$ and $c_1.S \neq \mathbf{J}^k.S$. Moreover, we can define also a *valid counterexample* as a counterexample c_i that predicts the correct solution for P_k, i.e. $c_i.S = S_k$.

Definition: The *refutation set* $R_{\mathbf{J}^k}$ of an incorrect JER $\mathbf{J}^k$ is defined as the set of cases from C^u that are valid counterexamples of $\mathbf{J}^k$. Formally: $R_{\mathbf{J}^k} = \{c_i \in C^u | \mathbf{J}^k.J \sqsubseteq c_i.P \land c_i.S = S_k\}$, where S_k is the correct solution class for the problem $\mathbf{J}^k.P = P_k$.

The examples in a refutation set $R_{\mathbf{J}^k}$ are the examples that can potentially prevent the system from making similar errors in the future and therefore they are candidate examples to be added to C^r. The collection of the refutation sets for all the incorrect JERs $\mathbf{J}_E^-$ will be noted as $\mathbf{R} = \{R_{\mathbf{J}^k} | \mathbf{J}^k \in \mathbf{J}_E^-\}$. Finally, we define the *belying set* as follows:

Definition: The *belying set* B is the minimum set of counterexamples that belies all the incorrect justifications built by the CBR system over an exam E using the case base C^r. Formally, the belying set is the collection of cases $B \subseteq C^u$ such that $\forall R_{\mathbf{J}^k} \in \mathbf{R} : B \cap R_{\mathbf{J}^k} \neq \emptyset$ and that $\nexists B' | \forall R_{\mathbf{J}^k} \in \mathbf{R} : B' \cap R_{\mathbf{J}^k} \neq \emptyset \land B' \subset B$. Notice

Function JUST $(C, \mathcal{T}, m)$
    $t = 0;\ C_0^r = \emptyset;\ C_0^u = C;$
    <u>Do</u>
        $E_t = \underline{\text{select-exam}}(C_t^u, m);$
        $\mathbf{J}_{E_t} = \underline{\text{build-JERs}}(E_t);$
        $\mathbf{J}_{E_t}^- = \{\mathbf{J}^k | \mathbf{J}^k \in \mathbf{J}_{E_t} \wedge \mathbf{J}^k.S \neq S_k\};$
        $\mathbf{R}_t = \underline{\text{build-refutation-sets}}(\mathbf{J}_{E_t}^-, C_t^u);$
        $B_t = \underline{\text{build-belying-set}}(\mathbf{R}_t);$
        $C_{t+1}^r = C_t^r \cup B_t;\ t = t + 1;$
    <u>While</u>(not $\mathcal{T}$);
    <u>Return</u>(C_t^r);
End-Function

Fig. 2. The JUST algorithm, where C is the initial case base, $\mathcal{T}$ is the termination criterion and m is the exam size.

that a) the belying set contains at least one counterexample that belies each one of the incorrect justifications and b) the belying set contains the minimum number of counterexamples that belie all incorrect justifications. For instance, if two refutation sets for two JERs $\mathbf{J}^k$ and $\mathbf{J}_j$ share a counterexample c_i, including c_i into B is enough to belie both incorrect justifications.

After introducing these definitions we can now present the JUST method. Figure 2 shows the JUST iterative algorithm. At each iteration t, JUST will select some cases from C to be added to the new reduced case base. We will define three sets of cases at each iteration t: C_t^r is the reduced case base created by JUST (containing all the cases selected in the previous iterations), $C_t^u = C - C_t^r$ are the cases from C that are not in C_t^r and finally B_t is the set of cases selected by JUST from C to be added to C_t^r in the iteration t.

The JUST method works as follows: Initially, $t = 0$, $C_0^r = \emptyset$ and $C_0^u = C$. At each iteration t, JUST builds an exam $E_t \subseteq C_t^u$ of size m. The size m of the exams is a parameter of JUST, in Section 4 we will analyze the effect of varying the parameter m. The CBR system solves all the problems in E_t using the case base C_t^r and builds the set of JERs $\mathbf{J}_{E_t}$. Then, the set $\mathbf{J}_{E_t}^-$ containing all the incorrect JERs in $\mathbf{J}_{E_t}$ is built. Notice that JUST can determine whether a JER $\mathbf{J}^k \in \mathbf{J}_{E_t}$ is correct or not because the solution for each problem in E_t is known (since they are problems extracted from cases of C_t^u). Next, JUST builds a refutation set for each incorrect JER in $\mathbf{J}_{E_t}^-$, obtaining the collection of refutation sets $\mathbf{R}_t$. Finally, the belying set B_t is built; B_t is the set of cases that JUST will add to C_t^r in the iteration t: therefore, $C_{t+1}^r = C_t^r \cup B_t$. If the termination criterion $\mathcal{T}$ is still not met, a new iteration starts.

There is a special situation for JUST when the belying set B_t is empty and the termination criterion is not met: then JUST selects a single random case from C_t^u and adds it to C_t^r. This is done to ensure convergence, avoiding an unbounded number of iterations. This way, the maximum number of iterations of JUST is exactly n (the number of cases in C), since at each iteration, at least one case is added to C_t^r.

When the termination criterion is met (at an iteration t) the case base C_t^r is considered the target case base C^r, and C_t^r is returned. If the set C_t^u is empty, this means that all the cases from C have been selected, and that C^r contains all the cases from C, and the process is also terminated.

3.1   Termination Criterion

In our experiments we have used two different termination criteria $\mathcal{T}$. If the termination criterion is to obtain a case base C^r of a given size M, JUST will finish once C_t^r has reached the size M. In fact, JUST will output C_{t-1}^r when it detects at iteration t that $size(C_t^r) > M$.

When the termination criterion is to obtain a case base C^r with a minimum accuracy level α, JUST uses the answers of the exams as an estimation of the current classification accuracy. However, depending on the size of the exam, this estimation may not be very reliable. If the size of the exam is large, the accuracy obtained on that exam is a good estimation of the classification accuracy of the CBR system; thus, when the accuracy obtained by the system in a large exam is above α, the JUST process can terminate. In our experiments, α takes values around 90%. Moreover, if the size of the exam is small, JUST needs more than one exam to have a good estimate of the accuracy.

The number of exams needed to have a good estimation can be determined assuming that the correctness of an answer can be modeled as a binomial distribution. Using the binomial distribution, for estimating accuracy values around $\alpha = 90\%$, 60 answers are enough to have a 66% certainty of having an error smaller than the 4% in the estimation of the accuracy. For instance, for an exam size $m = 20$, 3 exams are enough for being 66% sure that the accuracy of the CBR system does not differ more than a 4% from the estimated one. Thus, if the average accuracy α' of 3 consecutive exams of size $m = 20$ is higher than α, JUST can terminate with a 66% certainty that the accuracy of the CBR system is in a $\pm 4\%$ margin around α'. For an exam size of $m = 10$, 6 consecutive exams are needed for the same result. Summarizing, the termination policy is the following: if the average accuracy in the last $60/m$ exams is above α, JUST will stop.

3.2   ▭▭ ▯▯ in a Nutshell

The idea behind JUST is quite simple: at each iteration, the system tests which are the weak points (or competence holes) of the new reduced case base C^r by solving an exam. The justification J given for an incorrectly answered problem P in an exam is an incorrect local approximation of the neighborhood of P. Moreover, since a justification J is also a symbolic description, it can be used to find a case (a counter example) that satisfies that description and that proves that J is incorrect (i.e. the case has a solution different from the predicted by J). Adding that case into the reduced case base prevents the incorrect local approximation to be generated again, thus improving problem solving in that area of the problem space.

In fact, JUST selects the minimum set of cases that are counterexamples of all the incorrect justifications (the belying set) in order to minimize the number of cases of the reduced case base. Therefore, JUST iteratively constructs a case base that is more competent at each iteration, and this increase of competence is done trying to minimize the number of cases needed. Of course, all the process strongly depends on the ability of JUST to detect the weak points in the case base C^r. Therefore, we expect that the larger the exam size, the better JUST will work. In the extreme, all the remaining cases in C_t^u can be used as the exam in iteration t to obtain the smallest case base that JUST can obtain.

4   Experimental Results

This section presents the experimental results comparing the performance achieved by a CBR system after using the JUST case base reduction technique with the performance of the system without reducing the case base.

The lazy learning method we use is LID [3], a CBR method that is able to generate justifications and that can work both with propositional and relational data. We have used three different datasets to test out approach: *soybean*, a well known propositional dataset, *zoo*, another propositional data set from the UCI machine learning repository, and *marine sponges*, a complex relational data set [3]. Sponges have a complex structure, making them amenable to build complex justifications. The soybean data set consists of 307 examples, each one with 35 attributes (some of them with missing values), and there are 19 possible solution classes. the zoo data set consists of 101 examples, each one with 17 attributes and 7 solution classes. The sponges data set consists of 280 examples, each one with between 10 and 50 attributes (depending on its structure), and there are 3 solution classes.

The presented results are an average of 5 10-fold cross validation runs. Each 10-fold cross validation run involves 10 experimental runs. In an experimental run, a 10% of the cases are separated from the rest and will be used as the test set. The other 90% of the cases is used as the system case base, then the accuracy is measured after applying the case base reduction technique.

We have made experiments comparing the JUST technique with two base strategies: a base CBR system that does not use any case base reduction technique, and a CBR system that uses the CB2 [1] case base reduction technique. The idea of CB2 is simple: as with JUST we have two case bases C and C^r, individual cases are randomly selected from C, if the system can solve them using the cases in C^r, then they are discarded, otherwise they are added to C^r. The process is iterated until all the cases in C have been selected. Therefore, we will use no termination criteria for CB2 (as the ones used in JUST) but let it execute till the end.

Table 1 shows the results obtained by three CBR systems, one using the JUST case base reduction technique, another using the CB2 case base reduction technique and the third one using the complete case base for the three datasets (sponges, soybean and zoo). We have used JUST with an exam size of $m =$

Table 1. Comparison of the classification accuracy and case base size of JUST agains CB2 and with the complete case base.

	Sponges		Soybean		Zoo	
	Accuracy	CB size	Accuracy	CB size	Accuracy	CB size
JUST (m=20)	88.12%	32.34%	88.59%	55.00%	95.44%	38.86%
CB2	82.14%	22.71%	81.00%	28.62%	95.24%	18.59%
Complete CB	88.21%	100.00%	88.50%	100.00%	95.45%	100.00%

20, and a termination criterion of reaching an accuracy of about 90% for the sponges and soybean data sets, and of about 96% in the zoo data set (we have chosen those parameters as slightly greater values than the accuracy values of the complete case bases).

The table shows that JUST has been able to reduce the size of the case bases to the 32.34% of the total number of cases in the sponges case base, to the 55.00% in the soybean case base and to the 38.86% in the zoo case base. This reduction is achieved without losing classification accuracy: notice that the accuracy for JUST in the sponges data set is 88.12% while the accuracy without case reduction is 88.21%, the difference being not statistically significant. For the soybean data set, JUST has achieved a classification accuracy of 88.59% while the CBR system without case reduction achieves a 88.50% of classification accuracy; again the difference is not statistically significant. In the zoo data set, the accuracy achieved by JUST is 95.44%, and the accuracy achieved with the complete case base is 95.45%. Moreover, the termination criterion of JUST requested case bases with a 90% of classification accuracy in soybean and sponges and 96% in the zoo data set. Notice that JUST has stopped before reaching that accuracy in all the case bases. The reason is that the termination criterion used in our experiments has a margin of error of ±4% (see Section 3.1). A termination criterion with a lower margin of error could be used if need be.

Comparing JUST with CB2 in Table 1, notice that CB2 obtains reduced case bases that are even smaller than the achieved by JUST: 22.71% in the sponges data set, 28.62% in the soybean data set and 18.59% in the zoo data set versus 32.34%, 55.00% and 38.86% achieved with JUST. However, CB2 reduces the case base without preserving the classification accuracy in two of the three data sets; CB2 has been able to keep the degree of accuracy of the complete case base only in the zoo data set, in the other two data sets, the accuracy achieved by CB2 is appreciably lower than that of the complete case base: 82.14% in the sponges data set and 81.00% in the soybean data set. JUST, however, maintains the accuracy of the complete case base, namely 88.12% and 88.59% respectively. CB2 has problems in two data sets because cases are discarded in a very eager way. JUST, however, has a broader view of the problem and never discards any case until termination is decided. Thus, JUST is able to discard a considerable number of cases while maintaining the accuracy levels of the complete case base.

In order to test the effects of the size of the exams in JUST we have experimented with several exam sizes: 1, 5, 10, 20 and unlimited (when exam size is

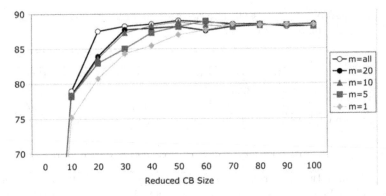

Fig. 3. Comparison of the accuracy evolution in the reduced case bases for several exam sizes in the sponges dataset using JUST.

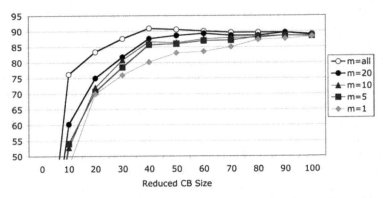

Fig. 4. Comparison of the accuracy evolution in the reduced case bases for several exam sizes in the soybean dataset using JUST.

unlimited, the whole set of cases C_t^u is used as the exam). Figures 3 and 4 show the accuracy results for JUST in the sponges and soybean data sets for several exam sizes. The unlimited exam size is shown in the figures as $m = all$. This experiments are performed using the case base size termination criterion (see Section 3.1) for sizes 10%, 20%, ..., and up to 100% percentage of the complete case base. Figures 3 and 4 plot the accuracy achieved by JUST varying the desired size of the reduced case base. For each exam size, a different plot is shown. We have made experiments with the three data sets but, for lack of space, we only present here results concerning marine sponges and soybean data set.

Figure 3 shows that as the exam size increases, JUST is able to reach higher accuracies with smaller case bases. For instance, reaching an accuracy higher than 85% with an exam size $m = 1$, JUST needs a case base of the 40% of the size of the complete case base, while with the exam size is $m = 5$, only a 30% of the original cases are needed. In the extreme, when the exam size is unlimited (i.e. all the cases in C_t^u are used as the exam at each iteration), only a 20% of the cases are needed. This is because when the exam size is larger, JUST can obtain

Table 2. Empirical JUST complexity analysis.

m	1	5	10	20	all
retrievals	256.8	713.0	458.0	1158.0	1627.7
iterations	256.8	142.6	45.8	57.9	8.2

more information of the weak points in the reduced case base C_t^r, and therefore make a more accurate choice of which cases to select to add to the reduced case base C_t^r. Moreover, notice that when the termination criterion is to obtain a case base with more than the 70% of the cases in the complete case base, there is no difference in the classification accuracy by varying the exam size. Notice also that in some experiments JUST has been able to obtain case bases that reach higher accuracy than the complete case base. For instance, when the exam size is unlimited, the accuracy achieved with a case base with the 50% of the cases of the complete sponges case base is 89.00% while the accuracy of the complete case base is 88.21%.

Figure 4 shows the experiments using the soybean data set. Notice that as the exam size increases, as before, the accuracy achieved by JUST also increases. However, the accuracy achieved by JUST in the soybean data set with an unlimited exam size is much higher than the accuracy with smaller exam sizes. For instance, with a case base containing the 40% of the cases in the complete case base, JUST with an unlimited exam size achieves an accuracy of 90.88% while the complete case base accuracy is 88.50%. This means that the exam size needed by JUST in the soybean data set to achieve a good performance is larger than the exam size needed in the sponges data set. The reason seems to be that the soybean data set has 19 solution classes and the sponges data set only 3. The larger the number of classes, the larger the exams should be in order to obtain representative information of the weak points of the reduced case base.

The overall conclusion is that the larger the exam size, the higher the performance of JUST, i.e. as we increase the exam size, we will obtain reduced case bases that are smaller and more accurate. However, as we increase the exam size, we also increase the computational cost of JUST. Let us analyze JUST in computational cost as the number of retrievals performed during the case base reduction process. The cost of JUST can be divided in two costs: the cost of solving the exams, and the cost of building the belying sets. Let T be the number of iterations that JUST has executed, n the number of cases in the complete case base C, and m the exam size. The cost of solving the exams is at most $T \times min(m, n)$ retrievals, and the cost of building the belying set is also at most $T \times min(m, n)$. Therefore, the complexity of JUST is of order $T \times min(m, n)$. As explained in Section 3, the maximum number of iterations is n, the number of cases in the complete case base C. Therefore, the worst case complexity is $n \times min(m, n)$, i.e. $O(n^2)$.

We have also performed an empirical evaluation of the JUST complexity varying the exam size in the soybean data set, as Table 2 shows.

The termination criterion used to perform those experiments is to reach an accuracy of the 90%. We see that the number of retrievals increases as the exam size increases (as predicted by the theoretical complexity of $n \times min(m, n)$). However, the practical complexity is much lower than the theoretical complexity, specially for large exam sizes, where the number of iterations is much smaller than the theoretical maximum n. This results point out that JUST can be used with large exam sizes without having to pay a high computational cost. Notice that the practical cost for an unlimited exam size, is 1627.7 retrievals in average, while the theoretical bound is $n^2 = 276 \times 276 = 76{,}176$ retrievals, since in the soybean data set the complete case base C has 276 cases (the other 10% is reserved as the test set). We can conclude that if the computational cost is not a problem in our CBR system an unlimited exam size should be used in order to obtain the maximum benefit from JUST. Moreover, although the cost of JUST with large exam sizes is not prohibitive (as we have seen in our experiments), smaller exam sizes may be used in order to reduce the computational cost if need be.

5 Conclusions and Future Work

In this paper we have presented JUST, a case base reduction technique based in the notion of justifications. In our experiments we have used LID as a CBR method that is able to generate justifications, but our work is not restricted to LID. Many other CBR methods can be adapted to generate justifications, for instance CBR systems using case indexing based on decision trees can return the portion of the decision tree used to solve a problem as the justification. We have seen that a justification J can be considered a local approximation of the neighborhood of the problem to solve, i.e. as a generalization of all the retrieved cases to solve a problem. Therefore, as future work, we plan to apply JUST to other CBR methods, such as nearest neighbor, that cannot provide justifications. How to adapt a nearest neighbor classifier is not obvious. However, we can see the set of retrieved cases as a local approximation to solve a problem P. From that local approximation an ad-hoc justification can be built by computing some generalization(s) of all or some of the retrieved cases. These generalizations could then be used by JUST to compute the belying sets. An interesting question here is whether this approach will work for any type of lazy classification method.

We have also seen that JUST is a parametric case base reduction method. By varying the exam size m, we can modify the behavior of JUST: with small exam sizes we can obtain moderate case base reductions at a low cost, and with large exam sizes we can obtain large case base reductions, but at a higher computational cost. This is clearly an advantage with respect to other case base reduction methods that are not parametric, since JUST can be adapted to several CBR systems that have different size and computational time restrictions. Moreover, JUST can accept another parameter: the termination criterion. By changing the termination criterion, we can request JUST to obtain reduced case bases that satisfy any desired conditions.

Finally, we have seen in the experiments section that there are reduced case bases that achieve higher accuracies than the complete case base. For instance, in Figure 4, the optimal point (with an unlimited exam size) is to build a reduced case base with the 40% of the original cases (since this is where the maximum accuracy was reached). Instead than by looking at the plot as we have done now, it remains as future work to automatically find the optimal accuracy point.

Acknowledgements

The authors thank Eva Armengol and Josep-Lluís Arcos of the IIIA-CSIC for the development of the LID and of the Noos agent platform respectively. Support for this work came from CIRIT FI/FAP 2001 grant and project SAMAP (MCYT-FEDER) TIC2002-04146-C05-01.

References

1. David W. Aha. Case-based learning algorithms. In *DARPA Case-Based Reasoning Workshop*, pages 147–158, 1991.
2. David W. Aha, Dennis Kibler, and Marc K. Albert. Instance-based learning algorithms. *Machine Learning*, 6(1):37–66, 1991.
3. E. Armengol and E. Plaza. Lazy induction of descriptions for relational case-based learning. In Luc de Raedt and Peter Flach, editors, *EMCL 2001*, number 2167 in Lecture Notes in Artificial Intelligence, pages 13–24. Springer-Verlag, 2001.
4. P. Hart. The condensed nearest neighbor rule. *IEEE Transactions on Information Theory*, 14:515–516, 1967.
5. David B. Leake and David C. Wilson. Remembering why to remember: Performance-guided case-base maintenance. In *EWCBR*, pages 161–172, 2000.
6. Elisabet Golobardes Maria Salamó. Hybrid deletion policies for case base maintenance. In *FLAIRS'2003*, pages 1150–155, 2003.
7. B. Smyth. The utility problem analysed: A case-based reasoning persepctive. In *Third European Workshop on Case-Based Reasoning EWCBR-96*, Lecture Notes in Artificial Intelligence, pages 234–248. Springer Verlag, 1996.
8. Barry Smyth and Mark T. Keane. Remenbering to forget: A competence-preserving case deletion policy for case-based reasoning systems. In *Proceedings of IJCAI-95*, pages 377–382, 1995.
9. Barry Smyth and Elizabeth McKenna. Building compact competent case-bases. *Lecture Notes in Computer Science*, 1650:329–342, 1999.
10. Jun Zhu and Qiang Yang. Remembering to add: Competence-preserving case-addition policies for case base maintenance. In *IJCAI*, pages 234–241, 1999.

Using Feature Conjunctions Across Examples for Learning Pairwise Classifiers

Satoshi Oyama[1] and Christopher D. Manning[2]

[1] Department of Social Informatics, Kyoto University,
Kyoto 606-8501, Japan
oyama@kuis.kyoto-u.ac.jp
http://www.dl.kuis.kyoto-u.ac.jp/~oyama/
[2] Department of Computer Science, Stanford University,
Stanford, CA 94305-9040, USA
manning@cs.stanford.edu
http://www-nlp.stanford.edu/~manning/

Abstract. We propose a kernel method for using combinations of features across example pairs in learning pairwise classifiers. Identifying two instances in the same class is an important technique in duplicate detection, entity matching, and other clustering problems. However, it is a difficult problem when instances have few discriminative features. One typical example is to check whether two abbreviated author names in different papers refer to the same person or not. While using combinations of different features from each instance may improve the classification accuracy, doing this straightforwardly is computationally intensive. Our method uses interaction between different features without high computational cost using a kernel. At medium recall levels, this method can give a precision 4 to 8 times higher than that of previous methods in author matching problems.

1 Introduction

Pairwise classifiers, which identify whether two instances belong to the same class or not, are important components in duplicate detection, entity matching, and other clustering applications. For example, in citation matching [8], two citations are compared and determined whether they refer to the same paper or not (Figure 1).

In early work, these classifiers were based on fixed or manually tuned distance metrics. In recent years, there have been several attempts to make pairwise classifiers automatically from labeled training data using machine learning techniques [1, 2, 11, 14]. Most of them are based on string edit distance or common features between two examples.

These methods are effective when two instances from the same class have many common features like two variant citations to the *same* paper. However, if two instances from the same class have few common features, these methods have difficulties in finding these pairs and achieving high recall. An instance of this is trying to identify the same author across *different* papers.

J.-F. Boulicaut et al. (Eds.): ECML 2004, LNAI 3201, pp. 322–333, 2004.

Gupta, A., Mumick, I, Subrahmanian, V. 1993. Maintaining Views Incrementally. In Proc. of ACM SIGMOD, pp. 157-166

A. Gupta, I. S. Mumick, V. S. Subrahmanian: Maintaining Views Incrementally. SIGMOD Conference 1993: 157-166

A. Gupta, I. S. Mumick, K. A. Ross: Adapting Materialized Views after Redefinitions. SIGMOD Conference 1995: 211-222

Fig. 1. Matching citations

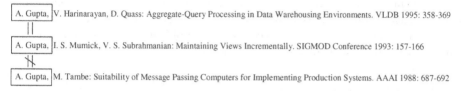

A. Gupta, V. Harinarayan, D. Quass: Aggregate-Query Processing in Data Warehousing Environments. VLDB 1995: 358-369

A. Gupta, I. S. Mumick, V. S. Subrahmanian: Maintaining Views Incrementally. SIGMOD Conference 1993: 157-166

A. Gupta, M. Tambe: Suitability of Message Passing Computers for Implementing Production Systems. AAAI 1988: 687-692

Fig. 2. Matching authors

First names of authors are abbreviated to initials in many citations. As shown in Figure 2, identifying the same authors among abbreviated names is another important problem in citation analysis or evaluating researchers. However, fielded citation databases such as ISI Citation Index[1] or "Most Cited Authors in Computer Science" in CiteSeer[2] cannot distinguish different authors with the same first initial and the same last name. Distinguishing these authors is important for treating people as first class entities in citation databases.

Matching authors is a harder problem than matching citations. As we can see in Figure 1, two citations to the same paper have many common keywords. Conversely, if two citation strings are the same or have many common keywords, we can suspect the two citations refer to the same paper. On the other hand, even if two strings of author names are exactly same, we cannot conclude these names refer to the same person in the real world. To disambiguate author names, we have to look into other fields in citations than author names themselves.

However, there is another difficulty in this problem. The first two records in Figure 2 have no common words other than the names of the first authors even though these two authors are the same person. Humans can somehow infer the identity of these two persons by considering the strong connection between the two conferences and the topical similarity between words in the titles. However, in such a case, where pairs from the same class have few common features, it is difficult to automatically determine these pairs using pairwise classifiers based on string similarity or common features.

One approach to solving this problem is using conjunctions of features across examples. In the case of Figure 2, we could give similarities to different words across examples like "SIGMOD" and "VLDB", and compute the overall similarity based on them. This helps avoiding zero similarity and breaking orthogonality. If there are many pairs where one paper is published in VLDB and the other

---

[1] http://isiknowledge.com/
[2] http://citeseer.ist.psu.edu/mostcited.html

paper is published in SIGMOD in labeled positive data (pairs of papers authored by the same person), we can expect that the learning algorithm incorporates this feature into the classifier. However, if we straightforwardly make all pairs from original features, the dimension of the resulting feature space become large and we cannot apply learning algorithms to real problems with many features.

In this paper, we propose a method for using feature conjunctions across examples in learning pairwise classifiers without causing excessive computational cost by using kernel methods [12, 13]. By using our kernel, learning algorithms can use feature conjunctions across examples without actually computing them. This results in high classification accuracy for problems with few common features, which are difficult for existing methods.

2   Pairwise Classification

2.1   Problem Definition

Pairwise classification is the problem of determining whether a pair of instances, x^α and x^β, belong to the same class or not. In a binary classification case, we look for the following function:

$$f(x^\alpha, x^\beta) = \begin{cases} 1 & \text{(if } x^\alpha \text{ and } x^\beta \text{ belong to the same class),} \\ -1 & \text{(otherwise).} \end{cases}$$

Pairwise classification and pairwise similarity have a close relation. We can also consider a problem where the function f outputs continuous values such as $f(x^\alpha, x^\beta) \in [0, 1]$, which give similarities between instances. We can change this into a binary classifier by introducing a certain threshold. On the other hand, many binary classifiers can be converted to a classifier that outputs continuous values [2]. Therefore, we will sometimes use the terms pairwise classification and pairwise similarity interchangeably.

Pairwise classification is an important component in duplicate detection, identity matching, and many other clustering problems. We make a global clustering decision based on pairwise classifications, for instance, by making the transitive closure of guessed positive pairs [2].

2.2   Making Pair Instances from the Original Data

It is a difficult problem to define accurate pairwise classifiers by hand. Thus there have been many works on inducing classifiers automatically from data using machine learning techniques. Many earlier methods first sample pair instances from the data and have humans label them according to whether they belong to the same class or not. Then these training examples are fed to binary classifier learning algorithms such as Support Vector Machines (SVMs) [15].

For example, Bilenko and Mooney [2] represent an original instance by a feature vector $x^\alpha = (x_1^\alpha, x_2^\alpha, \ldots, x_n^\alpha)$, where each feature corresponds to whether a word in a vocabulary appears in the string representation of the instance and the dimension of feature vectors n is the number of words in the vocabulary. From two original instances $\boldsymbol{x}^\alpha = (x_1^\alpha, x_2^\alpha, \ldots, x_n^\alpha)$ and $\boldsymbol{x}^\beta = (x_1^\beta, x_2^\beta, \ldots, x_n^\beta)$, they make a pair instance $\hat{\boldsymbol{x}} = (\boldsymbol{x}^\alpha, \boldsymbol{x}^\beta)$ and represent it as a vector in an n dimensional feature space:

$$\hat{\boldsymbol{x}}_{common} = (x_1^\alpha x_1^\beta, x_2^\alpha x_2^\beta, \ldots, x_n^\alpha x_n^\beta) \ . \tag{1}$$

(They also do normalization by dividing the value of each feature by $|\boldsymbol{x}^\alpha||\boldsymbol{x}^\beta|$.)

This method is effective for a problem like citation matching, where two instances from the same class have many common features. However, in the problem where two instances from the same class have few common features, this method cannot achieve high classification accuracy. For example, in Figure 2, the first and the second papers have no common words other than "A. Gupta" even though they are actually written by the same person. The representation of this pair instance by Equation (1) becomes a zero vector. This phenomenon is not rare in papers written by the same author, and the method based on common features cannot distinguish these pairs from the many negative examples that also have zero vectors as their representation.

One approach to avoiding the problem of zero vectors is using conjunctions of different features across examples $x_i^\alpha x_j^\beta$ and representing a pair instance as

$$\hat{\boldsymbol{x}}_{Cartesian} = (x_1^\alpha x_1^\beta, \ldots, x_1^\alpha x_n^\beta, x_2^\alpha x_1^\beta, \ldots, x_2^\alpha x_n^\beta, \ldots, x_n^\alpha x_1^\beta, \ldots, x_n^\alpha x_n^\beta) \ . \tag{2}$$

That is, the set of mapped features, $\{x_i^\alpha x_j^\beta | i = 1, \ldots, n; j = 1, \ldots, n\}$, is a Cartesian product between the sets of original features of $\boldsymbol{x}^\alpha$ and $\boldsymbol{x}^\beta$. In this feature space, a pair instance does not become a zero vector unless one of the original instances is a zero vector. If there are many positive pairs in which "VLDB" appears in one citation and "SIGMOD" appears in the other, we can expect that a learning algorithm incorporates the conjunction of these two features into the learned classifier, and it successfully classifies the case of Figure 2.

However, implementing this idea straightforwardly causes the following problems. One is that the dimension of the feature space becomes n^2 and the computational cost becomes prohibitive for practical problems with many features. Moreover, learning in a high dimensional feature space is in danger of overfitting, that is, the "curse of dimensionality."

3   Kernel Methods
for Using Feature Conjunctions Across Examples

3.1   Kernel Methods

Some learning algorithms such as SVMs can be written in forms where examples always appear as inner products $\langle \boldsymbol{x} \cdot \boldsymbol{z} \rangle$ of two examples and never appear individually [12, 13]. Kernel methods enable classification in higher dimensional space by substituting kernel functions $K(\boldsymbol{x}, \boldsymbol{z})$ for inner products $\langle \boldsymbol{x} \cdot \boldsymbol{z} \rangle$ in these algorithms.

Let us consider the following kernel function:

$$K(\boldsymbol{x}, \boldsymbol{z}) = \langle \boldsymbol{x} \cdot \boldsymbol{z} \rangle^2 \ . \tag{3}$$

Learning with this kernel function is equivalent to mapping examples into the following higher dimensional feature space,

$$\phi(\boldsymbol{x}) = (x_1 x_1, \ldots, x_1 x_n, x_2 x_1, \ldots, x_2 x_n, \ldots, x_n x_1, \ldots, x_n x_n) \ ,$$

and then applying the learning algorithm. We can show this as follows:

$$\langle \boldsymbol{x} \cdot \boldsymbol{z} \rangle^2 = \left(\sum_{i=1}^n x_i z_i \right) \left(\sum_{j=1}^n x_j z_j \right) = \sum_{i=1}^n \sum_{j=1}^n x_i z_i x_j z_j$$

$$= \sum_{i=1}^n \sum_{j=1}^n (x_i x_j)(z_i z_j) = \langle \phi(\boldsymbol{x}) \cdot \phi(\boldsymbol{z}) \rangle \ .$$

The kernel above is called a quadratic polynomial kernel. Previous work has also used another popular kernel, the Gaussian kernel, $K(\boldsymbol{x}, \boldsymbol{z}) = \exp\left(-\frac{\|\boldsymbol{x} - \boldsymbol{z}\|^2}{2\sigma^2} \right)$, which corresponds to a feature mapping into an infinite dimensional space. Using kernels, the algorithms can learn classifiers in a high dimensional feature space without actually doing feature mappings, which are computationally expensive. Moreover, SVMs with kernels are known to be robust against the overfitting problem of learning in a high dimensional feature space.

3.2   Using Kernels for Feature Conjunctions

A straightforward way to conjoin different features across examples is using the polynomial kernel mentioned above. We represent a pair instance as a vector with $2n$ dimensions,

$$\hat{\boldsymbol{x}} = (\boldsymbol{x}^\alpha, \boldsymbol{x}^\beta) = (x_1^\alpha, \ldots, x_n^\alpha, x_1^\beta, \ldots, x_n^\beta) \ , \tag{4}$$

and then apply the kernel of Equation (3) on this feature space.

The set of conjoined features resulting from the corresponding feature mapping is $\{x_i^\alpha x_j^\alpha\} \cup \{x_i^\alpha x_j^\beta\} \cup \{x_i^\beta x_j^\alpha\} \cup \{x_i^\beta x_j^\beta\}$ and it includes the set of features in Equation (2). However, it also includes features from the same example, $\{x_i^\alpha x_j^\alpha\}$ and $\{x_i^\beta x_j^\beta\}$. These features are clearly irrelevant to pairwise classification because they are related to only one party of the pair. When the frequencies of original instances are different between the set of positive pairs and the set of negative pairs, there is a possibility that a learning algorithm give weight to joint features from single parties and the generalization performance deteriorates.

What we want is the following feature mapping, which generates conjunctions of features only across the two original instances:

$$\phi(\hat{\boldsymbol{x}}) = \phi((\boldsymbol{x}^\alpha, \boldsymbol{x}^\beta))$$

$$= (x_1^\alpha x_1^\beta, \ldots, x_1^\alpha x_n^\beta, x_2^\alpha x_1^\beta, \ldots, x_2^\alpha x_n^\beta, \ldots, x_n^\alpha x_1^\beta, \ldots, x_n^\alpha x_n^\beta) \ . \tag{5}$$

So we propose using the following kernel for pair instances:

$$K(\hat{x}, \hat{z}) = K((x^\alpha, x^\beta), (z^\alpha, z^\beta)) = \langle x^\alpha \cdot z^\alpha \rangle \langle x^\beta \cdot z^\beta \rangle \ . \tag{6}$$

This kernel first computes the inner product of x^α and z^α and that of x^β and z^β respectively, then computes the product of these two real values.

We can show that this kernel does the feature mapping of Equation (5):

$$\langle x^\alpha \cdot z^\alpha \rangle \langle x^\beta \cdot z^\beta \rangle = \left(\sum_{i=1}^{n} x_i^\alpha z_i^\alpha \right) \left(\sum_{j=1}^{n} x_j^\beta z_j^\beta \right) = \sum_{i=1}^{n} \sum_{j=1}^{n} x_i^\alpha z_i^\alpha x_j^\beta z_j^\beta$$

$$= \sum_{i=1}^{n} \sum_{j=1}^{n} (x_i^\alpha x_j^\beta)(z_i^\alpha z_j^\beta) = \langle \phi((x^\alpha, x^\beta)) \cdot \phi((z^\alpha, z^\beta)) \rangle = \langle \phi(\hat{x}) \cdot \phi(\hat{z}) \rangle \ .$$

This kernel is a tensor product [6] of two linear kernels (inner products) on the original feature space. An intuitive explanation of this kernel is the following. A kernel defines similarity in an input space. In our case, the input space is the space of pair instances. The kernel of Equation (6) defines the similarity between pair instances so that it yields a high value only if each of the original instances in one pair has high similarity (a large value for the inner product) with the corresponding original instance in the other pair. For example, if the value of $\langle x^\alpha \cdot z^\alpha \rangle$ is 0, the overall value of Equation (6) always becomes 0 even if the value of $\langle x^\beta \cdot z^\beta \rangle$ is large. This is a desirable property because a pairwise classification decision should be based on both examples in a pair.

The feature mapping of Equation (5) depends on the order of instances, that is, $\phi((x^\alpha, x^\beta)) \neq \phi((x^\beta, x^\alpha))$. We can also make a product between two pair instances by making inner products between instances with different superscripts as $\langle x^\alpha \cdot z^\beta \rangle \langle x^\beta \cdot z^\alpha \rangle$. However, if we have both (x^α, x^β) and (x^β, x^α) in the training set, both definitions of kernels are equivalent in terms of learned classifiers.

4   Experiments

4.1   Datasets and Code

We show experimental results on the following two datasets. One is the DBLP dataset which is a bibliography of more than 400,000 computer science papers[3]. The data is publicly available in XML format. We used journal papers and conference papers as the data for our experiments. Bibliographic entries in DBLP were entered by humans and many author names are given as their full names. To make a training set and a test set for the author matching problem, we abbreviated first names into initials and removed middle names. We used words in titles, journal names, and names of coauthors as features.

---

[3] http://dblp.uni-trier.de/

The other is the Cora Citation Matching dataset provided by Andrew Mc-Callum[4]. We used these data for citation matching problems. They are also used in [2] and [3]. The dataset is composed of 1,879 citations to 191 papers in Cora, a computer science research paper search engine. We used each word appearing in citations as a feature.

We used SVM^{light}, an implementation of an SVM learning algorithm developed by Thorsten Joachims [7]. SVM^{light} provides basic kernels such as polynomial and Gaussian, and allow use of user-defined kernels. We implemented the kernel of Equation (6) for our experiments.

4.2   Results

From among the top 20 "Most Cited Authors in Computer Science,"[5] we selected four cases of first-initial-plus-surname names which involve a collapsing of many distinct authors (that is, we select names like *J. Smith* but not *J. Ullman*). To make a training set and a test set for each abbreviated name, we retrieved papers written by authors with the same last name and the same first initial from the DBLP data. If we make all pairs of instances, the number of negative examples becomes much larger than that of positive examples because the number of pairs from different classes is larger than that of pairs from same classes. To assess the effect of the imbalance between the numbers of positive and negative data, we prepared two different datasets. One is the *imbalanced data sets*, for which we generated pair instances from all combinations of two papers. The other is the *balanced data sets*, for which we first generated positive examples by making all combinations of papers in same classes, and then we generated negative examples by randomly sampling pairs from different classes. We evaluated classifiers learned from (im)balanced training sets by (im)balanced test sets respectively.

We trained classifiers on the training sets and evaluated them on the test sets in terms of precision and recall. In [2], the precision and recall are evaluated after making the transitive closure of guessed positive pairs. To make evaluation focused on the accuracy of pairwise classifiers, we calculated the precision and recall simply based on how many positive pairs classifiers can find. As suggested in [3], we drew precision-recall curves by shifting the decision boundary induced by SVMs and evaluating precision values on 20 different recall levels.

We evaluated the performance of classifiers with three different kernels.

Common. The Gaussian kernel applied to pair instances of Equation (1), which uses only common features across examples. The parameter of the Gaussian kernel is set to $\sigma = 10$, according to the preceding work [2].

Polynomial. The quadratic polynomial kernel applied to pair instances of Equation (4)

Cartesian. Our kernel of Equation (6)

Figure 3 shows the results with the balanced data sets. For low recall levels, **Common** yields high precision values. However, when recall levels become

---

[4] http://www.cs.umass.edu/~mccallum/code-data.html
[5] http://citeseer.ist.psu.edu/mostcited.html

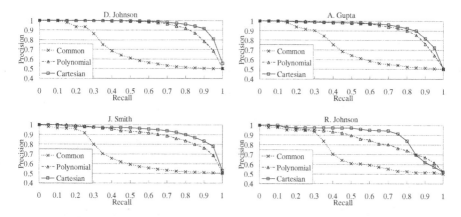

Fig. 3. Results of author matching problems with the balanced data sets

larger than a certain threshold, the precision start to decrease drastically. This seems to be because there are many (nearly) zero vectors among positive pairs generated by Equation (1) and these positive examples cannot be distinguished from negative pairs. On the other hand, **Polynomial** and **Cartesian** keep high precision in higher recall levels. Among the two kernels, **Cartesian** generally yields higher precision than **Polynomial**. Figure 4 shows the results with the imbalanced data sets. As in the case of the balanced data sets, the methods using feature conjunctions are much superior to the method using only common features. **Cartesian** can give a precision 4 to 8 times higher than that of **Common** at medium recall levels.

In the above experiments, we trained different classifiers for each abbreviated author name. A general classifier, which can identify papers written by the same author, given any pair of papers, is preferable because we need not train many classifiers. It could also classify papers by new authors, for which we do not have enough training data. We trained a general classifier in the following steps. First, we listed 50,000 authors who have more than one paper in the DBLP dataset, according to their alphabetical order. For each author, we chose two papers randomly and use the pair as a positive training example. Then we made pairs of papers written by different authors and prepared the same number of negative training examples. We used the same test data that was used in the experiments in Figure 4. We present the results by a general classifier in Figure 5. In the region where recall is smaller than 0.3, **Common** get better results than the others. For the higher recall levels, however, it gives worse results than **Cartesian** and **Common**, among which **Cartesian** generally yields better precision. The overall results are not as good as those of specific classifiers. This seems to be because the word distributions in the test sets for the specific abbreviated names are different from the distribution in the training set collected using many different names. Similar phenomena are also reported in [2].

Figure 6 shows the results of *citation* matching (as opposed to *author* matching) with the Cora dataset. We tried two different methods for splitting the data

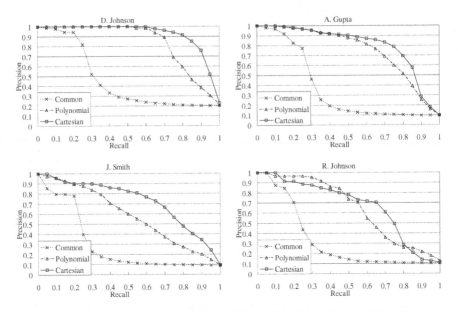

Fig. 4. Results of author matching problems with the imbalanced data sets

into a training set and a test set according to [3]. One method simply assigns each citation into the training set or the test set without considering the paper it refers to. The other method first assigns each paper into the training or the test set, then assigns all citations to the paper to the same set. For the Cora dataset, **Common** works as well as **Cartesian**. In citation matching, two citations to the same paper usually have many common words and the learning algorithm can find clues to identify these examples by only using their common features.

5   Related Work

A general definition of a tensor product between two kernels can be found in [6]. A tensor product between kernels on input space and output space is used in [16] for inducing metrics both Euclidean and Fisher separable spaces, on which the triangle inequality is satisfied and a distance between examples from different classes is always larger than a distance between examples from the same class. On the other hand, our work uses a tensor product between two kernels both on input space for solving the problem of zero similarities between examples, which has not been addressed in the preceding work.

Duplicate detection and entity matching have been studied for a long time in the database community. Recently these problems have attracted interest from machine learning researchers. We refer to only recent literature using machine learning technologies. Other conventional approaches are summarized by Bilenko *et al.* [1].

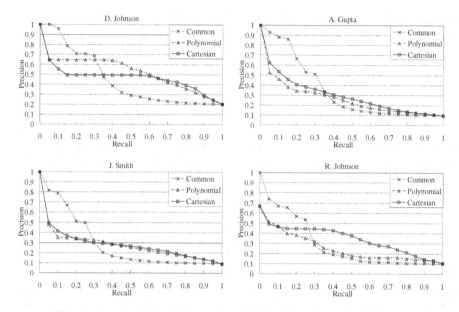

Fig. 5. Results of author matching problems by a general classifier

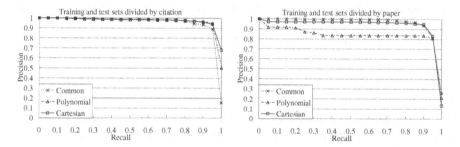

Fig. 6. Results of citation matching problems with the Cora dataset

The work by Bilenko and Mooney [2] is most relevant to our research. They proposed using learnable domain-specific string similarities for duplicate detection and showed the advantage of their approach against fixed general-purpose similarity measures. They trained a different similarity metric for each database field and calculated similarities between records composed of multiple fields by combining these field level similarities. In our work, we treated examples as single field datasets and focused on improving single level similarity measures. Sarawagi and Bhamidipaty [11] and Tejada *et al.* [14] used active learning for interactively finding informative training examples when learning classifiers that distinguish between duplicated pairs and non-duplicated ones. Their method need only a small number of training examples to obtain high accuracy classifiers. Bilenko and Mooney [3] advocated using precision-recall curves in evaluation of duplicate detection methods, and they also discussed different methods of collecting training examples for learnable duplicate detection systems.

6   Future Work

In this paper, we presented entity matching in citation databases as an application of our method. Entity matching has been also studied in natural language processing under the name of coreference resolution, where coreferent terms in texts are to be identified [9, 10]. Our future work includes application of the proposed method for this problem.

Our approach is applicable to the problem of matching different kinds of object. For example, English texts and Japanese texts have few common words. However, our method could learn a matching function between them without using external information sources like dictionaries. Our method can learn similarities between objects of different kinds based on similarities between objects of the same kind. This indicates great potential of our approach because there is no straightforward way to define similarity between completely different kinds of objects like texts and images while defining similarities between two texts and similarities between two images is much easier.

As mentioned in Section 4, learning pairwise classifiers faces the problem of imbalanced data. Employing techniques for handling imbalanced data [4] could improve the accuracy. We will also compare our supervised approach with unsupervised dimension reduction approaches such as LSI [5] for sparse data.

7   Conclusion

Pairwise classification is an important technique in entity matching. Preceding methods have difficulty in learning precise classifiers for problems where examples from the same class have few common features. Since similarities between examples from the same class become small, classifiers fail to distinguish positive pairs from negative pairs. To solve this problem, we proposed using conjunctions of features across examples in learning pairwise classifiers. Using a kernel on pair instances, our method can use feature conjunctions without causing a large computational cost. Our experiments on the author matching problem show that the new kernel introduced here yields higher precision than existing methods at middle to high recall levels.

Acknowledgements

This research was partially supported by the Informatics Research Center for Development of Knowledge Society Infrastructure (Kyoto University 21st Century COE Program) and by a Grants-in-Aid for Scientific Research (16700097) from the Ministry of Education, Culture, Sports, Science and Technology of Japan.

References

1. M. Bilenko, W. W. Cohen, S. Fienberg, R. J. Mooney, and P. Ravikumar. Adaptive name-matching in information integration. *IEEE Intell. Syst.*, 18(5):16–23, 2003.
2. M. Bilenko and R. J. Mooney. Adaptive duplicate detection using learnable string similarity measures. In *Proc. KDD-2003*, pages 39–48, 2003.
3. M. Bilenko and R. J. Mooney. On evaluation and training-set construction for duplicate detection. In *Proc. KDD-2003 Workshop on Data Cleaning, Record Linkage, and Object Consolidation*, pages 7–12, 2003.
4. N. Chawla, N. Japkowicz, and A. Kolcz, editors. *Special Issue on Learning from Imbalanced Datasets, SIGKDD Explorations*, 6(1), 2004.
5. S. C. Deerwester, S. T. Dumais, T. K. Landauer, G. W. Furnas, and R. A. Harshman. Indexing by latent semantic analysis. *J. Am. Soc. Inf. Sci.*, 41(6):391–407, 1990.
6. D. Haussler. Convolution kernels on discrete structures. Technical Report UCSC-CRL-99-10, Baskin School of Engineering, University of California, Santa Cruz, 1999.
7. T. Joachims. Making large-scale SVM learning practical. In B. Schölkopf, C. Burges, and A. Smola, editors, *Advances in Kernel Methods - Support Vector Learning*. MIT-Press, 1999.
8. S. Lawrence, K. Bollacker, and C. L. Giles. Autonomous citation matching. In *Proc. Third International Conference on Autonomous Agents*, 1999.
9. A. McCallum and B. Wellner. Toward conditional models of identity uncertainty with application to proper noun coreference. In *Proc. IJCAI Workshop on Information Integration on the Web*, pages 79–84, 2003.
10. T. S. Morton. Coreference for NLP applications. In *Proc. ACL-2000*, 2000.
11. S. Sarawagi and A. Bhamidipaty. Interactive deduplication using active learning. In *Proc. KDD-2002*, pages 269–278, 2002.
12. B. Schölkopf and A. Smola. *Learning with Kernels: Support Vector Machines, Regularization, Optimization and Beyond*. MIT Press, 2002.
13. J. Shawe-Taylor and N. Cristianini. *Kernel Methods for Pattern Analysis*. Cambridge University Press, 2004.
14. S. Tejada, C. A. Knoblock, and S. Minton. Learning domain-independent string transformation weights for high accuracy object identification. In *Proc. KDD-2002*, pages 350–359, 2002.
15. V. N. Vapnik. *The Nature of Statistical Learning Theory*. Springer, 2nd edition, 1999.
16. Z. Zhang. Learning metrics via discriminant kernels and multidimensional scaling: Toward expected euclidean representation. In *Proc. ICML-2003*, pages 872–879, 2003.

Feature Selection Filters Based on the Permutation Test

Predrag Radivojac[1], Zoran Obradovic[2], A. Keith Dunker[1], and Slobodan Vucetic[2]

[1] Center for Computational Biology and Bioinformatics, Indiana University,
Indianapolis, IN 46202, USA
[2] Center for Information Science and Technology, Temple University,
Philadelphia, PA 19122, USA

Abstract. We investigate the problem of supervised feature selection within the filtering framework. In our approach, applicable to the two-class problems, the feature strength is inversely proportional to the p-value of the null hypothesis that its class-conditional densities, $p(X|Y = 0)$ and $p(X|Y = 1)$, are identical. To estimate the p-values, we use Fisher's permutation test combined with the four simple filtering criteria in the roles of test statistics: sample mean difference, symmetric Kullback-Leibler distance, information gain, and chi-square statistic. The experimental results of our study, performed using naive Bayes classifier and support vector machines, strongly indicate that the permutation test improves the above-mentioned filters and can be used effectively when sample size is relatively small and number of features relatively large.

1 Introduction

The increasing trend of high dimensional data collection and problem representation calls for the use of feature selection algorithms in many machine learning tasks. Real-life datasets are often characterized by a large number of irrelevant features that, if not properly isolated, may significantly hamper model accuracy and learning speed. In addition, feature selection algorithms can be handy in explaining and visualizing data.

Traditionally, methods for selecting subsets of features that provide best performance results are divided into wrappers and filters [1]. Wrappers utilize the learning machine as a fitness (evaluation) function and search for the best features in the space of all feature subsets. This formulation of the problem allows the use of standard optimization techniques, with an additional complication that the fitness function has a probabilistic nature. Despite their simplicity and often having the best performance results, wrappers highly depend on the inductive principle of the learning model and may suffer from excessive computational complexity since the problem itself is NP-hard.

In contrast to wrappers, filters are typically based on selecting the best features in one pass, although more complex approaches have also been studied [2]. Filters are model independent and are applied as a preprocessing step to model selection and learning. In domains such as text categorization or gene selection filters are still dominant [3]. Evaluating one feature at a time, filters estimate its usefulness for the prediction process according to various metrics [4-7].

J.-F. Boulicaut et al. (Eds.): ECML 2004, LNAI 3201, pp. 334–346, 2004.

Besides wrappers and filters, some authors distinguish embedded methods as a separate category of feature selection algorithms [3, 8]. Embedded methods are incorporated into the learning procedure, and hence are also dependent on the model. Many such algorithms have been proposed in learning logical expressions or in the PAC setting. In fact, almost any learner can be considered some form of an embedded feature selection algorithm, where the particular estimation of features' usefulness may result in their weighting [9], elimination [10] or construction of new features [11].

In this paper we focus on the problem of supervised feature selection. We extend the work of Frank and Witten [12] and present a permutation-based filtering framework which is effective when the number of available examples is relatively small. In particular, we adopt a statistical approach with the goals of testing the null hypothesis that the class-conditional densities of individual features are equal and of using the test p-value for their comparison. The features are ranked in the increasing order of their estimated p-values and the top-ranked features are used for classification. To estimate p-values we used Fisher's permutation test. A simple procedure for feature ranking is then proposed that introduces only a moderate computational overhead over the standard filters. Finally, we performed extensive experimentation to evaluate the proposed permutation-based methodology.

The rest of the paper is organized as follows. Section 2 describes previous work relevant to our approach. In Section 3 we present our framework in detail. Section 4 gives experimental setting and most important results of our study. Finally, concluding remarks are contained in Section 5.

2 Related Work

A significant body of research has been produced in the feature selection area. Excellent surveys, systematizations, and journal special issues on feature selection algorithms have been presented in the recent past [1, 3, 8, 13]. Searching for the best features within the wrapper framework, Kohavi and John [1] define an optimal subset of features with respect to a particular classification model. The best feature subset given the model is the one that provides the highest accuracy. Numerous wrappers have been proposed to date. These techniques include heuristic approaches such as forward selection, backward elimination [14], hill-climbing, best-first or beam search [15], randomized algorithms such as genetic algorithms [16] or simulated annealing [17], as well as their combinations [18]. In general, wrappers explore the power set of all features starting with no features, all features, or a random selection thereof.

Optimality criterion was also tackled within the filtering framework. Koller and Sahami select the best feature subset based strictly on the joint probability distributions [19]; a feature subset $Z \subseteq X$ is optimal if $p(Y|X) = p(Y|Z)$. The difference between the probability distributions was measured by the relative entropy or Kullback-Leibler distance. This problem formulation naturally leads to the backward elimination search strategy. Since the true conditional distribution $p(Y|X)$ is generally unknown, Koller and Sahami proposed an efficient approximation algorithm based on Markov blankets.

In addition to the optimality criterion, many authors also discuss relevancy of features [1, 8, 20]. John et al. [20] define relevancy in the following way: feature j is strongly relevant to the target concept and distribution D iff there exists a pair of examples $\mathbf{x}_1$ and $\mathbf{x}_2$ in the instance space with non-zero probability over D, such that $\mathbf{x}_1$ and $\mathbf{x}_2$ differ only in their assignment to feature j and have different class labels. Additionally, feature j is weakly relevant to the target concept and distribution D, if there is a subset of features that can be removed such that feature j becomes strongly relevant. The fact that a feature is irrelevant according to some criterion, however, does not automatically imply that it is not useful in the model construction process. An example of such a situation is XOR task where none of the relevancy definitions can detect all truly relevant features [1]. Hence, relevance and optimality do not imply each other.

Naturally, in cases of high-dimensional datasets containing thousands of features, filters are preferred to wrappers. The domains most commonly considered within the filtering framework are text categorization [3] and gene expression [21, 22]. A significant difference between the two models is that text categorization systems typically contain both a large number of features and a large number of examples; while gene expression data usually contain a limited number of examples pushing the problem toward statistically underdetermined. Most commonly used filters are based on information-theoretic or statistical principles. For example, information gain or χ^2 goodness-of-fit tests have become baseline methods. However, both require discretized features and are difficult to "normalize" when features are multi-valued. Kononenko explored biases of several feature selection filters and showed that even normalized versions of the information gain and χ^2-test are significantly biased against the features with fewer values [4]. In addition, χ^2-test requires >30 examples in each field of the contingency table in order for the probability distribution to be well approximated by the χ^2 distribution. Thus, in many cases the application of both methods is limited. Several other approaches frequently used are Relief [23, 24], gini-index [11], relevance [25], average absolute weight of evidence [26], bi-normal separation [6] etc. Various benchmarking studies across several domains are provided in [5-7].

Some examples of embedded methods are decision tree learners such as ID3 [27] and CART [11] or the support vector machine approaches of Guyon et al. [10] and Weston et al. [28]. For example, in the recursive feature elimination approach of Guyon et al. [10], an initial model is trained using all the features. Then, features are iteratively removed in a greedy fashion until the largest margin of separation is reached. Good surveys of embedded techniques are given by Blum and Langley [8] and Guyon and Elisseeff [3].

2.1   Statistical Tests in Feature Selection

Statistical tests are straightforward choices for the feature selection algorithms, especially filters. Methods such as the F-test, measuring the ratio of standard deviations between the classes, or the t-test, in cases when the distribution of features is near Gaussian, have been used for feature selection in the statistical community. Several other approaches were also proposed as splitting criteria in decision tree training. For example, White and Liu [29] used a χ^2-goodness-of-fit test, while Martin [30] used an exact probability of a contingency table. In a study by Frank and Witten [12] it was shown that Fisher's permutation test [31] used on contingency tables can be effectively implemented as a decision-tree pre-pruning strategy. This algorithm represents a Monte Carlo approximation of Freeman and Halton's exact test and its significance lies in the bias correction of the exact probability of the contingency table. Frank and Witten also traced that the first use of the permutation test in machine learning was probably by Gaines [32], who used Fisher's exact test in rule learning. Excellent coverage of permutation tests and other non-parametric methods is provided by Efron and Tibshirani [31].

2.2 Classification Models in Evaluating Feature Selection Algorithms

Speed of the learning process in real-life conditions often dictates that the classification model be pre-selected. Thus, in the applications for high-dimensional datasets filtering methods are often combined with the simplest or fastest learners. This is due to the fact that learning parameters usually involved in choosing complex learners may make the selection process infeasible or may result in overfitting [33]. Consequently, most frequently used models have historically been naive Bayes [34], K-nearest neighbor models or decision trees, typically C4.5 [35]. Recently, embedded methods and increases in computational power have also enabled the choice of support vector machines [36].

3 Methods

We constrain our discussion to a class of binary classification problems. Let $D = \{(\mathbf{x}_i, y_i) | i = 1...n\}$ be the set of n labeled data points, where $\mathbf{x}_i = (x_{i,1}, x_{i,2}, ..., x_{i,k})^T$ represents an assignment of values to a set of k features $X = (X_1, X_2, ..., X_k)^T$ and $y_i \in \{0, 1\}$ is the realization of the class label Y. Let X_j be the domain for feature X_j. As real-life datasets may contain a large number of irrelevant features, the task of estimating the relevance of a feature in a single pass is gaining importance.

Definition 1. The relevance of feature X is measured as the difference between class-conditional distributions $p(X | Y = 0)$ and $p(X | Y = 1)$.

We consider the following distance measures between $p(X | Y = 0)$ and $p(X | Y = 1)$:

1. The difference in sample means
$$r_M(X) = E[X | Y = 0] - E[X | Y = 1]. \tag{1}$$

2. Symmetric variant of the Kullback-Leibler distance, called J-measure [37]
$$r_J(X) = \sum_x \{p(X = x | Y = 0) - p(X = x | Y = 1)\} \cdot \log_2 \frac{p(X = x | Y = 0)}{p(X = x | Y = 1)}. \tag{2}$$

3. Information gain

$$r_{IG}(X) = \sum_x \sum_y p(X = x, Y = y) \cdot \log_2 \frac{p(X = x, Y = y)}{p(X = x) \cdot p(Y = y)}. \tag{3}$$

4. χ^2 statistics-based measure

$$r_{CHI}(X) = \sum_x \sum_y \frac{\{p(X = x, Y = y) - p(X = x) \cdot p(Y = y)\}^2}{p(X = x) \cdot p(Y = y)}. \tag{4}$$

While r_{IG} and r_{CHI} have been often and successfully used for feature selection we consider r_M and r_J as interesting alternatives; r_M as a simple measure for selection of real-valued attributes, and r_J as an information-based measure of the difference between two probability distributions. It should be noted that r_M measure is suitable for real-valued or binary features while r_J, r_{IG}, r_{CHI} are suitable for categorical features. Therefore, if r_M is used, categorical features with $C > 2$ categories are transformed into C binary features. On the other hand, if r_J, r_{IG}, r_{CHI} are used, real-valued features are discretized and transformed into categorical attributes. Note that when $p(X|Y=0) = p(X|Y=1)$ all the measures result in zero values.

r_{CHI} measure has an interpretation particularly relevant to our study. The quantity $n \cdot r_{CHI}$ represents χ^2-statistic that is used in the χ^2 goodness-of-fit test of independence between a feature X and target Y, or, equivalently, of the equality between distributions $p(X|Y=0)$ and $p(X|Y=1)$. It can be shown that, for a sufficiently large sample size n, the χ^2-statistic follows the χ^2 distribution with $|X| - 1$ degrees of freedom. This allows easy estimation (using a lookup table) of the *p-value*, defined as the lowest significance level at which the null hypothesis H_0: $p(X|Y=0) = p(X|Y=1)$ can be rejected. Therefore, r_{CHI} is proportional to the p-value of the hypothesis test H_0, i.e. the feature relevance is inversely proportional to its p-value. We extend this notion to the novel framework for feature selection filters.

Let us define $D_j^0 = \{x_{i,j} | y_i = 0\}$ and $D_j^1 = \{x_{i,j} | y_i = 1\}$ as samples containing values of the j-th feature of all data points with class 0 and 1, respectively. Let us also denote $\theta(D_j^0, D_j^1)$ as a test statistic obtained as a function of samples D_j^0 and D_j^1, and π_j as the p-value of the hypothesis test H_0: $p(X_j|Y=0) = p(X_j|Y=1)$ based on $\theta(D_j^0, D_j^1)$.

Definition 2. The relevance of feature X_j is inversely proportional to the p-value π_j of the hypothesis test H_0: $p(X_j|Y=0) = p(X_j|Y=1)$ based on the test statistic $\theta(D_j^0, D_j^1)$.

Our goal is to empirically test whether Definition 2 results in a successful feature selection procedure. It should be observed that the measures in (1-4) can be interpreted as test statistics θ since they can be estimated from D_j^0 and D_j^1. Similarly, one could think of a number of different test statistics that could be used within the flexible framework provided by Definition 2.

As already mentioned, the test statistic r_{CHI} applied to large samples allows easy calculation of the p-value. However, for the small sample size and/or for an arbitrary test statistic θ, it is difficult to derive its distribution under the null hypothesis. Therefore, to estimate the p-value we use Fisher's permutation test. This reduces the feature selection algorithm to the application of a standard statistical tool with the test statistic chosen according to the criteria from Definition 1. In Section 3.1 we describe the permutation test used for feature selection according to Definition 2.

3.1 Permutation Test

The algorithm begins by choosing and calculating a test statistic θ, e.g. difference of means, J-measure, information gain, χ^2-statistic, for a given dataset. Without loss of generality, we consider only the cases where θ is non-negative. Then, assuming the null hypothesis H_0 is true, i.e. that samples D_j^0 and D_j^1 of lengths l and m were generated according to the same probability distribution, they are concatenated into a single sample $W = (D_j^0, D_j^1)$ of size $l + m$. There are $(l + m)!/(l! \cdot m!)$ possible splits of W into two parts of sizes l and m, each of which is equally likely under H_0. The achieved significance level, or the p-value, of the statistical test is defined to be the probability that the test statistic of a random permutation is at least as large as θ. However, due to the sizes of samples D_j^0 and D_j^1, the exact p-value, calculated by evaluating all possible permutations, cannot be computed in most practical situations. In such cases, it is estimated using a fixed number of permutations (B) of the combined sample W, as shown in Figure 1. In each step b ($b = 1 \ldots B$), W is randomly shuffled and split into two parts $U^*(b)$ and $V^*(b)$ of lengths l and m. The test statistic $\theta^*(b)$ is calculated for each pair $U^*(b)$ and $V^*(b)$, and the p-value is finally estimated as the fraction of times $\theta^*(b) \geq \theta$. The actually observed permutation W is included as the iteration $B + 1$.

After the p-values of all k features are calculated, the features are ranked according to the ascending level of their estimated p-values. Therefore, the most important features are the ones whose probability distributions of the components having different class labels are least likely to be identical.

3.2 Practical Implementation of the Permutation Test

Given the actual p-value π_j and the number of permutations B, the number of times n_j the test statistic of the random permutation is at least as large as $\theta(D_j^0, D_j^1)$ is a random variable with a binomial distribution $b(B, \pi_j)$. Therefore, to estimate π_j within 10% of its true value, the coefficient of variation $CV = ((1 - \pi_j)/(\pi_j \cdot B))^{1/2}$ should be set to 0.1. As a result, for an accurate estimate of the p-value $\pi_j = 0.05$, approximately $B = 2,000$ random permutations are required. However, for highly relevant features, π_j

Input: $D = \{(\mathbf{x}_i, y_i) \mid i = 1 \ldots n\}$; B – number of permutations

for each feature $j \in \{1, 2, \ldots k\}$
    split feature j into D_j^0 and D_j^1, where $D_j^0 = \{\mathbf{x}_{i,j} \mid y_i = 0\}$
    and $D_j^1 = \{\mathbf{x}_{i,j} \mid y_i = 0\}$ and $l = |D_j^0|$ and $m = |D_j^1|$
    calculate test statistic $\theta(D_j^0, D_j^1)$
    counter = 1
    for $b = 1$ to B
        randomly shuffle feature j and split it into two parts
        $U^*(b)$ and $V^*(b)$, where $|U^*(b)| = l$ and $|V^*(b)| = m$
        calculate $\theta(U^*(b), V^*(b))$
        if $\theta(U^*(b), V^*(b)) \geq \theta(D_j^0, D_j^1)$
            counter = *counter* + 1
        end
    end
    $\hat{\pi}_j$ = *counter* / $(B + 1)$
end

Output: $\hat{\pi}_1, \hat{\pi}_2, \ldots, \hat{\pi}_k$ – estimated p-values for features $1 \ldots k$

Fig. 1. Steps of the permutation-test based algorithm applied to the feature selection.

could be extremely small which would, in turn, require a very large number of permutations.

To reduce computational cost, we limit the total number of permutations, e.g. to B = 2,000, and propose the following procedure for feature ranking. Feature X_j is classified as *weak* if $n_j \geq 0.05B$ and its p-value is estimated as $\hat{\pi}_j = (n_j + 1)/(B + 1)$. Alternatively, if $n_j < 0.05B$, feature X_j is classified as *strong*. For the strong features, n_j is close or equal to zero and their p-value estimates $\hat{\pi}_j$ are highly unreliable. For such features, we calculate Z-scores $Z_j = \{\theta(D_j^0, D_j^1) - mean(\theta(U^*, V^*))\}/std(\theta(U^*, V^*))$, where Z_j measures the distance between $\theta(D_j^0, D_j^1)$ and the distribution of the test statistic of a random permutation. Finally, strong features are ranked in the upper tier based on their estimated Z-scores, while the weak features are ranked in the lower tier based on their estimated p-values. Note that for most irrelevant features the coefficient of variation may quickly reach the pre-specified threshold in which case much less than 2,000 permutations may be required.

The computational cost of the permutation test is $O(k \cdot n)$, linear in the number of features and data points.

4 Experiments and Results

4.1 Datasets

Our experiments were performed on eleven datasets summarized in Table 1. The first nine were downloaded from the UCI repository [38], with dataset HOUSING converted into a binary classification problem according to the mean value of the target. Datasets MAMMOGRAPHY and OIL were constructed in [39] and [40], respectively, and provided to us by the authors.

Table 1. Datasets: basic characteristics. *NF* and *CF* indicate the number of numerical and categorical features, respectively.

Dataset	Size	Size of class 1	NF	CF
IONOSPHERE	351	225	34	0
VOTES	435	267	0	48
GLASS	214	163	9	0
HEART	303	139	6	7
LABOR	57	37	8	21
HOUSING	506	250	13	0
CREDIT	690	307	6	41
PIMA	768	268	9	0
ZOO	78	41	1	15
MAMMOGRAPHY	11,183	260	6	0
OIL	937	41	49	0

4.2 Data Preprocessing

The datasets were preprocessed such that each categorical feature with $C > 2$ categories was represented using C binary features. This resulted in datasets that allowed consistent comparison of different feature selection methods with naive Bayes and SVM algorithms. To allow application of r_J, r_{IG}, and r_{CHI} test statistics, prior to the feature selection process, real-valued features were discretized using the method by Fayyad and Irani [41]. This is a supervised, entropy-based algorithm that mimics recursive splitting of a decision tree construction. It automatically decides on the number of quantization intervals.

Given a real-valued feature X and a threshold t the set $S = \{(x_i, y_i) \mid i = 1...n\}$ is divided into two subsets $S_1 = \{(x_i, y_i) \mid x_i \in I_1\}$ and $S_2 = \{(x_i, y_i) \mid x_i \in I_2\}$, where $I_1 = (-\infty, t)$ and $I_2 = [t, \infty)$. The optimal threshold t is the one that maximizes the information gain defined as $G(S,t) = H(S) - E(S,t)$, where

$$H(S) = \sum_y p(y \mid x \in I) \cdot \log_2 \frac{1}{p(y \mid x \in I)}; \quad E(S,t) = \sum_{i=1}^{2} \frac{|S_i|}{|S|} \cdot H(S_i). \tag{6}$$

The procedure is recursively repeated for each newly created interval $I \subset X$ until the stopping criterion is met. To determine whether a partition should be accepted, we use a simple stopping criterion based on the minimum description length [41]. That is, the split is allowed if

$$G(S,t) > \frac{\log_2(|S|-1)}{|S|} + \frac{\log_2(3^c - 2) - cH(S) + c_1 H(S_1) + c_2 H(S_2)}{|S|}, \tag{7}$$

where c, c_1, and c_2 are the numbers of distinct classes present in samples S, S_1, and S_2, respectively.

4.3 Evaluation Strategy and Learners

In order to evaluate different filters, we used 10 cross-validation. A dataset D is randomly divided into 10 equal-sized subsets D_1, D_2, ... D_{10} and the following procedure is repeated 10 times. In each step i, $i = 1$, 2, ...10, $D - D_i$ is used to rank the features and then to build a classifier, while D_i is used to test the accuracy of the classifier. The aggregate accuracy over the 10 steps represents the estimate of the accuracy. To eliminate the influence of a particular split on the performance results, we repeated the 10 cross-validation for 15 different partitions of D into 10 subsets. Finally, the average accuracy over 15 experiments is reported as the classification accuracy estimate.

Due to a considerable class-imbalance in some datasets, all models were trained and tested using balanced class sizes. During construction of the dataset D from the original data, in each of the 15 cross validation repetitions, all examples of the minority class were retained together with the same number of examples randomly selected from the majority class.

We examined two learning algorithms with different inductive biases: (i) naive Bayes and (ii) support vector machines. Naive Bayes is a MAP classifier based on the assumption that feature values are conditionally independent given the class label. In the case of categorical features, we estimated probabilities via the Laplace correction approach. For numerical features, we used the assumption of a normal distribution [7, 42]. Support vector classifiers are learning algorithms whose goal is to find class boundaries which maximize margin of class separation. For the experimental evaluation we used support vector machines with linear kernel and regularization parameter $C = 0.1$.

We examined eight feature selection methods; the first four of them are directly using measures r_M, r_J, r_{IG}, r_{CHI} for feature ranking, while the second four are ranking features according to the p-values of the hypothesis test that uses r_M, r_J, r_{IG}, r_{CHI} as test statistics, as described in Definition 2. Thus, the first four methods correspond to the traditional approach to feature ranking, while the second four correspond to the proposed framework.

For each of the eight feature selection filters, we trained naive Bayes and SVM classifiers using only the highest ranked features, then the two highest ranked features, up to the M highest ranked features, where $M = min(15, k/2)$ and k is the number of features in the dataset. This allowed us to provide a comprehensive evaluation of the proposed feature selection framework in which the datasets were similarly weighted. We observe that, to accomplish the proposed extensive evaluation, we trained $10 \cdot 15 \cdot 8 \cdot 2 \cdot M$ classifiers for each dataset.

4.4 Experimental Results

In Table 2 we show the maximum achieved accuracies for each dataset and feature selection algorithm. In each field of the table, accuracies of the two classifiers trained on $i = 1, 2, \ldots M$ highest ranked features were compared and the highest achieved accuracy is reported. These results provide a weak indication that the permutation-test based approaches result in higher accuracy. However, considering small differences between the methods and a possibility of overfitting, the results were not conclusive.

Table 2. Maximum achieved accuracy [%], with the number of selected features (in parentheses), for the eight feature selection criteria. Notation: r_{IG} – information gain, r_{CHI} – chi-square statistic, r_M – sample mean difference, r_J – J-divergence. Corresponding methods based on the permutation test are denoted as $p\text{-}r_{IG}$, $p\text{-}r_{CHI}$, $p\text{-}r_M$, and $p\text{-}r_J$. Symbols * and $^\square$ indicate that the maximum accuracy was achieved using naive Bayes classifier and SVM, respectively. The absence of any symbol indicates a tie between the two classification algorithms. Values in bold indicate the winning algorithm between each measure and its permutation-based variant.

Dataset	Feature selection method							
	r_{IG}	$p\text{-}r_{IG}$	r_{CHI}	$p\text{-}r_{CHI}$	r_M	$p\text{-}r_M$	r_J	$p\text{-}r_J$
IONOSPHERE	84.8 (15)*	**85.6 (11)***	83.9 (8)*	**84.8 (11)***	84.8 (13)$^\square$	**86.2 (4)***	87.2 (13)*	**87.7 (13)***
VOTES	96.0 (2)*	96.0 (2)*	96.0 (2)*	96.0 (2)*	96.0 (2)*	96.0 (2)*	96.0 (2)*	96.0 (2)*
GLASS	90.0 (2)*	**90.4 (4)$^\square$**	90.1 (3)*	90.1 (3)	**91.0 (3)***	90.7 (4)$^\square$	89.7 (4)$^\square$	**90.3 (1)$^\square$**
HEART	83.9 (9)$^\square$	83.9 (8)$^\square$	83.9 (9)$^\square$	83.9 (9)$^\square$	83.5 (11)*	**83.9 (9)$^\square$**	83.8 (9)$^\square$	83.9 (9)$^\square$
LABOR	**93.2 (8)***	93.0 (7)*	93.2 (8)$^\square$	93.2 (7)*	93.2 (13)$^\square$	**93.5 (9)***	93.0 (8)$^\square$	93.2 (6)*
HOUSING	84.9 (4)$^\square$	**85.1 (4)$^\square$**	84.9 (6)$^\square$	**85.0 (7)$^\square$**	82.3 (5)$^\square$	**84.9 (7)$^\square$**	85.0 (7)$^\square$	**85.1 (3)***
CREDIT	86.2 (1)	86.2 (1)	86.2 (1)	86.2 (1)	**86.6 (15)$^\square$**	86.4 (15)$^\square$	86.2 (1)	86.2 (1)
PIMA	72.8 (4)$^\square$	**73.7 (3)***	72.7 (4)*	**73.7 (3)***	72.6 (4)$^\square$	**73.6 (3)***	72.8 (3)*	**73.6 (3)***
ZOO	100.0 (1)*	100.0 (3)*	100.0 (1)*	100.0 (3)*	100.0 (3)$^\square$	**100.0 (1)***	**100.0 (1)***	99.8 (1)*
MAMMOGRAPHY	85.8 (3)*	**85.9 (3)***	85.8 (3)*	**85.9 (3)***	84.2 (3)$^\square$	**86.0 (3)***	85.9 (3)*	85.9 (3)*
OIL	81.5 (2)*	**81.7 (2)***	**81.8 (2)***	81.6 (2)*	80.4 (11)$^\square$	**81.3 (2)***	**80.8 (14)$^\square$**	80.5 (2)$^\square$

To provide a more detailed evaluation we used a win/loss counting method often applied by machine learning researchers, e.g. in [7]. The objective was to compare the performance of each traditional feature ranking measure with its permutation test counterpart. Since for each dataset we estimated accuracy of M naive Bayes and M SVM classifiers, this provided us with 103 comparisons for both classifiers. In Table 3 we list the number of wins and losses by the permutation-based method over its traditional counterpart, where the comparison is counted as a tie if the accuracies differed by less than 0.1%. It can be seen that permutation-based methods are consistently better for all four test statistics and for both classification algorithms. This provides a strong indication that the permutation-based approach is superior to traditional feature ranking.

Finally, we used a similar win/loss methodology to find the most successful among the eight feature ranking algorithms. Here, for each tuple (*dataset, learning method, number of selected features*) we compared a given feature ranking algorithm with the remaining ones and reported the number of wins (that could range from −7 to 7). The results shown in Table 4 indicate that each of the four permutation-based algorithms outperforms each of the four traditional algorithms. There is only a slight difference in the results obtained with naive Bayes and SVM classifiers. It is interesting to observe that while traditional use of r_M and r_J measures results in clearly inferior feature ranking as compared to the more popular r_{IG} and r_{CHI} measures, they appear to be superior if used as test statistics in a permutation-based approach.

Table 3. Relative comparisons between four feature selection filters and their permutation-test versions. The number of wins and losses are calculated using pairwise comparisons between each pair of filters. The score is calculated as the number of wins minus the number of losses.

Filters	Naive Bayes Classifier			Support Vector Machine		
	Score	Wins	Losses	Score	Wins	Losses
p-r_{IG} vs. r_{IG}	+33	50	17	+28	44	16
p-r_{CHI} vs. r_{CHI}	+20	44	24	+30	46	16
p-r_M vs. r_M	+79	88	9	+52	69	17
p-r_J vs. r_J	+42	54	12	+31	51	20

Table 4. Relative comparisons between eight feature selection filters. Each filter below is ranked according to its score, i.e. the number of wins − losses in pairwise comparisons to all other methods over all datasets and numbers of retained features.

Filters	Naive Bayes Classifier			Filters	Support Vector Machine		
	Score	Wins	Losses		Score	Wins	Losses
p-r_J	396	744	348	p-r_M	476	798	322
p-r_{IG}	354	700	346	p-r_J	180	618	438
p-r_M	268	744	476	p-r_{CHI}	156	566	410
p-r_{CHI}	180	624	444	p-r_{IG}	146	556	410
r_{CHI}	−8	524	532	r_{IG}	−156	408	564
r_{IG}	−30	518	548	r_{CHI}	−218	380	598
r_J	−178	482	660	r_J	−292	374	666
r_M	−982	196	1178	r_M	−292	464	756

5   Conclusions

In this study we investigated feature selection filters and the effects of the permutation test on various filtering metrics. Our experimental results suggest that sample mean difference and symmetric Kullback-Leibler distance (J-measure) can be used effectively for the feature selection and that, overall, they achieve better performance than information gain or χ^2-test. The permutation test was shown to improve all four metrics, but the improvement comes at a cost of increased computational complexity. The success of the proposed method on the diverse datasets selected for this study strongly suggests the applicability of the permutation-based framework to a wide range of real-life problems.

Acknowledgement

This study was supported by NIH grant 1R01 LM07688 awarded to AKD and ZO and by NSF grant IIS-0219736 awarded to ZO and SV. We thank Nitesh V. Chawla and Robert C. Holte for the datasets and Natascha A. Karlova for proofreading the manuscript.

References

1. Kohavi, R. and G. John, Wrappers for feature selection. *Artificial intelligence*, 1997. **97**(1-2): p. 273-324.
2. Almuallim, H. and T.G. Dieterich. Learning with many irrelevant features. *National Conference on Artificial Intelligence*. 1992: p. 547-552.
3. Guyon, I. and A. Elisseeff, An introduction to variable and feature selection. *Journal of Machine Learning Research*, 2003. **3**: p. 1157-1182.
4. Kononenko, I. On biases in estimating multi-valued attributes. *International Joint Conference on Artificial Intelligence*. 1995. p. 1034-1040.
5. Yang, Y. and J.P. Pedersen. A comparative study on feature selection in text categorization. *International Conference on Machine Learning*. 1997, p. 412-420.
6. Forman, G., An extensive empirical study of feature selection metrics for text classification. *Journal of Machine Learning Research*, 2003. **3**: p. 1289-1305.
7. Hall, M.A. and G. Holmes, Benchmarking attribute selection techniques for discrete class data mining. *IEEE Trans. Knowledge and Data Engineering*, 2003. **15**(6): p. 1437-1447.
8. Blum, A.L. and P. Langley, Selection of relevant features and examples in machine learning. *Artificial Intelligence*, 1997. **97**(1-2): p. 245-271.
9. Littlestone, N., Learning quickly when irrelevant attributes abound: a new linear threshold algorithm. *Machine Learning*, 1988. **2**: p. 285-318.
10. Guyon, I., et al., Gene selection for cancer classification using support vector machines. *Machine Learning*, 2002. **46**(1-3): p. 389-422.
11. Breiman, L., Classification and regression trees. 1984, Belmont, CA.
12. Frank, E. and I.H. Witten. Using a permutation test for attribute selection in decision trees. *International Conference on Machine Learning*. 1998. p. 152-160.
13. Dash, M. and H. Liu, Feature selection for classification. *Intelligent Data Analysis*, 1997. **1**(3): p. 131-156.
14. Bishop, C.M., Neural networks for pattern recognition. 1995, Oxford University Press.
15. Caruana, R. and D. Freitag. Greedy attribute selection. *International Conference on Machine Learning*. 1994, p. 28-36.
16. Vafaie, H. and I.F. Imam. Feature selection methods: genetic algorithms vs. greedy like search. *International Conference on Fuzzy and Intelligent Control Systems*. 1994.
17. Doak, J., An evaluation of feature selection methods and their application to computer security. 1992, Techical Report CSE-92-18. University of California at Davis.
18. Brassard, G. and P. Bratley, Fundamentals of algorithms. 1996, Prentice Hall.

19. Koller, D. and M. Sahami. Toward optimal feature selection. *International Conference on Machine Learning.* 1996. p. 284-292.

20. John, G.H., R. Kohavi, and K. Pfleger. Irrelevant features and the subset selection problem. *International Conference on Machine Learning.* 1994. p. 121-129.

21. Li, J. and L. Wong, Identifying good diagnostic gene groups from gene expression profiles using the concept of emerging patterns. *Bioinformatics*, 2002. **18**(5): p. 725-734.

22. Bhattacharyya, C., et al., Simultaneous relevant feature identification and classification in high-dimensional spaces: application to molecular profiling data. *Signal Processing*, 2003. **83**: p. 729-743.

23. Kira, K. and L.A. Rendell. The feature selection problem: traditional methods and a new algorithm. *National Conference on Artificial Intelligence.* 1992, p. 129-134.

24. Kononenko, I. Estimating attributes: analysis and extension of RELIEF. *European Conference on Machine Learning.* 1994, p. 171-182.

25. Baim, P.W., A method for attribute selection in inductive learning systems. *IEEE Transactions on PAMI*, 1988. **10**: p. 888-896.

26. Michie, D., Personal models of rationality. *Journal of Statistical Planning and Inference*, 1990. **21**, p. 381-399.

27. Quinlan, J.R., Learning efficient classification procedures and their application to chess and games, Machine learning:an artificial intelligence approach 1983, Morgan Kaufmann.

28. Weston, J., et al. Feature selection for SVMs. *Neural Information Processing Systems.* 2000, p. 668-674.

29. White, A.P. and W.Z. Liu, Bias in information-based measures in decision tree induction. *Machine Learning*, 1994. **15**(3): p. 321-329.

30. Martin, J.K., An exact probability metric for decision tree splitting and stopping. *Machine Learning*, 1997. **28**(2-3): p. 257-291.

31. Efron, B. and R.J. Tibshirani, An introduction to the bootstrap. 1993, Chapman & Hall.

32. Gaines, B. An ounce of knowledge is worth a ton of data. *International Workshop on Machine Learning.* 1989, p. 156-159.

33. Dietterich, T.G., Overfitting and undercomputing in machine learning. *Computing Surveys*, 1995. **27**: p. 326-327.

34. Mitchell, T.M., Machine learning. 1997, McGraw-Hill.

35. Quinlan, J., C4.5: programs for machine learning. 1992, Morgan Kaufmann.

36. Burges, C.J.C., A tutorial on support vector machines for pattern recognition. *Data Mining and Knowledge Discovery*, 1998. **2**(2): p. 121-167.

37. Lin, J., Divergence measures based on the Shannon entropy. *IEEE Transactions on Information Theory*, 1991. **37**(1): p. 145-151.

38. Blake, C.L. and C.J. Merz, UCI Repository of machine learning databases. 1998, UC Irvine.

39. Chawla, N.V., et al., SMOTE: synthetic minority over-sampling technique. *J. Artif. Intell. Res.*, 2002. **16**(2002): p. 321-357.

40. Kubat, M., R.C. Holte, and S. Matwin, Detection of oil spills in satellite radar images of sea surface. *Machine Learning*, 1998. 30: p. 195-215.

41. Fayyad, U.M. and K.B. Irani. Multiinterval discretisation of continuous-valued attributes. *International Joint Conference on Artificial Intelligence.* 1993. p. 1022-1029.

42. Langley, P., W. Iba, and K. Thompson. An analysis of Bayesian classifiers. *National Conference on Artificial Intelligence.* 1992. p.223-228.

Sparse Distributed Memories
for On-Line Value-Based Reinforcement Learning

Bohdana Ratitch[1] and Doina Precup[1]

McGill University, Montreal, Canada
{bohdana,dprecup}@cs.mcgill.ca

Abstract. In this paper, we advocate the use of Sparse Distributed Memories (SDMs) for on-line, value-based reinforcement learning (RL). SDMs provide a linear, local function approximation scheme, designed to work when a very large/ high-dimensional input (address) space has to be mapped into a much smaller physical memory. We present an implementation of the SDM architecture for on-line, value-based RL in continuous state spaces. An important contribution of this paper is an algorithm for dynamic on-line allocation and adjustment of memory resources for SDMs, which eliminates the need for choosing the memory size and structure a priori. In our experiments, this algorithm provides very good performance while efficiently managing the memory resources.

1   Introduction

The use of function approximators with on-line, value-based reinforcement learning (RL) algorithms is the subject of much recent research and presents important theoretical and practical challenges. For various reasons, detailed in Sect.2, linear, local approximators are often the preferred choice. Many practical RL applications have been built around such approximators, e.g., CMACs [27], variable-resolution discretizations [18, 23, 32] and memory-based methods [3, 8, 24, 26]. Radial basis function networks (RBFNs) with fixed centers and widths have been used much less [10, 27], the main difficulty being in the choice of parameters for the basis functions. Most of these methods, however, still face important difficulties when applied to on-line learning in large domains. For example, CMACs and variable-resolution discretization approaches do not scale well to high dimensions; related methods proposed in [18, 32] are intended for off-line learning; the memory-based methods in [3, 26] do not address the issue of limiting the memory size, which can grow very big during on-line reinforcement learning. Global and/or nonlinear approximators, e.g., Neural Networks (NNs) and Support Vector Machines (SVMs) scale better, in principle. However, with on-line reinforcement learning, they have no convergence guarantees and are subject to some other practical problems. For example, NNs suffer from catastrophic forgetting and are notoriously hard to tune when combined with RL algorithms; SVMs (even with recent incremental training methods) rely on batches of previously seen data [5, 6, 16, 17, 20] which can be problematic with on-line RL due to the non-stationary data distribution.

In this paper, we revive older ideas [27, 24, 8] of using Sparse Distributed Memories (SDMs) [13] and instance-based training [2] for value-function approximation in on-line RL. SDMs provide a linear, local architecture, designed for the case where a

J.-F. Boulicaut et al. (Eds.): ECML 2004, LNAI 3201, pp. 347–358, 2004.

very large input space has to be mapped into a much smaller physical memory. One of the advantages of instance-based methods is that they do not require choosing the size or the structure of the approximator in advance, but shape it based on the observed data. In general, local architectures, SDMs included, can be subject to the curse of dimensionality, as an exponential number of local units may be required in order to approximate some target functions accurately across the entire input space. However, many researchers believe that most decision-making systems need high accuracy only around low-dimensional manifolds of the state space or important state "highways". The SDM model enables us to take advantage of this fact.

In this paper, we explore the flexibility of the SDM model and some principles of the instance-based learning to provide a function approximator that automatically allocates resources only as needed based on the observed data. We propose a new approach for such allocation and adaptation of SDMs, which unlike many methods from supervised learning, is capable of adapting limited memory resources to the changing data distribution as the control strategies evolve during reinforcement learning. Based on our experimental results, the proposed approach has great practical potential by providing high levels of performance while being very efficient both in terms of the resulting memory sizes and computational time. It also remains close to the scope of existing theoretical convergence guarantees.

The paper is organized as follows. In Sect.2, we introduce the notation for value-based RL algorithms. We summarize the standard framework of SDMs and then present our implementation of the SDM idea for the case of RL tasks in continuous state spaces in Sect.3. In Sect.4, we describe our approach for dynamic memory allocation and adjustment in SDMs, designed to work with on-line RL algorithms. Experimental results are presented in Sect.5. We end with conclusions and future work in Sect.6.

2   Reinforcement Learning

In the standard RL framework, a learning agent interacts with a stochastic environment at discrete time steps. On each time step t, the environment assumes some state s from the *state space* S and the agent picks an action a from the *action space* A. As a result, the environment transitions to a new state s' and the agent receives a numerical (stochastic) *reward* r. In a Markovian environment, the state transition distribution and the rewards depend only on $\langle s, a \rangle$. The goal of the agent is to find a *policy* $\pi : S \times A \rightarrow [0, 1]$ (a way of choosing actions) that optimizes a *long-term performance* criterion, called *return*. Returns are usually defined as a cumulative function of rewards received over time. Many RL algorithms compute *value functions*, which are *expected returns*. For instance, the *optimal action-value function* with a discount factor $\gamma \in (0, 1]$ is $Q^*(s, a) = \max_\pi E_\pi \{ r_{t+1} + \gamma r_{t+2} + \ldots | s_t = s, a_t = a \}$.

In this paper, we focus on RL algorithms that iteratively compute estimates of the optimal action-value function from samples obtained by interacting with the environment. For example, at each time step, the SARSA algorithm [27] updates the value of the current state-action pair $\langle s, a \rangle$ based on the observed reward r and the next state-action pair $\langle s', a' \rangle$, using learning rate $\alpha \in (0, 1)$, as follows:

$$Q(s, a) \leftarrow (1 - \alpha)Q(s, a) + \alpha[r + \gamma Q(s', a')] \tag{1}$$

In domains with large or continuous state spaces, value functions can be represented by function approximators. In this case, RL methods sample state-action pairs $\langle s, a \rangle$, which represent inputs, and estimates of the action-value function, e.g., $[r + \gamma Q(s', a')]$, representing targets. However, the problem of function approximation is more difficult in the context of RL. Targets do not come from the true optimal value function, they are "guesses" based on the current approximation (see Eq.1). Also, in on-line RL, the agent's action choices typically depend on the current value estimates in a (semi) greedy manner. Hence, both the input distribution and the target function are non-stationary. Moreover, during on-line learning, the training samples are not independent.

Some researchers (see, e.g., [3, 19]) argue that local methods are more suitable for RL than global ones. Local approximators allow only a few local parameters to be updated on every step, based on a distance to the current input. This is in contrast with global models (e.g., sigmoid NNs), in which all parameters are updated on every step. Local approximators do not suffer from catastrophic forgetting, which can be caused by non-independent and non-stationary sampling in RL. Also, they quickly incorporate new data in a local region of the input space, thus adjusting faster to the non-stationarity.

Theoretically, convergence properties are best understood for linear approximators, which compute the state value as a linear combination of some features of the state. Relevant results include the convergence of policy evaluation [31], the convergence of approximate dynamic programming with averagers [10], and non-divergence of SARSA(λ) [11]. The behavior of non-linear approximators is still poorly understood in theory, while practical evidence is not consistent.

3   Sparse Distributed Memory

The Sparse Distributed Memory architecture [13] was originally proposed for learning input-output associations between data drawn from a binary space. The input can be viewed as an "address" and the output is the desired content to be stored at that address. The physical memory available is typically much smaller than the space of all possible inputs, so the physical memory locations have to be distributed sparsely.

In SDMs, a sample of addresses is chosen (in any suitable manner) and physical memory *locations* are associated only with these addresses. When some address $\mathbf{x}$ has to be accessed, a set of the *nearby* locations is activated, as determined by a *similarity measure* (e.g. Hamming distance, if addresses are binary). The original SDM design assumes that the data to be memorized consists of bit vectors (with 0s substituted by -1s). When such a vector $f(\mathbf{x})$ needs to be stored, it is distributed between all the locations activated by $\mathbf{x}$, using bitwise addition. When the value for input (address) $\mathbf{x}$ is retrieved, the content of all active locations is combined by summation and thresholding.

In this paper, we focus on the case in which the inputs are vectors of real values and the outputs are also reals: $f(\mathbf{x}) : R^n \rightarrow R$. In this case, other popular approximators, e.g., CMACs and RBFNs, can be related to SDMs. In RBFNs, each RBF unit can be viewed as a memory location, where the center of the unit is the address and the similarity measure is determined by the widths of the basis functions. The relationship between CMACs and SDMs is discussed in Sect.5.

For presentation purposes and for our experiments, we chose a similarity measure based on symmetric triangular functions. The similarity between input vector $\mathbf{x} = \langle x_1, ..., x_n \rangle$ and location $\mathbf{h} = \langle h_1, ..., h_n \rangle$ is given by:

$$\mu(\mathbf{h}, \mathbf{x}) = \min_{i=1,...,n} \mu_i(\mathbf{h}, \mathbf{x})$$

$$\mu_i(\mathbf{h}, \mathbf{x}) = \begin{cases} 1 - \frac{|x_i - h_i|}{\beta_i} & \text{if } |x_i - h_i| \le \beta_i \\ 0 & \text{otherwise} \end{cases} \tag{2}$$

Here, $\langle h_1, ..., h_n \rangle$ represents the *location address* and β_i are the *activation radii* in each dimension. The similarity measure directly translates into the location's degree of activation, which, in this case, is continuous in $[0, 1]$. This factorized similarity function allows an immediate symbolic interpretation of the location's semantics with respect to each input dimension. Of course, the similarity measure can be defined in many different ways (see, e.g., [2, 25]). It is possible to implement SDMs efficiently so that isolating active locations does not require computing the similarity of a data point to all locations, for example, by using *kd*-trees as in instance-based learning [26], or by inverted indexing.

To predict the value of input $\mathbf{x}$, we first find the set of active locations, $H_\mathbf{x}$. Let $\mu^k = \mu(\mathbf{h}^k, \mathbf{x})$ be the similarity between input $\mathbf{x}$ and the kth location, $\mathbf{h}^k$, as in (2). Let w_k be a value stored at $\mathbf{h}^k$. Then the predicted value of $\mathbf{x}$ is:

$$\hat{f}(\mathbf{x}) = \frac{\sum_{k \in H_\mathbf{x}} \mu^k w_k}{\sum_{k \in H_\mathbf{x}} \mu^k} \tag{3}$$

This representation is equivalent to Normalized RBFNs. Using normalization provides a better support (i.e., reduces non-smoothness in the approximate function) in the regions of the input space where the basis functions overlap only little [15]. The normalized activations of the memory locations, $\frac{\mu^m}{\sum_{k \in H_\mathbf{x}} \mu^k}$, can be viewed as features of the input $\mathbf{x}$. Hence, the prediction is computed as a linear combination of local features.

Upon receiving a training sample $\langle \mathbf{x}, f(\mathbf{x}) \rangle$, the values stored in all active locations are updated using the standard gradient descent algorithm for linear approximation:

$$w_m := w_m + \alpha \frac{\mu^m}{\sum_{k \in H_\mathbf{x}} \mu^k} \left[f(\mathbf{x}) - \hat{f}(\mathbf{x}) \right], \forall m \in H_\mathbf{x} \tag{4}$$

where $\hat{f}(\mathbf{x})$ is the prediction for input $\mathbf{x}$ and $\alpha \in (0, 1)$ is the learning rate. In Sect.4, we discuss how the addresses of the memory locations can be selected and updated.

SDMs can be incorporated into RL algorithms in a straightforward way. For instance, in order to combine SDMs with SARSA(λ) [27], one approximator is used to represent the action-value function, $Q(s, a)$, for each action. The values stored in the SDMs are updated after every transition $\langle s, a \rangle \xrightarrow{r} \langle s', a' \rangle$:

$$w_m(\bar{a}) := w_m(\bar{a}) + \alpha e_m(\bar{a})[r + \gamma Q(s', a') - Q(s, a)], \forall \bar{a} \in A \text{ and } m = 1, ..., M_{\bar{a}}$$

Here, $e_m(\bar{a})$ are the eligibility traces associated with each location. For the replacing traces method, they decay by $\gamma\lambda$, $\lambda \in [0, 1]$, for all $\bar{a} \ne a$, and are reset to $\frac{\mu^m}{\sum_{k \in H_s(a)} \mu^k}$ for the performed action a. If the memory is big, a list of locations with traces greater than some threshold can be maintained in order to perform this update efficiently.

4 Dynamic Resource Allocation

The distribution of the memory locations is crucial for the performance of SDMs and related models, such as RBFNs. It is usually assumed that the memory size is fixed at the beginning of learning and locations are either distributed uniformly randomly across the input space, or determined by unsupervised learning methods, such as clustering. In the second case, a batch of training data is assumed to exist from the beginning. Then the parameters of the local units can be additionally adjusted during learning. Both in the SDM and RBFN literature, there are several methods for doing this automatically.

For SDMs, the methods in [9, 12] periodically delete some units based on their activation frequencies to free up resources for allocation elsewhere: rarely activated locations are removed. According to our past experiments, this approach does not work well with RL, as it often results in the removal of units associated with very important states, such as goal states and catastrophic states, which usually have relatively low activation frequencies for some time after they have been initially discovered.

Memory layout can also be adjusted using on-line, unsupervised learning methods, as in [21, 28]. The approach introduced in [28] for binary SDMs slowly moves the existing memory locations toward observed data. If the number of active locations for a given training sample is too small, an inactive location is selected at random and moved toward the current input in one, randomly selected, dimension. A symmetric adjustment is made if too many locations are active. We implemented a version of this algorithm, but it did not allow stable learning, despite significant tuning because it was unable to track quickly the non-stationary data distribution produced by changing policies.

For RBFNs, one standard approach is to use gradient descent on the mean squared error to adjust the centers and widths of RBFs [7, 15]. Interestingly, it was observed in [15] that with RL, basis functions tend to move to regions in the state space with small temporal-difference errors while leaving large portions of the state space uncovered and failing to provide a good policy. As suggested in [15], a better method should also incorporate information about the density of the visited states.

Resource-allocating RBF networks [4, 19, 1] are initially empty, and new units are added based on the distance between the new data and the existing units, as well as based on the prediction error on the new data (with different variations on how the error is measured). These methods require lots of parameters to be chosen by the user, and it is not clear, in general, whether reliance on the prediction error is robust in on-line RL, because the error can vary a lot with changes in policy.

We propose a new method for determining automatically the SDM size and location addresses based on the observed data. In this paper, we assume that the activation radii of the memory locations are uniform and fixed by the user. The approach in [8], formulated in the instance-based learning framework, is conceptually similar to ours. However, technical differences between the two algorithms have some important implications, which we will discuss in more detail after the presentation of our method.

Our *dynamic allocation* algorithm starts with an empty memory, and locations are added based on the observed data. Since the samples obtained during on-line RL are correlated, memorizing all samples until the memory is filled can create unnecessary densely populated areas, while leaving other parts of the state space uncovered. Our goal is to add locations only if the memory is too sparse around the training samples.

Our algorithm has only one parameter, denoted N, which is the minimum number of locations that we would like to see activated for a data sample. It is important to ensure that these locations are "evenly distributed" across their local neighborhoods. Hence, we do not allow locations to be too close. More specifically, for any pair of locations $\mathbf{h}^i, \mathbf{h}^j$, we enforce a condition on their similarity:

$$\mu(\mathbf{h}^i, \mathbf{h}^j) \leq \begin{cases} 1 - \frac{1}{N-1} & N \geq 3 \\ 0.5 & N = 2 \end{cases} \tag{5}$$

This condition means that the fewer locations are required in a neighborhood (the smaller N), the farther apart these locations should be.

A new location can be added upon observing any new sample $\langle (s,a), \bar{Q}(s,a) \rangle$, where $s = \langle s_1, ..., s_n \rangle$ represents the input to the SDM for the action-value function of action a, and $\bar{Q}(s,a)$ represents the target for the current state-action pair (s,a). For example, $\bar{Q}(s,a) = r + \gamma Q(s',a')$ in the case of SARSA algorithm. The following N-based heuristic is aimed at ensuring a minimum of N active locations in the vicinity of s:

Rule 1: If fewer than N locations are activated by the input s, add a new location centered at s, if its addition does not violate condition (5). The current target value, $\bar{Q}(s,a)$, is stored in this location.

If during learning there is not enough exploration to ensure a good spread of the visited states, the allocation using only the above heuristic proceeds very slowly, and learning can be stalled for a long time (a phenomenon we observed in preliminary experiments). To counteract this problem, we use an extension of the above heuristic, which sets up memory resources faster, while still allocating them close to the actual data samples:

Rule 2: If after applying Rule 1, the number of active locations is $N' < N$, then $(N - N')$ locations are randomly placed in the neighborhood of the current sample. The addresses of new locations are sampled uniformly randomly from the intervals $[s_i - \beta_i, s_i + \beta_i]$ in each dimension, while enforcing condition (5). The value currently predicted by the memory for the corresponding address is stored in such a location.

The parameter N in the above heuristics is reminiscent of the parameter k in the k-nearest-neighbor methods, which determines the number of instances that are used for locally weighted learning. Unlike the classical instance-based approach, our method provides a way to selectively store training samples to obtain a good space coverage with respect to this parameter while controlling the memory size.

If the memory size limit is reached but we still encounter a data sample for which the number of active locations N' is smaller than the minimum desired number N, we also allow existing locations to move around. Unlike the approach described in [28], we do not adjust the existing addresses slowly. Instead, we pick at random and remove one inactive location (or $(N - N')$, if Rule 2 is used). The corresponding number of new locations are added to the neighborhood of the current sample using Rule 1 or 2. When a location $\mathbf{h}$ is to be removed, we first find, among locations in the active set $H_\mathbf{h}(a)$, the location $\mathbf{h}'$ that is closest to $\mathbf{h}$. Then, $\mathbf{h}$ and $\mathbf{h}'$ are both replaced by another location, $\mathbf{h}''$, placed midway between them. The value of $\mathbf{h}''$ is set to the average of the values of $\mathbf{h}$ and $\mathbf{h}'$. This approach, which we call *randomized reallocation*, allows the memory to react quickly to the lack of resources in the regions visited under the current behavior policy. At the same time, the randomized nature of the removals and the fact that there are sufficient locations in most of the previously visited regions ensure that it does not affect dramatically any particular area of the input space. The method is cheap both in terms of computation and space, since the choice of locations to be removed is not based on any extra information, like in other algorithms [9, 12, 14, 8].

Resource allocation proceeds in parallel with learning the memory content. On each learning step, new locations are added or moved, if necessary, then the values stored in the memory are updated as presented in Sect. 3. The resource adjustments can be performed on prediction steps as well. If a new location is added in this case, the value currently predicted for the corresponding address is stored in it. In our experiments, this proved to be very beneficial, as it allowed the memory layout to adapt faster. It allows the SDMs for all actions to get adjusted to the current state distribution, as opposed to adjusting only the SDM for the performed action.

Our approach is conceptually similar to the instance-based approach presented in [8], which also uses heuristics for selectively adding new instances to the memory and for removing some of them when the memory capacity limit is reached. The method was formulated in the classical instance-based framework [2], based on the definition of two functions: a distance metric in the input space, e.g., the Euclidean distance, and weighting functions, e.g., Gaussian, that transform the distances into weights to be used in locally weighted regression. In [8], as well as earlier in [24], new instances are added to the memory if they are farther away from the existing instances than a specified threshold. Such a threshold is defined in terms of the distance metric and is not related to the bandwidths of the weighting functions. If this correspondence is not explicitly addressed, the obtained memory can be too sparse. While it is easy to prevent this in the case of a uniform, fixed bandwidth of the weighting functions, the approach does not generalize to varying bandwidths. Although adaptive bandwidths were claimed to be used in [8], no discussion was provided for the practical behavior of the method and its parameter settings.

Our approach, on the other hand, is directly related to the similarity function. It ensures that the memory locations are spread appropriately with respect to the radii of the similarity function and allows a coherent extension to the case of variable radii. In our approach, the similarity threshold is implied by the parameter N (minimum desired number of activated locations). This may seem to be equivalent; however, more than N training samples can satisfy the similarity threshold and thus be added to the memory. Thus, using the parameter N provides a more conservative way to control the size of the memory, as was confirmed by our experiments (see Sect.5).

The heuristic in [8] for removing instances in the case when the memory capacity limit is reached is also different from ours. It suggests discarding the instances whose removal introduces the least error in the prediction of the values of their neighbors:

$$error_m = \frac{1}{|H_{\mathbf{h}_m}|} \sum_{k \in H_{\mathbf{h}_m}} |Q(\mathbf{h}_k, a) - Q_{-m}(\mathbf{h}_k, a)| \qquad (6)$$

where $Q_{-m}(\mathbf{h}_k, a)$ is the prediction for input $\mathbf{h}_k$ without the instance $\mathbf{h}_m$. In Sect.5, we experimentally show that this *error-based heuristic* and the randomized heuristic behave differently in practice. The former is also more expensive computationally: it requires either to perform a complete memory sweep when reallocation is necessary, or to perform $(|H_{\mathbf{h}_m}| - 1)$ additional predictions on every memory access in order to maintain (approximate) error estimates. The cost of the randomized heuristic, on the other hand, is that of generating a random number and applies only when a new location actually has to be added in an underrepresented region of the input space.

5   Experimental Results

We tested SDMs incorporated into the SARSA(0) algorithm with ε-greedy exploration. In this paper, we provide detailed experimental results on the standard Montain-Car benchmark [27], commonly used in the RL community. Due to the space limitation, we cannot include here the results on other domains, but we refer the reader to [22] for case studies on two other tasks: a variant of the hunter-prey domain with up to 11 state variables and an instance of a swimmer motor-control task with 6 state variables.

Mountain-Car is an episodic task, with a two-dimensional continuous state space, where the agent has to learn to drive up a hill from a valley. Episodes were terminated when the goal was reached, or after 1000 steps. To obtain a baseline for performance, we used the popular CMAC (tile coding) approximator [27], which is particularly successful on this domain. CMACs are related to SDMs, but the memory layout is fixed a priori, with the locations (tiles) arranged in several superimposed grids (tilings). Each input activates one tile in each tiling, and the activation mechanism is binary. Since CMACs rely on the discretization of the input space, their size scales exponentially with the input dimensionality. We used CMACs and SDMs of "similar resolutions": If a CMAC had T tilings, we set the parameter for dynamic memory allocation with the N-based heuristic as $N = T$. The activation radii of the SDMs were set equal to the size of the CMAC tiles. We also tested a dynamic allocation method in the style of [8], where a new location was added when the similarity of the new sample to all existing locations was below some threshold μ^*, whithout checking whether the number of active locations already exceeds N. We will refer to it as the *threshold-based heuristic*. In this case, we set the similarity thresholds μ^* to the values that would be obtained from Eq.(5) for the values of N and the activation radii used in the corresponding experiments with the N-based heuristic. The objective was to investigate the resulting memory sizes, layouts and the performance based on the two heuristics.

We conducted two sets of experiments as follows. In the first set, the start state of each episode was chosen uniformly randomly. This is the most popular setting and it is "easier" because the starting distribution ensures good exploration. Graphs (a), (b) and (c) of Fig.1 present the returns of the greedy policies learned by CMACs and dynamically allocated SDMs with the N-based and the threshold-based heuristics respectively. In these experiments, the memory size limit was set sufficiently high to ensure that it would not be reached and we could test the dynamic allocation method alone. The performance of the SDMs is either the same or (in most cases) much better than that of CMACs. It degrades more gracefully with the decrease in resolution. Moreover, SDMs with the N-based heuristic always consume fewer resources, as shown in the legends of the graphs. The asymptotic performance of the SDMs with the threshold-based heuristic is similar to that of the N-based heuristic, but learning is slower. The resulting memories are between 2-4 times larger with the threshold-based heuristic, which slows down learning, because more training is required for larger architectures. As mentioned before, the N-based heuristic allows better control over the amount of allocated resources and, as the experiments show, results in faster learning.

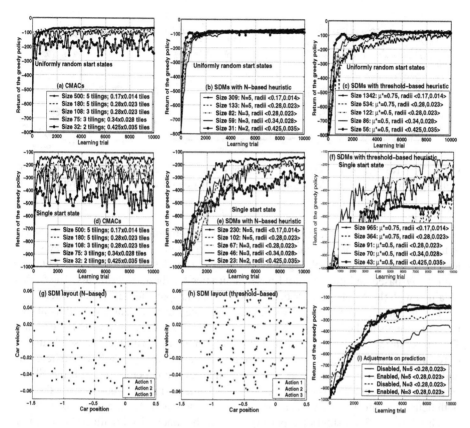

Fig. 1. Dynamic allocation method. Returns of the greedy policies are averaged over 30 runs. On graphs (a)-(c), returns are also averaged over 50 fixed starting test states. SDM sizes represent maximum over 30 runs. The exploration parameter ε and the learning step α were optimized for each architecture. Graphs (g) and (h) are for SDMs with radii $\langle 0.34, 0.028 \rangle$, and $N = 5$ and $\mu^* = 0.5$ respectively.

In the second set of experiments, we used a single start state where the car starts at the bottom of the hill with zero velocity. In this setting, exploration is much more difficult. We specifically wanted to test the performance of SDMs when the training samples are highly correlated and distributed non-uniformly. The results are shown in the middle row of Fig.1. SDMs with the N-based heuristic (using `Rule 1` and 2) generally learn better policies than CMACs and take advantage of the fact that not all states are visited. The resulting memory sizes for SDMs (graph (e)) are roughly 30% smaller than in the previous experiment (graph (b)). SDMs with the threshold-based heuristic, however, were much slower and exhibited much higher variance (not shown here) with this single start-state training, even though they had a large number of locations placed exactly along the followed trajectories. This demonstrates that, with restricted exploration, `Rule 2` of our approach, which allows adding locations close to but not exactly on trajectories, helps to build quickly a compact model with good

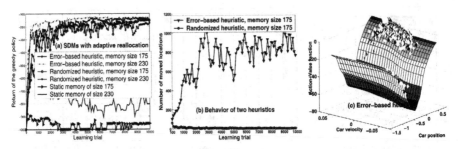

Fig. 2. Adaptive reallocation method. Each point on graph (b) represents the average over 100 trials and 30 runs. Graph (c) depicts an action-value function for action "positive throttle".

generalization capabilities. Also, under limited exploration, smaller architectures (as obtained with the N-based heuristic) should be expected to learn better as they suffer less from over-fitting. Graphs (g) and (h) show examples of SDM layouts obtained with the N-based and the threshold-based heuristics for these experiments. The SDMs obtained with the N-based heuristic are less dense and span the state space better.

Finally, graph (i) of Fig.1 shows the performance improvement achieved by allowing adjustments to the memory layout during predictions as well as during RL updates. The graph shows results for the dynamic allocation method with the N-based heuristic only, but performance improvements were observed with the threshold-based heuristic and the reallocation algorithm as well. Note that all the experiments with the SDMs (for both heuristics) discussed above were performed with this option enabled. With both heuristics, most memory locations ($\sim 85\%$) where added in the first 200 trials.

Graph (a) of Fig.2 shows the performance of the randomized reallocation method, which allows moving the existing locations when the memory size limit is reached. The experiments were performed for the single start-state problem using the N-based heuristic for location additions. We tested two removal approaches: the randomized one, introduced in this paper and the error-based, suggested in [8]. This graph shows experiments with memory parameters $N = 5, \beta = \langle 0.17, 0.014 \rangle$. The memory size limits were chosen to be equal to 230 and 175 which is 100% and 75% of the size obtained for the same memory resolution with the dynamic allocation method and the N-based heuristic in the previous experiments. The SDMs were initialized with all locations distributed uniformly randomly across the state space and then allowed to move according to the heuristics used. Note that the static memories of the same sizes were not able to learn a good policy. As can be seen from graph (a), both removal heuristics exhibit very similar performance. However, as shown on graph (b), the behavior of the two heuristics is quite different. With the randomized heuristic, most reallocations happen at the beginning of learning and then their number decreases almost to zero. With the error-based heuristic the number of reallocations is much higher. This happens because the addition heuristic is density-based and the removal heuristic is error-based, and their objectives are not "in agreement". Graph (c) depicts 3000 location moves at the end of one training run, where removed locations are plotted with black dots and added locations with white. A mixed black-and-white cloud in one region of the state space shows that most removals happen in a particular region where the value function is relatively flat. But the same region is then visited and found to be too sparsely populated, so locations are added back. Apparently such a cycle repeats itself. As mentioned earlier, with the randomized heuristic, no specific area of the input space is affected by removals more than others, so cyclic behavior is minimized. The randomized heuristic is computationally much cheaper while showing more stable behavior and providing good policies. The error-based heuristic can still be an interesting choice, provided that it is in tune with the addition heuristic.

6   Conclusion and Future Work

In this paper, we combined on-line value-based RL with a function approximation model based on SDMs. This model is local and linear, which is often preferred in RL and has enough flexibility to scale well with large and highly dimensional input spaces. Our main contribution is a new approach for dynamic allocation and adaptation of the memory resources specifically suited for on-line value-based RL. Our approach to adding new memory locations provides a disciplined way to control the memory size and density taking into account the location activation mechanism and can be readily used in the future with activation functions that have variable bandwidth across locations. Moreover, our method facilitates learning under constrained exploration scenarios. We demonstrated the importance of agreement between the methods for adding and removing the memory locations which have to be used together if the memory limit is reached. Our randomized approach to adaptive reallocation of the memory resources provides good performance and a stable behavior. Our algorithm allows learning good control policies while being simple to implement and efficient computationally and memory-wise.

One of the issues that we will address in the future is the automatic selection of the activation radii for the SDM locations while allowing them to vary across the state space. Our resource allocation mechanism is based only on the distribution of the inputs. In the future, we also plan to explore mechanisms that also use information about the function shape (e.g., function linearity, decision boundaries, as in [18]), so that the memory layout is adjusted taking into account the complexity of the target function. Finally, we will investigate the theoretical properties of the SDM model starting from currently available results in [29, 30].

References

1. Anderson, C. (1993). Q-learning with hidden-unit restarting. *NIPS*, 81-88.
2. Atkeson, C.G, Moore, A.W. & Schaal, S. (1997). Locally weighted learning *Artificial Intelligence Review*, 11-73.
3. Atkeson, C. G., Moore, A. W., & Schaal, S. (1997). Locally weighted learning for control. *Artificial Intelligence Review*, 75–113
4. Blanzieri, E., & Katenkamp, P. (1996). Learning RBFNs on-line. *ICML*, 37-45.
5. Dietterich, T. G., & Wang, X. (2001). Batch value function approximation via support vectors. *NIPS*, 444-450.
6. Engel, Y., Mannor, S. & Meir, R. (2003). Bayes meets Bellman: The Gaussian process approach to temporal difference learning. *ICML*, 154-161.

7. Flachs, B., & J.Flynn, M. (1992). *Sparse adaptive memory* (Tech. Rep. 92-530). Computer Systems Lab., Dptm. of Electrical Engineering and Computer Science, Stanford University.
8. Forbes,J.R.N. (2002). *Reinforcement learning for autonomous vehicles*. Ph.D. Thesis, Computer Science Department, University of California at Berkeley.
9. Fritzke, B. (1997). A self-organizing network that can follow non-stationary distributions. *ICANN*, 613-618.
10. Gordon, G.J. (1995). Stable function approximation in dynamic programming. *ICML*, 261-268.
11. Gordon, G.J. (2000). Reinforcement learning with function approximation converges to a region. *NIPS*, 1040-1046.
12. Hely, T.A., Willshaw, D.J. & Hayes, G.M.(1997). A new approach to Kanerva's sparse distributed memory. *Neural Networks, 3*, 791-794.
13. Kanerva, P. (1993). Sparse distributed memory and related models. In M. Hassoun (Ed.), *Associative neural memories: Theory and implementation*, Oxford University Press, 50-76.
14. Kondo, T., & Ito, K. (2002). A reinforcement learning with adaptive state space recruitment strategy for real autonomous mobile robots. *IROS*.
15. Kretchmar, R. & Anderson, C. (1997). Comparison of CMACs and RBFs for local function approximators in reinforcement learning. *IEEE Int. Conf. on Neural Networks*, 834-837.
16. Lagoudakis, M.G., & Parr, R. (2003). Reinforcement learning as classification: Leveraging modern classifiers. *ICML*, 424-431.
17. Martin, M. (2002). On-line support vector machine regression. *ECML*, 282-294.
18. Munos, R., & Moore, A. (2000). Variable resolution discretization in optimal control. *Machine learning, 49*, 291-323.
19. Platt, J. (1991). A resource-allocating network for function interpolation. *Neural Computation, 3*, 213–225.
20. Ralaivola, L., & d'Alche Buc, F. (2001). Incremental support vector machine learning: a local approach. *ICANN*.
21. Rao, R. P.N., & Fuentes, O. (1998). Hierarchical learning of navigational behaviors in an autonomous robot using a predictive SDM. *Autonomous Robots, 5*, 297-316.
22. Ratitch, B., Mahadevan, S. & Precup, D. (2004). Sparse distribute memories as function approximators in value-based reinforcement learning: Case studies. *AAAI Workshop on Learning and Planning in Markov Processes*.
23. Reynolds, S. I. (2000). Decision boundary partitioning: variable resolution model-free reinforcement learning. *ICML*, 783-790.
24. Santamaria, J. C., Sutton, R. S., & Ram, A. (1998). Experiments with reinforcement learning in problems with continuous state and action spaces. *Adaptive Behavior, 6*, 163–218.
25. Scholkopf, B. (2000). The kernel trick for distances. *NIPS*, 301–307
26. Smart, W. & Kaelbling, L.P. (2000). Practical reinforcement learning in continuous spaces *ICML*, 903-910.
27. Sutton, R. S., & Barto, A. G. (1998). *Reinforcement learning. An introduction*. The MIT Press.
28. Sutton, R. S., & Whitehead, S. D. (1993). Online learning with random representations. *ICML*, 314–321.
29. Szepesvari, C. & Smart, W. D. (2004). Convergent value function approximation methods. http://www.sztaki.hu/~szcsaba/papers/szws_icml2004_rlfapp.pdf
30. Tsitsiklis, J.N. & Van Roy, B. (1996). Feature-based methods for large scale dynamic programming. *Machine Learning*, pages 59-94.
31. Tsitsiklis, J.N. & Van Roy, B. (1997). An analysis of temporal difference learning with function approximation. *IEEE Transactions on Automatic Control, 42*, 674-690.
32. Uther, W. T. B. & Veloso, M. M. (1998). Tree based discretization for continuous state space reinforcement learning *AAAI*, 769–774.

Improving Random Forests

Marko Robnik-Šikonja

University of Ljubljana,
Faculty of Computer and Information Science,
Tržaška 25, 1001 Ljubljana, Slovenia
tel.: +386 1 4768459, fax: +386 1 4768498
Marko.Robnik@fri.uni-lj.si

Abstract. Random forests are one of the most successful ensemble methods which exhibits performance on the level of boosting and support vector machines. The method is fast, robust to noise, does not overfit and offers possibilities for explanation and visualization of its output. We investigate some possibilities to increase strength or decrease correlation of individual trees in the forest. Using several attribute evaluation measures instead of just one gives promising results. On the other hand replacement of ordinary voting with voting weighted with margin achieved on most similar instances gives improvements which are statistically highly significant over several data sets.

1 Introduction

Several authors have noted that constructing ensembles of base learners can significantly improve the performance of learning. Bagging [1], boosting [6], random forests [2] and their variants are the most popular examples of this methodology. Boosting and random forests are comparable and sometimes better than state-of-the-art methods in classification and regression [10].

The success of ensemble methods is usually explained with the margin and correlation of base classifiers [14, 2]. To have a good ensemble one needs base classifiers which are diverse (in a sense that they predict differently), yet accurate. The voting mechanism which operates on the top of base learners then ensures highly accurate predictions of the ensemble.

The AdaBoost algorithm constructs a series of base learners by weighting their training set of examples according to the correctness of the prediction. Correctly predicted examples have their weights decreased, and incorrect prediction results in the increased weight of an instance. In this way the subsequent base learners receive effectively different learning sets and gradually focus on the most problematic instances. Usually tree based models are used as base learners.

Random forests construct a series of tree-based learners. Each base learner receives different training set of n instances which are drawn independently with replacement from the learning set of n instances. The bootstrap replication of training instances is not the only source of randomness. In each node of the tree the splitting attribute is selected from a randomly chosen sample of attributes. Random forests are computationally effective and offer good prediction performance. They are proven not to overfit,

J.-F. Boulicaut et al. (Eds.): ECML 2004, LNAI 3201, pp. 359–370, 2004.

and are less sensitive to noisy data compared to boosting. As the training sets of individual trees are constructed by bootstrap replication, there is on average $1/e \approx 36.8\%$ of instances not taking part in construction of the tree[1]. These instances, called out-of-bag instances are the source of data for useful internal estimates of error, strength and correlation. Breiman's homepage offers several tools for exploiting the power of these estimates and random forests.

In spite of apparent success of random forests methodology, we believe there is room for improvement. This paper describes some successful and some unsuccessful attempts to do so.

Individually, each of the base learners is a poor predictor. The random selection of attributes makes individual trees rather weak. Our first aim was to strengthen individual trees, without sacrificing variety between them or, alternatively increase variance without sacrificing strength. We partly succeeded in the first goal by using ReliefF algorithm for attribute estimation and in the second by using several different attribute evaluation measures for split selection. Another improvements stems from the voting mechanism. Not all trees are equally successful in labeling all instances. We use internal estimates to identify instances most similar to the one we wish to label and then weight the votes of the trees with the strength they demonstrate on these near instances. Improvements are demonstrated on several classification data sets.

Throughout the paper we use the notation where each learning instance is represented by an ordered pair $(\mathbf{x}, y)$, where each vector of attributes $\mathbf{x}$ consists of individual attributes A_i, $i = 1, ..., a$, (a is the number of attributes) and is labeled with the target value y_j, $j = 1, ..., c$ (c is the number of class values). The correct class is denoted as y, without index. Each discrete attribute A_i has values v_1 through v_{m_i} (m_i is the number of values of attribute A_i). We write $p(v_{i,k})$ for the probability that the attribute A_i has value v_k, $p(y_j)$ is the probability of the class y_j, and $p(y_j|v_{i,k})$ is the probability of the class y_j conditioned by the attribute A_i having the value v_k.

The paper is organized into 6 sections. Section 2 contains some background on random forests, describes how strength and correlation are measured and shortly presents the databases and methodology we used to evaluate improvements. In Section 3 we propose using several attribute evaluation measures as split selectors to decrease correlation of trees in the forest. In Section 4 we analyze weighted voting. Section 5 contains evaluation of the proposed improvements on fresh data sets not used during development and Section 6 concludes the work.

2   Random Forests

Random forests as used by Breiman [2] consist of ensemble of K classifiers $h_1(\mathbf{x})$, $h_2(\mathbf{x}), ..., h_K(\mathbf{x})$. Each classifier votes for one of the classes and an instance being classified is labeled with the winning class. We denote the joint classifier as $h(\mathbf{x})$. Each training set of n instances is drawn at random with replacement from the training set of n instances. With this sampling called bootstrap replication, on average 36.8% of training instances are not used for building each tree. These out-of-bag instances come handy for computing an internal estimate of the strength and correlation of the forest.

---

[1] Constant $e \approx 2.718$ stands for the base of the natural logarithms.

Denote the set of out-of-bag instances for classifier h_k as O_k. Let $Q(\mathbf{x}, y_j)$ be the out-of-bag proportion of votes for class y_j at input $\mathbf{x}$ and an estimate of $P(h(\mathbf{x}) = y_j)$:

$$Q(\mathbf{x}, y_j) = \frac{\sum\limits_{k=1}^{K} I(h_k(\mathbf{x}) = y_j; (\mathbf{x}, y) \in O_k)}{\sum\limits_{k=1}^{K} I(h_k(\mathbf{x}); (\mathbf{x}, y) \in O_k)} \tag{1}$$

where $I(\cdot)$ is the indicator function. The margin function measures the extent to which the average vote for the right class y exceeds the average vote for any other class:

$$mr(\mathbf{x}, y) = P(h(\mathbf{x}) = y) - \max_{\substack{j=1 \\ j \neq y}}^{c} P(h(\mathbf{x}) = y_j) \tag{2}$$

It is estimated with $Q(\mathbf{x}, y)$ and $Q(\mathbf{x}, y_j)$. Strength is defined as the expected margin, and is computed as the average over the training set:

$$s = \frac{1}{n} \sum_{i=1}^{n} \left(Q(\mathbf{x}_i, y) - \max_{\substack{j=1 \\ j \neq y}}^{c} Q(\mathbf{x}_i, y_j) \right) \tag{3}$$

The average correlation is computed as the variance of the margin over the square of standard deviation of the forest:

$$\bar{\rho} = \frac{var(mr)}{sd(h())^2} = \frac{\frac{1}{n} \sum\limits_{i=1}^{n} \left(Q(\mathbf{x}_i, y) - \max\limits_{\substack{j=1 \\ j \neq y}}^{c} Q(\mathbf{x}_i, y_j) \right)^2 - s^2}{\left(\frac{1}{K} \sum\limits_{t=1}^{K} \sqrt{p_k + \hat{p}_k + (p_k - \hat{p}_k)^2} \right)^2} \tag{4}$$

where

$$p_k = \frac{\sum\limits_{(\mathbf{x}_i, y) \in O_k} I(h_k(\mathbf{x}) = y)}{\sum\limits_{(\mathbf{x}_i, y) \in O_k} I(h_k(\mathbf{x}))}$$

is an out-of-bag estimate of $P(h_k(\mathbf{x}) = y)$ and

$$\hat{p}_k = \frac{\sum\limits_{(\mathbf{x}_i, y) \in O_k} I(h_k(\mathbf{x}) = \hat{y}_j)}{\sum\limits_{(\mathbf{x}_i, y) \in O_k} I(h_k(\mathbf{x}))}$$

is an out-of-bag estimate of $P(h_k(\mathbf{x}) = \hat{y}_j)$ and

$$\hat{y}_j = \arg\max_{\substack{j=1 \\ j \neq y}}^{c} Q(\mathbf{x}, y_j)$$

is estimated for every instance $\mathbf{x}$ in the training set with $Q(\mathbf{x}, y_j)$.

Breiman [2] uses unpruned decision trees as base classifiers and introduces additional randomness into the trees. Namely, in each interior node of each tree a subset of r attributes is randomly selected and evaluated with the Gini index heuristics. The attribute with the highest Gini index is chosen as split in that node.

We have implemented the random forests methodology in the framework of our learning system[2]. All presented tests were executed with the recommended values of the parameters for the forests (number of trees $K = 100$, number of randomly selected attributes in each node $r = \sqrt{a}$, tree building is stopped when the number of instances in a node is 5 or less).

For evaluation of improvements we use the UCI data sets [11] from Breiman's paper and two additional parity problems: parity2 with two parity attributes, and parity3 with three parity attributes. Each of these parity problems contains also 10 random binary attributes. The characteristics of data sets are collected in Table 1 which contains information on the number of instances (n), number of classes (c), number of attributes (a), number of numeric (num) and nominal (nom) attributes, and the percentage of missing values (miss). All problems except three larger ones were evaluated with 10-fold cross-validation. For three larger problems we used predefined fixed splits to training and testing sets; for letters 15000 instances for learning, 5000 for testing, for sat 4435 for learning, 2000 for testing, and for zip 7291 for learning, 2007 for testing.

Table 1. Characteristics of the problems used during the development process.

name	n	c	a	num	nom	miss
breast-cancer	699	2	9	9	0	0.25
bupa	345	2	6	6	0	0
diabetes	768	2	8	8	0	0
ecoli	336	8	7	7	0	0
german-numeric	1000	2	24	24	0	0
glass	214	7	9	9	0	0
ionosphere	351	2	34	34	0	0
letter	20000	26	16	16	0	0
parity2	200	2	12	0	12	0
parity3	200	2	13	0	13	0
sat	6435	6	36	36	0	0
segmentation	2310	7	19	19	0	0
sonar	208	2	60	60	0	0
soybean	683	19	35	0	35	9.78
vehicle	846	4	18	18	0	0
vote	435	2	16	0	16	5.63
vowel	990	11	11	10	1	0
zip	9298	10	256	256	0	0

For comparison of classifiers we use Wilcoxon signed-rank test, a non-parametric equivalent of paired t-test. Its advantage is that it does not require normal distributions

---

[2] All algorithms and programs are available at http://lkm.fri.uni-lj.si/rmarko/

or homogenity of variance. The price we pay for this is lower power of the test, so we risk that some differences will not be recognized as significant. Details of the tests can be found in [15], and a discussion of their use in machine learning context in [4]. We compare the classification accuracy and the area under the ROC curve (AUC). For problems with more than two classes the AUC extension proposed by [7] is used. This extension evaluates separation of pairs of classes, which could be misleading in certain situations, e.g., in some folds we have noticed cases with perfect AUC score (1.0) but less than 100% classification accuracy.

Throughout the paper and our work with random forests we have used these data sets several times to evaluate improvements, which could lead to overfitting. To avoid this danger we introduce another set of learning problems, not used during the development, in Section 5 and test the final methods on them.

Our first aim was to increase strength or reduce correlation of the forests. We tackled this challenge with attribute evaluation.

3   Attribute Evaluation

Breiman uses Gini index as the feature evaluation measure in random forests. Gini index is fast but has some drawbacks compared to other heuristics (see [9] for detailed analysis), in particular it cannot detect strong conditional dependencies among attributes. If the problem is described with attributes where such dependencies arise (e.g., XOR type of attributes) the evaluation will be incorrect and resulting performance of classifier could be poor. The reason for this deficiency of Gini index is that it measures the impurity of the class value distribution before and after the split on evaluated attribute. In this way it assumes the conditional (upon the class) independence of attributes, evaluates each attribute separately and does not take the context of other attributes into account. The same behavior is typical for all impurity based measures (e.g., Gain ratio, DKM, MDL, j-measure). In problems which possibly involve much feature interactions these measures are not appropriate. The measure which solves this problem for classification problems is ReliefF [13].

My first idea of using ReliefF in random forests was to evaluate attributes in the preprocessing step, and use the quality estimates as weights in the process of selecting subsample of attributes in each interior node of the tree. While this approach worked well for artificial problems with highly dependent attributes (parity problems) it on average increased the correlation between the trees and resulted in decreased performance. Another idea was to replace Gini as the sole attribute evaluation measure with several others and thereby decrease correlation but retain strength. This indeed was the case and we describe the exact procedure below.

The problem of attribute evaluation has received much attention in the machine learning and there are several measures for estimating attributes' quality. In classification problems the most popular are e.g., Gini index [3], Gain ratio [12], ReliefF [8], MDL [9], and DKM [5]. DKM is suitable only for two class problems, so we did not use it in our study.

Except ReliefF all these measures are impurity based, meaning that they measure impurity of the class value distribution. They are fast, demanding $O(n \cdot a)$ steps for the evaluation of a attributes. We included also Myopic ReliefF, which contrary to ReliefF, is also impurity based and possesses some interesting biases [9]. The general form of all impurity based measures is:

$$I(A_i) = i(y) - \sum_{j=1}^{m_i} p(v_{i,j}) i(y|v_{i,j}) \; ,$$

where $i(y)$ is the impurity of class values before the split, and $i(y|v_{i,k})$ is the impurity of class values after the split on $A_i = v_{k,j}$. By subtracting the weighted impurity of the splits from the impurity of unpartitioned instances we measure gain in the purity of class values resulting from the split. Larger values of $I(A_i)$ imply pure splits and therefore good attributes. We cannot directly apply these measures to numerical attributes, but we can use any of the number of discretization techniques first and then evaluate discretized attributes, or, as in our case where the binary trees are built, we simply take the maximum purity gain over all possible splits of the numeric attribute.

We briefly present measures we used, first the ones based on impurity followed by ReliefF.

Gini index is used in CART learning system [3] and because of its simplicity it is also the measure chosen by Breiman for random forests.

$$Gini(A_i) = - \sum_{i=1}^{c} p(y_i)^2 + \sum_{j=1}^{m_i} p(v_{i,j}) \sum_{i=1}^{c} p(y_i|v_{i,j})^2 \qquad (5)$$

Gain ratio [12] is implemented in C4.5 program and is the most often used impurity based measure. It is defined as

$$GR(A_i) = \frac{\sum_{i=1}^{c} p(y_i) \log p(y_i) - \sum_{j=1}^{m_i} \sum_{i=1}^{c} p(y_i|v_{i,j}) \log p(y_i|v_{i,j})}{\sum_{j=1}^{m_i} p(v_{i,j}) \log p(v_{i,j})} \; . \qquad (6)$$

Its gain part tries to maximize the difference of entropy (which serves as the impurity function) before and after the split. To prevent excessive bias towards multiple small splits the gain is normalized with the attribute's entropy.

MDL is based on the Minimum Description Length principle and measures the quality of attributes as their ability to compress the data. The difference in coding length before and after the value of the attribute is revealed corresponds to the difference in impurity. Kononenko [9] has shown empirically that this criterion has the most appropriate bias concerning multi-valued attributes among a number of other impurity-based measures. It is defined as:

$$MDL(A_i) = \frac{1}{n} \left(\log_2 \binom{n}{n_{1.}, \ldots, n_{c.}} - \sum_{j=1}^{m_i} \log_2 \binom{n_{.j}}{n_{1j}, \ldots, n_{cj}} \right.$$
$$\left. + \log_2 \binom{n+c+1}{c-1} - \sum_{j=1}^{m_i} \log_2 \binom{n_{.j}+c-1}{c-1} \right) \qquad (7)$$

Here n is the number of training instances, n_i the number of training instances from class i, $n_{.j}$ the number of instances with j-th value of given attribute, and n_{ij} the number of instances from class i with j-th value of the attribute.

Myopic ReliefF [9, 13] is a byproduct of the analysis of ReliefF' behavior with large number of near instances. It is strongly correlated to Gini index but has additional normalization against multi-valued attributes and in case of multi-class problems:

$$MR(A_i) = \frac{\left(\sum_{j=1}^{m_i} p(v_{i,j})^2 \sum_{i=1}^{c} p(y_i|v_{i,j})^2\right) - \left(\sum_{j=1}^{m_i} p(v_{i,j})^2\right) \sum_{i=1}^{c} p(y_i)^2}{\left(\sum_{i=1}^{c} p(y_i)^2\right)\left(1 - \sum_{i=1}^{c} p(y_i)^2\right)} \tag{8}$$

ReliefF evaluates partitioning power of attributes according to how well their values distinguish between similar instances. An attribute is given a high score if its values separate similar observations with different class and do not separate similar instances with the same class values. ReliefF samples the instance space, computes the differences between predictions and values of the attributes and forms a statistical measure for the proximity of the probability densities of the attribute and the class. Its quality estimates can be explained as the the proportion of the explained class values. Assigned quality evaluations are in the range $[-1, 1]$. The computational complexity for evaluation of a attributes is $O(m \cdot n \cdot a)$, where m is the number of iterations. Details of the algorithm and its analysis can be found in [13]. We use it throughout this paper with its default settings, except for the number of iterations m, which we set to the $\log n$ to ensure fast execution needed for large number of evaluations in the trees. Nevertheless ReliefF is slower than impurity functions as it has to find nearest neighbors in $O(n \cdot a)$ steps even when the sample of attributes contains less than a attributes.

3.1   Forests with Several Evaluation Measures

In Table 2 we compare performance of two random forests variants. The standard one which uses Gini index as the sole attribute evaluation heuristic, and the modified one which uses five attribute evaluation measures (each fifth of the trees is build with different heuristics: Gini index, Gain ratio, MDL, Myopic ReliefF, or ReliefF). We present results for classification accuracy and AUC. For accuracy the difference over all data sets is significant at 0.2 level using Wilcoxon signed-rank test, while for AUC the differences are not significant.

While some improvement has been achieved we cannot be satisfied. Our further investigation were in the area of classification with the forests.

4   Weighted Voting

A close investigation of the performance of individual trees on artificial data sets have shown that not all trees are equally responsible for incorrect classification of individual instances. This simple observation led to the idea that it would be useful to use only

Table 2. Random forests performance for sole Gini and 5 estimators.

name	Gini index accuracy	AUC	5 estimators accuracy	AUC
breast-cancer	0.966	0.992	0.967	0.991
bupa	0.734	0.760	0.716	0.777
diabetes	0.762	0.756	0.770	0.747
ecoli	0.869	0.899	0.872	0.897
german-numeric	0.750	0.638	0.750	0.601
glass	0.763	0.942	0.776	0.940
ionosphere	0.937	0.958	0.937	0.963
letter	0.957	0.999	0.963	0.999
parity2	0.820	0.912	0.865	0.941
parity3	0.575	0.644	0.635	0.681
sat	0.910	0.985	0.908	0.984
segmentation	0.982	0.999	0.981	0.999
sonar	0.817	0.903	0.793	0.891
vehicle	0.750	0.926	0.752	0.926
vote	0.957	0.990	0.956	0.990
vowel	0.979	0.999	0.977	0.999
zip	0.934	0.995	0.938	0.995

some selected trees in classification. The selection of trees was based on their performance on similar instances, but without success. Further refinement of this idea has led to weighted voting.

For each instance we want to classify with the forest, we first find some of its most similar instances. Similarity is measured with the forests as in [2]. For that matter we keep track of the similarity for all the training instances. When classifying an instance I with one of the trees, all the training instances from the leaf node where I is classified into have their similarity score increased by one. As we repeat the procedure for all the trees the frequency of co-occurrence forms a measure of instance similarity. The same procedure is used by Breiman to detect prototypes and outliers. We select t most similar training instances and classify them with each tree where they are in the out-of-bag set. For each tree in the forest we measure margin (see Eq. (2)) on these similar out-of-bag instances. The trees with negative average margin are left out of classification. For final classification we use weighted voting of the remaining trees where weights are average margins on the similar instances when they are in the out-of-bag set. The algorithm demands $O(n \cdot K)$ additional space for saving information about n training instances in the leaves of the K trees. While learning time remains unchanged, the classification takes on average t/e times more time to classify t instances with the trees where they are in the out-of-bag set (this happens on average in $1/e \approx 36.8\%$ of the trees).

A few tests have shown that algorithm is quite robust to the selection of t, so we have set $t = 30$ which works satisfactory, but no systematic study was performed. In the left-hand side of Table 3 we present the accuracy and AUC of the forests with weighted voting (Gini with wv). If we compare these results with ordinary voting (see Gini columns in Table 2), we see that weighted voting is mostly better and never worse than ordinary voting.

Table 3. Random forests performance for weighted voting and 5 estimators with weighted voting.

name	Gini with wv accuracy	AUC	5est with wv accuracy	AUC
breast-cancer	0.967	0.992	0.967	0.991
bupa	0.739	0.770	0.719	0.781
diabetes	0.770	0.759	0.773	0.750
ecoli	0.869	0.902	0.866	0.896
german-numeric	0.760	0.641	0.758	0.613
glass	0.795	0.944	0.781	0.947
ionosphere	0.940	0.960	0.940	0.964
letter	0.958	0.999	0.964	0.999
parity2	0.875	0.940	0.910	0.971
parity3	0.625	0.691	0.740	0.841
sat	0.910	0.985	0.908	0.984
segmentation	0.982	0.999	0.981	0.999
sonar	0.865	0.936	0.841	0.922
vehicle	0.755	0.927	0.746	0.927
vote	0.957	0.991	0.956	0.990
vowel	0.979	0.999	0.977	0.999
zip	0.934	0.995	0.939	0.995

We executed Wilcoxon signed-ranks test to establish significance of the difference with ordinary voting. The results for accuracy and AUC are significant even at 0.001 level!

An obvious thing to do is to combine the two successful improvements: several attribute estimators and weighted voting. We present these results in the right-hand side of Table 3. Some improvements are observed but also slight degradation of performance on others. The differences are significant only compared to plain random forests (0.1 for accuracy and 0.2 for AUC) or random forests with 5 estimators (0.1 for accuracy, non significant for AUC) while they are nonsignificant compared to weighted voting.

The results indicate that weighted voting is clearly and significantly beneficial, while the positive effect of multiple estimators is not so convincing. Next Section tries to clarify this issue.

5   Evaluation on Fresh Data Sets

To avoid the overfitting resulting from the persistent use of data sets described in Table 1, we introduce another set of 17 learning problems from UCI repository, not used during development. The criterion for choosing particular data sets is their availability in the format our system could read (or little effort to transform them into such format). Their characteristics are contained in Table 4.

We compare the performance of plain random forests with random forests with one or both of successful improvements: several attribute evaluation heuristics and voting weighted with the average margin on similar instances. The accuracy and AUC figures collected in Table 5 are calculated with 10-fold cross validation.

Table 4. Characteristics of the new data sets.

name	n	c	a	num	nom	miss
adult	5908	2	14	6	8	1.05
audiology	226	24	69	0	69	2.03
banding	138	2	29	19	10	6.85
credit aus	690	2	15	6	9	0.65
heart	270	2	13	7	6	0
hepatitis	155	2	19	6	13	5.67
house	91	2	16	0	16	4.53
iris	150	3	4	4	0	0
lymphography	148	4	18	0	18	0.04
mushroom	8124	2	22	0	22	1.39
post-operative	90	3	8	1	7	0.42
primary tumor	339	22	17	0	17	3.9
promoter	106	2	57	0	57	0
rheumatism	355	6	32	21	11	0.04
spambase	4601	2	57	57	0	0
splice-jxn	3190	3	60	0	60	0.03
yeast	1484	10	8	8	0	0

We can observe similar effects as before. The weighted voting causes strong boost in performance (significant at 0.001 level for accuracy and 0.01 for AUC), while several estimators show only a moderate nonsignificant improvement. The combination of both is significantly different to plain variant at 0.005 level for accuracy and at 0.1 level for AUC; it is different to several estimators variant at 0.1 level for accuracy and AUC. The overall best method is therefore weighted voting, while it looks that using several estimators is beneficial only for problems with strong conditional dependencies.

The t-test for this comparisons (and for the differences on the development data sets as well) would declare all the differences more significant.

6   Conclusions

We investigate possibilities to improve the performance of random forests. First we propose the use of several attribute evaluation measures for split selection in the process of building the trees. This procedure decreases the correlation between the trees and retains their strength which results in slight increase of the method's performance. The improvement is especially visible on data sets with highly dependent attributes and the reason for this is the use of ReliefF algorithm.

The most important improvement in the performance of random forests is achieved by changing the mechanism of voting. When classifying a new instance with ordinary voting each tree casts a vote for one of the classes and the forest predicts the winning class. We propose first to estimate the average margin of the trees on the instances most similar to the new instance and then, after discarding the trees with negative margin, weight the trees' votes with the margin. Evaluation on several data sets has shown that this approach significantly improves accuracy and AUC.

Table 5. Random forests performance on fresh data sets.

name	Gini accuracy	AUC	5 estimators accuracy	AUC	weighted voting accuracy	AUC	5est & wv accuracy	AUC
adult	0.849	0.835	0.858	0.808	0.849	0.835	0.857	0.797
audiology	0.736	0.862	0.726	0.889	0.784	0.883	0.779	0.913
banding	0.738	0.606	0.716	0.553	0.796	0.687	0.760	0.677
credit aus	0.867	0.936	0.874	0.936	0.868	0.937	0.871	0.937
heart	0.830	0.886	0.837	0.890	0.833	0.889	0.848	0.897
hepatitis	0.833	0.717	0.858	0.735	0.858	0.755	0.851	0.769
house	0.956	0.988	0.956	0.988	0.956	0.988	0.956	0.988
iris	0.953	0.990	0.953	0.990	0.960	0.991	0.960	0.991
lymphography	0.817	0.895	0.824	0.884	0.824	0.909	0.857	0.916
mushroom	1.000	1.000	1.000	1.000	1.000	1.000	1.000	1.000
post-operative	0.656	0.669	0.700	0.669	0.678	0.689	0.711	0.669
primary tumor	0.440	0.740	0.439	0.723	0.460	0.722	0.481	0.701
promoter	0.914	0.943	0.885	0.955	0.923	0.961	0.953	0.991
rheumatism	0.698	0.668	0.690	0.682	0.701	0.680	0.690	0.692
spambase	0.952	0.985	0.953	0.984	0.952	0.985	0.952	0.984
splice-jxn	0.970	0.994	0.969	0.994	0.970	0.994	0.966	0.994
yeast	0.611	0.815	0.619	0.823	0.611	0.821	0.614	0.811

Systematical testing of the number of similar instances used in the weighting remains further work. The results indicate that there is a room for improvement when using several attribute evaluation measures, but a further study of which estimators to use and how to combine them is necessary. Also a verification of the performance of weighted voting in the regression context is needed.

Acknowledgements

I thank Leo Breiman for valuable insights into the inner workings of the method published at his web site and for invited talk he gave at ECML/PKDD 2003 which initiated my interest in random forests. This work was supported by Slovene Ministry of Education, Science and Sport through the research programme P2-0209.

Bibliography

[1] Leo Breiman. Bagging predictors. *Machine Learning Journal*, 26(2):123–140, 1996.

[2] Leo Breiman. Random forests. *Machine Learning Journal*, 45:5–32, 2001.

[3] Leo Breiman, Jerome H. Friedman, Richard A. Olshen, and Charles J. Stone. *Classification and regression trees*. Wadsworth Inc., Belmont, California, 1984.

[4] Janez Demšar. Statistically correct comparison of classifiers over multiple datasets, 2004. (submitted).

[5] Thomas G. Dietterich, Michael Kerns, and Yishay Mansour. Applying the weak learning framework to understand and improve C4.5. In Lorenza Saitta, editor, *Machine Learning: Proceedings of the Thirteenth International Conference (ICML'96)*, pages 96–103. Morgan Kaufmann, San Francisco, 1996.

[6] Yoav Freund and Robert E. Shapire. Experiments with a new boosting algorithm. In Lorenza Saitta, editor, *Machine Learning: Proceedings of the Thirteenth International Conference (ICML'96)*. Morgan Kaufmann, 1996.

[7] David J. Hand and Robert J. Till. A simple generalisation of the area under the ROC curve for multiple class classification problems. *Machine Learning Journal*, 45:171–186, 2001.

[8] Igor Kononenko. Estimating attributes: analysis and extensions of Relief. In Luc De Raedt and Francesco Bergadano, editors, *Machine Learning: ECML-94*, pages 171–182. Springer Verlag, Berlin, 1994.

[9] Igor Kononenko. On biases in estimating multi-valued attributes. In *Proceedings of the International Joint Conference on Artificial Intelligence (IJCAI'95)*, pages 1034–1040. Morgan Kaufmann, 1995.

[10] David Meyer, Friedrich Leisch, and Kurt Hornik. The support vector machine under test. *Neurocomputing*, 55:169–186, 2003.

[11] Patrick M. Murphy and David W. Aha. UCI repository of machine learning databases, 1995. http://www.ics.uci.edu/ mlearn/MLRepository.html.

[12] J. Ross Quinlan. *C4.5: Programs for Machine Learning*. Morgan Kaufmann, San Francisco, 1993.

[13] Marko Robnik-Šikonja and Igor Kononenko. Theoretical and empirical analysis of ReliefF and RReliefF. *Machine Learning Journal*, 53:23–69, 2003.

[14] Robert E. Schapire, Yoav Freund, Peter Bartlett, and Wee Sun Lee. Boosting the margin: a new explanation for the effectiveness of voting methods. In Douglas H. Fisher, editor, *Machine Learning: Proceedings of the Fourteenth International Conference (ICML'97)*, pages 322–330. Morgan Kaufmann, 1997.

[15] Jerrold H. Zar. *Biostatistical Analysis (4th Edition)*. Prentice Hall, Englewood Clifs, New Jersey, 1998.

The Principal Components Analysis of a Graph, and Its Relationships to Spectral Clustering

Marco Saerens[1], Francois Fouss[1], Luh Yen[1], and Pierre Dupont[2]

[1] Information Systems Research Unit, IAG, Université catholique de Louvain,
Place des Doyens 1, B-1348 Louvain-la-Neuve, Belgium
{saerens,fouss,yen}@isys.ucl.ac.be
[2] Department of Computing Science and Engineering, INGI,
Université catholique de Louvain,
Place Sainte Barbe 2, B-1348 Louvain-la-Neuve, Belgium
pdupont@info.ucl.ac.be

Abstract. This work presents a novel procedure for computing (1) distances between nodes of a weighted, undirected, graph, called the Euclidean Commute Time Distance (ECTD), and (2) a subspace projection of the nodes of the graph that preserves as much variance as possible, in terms of the ECTD – a principal components analysis of the graph. It is based on a Markov-chain model of random walk through the graph. The model assigns transition probabilities to the links between nodes, so that a random walker can jump from node to node. A quantity, called the **average commute time**, computes the average time taken by a random walker for reaching node j for the first time when starting from node i, and coming back to node i. The square root of this quantity, the ECTD, is a distance measure between any two nodes, and has the nice property of decreasing when the number of paths connecting two nodes increases and when the "length" of any path decreases. The ECTD can be computed from the pseudoinverse of the Laplacian matrix of the graph, which is a kernel. We finally define the **Principal Components Analysis** (PCA) of a graph as the subspace projection that preserves as much variance as possible, in terms of the ECTD. This graph PCA has some interesting links with spectral graph theory, in particular spectral clustering.

1 Introduction

This work introduces a general procedure allowing (1) to compute dissimilarities between nodes of a **weighted, undirected, graph** and (2) to represent the nodes of the graph in an Euclidean space of reduced dimensionality. Computing dissimilarities between pairs of nodes allows to determine the item that is most relevant (that is, similar) to a given item and allows, for instance, to cluster them. We present an application of this technique to collaborative filtering, with promising results, in a related paper [31].

The procedure used to compute the dissimilarities is based on a Markov-chain model. We define a **random-walk model** through the graph by assigning a transition probability to each edge. Thus, a random walker can jump from

J.-F. Boulicaut et al. (Eds.): ECML 2004, LNAI 3201, pp. 371–383, 2004.
© Springer-Verlag Berlin Heidelberg 2004

node to node, and each node therefore represents a state of the Markov model. From this Markov-chain model, we then compute a quantity, $m(j|i)$, called the **average first-passage time** (see for instance [17]), which is the average number of steps needed by a random walker for reaching state j for the first time, when starting from state i. The symmetrized quantity, $n(i,j) = m(j|i) + m(i|j)$, called the **average commute time** (see for instance [14]), provides a distance measure between any pair of states/nodes. The fact that this quantity is indeed a distance on a graph has been proved independently by Klein & Randic [18] and Gobel & Jagers [14]. Moreover, we show that $[n(i,j)]^{1/2}$, which is also a distance between nodes, takes a remarkable form and will be referred to as the **Euclidean Commute Time Distance** (ECTD). The ECTD can easily be computed from the pseudoinverse of the Laplacian matrix of the graph, which is shown to be a valid kernel.

These quantities have the nice property of decreasing when the number of paths connecting the two nodes increases and when the "length" of any path decreases (the communication is facilitated [11]). In short, two nodes are considered similar if there are many short paths connecting them. On the contrary, the "shortest path" (also called "geodesic" or "Dijkstra") distance does not necessarily decrease when connections between nodes are added, and thus does not capture the fact that strongly connected nodes are at a smaller distance than weakly connected nodes. This fact has already been recognized in the field of mathematical chemistry where there were attempts to use the "commute time" distance instead of the "shortest path" distance [18]. To our knowledge, while being interesting alternatives to the well-known "shortest path" or "geodesic" distance on a graph [6], these quantities have not been exploited as-is in the context of pattern recognition and machine learning. They have, however, been indirectly used in the framework of spectral clustering as will be shown in Section 6. This work therefore provides a new interpretation for spectral clustering since we will show that spectral clustering can be interpreted in terms of ECTD.

We further show that we can project the nodes space of the graph into an Euclidean subspace that maximaly preserves ECTD among all linear subspace projections. This subspace is optimal in the following sense: it keeps as much variance of the projected data as possible (in terms of the ECTD). It is therefore an equivalent of principal component analysis in terms of the ECTD; we call this technique the **principal components analysis of the graph**.

In summary, this paper has five main contributions: (1) it suggests the use of the average first-passage time and the ECTD between nodes of a graph as a useful pattern recognition tool; (2) it shows that the average first-passage time and the ECTD can be computed in terms of the pseudoinverse $\mathbf{L}^+$ of the Laplacian matrix of the graph, from the definition of the average first-passage time; (3) it shows that $\mathbf{L}^+$ is a kernel and could be used as such for SVM classification; (4) it introduces the PCA of a graph which is a principal component analysis computed on the ECTD matrix; (5) it provides an elegant interpretation of both spectral clustering and spectral embedding in terms of random walks on a graph.

Section 2 introduces the random-walk model – a Markov chain model. Section 3 develops our dissimilarity measures as well as the iterative formulae to compute them. Section 4 gives details for the computation of the average first-passage time and the average commute time from the Laplacian matrix of the graph. It also derives a number of interesting properties of the Laplacian pseudoinverse. Section 5 introduces an eigenvector decomposition of the pseudoinverse of the Laplacian matrix that maximizes the variance of the projected data. It also shows that this pseudoinverse is a valid kernel. Section 6 summarizes related work and develops some interesting relationships with spectral clustering, among others. Section 7 is the conclusion.

2 A Markov-Chain Model of Random Walk on a Graph

2.1 The Laplacian Matrix of a Weighted Graph

Let us consider that we are given a weighted, undirected, graph, G, with symmetric weights $w_{ij} > 0$ between every couple of nodes, i and j, which are linked by an edge (say G has n nodes in total). The weight w_{ij} of the edge connecting node i and node j should be set to some meaningful value, with the following convention: the more important the relation between node i and node j, the larger the value of w_{ij}, and consequently the easier the communication through the edge. Notice that we require that the weights are both positive ($w_{ij} > 0$) and symmetric ($w_{ij} = w_{ji}$). The elements a_{ij} of the adjacency matrix $\mathbf{A}$ of the graph are defined in a standard way as

$$a_{ij} = \begin{cases} w_{ij} \text{ if node } i \text{ is connected to node } j \\ 0 \text{ otherwise} \end{cases} \tag{1}$$

where $\mathbf{A}$ is symmetric. We also introduce the Laplacian matrix $\mathbf{L}$ of the graph, defined in the usual manner: $\mathbf{L} = \mathbf{D} - \mathbf{A}$, where $\mathbf{D} = \mathrm{diag}(a_{i.})$ is the degree matrix, and $d_{ii} = [\mathbf{D}]_{ii} = a_{i.} = \sum_{j=1}^{n} a_{ij}$. Furthermore, the volume of the graph is defined as $V_G = vol(G) = \sum_{i=1}^{n} d_{ii} = \sum_{i,j=1}^{n} a_{ij}$.

We suppose that the graph has a single connected component; that is, any node can be reached from any other node of the graph. In this case, $\mathbf{L}$ has rank $n - 1$, where n is the number of nodes [9]. If $\mathbf{e}$ is a column vector made of 1 (i.e., $\mathbf{e} = [1, 1, \ldots, 1]^{\mathrm{T}}$, where T denotes the matrix transpose) and $\mathbf{0}$ is a column vector made of 0, $\mathbf{Le} = \mathbf{0}$ and $\mathbf{e}^{\mathrm{T}}\mathbf{L} = \mathbf{0}$ hold: $\mathbf{L}$ is doubly centered. The null space of $\mathbf{L}$ is therefore the one-dimensional space spanned by $\mathbf{e}$. Moreover, one can easily show that $\mathbf{L}$ is symmetric and positive semidefinite (see for instance [4] or [9]).

2.2 A Random Walk Model on the Graph

The Markov chain describing the sequence of nodes visited by a random walker is called a random walk on a weighted graph (see for instance [14]). We associate a state of the Markov chain to every node; we also define a random variable, $s(t)$, representing the state of the Markov model at time step t. If the random walker is in state i at time t, we say $s(t) = i$. We define a random walk by the following single-step transition probabilities $P(s(t+1) = j|s(t) = i) = a_{ij}/d_{ii} = p_{ij}$.

In other words, to any state or node i, we associate a probability of jumping to an adjacent node, $s(t+1) = j$, which is proportional to the weight w_{ij} of the edge connecting i and j. The transition probabilities only depend on the current state and not on the past ones (first-order Markov chain). Since the graph is connected, the Markov chain is irreducible, that is, every state can be reached from any other state.

Now, if we denote the probability of being in state i at time t by $x_i(t) = P(s(t) = i)$ and we define $\mathbf{P}$ as the transition matrix whose entries are $p_{ij} = P(s(t+1) = j|s(t) = i)$, we have $\mathbf{P} = \mathbf{D}^{-1}\mathbf{A}$ and the evolution of the Markov chain is characterized by

$$\begin{cases} \mathbf{x}(0) = \mathbf{x}^0 \\ \mathbf{x}(t+1) = \mathbf{P}^T\mathbf{x}(t) \end{cases} \tag{2}$$

This provides the state probability distribution $\mathbf{x}(t) = [x_1(t), x_2(t), \ldots, x_n(t)]^T$ at time t once the initial probability distribution, $\mathbf{x}^0$, is known (see [5], [17], [26] for more details).

3   Average First-Passage Time and Average Commute Time

In this section, we review two basic quantities that can be computed from the definition of the Markov chain, that is, from its probability transition matrix: the average first-passage time and the average commute time.

The **average first-passage time**, $m(k|i)$ is defined as the average number of steps a random walker, starting in state i, will take to enter state k for the first time [26]. More precisely, we define the minimum time until hitting state k as $T_{ik} = \min(t \geq 0 \mid s(t) = k \text{ and } s(0) = i)$ for one realization of the stochastic process. The average first-passage time is the expectation of this quantity, when starting from state i: $m(k|i) = E[T_{ik}|s(0) = i] = E_i[T_{ik}]$. The $m(k|i)$ verify the following recurrence relations (see for instance [26])

$$\begin{cases} m(k|i) = 1 + \displaystyle\sum_{\substack{j=1 \\ j \neq k}}^{n} p_{ij}\, m(k|j), \text{ for } i \neq k \\ m(k|k) = 0 \end{cases} \tag{3}$$

These equations can be used in order to iteratively compute the average first-passage times [26]. The meaning of these formulae is quite obvious: in order to go from state i to state k, one has to go to any adjacent state j and proceed from there.

We now introduce a closely related quantity, the **average commute time**, $n(i,j)$, which is defined as the average number of steps a random walker, starting in state i, will take before entering a given state j for the first time, and go back to i. That is, $n(i, j) = m(j|i) + m(i|j)$. Notice that, while $n(i, j)$ is symmetric by definition, $m(i|j)$ is not.

As shown by several authors [14], [18], the average commute time is a distance measure, since, for any states i, j, k: $n(i, j) \geq 0$, $n(i, j) = 0$ if and only if $i = j$, $n(i, j) = n(j, i)$ and $n(i, j) \leq n(i, k) + n(k, j)$. In Section 4, we show that $[n(i, j)]^{1/2}$, which is also a distance on the graph, takes a remarkable form. Both the average first-passage time and the average commute time provide dissimilarity measures on any pairs i, j of nodes.

4   Computation of the Basic Quantities by Means of $\mathbf{L}^+$

Methods for computing these two quantities are based on matrix pseudoinverses or on iterative procedures. If the matrices are too large, the computation by pseudoinverse becomes untractable; in this case, one may use iterative techniques based on Equation 3 and on the sparseness of the probability transition matrix.

In this section, we will show how the average first-passage time and the average commute time can be computed from Equation 3, by using the pseudoinverse of the Laplacian matrix of the graph, which plays a fundamental role and has a number of interesting properties. The developments in this section are inspired by the work of Klein & Randic [18] which showed, based on an electrical equivalence (see last paragraph of Section 6), that the effective resistance (which is equivalent to the average commute time [8]) can be computed from the Laplacian matrix. We thus extend their results by showing that the formula computing the average commute time can be directly derived from 3, and by providing formulae for the average first-passage time as well.

Let us denote by l_{ij} element i, j of the Laplacian matrix $\mathbf{L}$; in other words, $l_{ij} = [\mathbf{L}]_{ij}$. The Moore-Penrose pseudoinverse of $\mathbf{L}$ (see [1]) will be denoted by $\mathbf{L}^+$, with elements $l_{ij}^+ = [\mathbf{L}^+]_{ij}$. In Appendix A, we prove some useful properties of $\mathbf{L}^+$.

In [31], we show[1] that the computation of the average first-passage time in terms of $\mathbf{L}^+$ can be obtained from Equation 3:

$$m(k|i) = \sum_{j=1}^{n} \left(l_{ij}^+ - l_{ik}^+ - l_{kj}^+ + l_{kk}^+ \right) d_{jj} \tag{4}$$

For $n(i, j)$, we obtain from Equation 4:

$$n(i, j) = V_G \left(l_{ii}^+ + l_{jj}^+ - 2l_{ij}^+ \right) \tag{5}$$

This formula has already been obtained by using the electrical equivalent of commute times (the effective resistance) [18], [31]. If we further define $\mathbf{e}_i$ as the ith column of $\mathbf{I}$, $\mathbf{e}_i = [0, \ldots, \underset{i-1}{0}, \underset{i}{1}, \underset{i+1}{0}, \ldots, \underset{n}{0}]^\mathrm{T}$, Equation 5 can be rewritten in the form:

$$n(i, j) = V_G \left(\mathbf{e}_i - \mathbf{e}_j \right)^\mathrm{T} \mathbf{L}^+ \left(\mathbf{e}_i - \mathbf{e}_j \right) \tag{6}$$

---

[1] We do not provide the proof here because it is both lengthy and technical.

where each node i is represented by a unit basis vector, $\mathbf{e}_i$, of the node space. We easily observe that $[n(i,j)]^{1/2}$ is a distance in the Euclidean space of the nodes of the graph since $\mathbf{L}^+$ is positive semidefinite. As already mentioned, it will therefore be called the **Euclidean Commute Time Distance** (ECTD).

5   The Principal Components Analysis of a Graph

In this section, we show that, based on the eigenvector decomposition, the nodes vectors, $\mathbf{e}_i$, can be mapped into a new Euclidean space that preserves the ECTD, or a subspace keeping as much variance as possible, in terms of ECTD.

5.1   Transformation to an Euclidean Space Preserving the ECTD

Let us first show that the node vectors $\mathbf{e}_i$ can be mapped into an Euclidean space that preserves the ECTD. Indeed, every positive semidefinite matrix can be transformed to a diagonal matrix, $\mathbf{\Lambda} = \mathbf{U}^T\mathbf{L}^+\mathbf{U}$, where $\mathbf{U}$ is an orthonormal matrix made of the eigenvectors of $\mathbf{L}^+$, $\mathbf{U} = [\mathbf{u}_1, \mathbf{u}_2, \ldots, \mathbf{u}_{n-1}, \mathbf{u}_n = \mathbf{0}]$: the column vectors $\mathbf{u}_k$ are the orthonormal eigenvectors of $\mathbf{L}^+$, $\mathbf{u}_i^T\mathbf{u}_j = \delta_{ij}$ or $\mathbf{U}^T\mathbf{U} = \mathbf{I}$ (see for instance [25]). The diagonal matrix $\mathbf{\Lambda}$ contains the eigenvalues of $\mathbf{L}^+$ in decreasing order of importance. Hence we have

$$n(i,j) = V_G\,(\mathbf{e}_i - \mathbf{e}_j)^T\mathbf{L}^+(\mathbf{e}_i - \mathbf{e}_j) = V_G\,(\mathbf{x}_i - \mathbf{x}_j)^T\mathbf{U}^T\mathbf{L}^+\mathbf{U}(\mathbf{x}_i - \mathbf{x}_j)$$
$$= V_G\,(\mathbf{x}_i - \mathbf{x}_j)^T\mathbf{\Lambda}(\mathbf{x}_i - \mathbf{x}_j) = V_G\,(\mathbf{x}_i - \mathbf{x}_j)^T(\mathbf{\Lambda}^{1/2})^T\mathbf{\Lambda}^{1/2}(\mathbf{x}_i - \mathbf{x}_j)$$
$$= V_G\,(\mathbf{x}_i' - \mathbf{x}_j')^T(\mathbf{x}_i' - \mathbf{x}_j')$$

where we made the transformations

$$\mathbf{x}_i = \mathbf{U}^T\mathbf{e}_i \text{ and } \mathbf{x}_i' = \mathbf{\Lambda}^{1/2}\mathbf{x}_i \tag{7}$$

So, in this n-dimensional Euclidean space, the transformed node vectors, $\mathbf{x}_i'$, are exactly separated by ECTD. In Appendix B, we show that $\mathbf{L}^+$ is a kernel since it corresponds to the matrix of the inner products of the $\mathbf{x}_i'$. Moreover, one can easily show [31] that the $\mathbf{x}_i'$ are centered (their center of gravity is $\mathbf{0}$): $\sum_{i=1}^n \mathbf{x}_i' = \mathbf{0}$.

5.2   Approximate ECTD Based on the Projection in a Subspace

However, the transformed space introduced in previous section has dimensionality n (the graph order), which is untractable for most applications. We therefore define an approximation of this transformation that preserves as much information as possible.

The so-called spectral (or eigenvector) decomposition of $\mathbf{L}^+$ is defined as (see any textbook on linear algebra, for instance, [20]) $\mathbf{L}^+ = \mathbf{U}\mathbf{\Lambda}\mathbf{U}^T = \sum_{k=1}^{n-1} \lambda_k\,\mathbf{u}_k\mathbf{u}_k^T$ where $\lambda_1 > \lambda_2 > \ldots > \lambda_{n-1} > \lambda_n = 0$ are the eigenvalues of $\mathbf{L}^+$. As in previous section, the column vectors $\mathbf{u}_k$ are the orthonormal eigenvectors of $\mathbf{L}^+$, $\mathbf{u}_i^T\mathbf{u}_j = \delta_{ij}$.

Suppose now that we compute the eigenvector expansion of $\mathbf{L}^+$ up to $m <$ $n - 1$: $\mathbf{L}^+ = \sum_{k=1}^{m} \lambda_k \mathbf{u}_k \mathbf{u}_k^{\mathrm{T}} = \widetilde{\mathbf{U}} \widetilde{\mathbf{\Lambda}} \widetilde{\mathbf{U}}^{\mathrm{T}}$ where $\widetilde{\mathbf{U}} = [\mathbf{u}_1, \mathbf{u}_2, \ldots, \mathbf{u}_m, \mathbf{0}, \ldots, \mathbf{0}]$ and $\widetilde{\mathbf{\Lambda}} = \mathrm{diag}[\lambda_1, \lambda_2, \ldots, \lambda_m, 0, \ldots, 0]$. Let us compute the corresponding distance between nodes i and j: $\widetilde{n}(i, j) = V_G (\mathbf{e}_i - \mathbf{e}_j)^{\mathrm{T}} \widetilde{\mathbf{L}}^+ (\mathbf{e}_i - \mathbf{e}_j)$.

By $\widetilde{\mathbf{L}}^+ = \widetilde{\mathbf{U}} \widetilde{\mathbf{\Lambda}} \widetilde{\mathbf{U}}^{\mathrm{T}}$ and using the same reasoning as in previous section, we can recompute the distance as follows: $\widetilde{n}(i, j) = V_G (\widetilde{\mathbf{x}}'_i - \widetilde{\mathbf{x}}'_j)^{\mathrm{T}} (\widetilde{\mathbf{x}}'_i - \widetilde{\mathbf{x}}'_j)$, where, this time, the $\widetilde{\mathbf{x}}'_i$ are column vectors containing zeroes from the $m + 1$ position: $\widetilde{\mathbf{x}}' = [\widetilde{x}'_1, \widetilde{x}'_2, \ldots, \widetilde{x}'_m, 0, \ldots, 0]^{\mathrm{T}}$. The transformation is therefore defined by

$$\widetilde{\mathbf{x}}_i = \widetilde{\mathbf{U}}^{\mathrm{T}} \mathbf{e}_i \text{ and } \widetilde{\mathbf{x}}'_i = \widetilde{\mathbf{\Lambda}}^{1/2} \widetilde{\mathbf{x}}_i \tag{8}$$

This subspace is an m-dimensional space where the commute time distances are approximately preserved. A bound on this approximation is provided in [31]: $\|n(i, j) - \widetilde{n}(i, j)\| \leq V_G \sum_{k=m+1}^{n-1} \lambda_k$.

Now, we easily observe from (7) that if u_i^k is coordinate i of eigenvector $\mathbf{u}_k$ ($[\mathbf{u}_k]_i = u_i^k$) corresponding to eigenvalue λ_k of $\mathbf{L}^+$, and if x_k^i is coordinate k of vector $\mathbf{x}_i$ ($[\mathbf{x}_i]_k = x_k^i$), $x_k^i = u_i^k$ holds. We thus have $x_k'^i = \sqrt{\lambda_k} u_i^k$ where $x_k'^i$ is coordinate k of vector $\mathbf{x}'_i$ ($[\mathbf{x}'_i]_k = x_k'^i$).

In other words, the first coordinate of the n node vectors, $\mathbf{x}_i, i = 1 \ldots n$, corresponding to the **first axis** ($k = 1$) of the transformed space, are $x_1'^1, x_1'^2, \ldots, x_1'^n$, or $\sqrt{\lambda_1} u_1^1, \sqrt{\lambda_1} u_2^1, \ldots, \sqrt{\lambda_1} u_n^1$. Thus, the first coordinate of these n node vectors is simply the projection of the original node vectors, $\mathbf{e}_1, \mathbf{e}_2, \ldots, \mathbf{e}_n$, on the first eigenvector, $\mathbf{u}_1$, weighted by $\sqrt{\lambda_1}$. More generally, coordinate k of the node vectors in the transformed space is simply the projection of the original node vectors, $\mathbf{e}_1, \mathbf{e}_2, \ldots, \mathbf{e}_n$, on $\mathbf{u}_k$, weighted by $\sqrt{\lambda_k}$. The idea is thus to discard the axes corresponding to the smallest eigenvalues of $\mathbf{L}^+$.

5.3   Relations to Principal Components Analysis

We will now show that this decomposition is similar to principal components analysis in the sense that the projection has maximal variance among all the possible candidate projections. If $\mathbf{X}'$ denotes the data matrix containing the coordinates of the nodes in the transformed space, $\mathbf{x}_i'^{\mathrm{T}}$, on each row (see Appendix B), we easily deduce from (7) that $\mathbf{X}' = \mathbf{U} \mathbf{\Lambda}^{1/2}$.

Now, it is well-known that the principal components analysis of a data matrix $\mathbf{X}'$ yields, as kth principal component, the eigenvector, $\mathbf{v}_k$, of $(\mathbf{X}')^{\mathrm{T}} \mathbf{X}'$ (which is the variance-covariance matrix, since the $\mathbf{x}'_i$ are centered). But $(\mathbf{X}')^{\mathrm{T}} \mathbf{X}' = (\mathbf{U} \mathbf{\Lambda}^{1/2})^{\mathrm{T}} \mathbf{U} \mathbf{\Lambda}^{1/2} = \mathbf{\Lambda}$. Since $\mathbf{\Lambda}$ is a diagonal matrix, we deduce that the $\mathbf{x}'_i$ are already expressed in the principal components coordinate system – the eigenvectors of $(\mathbf{X}')^{\mathrm{T}} \mathbf{X}'$ are the basis vectors of the transformed space. Thus, if $x_k'^i$ is coordinate k of vector $\mathbf{x}'_i$, it corresponds to the projection of node i on the kth principal component. The variance, in terms of ECTD, of the nodes cloud on each principal component k is therefore λ_k.

We thus conclude that this projection can be viewed as a principal components analysis in the Euclidean space where the nodes are exactly separated by

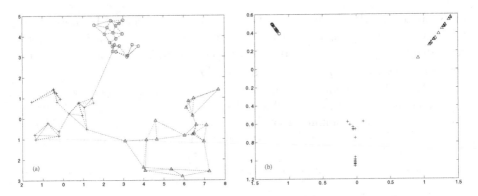

Fig. 1. One example of principal components analysis based on the ECTD. The original graph (the weight of each edge is inversely proportional to 1/(its length)) is shown on the left (a); its projection on the two first principal components is shown on the right (b).

ECTD. This decomposition therefore defines the projection of the node vectors that has maximal variance (in terms of the ECTD) among all the possible candidate projections. An exemple of PCA is provided in Figure 1. Notice that it can be shown that performing a multidimensional scaling on the ECTD gives exactly the same results as the principal components analysis.

Furthermore, since $\mathbf{L}$ and $\mathbf{L}^+$ both have rank $(n-1)$ and have the same set of eigenvectors but inverse eigenvalues (if λ_i^l are the eigenvalues of $\mathbf{L}$ and λ_i^+ are the eigenvalues of $\mathbf{L}^+$, $\lambda_i^l = 1/\lambda_i^+$, for $i \neq n$; $\lambda_n^l = \lambda_n^+ = 0$; see Appendix A) we do not need to explicitly compute the pseudoinverse of $\mathbf{L}$ in order to compute the projection. We only need to compute the m smallest (except $\lambda_n^l = 0 = \lambda_n^+$) eigenvectors (that is, with lowest eigenvalues) of $\mathbf{L}$, which become the largest of $\mathbf{L}^+$.

6   Related Work

There is a vast literature on *spectral graph theory* (see [9] for a monograph) and several results about the *Laplacian spectrum* of (hyper-)graphs are summarized in [22, 23]. Spectral techniques have been applied in a wide variety of contexts including high performance computing [28], image segmentation [33], web page ranking [27, 19], information retrieval [10], RNA motif classification [13], data clustering [24, 37], and dimensionality reduction [2].

In particular, *spectral clustering* refers to a collection of techniques that cluster n data points using eigenvectors of a matrix derived from the $n \times n$ *affinity matrix* $\mathbf{W}$: $w_{ij} = \exp[-d^2(\mathbf{x}_i, \mathbf{x}_j)/2\sigma^2]$, where $d(\mathbf{x}_i, \mathbf{x}_j)$ denotes the dissimilarity between the points $\mathbf{x}_i$ and $\mathbf{x}_j$, and σ is a free parameter (see [36] for a review). A common choice is $d^2(\mathbf{x}_i, \mathbf{x}_j) = ||\mathbf{x}_i - \mathbf{x}_j||^2$. An automatic procedure for determining σ so as to minimize the cluster distortion is proposed in [24].

Spectral clustering is a graph-theoretic approach to clustering and the affinity matrix precisely corresponds to the (weighted) adjacency matrix $\mathbf{A}$ defined in section 2.1. In the context of image segmentation, Shi and Malik [33] introduced the *normalized cut* (NCut) criterion to define an optimal bipartitioning of a graph:

Let $\{A, \overline{A}\}$ denotes a bipartition of the set of vertices V of a graph G ($A \neq \varnothing$, $\overline{A} \neq \varnothing$, $A \cap \overline{A} = \varnothing$ and $A \cup \overline{A} = V$). The *cut* is the total weight of edges connecting the two disjoint sets A and $\overline{A}$: $cut(A, \overline{A}) = \sum_{i \in A, j \in \overline{A}} w_{ij}$. The NCut criterion aims at finding the bipartition minimizing: $NCut(A, \overline{A}) = ((1/V_A) + (1/V_{\overline{A}})) \, cut(A, \overline{A})$ where $V_A = vol(A)$ is the subgraph volume. This criterion seeks a balance between the goal of clustering (finding tight clusters) and segmentation (finding well separated clusters). A very similar notion of *conductance* $\phi(A, \overline{A})$ of a cut is presented in [29]: $\phi(A, \overline{A}) = cut(A, \overline{A}) / \min(V_A, V_{\overline{A}})$. Finding the optimal NCut is NP-complete even for a graph on a regular grid but an approximation can be found by computing the eigenvalues of the *normalized Laplacian* $\mathbf{D}^{-1/2} \mathbf{L} \mathbf{D}^{-1/2} = \mathbf{I} - \mathbf{D}^{-1/2} \mathbf{A} \mathbf{D}^{-1/2}$ [33]. In particular, the eigenvector associated to the second smallest eigenvalue (also known as the *algebraic connectivity* or *Fiedler value* [12]) is used to bipartition the graph. Note that the standard spectral graph partitioning uses the Laplacian matrix $\mathbf{L}$ (instead of its normalized version). This corresponds to the minimization of the *average cut criterion*: $AverageCut(A, \overline{A}) = ((1/|A|) + (1/|\overline{A}|)) \, cut(A, \overline{A})$ where $|A|$ is the graph order. This last version is exactly similar to our method since we showed, in the previous section, that computing the largest eigenvalues/eigenvectors of $\mathbf{L}^+$ is equivalent to computing the smallest non-trivial eigenvalues/eigenvectors of $\mathbf{L}$.

Meila and Shi present links between spectral segmentation and *Markov random walks* [21]. Their random walk model is identical to the one defined in Section 2 but different properties are stressed. It is shown in particular that $NCut(A, \overline{A}) = p_{A\overline{A}} + p_{\overline{A}A}$, where p_{AB} denotes the probability of a random walk transiting from state set A to state set B in one step, given the current state is in A and the random walk is started according to the stationary distribution of the Markov chain.

An application of the same random walk model to partially labeled classification is proposed in [35]. In this learning framework (also known as *transductive learning*), unlabeled examples provide information of the structure of the domain while the class labels of a few examples are known. As for spectral clustering, each data point is associated to a graph vertex, *i.e.* a state of the associated Markov chain. The model assumes a uniform initial distribution and includes a distribution $p(y|i)$ of class label y given state i. $p(y|i)$ can be estimated with EM or a margin-based criterion. Classification of point k is performed so as to maximize the posterior probability $p(y|k) = \sum_i p(y|i)[\mathbf{P}^r]_{ik}$, where $\mathbf{P}^r$ denotes power r of the transition matrix $\mathbf{P}$. Thus the classification of the example k depends on $[\mathbf{P}^r]_{ik}$, the probability that the Markov process started from the state i given that it ended up in k after r steps. The value of r is a parameter controlling the smoothness of the random walk representation. Another work using the Laplacian spectrum for transductive learning is described in [15].

The random walk model presented in Section 2 defines the transition matrix $\mathbf{P}$ of a Markov process from the adjacency (or affinity) matrix $\mathbf{A}$ as $\mathbf{P} = \mathbf{D}^{-1}\mathbf{A}$. Let us mention that several alternative definitions of the Markov transition matrix are proposed in [16], in the context of supervised or unsupervised classification.

Laplacian eigenmaps (also called spectral embedding) is a dimensionality reduction procedure that has been proposed recently by Belkin and Niyogi [3]. The authors solve the following related eigenproblem: $\mathbf{Lu} = \lambda \mathbf{Du}$. The smallest eigenvalue is left out and the other small eigenvalues are used for the embedding. This is the same embedding that is computed with the spectral clustering algorithm from Shi and Malik [33]. As noted in [36], an equivalent result can be obtained by renormalizing the adjacency matrix: $\mathbf{D}^{-1/2}\mathbf{A}\mathbf{D}^{-1/2}$ and computing the eigenvectors/eigenvalues of $\mathbf{L}$ instead. It should be clear that, once more, this reduction technique is closely related to our definition of the principal components analysis of a graph.

Smola and Kondor present connections between spectral graph theory and *graph kernels* [34]. In particular, they define a graph regularization, which aims to emphasize the role of the smallest non-trivial eivenvalues of $\mathbf{L}$ and, on the contrary, discard the largest ones. Once more, this has interesting links with our definition of the PCA of a graph, since the PCA discard the smallest nontrivial eivenvalues/eigenvectors of $\mathbf{L}^{+}$ (which, as already stressed, correspond to the largest of $\mathbf{L}$). They also stress the links between these techniques and web page ranking algorithms such as PageRank [27], HITS [19] and randomized HITS [38].

Finally, there is an intriguing correspondence between random walk on a graph and electrical networks theory, as popularized by Doyle and Snell in their nice book [11] (see also [4]). Average commute time has an equivalent in terms of electrical networks. Indeed, in [8], it is shown that $n(i,j) = V_G \, r_{ij}^e$, where r_{ij}^e is the effective resistance between node i and node j. In other words, average commute time and effective resistance basically measure the same quantity (see [31] for more details).

7   Conclusion and Further Work

We introduced a general procedure for computing dissimilarities between nodes of a graph. It is based on a particular Markov-chain model of random walk through the graph. More precisely, we compute a quantity, called the Euclidean Commute Time Distance, that provides a distance measure between any pair of nodes. We also introduced a subspace projection method preserving as much variance (in terms of the ECTD) as possible; it therefore defines a principal components analysis on a graph. We are now exploiting this ECTD in various problems, including inexact graph matching, collaborative filtering [31], supervised classification and clustering. We are also working on the definition of a discriminant analysis of a graph, with application to graph vizualisation.

Acknowledgments

We thank Prof. Van Dooren and Prof. Blondel, from the "Département d'Ingénierie Mathématique" of the Université catholique de Louvain, for insightful discussions.

References

1. S. Barnett. *Matrices: Methods and Applications*. Oxford University Press, 1992.
2. M. Belkin and P. Niyogi. Laplacian eigenmaps and spectral techniques for embedding and clustering. In T. G. Dietterich, S. Becker, and Z. Ghahramani, editors, *Advances in Neural Information Processing Systems*, volume 14, pages 585–591. MIT Press, 2001.
3. M. Belkin and P. Niyogi. Laplacian eigenmaps for dimensionality reduction and data representation. *Neural Computation*, 15:1373–1396, 2003.
4. B. Bollobas. *Modern graph theory*. Springer, 1998.
5. P. Bremaud. *Markov Chains: Gibbs Fields, Monte Carlo Simulation, and Queues*. Springer-Verlag, 1999.
6. F. Buckley and F. Harary. *Distance in graphs*. Addison-Wesley Publishing Company, 1990.
7. S. Campbell and C. Meyer. *Generalized inverses of linear transformations*. Pitman Publishing Company, 1979.
8. A. K. Chandra, P. Raghavan, W. L. Ruzzo, R. Smolensky, and P. Tiwari. The electrical resistance of a graph captures its commute and cover times. *Annual ACM Symposium on Theory of Computing*, pages 574–586, 1989.
9. F. R. Chung. *Spectral Graph Theory*. American Mathematical Society, 1997.
10. S. Deerweester, S. Dumais, G. Furnas, T. Landauer, and R. Harshman. Indexing by latent semantic analysis. *Journal of the American Society for Information Science*, 41:391–407, 1990.
11. P. G. Doyle and J. L. Snell. *Random Walks and Electric Networks*. The Mathematical Association of America, 1984.
12. M. Fiedler. A property of eigenvectors of nonnegative symmetric matrices and its applications to graph theory. *Czech. Math. J.*, 25(100):619–633, 1975.
13. H. Gan, D. Fera, J. Zorn, N. Shiffeldrim, M. Tang, U. Laserson, N. Kim, and T.Schlick. RAG: RNA-As-Graphs Database - Concepts, Analysis, and Features. to appear in Bioinformatics, 2004.
14. F. Gobel and A. Jagers. Random walks on graphs. *Stochastic Processes and their Applications*, 2:311–336, 1974.
15. T. Joachims. Transductive learning via spectral graph partitioning. In *Proceedings of the 20th International Conference on Machine Learning*, Washington DC, 2003.
16. S. Kamvar, D. Klein, and C. Manning. Spectral learning. In *Proceedings of the International Joint Conference of Artificial Intelligence*, April 2003.
17. J. G. Kemeny and J. L. Snell. *Finite Markov Chains*. Springer-Verlag, 1960.
18. D. J. Klein and M. Randic. Resistance distance. *Journal of Mathematical Chemistry*, 12:81–95, 1993.
19. J. M. Kleinberg. Authoritative sources in a hyperlinked environment. *Journal of the ACM*, 46(5):604–632, 1999.
20. D. Lay. *Linear algebra and its applications, 3th ed.* Addison-Wesley, 2003.
21. M. Meila and J. Shi. A random walks view of spectral segmentation. In *Proceedings of AISTATS*, 2001.

22. B. Mohar. The Laplacian spectrum of graphs. In Y. Alavi, G. Chartrand, and A. S. O.R. Oellermann, editors, *Graph Theory, Combinatorics, and Applications*, volume 2, pages 871–898. Wiley, 1991.

23. B. Mohar. Laplace eigenvalues of graphs – a survey. *Discrete Mathematics*, 109:171–183, 1992.

24. A. Y. Ng, M. I. Jordan, and Y. Weiss. On spectral clustering: Analysis and an algorithm. In T. Dietterich, S. Becker, and Z. Ghahramani, editors, *Advances in Neural Information Processing Systems*, volume 14, pages 849–856, Vancouver, Canada, 2001. MIT Press.

25. B. Noble and J. Daniels. *Applied linear algebra, 3th ed.* Prentice-Hall, 1988.

26. J. Norris. *Markov Chains*. Cambridge University Press, 1997.

27. L. Page, S. Brin, R. Motwani, and T. Winograd. The pagerank citation ranking: Bringing order to the web. *Technical Report, Computer System Laboratory, Stanford University*, 1998.

28. A. Pothen, H. Simon, and K.-P. Liou. Partitioning sparse matrices with eigenvectors of graphs. *SIAM Journal of Matrix Analysis*, 11(3):430–452, 1990.

29. A. V. R. Kannan, S. Vempala. On clusterings: Good, bad and spectral. In *Proceedings of the 41st Annual Symposium on Foundations of Computer Science*, 2000.

30. C. Rao and S. Mitra. *Generalized inverse of matrices and its applications*. John Wiley and Sons, 1971.

31. M. Saerens, A. Pirotte, and F. Fouss. Computing dissimilarities between nodes of a graph: Application to collaborative filtering. *Technical Report, IAG, Universite catholique de Louvain (www.isys.ucl.ac.be/staff/francois/Articles)*, 2004.

32. B. Scholkopf and A. Smola. *Learning with kernels*. The MIT Press, 2002.

33. J. Shi and J. Malik. Normalised cuts and image segmentation. *IEEE Transactions on Pattern Matching and Machine Intelligence*, 22:888–905, August 2000.

34. A. J. Smola and R. Kondor. Kernels and regularization on graphs. In M. Warmuth and B. Schölkopf, editors, *Proceedings of the Conference on Learning Theory and Kernels Workshop*, 2003.

35. M. Szummer and T. Jaakkola. Partially labeled classification with markov random walks. In T. Dietterich, S. Becker, and Z. Ghahramani, editors, *Advances in Neural Information Processing Systems*, volume 14, Vancouver, Canada, 2001. MIT Press.

36. Y. Weiss. Segmentation using eigenvectors: a unifying view. In *International Conference on Computer Vision*, 1999.

37. H. Zha, C. Ding, M. Gu, X. He, and H. Simon. Spectral relaxation for K-means clustering. In T. Dietterich, S. Becker, and Z. Ghahramani, editors, *Advances in Neural Information Processing Systems*, volume 14, pages 1057–1064, Vancouver, Canada, 2001. MIT Press.

38. A. X. Zheng, A. Y. Ng, and M. I. Jordan. Stable eigenvector algorithms for link analysis. *Proceedings of the 24th International Conference on Research and Development in Information Retrieval*, pages 258–296, 2001.

A   Appendix: Some Useful Properties of the Laplacian Matrix

(1) $\mathbf{L}^+$ is symmetric. Since $\mathbf{L}$ is symmetric and, for any matrix $\mathbf{A}$, $(\mathbf{A}^\mathrm{T})^+ = (\mathbf{A}^+)^\mathrm{T}$ (see [1]), we easily obtain $\mathbf{L}^+ = (\mathbf{L}^\mathrm{T})^+ = (\mathbf{L}^+)^\mathrm{T}$. Therefore, $\mathbf{L}^+$ is symmetric.

(2) $\mathbf{L}$ is an EP-matrix. An EP matrix $\mathbf{A}$ is a matrix which commutes with its pseudoinverse, i.e. $\mathbf{A}^+\mathbf{A} = \mathbf{A}\mathbf{A}^+$. Since $\mathbf{L}$ is real symmetric, it is automatically an EP-matrix (see [1], p.253). In particular, it is worth mentioning the following properties of EP-matrices:

1. If $(\lambda_i^l \neq 0, \mathbf{u}_i)$ are (eigenvalues, eigenvectors) of $\mathbf{L}$, then $(\lambda_i^{-1} \neq 0, \mathbf{u}_i)$ are corresponding (eigenvalues, eigenvectors) of $\mathbf{L}^+$. On the other hand, if $(\lambda_j^l = 0, \mathbf{u}_j)$ are (eigenvalues, eigenvectors) of $\mathbf{L}$, then they are also (eigenvalues, eigenvectors) of $\mathbf{L}^+$.
2. In particular, $\mathbf{L}^+$ has rank $n-1$ and has the same null space as $\mathbf{L}$: $\mathbf{L}^+\mathbf{e} = 0$.
3. The previous property implies that $\mathbf{L}^+$ is doubly centered (the sum of the columns and rows of $\mathbf{L}^+$ is zero), just as $\mathbf{L}$ (see also [30], chapter 10, for a discussion of this topic).
4. Other properties of EP-matrices are described in [1] or [7].

(3) $\mathbf{L}^+$ is positive semidefinite. Indeed, from the previous property, the eigenvalues of $\mathbf{L}$ and $\mathbf{L}^+$ have the same sign and $\mathbf{L}$ is positive semidefinite; therefore $\mathbf{L}^+$ is also positive semidefinite.

B   Appendix: $\mathbf{L}^+$ Is a Kernel

In this section, we show that $\mathbf{L}^+$ is a kernel (see for instance [32]). Indeed, $\mathbf{L}^+$ is the matrix containing the inner products of the transformed vectors $\mathbf{x}_i'$:

$$\mathbf{x}_i'^{\mathrm{T}}\mathbf{x}_j' = (\Lambda^{1/2}\mathbf{x}_i)^{\mathrm{T}}\Lambda^{1/2}\mathbf{x}_j = \mathbf{x}_i^{\mathrm{T}}\Lambda\mathbf{x}_j = \mathbf{e}_i^{\mathrm{T}}\mathbf{U}\Lambda\mathbf{U}^{\mathrm{T}}\mathbf{e}_j = \mathbf{e}_i^{\mathrm{T}}\mathbf{L}^+\mathbf{e}_j = l_{ij}^+$$

Thus, if $\mathbf{X}'$ denotes the data matrix containing the coordinates of the nodes on each row, $\mathbf{X}' = [\mathbf{x}_1', \mathbf{x}_2', ..., \mathbf{x}_n']^{\mathrm{T}}$, we have $\mathbf{L}^+ = \mathbf{X}'(\mathbf{X}')^{\mathrm{T}}$ with elements $l_{ij}^+ = \mathbf{x}_i'^{\mathrm{T}}\mathbf{x}_j'$.

Using String Kernels to Identify Famous Performers from Their Playing Style

Craig Saunders[1], David R. Hardoon[1],
John Shawe-Taylor[1], and Gerhard Widmer[2]

[1] School of Electronics & Computer Science,
ISIS Research Group, Building 1, Highfield, University of Southampton,
Southampton, SO17 1BJ, UK
{cjs,drh,jst}@ecs.soton.ac.uk
[2] Department of Medical Cybernetics and Artificial Intelligence,
Medical University of Vienna, Freyung 6/2, A-1010 Vienna, Austria
and Austrian Research Institute for Artificial Intelligence Freyung 6/6/7,
A-1010 Vienna, Austria
gerhard@ai.univie.ac.at

Abstract. In this paper we show a novel application of string kernels: that is to the problem of recognising famous pianists from their style of playing. The characteristics of performers playing the same piece are obtained from changes in beat-level tempo and beat-level loudness, which over the time of the piece form a *performance worm*. From such worms, general performance alphabets can be derived, and pianists' performances can then be represented as strings. We show that when using the string kernel on this data, both kernel partial least squares and Support Vector Machines outperform the current best results. Furthermore we suggest a new method of obtaining feature directions from the Kernel Partial Least Squares algorithm and show that this can deliver better performance than methods previously used in the literature when used in conjunction with a Support Vector Machine.

1 Introduction

This paper focuses on the problem of identifying famous pianists using only minimal information obtained from audio recordings of their playing. A technique called the performance worm which plots a real-time trajectory over 2D space is used to analyse changes in tempo and loudness at the beat level, and extract features for learning. Previous work on this data has compared a variety of machine learning techniques whilst using as features statistical quantities obtained from the performance worm. It is possible however to obtain a set of cluster prototypes from the worm trajectory which capture certain characteristics over a small time frame, say of two beats. These cluster prototypes form a 'performance alphabet' and there is evidence that they capture some aspects of individual playing style. For example a performer may consistently produce loudness/tempo changes unique to themselves at specific points in a piece, e.g.

J.-F. Boulicaut et al. (Eds.): ECML 2004, LNAI 3201, pp. 384–395, 2004.

at the loudest sections of a piece. Once a performance alphabet is obtained, the prototypes can each be assigned a symbol and the audio recordings can then be represented as strings constructed from this alphabet. We show that using this representation delivers an improvement in performance over the current best results obtained using a feature-based approach. The ability of the string kernel to include non-contiguous features is shown to be key in the performance of the algorithm.

The rest of this paper is laid out as follows. In the following section we provide background details on the performance worm representation used for the music data. Section 3 outlines the Partial Least Squares (PLS) algorithm and string kernel function used to analyse the data. Section 4 then presents the Kernel variant of PLS algorithm and gives a formulation for extracting features which are then used in conjunction with support vector machines (SVMs). We then present experimental results in Section 5 and end with some analysis and suggestions for future research.

2   A Musical Representation

The data used in this paper, first described in [1], was obtained from recordings of sonatas by W.A. Mozart played by six famous concert pianists. In total the performances of 6 pianists were analysed across 12 different movements of Mozart sonatas. The movements represent a cross section of playing keys, tempi and time signatures, see Table 1 for details. In many cases the only data available for different performances are standard audio recordings (as opposed to for example MIDI format data from which more detailed analysis is possible), which poses particular difficulties for the extraction of relevant performance information. A tool for analysing this type of data called the performance worm has recently been developed [2, 1, 3]. The performance worm extracts data from audio recordings by examining tempo and general loudness of the audio when measured at the beat level. An interactive beat tracking program [4] is used to find the beat from which changes in beat-level tempo and beat-level loudness can be calculated. These two types of changes can be integrated to form trajectories over tempo-loudness space that show the joint development of tempo and dynamics over time. As data is extracted from the audio the 2D plot of the performance curve can be constructed in real time to aid in visualisation of these

Table 1. Movements of Mozart piano sonatas selected for analysis.

Sonata	Movement	Key	Time sig.	Sonata	Movement	Key	Time sig.
K.279	1st mvt.	C major	4/4	K.281	1st mvt.	Bb major	2/4
K.279	2nd mvt.	C major	3/4	K.282	1st mvt.	Eb major	4/4
K.279	3rd mvt.	C major	2/4	K.282	2nd mvt.	Eb major	3/4
K.280	1st mvt.	F major	3/4	K.282	3rd mvt.	Eb major	2/4
K.280	2nd mvt.	F major	6/8	K.330	3rd mvt.	C major	2/4
K.280	3rd mvt.	F major	3/8	K.332	2nd mvt.	F major	4/4

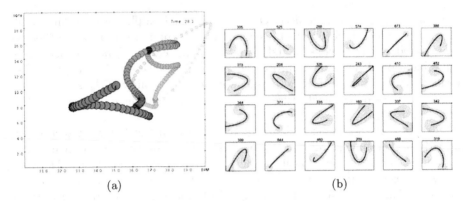

(a)   (b)

Fig. 1. (a) The performance worm: A 2D representation of changes in beat-level tempo and loudness can be plotted in realtime from an audio recording. (b) The performance alphabet: A set of cluster prototypes extracted from the performance worm.

dynamics, and this is called the performance worm. Figure 1(a) shows a screen-shot of the worm in progress. Note that this is the only information used in the creation of the worm, more detailed information such as articulation, individual voicing or timing details of that below the level of a beat is not available.

2.1   A Performance Alphabet

From the performance worm, patterns can be observed which can help charac-terise the individual playing styles of some pianists. For example, in [3] a set of tempo-loudness shapes typical of the performer Mitsuko Uchida were found. These shapes represented a particular way of combining a crescendo-decrescendo with a slowing down during a loudness maximum. These patterns were often re-peated in Mozart performances by Mitsuko Uchida, but were rarely found when analysing the recordings of other performers.

In order to try and capture more of these types of characterisations a 'Mozart Performance Alphabet' can be constructed in the following way. The trajectories of the performance worm are cut into short segments of a fixed length (e.g. 2 beats) and clustered into groups of similar patterns to form a series of proto-types (see Figure 1(b)). Recordings of a performance can then be transcribed in terms of this alphabet which can then be compared using string matching techniques. The list of pianists and the recordings used to obtain the data can be found in Table 2. For more detailed information on the performance worm and constructing a performance alphabet of cluster prototypes, please refer to [1, 3]. The task addressed in this paper is to learn to recognise pianists solely from characteristics of their performance strings. The ability of kernel methods to operate over string-like structures using kernels such as the n-gram kernel and the string kernel will be evaluated on this task. In addition to simply applying an SVM to the data however, we will also examine the ability of dimension reduc-tion methods such as Kernel PCA and Kernel Partial Least Squares (KPLS) to

Table 2. List of pianists and recordings used.

ID	Name	Recording
DB	Daniel Barenboim	EMI Classics CDZ 7 67295 2, 1984
RB	Roland Batik	Gramola 98701-705, 1990
GG	Glenn Gould	Sony Classical SM4K 52627, 1967
MP	Maria João Pires	DGG 431 761-2, 1991
AS	András Schiff	ADD (Decca) 443 720-2, 1980
MU	Mitsuko Uchida	Philips Classics 464 856-2, 1987

extract relevant features from the data before applying an SVM, which will hopefully lead to improved classification performance. KPCA is well known method and has often been used to extract features from data (see e.g. [5]). Partial least squares and its kernel-based variant KPLS has recenlty gained popularity within the machine learning community [6–8] and either can be used as a method for regression or classification, or as a method for dimension reduction. It is not always clear however, how to use the PLS-based methods to generate new input features for training and test data, so we shall briefly review the methods here.

3   Previous Results

3.1   String Kernels

The use of string kernels for analysing text documents was first studied by Lodhi et al. [9]. We briefly review the approach to creating a feature space and associated kernel.

The key idea behind the gap-weighted subsequences kernel is to compare strings by means of the subsequences they contain – the more subsequences in common, the more similar they are – rather than only considering contiguous n-grams, the degree of contiguity of the subsequence in the input string s determines how much it will contribute to the comparison.

In order to deal with non-contiguous substrings, it is necessary to introduce a decay factor $\lambda \in (0, 1)$ that can be used to weight the presence of a certain feature in a string. For an index sequence $\mathbf{i} = (i_1, \ldots, i_k)$ identifying the occurrence of a subsequence $u = s(\mathbf{i})$ in a string s, we use $l(\mathbf{i}) = i_k - i_1 + 1$ to denote the length of the string in s. In the gap-weighted kernel, we weight the occurrence of u with the exponentially decaying weight $\lambda^{l(\mathbf{i})}$.

Definition 1 (Gap-weighted subsequences kernel). *The feature space associated with the gap-weighted subsequences kernel of length p is indexed by $I = \Sigma^p$ (i.e. subsequences of length p from some alphabet Σ), with the embedding given by*

$$\phi_u^p(s) = \sum_{\mathbf{i}:\, u=s(\mathbf{i})} \lambda^{l(\mathbf{i})}, \ u \in \Sigma^p.$$

The associated kernel is defined as

$$\kappa_p(s,t) = \langle \phi^p(s), \phi^p(t) \rangle = \sum_{u \in \Sigma^p} \phi_u^p(s) \phi_u^p(t).$$

Example 1. Consider the simple strings "cat", "car", "bat", and "bar". Fixing $p = 2$, the words are mapped as follows:

ϕ	ca	ct	at	ba	bt	cr	ar	br
cat	λ^2	λ^3	λ^2	0	0	0	0	0
car	λ^2	0	0	0	0	λ^3	λ^2	0
bat	0	0	λ^2	λ^2	λ^3	0	0	0
bar	0	0	0	λ^2	0	0	λ^2	λ^3

So the unnormalised kernel between "cat" and "car" is $\kappa(\text{"cat"},\text{"car"}) = \lambda^4$, while the normalised version is obtained using

$$\kappa(\text{"cat"},\text{"cat"}) = \kappa(\text{"car"},\text{"car"}) = 2\lambda^4 + \lambda^6$$

as $\hat{\kappa}(\text{"cat"},\text{"car"}) = \lambda^4/(2\lambda^4 + \lambda^6) = (2 + \lambda^2)^{-1}$.

We omit a description of the efficient dynamic programming algorithms for computing this kernel referring the reader to Lodhi et al. [9].

3.2 Partial Least Squares

Partial Least Squares (PLS) was developed by Herman Wold during the 1960's in the field of econometrics [10]. It offers an effective approach to solving problems with training data that has few points but high dimensionality, by first projecting the data into a lower-dimensional space and then utilising a Least Squares (LS) regression model. This problem is common in the field of Chemometrics where PLS is regularly used. PLS is a flexible algorithm that was designed for regression problems, though it can be used for classification by treating the labels $\{+1, -1\}$ as real outputs. Alternatively it can also be stopped after constructing the low-dimensional projection. The resulting features can then be used in a different classification or regression algorithm. We will also adopt this approach by applying an SVM in this feature space, an approach pioneered by Rosipal et al. [8]. The procedure for PLS feature extraction is shown in Algorithm 1. The algorithmic procedure iteratively takes the first singular vector $\mathbf{u}_i$ of the matrix $\mathbf{X}_i'\mathbf{Y}$, and then deflates the matrix $\mathbf{X}_i$ to obtain $\mathbf{X}_{i+1}$. The deflation is done by projecting the columns of $\mathbf{X}_i$ into the space orthogonal to $\mathbf{X}_i\mathbf{u}_i$. The difficulty with this simple description is that the feature directions $\mathbf{u}_j$ are defined relative to the deflated matrix. We would like to be able to compute the PLS features directly from the original feature vector.

If we now consider a test point with feature vector $\phi(\mathbf{x})$ the transformations that we perform at each step should also be applied to $\phi_1(\mathbf{x}) = \phi(\mathbf{x})$ to create a series of feature vectors

$$\phi_{j+1}(\mathbf{x})' = \phi_j(\mathbf{x})'(\mathbf{I} - \mathbf{u}_j \mathbf{p}_j'),$$

Algorithm 1 The PLS feature extraction algorithm.

The PLS feature extraction algorithm is as follows:

input	Data matrix $\mathbf{X} \in \mathbb{R}^{\ell \times N}$, dimension k, target vectors $\mathbf{Y} \in \mathbb{R}^{\ell \times m}$.
process	$\mathbf{X}_1 = \mathbf{X}$
	for $j = 1, \ldots, k$
	let $\mathbf{u}_j, \sigma_j$ be the first singular vector/value of $\mathbf{X}'_j \mathbf{Y}$,
	$\mathbf{X}_{j+1} = \mathbf{X}_j \left(\mathbf{I} - \frac{\mathbf{u}_j \mathbf{u}'_j \mathbf{X}'_j \mathbf{X}_j}{\mathbf{u}'_j \mathbf{X}'_j \mathbf{X}_j \mathbf{u}_j} \right)$
	end
output	Feature directions $\mathbf{u}_j$, $j = 1, \ldots, k$.

---

where
$$\mathbf{p}_j = \frac{\mathbf{X}'_j \mathbf{X}_j \mathbf{u}_j}{\mathbf{u}'_j \mathbf{X}'_j \mathbf{X}_j \mathbf{u}_j},$$

This is the same operation that is performed on the rows of $\mathbf{X}_j$ in Algorithm 1. We can now write

$$\phi(\mathbf{x})' = \phi_{k+1}(\mathbf{x})' + \sum_{j=1}^{k} \phi_j(\mathbf{x})' \mathbf{u}_j \mathbf{p}'_j.$$

The feature vector that we need for the regression $\hat{\phi}(\mathbf{x})$ has components

$$\hat{\phi}(\mathbf{x}) = \left(\phi_j(\mathbf{x})' \mathbf{u}_j \right)_{j=1}^{k},$$

since these are the projections of the residual vector at stage j onto the next feature vector $\mathbf{u}_j$. Rather than compute $\phi_j(\mathbf{x})'$ iteratively, consider using the inner products between the original $\phi(\mathbf{x})'$ and the feature vectors $\mathbf{u}_j$ stored as the columns of the matrix $\mathbf{U}$:

$$\phi(\mathbf{x})' \mathbf{U} = \phi_{k+1}(\mathbf{x})' \mathbf{U} + \sum_{j=1}^{k} \phi_j(\mathbf{x})' \mathbf{u}_j \mathbf{p}'_j \mathbf{U}$$

$$= \phi_{k+1}(\mathbf{x})' \mathbf{U} + \hat{\phi}(\mathbf{x})' \mathbf{P}' \mathbf{U},$$

where $\mathbf{P}$ is the matrix whose columns are $\mathbf{p}_j$, $j = 1, \ldots, k$. Finally, it can be verified that

$$\mathbf{u}'_i \mathbf{p}_j = \delta_{ij} \quad \text{for } i \leq j. \tag{1}$$

Hence, for $s > j$, $(\mathbf{I} - \mathbf{u}_s \mathbf{p}'_s) \mathbf{u}_j = \mathbf{u}_j$, while $(\mathbf{I} - \mathbf{u}_j \mathbf{p}'_j) \mathbf{u}_j = 0$, so we can write

$$\phi_{k+1}(\mathbf{x})' \mathbf{u}_j = \phi_j(\mathbf{x})' \prod_{i=j}^{k} (\mathbf{I} - \mathbf{u}_i \mathbf{p}'_i) \mathbf{u}_j = 0, \text{ for } j = 1, \ldots, k.$$

It follows that the new feature vector can be expressed as

$$\hat{\phi}(\mathbf{x})' = \phi(\mathbf{x})' \mathbf{U} (\mathbf{P}' \mathbf{U})^{-1}.$$

These feature vectors can now be used in conjunction with a learning algorithm. If one wished to calculate the overall regression coefficients as in the full PLS algorithm, these can be computed as:

$$\mathbf{W} = \mathbf{U}\left(\mathbf{P}'\mathbf{U}\right)^{-1}\mathbf{C}', \tag{2}$$

where $\mathbf{C}$ is the matrix with columns

$$\mathbf{c}_j = \frac{\mathbf{Y}'\mathbf{X}_j\mathbf{u}_j}{\mathbf{u}_j'\mathbf{X}_j'\mathbf{X}_j\mathbf{u}_j}.$$

4   Kernel PLS

In this section we set out the kernel PLS algorithm and describe its feature extraction stage. The kernel PLS algorithm is given in Algorithm 2. The vector β_i is a rescaled dual representation of the primal vectors $\mathbf{u}_i$:

$$a_i\mathbf{u}_i = \mathbf{X}_i'\beta_i,$$

the rescaling arising because of the different point at which the renormalising is performed in the dual. We can now express the primal matrix $\mathbf{P}'\mathbf{U}$ in terms of the dual variables as

---

Algorithm 2 Pseudocode for kernel-PLS.

Input: Data $S = x_1, \ldots, x_l$ dimension k target outputs $Y \in \mathbb{R}^{l \times m}$

$\quad K_{ij} = \kappa\left(x_i, x_j\right)$
$\quad K_1 = K$
$\quad \hat{Y} = Y$

$\quad$**for** $i = 1, \ldots, k$ **do**
$\quad\quad \beta_i = $ first column of $\hat{Y}$
$\quad\quad$ normalise β_i
$\quad\quad$**repeat**
$\quad\quad\quad \beta_i = YY'K_i\beta_i$
$\quad\quad\quad$ normalise β_i
$\quad\quad$**until** convergence
$\quad\quad \tau_i = K_i\beta_i$
$\quad\quad c_i = \hat{Y}'\tau_i$
$\quad\quad \hat{Y} = \hat{Y} - \tau_i c_i'$
$\quad\quad K_{i+1} = \left(I - \tau_i\tau_i'\right)K_i\left(I - \tau_i\tau_i'\right)$
$\quad$**end for**

$\quad B = [\beta_i, \ldots, \beta_k]$
$\quad T = [\tau_i, \ldots, \tau_k]$
$\quad \alpha = B(TKB)^{-1}T'Y$

Output: Training outputs $Y - \hat{Y}$ and dual regression coefficients α

$$\mathbf{P'U} = \text{diag}\,(\mathbf{a})\,\text{diag}\,(\tau_i'\tau_i)^{-1}\,\mathbf{T'XX'B}\text{diag}\,(\mathbf{a})^{-1}$$
$$= \text{diag}\,(\mathbf{a})\,\text{diag}\,(\tau_i'\tau_i)^{-1}\,\mathbf{T'KB}\text{diag}\,(\mathbf{a})^{-1}.$$

Here $\text{diag}\,(\tau_i'\tau_i)$ is the diagonal matrix with entries $\text{diag}\,(\tau_i'\tau_i)_{ii} = \tau_i'\tau_i$, where $\tau_i = K_i\beta_i$. Finally, again using the orthogonality of $\mathbf{X}_j\mathbf{u}_j$ to τ_i, for $i < j$, we obtain

$$\mathbf{c}_j = \frac{\mathbf{Y}_j'\mathbf{X}_j\mathbf{u}_j}{\mathbf{u}_j'\mathbf{X}_j'\mathbf{X}_j\mathbf{u}_j} = \frac{\mathbf{Y'X}_j\mathbf{u}_j}{\mathbf{u}_j'\mathbf{X}_j'\mathbf{X}_j\mathbf{u}_j} = a_j\frac{\mathbf{Y'}\tau_j}{\tau_j'\tau_j},$$

making

$$\mathbf{C} = \mathbf{Y'T}\text{diag}\,(\tau_i'\tau_i)^{-1}\,\text{diag}\,(\mathbf{a}).$$

Putting the pieces together we can compute the dual regression variables as

$$\alpha = \mathbf{B}\,(\mathbf{T'KB})^{-1}\,\mathbf{T'Y}.$$

It is tempting to assume like [8] that a dual representation of the PLS features is then given by

$$\mathbf{B}\,(\mathbf{T'KB})^{-1},$$

but in fact

$$\mathbf{U}\,(\mathbf{P'U})^{-1} = \mathbf{X'B}\text{diag}\,(\mathbf{a})^{-1}\left(\text{diag}\,(\mathbf{a})\,\text{diag}\,(\tau_i'\tau_i)^{-1}\,\mathbf{T'KB}\text{diag}\,(\mathbf{a})^{-1}\right)^{-1}$$

so that the dual representation is

$$\mathbf{B}\,(\mathbf{T'KB})^{-1}\,\text{diag}\,(\mathbf{a})^{-1}\,\text{diag}\,(\tau_i'\tau_i) = \mathbf{B}\,(\mathbf{T'KB})^{-1}\,\text{diag}\,(\tau_i'\tau_i)\,\text{diag}\,(\mathbf{a})^{-1}.$$

The missing diagonal matrices perform a rescaling of the features extracted, which skews the geometry of the space and affects the performance of for example an SVM. The quantities a_i are difficult to assess, though these should not vary significantly over similar adjacent features since they will be related to the corresponding singular values. In our experiments we have compared the results that can be obtained ignoring both diagonal matrices with those obtained including $\text{diag}\,(\tau_i'\tau_i)$.

5   Experiments

In our experiments we followed the setup given in [1]. For each pair of performers a leave-one-out procedure was followed where on each iteration one movement played by each of a pair of performers was used for testing and the rest of the data was used for training. That is, for a given pair of performers, say Mitsuko Uchida and Daniel Barenboim (MU-DB), a total of 12 runs of an algorithm were performed (there are 12 movements and each time one movement by both performers was left out of the training set and tested upon). This was repeated for each of the possible 15 pairings of performers. Note that in all results the number reported is the number of *correct* classifications made by the algorithm.

5.1   Previous Results

Previous results on the data (as described in [1]) used a feature-based representation and considered a range of machine learning techniques by using the well-known Waikato Environment for Knowledge Analysis (WEKA) software package [11] to compare bayesian, rule-based, tree-based and nearest-neighbour methods. The best results obtained previously on the data are for a classification via regression meta-learner. These results are reported as FB (feature-based) in the results table. The feature-based representation used in the experiments included the raw measures of tempo and loudness along with various statistics regarding the variance and standard deviation of these and additional information extracted from the worm such as the correlation of tempo and loudness values.

5.2   Results

Experiments were conducted using both the standard string kernel and the n-gram kernel and several algorithms. In both cases experiments were conducted using a standard SVM on the relevant kernel matrix. Kernel Partial Least Squares and Kernel Principal Component Regression were also used for comparison. Finally, an SVM was used in conjunction with the projected features obtained from the iterative KPLS deflation steps. For these features there were two options, either to use the features as described in [8] or to include the extra reweighting factors diag $(\tau_i' \tau_i)$ described above. We first performed a comparison of these two options by counting the total number of correct predictions across all splits for different feature dimensions (T) for the original weighting (ORIG) and the reweighted (REW) features. Table 3 shows the results obtained. There is a clear advantage shown for the reweighting scheme and so we adopted this method for the remaining experiments.

Table 3. Total number of correct predictions across all splits against number of feature directions used (T) for both the feature projection method described in this paper (REW) and that in previous work (ORIG). The parameters used in this were those optimal for the KP-SV combination ($k = 5, \lambda = 0.9$).

Method/T	1	2	3	4	5	6	7	8	9	10
ORIG	287	265	248	251	253	250	256	252	246	238
REW	287	295	293	293	296	296	295	295	295	295

In the remaining experiments we chose one pair of composers (RB–DB) to select the various parameters. These included the number of characters used by the string kernel, the decay parameter and the number of PLS features extracted where appropriate. Substring lengths of $k = 1, \ldots, 10$ were tried for both the n-gram and string kernels, $\lambda = \{0.2, 0.5, 0.9\}$ decay parameters were used for the string kernel and for both KPLS and KPCR methods the number of feature directions (T) ranged from 1 to 10. All kernel matrices were normalised and whenever an SVM was used, the parameter C was set to one. In each case the parameters that delivered the best performance on the RB–DB data were chosen. Once selected the settings of these parameters were fixed for the remaining test experiments for all of the results reported in Table 4 – note that the RB–DB row is deliberately left blank to emphasise this.

The results obtained from using these methods and kernels show an improvement over the previous best results using statistical features extracted from the performance worm. We use the following shorthand to refer to the relevant algorithm/kernel combinations; **FB**: Previous best method using statistical features, **KPLS**: Kernel Partial Least Squares, **SVM**: Support Vector Machine, **KP-SV**: SVM using KPLS features, **KPCR**: Kernel Principal Components regression. If an n-gram kernel is used rather than a string kernel we append '-n' to the method name.

Table 4. Comparison of algorithms across each pairwise coupling of performers. Note that in all case the figures given are the number of movements correctly identified out of a maximum of 24. FB represents the previous best results using a feature-based representation rather than the 'performance alphabet' used for the other approaches.

Pairing	FB	String Kernel				n-gram Kernel			
		KPLS	SVM	KP-SV	KPCR	KPLS-n	SVM-n	KP-SV-n	KPCR-n
RB - DB	–	–	–	–	–	–	–	–	–
GG - DB	15	19	21	22	21	18	18	22	14
GG - RB	17	24	22	23	24	21	21	20	11
MP - DB	17	18	18	20	17	16	16	18	17
MP - RB	21	22	22	23	19	18	15	17	12
MP - GG	17	23	23	23	23	20	20	22	18
AS - DB	15	19	19	19	18	15	16	16	10
AS - RB	16	23	23	21	16	17	17	20	14
AS - GG	17	17	18	18	17	18	15	18	13
AS - MP	20	23	23	22	22	20	17	22	14
MU - DB	17	15	15	15	13	13	13	14	12
MU - RB	16	17	17	14	11	18	16	17	12
MU - GG	16	19	19	19	20	16	16	20	14
MU - MP	15	18	19	17	17	17	17	21	16
MU - AS	17	16	16	18	16	16	15	16	17
Total	236	273	275	274	254	243	232	263	194
Average (%)	70.2	81.3	81.9	81.6	75.6	72.3	69.5	78.2	57.7

The use of the methods in this paper in conjunction with the n-gram kernel offer a clear performance advantage over the feature-based approach. Interestingly, KPLS outperforms an SVM when using this kernel. This may suggest that for this kernel, projecting into a lower subspace is beneficial. Indeed, the performance of KPCR is also close to the SVM. The ability of KPLS however to correlate the feature directions it selects with the output variable gives it a clear advantage over KPCR and as expected from previous results on other data [6, 7], a performance gain is achieved. When using the SVM in conjunction with the features obtained from the KPLS deflation steps, the performance improves further which has also been the case on other data sets [8]. In all cases short substrings achieved the best performance (with substring lengths of only 1 or 2 characters, which would perhaps indicate that complex features are not used). It is interesting to note that in the experiments KPCR requires more feature directions to achieve good performance, whereas KPLS consistently requires fewer directions to perform well.

The string kernel operating over the performance alphabet provides significantly better classification performance than the feature-based method and in every case also outperforms the n-gram kernel. This would indicate that the ability of the string kernel to allow gaps in matching subsequences is a key benefit for this data, and that complex features are indeed needed to obtain good performance. This is in contrast to results reported using the string kernel for text, where the classification rate of n-gram kernels using contiguous sequences is equal to that of the string kernel if not superior [9]. For the string kernel however, the use of KPLS features did not improve the performance of the support vector machine (in fact over all of the data it made 1 more misclassification). It is therefore not clear in which situations the use of KPLS features in conjunction with an SVM will produce a performance gain.

6   Conclusions

In this paper we have presented a novel application of the string kernel: to classify pianists by examining their playing style. This is an extremely complex task and has previously been attempted by analysing statistical features obtained from audio recordings. Here we have taken a different approach and have examined using feature-projection methods in conjunction with kernels which operate on text. These can be applied to the performer recognition problem by representing the performance as a string of characteristic tempo-loudness curves, which are obtained by analysing a performance worm. We have reviewed the Kernel Partial Least Squares method and shown how this can be successfully used to generate new features which can then be used in conjunction with learning methods such as an SVM. We have also shown a reweighting scheme for obtaining feature directions from KPLS that peforms better than the technique used in current literature. All algorithms tested in this paper provided higher performance than the previous state of the art results on the data. We have also shown that the ability of the string kernel to consider and match non-contiguous substrings of input sequence has a real performance benefit over only considering contiguous substrings. This is in contrast to many applications of the string kernel to text, where the relative performance of the string kernel to the n-gram kernel tends to be very close or even slightly worse. It is an open problem to determine in what circumstances using KPLS to obtain features will result in an improvement in generalisation performance. Also, currently the number of dimensions has to be chosen via cross-validation or some other method, therefore an automatic selection method for this parameter would also be beneficial. These two problems will be addressed in future research.

Acknowledgements

This work was supported in part by EPSRC grant no GR/S22301/01 ("Development and Application of String-Type Kernels"), the IST Programme of the European Community, under the PASCAL Network of Excellence, IST-2002-506778 and by the Austrian Fonds zur Förderung der Wissenschaftlichen Forschung (FWF) under grant Y99-INF. The Austrian Research Institute for Artificial Intelligence is supported by the Austrian Federal Ministry for Education, Science, and Culture, and by the Austrian Federal Ministry for Transport, Innovation, and Technology.

References

1. Zanon, P., Widmer, G.: Learning to recognise famous pianists with machine learning techniques. In: Proceedings of the Stockholm Music Acoustics Conference (SMAC '03). (2003)
2. Dixon, S., Goebl, W., Widmer, G.: The performance worm: Real time visualisation of expression based on langner's tempo-loudness animation. In: Proceedings of the International Computer Music Conference (ICMC 2002). (2002)
3. Widmer, G., Dixon, S., Goebel, W., Pampalk, E., Tobudic, A.: In search of the horowitz factor. AI Magazine **3** (2003) 111–130
4. Dixon, S.: Automatic extraction of tempo and beat from expressive performances. Journal of New Music Research **30** (2001) 39–58
5. Schölkopf, B., Smola, A., Müller, K.R.: Nonlinear component analysis as a kernel eigenvalue problem. Neural Computation (1998)
6. Rosipal, R., Trejo, L.: Kernel partial least squares regression in reproducing kernel hilbert space. In: Journal of Machine Learning Research 2. (2001) 97–123
7. Bennett, K.P., Embrechts, M.J.: An optimization perspective on kernel partial least squares regression. Advances in Learning Theory: Methods, Models and Applications. NATO Science Series III: Computer & Systems Science **190** (2003) 227–250
8. Rosipal, R., Trejo, L., Matthews, B.: Kernel pls-svc for linear and nonlinear classification. In: Proceedings of the Twentieth International Conference on Machine Learning (ICML-2003). (2003)
9. Lodhi, H., Saunders, C., Shawe-Taylor, J., Cristianini, N., Watkins, C.: Text classification using string kernels. Journal of Machine Learning Research (2002) 419–444
10. Wold, H.: Estimation of principal components and related models by iterative least squares. Multivariate Analysis (1966) 391–420
11. Witten, I., Frank, E.: Data Mining. Morgan Kaufmann, San Francisco, CA (1999)

Associative Clustering

Janne Sinkkonen[1], Janne Nikkilä[1], Leo Lahti[1], and Samuel Kaski[2,1]

[1] Helsinki University of Technology, Neural Networks Research Centre,
P.O. Box 5400, FIN-02015 HUT, Finland
{Janne.Sinkkonen,Janne.Nikkila,Leo.Lahti,Samuel.Kaski}@hut.fi
http://www.cis.hut.fi/projects/mi
[2] Department of Computer Science,
P.O. Box 68, FIN-00014 University of Helsinki, Finland

Abstract. Clustering by maximizing the dependency between two paired, continuous-valued multivariate data sets is studied. The new method, *associative clustering (AC)*, maximizes a Bayes factor between two clustering models differing only in one respect: whether the clusterings of the two data sets are dependent or independent. The model both extends Information Bottleneck (IB)-type dependency modeling to continuous-valued data and offers it a well-founded and asymptotically well-behaving criterion for small data sets: With suitable prior assumptions the Bayes factor becomes equivalent to the hypergeometric probability of a contingency table, while for large data sets it becomes the standard mutual information. An optimization algorithm is introduced, with empirical comparisons to a combination of IB and K-means, and to plain K-means. Two case studies cluster genes 1) to find dependencies between gene expression and transcription factor binding, and 2) to find dependencies between expression in different organisms.

1 Introduction

Distributional clustering by the information bottleneck (IB) principle [21] groups nominal values x of a random variable X by maximizing the dependency of the groups with another, co-occurring discrete variable Y. Clustering documents x by the occurrences of words y in them is an example. For continuous-valued X, the analogue of IB is to *partition* the space of possible values $\boldsymbol{x} \in \mathbb{R}^{d_x}$ by discriminative clustering (DC); then the dependency of the partitions and y is maximized [16].

Both DC and IB maximize dependency between representations of random variables. Their dependency measures are asymptotically equivalent to mutual information (MI)[1]; the empirical mutual information used by IB and some variants of DC is problematic for finite data sets, however. A likelihood interpretation of empirical MI (see [16]) opens a way to probabilistic dependency measures that

---

[1] Yet another example of dependency maximization is canonical correlation analysis, which uses a second-moment criterion equivalent to mutual information assuming normally distributed data [11].

J.-F. Boulicaut et al. (Eds.): ECML 2004, LNAI 3201, pp. 396–406, 2004.

are asymptotically equivalent to MI but perform better for finite data sets [17]. The current likelihood formulation, however, breaks down when both margins are clustered simultaneously.

In this paper we introduce a novel method, *associative clustering (AC)*, for clustering of paired continuous-valued data by maximizing the dependency between the clusters of X and Y, later called *margin clusters*. A sample application is search for different types of city districts, by partitioning a city into demographically homogeneous regions (Fig. 1**B**). Here the paired data are the coordinates and demographics of the buildings of the city.

As a measure of dependency between the cluster sets, we suggest using a Bayes factor, extended from an optimization criterion for DC [17]. The criterion compares evidence for two models, one assuming independent margin clusters (clusters for x and y), and the other allowing more general dependency of the margin clusters in generating data. With suitable prior assumptions the Bayes factor is equivalent to a hypergeometric probability commonly used as a dependency measure for contingency tables. It is well justified for finite data sets, avoiding the problems of empirical mutual information due to sampling uncertainty. Yet it is asymptotically equivalent to mutual information for large data sets. The Bayes factor is also usable as the cost function of IB [14].

AC will be applied for finding dependencies in gene expression data. It will be compared with standard K-means, computed independently for the two margins, which provides a baseline result. The comparison relevals how much is gained by explicit dependency modeling.

AC will additionally be compared with a new variant of IB. IB operates on discrete data, and therefore the continuous multivariates need first to be discretized into atomic regions, for example with K-means. The symmetric IB [5] can then compose discrete representations for the margins as combinations of the atomic regions. Again dependence of the representations is the criterion for clustering, and a dependency-maximized contingency table spanned by the margin clusters results. K-means discretization was chosen because its parameterization is similar to AC and, more importantly, because it is perhaps the most obvious alternative for multidimensional discretization[2].

In IB, dependency has classically been measured by the (empirical) mutual information. As margin clusters are here combinations of very small Voronoi regions, IB finds dependencies between the data sets well, but on the other hand produces clusters that are potentially less local than those obtained by AC or standard K-means. We will evaluate the average dispersion of the clusters in the empirical tests of Section 4.

Both mixture models for discrete data [2, 3, 8] and Mixture Discriminant Analysis (MDA)-like [7, 13] models for continuous data have common elements with our approach, and can readily be extended for the double-margin case.

---

[2] Note that discretizing the dimensions independently of each other and using the Cartesian product as the multidimensional partitioning would fail badly for high-dimensional x or y. As far as we know, better discretization methods or other comparable methods for co-clustering of continuous data have not been published.

A

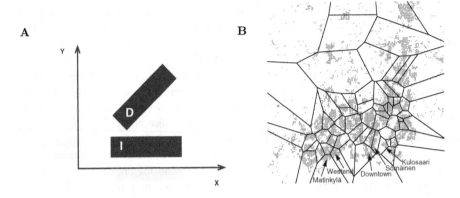

B

Fig. 1. A Demonstration of the difference between dependency modeling and joint density modeling. The hypothetical joint density of two one-dimensional variables x and y is plotted with black, and the respective marginal densities are depicted as histograms (*grey*). The marginals, here for simplicity univariate, correspond to the paired data of the AC setting. The visualized joint distribution consists of two equally-sized parts: a block in which x and y are independent (denoted by I) and another block (D) where x and y are dependent. Models for the joint distribution would focus equally on both blocks, whereas AC and IB focus on the dependent block D not explainable as products of the marginals, and neglect the independent block I. **B** Partitioning of Helsinki region into demographically homogeneous regions with AC. Here x contains geographic coordinates of buildings and y demographic information about inhabitants indicating social status, family structure, etc. Spatially relatively compact yet demographically homogeneous clusters emerge. For instance downtown and close-by relatively rich (Kulosaari, Westend) areas become separated from less well-off areas

An important difference is that our optimization criterion (as well as that of the Information Bottleneck) focuses only on the *dependencies* between the variables, skipping the parts of the joint distribution representable as a product of margins. Both goals are rigorous but different, as illustrated in Figure 1**A**.

2   Associative Clustering

2.1   Bayes Factor for Maximizing Dependency Between Two Sets of Clusters

The dependency between two clusterings, indexed by i and j, for the same set of objects can be measured by mutual information if their joint distribution p_{ij} is known. If only a *contingency table* of co-occurrence frequencies n_{ij} computed from a finite data set is available, the mutual information computed from the empirical distribution would be a biased estimate. A *Bayes factor*, to be introduced below, then has the advantage of properly taking into account the finiteness of the data while still being asymptotically equivalent to mutual information. Bayes factors have been classically used as dependency measures for contingency tables (see, e.g., [6]) by comparing a model of dependent margins to another one for independent margins. We will use the classical results as building blocks to derive an optimizable criterion for associative clustering; the novelty here is that the Bayes factor is optimized instead of only using it to measure dependency in a fixed table.

In general, frequencies over the cells of a contingency table are multinomially distributed. The model M_i of *independent margins* assumes that the multinomial parameters over cells are outer products of posterior parameters at the margins: $\theta_{ij} = \theta_i \theta_j$. The model M_d of *dependent margins* ignores the structure of the cells as a two-dimensional table and samples cell-wise frequencies directly from a table-wide multinomial distribution θ_{ij}. Dirichlet priors are assumed for both the margin and the table-wide multinomials.

Maximization of the Bayes factor

$$BF = \frac{p(\{n_{ij}\}|M_d)}{p(\{n_{ij}\}|M_i)}$$

with respect to the margin clusters then gives a contingency table where the margins are maximally dependent, that is, which cannot be explained as a product of independent margins. In the associative clustering introduced in this paper, the data counts are defined by the training data set and the parameters that determine how the continuous data spaces are partitioned into margin clusters. Then BF is maximized with respect to the parameters. If this principle were applied to two-way IB, the margins would be determined as groupings of nominal values of the discrete margin variables, and the BF would be maximized with respect to different groupings.

After marginalization over the multinomial parameters, the Bayes factor can be shown to take the form

$$BF = \frac{\prod_{ij} \Gamma(n_{ij} + n^{(d)})}{\prod_i \Gamma(n_{i.} + n^{(x)}) \prod_j \Gamma(n_{.j} + n^{(y)})} \,, \tag{1}$$

with $n_{i.} = \sum_j n_{ij}$ and $n_{.j} = \sum_i n_{ij}$ expressing the margins. The parameters $n^{(d)}$, $n^{(x)}$, and $n^{(y)}$ arise from Dirichlet priors. We have set all three parameters to unity, which makes BF equivalent to the hypergeometric probability classically used as a dependency measure of contingency tables. In the limit of large data sets, (1) becomes mutual information of the margins; [17] outlines the proof for the case of one fixed and one parameterized margin.

2.2   Optimization of AC

For paired data $\{(\boldsymbol{x}_k, \boldsymbol{y}_k)\}$ of real vectors $(\boldsymbol{x}, \boldsymbol{y}) \in \mathbb{R}^{d_x} \times \mathbb{R}^{d_y}$, we search for partitionings $\{V_i^{(x)}\}$ for $\boldsymbol{x}$ and $\{V_j^{(y)}\}$) for $\boldsymbol{y}$. The partitions can be interpreted as clusters in the same way as in K-means; they are Voronoi regions parameterized by their centroids $\boldsymbol{m}_i$: $\boldsymbol{x} \in V_i^{(x)}$ if $\|\boldsymbol{x} - \boldsymbol{m}_i\| \leq \|\boldsymbol{x} - \boldsymbol{m}_k\|$ for all k, and correspondingly for $\boldsymbol{y}$. The Bayes factor (1) will be maximized with respect to the Voronoi centroids.

The optimization problem is combinatorial for hard clusters, but gradient methods are applicable after the clusters are smoothed. Gradients for the simpler one-margin problem have been derived in [17], and are analogous here. An extra trick, found to improve the optimization in the fixed-margin case [10], is applied here as well: The denominator of the Bayes factor is given extra weight. A choice of $\lambda^{(\cdot)} > 1$ introduces a regularizing term to the cost function that for large sample sizes approaches margin cluster entropy, and thereby in general favors solutions with uniform margin distributions.

The smoothed BF, here called BF', is then optimized with respect to the $\{m\}$ by a conjugate-gradient algorithm (see, for example [1]). We have

$$\log BF' = \sum_{ij} \log \Gamma \left(\sum_k g_i^{(x)}(\boldsymbol{x}_k) g_j^{(y)}(\boldsymbol{y}_k) + n^{(d)} \right)$$

$$- \lambda^{(x)} \sum_i \log \Gamma \left(\sum_k g_i^{(x)}(\boldsymbol{x}_k) + n^{(x)} \right) - \lambda^{(y)} \sum_j \log \Gamma \left(\sum_k g_j^{(y)}(\boldsymbol{y}_k) + n^{(y)} \right) ,$$

$$g_i^{(x)}(\boldsymbol{x}) \equiv Z^{(x)}(\boldsymbol{x})^{-1} \exp\left(-\|\boldsymbol{x} - \boldsymbol{m}_i^{(x)}\|^2 / \sigma_{(x)}^2 \right) ,$$

and similarly for $g^{(y)}$. The $g(\cdot)$ are the smoothed Voronoi regions at the margins. The $Z(\cdot)$ is set to normalize $\sum_i g_i^{(x)}(\boldsymbol{x}) = \sum_j g_j^{(y)}(\boldsymbol{y}) = 1$. The parameters σ control the degree of smoothing of the Voronoi regions.

The gradient of $\log BF'$ with respect to an X-prototype $\boldsymbol{m}_i^{(x)}$ is

$$\nabla_{\boldsymbol{m}_i^{(x)}} \log BF' = \frac{1}{\sigma_{(x)}^2} \sum_{k,i'} (\boldsymbol{x}_k - \boldsymbol{m}_i^{(x)}) g_i^{(x)}(\boldsymbol{x}_k) g_{i'}^{(x)}(\boldsymbol{x}_k) \left(L_i^{(x)}(\boldsymbol{y}_k) - L_{i'}^{(x)}(\boldsymbol{y}_k) \right) ,$$

where

$$L_i^{(x)}(\boldsymbol{y}) \equiv \sum_j \Psi \left(\sum_k g_i^{(x)}(\boldsymbol{x}_k) g_j^{(y)}(\boldsymbol{y}_k) + n^{(d)} \right) g_j^{(y)}(\boldsymbol{y}) - \lambda^{(x)} \Psi \left(\sum_k g_i^{(x)}(\boldsymbol{x}_k) + n^{(x)} \right) ,$$

and for y accordingly. In the gradient, $\Psi(\cdot)$ is the digamma function.

Note that the smoothing is used during optimization only. Results are evaluated with hard clusters and the original BF.

3   Reference Methods

3.1   Information Bottleneck with K-Means (K-IB)

For discrete X and Y, AC-type of clustering translates to grouping the nominal margin values to two sets of clusters that are maximally dependent. The setup is that of the information bottleneck [18, 21].

Our continuous data must be discretized before IB can be applied. One approach is to first quantize the vectorial margins $\boldsymbol{x}$ and $\boldsymbol{y}$ separately by, for instance., K-means, without paying attention to possible dependencies between the two margins. This results in two sets of margin partitions which span a large, sparse contingency table that can be filled with frequencies of training data pairs $(\boldsymbol{x}_k, \boldsymbol{y}_k)$. The number of elementary Voronoi regions is chosen by a validation set, as detailed in Section 4. In the second phase, the large table is compressed by standard IB to the desired size by aggregating the atomic margin clusters. At this stage, joins at the margins are made to explicitly maximize the dependency of margins in the resulting smaller contingency table.

IB algorithms are well described in the literature. We have used the symmetric sequential information bottleneck, described fully in [18]. The algorithm measures dependency of the margins by empirical mutual information, and it is optimized by re-assigning of individual samples (here atomic margin partitions) to clusters until a differential, local version of the cost function does not decrease. Optimization is robust and fast.

The final partitions obtained by the combination of K-means and IB are of a very flexible form, and therefore the method is expected to model the dependencies of the margin variables well – as long as one does not overfit to the data with too many K-means clusters. As a drawback, the final margin clusters will consist of many atomic Voronoi regions, and they are therefore not guaranteed to be especially homogeneous with respect to the original continuous variables ($\boldsymbol{x}$ or $\boldsymbol{y}$). Interpretation of the clusters may then be difficult. Our empirical results support both the good performance of K-IB and the non-localness of the resulting clusters.

3.2 K-Means

The data sets will also be clustered by independent K-means clusterings in both data spaces. Results will represent a kind of a baseline, with no attempt to model dependency.

4 Experiments

4.1 Dependencies Between Gene Expression Patterns and TF Binding Patterns

We sought gene regulation patterns by exploring dependencies between gene expression on the one hand, and measurement data about potential regulatory interactions on the other. The latter was measurements of binding patterns of putative regulatory proteins, transcription factors (TFs), in the promoter regions of the same genes. Associative clustering, K-IB, and K-means were applied to 6185 genes of the common yeast, *Saccharomyces cerevisiae*. The first margin data ($\boldsymbol{x}$) was 300-dimensional, consisting of expressions after 300 knock-out mutations[3] [9]. The second margin data ($\boldsymbol{y}$) consisted of 113-dimensional patterns of binding intensities of TFs [12]. Margin clusters would then ideally be

---

[3] Knocking out means elimination of single genes. In all the data sets, missing values were imputed by gene-wise averages, and variances of dimensions were each separately normalized to unity.

internally homogeneous sets of expressions and TFs, selected to produce combinations (contingency table cells) with unexpectedly high or low numbers of genes.

For AC, the numbers of margin clusters were chosen to produce cross clusters (contingency table cells) with ten data samples on average. During the cross-validation runs margin clusters were initialized by K-means, and in each fold the best of three AC runs was chosen as the final AC clustering. The parameters $\sigma_{(\cdot)}$ were chosen with a validation set (half of the data as a training set, and half of the data as validation set), and based on the previous experiments $\lambda^{(\cdot)} = 1.2$.

Essentially the same test was conducted for the combination of K-means and information bottleneck (K-IB). Now the number of atomic K-means clusters was chosen with a validation set, resulting in 400 clusters for the expression space and 300 clusters for the transcription factor binding space. In the cross-validation runs, the atomic clusters were computed by K-means from three different random initializations, and for each of these a symmetric IB was sequentially optimized [18]. Of the three runs the best clustering (in the sense of IB cost) was chosen.

K-IB and AC tables were compared to each other and to tables obtained by bare margin K-means (10-fold cross validation, tables evaluated by equation 1, paired t-test). For this data, AC outperformed K-IB (p<0.01) and found more dependent clusters. Not surprisingly, significant differences to K-means were found (p<0.01) for both AC and K-IB.

The internal dispersion of the margin clusters was measured for all methods by the sum of intra-cluster component-wise variances. As expected, K-IB clusters are more scattered (Figure 2**A**) in both data spaces. Significant difference was found between AC and K-IB, but not between AC and K-means, nor between the random partitioning and K-IB.

Finally, data from the AC cross clusters was studied more closely to find potential biologically interesting gene concentrations, focusing on contingency table cells with the most unexpectedly high data counts. In two of the cells, for example, genes showed a clear and significant bias towards an over-representation of ribosomal protein coding genes. In the one cell, most of the genes coding for constituent proteins of the cellular ribosomal complex are present. In the other cell several genes coding for the mitochondrial ribosomal subunits are present, and also another set of genes coding for cellular ribosomal protein subunits.

4.2   Of Mice and Men

As a second test, we clustered human-mouse expression profiles of putative orthologs, that is, gene pairs sequence-wise similar enough to be suspected to have the same evolutionary origin (see Figure 3). Ideal margin clusters would be internally homogeneous by expression in at least one species. Cross clusters (cells of the contingency table formed from margin clusters) would then be cross-species clusters and will be optimized to detect cross-species regularities in gene expression.

Gene expression from 46 and 45 cell-lines (tissues) of human and mouse were available, respectively [19]. After removing non-expressed genes (Affymetrix

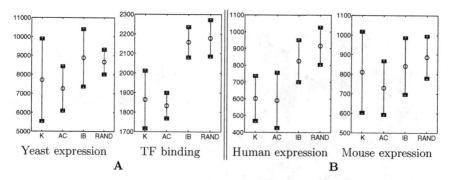

Yeast expression   TF binding   Human expression   Mouse expression

A   B

Fig. 2. Average internal dispersion of expression and TF margin clusters obtained by four methods. 'K' denotes independent K-means for the margins, and is supposed to produce very compact clusters. Clusters in 'RAND' are produced by random assignment and therefore represent an upper limit of dispersion. The AC and K-means clusters are more condensed in the expression and in the TF binding space than the IB clusters. Circles denote the average component-wise intra-cluster variances in left-out data of cross-validation folds (n=10), and squares show the approximate 99 percent confidence interval for the means over the cross validation folds. **A**: Yeast expression and TF binding. The differences between neither AC and K-means, nor between IB and RAND are statistically significant (p>0.1, 10-fold cross validation, paired t-test), but the difference between IB and AC is significant for both expression and TF binding (p<0.01). **B**: Homologous genes of human and mouse. The AC and K-means clusters seem to be more condensed in human and in mouse expression space than the IB or RAND clusters (p<0.05; paired t-test). Differences between AC and K-means or between IB and RAND are not statistically significant (p>0.1)

AD<200), 4499 putative orthologs from the the HomoloGene [15] data base were available. After experiments analogous to those of Section 4.1, we found the human-mouse orthologs of left-out data to be significantly dependent according to both K-IB and AC (10-fold cross validation against K-means, paired t-test, p<0.001). Differences between AC and K-IB were not very clear. AC clusters, however, were probably more condensed (p<0.05; Fig. 2**B**) while tables obtained by K-IB were more dependent (p<0.02).

To illustrate the use of AC for finding interesting relationships, that is, groups of genes with functional similarity, we picked some cross clusters with significant deviation from the null hypothesis of independent margin clusters (see also Figure 3).

In the first example AC found a gene pair with a rare and potentially interesting functional relationship. This cell had unexpectedly few genes (p<0.01), in fact only a single gene pair (LocusIDs 1808 and 12934). Average margin profiles of the cluster suggested activity in the human brain co-occurring with no activity in the mouse at all. Combining the margin profile information and the fact that only one this kind of gene exists in the contingency table, we may deduce that homologues which are active in human brain but totally silent in the mouse are very rare. Examples of such gene pairs may highlight interesting functional

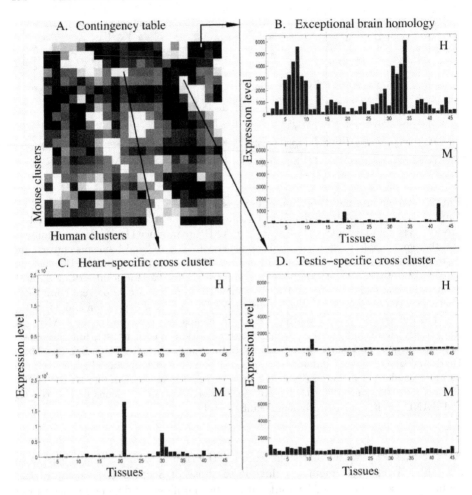

Fig. 3. A The contingency table from associative clustering of orthologous human-mouse gene pairs (orthologous genes are supposed or known to have a common evolutionary ancestor gene). *White cross clusters* contain an unexpectedly high number of genes compared to the margin-based expectation. *Black cross clusters* contain examples of exceptional gene pairs. **B** An example of an interesting outlier homology from a black cross cluster: the gene is highly active in most human tissues but is hardly expressed at all in mouse. The first 21 tissues are common for both species in B, C and D. **C** Cluster-wide average profiles reveal activity in heart tissue, and additional strong activity in mouse skeletal muscle. Measuring human skeletal muscle would reveal either a more complete homology or a species difference. **D** A densely populated cross cluster of testis-specific genes

differences between the species. Indeed, the function of the gene was found to be related to embryo-stage brains *and* later brain activity only in humans (see Figure 3B).

In another example, a cross cluster contained unexpectedly many genes (p<0.01), most of them testis-specific (see Figure 3D). Due to their tissue specificity and importance for reproduction, they may have sustained their function during evolution.

5   Discussion

We have presented a novel method, associative clustering (AC), for clustering continuous paired data. It maximizes a Bayes factor between two sets of clusters. AC was found to perform better or equally well than a combination of K-means and information bottleneck (IB), and better than standard K-means. AC was also capable of extracting biologically interesting structure from paired gene expression data sets.

Maximization of the suggested Bayes factor is asymptotically equivalent to maximization of mutual information, and could therefore be seen as a dependency criterion alternative to empirical mutual information. It additionally gives information bottleneck-type dependency modeling a new justification that is clearly different from joint distribution models but still rigorously probabilistic. The Bayes factor could probably replace mutual informaton in the Information-Theoretic Co-Clustering Algorithm [4] as well.

The work could possibly be extended towards a compromise between strict dependency modeling and a model of the joint density (as has been done for one-sided clustering, [10]). Then the margins could be estimated in part from non-paired data. This would be analogous to "semisupervised learning" from partially labeled data (see e.g. [20]), the labels having been replaced by samples of co-occurring paired data.

Acknowledgments. This work has been supported by the Academy of Finland, decisions #79017 and #207467. We thank Jaakko Peltonen for the code for sequential IB, and Juha Knuuttila and Christophe Roos for help with biological interpretation of the results.

References

1. Bazaraa, M.S., Sherali, H.D., Shetty, C.M.: Nonlinear Programming: Theory and Algorithms (1993). Wiley, New York
2. Blei, D., Ng, A.Y., Jordan, M.I.: Latent Dirichlet allocation. J. Machine Learning Res. **3** (2003) 993–1022
3. Buntine, W.: Variational extensions to EM and multinomial PCA. In: Elomaa, T., Mannila, H., Toivonen, H. (eds.): Proc. of the ECML'02, Lecture Notes in Artificial Intelligence, 2430 (2002). Springer, Berlin, pp. 23–34
4. Dhillon, I.S., Mallela, S., Kumar, R.: A divisive information-theoretic feature clustering algorithm for text classification. J. Machine Learning Res. **3** (2003) 1265–1287
5. Friedman, N., Mosenzon, O., Slonim, N., Tishby, N.: Multivariate information bottleneck. In: Proc. of UAI'01, The 17th Conference on Uncertainty in Artificial Intelligence (2001). Morgan Kaufmann Publishers, San Francisco, CA, pp. 152–161

6. Good, I.J.: On the application of symmetric Dirichlet distributions and their mixtures to contingency tables. Annals of Statistics, **4** (1976) 1159–1189
7. Hastie, T., Tibshirani, R.: Discriminant analysis by Gaussian mixtures. J. of the R. Stat. Soc. B **58** (1996) 155–176
8. Hofmann, T.: Unsupervised learning by probabilistic latent semantic analysis. Machine Learning **42** (2001) 177–196
9. Hughes, T.R., Marton, M.J., Jones, A.R., Roberts, C.J., Stoughton, R., Armour, C.D., Bennett, H.A., Coffrey, E., Dai, H., He, Y.D., Kidd, M.J., King, A.M., Meyer, M.R., Slade, D., Lum, P.Y., Stepaniants, S.B., Shoemaker, D.D., Gachotte, D., Chakraburtty, K., Simon, J., Bard, M., Friend, S.H.: Functional discovery via a compendium of expression profiles. Cell **102** (2000) 109–126
10. Kaski, S., Sinkkonen, J., and Klami, A.: Regularized discriminative clustering. In: Molina, C., Adali, T., Larsen, J., van Hulle, M., Douglas, S., Rouat, J. (eds.): Neural Networks for Signal Processing XIII (2003). IEEE, New York, NY, pp. 289–298
11. Kay, J.: Feature discovery under contextual supervision using mutual information. In: Proc. of IJCNN'92, International Joint Conference on Neural Networks (1992). IEEE, Piscataway, NJ, pp. 79–84
12. Lee, T.I., Rinaldi, N.J., Robert, F., Odom, D.T., Bar-Joseph, Z., Gerber, G.K., Hannett, N.M., Harbison, C.T., Tomphson, C.M., Simon, I., Zeitlinger, J., Jennings, E.G., Murray, H.L., Gordon, D.B., Ren, B., Wyrick, J.J., Tagne, J.-B., Volkert, T.L., Fraenkel, E., Gifford, D.K., Young, R.A.: Transcriptional regulatory networks in saccharomyces cerevisiae. Science **298** (2002) 799–804
13. Miller, D.J., Uyar, H.S.: A mixture of experts classifier with learning based on both labelled and unlabelled data. In: Mozer. M, Jordan, M., Petsche, T. (eds.): Advances in Neural Information Processing Systems, 9 (1997). MIT Press, Cambridge, MA, pp. 571–577
14. Peltonen, J., Sinkkonen, J., and Kaski, S.. Sequential information bottleneck for finite data. In: Proc. of the International Conference on Machine Learning (to appear)
15. Pruitt, K.D., Maglott, D.R.: RefSeq and LocusLink: NCBI gene-centered resources. Nucleic Acids Research **29** (2001) 137–141
16. Sinkkonen, J. and Kaski, S.: Clustering based on conditional distributions in an auxiliary space. Neural Computation **14** (2002) 217–239
17. Sinkkonen, J., Kaski, S., and Nikkilä, J.: Discriminative clustering: Optimal contingency tables by learning metrics. In Elomaa, T., Mannila, H., Toivonen, H. (eds.): Proc. of the ECML'02, 13th European Conference on Machine Learning (2002). Springer, Berlin, pp. 418–430
18. Slonim, N.: The information bottleneck: theory and applications (2002). PhD thesis, Hebrew University, Jerusalem
19. Su, A.I., Cooke, M.P., Ching, K.A., Hakak, Y., Walker, J.R., Wiltshire, T., Orth, A.P., Vega, R.G., Sapinoso, L.M., Moqrich, A., Patapoutian, A., Hampton, G.M., Schultz, P.G., and Hogenesch, J.B.: Large-scale analysis of the human and mouse transcriptomes. PNAS **99** (2002) 4465–4470
20. Szummer, M. and Jaakkola, T.: Kernel expansions with unlabeled examples. In: Leen, T, Dietterich, T., Tresp, V. (eds.): Advances in Neural Information Processing Systems, 13 (2001). MIT Press, Cambridge, MA, pp. 626–632
21. Tishby, N., Pereira, F.C., Bialek, W.: The information bottleneck method. In: Hajek, B. and Sreenivas, R.S. (eds.): Proc. of The 37th Annual Allerton Conference on Communication, Control, and Computing (1999). University of Illinois, Urbana, Illinois, pp. 368–377

Learning to Fly Simple and Robust

Dorian Šuc[1], Ivan Bratko[1], and Claude Sammut[2]

[1] Faculty of Computer and Information Science, University of Ljubljana,
Tržaška 25, 1000 Ljubljana, Slovenia
{dorian.suc,ivan.bratko}@fri.uni-lj.si
[2] School of Computer Science and Engineering, University of New South Wales,
Sydney, Australia
claude@cse.unsw.edu.au

Abstract. We report on new experiments with machine learning in the reconstruction of human sub-cognitive skill. The particular problem considered is to generate a clone of a human pilot performing a flying task on a simulated aircraft. The work presented here uses the human behaviour to create constraints for a search process that results in a controller – pilot's clone. Experiments in this paper indicate that this approach, called "indirect controllers", results in pilot clones that are, in comparison with those obtained with traditional "direct controllers", simpler, more robust and easier to understand. An important feature of indirect controllers in this paper is the use of qualitative constraints.

1 Introduction

Reconstructing sub-cognitive human skills from human experts' behavioural traces is one of the most fascinating applications of machine learning, also known as behavioural cloning. Learning to fly a fixed-wing aircraft in a flight simulator has become a benchmark for behavioural cloning [1, 2]. As well as providing complex control problems, flying also requires learning different kinds of manoeuvres for different flight stages and combining these manoeuvres to create a complete flight plan.

Early experiments in behavioural cloning adopted a "situation-action" approach in which control rules map the current state of the world directly into control actions [1, 2]. While these experiments were successful in constructing auto-pilots that could complete a flight, the situation-action approach had several problems. The control rules were not understandable nor were they very robust to noise and variations in the flight plan.

Subsequently, more "goal-directed" approaches have been employed [3, 4], giving greater readability and robustness. These methods first learn goal settings for different stages in a flight and then learn control rules to achieve those settings. The controllers are still directly derived from the human behaviour. In contrast, the work presented here uses the human behaviour to create constraints for a search process that results in the controller. We show in this paper that applying this approach, called "indirect controllers" [5], results in pilot clones that are comparatively much simpler, more robust and easier to understand than

J.-F. Boulicaut et al. (Eds.): ECML 2004, LNAI 3201, pp. 407–418, 2004.
© Springer-Verlag Berlin Heidelberg 2004

direct controllers. An important feature of indirect controllers in this paper is the use of qualitative constraints.

In the sequel we first outline the idea of indirect controllers that employ qualitative constraints. We then present the details of the flying task and experiments in extracting flying skills, and analyse the resulting clones with respect to their understandability and performance.

2 Indirect Controllers and Qualitative Strategies

2.1 Learning Direct and Indirect Controllers

The following is the usual procedure of applying Machine Learning to recover a control strategy from example execution traces. A continuous trace is sampled so that we have a sequence of pairs $(State_i, Action_i)$ ordered according to time. $State_i$ is the state of the system at time i, and $Action_i$ is the operator's action performed at time i. Then, usually, the sequence of these pairs is viewed as a *set* of examples, thereby ignoring the time order. The state is a vector of state variables: $State = (x_1, x_2, ...)$. A standard ML method is applied to induce the mapping from states to actions, whereby the state variables $x_1, x_2, ...$ correspond to attributes, and the actions are the class values. In continuous domains, both the state variables and the class are real-valued, therefore a numerical learning method, such as regression tree learning is appropriate for this. The result of learning, using this formulation of the learning problem, is a controller in the form of a function from system states to actions:

$$Action = f(State) = f((x_1, x_2, ...))$$

This controller maps the system's current state into an action directly, without any intermediate, auxiliary result. Therefore such controllers will be called *direct controllers*, to be distinguished from "indirect" controllers used in this paper.

We say that a controller is "indirect" if it does not compute the next action directly from the current system's state, but uses in addition to the state some additional information. Typical such additional information is a sub-goal to be attained before attaining the final goal. One idea to obtain such additional information, appropriate for handling dense sub-goals, is to generalise the operator's trajectory [5,6]. Such a generalised trajectory can be viewed as defining a continuously changing sub-goal.

Subgoals or generalised trajectories are not sufficient to define a controller. A model of the system's dynamics is also required. Therefore, in addition to inducing subgoals or a generalised trajectory, this approach also requires the learning of approximate system's dynamics, that is a model of the controlled system. The next action is then computed "indirectly", targeting the sub-goals as follows: (1) compute the desired next state on the generalised trajectory (i.e. next sub-goal), and (2) determine an action that brings the system closer to the desired next state. This amounts to trying to follow a generalised trajectory as follows. The next action is determined indirectly as: using the model of the system's dynamics, and the generalised trajectory, find the action that will minimise the difference between the generalised trajectory and the state resulting from this action. So an indirect controller computes actions as:

$$Action = \arg\min_A(diff(model(State, A), Trajectory))$$

The point of indirect controllers is that the problem of behavioural cloning is decomposed into two learning problems: (1) learning trajectory, and (2) learning dynamics. It has been shown experimentally that this decomposition may result in much better performance than the induction of direct controllers [5, 6]. Related ideas of using subgoals in behavioural cloning in aeroplane flying were also discussed by Bain and Sammut [3].

2.2   Learning Qualitative Strategies

In earlier experiments [7, 6], we found that *qualitative* descriptions of generalised trajectories are particularly useful. We will refer to them as *qualitative generalised trajectories*. They are described in terms of monotonic qualitative constraints regularly used in the field of qualitative reasoning. For example, the constraint $Y = M^+(X)$ says that Y monotonically increases with X: if X increases then Y also increases. Analogously, $Y = M^-(X)$ says that Y monotonically decreases with X. These constraints can have multiple arguments. For example, $Z = M^{+,-}(X, Y)$ means that Z is monotonically increasing in X and decreasing in Y. If both X and Y increase then Z may increase, decrease, or stay unchanged.

Monotonicity constraints can be combined into if-then rules to express piecewise monotonic functional relationships. For example: *if $X < 0$ then $Y = M^-(X)$ else $Y = M^+(X)$* Nested if-then expressions can be represented as trees, called *qualitative trees* [7, 8]. Qualitative trees are similar to regression trees [9]. Both regression and qualitative trees describe how a numerical variable (class variable) depends on other (possibly numerical) variables (attributes). The difference between the two types of trees only occurs in the leaves. A leaf of a regression tree tells how the class variable numerically depends on the attributes within the scope of the leaf. On the other hand, a leaf in a qualitative tree only specifies the relation between the class and the attributes qualitatively, in terms of monotonic qualitative constraints.

In this paper we applied the learning of indirect controllers to the problem of reconstructing pilots' skills when flying an aircraft. Generalised trajectories were stated in terms of qualitative trees. To induce qualitative generalised trajectories from examples of pilots' flights, we used program QUIN [7, 8]. QUIN (Qualitative Induction) is a learning program that induces qualitative trees from numerical data. QUIN detects monotonic qualitative constraints that hold "sufficiently well" in the data. Roughly, QUIN employs a criterion of "qualitative fit" between a qualitative tree and the learning examples. In the spirit of the MDL principle, QUIN searches for "small" qualitative trees that fit the learning data well. These mechanisms also make QUIN relatively robust with respect to noisy data.

3   Learning to Fly

The flight simulator used in the following experiments is of a Pilatus two-seat turboprop PC-9 aerobatic training aircraft. The dynamic model was provided to us by the Aeronautical and Maritime Research Laboratory of the Australian Defence Science and Technology Organisation. The model was derived from wind-tunnel testing and data collection from an actual aircraft.

3.1   Flying an Aircraft

The main controls for a fixed-wing aircraft are: the elevator that controls pitching the nose up or down, the ailerons that control rolling of the aircraft, the rudder that controls the yawing of the nose left or right, the throttle controlling the thrust, and the flaps that increase lift when they are extended. Any change in aircraft attitude can be expressed in terms of the motion about three aircraft axes:

- *pitch* is the motion about the lateral axis;
- *roll* is the motion about the longitudinal axis (bank);
- *yaw* is the motion about the normal axis.

When the aircraft is in approximately level flight, these correspond respectively to lift the nose up or down, banking the aircraft and changing compass heading. *Roll* is mainly controlled by the ailerons. *Pitch* is mainly controlled by the elevator. *Yaw* is controlled by rudder and is affected by *roll*.

In our experiments, the control variables were: *flaps* and landing *gear*, *throttle* controlling the *airspeed*, stick x and y position ($stick_x$ and $stick_y$) controlling ailerons and elevators. As in previous experiments in learning to fly, we did not use the rudder.

Controlling the landing gear is very simple: raise the gear after take-off and lower the gear before landing. This rule is easily learned from any successful execution trace and will be omitted in the rest of the paper.

3.2   The Learning Task

The learning task is to do a standard left-hand circuit (see Figure 1) as described in the flying training manual [10]. The circuit consists of take-off, climb to a specified height, four left turns, descent to the runway and landing. The requirement to do some of the turns while climbing or descending makes the task more difficult. The success of the landing is score according to the descent rate, distance from the centre line of the runway and angle to the centre line. Since the visual field in the simulator is quite sparse and therefore provides few useful landmarks, we provided "windows in the sky" to help guide the pilot. These are squares whose centre marks the desired way point. When executing the task, pilots were supposed to fly through these windows. The side of each window is 200 feet (61m) in length[1]. This is intended to indicate a 100 ft tolerance when

---

[1] All units in the simulator are imperial since that is standard in commercial flight

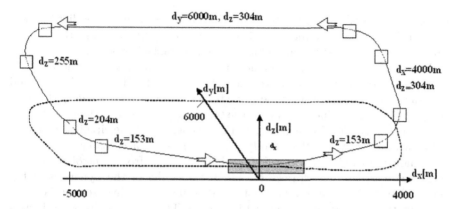

Fig. 1. The learning task: pilots were required to do the standard left-hand circuit, marked with 8 "windows". d_x and d_y denote the x and y distance from the runway and d_z denotes the altitude above the runway.

reaching a way point or goal. Each window (and the runway) defines the current goal for the pilot or the clone.

Pilots were considered to have flown successfully if they flew through all eight windows and land successfully. Successful landing requires low airspeed, near zero roll and pitch and landing gear down when the aircraft touches the runway.

4   Experiments

During a pilot's flight, the values of variables d_x, d_y, d_z, *roll*, *pitch*, *yaw*, *airspeed*, e_g, a_g, *stick$_x$*, *stick$_y$*, *throttle*, *flaps* were recorded. Here d_x, d_y and d_z stand for the distances in the three directions (in feet) from the starting position on the runway. The velocities of pitch, roll and yaw were not available. The attributes *goal elevation* e_g and *goal azimuth* a_g give the relative angles of the current goal window with respect to the current aircraft position. The goal elevation e_g is the difference between the current pitch of the goal window and the pitch to the aircraft. The goal azimuth a_g is the difference between the current direction of the goal window and the direction of the aircraft.

To make the clones independent of the runway/window positions we avoid using the variables d_x, d_y, d_z and *yaw*. However, controlling the airspeed of the aircraft requires some data about the aircraft position or the distance from the runway. For this reason, variables d_x, d_y, d_z were used while learning the control rule for airspeed, as will become clear later. Another representation that could be used is to convert absolute distances to distances relative to the target. This alternative is yet to be explored.

Flying an aircraft requires control rules for stick position (*stick$_x$* and *stick$_y$*), *throttle* and *flaps*. These rules are learned from successful execution traces. In our experiments, we used traces from three pilots. We learned the clones as indirect controllers [5, 7]. That is, we separately learned the generalized trajectory and the system dynamics model. We used the qualitative induction system QUIN to learn qualitative constraints on the generalized trajectory.

When estimating the performance of the clones we consider the clone to have completed the task *completely* if it flies through all eight windows and lands successfully. We consider the clone to perform the task *partially*, if it flies through at least five windows, misses the other windows by less than 100 ft. and lands successfully. Considering the fact that the length of the circuit is 9,000 ft., missing a window by less than 100 ft. is still considered acceptable.

To induce an indirect controller, we have to learn from control traces two things: (a) a generalised trajectory, and (b) a model of the dynamics of the controlled system (the aircraft). First, we describe in the next section how the approximate system dynamics model is learned. Then we describe experiments in learning qualitative constraints on the generalized trajectory, i.e. learning the qualitative strategy. Finally, we transform the learned qualitative strategies into quantitative control rules that can be applied to controlling the aircraft.

5   Learning Dynamics

First we used locally weighted regression (LWR) [11] to learn the approximate system dynamics model. The prediction errors of the induced locally linear models were sufficiently small, so that these models of system's dynamics in combination with the generalized trajectory were easily sufficient to control the aircraft.

We also experimented with much simpler, global linear models of the system's dynamics. An example of such a global linear model of the system's dynamics, induced from three example flights by linear regression with $\Delta t = 1s$, is:

$$r(t+\Delta) = 0.994\,r(t) - 0.003\,v(t) + 2.773\,s_x(t) + 0.155$$
$$p(t+\Delta) = 0.958\,p(t) - 0.029\,v(t) + 0.775\,s_y(t) - 0.040f(t) + 0.585 \qquad (1)$$
$$v(t+\Delta) = 0.071\,p(t) + 0.964\,v(t) + 1.803\,t(t) - 0.022f(t) + 2.109$$

Here r, p and v denote roll, pitch and airspeed, s_x and s_y the stick x and y position, f flaps and t throttle. The mean absolute errors of this linear model on a different flight trace are respectively (roll, pitch, airspeed) 0.429, 0.376, 0.378. Note that airspeed typically varies between 0 and 110 and roll and pitch are measured in degrees.

Although such a simple linear model is not perfect, we found that it is easily sufficient, in combination with a generalised trajectory, to control the system. Due to the simplicity and efficiency of the global linear model in comparison with locally linear models near the current state, we decided to use this linear model instead of LWR in the rest of our experiments. As found in our earlier work [5, 6], indirect controllers are in general not significantly affected by errors in the system's dynamics model as long as the model is qualitatively correct.

6   Learning Indirect Aircraft Controllers

To control the system with an indirect controller using a generalized trajectory, the generalized trajectory is combined with the learned dynamics model to constrain each of the control variables. An important criterion, when inducing the generalized trajectory, is comprehensibility. For example, if the generalized trajectory is induced through tree learning, the class values should be state variables that are intuitive to human thinking about controlling the particular dynamic system.

We decided to learn constraints on the aircraft's *roll*, *pitch*, *airspeed* and *flaps* with respect to the other variables. Constraints on these four variables will form the generalized trajectory. Such a trajectory, expressed in symbolic form, is usually easy to understand, as will be illustrated later. The constraints in the generalised trajectory determine the desired *roll*, *pitch*, *airspeed* and *flaps* for each aircraft position. Once the desired values of these four variables are known, it is possible to determine the control actions by the principle of indirect controllers using the model of the aircraft's dynamics.

In the remainder of this section, we describe experiments in learning generalized trajectories from example flights, and using these strategies in indirect controllers of the aircraft.

6.1   Learning Generalised Trajectories

In our case, a generalised trajectory consists of constraints on flaps, airspeed, roll and pitch. Here we describe the induction of these constraints from example execution traces. Constraints on each of the four "target" variables are expressed in terms of other state variables of the aircraft. We look at each target variable in turn, beginning with flaps.

Learning constraints on flaps. The flaps setting is a discrete variable with only three possible values, so it is appropriate to induce a decision tree that determines the flaps value from other state variables. An example of such a decision tree induced from one of the pilots' traces is:

$$airspeed \leq 84.75$$
$$| \quad airspeed \leq 62.35 : flaps = f_{land} \quad \{\text{flying slow, nose down}\}$$
$$| \quad airspeed > 62.35 : flaps = f_{normal} \quad \{\text{nose up}\} \tag{2}$$
$$airspeed > 84.75 : flaps = f_{off} \quad \{\text{flying fast, nose up}\}$$

This rule can be interpreted as follows. Extending the flaps increases the surface of the wing and hence provides greater lift. The aircraft used in our experiments has the following three settings for the flaps: f_{land}=40, f_{normal}=20 and f_{off}=0. When flaps are extended (f_{land}), less speed is required to achieve a positive climb rate. In our control traces, experienced pilots usually used f_{normal} or f_{land} during take off, f_{off} when airspeed was high and f_{land} during the landing. Correspondingly the decision trees for flaps usually had only three leaves. Note that the induced decision tree above can be used for control directly, without a model of the system's dynamics.

Learning constraints on airspeed. In the traces we experimented with, controlling the airspeed is qualitatively quite simple: increase it to take-off, hold it constant during the flight and decrease it when landing. A good pilot uses the throttle to control the aircraft's climb and descent rates during a flight. Our control strategy is relatively naive in its lack of fine control of the throttle. However, it does closely emulate the actions of our pilots who tended to leave the throttle setting more or less constant. In the sequel we present performance results with rules obtained from regression tree learning, applying rather severe pruning of trees that resulted in trees with 6 – 10 leaves. These trees have small training error, are easy to understand and usually control the airspeed adequately. However, they have limited generality as they define functions of the form: $airspeed = f(d_x, d_y, d_z)$. The attributes d_x, d_y, d_z are relative to the runway position, so the induced trees may not be appropriate for other flight plans.

Learning qualitative constraints on roll and pitch. We found experimentally, that flaps and airspeed can be handled easily by decision or regression tree learning. But pitch and roll are not so easily susceptible to regression trees. Sometimes, successful regression trees were more complex (up to 20 nodes), harder to interpret and not as effective in control. So it is the pitch and roll where learning qualitative constraints really mattered.

A very elegant qualitative strategy was learned from some of the traces:

$$roll = M^-(a_g)$$
$$pitch = M^-(e_g)$$

(3)

These two rules are quite intuitive and give a simple strategy to control pitch and roll by adjustment of the stick position. To explain this strategy, we first describe how roll and pitch affect the motion of the aircraft. Flying straight-and-level requires maintaining a constant heading and altitude. This can be achieved by keeping zero roll and near-zero pitch p_0. The exact pitch value p_0 that maintains the current aircraft height depends also on the airspeed and flaps. Roll and pitch angles are measured in the clockwise direction, whereas goal elevation and goal azimuth are measured in the standard anti-clockwise direction. To reach the goal with positive goal elevation and positive goal azimuth, the aircraft should climb and turn to the left. This is achieved by negative roll and negative ($< p_0$) pitch.

Now we explain how the qualitative strategy (rules 3) achieves the current goal. Consider straight-and-level flight, where the aircraft approaches the goal with positive goal azimuth and positive goal elevation. Since the aircraft's distance to the goal is decreasing, goal azimuth and goal elevation angles are increasing. The induced rules decrease roll and pitch, producing a left-turn and climb. That is exactly what is needed to achieve the goal. If the turn (climb) was too strong, goal azimuth (elevation) becomes negative and is decreasing (since the aircraft is approaching the goal). Now the induced rules increase roll (pitch) producing a right-turn (descent) to the goal. In this way, the induced rules tend to achieve zero goal azimuth and goal elevation, causing the aircraft to fly straight to the goal. The induced rules also command a tighter turn or steeper climb using a larger absolute roll or pitch, when the absolute goal azimuth or elevation is larger.

The qualitative strategy learned from a more experienced pilot is correspondingly more elaborate. Unlike a beginner, he also used flaps. This is reflected in the rule induced for pitch:

$$roll = M^-(a_g)$$
$$pitch = M^{-,+}(e_g, flaps)$$

(4)

When controlling the pitch to obtain the goal elevation, the flaps setting is also considered. The rule states that if the flaps setting is higher ($f_{land} = 40$, flaps extended for the landing), the pitch should be larger (nose further down). This actually describes the property of the flaps: extended flaps requires the stick to be further forward to achieve the same goal elevation. If flaps are off ($f_{off} = 0$), the wings provide less lift, requiring the stick to be pulled back further (assuming constant thrust).

6.2   Transforming Qualitative Strategy into Quantitative Strategy

A qualitative control strategy only imposes qualitative constraints on "target" variables. These are directly useful for explanation, but they cannot be immediately applied for control. First, qualitative constraints have to be transformed into quantitative functions.

The induced qualitative constraints (rules 4) were transformed into quantitative functions as follows. Let $roll$ denote a function $[-a_g^{mx}, a_g^{mx}] \mapsto [-roll^{mx}, roll^{mx}]$ and $pitch$ denote a function $[-e_g^{mx}, e_g^{mx}] \times [f_{off}, f_{land}] \mapsto [-pitch^{mx}, pitch^{mx}]$ satisfying the induced qualitative constraints given by rule 4. The superscripts mx indicate the extreme values of the corresponding variables. In this transformation, we used simple domain knowledge to define additional constraints on $roll$ and $pitch$:

- roll is 0 when goal azimuth is 0 ($roll(0) = 0$).
- pitch is 0 when goal elevation is 0 and flaps are normal ($pitch(0, f_{norm}) = 0$).
- flaps affect pitch for a small value f_{dif} ($|pitch(e_g, f_{land}) - pitch(e_g, f_{off})| = f_{dif}$, $0 \leq f_{dif} \leq 6deg$).
- maxima of corresponding variables used for $roll^{mx}$, $pitch^{mx}$, a_g^{mx} and e_g^{mx}.

Note that this domain knowledge is not perfect and is just a naive commonsense knowledge about flying an aircraft. For example, to maintain zero goal elevation with normal flaps, a near zero pitch p_0 is required. Its exact value depends also on the airspeed. Since the qualitative strategy is goal-directed, it is able to reduce the errors resulting from imperfect domain knowledge or imperfect model of system dynamics.

We used the procedure described in [7] to randomly generate the functions for $roll$ and $pitch$ so that the resulting randomly obtained functions satisfied the corresponding qualitative constraints stated above. We used the grid $C = 8$ and random $0 \leq f_{dif} \leq 6$. Out of 50 randomly generated functions, 27 (54 %) succeeded to fly completely or partially (the criteria of success as defined earlier). Figure 2 shows one such clone. As observed in our experiments in other

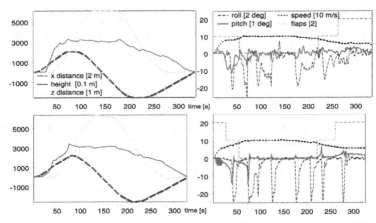

Fig. 2. Trace of the operator and trace of its clone. The upper two graphs show how the operator is flying. The lower graphs show a trace of a clone that controls roll and pitch according to the induced qualitative strategy (rule 4), and speed and flaps according to the induced trees. Eight negative local maxima of roll correspond to the eight windows where left-turn is required. Negative local maxima of pitch correspond to climbs (the first and second window) and positive local maxima to descent.

domains ([7, 6], for example) success of the clones could be improved by using more domain knowledge. In the flight domain, such additional domain knowledge could be the requirement that roll and pitch are small for small goal azimuth and goal elevation.

Note that we here used randomly generated functions satisfying induced qualitative constraints and simple domain knowledge. An alternative, described in [12], would be to use control traces to find a quantitative strategy that fits the control traces numerically and is consistent with the qualitative constraints.

6.3   Robustness of the Qualitative Strategy

To evaluate the robustness of the clones we performed two sets of experiments in which we tested:

- *the clone's robustness against the turbulence:* clones were tested in the simulator with turbulence added.
- *the clone's ability to complete different missions:* clones were tested with a modified flight plan that includes a right climbing turn, which is a maneuver not seen in the execution traces. The task also requires a sharper left-turn than any in the original flight plan.

We tested ten different clones that scored complete success on the original task. They control roll and pitch according to the induced qualitative strategy (rule 4) and speed and flaps according to the induced trees. Note that in this experiment, clones learned from traces of the original flight plan with no turbulence were required to deal with turbulence and a modified flight plan.

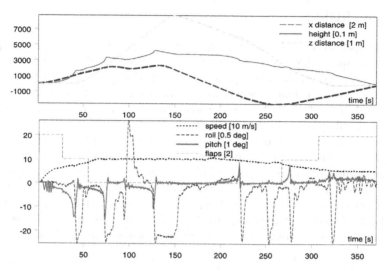

Fig. 3. Trace of a clone that does the modified flight task with strong turbulence. Positive maxima of roll corresponds to right-turn after third window. Oscillations in roll and pitch correspond to clone's adjustments to the turbulence. Note that this is the same clone as clone in Figure 2.

The results indicate good robustness of our clones in both respects. With turbulence, all the clones completed the task entirely or partially. Eight of ten clones also completed the modified plan entirely or partially. We obtained similar results, when the clones were tested with both modified flight plan and turbulence. Figure 3 shows a flight by a clone that carries out the modified task under turbulence.

6.4   Flying Simply

Here we give an example of a very simple controller that is consistent with the induced qualitative rules $roll = M^{-,+}(a_g, flaps)$ and $pitch = M^{-}(e_g)$. It uses linear quantitative rules:

$$
\begin{aligned}
roll &= -1.8\,a_g \\
pitch &= -1.0\,e_g + 0.02\,(flaps - f_{normal})
\end{aligned}
\tag{5}
$$

To compute the actions s_x and s_y aiming to achieve the desired roll and pitch linear dynamics (Eq. 1) is used. Flaps are controlled by the rule 2 and the airspeed by the induced regression tree with six leaves. Such a controller completes the original task, can perform the modified plan (and also other tasks) and is robust to turbulence. Note that the controller is also robust with respect to (reasonable) changes in coefficients in equations 5. For example, rules $roll = -3\,a_g$ and $pitch = -3.0\,e_g + 0.03\,(flaps - f_{normal})$ also do well.

7   Conclusions

In this paper we experimented in the well-known domain of cloning air pilots' skills. We applied the approach of inducing from pilots' performance data *indirect controllers* using qualitative representations of the generalised trajectories. In comparison with the more traditional learning of direct controllers in this domain on similar flying tasks, our results show that the indirect controller approach leads to simpler and more robust clones.

Two limitations of the work described in this paper that belong to future work are: (1) Human expert intervention was required in determining "target" variables featuring in constraints defining the generalised trajectory; it is a challenging problem to determine these variables automatically; (2) our induced controllers are rather task-dependent, in particular the rule for *airspeed* corresponds closely to the flight plan of the example flying task; in future experiments this should be generalised to an arbitrary specification of a flight plan.

Acknowledgements

The work reported in this paper was partially supported by the Slovenian Ministry of Education, Science and Sport. We thank the Aeronautical and Maritime Research Laboratory for providing the PC-9 model.

References

1. Sammut, C., Hurst, S., Kedzier, D., Michie, D.: Learning to fly. In: *Proc. 9th International Workshop on Machine Learning*, Morgan Kaufmann (1992) 385–393
2. Camacho, R.: Using machine learning to extract models of human control skill. In: *Proceedings of AIT'95. (1995)* Brno, Czech Republic
3. Bain, M., Sammut, C.: A framework for behavioural cloning. In: *Machine Intelligence 15*, Oxford University Press (1999) 103–129
4. Isaac, A., Sammut, C.: Goal-directed learning to fly. In: *Machine Learning, Proc. 20th International Conference (ICML 2003)*, AAAI Press (2003) 258–265
5. Šuc, D., Bratko, I.: Problem decomposition for behavioural cloning. In: *Proc. of the 11th European Conference on Machine Learning*, Springer (2000) 382–391
6. Šuc, D., Bratko, I.: Symbolic and qualitative reconstruction of control skill. *Electronic Transactions on Artificial Intelligence, Section B* **3** (1999) 1–22
7. Šuc, D.: *Machine Reconstruction of Human Control Strategies*. Frontiers in Artificial Intelligence and Applications, volume 99. IOS Press, Amsterdam, (2003)
8. Šuc, D., Bratko, I.: Induction of qualitative trees. In: *Proc. of the 12th European Conference on Machine Learning*, Springer (2001) 442–453
9. Breiman, L., Friedman, J., Olshen, R., Stone, C.: *Classification and Regression Trees*. Wadsworth, Belmont, California (1984)
10. Thom, T.: *The Air Pilot's Manual. 7 edn.* Air Pilot Publishing Ltd (2003)
11. Atkeson, C., Moore, A., Schaal, S.: Locally weighted learning. *Artificial Intelligence Review* **11** (1997) 11–73
12. Šuc, D., Vladušič, D., Bratko, I.: Qualitatively faithful quantitative prediction. *Artificial Intelligence* (2004), Accepted for publication.

Bayesian Network Methods for Traffic Flow Forecasting with Incomplete Data

Shiliang Sun[1], Changshui Zhang[1], Guoqiang Yu[1], Naijiang Lu[2], and Fei Xiao[2]

[1] State Key Laboratory of Intelligent Technology and Systems,
Department of Automation, Tsinghua University, Beijing, China, 100084
`sunsl02@mails.tsinghua.edu.cn`
`zcs@mail.tsinghua.edu.cn`, `ygq01@mails.tsinghua.edu.cn`
[2] Shanghai Cogent Biometrics Identification Technology Co. Ltd., China
`{lunj,xiaof}@cbitech.com`

Abstract. Traffic flow forecasting is an important issue in the field of Intelligent Transportation Systems. Due to practical limitations, traffic flows recorded can be partially missing or unavailable. In this case few methods can deal with forecasting successfully. In this paper two methods based on the concept of Bayesian networks are originally proposed to cope with this matter. A Bayesian network model and a two-step Bayesian network model are constructed respectively to describe the causal relationship among traffic flows, and then the joint probability distribution between the cause and effect nodes with its dimension reduced by Principal Component Analysis is approximated through a Gaussian Mixture Model. The parameters of the Gaussian Mixture Model are learned through the Competitive EM algorithm. Experiments show that the proposed Bayesian network methods are applicable and effective for traffic flow forecasting with incomplete data.

1 Introduction

In recent years, Intelligent Transportation Systems (ITS) have achieved great developments. However, many problems, including traffic management and congestion control, still remain unsolved. Precise analysis of historical trends of traffic flows or transportation forecasting therefore becomes fundamental tasks in order to progress successfully and smoothly in our daily routines. On the other hand, many approaches and methods in the machine learning field were presented recently and got highly developed, which can be instructive to the traffic flow forecasting problem. In this paper, we concentrate on using machine learning methods to deal with the application-orientated problem of short-term traffic flow forecasting in ITS.

Short-term traffic flow forecasting, which is to determine the traffic volume in the next time interval usually in the range of five minutes to half an hour, is an important problem in the research area of ITS. In the past few years, many theories and methods on this theme were proposed including those based on time series models (including ARIMA, seasonal ARIMA), Kalman filter theory,

J.-F. Boulicaut et al. (Eds.): ECML 2004, LNAI 3201, pp. 419–428, 2004.

neural network approaches, non-parametric methods, simulation models, local regression models and layered models [1]∼[6]. Although these theories and methods have alleviated difficulties in traffic flow modelling and forecasting to some extent, they hardly work when the data used for forecasting is partially missing or unavailable, while this case of incomplete data often occurs in practice. Although the historical average (fill up the incomplete data with their historical average) method is often applied to cope with this issue, the forecasting performance is quite limited.

The Bayesian network approach, as studied comprehensively in the community of machine learning, gives us some inspiration on traffic flow forecasting. Considering the nature of short-term traffic flows, we can draw the conclusion that the traffic flow at a given road link is closely related to those of its neighbors, and thus in order to forecast as accurately as possible, we should also take into account the information provided by neighbor links. This is consistent with the ideology of the Bayesian network model. Bayesian network is such a model that can fully take into account the causal relationship between random variables statistically and has the capability to encode incomplete data.

Our main contribution of the paper is that we introduce the concept and approach of Bayesian network in machine learning field to the area of ITS for the first time and effectively solve the traffic flow forecasting problem with incomplete data. For a given road net, we focus on constructing rational Bayesian networks, learn the statistical relations between the cause and effect nodes, and then based on the statistical relationship carry out forecasting. Experiments for real-world short-term vehicular flow forecasting in case of incomplete data are carried out to validate our methods. A comparison with the autoregressive (AR) model and the historical average method shows that our Bayesian network methods are appropriate and effective for this kind of traffic flow forecasting problem.

The remainder of this paper is organized as follows. After introducing Bayesian networks and our two Bayesian network methods for traffic flow forecasting briefly in section 2 and 3 respectively, we describe the approaches and techniques related with our methods in section 4. Section 5 reports the experimental results on real-world traffic flow data, and gives a performance comparison among several methods. Section 6 concludes the paper and discusses some directions of future research work.

2   Bayesian Networks

A Bayesian network, also known as a casual model, is simply a directed graphical model for representing conditional independencies between a set of random variables. In a Bayesian network, an arc from node A to B can be informally interpreted as indicating that A "causes" B [7]. Suppose we have several random variables denoted by $x_1, x_2, ..., x_m, y_1, y_2, ..., y_n$ and z respectively. $x_1, x_2, ..., x_m$ are used to forecast y_1 and $y_1, y_2, ..., y_n$ are used to forecast z in turn. Then considering the causal relations in variable forecasting, we can construct two

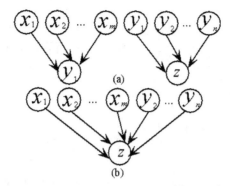

Fig. 1. (a) Two Bayesian networks. (b) A newly constructed Bayesian network

Bayesian networks as shown in Fig. 1.a where arrows start from the cause nodes and point to the effect nodes.

3   Two Bayesian Network Methods

Fig. 2.a is a patch of one urban traffic map. Each circle node denotes a road link. Each arrow shows the direction of the traffic flow on the corresponding road. We take road link D_d as an example to show our approach. From the view point of Bayesian Network, vehicle flows of C_e, C_g and C_h should have causal relations with vehicle flow of D_d. Similarly, vehicle flows of B_a and B_c should have causal relations with vehicle flow of C_h. Furthermore, considering the time factor, to predict the vehicle flow of D_d at time t (denoted by $D_d(t)$)we should use values $D_d(t-1), D_d(t-2), ..., D_d(t-d)$ as well. That is, some historical values of C_e, C_g, C_h and D_d could be regarded as the cause nodes of $D_d(t)$ in a Bayesian network. We show this causal relation in Fig. 2.b.

However, if traffic flow data $C_h(t-m)$ is missing, how can we forecast $D_d(t)$? We propose two methods to deal with this issue.

Method 1. Construct a new Bayesian network to model the whole causal relationship. We take Fig. 1.a as an example to show the procedure. Suppose data for random variable y_1 is missing while data for $x_1, x_2, ..., x_m, y_2, ..., y_n$ is complete (intact), we can construct another Bayesian network to describe the whole causal relation, which is given in Fig. 1.b. The new Bayesian network is constructed and expanded by absorbing the node y_1, and thus in the graph, $x_1, x_2, ..., x_m, y_2, ..., y_n$ serve as the cause nodes of z . Similarly, the newly constructed Bayesian network for forecasting $D_d(t)$ with missing data $C_h(t-m)$ can be obtained, as is shown in Fig. 3.

Method 2. Two-step Bayesian network method. That is, forecast $C_h(t-m)$ first and then using the result to forecast $D_d(t)$. Both steps use Bayesian network models to describe the causal relations among traffic flows.

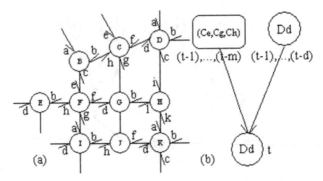

Fig. 2. (a) A patch taken from the whole map of Beijing City where UTC/SCOOT systems are placed. (b) The Bayesian network between the object road link and its cause neighbors

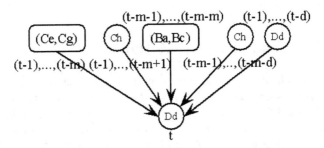

Fig. 3. The newly constructed Bayesian network for object road link D_d

4   Related Methods

4.1   PCA for Dimension Reduction

When using Bayesian networks, the joint probability distribution of related variables should be estimated. Usually the dimension of the joint probability distribution using Bayesian network is high and the data is not enough comparatively. So there might be a large error coming from the parameter learning stage. However, if we carry out parameter learning on a lower dimension with the same data, the estimation will be more accurate and efficient.

Principal Component Analysis (PCA) is such an effective tool for linear dimension reduction [8]. When using PCA for dimension reduction, we select some representative principal components from the input nodes, and then estimate the joint probability distribution among these components and the output node. Based on this new and concise relationship, we can carry out traffic flow forecasting more efficiently. In the paper, we using PCA to carry out dimension reduction for both the Bayesian network methods explained in section 3. More detail on how PCA is used will be given in the experiment section.

4.2   Representation and Parameter Learning of Joint Probability Distribution

How to estimate the joint probability density function (PDF) among all nodes in a constructed Bayesian network should be considered. The Gaussian Mixture Model (GMM), a combination of several Gaussian functions, is a widely used model applied to approximate an arbitrary PDF with enough accuracy. In this article, the joint probability distribution between cause nodes and effect node in a Bayesian network is approximated through GMM. Let x denote one random variable or multidimensional random vector, and then the GMM form of its probability distribution with M mixture components can be represented as:

$$p(x|\Theta) = \sum_{l=1}^{M} a_l G(x|\theta_l) \tag{1}$$

where the parameters are $\Theta = (a_1, ..., a_M, \theta_1, ..., \theta_M)$ and M, s.t. $\sum_{l=1}^{M} a_l = 1$. Each $G(.)$ is a Gaussian PDF parameterized by $\theta_l = (\mu_l, \Sigma_l), l = 1, ..., M$.

Usually we use Maximum Likelihood Estimation (MLE) to carry out parameter learning with given data. Although the EM algorithm is an effective method to carry out MLE, it usually converges to local maxima [9]. To find a global maximum is more significant in most cases. The Competitive EM (CEM) algorithm presented by Zhang et al. overcomes the drawbacks of the basic EM algorithm and can be used for parameter learning of GMM [10]. It includes stages of EM iteration (E-step and M-step), split, merge and annihilation operations. The intial component number and model parameters can be set arbitrarily, and the split and merge operation can be selected efficiently by a competitive mechanism the authors proposed. Using the annihilation operation, CEM algorithm overcomes the problem of converging to the boundaries of parameter space. In other words, CEM algorithm can easily escape all kinds of local extrema and automatically determine the appropriate component number and the model parameters [10]. In this article, the parameters of a GMM which describe the joint PDF of the cause nodes and effect node in a Bayesian network are estimated through CEM algorithm.

4.3   Forecasting in Bayesian Networks

Traffic flow forecasting here can be regarded as an inference problem in a Bayesian network. The main goal of inference in a Bayesian network is to estimate the values of hidden nodes, given the values of observed nodes. We use this mechanism to implement forecasting of traffic flows. Suppose (E, F) be a partitioning of the node indices of a Bayesian network into disjoint subsets, and (x_E, x_F) be a partitioning of the corresponding random variables. Under the rule of Minimum Mean Square Error (M.M.S.E.), the optimal estimation of x_F from x_E can be given as [11]:

$$\hat{x}_F = E(x_F|x_E) . \tag{2}$$

To deduce the representation of the optimal forecasting $\hat{x}_F$ under the GMM setting, we employ the following lemma.

Lemma [12] Let $G(x; \mu, \Sigma)$ denote a multidimensional normal density function with mean $\mu^T = (\mu_1^T, \mu_2^T)$ and covariance matrix $\Sigma = \begin{pmatrix} \Sigma_{11} & \Sigma_{12} \\ \Sigma_{21} & \Sigma_{22} \end{pmatrix}$. $x^T = (x_1^T, x_2^T)$ is a random vector. Then we have:

$$p(x) = G(x_1; \mu_1, \Sigma_{11}) G(x_2; \mu_{x_2|x_1}, \Sigma_{x_2|x_1}) ,$$

where

$$\mu_{x_2|x_1} = \mu_2 - \Sigma_{21} \Sigma_{11}^{-1} (\mu_1 - x_1) ,$$
$$\Sigma_{x_2|x_1} = \Sigma_{22} - \Sigma_{21} \Sigma_{11}^{-1} \Sigma_{12} .$$

If we rewrite $x^T = (x_F^T, x_E^T), \mu_l^T = (\mu_{lF}^T, \mu_{lE}^T), \Sigma_l = \begin{pmatrix} \Sigma_{lFF} & \Sigma_{lFE} \\ \Sigma_{lEF} & \Sigma_{lEE} \end{pmatrix}$, by the above lemma we can obtain:

$$p(x_F, x_E) = \sum_{l=1}^{M} a_l G(x; \mu_l, \Sigma_l)$$
$$= \sum_{l=1}^{M} a_l G(x_E; \mu_{lE}, \Sigma_{lEE}) G(x_F; \mu_{lF|E}, \Sigma_{lF|E}) .$$

The conditional probability density function can be represented as follows:

$$p(x_F|x_E) = \sum_{l=1}^{M} \beta_l G(x_F; \mu_{lF|E}, \Sigma_{lF|E}) ,$$

where

$$\beta_l = \frac{a_l G(x_E; \mu_{lE}, \Sigma_{lEE})}{\sum_{j=1}^{M} a_j G(x_E; \mu_{jE}, \Sigma_{jEE})} ,$$
$$\mu_{lF|E} = \mu_{lF} - \Sigma_{lFE} \Sigma_{lEE}^{-1} (\mu_{lE} - x_E) ,$$
$$\Sigma_{lF|E} = \Sigma_{lFF} - \Sigma_{lFE} \Sigma_{lEE}^{-1} \Sigma_{lEF} .$$

Thus the optimal forecasting $\hat{x}_F$ under the criterion of M.M.S.E. has the following form:

$$\hat{x}_F = E(x_F|x_E) = \sum_{l=1}^{M} \beta_l \mu_{lF|E} , \tag{3}$$

where β_l and $\mu_{lF|E}$ have the same meanings as above.

5   Experiments

The experimental data for analysis is the vehicle flow rates of discrete time series recorded every 15 minutes on many road links by the UTC/SCOOT system in Traffic Management Bureau of Beijing, whose unit is vehicles per hour (veh/hr). The data is from Mar. 1 to Mar. 25, 2002 and 2400 sample points totally. To evaluate our approach objectively, 2112 points (training set) of them are employed to learn parameters of GMM and the rest (test set) are employed to test the forecasting performance. Fig. 2.a shows the analyzed patch.

The flow chart of our forecasting procedure is described in Table 1.

Table 1. The Flow Chart of Our Forecasting Procedure

Step 1:
—Construct the Bayesian network models between input (cause nodes) and output (effect node) for a given road link using two methods explained in section 3.
Step 2:
—Approximate the joint probability distribution of all nodes in the network by PCA and GMM using methods explained in section 4.
Step 3:
—Carry out the optimal estimation of flow rates of the object road in the form of equation (3).

In the experiment, the forecasting orders from the object road link and from the neighbor links are respectively taken as 4 and 5 empirically (parameters $d = 4, m = 5$). Then for Fig. 3 the joint probability distribution is: $p(C_e(t - j), C_g(t - j), B_a(t - j - 5), B_c(t - j - 5), C_h(.), D_d(t - j + 1), j = 1, ..., 5$, where $C_h(.) = (C_h(t - l), C_h(t - l - 5), l = 1, ..., 4)$.

We can see the dimension of the joint probability distribution is very high (dimension=33), since the dimension for input nodes is high (input dimension=32). We should choose the reduced dimension number for input nodes by means of PCA. Fig. 4 shows the residual variance of PCA with different dimensions for the last joint probability distribution on the training data [13]. We see that using dimension 33 for forecasting is quite redundant and doesn't focus on the few essential dimensions. To effectively make use of data and gain well forecasting performance, we should look for the "elbow" where the curve ceases to decrease significantly with added dimensions. Based on the last curve of residual variance and the rectangle around the elbow, we apply PCA to the input nodes on the training data and select a few principal components (i.e. 5, 6, 7, 8 and 9) corresponding to the largest eigenvalues to represent the input data. Then, we respectively reduce the input data to these dimensions, built a GMM, carry out parameter learning through CEM algorithm and implement forecasting on the training set. From these several results, we can select the best one, and its corresponding reduced dimension of input data can also be identified. Experiments show that the best forecasting accuracy is obtained at input dimension 8 (i.e. the dimension of the joint probability distribution is 9). Thus, we use the parameter configuration corresponding to input dimension 8 to implement traffic flow forecasting on the test set. Fig. 5 gives the final forecasting result of Bayesian network method on the test set for road D_d.

For other road links, we also carry out dimension selection by PCA before the parameter estimation of GMM. The final forecasting performances using the Bayesian network method and the two-step Bayesian network method are listed in Table 2 evaluated by root Mean Square Error (RMSE). For a given road link of Table 2, the smaller RMSE corresponds to the better forecasting performance (accuracy).

For vector $X = [x_1, x_2, ..., x_n]$ and its estimation $Y = [y_1, y_2, ..., y_n]$, the performance measure RMSE can be given in the following form:

$$RMSE(X, Y) = [\frac{\sum_{i=1}^{n}(y_i - x_i)^2}{n}]^{1/2}.$$

Since the parameters d and m is just selected empirically, utilizing autoregressive (AR) model with the same parameter d for comparison is reasonable (AR model is comparable which only uses historical flow rates of the object road link to forecast). The forecasting results through AR model and the historical average method (using the the average value of the historical flow rates at the corresponding time to forecast) are also given in Table 2.

Table 2. A Performance comparison of four methods for short-term traffic flow forecasting of four different road links

Methods	D_d	J_f	G_d	C_f
Historical Average	84.20	140.69	213.39	112.50
AR	66.14	123.65	155.20	90.76
Bayesian network	57.44	110.88	138.39	86.31
Two-step Bayesian network	53.95	113.96	140.40	87.73

From the experimental results we can see the outstanding improvements of forecasting capability brought by using Bayesian networks. For each of the four road links analyzed, the performances of the two Bayesian network methods are quite similar; and they both outperform the other two methods significantly. The Bayesian network method and the two-step Bayesian network method are both appropriate and effective for incomplete short-term traffic flow forecasting.

6   Conclusions and Future Work

In this paper, we first successfully introduce the concept and approach of Bayesian networks in the machine learning field to the community of ITS for the application problem of incomplete data forecasting. In the short-term traffic

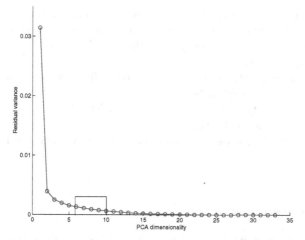

Fig. 4. Residual variance of PCA with different dimensions

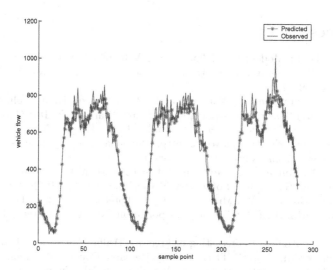

Fig. 5. Traffic flow forecasting result (veh/hr) for road D_d

flow forecasting theme, as vehicles usually keep travelling from one road link to its neighbor links, the traffic volume of one link at some given time can be regarded as the result of the historical flows of its neighbors and itself. The essence of traffic flow is consistent with the ideology of Bayesian networks. Besides, as Bayesian network encodes dependencies among all variables, it readily handles situations where some data entries are incomplete. Therefore, constructing Bayesian networks for traffic flow forecasting is reasonable. Experiments with real-world data also show that Bayesian network is applicable and effective for short-term traffic flow forecasting.

Though our proposed approach is more complicated than the AR model and some other models used for traffic flow forecasting, with the ever-increasing capability of digital computers coupled with a simultaneous decrease in the cost, the computation cost will not be a burden.

However, there are still some problems to be discussed and improved in the future, two of which are listed below.

1). How to elaborately select the prediction orders d and m for varying road conditions of different road links.

2). How to effectively combine Bayesian network with periodical information of traffic flows, etc.

Acknowledgements

This work was supported by National High Technology Research and Development Program of China (863 Program) under contract No. 2001AA114190.

References

1. William, B.M.: Modeling and Forecasting Vehicular Traffic Flow as a Seasonal Stochastic Time Series Process. Doctoral dissertation. University of Virginia, Charlottesville (1999)
2. Okutani, I., Stephanedes, Y.J.: Dynamic Prediction of Traffic Volume through Kalman Filter Theory. Transportation Research, Part B, Vol.18B (1984) 1-11
3. Edwards, T., Transley, D.S.W., Frank, R.J., Davey, N.: Traffic Trends Analysis using Neural Networks. http://homepages.feis.herts.ac.uk/~nngroup/pubs/papers/ed-wards-iwannt97.pdf (1997)
4. Davis, G.A., Nihan, N.L.: Non-Parametric Regression and Short-Term Freeway Traffic Forecasting. Journal of Transportation Engineering (1991) 178-188
5. Roland, C., Joachim, W., Michael, S.: Traffic Forecast Using Simulations of Large Scale Networks. IEEE Intelligent Transportation Systems Conference Proceedings (2001)
6. Davis, G.A.: Adaptive Forecasting of Freeway Traffic Congestion. Transportation Research Record, No.1287. TRB, National Research Council, Washing, D.C. (1990)
7. Kevin, P.M.: An Introduction to Graphical Models. http://www.ai.mit.edu/~murphyk/Papers/intro_gm.pdf (2001)
8. Jolliffe, I.T.: Principal Component Analysis. Springer-Verlag, New York (1986)
9. Jeff, A.B.: A Gentle Tutorial of the EM Algorithm and its Application to Parameter Estimation for Gaussian Mixture and Hidden Markov Models. International Computer Science Institute, Berkeley CA, TR-07-021 (1998)
10. Zhang, B.B., Zhang, C.S., Yi, X.: Competitive EM Algorithm for Finite Mixture Models. Pattern Recognition, Volume: 37, Issue: 1, January (2004) 131-144
11. Andrew, H.J.: Stochastic Processes and Filtering Theory . Academic Press, Inc., New York and London (1970)
12. Rao, C.R.: Linear Statistical Inference and Its Applications (Second Edition). John Wiley&Sons, Inc. (1973)
13. Tenenbaum, J.B., Silva, V.D., Langford, J.C.: A Global Geometric Framework for Nonlinear Dimensionality Reduction. Science (2000), 290, 2319

Matching Model Versus Single Model: A Study of the Requirement to Match Class Distribution Using Decision Trees

Kai Ming Ting

Gippsland School of Computing and Information Technology,
Monash University, Australia
kaiming.ting@infotech.monash.edu.au

Abstract. A tacit assumption in classifier induction is that the class distribution of the training set must match the class distribution of the test set. A direct implementation is to retrain a model using a data set with matching class distribution every time the operating condition changes (i.e., the matching model). The alternative is to modify the decision rule of a previous trained model to the new operating condition. The latter is the single model approach commonly used and recommended by many researchers. In this paper, we argue with empirical support using decision trees that learning using the matching class distribution is desirable. We also make explicit the differences and limitations of the two methods for the single model approach: rescaling and thresholding.

1 Introduction

In order to produce the best classifier for the test condition, conventional wisdom requires the class distribution of the training data to match that of the testing data. Strict compliance to this principle requires one to retrain a new model using a matching (class) distribution whenever the test class distribution changes. However, many opt to modify the decision output of a previously trained model to adjust to the new condition. We call the first approach *the matching model approach* and the second the *single model approach*. The second approach has a practical advantage because it uses a single model only for all operating conditions. Thus, many researchers (e.g., [2, 4, 7, 14]) use the single model approach by default or recommend others to use it.

However, despite its common application, it is unclear if the performance of the single model approach will match that of the matching model approach. This paper aims to answer this open question.

Both approaches have multiple variations. For the matching model approach, one may collect a separate training set with matching class distribution; or retrain using the same training set by re-weighting the instances according to new class distribution; or use over-sampling or under-sampling to reproduce a new training set from the original one. For the single model approach, one may *rescale* the output probability by a ratio of the changed prior probability [2, 4, 7]; or use

J.-F. Boulicaut et al. (Eds.): ECML 2004, LNAI 3201, pp. 429–440, 2004.

thresholding in which one determines the appropriate threshold of the previously trained model using ROC or cost curves [9, 12].

Previous analyses on rescaling have not taken into account the type of model employed. There are two types of models, depending on whether the learning algorithm is modeling posterior probability or class-conditional probability density function (or class density model, hereafter). Some suggest that one should rescale a model regardless of its type. We show that different model types can be treated differently when rescaling. Examples of posterior probability models are decision trees, logistic regression and neural networks; and class density models are Naive Bayesian classifiers and linear discriminant functions.

In addition, we show that model sensitivity is a necessary condition when considering rescaling a model. An algorithm that is insensitive to prior probability produces models with the same structure when trained using different class distributions. We reveal that a previous analysis on rescaling [7] is based on an implicit assumption of model insensitivity.

Because of differing and sometimes conflicting factors as described above, it is not always clear which is the most appropriate approach to produce the best model in accordance to the requirement of matching distribution. It is thus important to have a clear understanding of the relationship between different factors and provide a guide as to what to apply under different scenarios. This paper contributes toward this end.

Specifically, we investigate the following issues:
- Does the type of model influence what we do when rescaling?
- The limitations of rescaling.
- Does the single model perform comparably to the matching model?

We provide analyses on the first two issues and a comprehensive experiment comparing the two approaches.

Despite the now known fact that optimal learning can be achieved by using unmatched class distribution, it is still important to know which of the two matched class distribution approaches perform better because most of the current research is comparing optimal learning against the commonly used single model approach rather than the matching model approach. We show in this paper that the latter can be significantly better than the former.

The issue of optimal learning using unmatched class distribution has been explored elsewhere [12, 14]. This issue is not discussed in this paper. Another related issue is: what does one do when there is insufficient training data for reasonable estimation in the modeling process? For example, given a fixed training set with class distribution 1:99 while the test distribution is known to be 99:1. In this paper, we assume the training set has sufficient data to make reasonable estimation and focus on the stated issues, and leave the issue of insufficient data to be discussed elsewhere.

Bayes decision rules form the basis of this paper and are described in Section 2. We show that rescaling a class density model is simpler than rescaling a posterior probability model. Section 3 discusses the limitations of rescaling and its implicit assumption in a previous analysis. Section 4 describes thresholding and representing the performance of a model using cost curves. Section 5 shows the experimental result comparing the single model approach with the matching model approach. We provide a discussion of the related issues in Section 6 and conclude in the last section.

2   Bayes Decision Rules and Rescaling

Let $x = <x_1, x_2, ..., x_n>$ be a vector of attribute-values representing an example in a classification task; and $C \in \{1, 2\}$ is the class label of the task.

Given a model that produces the posterior probability $P(C|x)$ for a test example x, the Bayes decision rule used to make a final prediction is as follows:

$$\text{Predict class 1 if } P(1|x) > P(2|x), \tag{1}$$
$$\text{otherwise predict class 2.}$$

Alternatively, if it is the class density function $P(X|C)$ of the data that is being modeled, then the rule can be similarly described as:

$$\text{Predict class 1 if } P(x|1)P(1) > P(x|2)P(2), \tag{2}$$
$$\text{otherwise predict class 2.}$$

$P(C)$ is the prior probability for class C.

The second equation is derived from the first by applying the Bayes rule

$$P(C|x) = \frac{P(x|C)P(C)}{P(x)}. \tag{3}$$

$P(x)$ can be ignored in the Bayes decision rules because it is a constant independent of class.

Let M be the factor of the changed ratio of $P(C)$.

$$M = \frac{P'(1)}{P'(2)} : \frac{P(1)}{P(2)}, \tag{4}$$

where $P(C)$ and $P'(C)$ are the prior probabilities for class C in the training set and testing set, respectively.

Rescaling as suggested by some authors [4, 14] can be done by simply rescaling $P(C|x)$ of the previously trained model by the ratio of the changed $P(C)$. Following this suggestion, Equation (1) can be rescaled to the test condition as follows.

$$P(1|x)\frac{P'(1)}{P(1)} > P(2|x)\frac{P'(2)}{P(2)},$$
$$\frac{P(1|x)}{P(2|x)} > \frac{P(1)}{P(2)}\frac{P'(2)}{P'(1)},$$
$$\frac{P(1|x)}{P(2|x)} > \frac{1}{M}. \tag{5}$$

The same rescaling can be applied to both posterior probability models and class density models. The following rescaling for the class density model shows that it produces the same result as in the case for posterior probability model. Rescaling Equation (2) gives:

$$P(x|1)P(1)\frac{P'(1)}{P(1)} > P(x|2)P(2)\frac{P'(2)}{P(2)}$$

$$\frac{P(x|1)P(1)}{P(x|2)P(2)} > \frac{P(1)}{P(2)}\frac{P'(2)}{P'(1)},$$

$$> \frac{1}{M} \tag{6}$$

However, Equation (6) can be re-written and simplified as follows.

$$\frac{P(x|1)}{P(x|2)} > \frac{P'(2)}{P'(1)} \tag{7}$$

This means that *rescaling a class density model can be done without knowing the training prior probability.*

A caveat is in order here. The analysis thus far assumes that the algorithm, whether it is producing class density models or posterior probability models, is totally insensitive to the training prior probability. If this assumption does not hold, then the rescaled model cannot guarantee to produce the same output as that from the retrained matched model. We will have further discussion on this issue in the next section.

3   The Limitations of Rescaling

The above analyses do not take practical considerations into account which limit its applicability in practice. Here we list two practical constraints and reveal a limiting implicit assumption in a previous analysis on rescaling.

(a) Rescaling does not adapt to the output range of the model. For example, if the output range for $P(1|x)$ is between 0.3 and 0.7 (which is the typical range of values obtained using the Laplace estimate in decision trees in most of the experiments we conducted), then rescaling for $M > 2$ will always predict class 1 using (5)! An example is shown in Figure 1 in which rescaling a model trained with natural distribution performs poorly with respect to the models trained from the matching distribution using the default threshold = 0.5 in each operating condition $1 \leq M \leq 10$.

(b) Rescaling relies on accurate probability estimation. Many classifiers are poor probability estimators [10]. As a result, rescaling becomes an unreliable method to provide accurate prediction.

(c) The following analysis on rescaling has an implicit assumption that the learning algorithm is totally insensitive to prior probability.

"Theorem 1: To make a target probability threshold p' correspond to a given probability threshold p, the number of negative examples in the training set should be multiplied by $\frac{p'}{1-p'}\frac{1-p}{p}$." [7]

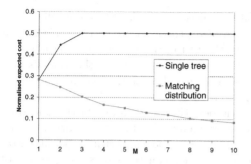

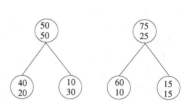

Fig. 1. An example of rescaling a single tree compared to trees trained from matching distribution (using threshold = 0.5) in the coding data set. Single tree is trained from the natural distribution ($M = 1$) and then rescaled to different operating conditions, $M > 1$.

Fig. 2. Retrain a model using a different class distribution: an example.

Two models with different thresholds will produce the same decision, if and only if the learning algorithm produces models with the same structure when trained using different class distributions. Figure 2 shows a simple example: a model is initially trained using 50:50 distribution; and then a second model is trained with the *same split* using a 75:25 distribution. Assuming p and p' are the corresponding thresholds in these models that produce the same prediction. Using Elkan's formulation, the relationship can be computed as $p' = 1.5p$. This is interpreted as: for the first model, predict class 1 if the output probability is more than $p = 0.5$ otherwise predict class 2; the second model can then use $p' = 0.75$ to produce the same prediction.

This is only true if the algorithm is totally insensitive to prior probability, or in the case of decision trees, the splitting criterion is totally insensitive to prior probability. The model insensitivity assumption is not true with decision tree learning algorithms, in general, as shown in the experimental results in [12, 14], for example.

It is important to point out that rescaling does not provide the kind of fine adjustment as in thresholding because thresholding adapts to the output range of the model, and can be determined for a wider range of M value. Thresholding using exactly the same model comes close to that of the matching distribution; thus, it is much better then rescaling as shown in Figure 1 (the plot for thresholding is eliminated to increase readability.) In addition, thresholding does not rely on accurate probability estimation, but only requires the class ranking to be correct (see [10] for a discussion of probability estimation trees.) We will describe thresholding in the next section.

4   Thresholding and Cost Curves

The key difference between thresholding and rescaling is that each threshold is determined empirically rather than an adjustment through a decision rule (based on Bayes rule), as described in the last two sections.

A decision threshold is the cut-off level used to decide the final prediction of a classification model. In a two-class problem, the final prediction is class positive if the model's posterior probability of a test example is above the threshold; otherwise it is class negative. When the threshold is changed, the model's performance also changes. The best threshold is usually determined empirically for each testing condition using a holdout set.

The procedure used to determine the best threshold can be further aided by either a cost curve [5] or a ROC curve [9], which represents the performance of a model. We use cost curves in this paper and describe the pertinent detail below.

The normalised expected cost of a classifier can be expressed in terms of true positive rate (TP), false positive rate (FP) and probability-cost function (PCF); it is defined by [5] as

$$NEC = (1 - TP)PCF + FP(1 - PCF) \qquad (8)$$
$$= (1 - TP - FP)PCF + FP,$$
$$\text{where } PCF = \frac{P'(1)C'(2|1)}{P'(1)C'(2|1) + P'(2)C'(1|2)}.$$

For the purpose of discussion in this paper, $PCF = P'(1)$ since we assume $C'(2|1) = C'(1|2)$, where $C(a|b)$ is the cost of misclassifying an example of class b as belonging to class a. This assumption is solely for ease of discussion and the result is by no means restricted to the cost-insensitive case only since doubling $P'(1)/P'(2)$ has the same effect of doubling $C'(2|1)/C'(1|2)$.

The performance of a classification model that uses a fixed decision threshold is represented by a pair $\{TP, FP\}$. Given the pair, it can be represented as a line in the cost space, which consists of the normalised expected cost in the y-axis and PCF in the x-axis, indicated by the second linear equation. Because both are normalised, they range from 0 to 1. Different cost lines are obtained by varying the decision threshold of the same model, as shown in Figure 3a. The cost curve representing the performance of the single model that uses varying decision thresholds is the lowest envelop of all cost lines produced by the model. Examples of cost curves produced from a single tree and multiple trees, using thresholding, are given in Figure 3b.

We compare the single model approach with the matching model approach, both using thresholding, in the following section.

5   Single Tree vs Trees Trained from Matching Distribution

5.1   Experimental Settings

The experiment is aimed to compared the performance of a single tree to that of trees trained from a matching distribution for different testing conditions. A cost curve is produced from each case; the latter uses 100 trees, one for each of the testing conditions (denoted by an integral value of M for 1 to 100), whereas the former is using one tree for all conditions.

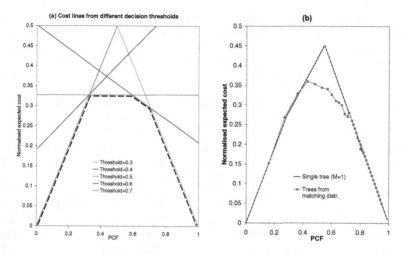

Fig. 3. (a) Cost lines and curves: each cost line is produced using a fixed decision threshold. The *cost curve* for the model is the lowest envelop of all the cost lines for the model, indicated as the dotted line. (b) Cost curves for a single tree trained from $M = 1$ and trees trained from matching distribution in the flare data set. Note that the cost curve for trees trained from matching distribution spans over the range corresponding to $1 \leq M \leq 100$, and not the entire range.

We use the decision tree induction algorithm C4.5 [11] and its default setting in all experiments, while taking the following modifications into consideration. The algorithm is modified to take M into consideration in the training process. For example, with $M=2$, every minority class training instance will be weighted twice as high as every majority class instance. Cost-sensitive pruning is done in accordance with the modified weights, though the default pruning method of C4.5 is used unaltered. We also added the DKM splitting criterion [3]. We report the results of pruned trees using the gain ratio criterion unless stated otherwise. Note that the probability estimates of decision trees are smoothed using the Laplace-estimate (as used by [10, 12]).

We use thirteen data sets obtained from the UCI repository [1]. The minority prior spans from 50% to about 1%, that is from balanced to highly skewed distributions; and the data sizes range from 1000 to about 49000. There are seven data sets which have more than two classes and they are converted to two classes (marked with ′). A stratified 10-fold cross-validation is conducted for each data set.

To compute cost curves, we use an algorithm provided by [9] to obtain all pairs of $\{TP, FP\}$ in one pass through a test set for all the different thresholds of a model. Note that although the test set we used to produce the cost curves is derived from the natural distribution, we can still compute the expected cost for different testing or operating conditions (denoted by PCF or its equivalent M) using Equation (8) since the resultant cost curve, like the ROC curve, is independent of prior probability and cost.

Table 1. Average AUCC for a single tree and matching trees trained for the testing condition $1 \leq M \leq 100$. Bold face indicates the lowest value in each data set.

Data set		Gain Ratio			DKM		
	%Minority prior	Single Tree $M = 1$	$M = M_b$	Matching Trees	Single Tree $M = 1$	$M = M_b$	Matching Trees
Coding	50.0	**3.39**	**3.39**	3.69	**3.45**	**3.45**	3.71
Kr-vs-kp	47.8	**0.26**	**0.26**	0.42	**0.26**	**0.26**	0.33
Abalone'	31.7	7.22	6.96	**6.58**	7.30	6.73	6.62
German	30.0	7.37	**5.77**	6.60	7.45	**5.50**	6.50
Adult	24.1	7.22	7.34	**6.01**	7.32	7.09	6.40
Splice'	24.0	2.16	2.65	**1.49**	2.28	2.46	1.53
Solar Flare	15.7	13.68	12.81	**12.62**	13.91	12.64	12.44
Satellite'	9.7	14.96	13.68	**13.25**	14.44	**13.71**	13.72
Pendigits'	9.6	2.65	1.93	**1.57**	2.37	2.39	2.08
Hypothyroid	4.8	4.94	4.03	**3.44**	3.76	4.14	3.38
Letter-a'	3.9	2.92	**2.28**	2.32	3.19	2.32	2.15
Nursery'	2.6	1.91	**1.27**	1.39	1.91	**1.27**	1.39
Nettalk-stress'	1.1	32.75	**21.94**	23.65	32.75	**20.19**	20.24
Win:loss ratio							
wrt matching trees		2:11	6:7		2:11	6:7	
wrt M_b tree		2:9			3:8		
wrt DKM tree		7:3	5:6	6:6			

The area under cost curve (AUCC) is used as a generic measure to compare the performance of different algorithms under all operating conditions, like that in the ROC curve [12, 14]. Here we limit ourselves to operating conditions $1 \leq M \leq 100$ for models trained from naturally skewed class distribution data sets (where class 1 in Equation (4) represents the minority class.) $M > 1$ allows us to concentrate on situations that bias the minority class which often occurs in practice. This is equivalent to assigning higher cost to the minority class in cost-sensitive learning.

All AUCC figures reported refer to a partial area under the cost curve. An algorithm which has smaller AUCC is performing better in general under those operating conditions. AUCC is computed by integrating over M rather than PCF because a precise value of performance is available for each M.

5.2   Experimental Results

Table 1 shows the average result for both the gain ratio and DKM splitting criteria. In addition to a single tree trained from the natural distribution, the results of a single tree trained from the balanced distribution (i.e., the M_b tree) are also provided. The last three rows show the ratios of the number of data sets in which one approach wins and loses with respect to (wrt) the other.

The gain ratio results, in the '$M = 1$' column, clearly show that a single tree trained from the natural distribution performs worse than trees trained from a matching distribution with a win:lose ratio of 2:11.

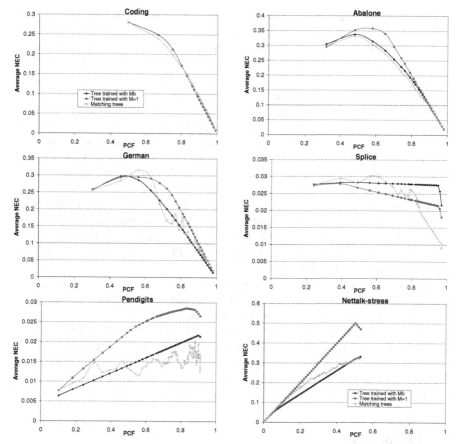

Fig. 4. Single tree versus matching trees: the detailed results for pruned trees using partial cost curves constructed from $M = 1$ (the left-most point) to $M = 100$ (the right-most point). Each point is an average over a 10-fold cross-validation. Coding and kr-vs-kp have identical cost curves for single trees trained with $M = 1$ and $M = M_b$ since they are naturally balanced. Not all results are presented because of space limitation.

It is interesting to note that there are two data sets in which a single tree performs better and the only data characteristic that stands out from the other data sets is that they have balanced distribution. If that is an important criterion, then a single tree trained from the balanced distribution will perform better than a single tree trained from the natural distribution. The results in the '$M = M_b$' column of Table 1 indeed demonstrates that with a win:lose ratio of 2:9. This result agrees with that obtained by Weiss & Provost [14] using the AUC measure for ROC curves though they are using sampling and we are using re-weighting to change the training priors.

Comparing to trees trained from the matching distribution, a single tree trained from the balanced distribution is a better contender than that trained from the natural distribution but it is still slightly in favour of matching trees, with the win:lose ratios of 6:7. This result shows that it is still advisable to train a tree that matches the operating condition.

We repeat the experiments using the DKM criterion. The results in Table 1 show similar trends for all the pair-wise comparisons as those for gain ratio.

Figure 4 shows the detailed results for gain ratio trees. It is interesting to note that the M_b tree almost always performs better than the $M = 1$ tree in most operating conditions in most data sets, and in many cases there is only a minor difference between the two in the natural distribution operating condition. Interestingly, M_b tree performs better than $M = 1$ tree in some cases even in the natural distribution operating condition (at the left-most point)! An example is in the pendigits data set. The only exception to the above overwhelming one-sided result is in the splice data set.

The matching model is always better than the single model in abalone and adult. Compared to the single model trained from the balanced distribution, the matching model is significantly better in a substantial part of the testing conditions in splice, pendigits and hypothyroid. The reverse is true in kr-vs-kp, german, nursery and nettalk-stress.

The cost curves for matching trees are not "smooth" because there are two variables: a different tree and a different threshold for each point in the curve. Single tree has only one variable, that is the threshold.

Note that the above discussion on the detailed results are for the gain ratio trees only. The relative results between the two approaches correspond to the summarised results shown in Table 1, whether it is for the gain ratio trees or the DKM trees. However, one can expect some variation in local operating points as shown in Figure 4 and unsmooth curves for matching trees in all cases.

6   Discussion

We begin this investigation assuming that the single model approach will perform comparable to the matching model approach at its best, but will never perform better. The assumption turns out to be incorrect, as shown in the experimental results in Section 5.2 in which the single model can sometimes outperform the matching model when the training class distribution is balanced. This unintuitive result is a direct result of the now known fact that the best classifier can be induced from an unmatching class distribution [5, 12, 14].

Quite a few researchers (e.g., [8, 14]) have shown that models trained from the balanced distribution perform better than models trained from the natural distribution, using either rescaling or thresholding. However, none of them has compared them with matching models. Our result shows that matching models cannot be ignored by assuming that single models will perform comparably to matching models.

The re-weighting method is best suited for scenarios in which a skewed distribution data set is readily available and misclassifying a minority class is more costly than misclassifying a majority class. The main advantage of the re-weighting method over the sampling methods is that for any class distribution we obtain a training set with the same data size, using all the examples.

This is achieved through weight normalization in which the total weight is always equal to the total size of the original data [13]. This effectively uses a mixture of up-weighting for one class and down-weighting for another in each class distribution modification.

If the test condition is expressed as misclassification cost, one common method is to apply the minimum expected cost criterion to a previously trained model and make the final decision with a class that has the minimum expect cost. It can be easily shown that this is equivalent to rescaling.

7   Conclusions and Future Work

This paper's first contribution is establishing the relationship among different methods for the single model approach and their limitations. Its second contribution is answering the open question of whether the single model approach is sufficient to implement the matching distribution assumption, in comparison to the matching model approach using decision trees.

Specifically for the first contribution, we show that

- Rescaling for a class density model is easier than rescaling a posterior probability model because no knowledge of the training prior probability is required. It is also simpler than rescaling by a ratio of changed probability. This result suggests that when using class density models such as Naive Bayes, prior probability needs not be estimated during training; and then apply Equation (7) which uses the appropriate prior probability for classification.
- Rescaling is not a recommended approach because it relies on accurate probability estimation and does not adapt to the output range of the model. We also reveal that a previous analysis advocating the use of rescaling has an implicit strong assumption, that is, the learning algorithm must be totally insensitive to prior probability. We argue that the rescaled model cannot guarantee to produce the same output as that from the matching model, as claimed by the analysis when this assumption is violated; which is the case for decision trees, in general.
- Thresholding is the preferred method for the single model approach because it determines the threshold empirically that avoids the limitations of rescaling.

For the second contribution, we show using decision trees that there is no foolproof substitute for the matching model approach that recommends training a model using data whose class distribution matches the testing condition. Using matching model is usually better than a single model trained from the natural distribution. One possible substitute for the matching model is to train a single model using a balanced distribution (either natural or derived). The single model trained from the derived balanced distribution is only likely to work better than the matching model when the original distribution is highly skewed.

We show that model sensitivity, as exhibited by using two different splitting criteria with different degrees of sensitivity to priors in decision trees, does not play a role in determining whether the single model approach or the matching model approach should be used.

Our experiments have been limited to decision trees. It is possible that other learning algorithms which are designed for probability estimation might behave quite differently from the results presented. Also, we have limited this study to the case of changed class distribution that happens uniformly across the sample space. It is possible that class distribution changes non-uniformly; in which case re-weighting instances uniformly as we have done for the matching model here is an inappropriate method. The analysis is restricted to the two-class case because of the current limitation of the cost space or ROC analysis that we employed. We intend to explore these issues in the near future.

Acknowledgement

Discussion with Phil Rayment, Geoff Webb and David Albrecht has helped to develop the material presented in this paper. Ross Quinlan provides C4.5. The anonymous reviewers have helped to improve the presentation of this paper.

References

1. Blake, C. & Merz, C.J.: UCI Repository of machine learning databases. [www.ics. uci.edu/~mlearn/MLRepository.html]. Irvine, CA: University of California (1998)
2. Breiman, L., Friedman, J.H., Olshen, R.A. & Stone, C.J.: Classification And Regression Trees. Chapman & Hall. (1993)
3. Dietterich, T.G., Kearns, M., & Mansour, Y.: Applying the weak learning framework to understand and improve C4.5. Proceedings of Thirteenth International Conference on Machine Learning (1996) 96–104. San Francisco: Morgan Kaufmann
4. Duda, O.R., Hart, P.E. & Stork, D.G.: Pattern Classification. John Wiley (2001)
5. Drummond, C. & Holte, R.C.: Explicitly Representing Expected Cost: An Alternative to ROC Representation. Proceedings of the Sixth International Conference on Knowledge Discovery and Data Mining (2000) 198–207
6. Drummond, C. & Holte, R.C.: Exploiting the Cost (In)sensitivity of Decision Tree Splitting Criteria. Proceedings of The Seventeenth International Conference on Machine Learning (2000) 239–246. San Francisco: Morgan Kaufmann
7. Elkan, C.: The Foundations of Cost-Sensitive Learning. Proceedings of the Seventeenth International Joint Conference on Artificial Intelligence (2001) 973–978
8. Hooper, P.M.: Reference Point Logistic Regression and the Identification of DNA Functional Sites. Journal of Classification. 18 (2001) 81–107
9. Provost, F. & Fawcett, T.: Robust Classification for Imprecise Environments. Machine Learning. 42 (2001) 203–231
10. Provost, F. & Domingos, P.: Tree-Induction for Probability-based Ranking. Machine Learning. 52 (2003) 199–215
11. Quinlan, J.R.: C4.5: Program for Machine Learning. Morgan Kaufmann (1993)
12. Ting, K.M.: Issues in Classifier Evaluation using Optimal Cost Curves. Proceedings of The Nineteenth International Conference on Machine Learning (2002) 642–649
13. Ting, K.M.: An Instance-Weighting Method to Induce Cost-Sensitive Trees. IEEE Transactions on Knowledge and Data Engineering. Vol.14 No.3 (2002) 659–665
14. Weiss, G. & Provost, F.: Learning when Training Data are Costly: The Effect of Class Distribution on Tree Induction. Journal of Artificial Intelligence Research. 19 (2003) 315–354

Inducing Polynomial Equations for Regression

Ljupčo Todorovski, Peter Ljubič, and Sašo Džeroski

Department of Knowledge Technologies, Jožef Stefan Institute
Jamova 39, SI-1000 Ljubljana, Slovenia
Ljupco.Todorovski@ijs.si

Abstract. Regression methods aim at inducing models of numeric data. While most state-of-the-art machine learning methods for regression focus on inducing piecewise regression models (regression and model trees), we investigate the predictive performance of regression models based on polynomial equations. We present CIPER, an efficient method for inducing polynomial equations and empirically evaluate its predictive performance on standard regression tasks. The evaluation shows that polynomials compare favorably to linear and piecewise regression models, induced by standard regression methods, in terms of degree of fit and complexity. The bias-variance decomposition of predictive error shows that CIPER has lower variance than methods for inducing regression trees.

1 Introduction

Regression methods [9] aim at inducing accurate predictive models that relate the value of a target or dependent numeric variable to the values of a set of independent variables. In the last decade or so, most machine learning studies of regression as well as most state-of-the-art regression methods are concerned with inducing piecewise models. These methods partition the training set and induce a simple model in each part. Piecewise models are typically based on simple constant and linear models (as in regression and model trees [15] and MARS models [7]) or polynomials [2].

In this paper, we evaluate the usability and performance of simple models based on polynomial equations on standard regression tasks. Despite the fact that piecewise regression models prevail over simple ones in machine learning literature, we claim here that simple polynomial equations can be efficiently induced and have competitive performance with piecewise models. To approach the regression task efficiently, we develop CIPER[1], a method for inducing polynomial equations. The method performs heuristic search through the space of candidate polynomial equations. The search heuristic combines model degree of fit to the data with model complexity. We evaluate the performance of CIPER on thirteen standard regression data sets from two public repositories [1, 13]. Empirical evaluation includes comparison with standard regression methods for inducing linear and piecewise linear models, implemented within WEKA data mining suite [6].

---

[1] The acronym CIPER stands for "Constrained Induction of Polynomial Equations for Regression".

J.-F. Boulicaut et al. (Eds.): ECML 2004, LNAI 3201, pp. 441–452, 2004.
© Springer-Verlag Berlin Heidelberg 2004

We compared different methods in terms of predictive error and complexity of the induced models. We also performed empirical bias-variance decomposition of the predictive error on some of the data sets.

The paper is organized as follows. In Section 2, we present the CIPER method for heuristic search through the space of polynomial equations and discuss its relation to stepwise regression methods. Section 3 presents the results of the empirical evaluation of the proposed method and its comparison to standard regression methods. Section 4 discusses related work. Finally, Section 5 concludes the paper with a summary and directions for further work.

2   Inducing Polynomial Equations with CIPER

In this section, we present a heuristic search algorithm CIPER that searches through the space of polynomial equations and finds the one that has an optimal value of the heuristic function. First, we introduce a refinement operator that orders the space of polynomial equations. Then, we present the heuristic function used to measure the quality of each equation considered during the search along with the stopping criterion. After presenting the search algorithm based on beam search strategy, we discuss the relation of CIPER to stepwise regression methods.

2.1   The Language of Polynomial Equations

We focus here on inducing polynomial equations that can be used to predict the value of a dependent variable v_d. Given a set of variables V, and a dependent variable $v_d \in V$, a polynomial equation has the form $v_d = P$, where P is a polynomial over $V \setminus \{v_d\}$, i.e., $P = \sum_{i=1}^{r} \text{const}_i \cdot T_i$, where each T_i is a multiplicative term, r is the number of such terms, and const_i are real-valued constants. Each term is a finite product of variables from $V \setminus \{v_d\}$: $T_i = \prod_{v \in V \setminus \{v_d\}} v^{d_{v,i}}$, where $d_{v,i}$ is (a non-negative integer) degree of the variable in the term. The degree of 0 denotes that the variable does not appear in the term. The sum of degrees of all variables in a term is called the degree of the term, i.e., $\deg(T_i) = \sum_{v \in V \setminus \{v_d\}} d_{v,i}$. The degree of a polynomial is the maximum degree of a term in that polynomial, i.e., $\deg(P) = \max_{i=1}^{r} \deg(T_i)$. The length of a polynomial is the sum of the degrees of all terms in that polynomial, i.e., $\text{len}(P) = \sum_{i=1}^{r} \deg(T_i)$.

For example, consider a set of variables $V = \{x, y, z\}$, where z is chosen to be a dependent variable. The term x (that is equivalent to $x^1 y^0$) has degree 1, the term $x^2 y$ has degree 3, while $x^2 y^3$ is a term of degree 5. An example polynomial equation is $z = 1.2 x^2 y + 3.5 x y^3$. It has degree 4 and length 7.

2.2   The Refinement Operator

In order to apply heuristic search methods to the task of inducing polynomial equations, we first have to order the search space of candidate equations. We introduce a refinement operator that orders this space according to equation

Table 1. The refinement operator for ordering the space of polynomial equations.

original (current) equation
$v_d = \sum_{i=1}^{r} \text{const}_i \cdot T_i$
refined equations that increase r (one for each $v \in V \setminus v_d$)
$v_d = \sum_{i=1}^{r} \text{const}_i \cdot T_i + \text{const}_{r+1} * v$, where $\forall i : v \neq T_i$
refined equations that increase d (one for each T_j and $v \in V \setminus v_d$)
$v_d = \sum_{i=1, i \neq j}^{r} \text{const}_i \cdot T_i + T_j * v$, where $\forall i \neq j : T_j * v \neq T_i$

complexity. Starting with the simplest possible equation and iteratively applying the refinement operator, all candidate polynomial equations can be generated.

Assume we measure the complexity of the polynomial equation $v_d = P$ as $\text{len}(P)$. The refinement operator increases the complexity of the equation by 1, either by adding a new linear term or by adding a variable to an existing term. First, we can add an arbitrary linear (first degree) term (that is a single variable from $V \setminus \{v_d\}$) to the current equation as presented in the first (upper) part of Table 1. Special care is taken that the newly introduced term is different from all the terms in the current equation. Second, we can increase the complexity $\text{len}(P)$ by adding a variable to one of the terms T_j in the current polynomial equation. Again, care should be taken that the changed term is different from all the other terms in the current equation. Note that the refinements of a given polynomial P are super-polynomials of P. They are minimal refinements in the sense that they increase the complexity of P by one unit.

The branching factor of the presented refinement operator depends on the number of variables $|V|$ and number of terms in the current equation r. The upper bound of the branching factor is $\mathcal{O}((|V|-1)(r+1)) = \mathcal{O}(|V|r)$, since there are at most $|V| - 1$ possible refinements that increase r and at most $(|V| - 1)r$ possible refinements that increase d.

The ordering of the search space of polynomial equations, defined on the set of variables $V = \{x, y, z\}$, where z is the dependent variable, is presented in Figure 1. It shows that the defined refinement operator is not optimal, in sense that each polynomial equation can be derived more than once. This is due to the commutativity of the addition and multiplication operators. An optimal refinement operator can be easily obtained by taking into account the lexical ordering of the variables in V. Then, only variables (and/or terms) with higher lexical rank should be added to the terms and/or equations. The dotted nodes in the graph in Figure 1 denote equations that would not be generated by the refinement operator that takes into account lexical order. However, the redundancy due to the sub-optimality of the refinement operator can be avoided during the search procedure, as we will point out in the following section.

While an optimal refinement operator is desired for complete/exhaustive search, it may prevent the generation of good equations in greedy heuristic search. Suppose the polynomials x and z have low heuristic value, while y has a high heuristic value and $x + y$ is actually the best. Greedy search would choose y

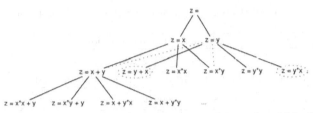

Fig. 1. The search space of polynomial equations over the set of variables $V = \{x, y, z\}$, where z is the dependent variable, as ordered by the refinement operator from Table 1. Note that for simplicity, real-valued constants are omitted from the equations.

and the optimal refinement operator that takes into account lexicographic order would not generate $x + y$.

2.3   The Search Heuristic

Each polynomial equation structure considered during the search contains a number of generic constant parameters (denoted by const_i). In order to evaluate the quality of an equation, the values of these generic constants has to be fitted against training data consisting of the observed values of the variables in V. Since the polynomial equations are linear in the constant parameters, the standard linear regression method can be used for this purpose.

The quality of the obtained equation is evaluated using a degree of fit measure that measures the discrepancy between the observed values of v_d and the values predicted using the equation. One such measure is mean squared error (MSE), calculated as: $\text{MSE}(v_d = P) = \frac{1}{m}\sum_{i=1}^{m}(v_d(i) - \hat{v}_d(i))^2$, where $v_d(i)$ is the value of v_d for the i-th training example, $\hat{v}_d(i)$ is the value of v_d for the same example, but predicted using equation $v_d = P$, and m is the number of training examples.

CIPER uses an MDL (minimal description length) based heuristic function for evaluating the quality of equations that combines the degree of fit with the complexity of the equation. In the literature, the following combination has been considered: based on Akaike and Bayesian information criteria for regression model selection [9]:

$$\text{MDL}(v_d = P) = \text{len}(P)\log m + m\log\text{MSE}(v_d = P).$$

where $\text{len}(P)$ is the length of the P, and m number of training examples. While the second term the MDL heuristic function measures the degree of fit of a given equation, the first term introduces a penalty for complexity of the equation. Through this penalty the MDL heuristic function introduces preference toward simpler equations.

2.4   The Search Algorithm

CIPER employs beam search through the space of possible equations using the search algorithm presented in Table 2. The algorithm takes as input a training

Table 2. A top-level outline of CIPER's beam search procedure.

---

procedure CIPER(D, v_d, b)
1 E_0 = simplest polynomial equation (v_d = const)
2 E_0.MDL = FITPARAMETERS(E_0, D)
3 $Q = \{E_0\}$
4 **repeat**
5   Q_r = {refinements of equation structures in Q}
6   **foreach** equation structure $E \in Q_r$ **do**
7   E.MDL = FITPARAMETERS(E, D)
8   **endfor**
9   Q = {best b equations from $Q \cup Q_r$}
10 **until** Q unchanged during the last iteration
11 **print** Q

---

data set D containing the values of independent variables and the dependent variable v_d. The output of CIPER consists of the b best polynomial equations according to the MDL heuristic function defined in the previous section.

Before the search procedure starts, the beam Q is initialized with the simplest possible polynomial equations of the form v_d = const. The value of the constant parameter const is fitted against the training data D using linear regression. In each search iteration, the refinements of the equations in the current beam are generated (using the refinement operator from Table 1) and collected in Q_r (line 5). In case when redundant equations are generated due to the sub-optimality of the refinement operator, the duplicate equations are filtered out from the set Q_r. Again, linear regression is used to fit the constant parameters of the refinements against the training data D (lines 6-8). Finally, at the end of each search iteration, only the best b equations, according to the MDL heuristic function, are kept in the beam (line 10). The search stops when the performed iteration does not change the beam.

2.5 Stepwise Regression

The CIPER search algorithm is similar in spirit to the forward stepwise method for linear regression [9]. As CIPER, the stepwise regression method also starts with the simplest model v_d = const and sequentially adds those independent variables to the model that most significantly improve its fit to the training data. To avoid overfitting, stepwise regression methods test the significance of the MSE improvement gained by refining the current equation and do not take into account those refinements that do not lead to significant improvements. The significance of the MSE improvement is based on F statistic:

$$F = \frac{\text{MSE}(v_d = P) - \text{MSE}(v_d = P')}{MSE(v_d = P')} \cdot (m - r - 2),$$

where $v_d = P$ is the current equation, $v_d = P'$ is the candidate equation with the newly added term, r is the number of terms in the current equation, and m is the number of training examples. The improvement is significant, if the obtained F value is greater than the 95th percentile of the $F(1, m - r - 2)$ distribution [9]. Stepwise regression method proceed with greedy search by choosing the best significant improvement and stops, if no significant improvement is available.

CIPER can be viewed as a stepwise method for polynomial regression with MDL heuristic function. However, there are several other important differences between CIPER and the stepwise regression method.

The refinement operator used in CIPER is better suited for polynomial regression. While the stepwise regression method can only refine the current equation by adding a new term to it, CIPER can also add a variable to an existing term in the current equation. Using this second kind of refinement, CIPER can generate polynomials of arbitrary degree. On the other hand, to use forward stepwise method for polynomial regression, terms of degree two and more have to be precomputed and introduced as new independent variables. However, this is a serious limitation of the stepwise method, since precomputation of higher degree terms requires user to specify their maximal degree of the introduced terms and it introduces potentially huge number of independent variables. The number of independent variables is of order $\mathcal{O}(|V|^d)$, where d is the maximal degree of precomputed terms.

The huge number of precomputed higher degree terms is reflected in the high branching factor of the stepwise refinement operator. Since it adds a new term to the current equation, its branching factor equals the number of independent variables, i.e., $\mathcal{O}(|V|^d)$. Note that the branching factor of CIPER's refinement operator ($\mathcal{O}(|V|r)$) is linear with regards to the number of independent variables. The lower branching factor of the refinement operator permits the use of higher beam widths in CIPER, which is in contrast with beam width of one used for stepwise regression methods.

3   Experimental Evaluation

The main goal of the performed experiments is to evaluate the predictive performance of CIPER especially in comparison with the standard regression methods for inducing linear and piecewise models, implemented in the data mining suite WEKA [6]. The performance of the methods is evaluated on thirteen data sets from the UCI Repository [1] and another publicly available collection of regression data sets [13]. These data sets have been widely used in other comparative studies. Table 3 presents the basic properties the data sets.

3.1   Experimental Methodology and Settings

In all the experiments presented here, we estimate the regression performance on unseen examples using 10-fold cross validation. The regression performance of a model M is measured in terms of relative mean squared error (RE) defined as $RE(M) = MSE(M)/VAR(v_d)$, where $VAR(v_d)$ is the variance of the dependent variable v_d. The normalization of the MSE with the variance of v_d allows for comparison of the performance measure across different data sets.

Table 3. Properties (number of variables n, number of examples m, and class variance $\mathrm{VAR}(v_d)$) of the thirteen regression data sets used in the experiments.

Data set	n	m	$\mathrm{VAR}(v_d)$
auto_price	16	159	$3.433 \cdot 10^7$
baskball	5	96	0.01173
bodyfat	15	252	69.76
cal_housing	9	20640	$1.331 \cdot 10^{10}$
elusage	3	55	566.0
fried_delve	11	40768	24.97
house_8l	9	22784	$2.792 \cdot 10^9$
housing	14	506	84.4196
kin_8nm	9	8192	0.06948
mbagrade	3	61	0.1063
pw_linear	11	200	19.92
quake	4	2178	0.03587
vineyard	4	52	18.94

We compare the performance of our approach based on polynomial equations to the performance of three standard regression methods implemented in WEKA [6]: linear regression, regression trees, and model trees. The tree-based models are induced with the M5' algorithm [15]. All algorithms have been used with their default parameters' settings. The default beam width in CIPER is 16. For pairwise comparison of methods, we calculate relative error reduction achieved for a given data set by using method M_1 as compared to using method M_2: $1 - \mathrm{RE}(M_1)/\mathrm{RE}(M_2)$. The statistical significance of the difference is tested using the paired t-test (with the sample size equal to the number of folds; the same folds are used for all methods) with significance level of 99%: $+/-$ to the right of a figure in the tables with results means that the difference is significant.

We also perform bias-variance decomposition of the predictive error following the Monte Carlo procedure from [8]. Following this procedure, we first randomly sample (with replacements) 100 sets from the original data set, build 100 models using method M, and use these models to obtain 100 predictions for each example in the training set. Let us denote with $v_d^k(i)$ the prediction of the model induced on the k-th sampled set and $v_d^*(i)$ the average prediction of these models. Then, the bias-variance decomposition of the squared error (SE) can be approximated as:

$$\mathrm{SE}_i(v_d = P) = (v_d^*(i) - v_d(i))^2 + \frac{1}{100} \sum_{k=1}^{100} (v_d^k(i) - v_d^*(i))^2,$$

where the first term represent the bias and the second term represents the variance of the regression method M. We calculate then the average percentage of variance in the mean squared error.

Table 4. Predictive performance of CIPER in terms of relative mean squared error (RE), as compared to stepwise regression (with maximal polynomial degree of 1, 2, and 3) and three other regression approaches implemented in WEKA: linear regression LR, model trees MT, and regression trees RT. Sign $+/-$ on the right hand side of the figure denotes that CIPER performed significantly better/worse.

| Data set | CIPER | Stepwise regression | | | WEKA | | |
		$d = 1$	$d = 2$	$d = 3$	LR	MT	RT
auto_price	0.1610	0.2426	0.1985	0.3966	0.2168	0.1351	0.2896 +
baskball	0.6334	0.6334	0.6397	0.6218	0.6672	0.6334	0.8351 +
bodyfat	0.0282	0.0285	0.0324	0.0286	0.0295	0.0260	0.1025 +
cal_housing	0.2901	0.3639 +	0.3339	0.3510	0.3639 +	0.2376 −	0.2664 −
elusage	0.2720	0.3604	0.2720	0.2720	0.3731	0.3312	0.4827
fried_delve	0.1021	0.2773 +	0.1128	0.0436	0.2773 +	0.0765	0.1271
house_8L	0.3793	0.6193 +	0.4370 +	16.1411	0.6191 +	0.3545	0.3932
housing	0.1768	0.2866 +	0.1676	0.1680	0.2858 +	0.1745	0.2550 +
kin_8nm	0.3631	0.5871 +	0.4390 +	0.2684 −	0.5871 +	0.3673	0.4711 +
mbagrade	0.8403	0.8403	0.8450	0.8502	0.8403	0.8403	1.0209
pw_linear	0.3936	0.2504	0.1162	0.6122	0.2377	0.1047	0.3264
quake	1.0000	0.9964	0.9964	0.9997	0.9966	1.0035	1.0102
vineyard	0.5347	0.7400	0.6674	0.7679	0.7116	0.7404	0.7207
Average	0.3980	0.4789	0.4044	1.6555	0.4774	0.3865	0.4847

3.2   Experimental Results

We present the results of the experiments in Tables 4–6. The first table compares the regression methods in terms of their predictive error, the second compares the complexity of the induced models, and the third percentage of variance in the bias-variance decomposition of the predictive error.

Predictive Error. CIPER clearly outperforms linear regression and stepwise linear regression ($d = 1$) on most of the experimental data sets (and significantly on five of them). The stepwise regression methods gain higher accuracy with increasing the maximal degree of precomputed terms d, but they tend to overfit the training data – compare, for example, the results on house_8l, pw_linear, and cal_housing data sets. Although insignificant, these differences are still considerably large, especially for $d = 3$. In terms of significant differences, they are comparable to CIPER. Results of stepwise regression indicate further improvement with increasing d, however this is intractable for large data sets. Also, as we show later, stepwise regression method tend to induce more complex models. Note also that the performance of stepwise polynomial regression is very sensitive to the value of d. Selecting the optimal d value for stepwise polynomial regression is a nontrivial problem, since it can differ from one data set to another and would be, for practical reasons, guided by computational complexity issues (number of precomputed higher degree terms). Note that the computational complexity of CIPER compares favorably to the stepwise regression method with $d = 3$: the CIPER search procedure, on average, considers 10 times fewer candidate equations then stepwise regression search procedure.

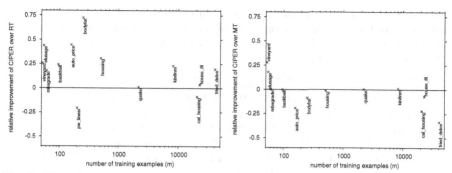

Fig. 2. The relation between number of training examples and relative accuracy improvement achieved with CIPER when compared to regression and model trees.

The overall accuracy of CIPER compares favorably to the accuracy of regression trees – CIPER is significantly better than RT in five data sets. The graph on the left-hand side of Figure 2 depicts the relative improvement of CIPER when compared to regression trees. It shows that the relative accuracy improvement is higher for smaller data sets. A possible explanation for this is that CIPER induces a single equation/model over the entire data set, as opposed to a number of partial models induced for data subsets in model trees. Finally, to our surprise, the overall accuracy of CIPER is comparable to the accuracy of model trees – note that model trees significantly outperform polynomial equations on a single data set.

Note that we also compared the predictive error of models induced using CIPER with MDL heuristic to the error of models induced using CIPER with F statistics as heuristic (used in stepwise regression methods, see Section 2.5). The results, which due to lack of space are not included in the paper, show that CIPER with MDL outperforms CIPER with F.

Model Complexity. We assess the complexity of models based on polynomial equations in terms of number of constant parameters #P, length LEN (as defined in Section 2.1), and polynomial degree DEG. The complexity of tree-based models is measured in number of constant parameters in the leaf nodes #P, and number of decision nodes #DN.

Table 5 presents the results of the model complexity comparison. CIPER produces less complex polynomials than stepwise regression method with maximal degree of precomputed terms $d = 2$. Despite the (two times) higher overall degree of equations induced with CIPER, they are shorter and have two times fewer number of parameters than the equations induced with stepwise regression methods. The complexity of the polynomial models is much lower than the complexity of piecewise tree-based models. The factor of complexity reduction is of order of a hundred for both regression and model trees.

Bias-Variance Decomposition. For eight of the thirteen data sets we performed bias-variance decomposition of the predictive error. As expected, the

Table 5. Complexities of the models induced with CIPER as compared to the stepwise, linear and tree-based models in terms of number of constant parameters in the equation #P, polynomial length LEN and degree DEG, as well as number of decision nodes #DN for tree-based piecewise models.

| | CIPER | | | Stepwise ($d = 2$) | | | Regr. Trees | | Model Trees | |
Data set	#P	LEN	DEG	#P	LEN	DEG	#P	#DN	#P	#DN
auto_price	5	5	2	7	10	2	8	7	19	6
baskball	3	2	1	3	3	2	2	1	3	0
bodyfat	8	11	3	4	5	2	16	15	12	5
cal_housing	24	81	17	40	71	2	499	498	898	268
elusage	3	3	2	3	3	2	3	2	6	1
fried_delve	7	7	2	66	120	2	1919	1918	2356	538
house_8l	35	163	13	34	60	2	266	265	434	127
housing	15	32	4	29	53	2	26	25	56	18
kin_8nm	13	16	2	33	56	2	264	263	409	105
mbagrade	3	2	1	3	2	1	1	0	3	0
pw_linear	10	12	2	13	18	2	14	13	12	1
quake	2	1	1	2	1	1	1	0	10	5
vineyard	4	4	2	3	3	2	4	3	6	1
Average	10.5	26.1	4.0	18.5	31.1	1.8	232.5	231.5	324.9	82.7

Table 6. Percentage of variance in the bias-variance decomposition of predictive error of CIPER as compared to tree-based piecewise models.

Data set	CIPER	Model Trees	Regr. Trees
auto_price	2.73	12.64	10.53
bodyfat	0.02	99.43	4.98
fried_delve	<0.01	51.88	37.92
house_8l	0.01	9.80	12.56
housing	1.75	4.72	2.17
kin_8nm	0.01	38.94	26.17
pw_linear	0.32	12.21	69.04
quake	0.04	1.91	2.61

results from Table 6 show that CIPER has much lower variance than methods for inducing tree-based models.

4   Related Work

Equation discovery [10] aims at developing methods for computational discovery of quantitative laws or models, expressed in the form of equations, in collections off measured numeric data. These methods are mainly used for automated modeling of real-world systems from measurements and observations. Since they operate on numeric data, they are strongly related to regression methods. However, note that there is an important difference in focus. While equation discovery methods focus on inducing *general*, *comprehensible*, and *explanatory* models of observed systems or phenomena [11, 5], regression methods focus on the task of inducing *accurate* model for predicting the value of a specific designated dependent variable. While the comprehensibility, generality, explanatory power of the induced model are more important for the performance of equation discovery methods than their accuracy and predictive power, the later is the most (or the only) important evaluation criterion for the regression methods.

The refinement operator in CIPER is very similar in spirit to forward stepwise methods for linear regression [9]. However, as discussed in Section 2.5, the CIPER refinement operator is much more suited for stepwise polynomial regression. Similar refinement operator has been also used in the MARS (multivariate adaptive regression splines) method [7]. The difference is however that the MARS refinement operator adds all possible *piecewise* linear terms of a form $\max(v - t, 0)$ or $\max(t - v, 0)$, where v is an independent variable $v \in V \setminus \{v_d\}$ and t is one of its values, to a current equation. Since each example in the training set defines a potential break point (knot) t in the piecewise linear term, the branching factor of MARS refinement operator is much higher since it also depends on the number of examples in the training set m. The branching factor of MARS refinement operator is of order $\mathcal{O}(|V|rm)$, which can be quite prohibitive for large data sets.

Finally, note that we have already presented other aspects of CIPER elsewhere. [12] focuses on the efficient implementation of the linear regression procedure (used in CIPER for constant parameter fitting) that benefits from the incremental nature of the refinement operator. In [4], we evaluate CIPER on the task of inducing ordinary differential equations.

5   Conclusions and Further Work

This paper presents CIPER, a method for efficient induction of polynomial equations that can be used as predictive regression models. CIPER employs heuristic beam search through the space of candidate polynomial equations. The search is based on a refinement operator with low branching factor that makes it much more suitable for polynomial regression compared to much complex refinement operators used in stepwise regression methods and MARS. Evaluation of CIPER on a number of standard predictive regression tasks shows that it is superior to linear regression and stepwise regression methods as well as regression trees. CIPER appears to be competitive to model trees too. The complexity of the induced polynomials, in terms of number of parameters, is much lower than the complexity of piecewise models. Finally, CIPER greatly reduce the variance of tree induction methods.

Directions for further research include integration of efficient methods for partitioning the data set in CIPER and use them to induce piecewise polynomial models (one piece for each partition). The partitioning of the data set can be based on Euclidean proximity of training examples: clustering methods can be used for this purpose as in [14, 5]. Furthermore, since linear regression method is used for fitting the model parameter in CIPER, it is fairly straightforward to develop a version of CIPER that is capable of incremental induction of regression models from numeric data streams. The development can be based on the incremental linear regression method presented in [3].

Acknowledgments

This work was supported in part by the project cInQ (Consortium on discovering knowledge with Inductive Queries), funded by the European Commission under the FET arm of the IST programme.

References

1. C. L. Blake and C. J. Merz. UCI repository of machine learning databases, 1998. http://www.ics.uci.edu/~mlearn/MLRepository.html.
2. P. Chaudhuri, M. C. Huang, W. Y. Loh, and R. Yao. Piecewise-polynomial regression trees. *Statistica Sinica*, 4:143–167, 1994.
3. Y. Chen, G. Dong, J. Han, B. Wah, and J. Wang. Multidimensional regression analysis of time-series data streams. In *Proceedings of the Twentyeighth International Conference on Very Large Data Bases*, pages 323–334. Morgan Kaufmann, 2002.
4. S. Džeroski, L. Todorovski, and P. Ljubič. Using constraints in discovering dynamics. In *Proceedings of the Sixth International Conference on Discovery Science*, pages 297–305, Berlin, 2003. Springer.
5. B. Falkenhainer and R. Michalski. Integrating quantitative and qualitative discovery in the ABACUS system. In *Machine Learning: An Artificial Intelligence Approach*, volume 3, pages 153–190. Morgan Kaufmann, San Mateo, CA, 1990.
6. E. Frank and I. H. Witten. *Data Mining: Practical Machine Learning Tools and Techniques with Java Implementations*. Morgan Kaufmann, San Mateo, CA, 1999.
7. J. Friedman. Multivariate adaptive regression splines (with discussion). *Annals of Statistics*, 19:1–141, 1991.
8. S. Geman, E. Bienenstock, and R. Doursat. Neural networks and the bias/variance dilemma. *Neural Computation*, 4:1–58, 1992.
9. T. Hastie, R. Tibshirani, and J. Friedman. *The Elements of Statistical Learning: Data Mining, Inference, and Prediction*. Springer, Berlin, 2001.
10. P. Langley, H. A. Simon, G. L. Bradshaw, and J. M. Żythow. *Scientific Discovery*. MIT Press, Cambridge, MA, 1987.
11. L. Todorovski and S. Džeroski. Using domain knowledge on population dynamics modeling for equation discovery. In *Proceedings of the Twelfth European Conference on Machine Learning*, pages 478–490. Springer, 2001.
12. L. Todorovski, S. Džeroski, and P. Ljubič. Discovery of polynomial equations for regression. In *Proceedings of the Sixth International Multi-Conference Information Society (Volume A)*, pages 151–154, Ljubljana, Slovenia, 2003. Jozef Stefan Institute.
13. L. Torgo. Regression data sets, 2001. http://www.liacc.up.pt/~ltorgo/Regression/DataSets.html.
14. L. Torgo and J. .P. da Costa. Clustered partial linear regression. In *Proceedings of the Eleventh European Conference on Machine Learning*, pages 426–436. Springer, 2000.
15. Y. Wang and I. H. Witten. Induction of model trees for predicting continuous classes. In *The Proceedings of the Poster Papers of the Eighth European Conference on Machine Learning*, pages 128–137, University of Economics, Faculty of Informatics and Statistics, Prague, 1997.

Efficient Hyperkernel Learning
Using Second-Order Cone Programming

Ivor W. Tsang and James T. Kwok

Department of Computer Science
The Hong Kong University of Science and Technology
Clear Water Bay, Hong Kong
{ivor,jamesk}@cs.ust.hk

Abstract. The kernel function plays a central role in kernel methods. Most existing methods can only adapt the kernel parameters or the kernel matrix based on empirical data. Recently, Ong *et al.* introduced the method of hyperkernels which can be used to learn the kernel function directly in an inductive setting [12]. However, the associated optimization problem is a semidefinite program (SDP), which is very computationally expensive even with the recent advances in interior point methods. In this paper, we show that this learning problem can be equivalently reformulated as a second-order cone program (SOCP), which can then be solved more efficiently than SDPs. Experimental results on both toy and real-world data sets show significant speedup. Moreover, in comparison with the kernel matrix learning method proposed by Lanckriet *et al.* [7], our proposed SOCP-based hyperkernel method yields better generalization performance, with a speed that is comparable to their formulation based on quadratically constrained quadratic programming (QCQP).

1 Introduction

In recent years, kernels have been successfully used in various aspects of machine learning, such as classification, regression, clustering, ranking and principal component analysis [14]. Because of the central role of the kernel, a poor kernel choice can lead to significantly impaired performance. Typically, the practitioner has to decide the kernel function before learning starts. The associated kernel parameters (such as the order in a polynomial kernel) can then be determined by optimizing a quality functional of the kernel [12], such as kernel target alignment, generalization error bounds, Bayesian probabilities and cross-validation error.

Instead of adapting only the kernel parameters, a recent development is on adapting also the form of the kernel itself. In a transductive setting, as all information on the feature space is encoded in the kernel matrix (with entries for both the training and test patterns), one can bypass the learning of the kernel function by just learning the kernel matrix instead. As the kernel matrix must be positive semidefinite (psd), Lanckriet *et al.* [7] used semidefinite programming (SDP) to optimize a cost function (such as the hard/soft margin[1]) on the train-

---

[1] When the kernel-target alignment [5] is used instead, [7] can be shown to be a generalization of the kernel learning method in [5].

J.-F. Boulicaut et al. (Eds.): ECML 2004, LNAI 3201, pp. 453–464, 2004.
© Springer-Verlag Berlin Heidelberg 2004

ing set, over the set of psd matrices. To avoid overfitting, capacity of the search space has to be controlled. Inspired from a generalization bound for transduction, Lanckriet *et al.* [7] constrained the kernel matrix to be in a convex subset of psd matrices with a fixed trace. Other kernel matrix learning methods, such as using boosting to optimize a weighted combination of base kernels [4], and the use of a Bayesian hierarchical model together with the Tanner-Wong data augmentation algorithm [16], have also been recently proposed.

However, transduction requires knowing the test patterns in advance and thus may not be always appropriate. In an inductive setting, a novel approach that learns the kernel *function* directly is the method of hyperkernels [12]. By introducing the notion of a hyper reproducing kernel Hilbert space, the desired kernel function can be obtained by minimizing a regularized quality functional, in which the capacity of the search space is explicitly controlled by a regularization term. It can be shown that the kernel function obtained is always a linear combination of a finite number of pre-specified hyperkernel evaluations. Often, this is further constrained to be a positive linear combination. As will be discussed in Section 2, learning with hyperkernels involves optimizing two sets of variables. The first set of variables, $\{\alpha_1, \ldots, \alpha_m\}$ where m is the number of training samples, are coefficients in the kernel expansion, while the second set, $\{\beta_1, \ldots, \beta_{m^2}\}$, are coefficients in the hyperkernel expansion. Originally, these two sets have to be optimized separately in an alternating manner [12]. Recently, simultaneous optimization of both sets of variables is made possible by formulating this as a SDP problem [11].

However, even with the recent advances in interior point methods, solving SDPs is still very computationally expensive. In the method of hyperkernels, this is further aggravated by the fact that $O(m^2)$ variables, instead of $O(m)$ variables as in other kernel methods, are involved. In [11, 12], this problem is partially alleviated by reducing the number of variables using a low rank approximation (e.g., [6]) on the hyperkernel matrix. While this often makes the SDP problem more tractable, an alternative formulation faster than SDP is still very desirable.

Moreover, as mentioned earlier, the kernel function obtained can be expressed as a positive linear combination of hyperkernels. Consequently, the training kernel matrix becomes a positive linear combination of some pre-specified matrices. By regarding this derived property rather as a constraint in the kernel learning process, the approach in [7] can also be applied in this inductive setting, and the computational problem reduces to solving a quadratically constrained quadratic programming (QCQP) problem, which is much faster than solving SDPs. Recently, Bousquet and Herrmann [3] proposed an even faster method based on gradient descent. Note that the hyperkernel method cannot be similarly reduced to a QCQP because it uses the hyperkernel prior, while [3, 7] use the trace of the kernel matrix for complexity control. However, although these QCQP-based and descent-based methods have significant speed advantages over the SDP-based hyperkernel method, our experiments in Section 5 show that the hyperkernel method has better generalization performance over all the real-world data sets tested.

In this paper, we attempt to improve the hyperkernel method so that its generalization performance is as good as that of the original SDP formulation, but with a speed that is closer to the QCQP-based method of [7]. In particular, we will show that the hyperkernel method can be equivalently formulated as a second-order cone program (SOCP) [1]. SOCPs are convex optimization problems in which a linear function is minimized over the intersection of an affine linear manifold with the Cartesian product of second-order cones. Moreover, interior-point methods for solving SOCPs have a much better worst-case complexity and run far more efficiently in practice than those for SDPs [1].

The rest of this paper is organized as follows. Section 2 reviews the method of hyperkernels and Section 3 gives a short introduction on SOCP. Section 4 describes the proposed general procedure for obtaining a SOCP formulation for the learning problem, which is then followed by some specific kernel method examples. Experimental results on both toy and real-world data sets are presented in Section 5, and the last section gives some concluding remarks.

2   Learning with Hyperkernels

In this section, we review the method of hyperkernels as introduced in [11–13]. Section 2.1 first introduces the concepts of reproducing kernel Hilbert space (RKHS) and regularized risk functional minimization, which are then extended to hyper-RKHS and regularized quality functional minimization in Section 2.2.

In the sequel, $\mathbf{A} \succeq 0$ means that the matrix $\mathbf{A}$ is symmetric and positive semidefinite (psd), $\mathbb{R}^k_+, \mathbb{R}^k_{++}$ denote the sets of non-negative and positive vectors in $\mathbb{R}^k$ respectively, and $\{(\mathbf{x}_1, y_1), \ldots, (\mathbf{x}_m, y_m)\}$ is the training set. Moreover, vector/matrix transpose is denoted by the superscript ^{T}.

2.1   Reproducing Kernel Hilbert Space

Given a nonempty set $\mathcal{X}$ and a Hilbert space $\mathcal{H}_k$ of functions $f : \mathcal{X} \to \mathbb{R}$, $\mathcal{H}_k$ is a *reproducing kernel Hilbert space* (RKHS) with kernel function $k : \mathcal{X} \times \mathcal{X} \to \mathbb{R}$ if

1. k has the reproducing property: $\langle f, k(\mathbf{x}, \cdot) \rangle_{\mathcal{H}_k} = f(\mathbf{x})$, $\forall f \in \mathcal{H}_k, \forall \mathbf{x} \in \mathcal{X}$, where $\langle \cdot, \cdot \rangle_{\mathcal{H}_k}$ denotes the dot product in $\mathcal{H}_k$; and
2. k spans $\mathcal{H}_k$.

The *regularized risk functional* is a sum of the empirical risk corresponding to a loss function $l : (\mathcal{X} \times \mathbb{R}^2)^m \to \mathbb{R} \cup \{\infty\}$, and a regularizer $\Omega : [0, \infty) \to \mathbb{R}$. Minimizing this regularized risk leads to the primal:

$$\min_{f \in \mathcal{H}_k} \frac{1}{m} \sum_{i=1}^m l(\mathbf{x}_i, y_i, f(\mathbf{x}_i)) + \frac{\lambda}{2} \Omega(\|f\|_{\mathcal{H}_k}), \tag{1}$$

where $\|f\|_{\mathcal{H}_k}$ is the RKHS norm of f and $\lambda \in \mathbb{R}_{++}$ is a user-defined constant. By the representer theorem, the minimizer f admits a representation of the form $f(\mathbf{x}) = \sum_{i=1}^m \alpha_i k(\mathbf{x}_i, \mathbf{x})$, where $\alpha_i \in \mathbb{R}$ for $1 \leq i \leq m$.

Instead of solving the primal in (1) directly, most kernel methods solve its dual instead, which is usually a quadratic programming (QP) problem of the form

$$\max_{\boldsymbol{\alpha}} \boldsymbol{\alpha}^T \mathbf{v} - \frac{1}{2} \boldsymbol{\alpha}^T \mathbf{G}(\mathbf{K}) \boldsymbol{\alpha} \text{ s.t. } \mathbf{A}\boldsymbol{\alpha} + \mathbf{b} \geq \mathbf{0}, \tag{2}$$

where $\boldsymbol{\alpha} = [\alpha_1, \cdots, \alpha_m]^T, \mathbf{v} \in \mathbb{R}^m, \mathbf{A} \in \mathbb{R}^{n \times m}, \mathbf{b} \in \mathbb{R}^n$, and $\mathbf{G}(\mathbf{K}) \in \mathbb{R}^{m \times m}$ is a matrix-valued function of the kernel matrix $\mathbf{K} = [k(\mathbf{x}_i, \mathbf{x}_j)]_{ij} \in \mathbb{R}^{m \times m}$ and is psd.

2.2   Hyper Reproducing Kernel Hilbert Space

Denote $\underline{\mathcal{X}} = \mathcal{X} \times \mathcal{X}$. Consider a Hilbert space of functions $k : \underline{\mathcal{X}} \to \mathbb{R}$. Analogous to a RKHS, the Hilbert space $\underline{\mathcal{H}}$ of functions $k : \underline{\mathcal{X}} \to \mathbb{R}$ is a *hyper reproducing kernel Hilbert space* (hyper-RKHS) if there exists a hyperkernel $\underline{k} : \underline{\mathcal{X}} \times \underline{\mathcal{X}} \to \mathbb{R}$ such that

1. $\underline{k}$ has the reproducing property: $\langle k, \underline{k}(\underline{\mathbf{x}}, \cdot) \rangle_{\underline{\mathcal{H}}} = k(\underline{\mathbf{x}}), \quad \forall k \in \underline{\mathcal{H}}, \forall \underline{\mathbf{x}} \in \underline{\mathcal{X}}$, where $\langle \cdot, \cdot \rangle_{\underline{\mathcal{H}}}$ denotes the dot product in $\underline{\mathcal{H}}$;
2. $\underline{k}$ spans $\underline{\mathcal{H}}$; and
3. For any fixed $\underline{\mathbf{x}} \in \underline{\mathcal{X}}$, the hyperkernel $\underline{k}$ is a valid kernel in its second argument.

The suitability of a kernel k in a particular training data set is measured by the *regularized quality functional*, which is a sum of the regularized risk functional and the norm $\|k\|_{\underline{\mathcal{H}}}$ of k in $\underline{\mathcal{H}}$. The desired kernel function is then obtained by minimizing this regularized quality functional over the entire space $\underline{\mathcal{H}}$ of kernels, which leads to the primal:

$$\min_{k \in \underline{\mathcal{H}}} \min_{f \in \mathcal{H}_k} \frac{1}{m} \sum_{i=1}^m l(\mathbf{x}_i, y_i, f(\mathbf{x}_i)) + \frac{\lambda}{2} \Omega(\|f\|_{\mathcal{H}_k}) + \frac{\lambda_Q}{2} \|k\|_{\underline{\mathcal{H}}}^2, \tag{3}$$

where $\lambda_Q \in \mathbb{R}_{++}$ is another user-defined constant. By the representer theorem for hyper-RKHS, the minimizer k admits a representation of the form

$$k(\mathbf{x}, \mathbf{x}') = \sum_{i,j=1}^m \beta_{ij} \underline{k}((\mathbf{x}_i, \mathbf{x}_j), (\mathbf{x}, \mathbf{x}')), \tag{4}$$

where $\beta_{ij} \in \mathbb{R}$ for $1 \leq i, j \leq m$. To ensure that k in (4) is a valid kernel, the expansion coefficients β_{ij}'s are often constrained to be non-negative. By defining $\underline{\mathbf{K}}_{ij} = [\underline{k}((\mathbf{x}_i, \mathbf{x}_j), (\mathbf{x}_k, \mathbf{x}_l))]_{kl} \in \mathbb{R}^{m \times m}$, (4) can be written in matrix form as:

$$\mathbf{K} = \sum_{i,j=1}^m \beta_{ij} \underline{\mathbf{K}}_{ij}, \quad \beta_{ij} \geq 0. \tag{5}$$

It is obvious that $\underline{\mathbf{K}}_{ij} \succeq 0$ from Property 3 of hyperkernels.

Combining (2) with the representer theorem for hyper-RKHS, the dual of (3) can be obtained as:

$$\min_{\beta} \max_{\alpha} \; \alpha^T \mathbf{v} - \frac{1}{2} \alpha^T \mathbf{G}(\mathbf{K}) \alpha + \frac{\lambda_Q}{2} \beta^T \underline{\mathbf{K}} \beta$$

$$\text{s.t.} \quad \mathbf{A}\alpha + \mathbf{b} \geq \mathbf{0}, \;\; \mathbf{1}^T \beta = c, \;\; \beta \geq \mathbf{0}, \;\; \mathbf{K} = \text{reshape}(\underline{\mathbf{K}}\beta), \qquad (6)$$

where $\beta = [\beta_{11}, \beta_{12}, \ldots, \beta_{1m}, \ldots, \beta_{m1}, \ldots, \beta_{mm}]^T$, $\underline{\mathbf{K}} = [\underline{k}((\mathbf{x}_i, \mathbf{x}_j), (\mathbf{x}_k, \mathbf{x}_l))]_{ijkl}$ $\in \mathbb{R}^{m^2 \times m^2}$, and $\mathbf{K} = \text{reshape}(\underline{\mathbf{K}}\beta)$ means reshaping the $m^2 \times 1$ vector $\underline{\mathbf{K}}\beta$ to a $m \times m$ matrix $\mathbf{K}$. Notice that an additional constraint $\mathbf{1}^T \beta = c$, where $\mathbf{1} = [1, \ldots, 1]^T \in \mathbb{R}^{m^2}$ and c is a constant, is imposed to avoid arbitrary scaling of the resultant $\mathbf{K}$ matrix. Finally, this can then be formulated and solved as a SDP [11].

3 Second-Order Cone Programming

In recent years, it has been found that many optimization problems can be formulated as second-order cone programs (SOCP) [1, 8, 10]. SOCP is a class of convex optimization problems in which a linear function is minimized over the intersection of an affine linear manifold with the Cartesian product of second-order cones[2]. Its standard primal form is:

$$\min_{\mathbf{x}_1, \ldots, \mathbf{x}_r} \; \mathbf{c}_1^T \mathbf{x}_1 + \ldots + \mathbf{c}_r^T \mathbf{x}_r \;\; \text{s.t.} \;\; \mathbf{A}_1 \mathbf{x}_1 + \ldots + \mathbf{A}_r \mathbf{x}_r = \mathbf{b}, \;\; \mathbf{x}_i \succeq_{\mathcal{Q}} \mathbf{0},$$

where $\mathbf{x}_i \in \mathbb{R}^{n_i}, \mathbf{c}_i \in \mathbb{R}^{n_i}, \mathbf{b} \in \mathbb{R}^m, \mathbf{A}_i \in \mathbb{R}^{m \times n_i}$ and inequalities of the form $\mathbf{x} \succeq_{\mathcal{Q}} \mathbf{y}$ means $\mathbf{x} - \mathbf{y} \in \mathcal{Q}$. The corresponding dual is

$$\max_{\mathbf{y}, \mathbf{z}_1, \ldots, \mathbf{z}_r} \; \mathbf{b}^T \mathbf{y} \;\; \text{s.t.} \;\; \mathbf{A}_i^T \mathbf{y} + \mathbf{z}_i = \mathbf{c}_i, \;\; \mathbf{z}_i \succeq_{\mathcal{Q}} \mathbf{0},$$

where $\mathbf{y} \in \mathbb{R}^m$ and $\mathbf{z}_i \in \mathbb{R}^{n_i}$. Denote $\mathbf{x} = (\mathbf{x}_1^T, \ldots, \mathbf{x}_r^T)^T, \mathbf{z} = (\mathbf{z}_1^T, \ldots, \mathbf{z}_r^T)^T$ and $\mathbf{c} = (\mathbf{c}_1^T, \ldots, \mathbf{c}_r^T)^T$. A duality theory, very similar to that for linear programs (LP), has been developed for SOCPs. In particular, the strong duality theorem [1] guarantees that if the primal and dual problems have strictly feasible solutions, then both have optimal solutions $\mathbf{x}^*, (\mathbf{y}^*, \mathbf{z}^*)$ with zero duality gap (i.e., $\mathbf{c}^T \mathbf{x}^* = \mathbf{b}^T \mathbf{y}^*$).

Moreover, it is well-known that standard optimization problems such as LPs, convex QPs, and QCQPs can all be solved as SOCPs. In turn, SOCP is a special case of SDP [15]. Thus, the complexity of SOCP falls between those of SDP and QCQP. While SOCPs can be solved as SDPs, it is however not recommended to do so [1, 8]. Interior point methods that solve SOCP directly have a much better worst-case complexity and run far more efficiently in practice than solving the corresponding SDP.

---

[2] The *second-order cone* $\mathcal{Q}$ is the norm cone for the Euclidean norm: $\mathcal{Q} = \{\mathbf{x} = [x_0, \tilde{\mathbf{x}}^T]^T \; : \; x_0 \geq \|\tilde{\mathbf{x}}\|\}$, where $\mathbf{x} = [x_0, x_1, \ldots, x_n]^T \in \mathbb{R}^n, \tilde{\mathbf{x}} = [x_1, \ldots, x_n]^T \in \mathbb{R}^{n-1}$ and $\| \cdot \|$ denotes the standard Euclidean norm.

4   SOCP Formulation

In Section 4.1, we will show that the general optimization problem in (6) can be equivalently formulated as a SOCP, which can then be solved more efficiently than a SDP. The specific SOCP formulations for two popular kernel classifiers, namely, C-SVM and ν-SVM, are then discussed in Section 4.2. Because of the lack of space, SOCP formulations for the other kernel methods, will be reported in a longer version of this paper.

4.1   General Formulation

First, the Lagrangian for (2) is $\mathcal{L}(\boldsymbol{\alpha}, \boldsymbol{\gamma}) = \boldsymbol{\alpha}^T \mathbf{v} - \frac{1}{2}\boldsymbol{\alpha}^T \mathbf{G}(\mathbf{K})\boldsymbol{\alpha} + \boldsymbol{\gamma}^T(\mathbf{A}\boldsymbol{\alpha} + \mathbf{b})$, where $\boldsymbol{\gamma} \in \mathbb{R}^n_+$. Setting its derivative w.r.t. $\boldsymbol{\alpha}$ to zero, we have[3]

$$\frac{\partial \mathcal{L}(\boldsymbol{\alpha}, \boldsymbol{\gamma})}{\partial \boldsymbol{\alpha}} = \mathbf{v} - \mathbf{G}(\mathbf{K})\boldsymbol{\alpha} + \mathbf{A}^T \boldsymbol{\gamma} \;\Rightarrow\; \boldsymbol{\alpha} = \mathbf{G}(\mathbf{K})^{-1}(\mathbf{A}^T \boldsymbol{\gamma} + \mathbf{v}).$$

Substituting this back into (6), we then obtain:

$$\min_{\boldsymbol{\beta}, \boldsymbol{\gamma}} \quad \frac{1}{2}(\mathbf{A}^T \boldsymbol{\gamma} + \mathbf{v})^T \mathbf{G}(\mathbf{K})^{-1}(\mathbf{A}^T \boldsymbol{\gamma} + \mathbf{v}) + \boldsymbol{\gamma}^T \mathbf{b} + \frac{\lambda_Q}{2}\boldsymbol{\beta}^T \underline{\mathbf{K}}\boldsymbol{\beta}$$

$$\text{s.t.} \quad \mathbf{1}^T \boldsymbol{\beta} = c, \;\; \boldsymbol{\beta}, \boldsymbol{\gamma} \geq \mathbf{0}, \;\; \mathbf{K} = \text{reshape}(\underline{\mathbf{K}}\boldsymbol{\beta})$$

$$= \min_{\boldsymbol{\beta}, \boldsymbol{\gamma}, t_1, t_2} \frac{1}{2}t_1 + \boldsymbol{\gamma}^T \mathbf{b} + \frac{\lambda_Q}{2}t_2$$

$$\text{s.t.} \quad t_1 \geq (\mathbf{A}^T \boldsymbol{\gamma} + \mathbf{v})^T \mathbf{G}(\mathbf{K})^{-1}(\mathbf{A}^T \boldsymbol{\gamma} + \mathbf{v}), \;\; t_2 \geq \boldsymbol{\beta}^T \underline{\mathbf{K}}\boldsymbol{\beta},$$

$$\mathbf{1}^T \boldsymbol{\beta} = c, \;\; \boldsymbol{\beta}, \boldsymbol{\gamma} \geq \mathbf{0}, \;\; \mathbf{K} = \text{reshape}(\underline{\mathbf{K}}\boldsymbol{\beta}). \tag{7}$$

Now, we will utilize two techniques on converting problems to SOCPs as discussed in [1, 10]. Let $\mathbf{y} \in \mathbb{R}^n$, $\mathbf{s} = [s_1, \ldots, s_k]^T \in \mathbb{R}^k_+$, and

$$\mathbf{M}(\mathbf{s}) = \sum_{i=1}^{k} s_i \mathbf{M}_i, \tag{8}$$

where each $\mathbf{M}_i \in \mathbb{R}^{n \times n}$ is psd. The first technique shows that inequality constraints on fractional quadratic functions of the form $t \geq \mathbf{y}^T \mathbf{M}(\mathbf{s})^{-1}\mathbf{y}$, where $t \in \mathbb{R}_+$, can be replaced by the system:

$$\sum_{i=1}^{k} \mathbf{D}_i \mathbf{w}_i = \mathbf{y}, \;\; t \geq \sum_{i=1}^{k} t_i, \;\; s_i t_i \geq \mathbf{w}_i^T \mathbf{w}_i,$$

where, for $i = 1, \ldots, k, t_i \in \mathbb{R}_+, \mathbf{w}_i \in \mathbb{R}^{r_i}, r_i = \text{rank}(\mathbf{M}_i)$ and $\mathbf{D}_i \in \mathbb{R}^{n \times r_i}$ such that $\mathbf{M}_i = \mathbf{D}_i \mathbf{D}_i^T$. As will be seen in Section 4.2, $\mathbf{G}(\mathbf{K})$ can be written in the form of (8) in many kernel methods, i.e.,

$$\mathbf{G}(\mathbf{K}) = \sum_{i,j=1}^{m} \beta_{ij} \mathbf{G}_{ij}, \tag{9}$$

---

[3] When $\mathbf{G}(\mathbf{K})$ is only positive semidefinite, we can use the pseudo-inverse $\mathbf{G}(\mathbf{K})^+$ instead of $\mathbf{G}(\mathbf{K})^{-1}$.

where $\beta_{ij} \in \mathbb{R}_+$ and $\mathbf{G}_{ij} \succeq 0$. We also decompose $\mathbf{G}_{ij}$ in the same form as for $\mathbf{M}_i$, i.e.,

$$\mathbf{G}_{ij} = \tilde{\mathbf{G}}_{ij}\tilde{\mathbf{G}}_{ij}^T, \tag{10}$$

which is always possible as $\mathbf{G}_{ij} \succeq 0$. The constraint $t_1 \geq (\mathbf{A}^T\boldsymbol{\gamma} + \mathbf{v})^T\mathbf{G}(\mathbf{K})^{-1}(\mathbf{A}^T\boldsymbol{\gamma} + \mathbf{v})$ in (7) can thus be replaced by

$$\sum_{i,j=1}^{m} \tilde{\mathbf{G}}_{ij}\mathbf{c}_{ij} = \mathbf{A}^T\boldsymbol{\gamma} + \mathbf{v}, \quad t_1 \geq \sum_{i,j=1}^{m} \tau_{ij}, \quad \beta_{ij}\tau_{ij} \geq \mathbf{c}_{ij}^T\mathbf{c}_{ij}, \tag{11}$$

where $\tau_{ij} \in \mathbb{R}_+, r_{ij} = \text{rank}(\mathbf{G}_{ij})$ and $\mathbf{c}_{ij} \in \mathbb{R}^{r_{ij}}$ for $i,j = 1,\ldots,m$.

The second technique converts hyperbolic constraints of the form $xy \geq \mathbf{w}^T\mathbf{w}$, where $x, y \in \mathbb{R}_+, \mathbf{w} \in \mathbb{R}^n$, to the equivalent second-order cone constraint $x + y \geq \left\|\begin{bmatrix} 2\mathbf{w} \\ x - y \end{bmatrix}\right\|$. Define $\underline{\mathbf{G}}$ by

$$\underline{\mathbf{K}} = \underline{\mathbf{G}}\,\underline{\mathbf{G}}^T. \tag{12}$$

Then, for the constraints $\beta_{ij}\tau_{ij} \geq \mathbf{c}_{ij}^T\mathbf{c}_{ij}$ in (11) and

$$t_2 \geq \boldsymbol{\beta}^T\underline{\mathbf{K}}\boldsymbol{\beta} = (\underline{\mathbf{G}}^T\boldsymbol{\beta})^T(\underline{\mathbf{G}}^T\boldsymbol{\beta}) \tag{13}$$

in (7), as $\beta_{ij}, \tau_{ij}, t_2 \in \mathbb{R}_+$, they can be rewritten as $\beta_{ij} + \tau_{ij} \geq \left\|\begin{bmatrix} 2\mathbf{c}_{ij} \\ \beta_{ij} - \tau_{ij} \end{bmatrix}\right\|$ and $t_2 + 1 \geq \left\|\begin{bmatrix} 2\underline{\mathbf{G}}^T\boldsymbol{\beta} \\ t_2 - 1 \end{bmatrix}\right\|$, respectively.

Finally, putting these and (11) back into (7), we obtain

$$\min_{\boldsymbol{\beta},\boldsymbol{\gamma},t_1,t_2,\boldsymbol{\tau},\mathbf{c}} \frac{1}{2}t_1 + \boldsymbol{\gamma}^T\mathbf{b} + \frac{\lambda_Q}{2}t_2$$

$$\text{s.t.} \quad \sum_{i,j=1}^{m} \tilde{\mathbf{G}}_{ij}\mathbf{c}_{ij} = \mathbf{A}^T\boldsymbol{\gamma} + \mathbf{v}, t_1 \geq \sum_{i,j=1}^{m} \tau_{ij},$$

$$\beta_{ij} + \tau_{ij} \geq \left\|\begin{bmatrix} 2\mathbf{c}_{ij} \\ \beta_{ij} - \tau_{ij} \end{bmatrix}\right\|, \quad t_2 + 1 \geq \left\|\begin{bmatrix} 2\underline{\mathbf{G}}^T\boldsymbol{\beta} \\ t_2 - 1 \end{bmatrix}\right\|,$$

$$\mathbf{1}^T\boldsymbol{\beta} = c, \quad \boldsymbol{\beta},\boldsymbol{\gamma},\boldsymbol{\tau} \geq \mathbf{0}, \tag{14}$$

where $\boldsymbol{\tau} = [\tau_{ij}]_{i,j=1}^m, \mathbf{c} = [\mathbf{c}_{ij}]_{i,j=1}^m$, and this is a SOCP.

In this kernel learning setting, it can be shown that the solving of SDP, SOCP and QCQP by interior point methods yield worst-case complexities of $O(n^{6.5})$, $O(n^5)$ and $O(n^5)$, respectively [7].

4.2   Examples

We first consider the C-SVM, whose dual is:

$$\max_{\boldsymbol{\alpha}} \boldsymbol{\alpha}^T\mathbf{1} - \frac{1}{2}\boldsymbol{\alpha}^T(\mathbf{K} \odot \mathbf{y}\mathbf{y}^T)\boldsymbol{\alpha} \quad \text{s.t.} \quad \boldsymbol{\alpha}^T\mathbf{y} = 0, \quad \mathbf{0} \leq \boldsymbol{\alpha} \leq C\mathbf{1},$$

where $\mathbf{1} = [1, \ldots, 1]^T \in \mathbb{R}^m, \mathbf{y} = [y_1, \ldots, y_m]^T \in \mathbb{R}^m$, $\odot$ denotes the Hadamard product and $C \in \mathbb{R}_+$ is a user-defined parameter. Comparing with (2), we have $\mathbf{v} = \mathbf{1}$ and $\mathbf{G}(\mathbf{K}) = \mathbf{K} \odot \mathbf{y}\mathbf{y}^T = (\sum_{i,j=1}^m \beta_{ij} \underline{\mathbf{K}}_{ij}) \odot \mathbf{y}\mathbf{y}^T = \sum_{i,j=1}^m \beta_{ij}(\underline{\mathbf{K}}_{ij} \odot \mathbf{y}\mathbf{y}^T)$, on using (5). Thus, $\mathbf{G}(\mathbf{K})$ is of the form in (9), with $\mathbf{G}_{ij} = \underline{\mathbf{K}}_{ij} \odot \mathbf{y}\mathbf{y}^T \succeq 0$. Moreover, $\mathbf{A} = [\mathbf{I}_m, -\mathbf{I}_m, -\mathbf{y}, \mathbf{y}]^T$ and $\mathbf{b} = [\mathbf{0}^T, C\mathbf{1}^T, 0, 0]^T$, where $\mathbf{I}_m$ is the $m \times m$ identity matrix and $\mathbf{0} = [0, \ldots, 0]^T \in \mathbb{R}^m$. Define $\tilde{\mathbf{G}}_{ij}$ and $\underline{\mathbf{G}}$ by (10) and (12) respectively, and $\boldsymbol{\gamma} = [\boldsymbol{\eta}, \boldsymbol{\xi}, b_1, b_2]^T$, (14) then becomes

$$\min_{\boldsymbol{\beta}, \boldsymbol{\eta}, \boldsymbol{\xi}, b, t_1, t_2, \boldsymbol{\tau}, \mathbf{c}} \frac{1}{2}t_1 + C\boldsymbol{\xi}^T\mathbf{1} + \frac{\lambda_Q}{2}t_2$$

$$\text{s.t.} \quad \sum_{ij} \tilde{\mathbf{G}}_{ij}\mathbf{c}_{ij} = -b\mathbf{y} + \boldsymbol{\eta} - \boldsymbol{\xi} + \mathbf{1}, \ t_1 \geq \sum_{ij} \tau_{ij},$$

$$\beta_{ij} + \tau_{ij} \geq \left\| \begin{bmatrix} 2\mathbf{c}_{ij} \\ \beta_{ij} - \tau_{ij} \end{bmatrix} \right\|, \ t_2 + 1 \geq \left\| \begin{bmatrix} 2\underline{\mathbf{G}}^T\boldsymbol{\beta} \\ t_2 - 1 \end{bmatrix} \right\|,$$

$$\mathbf{1}^T\boldsymbol{\beta} = c, \ \boldsymbol{\eta}, \boldsymbol{\xi}, \boldsymbol{\beta}, \boldsymbol{\gamma}, \boldsymbol{\tau} \geq \mathbf{0},$$

where $b = b_1 - b_2$ can be shown to be the bias in C-SVM.

Another popular kernel classifier is the ν-SVM, in which $\nu \in (0, 1)$ controls the fractions of errors and support vectors. Its dual is

$$\max_{\boldsymbol{\alpha}} -\frac{1}{2}\boldsymbol{\alpha}^T(\mathbf{K} \odot \mathbf{y}\mathbf{y}^T)\boldsymbol{\alpha} \ \text{s.t.} \ \boldsymbol{\alpha}^T\mathbf{y} = 0, \ \boldsymbol{\alpha}^T\mathbf{1} \geq 1, \ \mathbf{0} \leq \boldsymbol{\alpha} \leq \frac{1}{\nu m}\mathbf{1}.$$

Again, on comparison with (2), we have $\mathbf{v} = \mathbf{0}$, $\mathbf{G}(\mathbf{K}) = \mathbf{K} \odot \mathbf{y}\mathbf{y}^T$ (as for C-SVM), $\mathbf{A} = [\mathbf{I}_m, -\mathbf{I}_m, -\mathbf{y}, \mathbf{y}, \mathbf{1}]^T$ and $\mathbf{b} = [\mathbf{0}^T, \frac{1}{\nu m}\mathbf{1}^T, 0, 0, -1]^T$. Define $\tilde{\mathbf{G}}_{ij}$ and $\underline{\mathbf{G}}$ as for C-SVM, $\boldsymbol{\gamma} = [\boldsymbol{\eta}, \boldsymbol{\xi}, b_1, b_2, \rho]^T$ and $b = b_1 - b_2$, (14) then becomes

$$\min_{\boldsymbol{\beta}, \boldsymbol{\eta}, \boldsymbol{\xi}, \rho, b, t_1, t_2, \boldsymbol{\tau}, \mathbf{c}} \frac{1}{2}t_1 - \rho + \frac{1}{\nu m}\boldsymbol{\xi}^T\mathbf{1} + \frac{\lambda_Q}{2}t_2$$

$$\text{s.t.} \quad \sum_{ij} \tilde{\mathbf{G}}_{ij}\mathbf{c}_{ij} = -b\mathbf{y} + \boldsymbol{\eta} - \boldsymbol{\xi} + \rho\mathbf{1}, \ t_1 \geq \sum_{ij} \tau_{ij},$$

$$\beta_{ij} + \tau_{ij} \geq \left\| \begin{bmatrix} 2\mathbf{c}_{ij} \\ \beta_{ij} - \tau_{ij} \end{bmatrix} \right\|, \ t_2 + 1 \geq \left\| \begin{bmatrix} 2\underline{\mathbf{G}}^T\boldsymbol{\beta} \\ t_2 - 1 \end{bmatrix} \right\|,$$

$$\mathbf{1}^T\boldsymbol{\beta} = c, \ \rho, \boldsymbol{\eta}, \boldsymbol{\xi}, \boldsymbol{\beta}, \boldsymbol{\gamma}, \boldsymbol{\tau} \geq \mathbf{0}.$$

5   Experiments

The use of hyperkernels has been shown to produce SVMs that are always equally good, or better than, traditional SVMs tuned by cross-validation [11]. In this section, we demonstrate the speed-up that can be obtained by replacing the SDP formulation in [11] with our SOCP formulation. Because of the lack of space, only classification experiments using the C-SVM (Section 4.2) in an inductive setting are performed. We use the ARD (automatic relevance determination) hyperkernel, with the same setting as in [11]. For comparison, we also perform [7] under this setting. In particular, the candidate kernel matrix is *assumed* to be of the form in (5), with its trace fixed at $\sum_{ij} \text{trace}(\mathbf{K}_{ij})$. The mixing coefficients β_{ij}'s are to be learned, resulting in a QCQP. We use SDPT3 as the SDP solver[4], and MOSEK for solving SOCP and QCQP. All implementations are in Matlab, and the experiments are performed on a 2.4GHz Pentium 4 machine, with 1GB memory.

Comparison has also been made with the method proposed in [3] (which is adapted for the soft-margin C-SVM here). Analogous to the QCQP-based method, gradient descent is performed w.r.t. the β_{ij}'s in (5). However, because of the nonlinear nature of the optimization problem and also the large number (m^2) of β_{ij}'s to be learned[5], its performance turns out to be highly sensitive to the optimizer used. In particular, if a simple gradient descent scheme with a fixed learning rate is adopted, it can be faster than the QCQP-based method but the kernel solution has poor generalization performance, especially on the real-world data sets in Section 5.2. On the other hand, if a more sophisticated solver is used[6], its generalization performance becomes almost comparable to that of the hyperkernel method, but the learning is even much slower than hyperkernel's SDP formulation. Thus, because of this large variability, results on this descent-based method will not be reported in the sequel.

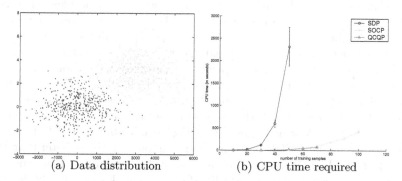

(a) Data distribution   (b) CPU time required

Fig. 1. The toy data set (Note that the y-axis in Figure 1(b) is in log scale)

5.1   Toy Data Set

The first experiment is performed on the two-class data used in [11] (Figure 1(a)). It is generated by two Gaussian distributions with highly non-isotropic variance (the standard deviation is 1 in one dimension and 1000 in the other). In order to better demonstrate the computational requirements of the different formulations, low rank approximation on the hyperkernel matrix is not used in this toy

---

[4] A recent benchmark study in [9] shows that SDPT3 is able to solve larger SDP problems than SeDuMi (used in [11]).

[5] Note that linear combinations of only three kernel matrices have been conducted in the experiments of [3].

[6] To be more specific, we used the fmincon function in Matlab's Optimization Toolbox.

problem. The number of training samples is varied from 10 to 100, and an independent set of 1000 samples are used for testing. To reduce statistical variability, results here are based on averages over 30 random repetitions.

Table 1. Test set accuracies (%) on the toy data set

# training samples	SDP	SOCP	QCQP
10	84.60 ± 10.60	84.60 ± 10.60	84.55 ± 12.41
20	95.83 ± 1.70	95.83 ± 1.70	94.99 ± 3.50
30	96.15 ± 1.45	96.15 ± 1.45	95.88 ± 3.93
40	97.02 ± 0.71	97.02 ± 0.71	97.21 ± 0.63
50	97.39 ± 0.51	97.39 ± 0.51	97.34 ± 0.71
60	-	97.35 ± 0.49	97.33 ± 0.61
70	-	97.49 ± 0.36	97.47 ± 0.38
80	-	97.34 ± 0.49	-
90	-	97.51 ± 0.36	-
100	-	97.36 ± 0.41	-

Table 1 compares the test set accuracies obtained. As both the SDP and SOCP formulations are derived from the same optimization problem, they yield identical kernel functions and identical C-SVMs. In practice, there may be minor differences due to the use of different optimization solvers. Notice that the QCQP-based method also yields comparable generalization performance on this simple toy problem. However, its implementation takes more storage and so has to stop at a training set size of 70. Moreover, we will see in Section 5.2 that there is also a significant difference in generalization performance on the real-world data sets. On the other hand, the speeds of the SDP and SOCP formulations are vastly different. As can be seen from Figure 1(b), our SOCP formulation, which is as fast as the QCQP-based method, is about 100 times faster than that of SDP. In fact, the SDP formulation is so slow that we have to stop when the training set size reaches 50. Empirically, the time complexities we obtained for SDP, SOCP and QCQP are $O(m^{4.27})$, $O(m^{3.38})$ and $O(m^{3.11})$ respectively.

5.2   Real-World Data Sets

The second set of experiments are performed on seven real-world data sets[7]. We use 60% of the data for training and the remaining 40% for testing. Results here are based on averages over 100 random repetitions. Moreover, we perform low rank approximation on the hyperkernel matrix as mentioned in [12,13]. We observe that the resultant matrix ranks obtained are in the range 10-20.

Results on the various methods are shown in Table 2. As can be seen, the test set accuracies obtained by the SDP and SOCP formulations are almost

---

[7] Data sets heart, ionosphere, liver, pima and sonar are from the UCI machine learning repository; while colon and lymphoma can be downloaded from http://www.kyb.tuebingen.mpg.de/bs/people/weston/l0.

Table 2. Test set accuracies and CPU time on the real-world data sets

	data set	SDP	SOCP	QCQP
accuracy	colon	84.08 ± 5.81	84.08 ± 5.81	83.04 ± 6.39
(in %)	heart	83.80 ± 2.80	83.80 ± 2.80	82.43 ± 2.82
	ionosphere	93.24 ± 1.55	93.24 ± 1.55	84.56 ± 3.76
	liver	64.80 ± 4.12	64.80 ± 4.12	64.55 ± 4.22
	lymphoma	90.24 ± 4.90	90.24 ± 4.90	82.30 ± 6.39
	pima	77.25 ± 1.71	77.25 ± 1.71	75.44 ± 1.69
	sonar	79.18 ± 4.41	79.18 ± 4.41	74.20 ± 3.94
CPU time	colon	1.15 ± 0.11	0.28 ± 0.17	0.22 ± 0.13
(in sec)	heart	17.25 ± 0.99	2.39 ± 0.18	0.71 ± 0.11
	ionosphere	27.50 ± 2.94	4.75 ± 0.26	1.41 ± 0.10
	liver	21.05 ± 0.82	3.17 ± 0.25	1.42 ± 0.17
	lymphoma	2.13 ± 0.20	0.39 ± 0.02	0.22 ± 0.04
	pima	224.54 ± 9.04	45.99 ± 2.21	9.58 ± 0.30
	sonar	8.91 ± 0.39	1.60 ± 0.15	0.53 ± 0.14

identical, while significant speedup can be achieved by using SOCP. Moreover, in terms of test set accuracy, both the SDP and SOCP formulations are better than the QCQP-based method on all data sets tested. Using the one-tailed paired t test, this difference is statistically significant at a 0.025 level of significance. In terms of speed, our SOCP formulation is very competitive with the QCQP-based method, with a running time of about 1.3 to 4.8 times that of the QCQP-based method on average.

6   Conclusion

In this paper, we show that the method of hyperkernels can be equivalently formulated as a SOCP, which can be solved more efficiently than the traditional SDP formulation. Experimental results on using the C-SVM on both toy and real-world data sets demonstrate significant speedups. We also demonstrate that the hyperkernel method yields better generalization performance than the QCQP-based method in [7]. The combination of this SOCP formulation with low rank approximation on the hyperkernel matrix will thus enable the method of hyperkernels to be efficiently applied even on large data sets, with good generalization performance.

In the experiments, we only used a straightforward implementation for the SOCP. In the future, we will further exploit potential structure and sparsity in our SOCP formulation, which have often provided substantial speedups in many convex optimization problems. Moreover, recently, Bach et al. [2] proposed a fast kernel learning method based on the sequential minimal optimization algorithm, and this will be also be studied in the future. Finally, note that the hyperkernel method can also be easily extended for transduction problems, and its comparison with the transductive method in [7] will be further explored.

References

1. F. Alizadeh and D. Goldfarb. Second-order cone programming. *Mathematical Programming, Series B*, 95:3–51, 2003.
2. F.R. Bach, G.R.G. Lanckriet, and M.I. Jordan. Multiple kernel learning, conic duality, and the SMO algorithm. In *Proceedings of the Twentieth-First International Conference on Machine*, Banff, Alberta, Canada, July 2004.
3. O. Bousquet and D.J.L. Herrmann. On the complexity of learning the kernel matrix. In S. Becker, S. Thrun, and K. Obermayer, editors, *Advances in Neural Information Processing Systems 15*, Cambridge, MA, 2003. MIT Press.
4. K. Crammer, J. Keshet, and Y. Singer. Kernel design using boosting. In S. Becker, S. Thrun, and K. Obermayer, editors, *Advances in Neural Information Processing Systems 15*, Cambridge, MA, 2003. MIT Press.
5. N. Cristianini, J. Shawe-Taylor, A. Elisseeff, and J. Kandola. On kernel-target alignment. In T.G. Dietterich, S. Becker, and Z. Ghahramani, editors, *Advances in Neural Information Processing Systems 14*, Cambridge, MA, 2002. MIT Press.
6. S. Fine and K. Scheinberg. Efficient SVM training using low-rank kernel representation. *Journal of Machine Learning Research*, 2:243–264, December 2001.
7. G.R.G. Lanckriet, N. Cristianini, P. Bartlett, L. El Ghaoui, and M.I. Jordan. Learning the kernel matrix with semidefinite programming. *Journal of Machine Learning Research*, 5:27–72, 2004.
8. M.S. Lobo, L. Vandenberghe, S. Boyd, and H. Lebret. Applications of second-order cone programming. *Linear Algebra Applications*, 284:193–228, 1998.
9. H.D. Mittelmann. An independent benchmarking of SDP and SOCP solvers. *Mathematical Programming Series B*, 95:407–430, 2003.
10. Y. Nesterov and A. Nemirovskii. *Interior-point Polynomial Algorithms in Convex Programming*. Society for Industrial and Applied Mathematics, Philadelphia, PA, 1994.
11. C.S. Ong and A.J. Smola. Machine learning with hyperkernels. In *Proceedings of the Twentieth International Conference on Machine Learning*, pages 568–575, Washington DC, USA, 2003.
12. C.S. Ong, A.J. Smola, and R.C. Williamson. Hyperkernels. In S. Becker, S. Thrun, and K. Obermayer, editors, *Advances in Neural Information Processing Systems 15*, Cambridge, MA, 2003. MIT Press.
13. C.S. Ong, A.J. Smola, and R.C. Williamson. Learning the kernel with hyperkernels, 2003. Submitted to Journal of Machine Learning Research.
14. B. Schölkopf and A.J. Smola. *Learning with Kernels*. MIT Press, Cambridge, MA, 2002.
15. L. Vandenberghe and S. Boyd. Semidefinite programming. *SIAM Review*, 38(1):49–95, 1996.
16. Z. Zhang, D.-Y. Yeung, and J.T. Kwok. Bayesian inference for transductive learning of kernel matrix using the Tanner-Wong data augmentation algorithm. In *Proceedings of the Twentieth-First International Conference on Machine Learning*, Banff, Alberta, Canada, July 2004.

Effective Voting of Heterogeneous Classifiers

Grigorios Tsoumakas, Ioannis Katakis, and Ioannis Vlahavas

Department of Informatics,
Aristotle University of Thessaloniki,
54124 Thessaloniki, Greece
{greg,katak,vlahavas}@csd.auth.gr

Abstract. This paper deals with the combination of classification models that have been derived from running different (heterogeneous) learning algorithms on the same data set. We focus on the Classifier Evaluation and Selection (ES) method, that evaluates each of the models (typically using 10-fold cross-validation) and selects the best one. We examine the performance of this method in comparison with the Oracle selecting the best classifier for the test set and show that 10-fold cross-validation has problems in detecting the best classifier. We then extend ES by applying a statistical test to the 10-fold accuracies of the models and combining through voting the most significant ones. Experimental results show that the proposed method, Effective Voting, performs comparably with the state-of-the-art method of Stacking with Multi-Response Model Trees without the additional computational cost of meta-training.

1   Introduction

A very active research area during the last years is the one involving methodologies and systems for the combination of multiple predictive models. It has attracted scientists from the fields of Statistics, Machine Learning, Pattern Recognition and Knowledge Discovery aiming at improving the predictive accuracy of a single classification or regression model. Within the Machine Learning community this area is commonly referred to as Ensemble Methods [6].

Models that have been derived from different executions of the same learning algorithm are often called Homogeneous. Such models can be induced by injecting randomness into the learning algorithm or through the manipulation of the training instances, the input attributes and the model outputs [7]. Homogeneous models are typically combined through weighted or unweighted voting. Models that have been derived from running different learning algorithms on the same data set are often called Heterogeneous.

This paper deals with the combination of Heterogeneous Classification Models and focuses on the Classifier Evaluation and Selection (ES) method. This method evaluates each of the models (typically using 10-fold cross-validation) and selects the best one. We examine the performance of ES in comparison with the Oracle selecting the best classifier for the test set and show that 10-fold cross-validation has problems in detecting the best classifier. We then extend

J.-F. Boulicaut et al. (Eds.): ECML 2004, LNAI 3201, pp. 465–476, 2004.
© Springer-Verlag Berlin Heidelberg 2004

ES by applying a statistical test to the 10-fold accuracies of the models and combining through voting the most significant ones in an attempt to alleviate this problem. Extensive experimental results show that the proposed method, Effective Voting, performs comparably with the state-of-the-art Heterogeneous Ensemble Method of Stacking with Multi-Response Model Trees [8] without the additional computational cost of meta-training.

The rest of this paper is organized as follows. The next section presents related work on combining Heterogeneous Classification Models. Section 3 describes in detail the proposed approach. Section 4 presents the experimental methodology and Section 5 the results and observations. Finally, Section 6 summarizes this paper and discusses issues for further investigation.

2   Combining Heterogeneous Classification Models

Unweighted and Weighted Voting are two of the simplest methods for combining not only Heterogeneous but also Homogeneous models. In Voting, each model outputs a class value (or ranking, or probability distribution) and the class with the most votes (or the highest average ranking, or average probability) is the one proposed by the ensemble. Note that this type of Voting is in fact called Plurality Voting, in contrast to the frequently used term Majority Voting, as the latter formally implies that at least 50% (the majority) of the votes should belong to the winning class. In Weighted Voting, the classification models are not treated equally. Each model is associated with a coefficient (weight), usually proportional to its classification accuracy.

Another simple method is Evaluation and Selection. Each of the classification models is evaluated (typically using 10-fold cross-validation) on the training set and the best one is selected for application on the test set. In [10,20], the accuracy of the models is estimated locally on the different examples that surround each test example. Such approaches belong to the family of Dynamic Classifier Selection introduced in [11], which was the first work discussing the idea of using a different function for classifier combination in different partitions of the training set.

Stacked Generalization [19], also known as Stacking in the literature, is a method that combines multiple classifiers by learning a meta-level model that predicts the correct class based on the decisions of the classifiers. This model is induced on a set of meta-level training data that are typically produced by a process similar to applying k-fold cross-validation on the training data. Specifically, k-1 folds are used for training the classifiers and one for recording their decisions along with the true class. This leads to a meta-level training data set of equal size to the original training data set. A meta-classifier is then induced from these data. When a new instance appears for classification, the output of all classifiers is first calculated and then propagated to the meta-level model, which outputs the final result. A recent study [9] has shown that Stacking with Multi-Response Model Trees [8] as the meta-level learning algorithm, is the most accurate heterogeneous classifier combining method of the Stacking family.

3   Effective Voting of Heterogeneous Classifiers

This paper presents a simple, yet effective extension to Classifier Evaluation and Selection. On top of the 10-fold cross-validation for the evaluation of the models we apply a paired t-test with a significance level of 0.05 for each pair of models to evaluate the statistical significance of their relative performance. We then combine the most significant ones through 3 different strategies. The whole process of the proposed method, called Effective Voting, is described in the following paragraphs.

Consider a set of classification models c_i, $i=1..N$. For each pair of models i,j we initially perform the paired t-test:

$$test(c_i, c_j) = \begin{cases} 1 & \text{if } c_i \text{ significantly better than } c_j \\ -1 & \text{if } c_j \text{ significantly better than } c_i \\ 0 & \text{otherwise} \end{cases}$$

Then for each model we calculate the overall significance index:

$$Sig(c_i) = \sum_{j=1}^{N} test(c_i, c_j)$$

Finally we try the following 3 strategies:

- EV_1: We select the model(s) with the highest significance index and combine their decisions through Weighted Voting (if more than one).
- EV_2: We select the model with the lowest error rate along with any others that are not significantly worse than this and combine their decisions through Weighted Voting (if more than one).
- EV_3: We select the three models with the highest significance index and combine their decisions through Voting. If there are ties, we brake them by selecting the most accurate ones.

Note that all of the above proposed strategies aim at selecting the most significantly accurate models, yet in a different way. The first gives priority to models with the highest statistical significance index taking into account their accuracies through the Weighted Voting process. The second gives priority to the most accurate model but also considers those that are not significantly worse than the best one. The last strategy always chooses the three models with the highest statistical significance index and combines them through simple Voting. However, it also takes into account the accuracy of the models, by selecting the most accurate ones when there are draws.

Table 1 exemplifies the operation of the three different strategies, based on a sample of the error rates and significance tests of 10 models from the experimental results. For each model in each row, the first 10 columns show the result of the paired t-test. The next two columns show the significance index and the average error rate. The last 3 columns show which models are selected by each strategy.

Table 1. Example of the operation of the three Effective Voting strategies

	c_1	c_2	c_3	c_4	c_5	c_6	c_7	c_8	c_9	c_{10}	Sig	Err. (%)	EV_1	EV_2	EV_3
c_1	0	1	1	1	0	0	1	0	0	0	4	23.53	√		
c_2	-1	0	-1	-1	-1	-1	-1	-1	-1	-1	-9	71.08			
c_3	-1	1	0	0	0	-1	0	0	-1	-1	-3	28.44			
c_4	-1	1	0	0	-1	-1	0	0	-1	-1	-4	29.42			
c_5	0	1	0	1	0	0	0	0	0	0	2	24.51		√	
c_6	0	1	1	1	0	0	1	1	0	0	5	20.59	√	√	√
c_7	-1	1	0	0	0	-1	0	0	-1	-1	-3	28.93			
c_8	0	1	0	0	0	-1	0	0	0	0	0	27.97			
c_9	0	1	1	1	0	0	1	0	0	0	4	22.55		√	√
c_{10}	0	1	1	1	0	0	1	0	0	0	4	21.57		√	√

We notice that EV_1 selects just one model, c_6, as it is the only one with the highest significance index, equal to 5. It is also the model with the lowest error rate. However, if we look at the line of c_6, we will see that models c_1, c_5, c_9 and c_{10} are not significantly worse. Therefore the decisions of all these models along with c_5 are combined by EV_2 through Weighted Voting. Finally EV_3 selects c_6 and then has to choose another two models from c_1, c_9 and c_{10} as they tie with a significant index of 4. From these it drops c_1, as it has the highest error rate and combines c_6 c_9 and c_{10} with Voting.

Effective Voting aims to stand in between methods that combine all models, such as Voting, Weighted Voting and Stacking and methods that just select a single model, like Evaluation and Selection. The former category of methods has the advantage of error correction through the contribution of different biases but also has the disadvantage of letting some models with potentially inferior predictive performance participate in the combination process. On the other hand the latter category excludes all models but one, which might not always be the most accurate one. Effective Voting attempts to first select the most significant models with the aid of statistical tests and then combine them through a voting process. It can therefore be considered as a pre-processing method, rather than an actual combination method.

4   Experimental Setup

This section provides information on the data sets, combining methods, participating algorithms and evaluation methodology that were used for the experiments. The WEKA machine learning software [18] was used as the platform for all the experiments.

4.1   Data Sets

The predictive performance of the combining methods was evaluated on 40 data sets from the UCI Machine Learning repository [3]. Table 2 presents the details

Table 2. Details of the data sets used in the experiments: Folder in UCI server, number of instances, classes, continuous and discrete attributes, (%) percentage of missing values

UCI Folder	Inst	Cls	Cnt	Dsc	MV
annealing	898	6	6	32	64.98
audiology	226	24	0	69	2.03
autos	205	7	15	10	1.15
balance-scale	625	3	4	0	0.00
breast-cancer	286	2	0	9	0.35
breast-cancer-wisconsin	699	2	9	0	0.25
car	1728	4	0	6	0.00
chess (kr-vs-kp)	3196	2	0	36	0.00
cmc	1473	3	2	7	0.00
dermatology	366	6	1	33	0.01
ecoli	336	8	7	0	0.00
glass	214	7	9	0	0.00
heart-disease (cleveland)	303	5	6	7	0.18
heart-disease (hungary)	294	5	6	7	20.46
heart-disease (switzerland)	123	5	6	7	17.07
heart-disease (va)	200	5	6	7	26.85
hepatitis	155	2	6	13	5.67
horse-colic	368	2	7	15	23.80
image	2310	7	19	0	0.00
ionosphere	351	2	34	0	0.00
iris	150	3	4	0	0.00
labor	57	2	8	8	35.75
lymphography	148	4	3	15	0.00
pima-indians-diabetes	768	2	8	0	0.00
primary-tumor	339	22	0	17	3.90
soybean	683	19	0	35	9.78
statlog (australian)	690	2	6	9	0.65
statlog (german)	1000	2	7	13	0.00
statlog (heart)	270	2	13	0	0.00
statlog (satimage)	6435	6	36	0	0.00
statlog (segment)	2310	7	19	0	0.00
statlog (vehicle)	846	4	18	0	0.00
thyroid-disease	3772	4	7	22	5.54
tic-tac-toe	958	2	0	9	0.00
undocumented (sonar)	208	2	60	0	0.00
undocumented (vowel-context)	990	11	10	3	0.00
voting-records	435	2	0	16	5.63
waveform	5000	3	40	0	0.00
wine	178	3	13	0	0.00
zoo	101	7	1	16	0.00

of the data sets (Folder in UCI server, number of instances, classes, continuous and discrete attributes, (%) percentage of missing values).

4.2   Combining Methods and Participating Algorithms

We compared the following classifier combining methods that were described in Sections 2 and 3: Stacking with Multi-Response Model Trees (SMT), Voting (V), Weighted Voting (WV), Effective Voting with the 3 different strategies (EV) and Evaluation and Selection (ES).

The comparison also includes the Oracle classifier selection method (ORA) that a-posteriori selects the classification algorithm with the highest accuracy on the test-set. This is not an actual combining method, but it is used to evaluate the ability of (ES) to select the best classifier on the test set. The predictive performance of ORA is the best performance that ES could achieve, if it always selected the best classifier for the test-set.

All the above methods are used in conjunction with the WEKA implementations of the following 10 base-level classification algorithms, which are run with default parameter values unless otherwise stated:

- DT: the decision table algorithm of [13].
- JRip: the RIPPER rule learning algorithm [5].
- PART: the PART rule learning algorithm [17].
- J48: the decision tree learning algorithm C4.5 [15].
- IBk: the k nearest neighbor algorithm [1].
- K*: an instance-based learning algorithm with entropic distance measure [4].
- NB: the Naive Bayes algorithm [12] using the kernel density estimator rather than assume normal distributions for numeric attributes.
- SMO: the sequential minimal optimization algorithm for training a support vector classifier using polynomial kernels [14].
- RBF: an algorithm for training a radial basis function network [2].
- MLR: the multi-response linear regression algorithm, as used in [16].

The meta-level training data for Stacking are produced using 10-fold stratified cross-validation on the training set. The same procedure is used for estimating the accuracy of the above base-level algorithms and their significance index through the paired t-tests. All combining methods operate on probability distributions of the base-level classifiers.

4.3   Evaluation Methodology

For the evaluation of the combining methods we perform a 10-fold stratified cross-validation experiment. In each of the 10 repetitions, the same 9 folds are used for training the different combining methods and 1 fold for evaluating their performance. The error rates are averaged over the 10 folds in order to obtain the average error $err_m(d_i)$ of each method m in each data set d_i.

A first indicator for pairwise comparisons, is the geometric mean of the average error of each method over all the data sets. Comparing the geometric means of each method we can get a general impression of the relationship between the methods. If the geometric mean of a method m_1 is greater than another method m_2 then this implies that method m_1 performs worse than method m_2, and vice versa. The ratio of their means gives a measure of how much better/worse is their relative performance.

In addition, we apply a paired t-test to the errors of the methods in the 10 folds of the cross-validation experiment with a significance level of 0.05. From the outcome of this test on all data sets we report the statistically significant wins and losses for each pair of methods.

5   Results and Discussion

Table 3 shows the significant wins and losses for each pair of combining methods on all data sets. Table 4, shows the average 10-fold cross-validation error rate of the combining methods for each data set. The geometric mean is presented in the last line.

Table 3. A symmetric matrix that presents the significant wins and losses (w:l) for each pair of combining methods

	SMT	V	WV	EV_1	EV_2	EV_3	ES	ORA
SMT		7:1	7:1	5:2	3:3	3:4	8:2	3:18
V	1:7		0:1	2:5	0:7	0:6	5:6	0:23
WV	1:7	1:0		2:5	0:4	0:5	5:6	0:22
EV_1	2:5	5:2	5:2		0:1	1:4	0:0	0:31
EV_2	3:3	7:0	4:0	1:0		1:1	3:1	0:17
EV_3	4:3	6:0	5:0	4:1	1:1		3:2	0:23
ES	2:8	6:5	6:5	0:0	1:3	2:3		0:29
ORA	18:3	23:0	22:0	31:0	17:0	23:0	29:0	

5.1   The Performance of Evaluation and Selection

The results show that ORA achieves by far the significantly best performance compared to the rest. However, ORA is a control method for comparison purposes. The ES method which should approximate it, actually performs much worse. This reveals the fact that the average accuracy of a classification algorithm based on a 10-fold cross-validation experiment on a training set is often an unsuccessful indicator of the algorithm's accuracy on a test set.

A more profound look into which algorithms are selected as best by ES against the true best as selected by ORA is given by the confusion matrix of Table 5. The total number of selections in the last column, shows how many times the algorithm of each row was selected by ES. The total number of selections at the bottom of the table, shows how many times the algorithm of each column was truly best. The number in row i and column j represents the number of times that the algorithm of row i was found to be the best by ES while the true best was the algorithm of column j. Note that the total number of selections is 400 (40 data sets * 10 folds of the cross-validation).

Table 4. Folder in UCI server, average error rate of each combining method on each of the 40 data sets and geometric mean of each combining method over all data sets

UCI Folder	SMT	V	WV	EV$_1$	EV$_2$	EV$_3$	ES	ORA
annealing	1.56	2.78	2.67	1.67	1.67	2.00	1.67	1.67
audiology	20.34	16.80	17.69	19.49	17.31	18.16	20.36	14.60
autos	15.48	16.02	16.00	19.83	18.40	16.45	21.76	14.57
balance-scale	5.44	10.24	9.92	8.00	8.32	9.91	8.00	8.00
breast-cancer	24.47	24.11	24.47	26.88	23.41	25.91	29.01	19.94
breast-cancer-wisconsin	3.01	3.00	3.00	2.86	3.00	3.00	2.72	2.00
car	1.74	5.09	4.92	4.75	4.74	4.46	5.32	3.88
chess (kr-vs-kp)	0.63	0.78	0.72	0.56	0.47	0.59	0.59	0.47
cmc	45.15	47.05	46.98	48.21	46.37	47.12	48.68	44.20
dermatology	1.64	1.91	2.18	3.00	2.46	2.46	2.73	0.82
ecoli	14.31	12.83	13.13	13.39	13.71	13.40	12.79	11.31
glass	22.40	23.79	23.31	23.81	23.29	24.29	27.51	17.77
heart-disease (cleveland)	16.46	18.19	18.19	15.84	17.19	14.85	16.81	11.57
heart-disease (hungary)	16.34	18.01	17.68	14.63	14.97	14.61	13.95	11.89
heart-disease (switzerland)	65.71	58.21	59.74	63.21	60.64	63.14	61.67	47.63
heart-disease (va)	68.50	66.50	68.00	69.50	66.00	64.00	64.50	57.50
hepatitis	19.46	14.88	14.88	14.25	14.88	14.25	14.21	8.38
horse-colic	16.29	14.67	14.67	16.00	16.82	15.46	16.00	12.21
image	2.08	1.90	1.86	2.21	1.90	1.65	2.25	1.73
ionosphere	7.12	7.68	7.97	8.83	7.12	5.13	7.99	4.28
iris	6.00	4.67	4.67	4.67	4.67	5.33	3.33	2.00
labor	7.00	5.33	5.33	8.33	5.33	7.00	10.33	0.01
lymphography	21.52	14.24	14.24	18.90	14.24	12.90	14.81	8.14
pima-indians-diabetes	22.91	23.30	23.04	22.91	23.04	23.17	23.56	20.83
primary-tumor	58.38	53.96	53.96	51.92	51.91	49.26	52.80	47.49
soybean	6.59	7.02	7.02	6.59	6.73	7.02	6.30	4.39
statlog (australian)	14.35	13.19	13.19	14.35	13.91	13.62	14.78	11.74
statlog (german)	22.80	24.00	23.90	25.00	24.60	24.50	25.20	22.40
statlog (heart)	14.81	15.93	16.30	15.19	15.19	15.56	15.19	11.85
statlog (satimage)	7.79	8.38	8.27	9.20	8.80	8.50	9.71	8.78
statlog (segment)	1.82	1.52	1.47	2.12	1.90	1.77	2.25	1.69
statlog (vehicle)	20.33	25.53	25.30	23.76	23.88	23.40	24.95	21.63
thyroid-disease	0.40	2.78	2.41	0.48	0.42	0.37	0.58	0.32
tic-tac-toe	0.83	3.13	3.13	1.56	1.67	1.67	0.94	0.94
undocumented (sonar)	17.79	15.90	15.43	14.31	11.50	11.50	15.29	8.62
undocumented (vowel-context)	0.91	1.21	0.71	0.71	0.71	0.71	0.71	0.51
voting-records	3.91	4.37	4.37	3.91	3.92	4.14	4.13	2.77
waveform	13.58	16.30	16.14	13.58	13.58	13.92	13.42	13.24
wine	1.70	0.56	0.56	2.78	1.11	1.70	2.78	0.01
zoo	5.91	2.91	2.91	6.00	2.91	5.00	7.00	2.00
geometric mean	7.93	8.60	8.45	8.58	7.81	8.00	8.57	4.59

Table 5. Confusion matrix: number of times each algorithm was selected by ES against true times being best

	DT	IBk	J48	JRip	K*	MLR	NB	PART	RBF	SMO	Total
DT	11	2	1	0	2	2	2	2	0	0	22
IBk	2	9	1	4	9	0	1	1	0	6	33
J48	5	0	7	5	2	3	2	5	1	3	33
JRip	4	6	9	21	8	5	4	9	1	2	69
K*	0	5	2	7	4	1	4	2	0	6	31
MLR	1	2	2	7	3	9	13	5	1	7	50
NB	5	7	8	6	4	10	18	3	1	11	73
PART	1	4	4	3	0	1	0	3	0	3	19
RBF	0	0	0	0	0	0	1	0	1	0	2
SMO	5	5	5	4	4	13	7	5	0	20	68
Total	34	40	39	57	36	44	52	35	5	58	
Ratio	0.32	0.23	0.18	0.37	0.11	0.16	0.35	0.09	0.20	0.34	

We firstly notice that RBF is only 5 times the best classifier out of the 400. This shows that in general it is not a very accurate classification learning algorithm with the default parameters as used in the experiments. The most accurate classifiers are JRip, NB and SMO. These are also the algorithms that are most of the times correctly identified by ES as it is given by the ratio of correct selections by ES over the actual selections by ORA, in the last line of Table 5. PART and K* are two algorithms that although together they are 71 times the best algorithms, yet ES only correctly identifies them 7 times.

5.2   The Performance of Effective Voting

The results in Table 3 show that the proposed approach manages to alleviate the problem of predicting the most accurate classification algorithm on a test set based on the average accuracies of a 10-fold cross-validation experiment on the training set. Strategy EV_1 is comparable to ES and has a lower geometric mean error. More importantly, strategies EV_2 and EV_3 have respectively two and one significant wins more than ES and a lower geometric mean error.

In addition, EV_2 is comparable to the state-of-the-art SMT method with a lower geometric mean error and EV_3 has one significant win more but a little higher geometric mean error. Moreover, Effective Voting is much faster than SMT as it does not involve any computational cost for meta-training. In fact, SMT is a very complex method since not only does it require meta-training, but it also learns one model for each class at the meta-level. It so creates a second Ensemble of homogeneous models at the meta-level, which in part justifies its increased performance.

It is interesting to mention the actual data sets where the significant wins/losses of the Effective Voting variants occur compared to the state-of-the-art SMT method. SMT is significantly better than all three methods in the data sets of *balance-scale* and *car* (which is in accordance with the results of [9]). In addition, in the *cmc* domain it wins all but EV_2 and in *statlog-satimage* all but EV_3. All variants of EV win SMT in the *primary-tumor* domain. In addition EV_1 wins SMT in the *hepatitis* domain, EV_2 in the *hepatitis* and *sonar* domains and EV_3 in the *lymphography, ionosphere* and *sonar* domains. This shows that the three different strategies of EV actually offer different merits.

5.3   Evaluating the Effect of Model Removal

In this part we evaluate the effect that the removal of a model has on the performance of the methods. We will remove in turn the different models, replacing them back to the ensemble before removing the next. The geometric mean error of the combining methods is presented in Table 6. Each column corresponds to one run and the header of the columns states the classification algorithm not used.

Table 6. Geometric mean error of combining methods with different ensemble compositions

	(ALL)	DT	IBk	J48	JRIP	K*	MLR	NB	PART	RBF	SMO
SMT	7.93	7.91	7.78	7.85	7.82	7.88	8.23	7.95	7.90	7.92	7.88
V	8.60	8.69	8.85	8.92	8.86	9.04	8.47	8.65	9.03	8.50	8.77
WV	8.45	8.47	8.63	8.48	8.74	8.78	8.27	8.40	8.70	8.28	8.43
EV_1	8.58	8.56	8.71	8.57	8.52	8.45	8.47	8.47	8.59	8.52	8.55
EV_2	7.81	7.81	7.69	7.84	7.98	7.92	7.89	8.01	7.93	7.84	7.76
EV_3	8.00	8.03	8.26	8.12	8.33	8.46	8.20	8.26	8.08	8.06	8.12
ES	8.57	8.88	8.62	8.59	8.81	8.48	8.71	8.79	8.74	8.74	8.70
ORA	4.59	5.34	4.77	4.73	4.75	4.68	4.64	5.38	4.72	4.56	4.66

The results show that from the three proposed strategies for Effective Voting, the most competitive one is EV_2. For all different model compositions of the ensemble it has a much lower geometric error mean. In addition the geometric mean of EV_2 is comparable with that of SMT.

6   Conclusions and Future Work

This paper has focused on the method of Classifier Evaluation and Selection (ES). It demonstrated that one of the weaknesses of this method derives from the inaccurate evaluation of the models' accuracies. To remedy this problem we proposed an extension to ES that makes use of statistical significance tests in order to select and combine the most accurate models. Through a large and thorough experimental study we showed that the proposed method, Effective Voting, is comparable in accuracy to recent state-of-the-art heterogeneous classifier combining methods, such as Stacking with Multi-Response Model Trees having at the same time reduced computational cost.

As a general conclusion, we believe that it is worth researching more into advancing simple heterogeneous ensemble methods such as evaluation and selection instead of complex methods that require a lot more computational cost. This conclusion is reinforced by the very good performance of the ORA method. On the other hand, ORA was significantly worse than SMT in the domains of *balance-scale* and *car*, which shows that in some cases more complex methods are definitely required to achieve better performance.

For future work, we intend to research into alternative methods for classifier performance evaluation, in order to further improve the Evaluation and Selection framework. In addition we intend to investigate the applicability of the proposed ideas to more complex Classifier Evaluation methods such as those that are based on local accuracy estimates.

References

1. D. Aha, D.W. Kibler, and M.K. Albert. Instance-based learning algorithms. *Machine Learning*, 6:37–66, 1991.
2. C.M. Bishop. *Neural Networks for Pattern Recognition*. Oxford University Press, 1995.
3. C.L. Blake and C.J. Merz. UCI repository of machine learning databases. http://www.ics.uci.edu/~mlearn/MLRepository.html.
4. J.G. Cleary and L.E. Trigg. K*: An instance-based learner using an entropic distance measure. In *Proceedings of the 12th International Conference on Machine Learning*, pages 108–114. Morgan Kaufmann, 1995.
5. W.W. Cohen. Fast effective rule induction. In *Proceedings of the 12th International Conference on Machine Learning*, pages 115–123. Morgan Kaufmann, 1995.
6. T. G. Dietterich. Machine-learning research: Four current directions. *AI Magazine*, 18(4):97–136, 1997.
7. T. G. Dietterich. Ensemble Methods in Machine Learning. In *Proceedings of the 1st International Workshop in Multiple Classifier Systems*, pages 1–15, 2000.
8. S. Dzeroski and B. Zenko. Stacking with multi-response model trees. In *Proceedings of the 3d International Workshop in Multiple Classifier Systems*. Springer, 2002.
9. S. Dzeroski and B. Zenko. Is Combining Classifiers with Stacking Better than Selecting the Best One? *Machine Learning*, 54:255–273, 2004.
10. G. Giacinto and F. Roli. Adaptive selection of image classifiers. In *Proceedings of the 9th International Conference on Image Analysis and Processing*, pages 38–45, 1997.
11. T.K. Ho, J.J. Hull, and S.N. Srihari. Decision combination in multiple classifier systems. *IEEE Transactions on Pattern Analysis and Machine Intelligence*, 16(1):66–75, 1994.
12. G.H. John and P. Langley. Estimating continuous distributions in bayesian classifiers. In *Proceedings of the 11th Conference on Uncertainty in Artificial Intelligence*, pages 338–345, San Francisco, 1995. Morgan Kaufmann.
13. R. Kohavi. The power of decision tables. In *Proceedings of the 12th European Conference on Machine Learning*, pages 174–189, 1995.
14. J. Platt. Fast training of support vector machines using sequential minimal optimization. In B. Scholkopf, C. Burges, and A. Smola, editors, *Advances in Kernel Methods - Support Vector Learning*. MIT Press, 1998.

15. R.J. Quinlan. *C4.5: Programs for Machine Learning.* Morgan Kaufman, San Mateo, 1993.
16. K.M. Ting and I.H. Witten. Issues in stacked generalization. *Journal of Artificial Intelligence Research*, 10:271–289, 1999.
17. I.H. Witten and E. Frank. Generating accurate rule sets without global optimization. In *Proceedings of the 15th International Conference on Machine Learning, ICML98*, pages 144–151, 1998.
18. I.H. Witten and E. Frank. *Data Mining: Practical machine learning tools with Java implementations.* Morgan Kaufmann, 1999.
19. D. Wolpert. Stacked generalization. *Neural Networks*, 5:241–259, 1992.
20. K. Woods, W. P. Kegelmeyer, and K. Bowyer. Combination of multiple classifiers using local accuracy estimates. *IEEE Transanctions on Pattern Analysis and Machine Intelligence*, 19(4):405–410, 1997.

Convergence and Divergence in Standard and Averaging Reinforcement Learning

Marco A. Wiering

Intelligent Systems Group
Institute of Information and Computing Sciences
Utrecht University
marco@cs.uu.nl

Abstract. Although tabular reinforcement learning (RL) methods have been proved to converge to an optimal policy, the combination of particular conventional reinforcement learning techniques with function approximators can lead to divergence. In this paper we show why off-policy RL methods combined with linear function approximators can lead to divergence. Furthermore, we analyze two different types of updates; standard and averaging RL updates. Although averaging RL will not diverge, we show that they can converge to wrong value functions. In our experiments we compare standard to averaging value iteration (VI) with CMACs and the results show that for small values of the discount factor averaging VI works better, whereas for large values of the discount factor standard VI performs better, although it does not always converge.

1 Introduction

Reinforcement learning algorithms [13, 7] are very suitable for learning to control an agent by letting it interact with an environment. In case of tabular representations of the state-action space, convergence with probability 1 to an optimal policy has been proved for different reinforcement learning (RL) algorithms [18, 6, 16, 11]. However, in case of very large or continuous spaces, a tabular representation of the value function is not suitable. Therefore, instead of tabular representations, function approximators (FA) for representing the value function are necessary. In particular cases the combination of function approximators (e.g. neural networks) with reinforcement learning has been very successful [15]. However, in some cases divergence of particular combinations of RL algorithms with function approximators has been demonstrated [4, 5, 2].

Although some light has been shed on this problem of divergence, the cause of this divergence has not yet been demonstrated in an illustrative way. In this paper we use a very illustrative example to show why off-policy RL methods (e.g., on-line value iteration and Q-learning [17]) combined with function approximators may lead to divergence if parameters are shared between different states and sufficient high exploration is used. The reason of this is that the agent can stay in the same state for a while due to exploration, while continuously updating the value function on the largest action value that also increases due to the update.

J.-F. Boulicaut et al. (Eds.): ECML 2004, LNAI 3201, pp. 477–488, 2004.

There are in principle two types of RL methods when combined with function approximators; (1) Standard RL updating, and (2) Averaging RL updating. In standard RL, parameters of the function approximator are updated using the difference between the reward plus the next state's value and the Q-value of the current state-action pair that is computed using all parameters. In averaging RL, parameters are updated using the difference between the reward plus the next state's value and the parameter value. Although averaging RL has stronger convergence properties [5, 9] than standard RL, we show that averaging RL and standard RL are very much related, but that co-operative parameter learning only is the case for standard RL and that averaging RL can converge to non-optimal value functions.

In our experiments, we compare averaging to standard dynamic programming (DP)[1], and show that the obtained value function can be much worse for using averaging DP compared to standard DP for very large values of the discount factor, whereas the obtained value function and policy is better for averaging DP for smaller values of the discount factor. This leaves us with the question which RL method would be most appropriate; one which always converges, but to a possibly bad value function approximation if the discount factor is large, or one that does not have to converge, but that sometimes converges to a better approximation of the optimal value function.

Outline of this paper. In Section 2 we will describe reinforcement learning algorithms and in Section 3 we present the combination of standard and averaging reinforcement learning with linear function approximators. In Section 4 we will show our example for which standard off-policy RL algorithms with linear function approximators will diverge. In Section 5 we will compare averaging dynamic programming to standard dynamic programming with CMACs on some maze problems. Finally, Section 6 concludes this paper.

2   Reinforcement Learning

Reinforcement learning algorithms are able to let an agent learn from its experiences generated by its interaction with an environment. We assume an underlying Markov decision process (MDP) which does not have to be known to the agent. A finite MDP is defined as; (1) The state-space $S = \{s^1, s^2, \ldots, s^n\}$, where $s_t \in S$ denotes the state of the system at time t; (2) A set of actions available to the agent in each state $A(s)$, where $a_t \in A(s_t)$ denotes the action executed by the agent at time t; (3) A transition function $P(s, a, s')$ mapping state-action pairs s, a to a probability distribution over successor states s'; (4) A reward function $R(s, a, s')$ which denotes the average reward obtained when the agent makes a transition from state s to state s' using action a, where r_t denotes the (possibly stochastic) reward obtained at time t; (5) A discount factor $0 \leq \gamma \leq 1$ which discounts later rewards compared to immediate rewards.

---

[1] As DP method we use value iteration which can be seen as an off-policy DP algorithm in contrast to policy iteration which is on-policy. When we mention DP in this paper we restrict our conclusions to value iteration.

2.1   Value Functions and Dynamic Programming

In optimal control or reinforcement learning, we are interested in computing or learning the optimal policy for mapping states to actions. We denote the optimal deterministic policy as $\pi^*(s) \to a^*|s$. It is well known that for each MDP, one or more optimal deterministic policies exist. The optimal policy is defined as the policy which receives the highest possible cumulative discounted rewards in its future from all states. In order to learn the optimal policy, value-function based reinforcement learning [13] uses value functions to summarize the results of experiences generated by the agent in the past. We denote the value of a state $V^\pi(s)$ as the expected cumulative discounted future reward when the agent starts in state s and follows a particular policy π:

$$V^\pi(s) = E(\sum_{i=0}^\infty \gamma^i r_i | s_0 = s, \pi)$$

The optimal policy is the one which has the largest state-value in all states: $\pi^* = \arg\max_\pi V^\pi$.

In most cases reinforcement learning algorithms used for learning to control an agent also make use of a Q-function for evaluating state-action pairs. Here $Q^\pi(s, a)$ is defined as the expected cumulative discounted future reward if the agent is in state s, executes action a, and follows policy π afterwards:

$$Q^\pi(s, a) = E(\sum_{i=0}^\infty \gamma^i r_i | s_0 = s, a_0 = a, \pi)$$

It is easy to see that if the optimal Q-function, Q^* is known, that the agent can select optimal actions by selecting the action with the largest value in a state: $\pi^*(s) = \arg\max_a Q^*(s, a)$. and furthermore the optimal value of a state should correspond to the highest action value in that state according to the optimal Q-function: $V^*(s) = \max_a Q^*(s, a)$.

It is also well-known that there exists a recursive equation known as the Bellman optimality equation [3] which relates a state-action value of the optimal value function to other optimal state-values which can be reached from that state using a single local transition:

$$Q^*(s, a) = \sum_{s'} P(s, a, s')(R(s, a, s') + \gamma V^*(s'))$$

The Bellman equation has led to very efficient dynamic programming (DP) techniques for solving known MDPs [3, 13]. One of the most used DP algorithms is value iteration which uses the Bellman equation as an update:

$$Q^{k+1}(s, a) := \sum_{s'} P(s, a, s')(R(s, a, s') + \gamma V^k(s'))$$

Where $V^k(s) = \max_a Q^k(s, a)$. In each step the Q-function looks ahead one step, using this recursive update rule. It can be easily shown that $\lim_{k \to \infty} Q^k = Q^*$, when starting from an arbitrary Q^0 containing only finite values.

2.2   Reinforcement Learning Algorithms

Although dynamic programming algorithms can be efficiently used for computing optimal solutions for particular MDPs they have some problems for more practical applicability; (1) The MDP should be known a-priori; (2) For large state-spaces the computational time would become very large; (3) They cannot be directly used in continuous state-action spaces.

Reinforcement learning algorithms can cope with these problems; first of all the MDP does not need to be known a-priori, all that is required is that the agent is allowed to interact with an environment which can be modelled as an MDP. Secondly, for large or continuous state-spaces, a RL algorithm can be combined with a function approximator for learning the value function. When combined with a function approximator, the agent does not have to compute state-action values for all states, but can generalize from experiences and concentrate itself on parts of the state-space where the best policies lead into.

One particular algorithm for learning a Q-function is Q-learning [17, 18]. Q-learning makes an update after an experience (s_t, a_t, r_t, s_{t+1}) as follows:

$$Q(s_t, a_t) := Q(s_t, a_t) + \alpha(r_t + \gamma \max_a Q(s_{t+1}, a) - Q(s_t, a_t))$$

Where $0 < \alpha \leq 1$ is the learning rate. Q-learning is an off-policy reinforcement learning algorithm [13], which means that the agent learns about the optimal value function while following another behavioral policy which usually includes exploration steps. This has as advantage that it does not matter how much exploration is used, as long as the agent visits all state-action pairs an infinite number of times, tabular Q-learning (with appropriate learning rate adaptation) will converge to the optimal Q-function [18, 6, 16]. On the other hand, Q-learning does not learn about its behavioral policy, so if the behavioral policy always receives low cumulative discounted rewards, the agent does not try to improve it.

Instead of Q-learning, the on-policy algorithm SARSA(0) for learning Q-values has been proposed in [10, 12]. SARSA(0) makes the following update after an experience $(s_t, a_t, r_t, s_{t+1}, a_{t+1})$:

$$Q(s_t, a_t) := Q(s_t, a_t) + \alpha(r_t + \gamma Q(s_{t+1}, a_{t+1}) - Q(s_t, a_t))$$

Tabular SARSA(0) converges to the optimal policy under some conditions on the learning rate after an infinite number of steps if the exploration policy is GLIE (greedy in the limit of infinite exploration), which means that the agent should always explore, but stop exploring after an infinite number of steps [11].

3   Reinforcement Learning with Function Approximation

To learn value functions for problems with many state variables, there is the curse of dimensionality; the number of states increases exponentially with the number of state variables, so that a tabular representation would quickly become infeasible in terms of storage space and computational time. Also for a problem having continuous states, a tabular representation requires a good discretization which has to be done a-priori using knowledge of the system, and a fine-grained discretization will also quickly lead to a large number of states. Therefore, instead of using tabular representations it is more appropriate to use function approximators to deal with large or continuous state spaces.

In this paper we will concentrate ourselves on linear function approximators where the state-vector s_t which is received by the agent at time t is mapped upon a feature-vector $\phi(s_t)$. Then we use a parametrized function approximator where the set of parameters is a vector $\boldsymbol{\theta}$. The value of a state-action pair is:

$$Q(s, a) = \sum_i \theta_{i,a} \phi_i(s)$$

Well-known function approximators (FA) of this type are CMACs, locally weighted learning, radial basis networks, and linear neural networks, but not multi-layer perceptrons since these change the mapping from input-space to feature-space.

Using reinforcement learning techniques, we can learn the parameter vector $\boldsymbol{\theta}$ which makes up the value function. There are two different types of RL updates; (1) Standard RL updating; (2) Averaging RL updating.

3.1   Standard RL with Linear Function Approximators

In case we use standard RL updating, we get the following algorithms:
Standard Q-learning. For Q-learning with linear function approximators, we use the following update after an experience (s_t, a_t, r_t, s_{t+1}) for all i:

$$\theta_{i,a_t} := \theta_{i,a_t} + \alpha(r_t + \gamma \max_a Q(s_{t+1}, a) - Q(s_t, a_t))\phi_i(s_t)$$

Q-learning using this update-rule may diverge to infinite values as we show in the following section, therefore no general convergence proofs can be obtained using standard Q-learning with linear function approximators.
Standard SARSA(0). For SARSA(0) with linear function approximators, we use the following update after an experience $(s_t, a_t, r_t, s_{t+1}, a_{t+1})$ for all i:

$$\theta_{i,a_t} := \theta_{i,a_t} + \alpha(r_t + \gamma Q(s_{t+1}, a_{t+1}) - Q(s_t, a_t))\phi_i(s_t)$$

SARSA(0) is an on-policy RL method, and Gordon (2002) proved that using this update for a fixed policy the parameters will converge, and for a changing policy the parameters will stay fixed in a bounded region. Furthermore Perkins and Precup (2002) proved that the parameters using SARSA(0) will converge if the policy improvement operator produces ϵ-soft policies and is Lipschitz continuous in the action values with a constant that is not too large.

3.2   Averaging RL with Linear Function Approximators

In averaging RL updates do not use the difference between two successor state-values, but between the successor state-value and the parameter's value itself.

As Reynolds (2002) has shown, averaging RL will not diverge if the feature-vector for each state is normalized, but the value functions will remain in some region. Reynolds did not prove convergence with averaging RL, but Szepesvari and Smart (2004) have proved convergence of averaging Q-learning with inter-polative function approximators, although the proof requires that the sampling distribution is fixed and follows the stationary distribution. In the following we assume normalized feature vectors, so we will use $\phi_i'(s)$ as the normalized feature-vector computed as: $\phi_i'(s) = \frac{\phi_i(s)}{\sum_j \phi_j(s)}$, where we assume all $\phi_i(s)$ are positive. Furthermore we define $Q(s, a)$ in terms of $\phi'(s)$.

Q-learning. The averaging Q-learning update looks as follows for all i:

$$\theta_{i,a_t} := \theta_{i,a_t} + \alpha(r_t + \gamma \max_a Q(s_{t+1}, a) - \theta_{i,a_t})\phi_i'(s_t)$$

The θ parameters learn towards the desired value and are not cooperating in the learning updates. The use of this averaging Q-learning rule will not lead to diver-gence [9]. Furthermore, under a fixed stationary distribution with interpolative function approximators, averaging Q-learning has been proved to converge [14]. The requirement that the function approximator is interpolative is quite strict, however, since locally weighted learning and CMACs do not fall in this class of function approximators.

SARSA(0). For SARSA(0), an averaging RL update looks as follows for all i:

$$\theta_{i,a_t} := \theta_{i,a_t} + \alpha(r_t + \gamma Q(s_{t+1}, a_{t+1}) - \theta_{i,a_t})\phi_i'(s_t)$$

So, what can we expect when we use averaging RL instead of standard RL? Their convergence properties seem stronger as averaging RL does at least not lead to divergence for all different RL algorithms, but averaging RL can learn wrong value functions, as we will show in the next subsection.

3.3 Sample-Based Dynamic Programming

In case we have a model of the environment, we can also use sample-based Dynamic Programming as was proposed by Boyan and Moore (1995) and Gordon (1995). Sample-based value iteration goes as follows. First we select a subset of states $S_0 \subset S$. Often S_0 is chosen arbitrarily, but in general S_0 should be large enough and be spread over the state space. Then we are going to use the states $s \in S_0$ for updating the value function using a model of the environment. Again this can be done by averaging methods or by standard methods.

Averaging Q-value iteration with linear FA. Averaging sample-based DP uses the following update, where $T(.)$ is the backup operator:

$$T(\theta_{i,a}) = \frac{1}{\sum_{s \in S_0} \phi_i'(s)} \sum_{s \in S_0} \phi_i'(s) \sum_{s'} P(s, a, s')(R(s, a, s') + \gamma \max_b \sum_j \phi_j'(s')\theta_{j,b})$$

This DP-update rule is obtained from the averaging Q-learning rule with linear function approximators (where we set the learning rate α to 1). Remember that we had: $\theta_{i,a_t} := \theta_{i,a_t} + (r_t + \gamma \max_a Q(s_{t+1}, a) - \theta_{i,a_t})\phi_i'(s_t)$. We rewrite this as:

$$\theta_{i,a_t} := \theta_{i,a_t} + (r_t + \gamma \max_a Q(s_{t+1}, a))\phi_i'(s_t) - \theta_{i,a_t}\phi_i'(s_t)$$

$$\theta_{i,a_t} := \frac{(r_t + \gamma \max_a Q(s_{t+1}, a))\phi_i'(s_t)}{\phi_i'(s_t)}$$

The Q-value iteration backup operator is obtained by averaging over all states in the sweep. Why is this averaging DP? Well, because we take the weighted average of all targets irrespective of other parameter values for the current state, so parameter estimation is done in a non co-operative way. Note that for a tabular representation, this would simply be conventional Q-value iteration. We note that averaging RL has a problem. Consider two examples $0.5 \to 1$ (which means that one feature value is 0.5 and the discounted cumulative reward is 1) and $1 \to 2$. Thus, the best value of the parameter would be 2, but averaging Q-value iteration will compute the value $\frac{5}{3}$. Note that this would also be the fixed point if averaging Q-learning is used: $(1 - 5/3)*0.5 + (2 - 5/3)*1 = 0$. So although it can be shown that averaging DP converges [5], averaging DP or RL does not have to converge to the best possible value function.

Standard Q-value iteration with linear FA. For standard value-iteration with linear function approximators, the resulting algorithm will look a bit non-conventional. First of all we introduce the value of a state if a particular parameter i is not used as:

$$Q_{-i}(s, a) = \sum_{j \neq i} \theta_{j,a}\phi_j'(s)$$

Now we have $Q(s, a) = Q_{-i}(s, a) + \theta_{i,a}\phi_i(s)$. Furthermore $Q_{-i}(s, a) = 0$ in case of tabular representations with only feature i active. The standard Q-value iteration algorithm that is co-operative, but may diverge, is:

$$T(\theta_{i,a}) = \frac{1}{\sum_{s \in S_0} \phi_i'(s)^2} \sum_{s \in S_0} \phi_i'(s) \sum_{s'} P(s, a, s')(R(s, a, s')$$

$$+ \gamma \max_b \sum_j \phi_j'(s')\theta_{j,b} - Q_{-i}(s, a))$$

This rule is obtained by closely examining the Standard Q-learning rule with linear function approximators (with $\alpha = 1$). Remember that we had:

$$\theta_{i,a} := \theta_{i,a} + (r_t + \gamma \max_b Q(s_{t+1}, b) - Q(s_t, a))\phi_i'(s_t)$$

We can rewrite this as:

$$\theta_{i,a} := \theta_{i,a} + (r_t + \gamma \max_b Q(s_{t+1}, b) - Q_{-i}(s_t, a))\phi_i'(s_t) - \theta_{i,a}\phi_i'(s_t)^2$$

$$\theta_{i,a} := \frac{(r_t + \gamma \max_b Q(s_{t+1}, b) - Q_{-i}(s_t, a))\phi_i'(s_t)}{\phi_i'(s_t)^2}$$

The standard Q-value iteration is the result from using the backup operator where all sample states are used together with a model. If we examine the same examples: $0.5 \to 1$ and $1 \to 2$, we can see that standard DP would compute the value 2, which is correct.

In the case of a tabular representation with only one state active, the resulting algorithm is again the same algorithm as conventional Q-value iteration. The problem of this standard value-iteration algorithm with function approximators, which is also similar (although it looks quite different) to the one used by Boyan and Moore (1995), is that it may diverge, just as Q-learning may diverge.

4   Divergence of Q-Learning with Function Approximators

Off-policy RL methods such as online value iteration or standard Q-learning can diverge for a large number of function approximators such as linear neural networks, locally weighted learning, and radial basis networks. We show an example which shows why divergence to infinite parameter values can be obtained by using online value iteration together with exploration. The online value iteration algorithm uses a model of the environment, but only updates on states visited by the agent. This divergence to infinite values will also happen for Q-learning by taking action values into account, but divergence will not happen for on-policy methods such as SARSA or TD-learning with standard updating, neither for averaging RL methods.

Our example is very simple; suppose there is one state s with value 0.5 or 1. The agent can select actions a_t from $\{0.1, 0.2, 0.3, \ldots, 0.9, 1.0\}$. An absorbing state has been reached if $s = 1$, else the next state s_{t+1} is influenced by the action a_t by setting $s_{t+1} = 0.5$ if $a_t < 1$ and $s_{t+1} = 1$ if $a_t = 1$. The reward on all transitions is 0, and we use a discount factor γ. The initial state $s_0 = 0.5$. We use one feature $\phi(s)$ which has the same value as the state s. It is clear that the optimal parameter $\theta^* = 0$. Suppose that we initialize θ to a positive value. Now the learning algorithm computes the following update if $s = 0.5$:

$$\theta = \theta + \alpha(\gamma\theta - 0.5\theta)0.5$$

And the following update if $s = 1$: $\theta = \theta + \alpha(0 - \theta)$

If the agent often selects random actions, in many cases the agent will be in state $s = 0.5$. Suppose it stays on average h times in state $s = 0.5$ before making a step to $s = 1$. Then it will make the following average update:

$$\theta = \theta + \alpha((\gamma\theta - 0.5\theta)0.5h - \theta)$$

This will lead to increasing values of θ if: $h > \frac{1}{0.5\gamma - 0.25}$. Thus, for large enough γ and exploration, the parameter will always increase.

If the next state and the current state share parameters, it is easy to see that if the estimated value of the current state grows, that the estimated value of the best next state grows at the same time. This may lead to divergence. If instead we use a Monte-Carlo return, and do not use bootstrapping at all, we will not have the problem. Also if we use the averaging RL update divergence is prevented. Finally, if we use on-policy algorithms such as SARSA or TD-learning divergence will not happen, because an increasing update is only made if the agent actually makes a transition to the higher valued state.

5   Experiments with Standard and Averaging DP

We executed a number of experiments to compare standard and averaging DP with CMACs [1] as a linear function approximator. For this, we always normalize the activity of all tile-cells which are active given a state so that the combined activity adds up to 1.0. We use Q-value iteration (as described in Subsection 3.3) using all states of the environment as sampling states.

The environment is a maze of size 51×51 with one goal state. Each state can be a starting state except for the goal state. There are deterministic single-step actions North, East, South, and West. The reward for every action is -1. The process stops if the agent is in the goal-location. The tilings we use divide the maze in horizontal slices and vertical slices. So there is one tile with 51 cells which denotes the X-position, and one tile with 51 cells which denotes the Y-position.

We executed 3 experiments; 1 with an empty maze, where we examine the obtained value functions of the different DP methods using CMACs. Furthermore, we examine convergence of the algorithms if we initialize the parameters to a range of larger randomly generated numbers. We also run experiments on a maze containing walls, which makes it impossible for the representation to come up with an optimal policy. Therefore we will examine the number of steps which results after the DP algorithm terminates (or after a large number of iterations in case of standard DP which does not always terminate).

5.1   Experiments on an Empty Maze

Although it is easy to come up with an optimal policy for an empty maze, it is interesting to study the resulting value function for standard and averaging RL with CMACs compared to the optimal value function. It should be clear that our representation does not always allow to represent the optimal value function for all different values of the discount factor. Therefore, we examined the cumulative absolute difference between the optimal value function and the obtained value functions of standard DP with CMACs and averaging DP with CMACs for a large range of values of the discount parameter $\gamma \in \{0, 0.05, \ldots, 0.95, 1.0\}$. The experimental results are shown in Figure 1(A), where we initialized all value-function parameters to random values between 0 and 100. Figure 1(A) shows: (1) For $\gamma = 0$, both algorithms compute the optimal value function. (2) For $\gamma = 1$, standard DP is able to compute the perfect value function, but averaging RL makes a large error. (3) For γ values in between 0.05 and 0.9 the value function obtained by averaging RL is slightly better than the one obtained with standard DP. Both algorithms always converged to a unique value function given the discount factor.

In Figure 1(B) the convergence on the empty maze with discount factor $\gamma = 1$ is shown to the unique final value function (which does not need to have 0-error compared to the optimal value function) of both algorithms. We can see that although standard DP converges faster, it sometimes increases the error, whereas averaging DP never increases the error. Although it is not shown in the figures, we note that for $\gamma = 0.8$ averaging DP converges faster. The fact that standard

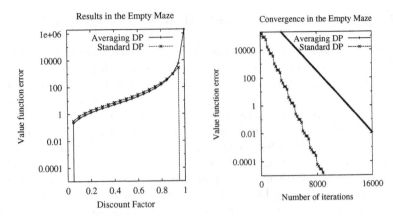

Fig. 1. (A) The error (cumulative absolute difference between V-values computed over all states) of the value functions computed by standard and averaging DP. (B) The convergence of both algorithms when $\gamma = 1.0$. Note that standard DP sometimes increases the error, although it is hard to see.

DP computes the optimal value function for the empty maze with $\gamma = 1$ is remarkable. It does this by computing 0, -2, -4, etc. for one tiling with distances to the goal of 0, 1, 2, etc. In this way the value of state (2,1) will be the average of -4 and -2 which is -3, which is optimal for $\gamma = 1$. For many other values of γ, standard DP cannot compute an optimal value function, and actually performs slightly worse than averaging DP. We also performed experiments with different initializations of the parameters of the value function where $\gamma = 1$. As expected averaging DP always converged to the same value function. For standard DP, initializations of 0 to 100 and 0 to 1000 led to convergence, but if we initialized the parameters to values between 0 and 10000, the parameters always diverged.

5.2   Experiments on a Maze Containing a Wall

The next experiment uses the maze shown in Figure 2(A). It is impossible for the value function obtained with CMACs and our chosen features to compute an optimal policy given all states as starting state. Instead we will examine how well the policy obtained by both algorithms after it converged (or a sufficient number of sweeps in case of standard DP) performs. The results are shown in Figure 2(B). It depicts the total number of steps the greedy policy needs to find the goal where not finding the goal is counted as 1000 steps (so that the maximum number would be $(51 \times 51 - 1) \times 1000$). We can see that averaging RL performs much better over a wide range of values for γ. Only when γ is 1.0, standard DP works better and in this case also obtains the best results. We can see that low values of γ do not harm averaging RL, but standard DP works better for $\gamma = 1$, since otherwise the subtraction of the other parameters in the standard DP update rule plays an important role. It should be said that averaging RL always converges, whereas standard DP with $\gamma = 1$ was constantly changing its

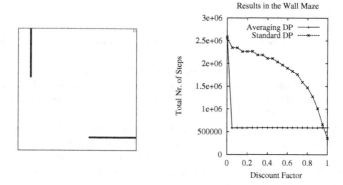

Fig. 2. (A) The second maze containing two walls: one wall is between $x = 5$ and $x = 6$ where $y > 30$ and the other wall is between $y = 5$ and $y = 6$ where $x > 30$. (B) The number of steps in this maze with the policy computed by standard or averaging DP.

policy, and did not converge, although the parameters did not diverge to infinite values (we used an initialization of parameter values between 0 and 100).

6   Conclusion

In this paper we have described two types of reinforcement learning algorithms when linear function approximators are used; standard RL is used in most applications of RL with function approximators [13], and averaging RL is another way which has received little attention. Since particular standard RL algorithms with function approximators may diverge, it is worth taking a look at averaging RL methods which have been proved not to diverge. We explained the reason why standard off-policy RL algorithms may diverge when combined with linear function approximators – if an agent stays in the same state due to exploration, it may increase parameters which are shared by the state and the best possible next state. This divergence will not happen for standard on-policy RL algorithms or averaging RL. Averaging sample-based dynamic programming techniques converge, although the resulting value function may not be the best possible value function, whereas standard sample-based (off-policy) dynamic programming does not have to converge. To compare standard RL to averaging RL, we executed some experiments on maze problems with Q-value iteration and CMACs as a linear function approximator. The results indicated a number of things. First averaging DP always converges (as expected) and standard DP also often converges, but can diverge if we set initial parameters to very large values. Furthermore, the resulting value function and policy of averaging DP may be better if the discount factor is not very large, whereas standard DP works best for very large values of the discount factor. In future work, we want to compare averaging and standard RL on a number of different problems. We are especially interested in comparing convergence speed of on-policy RL and averaging RL methods, since these methods seem most promising. Furthermore, we want to analyze the convergence of averaging RL methods with changing policies.

References

1. J. S. Albus. A theory of cerebellar function. *Mathematical Biosciences*, 10:25–61, 1975.
2. L. Baird. Residual algorithms: Reinforcement learning with function approximation. In A. Prieditis and S. Russell, editors, *Machine Learning: Proceedings of the Twelfth International Conference*, pages 30–37. Morgan Kaufmann Publishers, San Francisco, CA, 1995.
3. R. Bellman. *Dynamic Programming*. Princeton University Press, 1957.
4. J. A. Boyan and A. W. Moore. Generalization in reinforcement learning: Safely approximating the value function. In G. Tesauro, D. S. Touretzky, and T. K. Leen, editors, *Advances in Neural Information Processing Systems 7*, pages 369–376. MIT Press, Cambridge MA, 1995.
5. G.J. Gordon. Stable function approximation in dynamic programming. Technical Report CMU-CS-95-103, Carnegie Mellon University, 1995.
6. T. Jaakkola, M. I. Jordan, and S. P. Singh. On the convergence of stochastic iterative dynamic programming algorithms. *Neural Computation*, 6:1185–1201, 1994.
7. L. P. Kaelbling, M. L. Littman, and A. W. Moore. Reinforcement learning: A survey. *Journal of Artificial Intelligence Research*, 4:237–285, 1996.
8. T.J. Perkins and D. Precup. A convergent form of approximate policy iteration. In Todd K. Leen, Thomas G. Dietterich, and Volker Tresp, editors, *Advances in Neural Information Processing Systems 13*. MIT Press, 2002.
9. S.I. Reynolds. The stability of general discounted reinforcement learning with linear function approximation. In *Proceedings of the UK Workshop on Computational Intelligence (UKCI-02)*, pages 139–146, 2002.
10. G.A. Rummery and M. Niranjan. On-line Q-learning using connectionist sytems. Technical Report CUED/F-INFENG-TR 166, Cambridge University, UK, 1994.
11. S.P. Singh, T. Jaakkola, M.L. Littman, and C. Szepesvari. Convergence results for single-step on-policy reinforcement-learning algorithms. *Machine Learning*, 38(3):287–308, 2000.
12. R. S. Sutton. Generalization in reinforcement learning: Successful examples using sparse coarse coding. In D. S. Touretzky, M. C. Mozer, and M. E. Hasselmo, editors, *Advances in Neural Information Processing Systems 8*, pages 1038–1045. MIT Press, Cambridge MA, 1996.
13. R. S. Sutton and A. G. Barto. *Reinforcement Learning: An Introduction*. The MIT press, Cambridge MA, A Bradford Book, 1998.
14. C. Szepesvari and W.D. Smart. Convergent value function approximation methods. 2004. Accepted in the International Conference om Machine Learning (ICML'04).
15. G.J. Tesauro. Temporal difference learning and TD-Gammon. *Communications of the ACM*, 38:58–68, 1995.
16. J. N Tsitsiklis. Asynchronous stochastic approximation and Q-learning. *Machine Learning*, 16:185–202, 1994.
17. C. J. C. H. Watkins. *Learning from Delayed Rewards*. PhD thesis, King's College, Cambridge, England, 1989.
18. C. J. C. H. Watkins and P. Dayan. Q-learning. *Machine Learning*, 8:279–292, 1992.

Document Representation for One-Class SVM

Xiaoyun Wu, Rohini Srihari, and Zhaohui Zheng

University at Buffalo, Buffalo NY 14260, USA

Abstract. Previous studies have shown that one-class SVM is a rather weak learning method for text categorization problems. This paper points out that the poor performance observed before is largely due to the fact that the standard term weighting schemes are inadequate for one-class SVMs. We propose several representation modifications, and demonstrate empirically that, with the proposed document representation, the performance of one-class SVM, although trained on only small portion of positive examples, can reach up to 95% of that of two-class SVM trained on the whole labeled dataset.

1 Introduction

Like most multi-labeled classification problems, text categorization problems are usually converted to binary classification problems in "one-versus-rest" fashion, where examples that belong to category of interest are labeled as positive, and the others as negative. In a number of recent empirical studies [3, 15], Support Vector Machines (SVMs) have been shown to be among the most effective methods for such binary text categorization problems. Applying one-class SVM [11] on text categorization, which uses only the positive examples in the training phase, is worthy exploring for the following three reasons:

First, since negative examples are from many different categories, they are generally not as representative. It is logical to hypothesize that the resulting binary problems can be characterized mostly by their positive examples. And ideally, the classifier learned from positive examples should perform reasonably close to the classifier learned from fully labeled dataset. To the best of our knowledge, there is no empirical evidence for such conjecture. Applying one-class SVM on text categorization is one way of testing such hypothesis.

Second, the problem of learning with positive examples commonly arises in many real-world applications, particularly in information retrieval domain. For example, to learn a user's preference, pages in his bookmarks are readily available as positive examples, but it will be difficult to come up with enough representative negative examples. Effective learning methods that rely on only positive examples thus are of great practical interest.

Third, one characteristic for these binary problems is the skewness in the dataset, since frequently there are only a small number of positive examples but a very large number of negative examples. The time complexity of typical SVM training methods like sequential minimal optimization (SMO) is super-linear in the number of examples in the dataset [9]. The training of one-class SVMs

J.-F. Boulicaut et al. (Eds.): ECML 2004, LNAI 3201, pp. 489–500, 2004.

should be much more efficient than that of tw o-class SVMs since a large number
of negative examples are ignored. In the case where there is a stringent constrain
on the training time, highly effective one-class SVM can serve as an alternative
to its tw o-class courter-part.

A previous study [7] show ed empirically that performance of one-class SVMs
is nowhere near that of tw o-class SVMs. In this paper, we reveal that standard
document representation is inappropriate for one-class SVMs. We propose three
modifications of document representation, including removing negative features,
scaling dimensions and length normalization. We further demonstrate that the
category statistics needed to tailor the document representation for one-class
SVMs can be reliably estimated from both the fully labeled dataset and also
the datasets with only positive and unlabeled examples. Experiments show that
one-class SVM with the proposed representation modifications is effective for
text categorization problems.

The rest of the paper is structured as follows. Section 2 gives the background
of one-class SVMs, the problems of using the standard document representation
with one-class SVMs and their respective fixes are detailed in section 3. Section
4 lists the proof that the same modification is valid in learning with positiv e
and unlabeled examples. Section 5 provides the empirical results. We conclude
in section 6 with some discussion of the results.

2   Introduction to One-Class SVMs

One-class SVMs [11] are closely related to the so-called minimum volume estimators which try to find a small region containing most of the positive examples.
The goal is to find the boundary function that can be used for discrimination
purposes. Avoiding the densit yestimation problem, this region estimation approach is in line with Vapnik's principle of never solving a problem which is more
general than the one that actually needs to be solved. Similar to the tw o-class
SVMs, regularization is also used to balance the training errors
plexit y for better generalization. Since text categorization problems are generally
considered as linearly separable even in original feature space [15], we will focus
on hyperplane-based one-class SVMs and use only dot product (linear) kernel in
this paper.

Hyperplane-based one-class SVMs seeks a h yperplane that pushes positiv e
examples aw ay from origin as much as possible without leaving too many positive examples behind. Given a set of positive examples: $S = (x_1, \cdots, x_m)$, the
h yperplane (w, ρ) is given b y solving the follwing primal quadratic optimization
problem:

$$\text{minimize} : \frac{1}{2}\langle w \cdot w \rangle - \rho + \frac{1}{\nu m}\sum_{i=1}^{m}\xi_i$$

$$\text{subject to} : \langle w \cdot x_i \rangle \geq \rho - \xi_i$$

$$\xi_i \geq 0, i = 1, \cdots, m$$

Here, w is the weight vector for decision hyperplane, ρ is the functional distance from origin to hyperplane (w, ρ). The slack ξ_i is defined by how far a data point fails to stay away from origin with respect to boundary hyperplane (w, ρ). Like their two-class counter-part [11], there are two goals sought by its objective function: larger geometric distance defined by $\rho/||w||$ and smaller training errors approximated by $\sum \xi_i$.

Parameter $\nu \in (0, 1]$ is used to control the trade-off between these two possibly conflicting goals. It is an upper bound foaction of training margin errors and lower bound on the fraction of support vectors. With probability approaching 1, asymptotically, ν equals to both the fraction of support vectors and fraction of training margin errors. A training margin error occurs $\xi_i > 0$. We choose to work with this ν formulation because it is intuitive to pick the parameter ν due to its property.

Due to the nonsmoothness introduced by ξ in primal cost function, it is a common practice to solve the dual problem to find the coefficients αs. Using dot product as kernel, both one-class and two-class SVM training result in a linear decision function in the same form of:

$$f(x) = sign(\langle w \cdot x \rangle - \rho) = sign(\sum w^k x^k - \rho) \qquad (1)$$

Where the kth component of the weight vector w is defined as:

$$w^k = \sum \alpha_i y_i x_i^k, \; \alpha_i \geq 0 \qquad (2)$$

While $y_i \in (-1, +1)$ for two-class SVM, we have $y_i \in (+1)$ for one-class SVM since there are only positive examples available for one-class SVM training.

3   Document Representation Issues

Most text categorization studies use the term weighting scheme that is developed for information retrieval applications [10]. Such representation includes three components: term frequency, document frequency, and normalization component. Let x_i^k denote the k component for ith document x_i, we have $x_i^k \geq 0$ for the standard term weighting scheme. However, the following analysis holds for $x_i^k \leq 0$.

The document representation based on term weighting scheme reportedly works well with two-class SVM classifiers [3]. However, due to the lack of negative examples, such standard representation does not bring out the full potential of one-class SVMs. Our discussion on document representation in this section is based on a fully labeled dataset with both positive and negative examples. Document representation issues for partially labeled dataset with positive and unlabeled examples are addressed

3.1   Using Positive Features Only

In feature selection research, it is commonly known that there are two types of features: positive and negative features [16]. Positive features are positively correlated with the category of interest; occurrences of such features in a document basically add more support for the document belonging to the category. Similarly, occurrences of negative features in a document should decrease the probability of the document belonging to the category. When working with linear decision functions, one typically expects that weights for positiv efeatures stay positive and weigh ts for negatie features stay negative. This is because a positive weigh t for a negatie feature is deemed to degrade the performance of the linear classifier.

F rom expression (2), for one-class SVM, one easily has $w^k \geq 0$ since $y_i = +1$. So if there is a negative feature contained in one of the support v ectors, its influence on decision h yperplane will be positive instead of negative. This suggests that, for one-class SVMs, the document representation should only use positiv e features. Inclusion of negatie features will only degrade the performance of the learned classier.

T able 1. Contingency table for feature-category correlation, where category absent implies either not-in-class or lack the label information

	category present	category absent
feature present	a	b
feature absent	c	d

In this paper, w euse correlation coefficient (CC) to determine whether a feature is positively correlated with the category of interest. It is first used as a feature selection measure in [8] and is defined as:

$$(ad - bc)\sqrt{N}/\sqrt{(a+b)(a+c)(b+d)(c+d)}$$

where a, b, c, d are defined in table 1, and $N = a+b+c+d$. The sign of a feature can thus be easily decided based on the feature-category correlation contingency table if one works on fully labeled dataset.

It is the common knowledge that negative features are potentially useful for discrimination purpose. How ev er, from expression (2), one needs $\sum_{y_i=-1} \alpha_i x_i^k > \sum_{y_i=+1} \alpha_i x_i^k$ to have $w^k \leq 0$. This suggests that importance of negative features is mainly characterized by negative examples. It is difficult to model negative features with one-class SVMs since its training involves only positive examples. Luckily, as we will reveal later, the categories are largely characterized by their corresponding positive features.

3.2   Relative Importance of Features

With both positive and negative examples, tw o-class SVMs are generally capable of determining the importance of each feature. How ev er, with only positie examples, one-class SVMs lack some of the information needed to determine the importance of features. To see this, assume that there are tw o positie features,

f_1 and f_2, and these tw o features alwa ys occur together in the positive dataset. But feature f_1 occurs a lot more in negative examples. Although there is evidence for tw o-class SVMs to give feature f_2 more weight, for one-class SVMs, there is no reason to treat them differently.

Clearly, for one-class SVMs to work better, the relativ e importance of features, usually measured by feature selection metric, has to be embedded in document representation. We propose in this paper to scale each dimension based on correlation coefficient. The basic idea behind this proposed solution is simple: we want training process pay more attention to these important features. In another word, cost rooted from the less important feature should be penalized less.

Scaling features using feature weight is equivalen t to modifying the similarity measure, or equivalently, distance metric, k ernel function. Appropriate scaling can bring all positiv e examples closer th us make training discriminant model easier. For example, it is shown that performance of Nested Generalized Exampler(NGE) can be greatly improv ed when the Mutual Information (MI) is used to reweigh t features [12]. In general, it is hard to justify pi cking one feature selection metric ov er another theoretically. W e choose correlation coefficient based on empirical evidence, since preliminary experiments show that it is more effective comparing to other feature selection metric such as χ^2 and information gain.

3.3   Document Length Normalization Issue

Document length normalization is important for one-class SVM since only positive features are correctly modeled. To see this, assume we are to determine the class label for a long document d_l which contains multiple copies of a not-in-class document d_s (thus $\langle w \cdot d_s \rangle < \rho$). F or one-class SVM, we always hav e $\langle w \cdot d_s \rangle \geq 0$. So, the long document d_l with $\lceil \rho/d_s \rceil$ copies of d_s will be considered as in-class since one hav e $\langle w \cdot d_l \rangle \geq \rho$. Here, $\lceil \cdot \rceil$ denote the ceil function. For tw o-class SVM, since both positiv e and negative features are modeled, typically we will ha v e $\langle w \cdot d_s \rangle \leq 0$, which makes $\langle w \cdot d_d \rangle \leq 0$ as expected.

T o address this issue, we propose to apply the cosine normalization in test phase. Although the abov e analysis also holds when such normalization is applied in training phase, preliminary results show that normalization in training phase h urts the performance of one-class SVM. This is because normalization in training stage makes v alues of positive features depend on values of negative features, while the negative features are not correctly modeled by one-class SVM.

Normalization in test phase will only make the learned threshold value unusable. However, it is not a big issue since a separated thresholding component is needed for one-class SVM anywa y. To see this, note that the default threshold returned by one-class SVMs training tends to be too high as it touches all the positive support vectors.

4   Learning with Positive and Unlabeled Examples

Except for the document length normalization, the modifications we proposed in the last section are based on the assumption that we have access to the fully labeled dataset. We now show that the category statistics needed for proposed document representation modification can also be estimated from datasets with positiv e and unlabeled examples.

Learning with Positive and Unlabeled examples (LPU) itself is interesting researc h topic for both theoretical [2, 5] and practical [14, 5, 4, 6] reasons. Formally, learning with positive and unlabeled examples can be modeled as follows: positiv e examples are randomly labeled positie with probability $1 - \beta$, and are left unlabeled with probability β. With this model, if we label all unlabeled examples as negative, w e will never make an error on a negative example but will label positive examples as negative with probability β. In practice, β is generally unknown, effective solutions to this problem thus should not depend on the knowledge of β.

We have follo wing proposition that haracterizes the expectation of the quality of correlation coefficient estimated from positive and unlabeled examples.

Proposition 1 *L eta*, b*, c* and d* be corresponding entries in the contingency table for feature-category correlation with positive and unlabeled data, where positive examples are left unlabeled with probability β. Assume that feature occurrences are independent of the labeling pro cess. We have, first, the sign of a featur e is then expected to be the same as that of the expression $a^*d^* - b^*c^*$. Second, let CC^* be the correlation co efficient defined on table 1, the ratio between CC and CC^* is exp cted to be a constant that is feature independent.*

Proof sketch. For first part, from the independent assumption, w e ha ve $E(a^*) = a - \beta a$, $E(b^*) = b - \beta a$, $E(c^*) = c - \beta c$ and $E(d^*) = d - \beta a$. Here $E(\cdot)$ denotes the expected alue of a random variable. It is not difficult to see that $E(a^*d^* - b^*c^*) = (ad - bc)(1 - \beta)$. When $\beta < 1$, $a^*d^* - b^*c^*$ and $(ad - bc)$ is th us expected to have the same sign. For second part, using the expected value for a^*, b^*, c^*, d^* as before, it is not difficult to see:

$$E(CC^*/CC) = \sqrt{(b+d)(1-\beta)/(b+d+\beta a+\beta c)}$$

Note that both $a + c$ and $b + d$ are fixed for all features for each category, and β is also feature independent.

The proposition states that, on average, CC^* is a good replacement of CC since the ratio betw een them is expected to stay constant for each feature. The probability of such statement to hold, however, depends on both the dataset and feature. In general, the more positive examples labeled and the higher frequent of a feature, the higher the probability for these statements to sta y true. Moreover, less frequent word tend to have smaller impact on text categorization applications, as noted in [13].

Since both the quality of the representation modifications based on CC^* and the training for the one-class SVMs are independent of the percentage of the positiv eexamples left unlabeled, the performance of the one-class SVM with proposed representation modifications is arguably also independent of the percen tage of the positive examples left unlabeled. This is a highly desired property for obvious reasons. For example, to get an exact value for β for quality control purposes, one has to label the entire dataset. Note how ever, more positive examples are beneficial for both the estimating of CC^* and the training of one-class SVM.

5   Experiments

We conduct all our experiments on the standard text categorization dataset: Reuters-21578 compiled by David Lewis from Reuters newswire. The ModApte split we used has 90 categories. After removing all numbers, stop words and low frequency terms, there are about 10,000 unique
selection is done. Words occurring in the title are simplgoun ted three times. Baseline document representation is $log(1 + tf)$, where tf is the term frequency defined by the number of occurrences for that term. We use libSVM [1] to train both one-class and tw o-class SVMs in this paper. To compare the performance of linear classifiers based on the orientation of their decision hyperplane, and to sta y comparable with [15], we use both the micro-average F1 and macro-av erage F1 ov er Break-Even-Point(BEP) as performance measurement.

Experiments are organized in tw o different parts. In the next subsection, w e examine effectiveness of the three representation improvements on the fully labeled datasets. In the subsection that follows, the effectiveness of the improvements on the positive and unlabeled dataset is studied.

5.1   Effectiveness of Representation Improvements

T o test the effectiveness of the proposed modifications to document representation, we run both one-class SVMs (oc) and tw o-class SVMs(tc) on baseline document representation. We then modify the document representation for one-class SVMs by incorporating the following representation changes one at a time: removing negative features based on the sign of correlation coefficient (p), scaling dimensions based on the magnitude of correlation coefficient(s), and also normalization (m). Note the correlation coefficient is computed here based on the contingency table 1. To make our results comparable with previous reported results, we report results on both the first 10 most frequent categories and all 90 categories. From table 2, our results on all 90 categories with tw o-class SVMs are comparable with that of [15], and our results on first 10 most frequent categories with one-class SVMs are comparable with that of [7]. Table 2 suggest that these three modifications for document representation can provide significant performance improvements for one-class SVM. Using all three modification together, on all 90 categories, the performance gap betw een one-class and tw o-class is reduced from 0.364 to 0.048 measured in micro-av erage F1 that is an

Table 2. P erformance of different document representation methods on one-class and tw o-class SVMs, measured in micro-average F1(miF1) and macro-average F1(maF1) over BEP on both all 90 categories and first 10 most frequent categories on the Reuters-25718 dataset. Here, oc(tc) corresponds to one(tw o) class SVM

	90 categories		10 categories	
	miF1	maF1	miF1	maF1
oc	0.516	0.293	0.583	0.460
oc.pos	0.599	0.340	0.676	0.538
oc.scale	0.745	0.641	0.767	0.710
oc.norm	0.715	0.493	0.784	0.681
oc.pos.scale	0.763	0.651	0.792	0.755
oc.norm.scale	0.834	0.685	0.872	0.810
oc.norm.pos	0.750	0.499	0.823	0.722
oc.norm.pos.scale	0.835	0.686	0.873	0.817
tc	0.880	0.679	0.924	0.858
tc.scale	0.880	0.679	0.924	0.858
tc.pos	0.840	0.650	0.878	0.829
tc.norm	0.866	0.662	0.917	0.844

87% reduction. At same time, macro-average F1 is reduced from 0.386 to -0.006, which suggests that one-class SVMs are more effective on the rare categories.

It is in teresting that with appropriate representation, using only positive examples can result in a performance that is close to 95% of that of using both positiv e and negative examples. It suggests that binary text categorization problems reduced from multi-label problems in one-versus-rest fashion are mostly characterized by its positiv e examples.Moreover, if one works on positiv e features only, one-class SVMs with proposed document representation (oc.m.p.s) is as effective as tw o-class SVMs (tc.p). This provides the empirical evidence that the importance of positive features can mostly be modeled by positive examples. For tw o-class SVMs, the performance difference between using all features and using only positive features is rather small, again 5% difference. This is rather surprising, but it suggests that, for the purpose of discrimination, the additional information embedded in negative features is really small.

While the feature scaling can greatly improve theperformance ofie-class SVM(oc vs. oc.s), their influence on tw o-class SVMis not observable at all(tc vs tc.s). This suggests that tw o-classSVM has all the information needed to learn the importance of each feature and one-class SVM does not. Note that the identical performance of two-class SVM measured in average F1 before and after feature scaling is misleading, because stronger   h as AUC (Area Under Curve)reveals that scaling does provide some marginal improvement for two-class SVM. Both one-class and two-class SVM training return a different set of support vectors after the feature scaling. Furthermore, the number of support v ectors decreases noticeably in the scaled feature space for both one-class and two-class SVM training. For example, at $\nu = 0.01$, for category "earn", feature scaling reduces the number of positive/negative support vectors from 260/436 to 169/263 for two-class SVM training and from 99/0 to 44/0 for one-class SVM training. Due to the high dimensionality of the problem, it is difficult to understand exactly how the scaling influences the training process. But the fewer support vectors seems to suggest that data is easier to separate after feature scaling.

All the three document representations provide some meaningful performance gains when used alone, with scaling as the most effective factor and negative-feature removing the least. Furthermore, it seems that the discrimination power contained in the negative-feature removing is mostly contained in scaling. This is because scaling can greatly reduce   e features, since the absolute value of feature selection metric such as correlation coefficient is often much smaller than that of positive features, as noted [16].

There is no known close-form time-complexity analysis for SVM training as it depends on the dataset, termination criteria and parameter choices. To get a rough idea, we timed libSVM java implementation using Pentium-M 1.3Ghz Linux PC with 512M memory. Including the feature scoring for all 10 categories, it takes 90 minutes for two-class SVM training, and 2 minutes for one-class SVM. This is mostly because one-class SVM training only uses positive examples.

5.2   Learning from Positive and Unlabeled Examples

To test whether the performance of one-class with proposed modifications depends on β, the fraction of positive examples left unlabeled, we intentionally hide the label for 19, 36, 51, 64, 75, 84, 91, 96, and 99 percent of randomly selected positive examples. One-class SVMs are trained on the remaining positive examples. For the document representation, we removed negative features, scale features based on magnitude of correlation co   t computed from the contingency table 1. Document representation is normalized in the test phase.

Figure 1 reports both the micro and macro F1 (based on BEP) for first 10 most frequent categories. Notice that the performance of one-class stays virtually constant until there is only 4% ($\beta = 0.96$) positive examples left labeled. The significant performance drop of both micro and macro F1 at $\beta = 0.99$ is understandable, as 8 out of 10 categories are left with less than 6 positive examples. We believe that the performance of one-class SVMs positive   e and unlabeled dataset depends only on the number of positive examples used, not the fraction of positive examples used. To test this argument, we also report F1 over BEP) on the most frequent category "earn", which has 27 positive examples at $\beta = 0.99$. From figure 1, the performance of the category "earn" stays almost untouched even when only 1% of positive examples are used in the training. The results thus conform elegantly to the analysis we had in section 5.

We are able to compare the result directly with biased two-class SVM approach in [6] since we are using the same 10 categories from the same dataset. Note that when β increased from 0.3 to 0.7, the micro F1 stayed around 0.87 for one-class SVMs, the macro F1 dropped from 0.856 to 0.785 for biased two-class

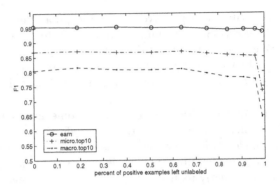

Fig. 1. performance of one-class SVMs versus β, the fraction of positive examples left unlabeled

Table 3. P erformance of one-class and tw o-class SVMs on differeit β value on 10 most frequent categories on Reuters-25718, measured in micro-average F1.

β	0.0	0.3	0.7
oc.n.p.s	0.873	0.867	0.881
tc	0.924	0.856	0.785

SVMs. It appears from this direct comparison on macro F1 that one-class SVM is a more effective method, particularly when β is approaching to 1.0.

6   Conclusion and Discussion

In this paper, we identify the "incompatibility" betw een the standard documeit representation and one-class SVMs. We propose several modifications to docu-ment representation that use the correlation coefficient, which can be estimated from not only the fully labeled dataset but also the dataset with positiv e and unlabeled examples. The experiments show that the proposed representation modifications can greatly improv e the performance of one-class SVMs.

As a case study on text categorization, this paper provides quantitativ e em-pirical evidence that for binary classification problems   v erted from multi-label problem, the category is mostly characterized by positive examples. Furthermore, we also reveal through experiment that the nature of category is mostly embed-ded in the feature space spanned by positiv efeatures. It is thus interesting to see whether these trends exist in other binary classification problems that are conv erted from multi-label problems.

In practice, it is usually difficult to obtain labeled data, but unlabeled data is often abundantly a vailable. This means that learning with positiv e and unlabeled examples is a much more realistic problem when β approaches to 1.0 than when it approaches to 0.0. Most previous studies assume at least some of unlabeled examples as negative examples so that they can use standard tw o-class learning methods. The probability for such assumption to hold is thus negatively corre-lated with β. These previous methods usually perform reasonably well when β is small and the performance degrades with an increasing β [5, 6]. Howev er, the performance of one-class SVM with proposed document representation is inde-pendent on β. While not impressive when β is small, it is very competitive when β is large. This makes one-class SVM a very useful method in many real-world applications.

Although the example applicatiumd   in this paper is text categorization problems, the only requirement for the proposed representation modifications is the sparseness of the data representation, which makes computing the correlation coefficient possible. In general, we believe that one-class SVM with the proposed modification can be directly used with any sparse data with appropriate data preprocessing.

Acknowledgments

We thank Dr. Zhixin Shi, Dr. Ajay Shekhaw atand anonymous reviewers for their v alue commerts.

References

1. C. Chang and C. Lin. LIBSVM: a library for support vector machines (version 2.3), 2001.
2. F ran çoisDenis. P A Clearning from positive statistical queries. In *A lgorithmic L earning Th@ry, 9th International Conference, ALT '98, Otzenhausen, Germany, October 1998, Proceeding*, volume 1501, pages 112–126. Springer, 1998.
3. Thorsten Joachims. *L earning T o Classify T ext Using Support V ector Machines*. Kluw er Academic Publishers, Boston, 2002.
4. Wee Sun Lee and Bing Liu. Learning with positive and unlabeled examples us-ing w eighted logistic regression. In *Proceedings of ICML-03, 20th International Conference on Machine Learning*. ACM Press, US, 2003.
5. B. Liu, W. Lee, P. Yu, and X. Li. Partially supervised classification of text doc-uments. In *Proc. 19th Intl. Conf. on Machine Learning*, Sydney, Australia, July 2002.
6. Bing Liu, Yang Dai, Xiaoli Li, Wee Sun Lee, and Philip S. Yu. Building text classifiers using positive and unlabeled examples. In *Proceedings of Thir dIEEE International Conference on Data Mining*, Melbourne, Florida, 2003.
7. Larry M. Manevitz and Malik Yousef. One-class svms for document classification. *Journal of Machine Learning Research*, 2:139–154, 2001.
8. Hwee T. Ng, Wei B. Goh, and Kok L. Low. Feature selection, perceptron learning, and a usability case study for text categorization. In Nicholas J. Belkin, A. De-sai Narasimhalu, and Peter Willett, editors, *Pr oceedings of SIGIR-97, 20th ACM International Conference on Research and Development in Information Retrieval*, pages 67–73, Philadelphia, US, 1997. ACM Press, New York, US.
9. J. Platt. Fast training of support vector machines using sequential minimal opti-mization. In B. Scholk opf, C. Burges, and A. Smola, editors, *Advances in kernel methods - support vector learning*. MIT Press, 1998.

10. Gerald Salton and Buckley C. Term weighting approaches in automatic text retrieval. *Information Processing and Management*, 24(5):513–523, 1988.
11. Bernhard Schölkopf and Alexander J. Smola. *Learning with Kernels: Support Vetor Machines, Regularization, Optimization and Beyond*. The MIT Press, Cambridge, Massachusetts, 2002.
12. Dietrich Wettschereck and Thomas G. Dietterich. An experimental comparison of the nearest-neighbor and nearest-hyperrectangle algorithms. *Machine Learning*, 19(1):5–27, 1995.
13. Yiming Yang and Jan O. Pedersen. A comparative study on feature selection in text categorization. In *Proc. 14th International Conference on Machine Learning*, pages 412–420. Morgan Kaufmann, 1997.
14. Hwanjo Yu, Jiawei Han, and K. C-C. Pebl: Positive example-based learning for web page classification using svm. In *Proc. ACM SIGKDD Int'l Conf. Knowledge Discovery in Databases (KDD02)*, pages 239–248, New York, 2002.
15. Tong Zhang and Frank J. Oles. Text categorization based on regularized linear classification methods. *Information Retrieval*, 4(1):5–31, 2001.
16. Zhaohui Zheng, Xiaoyun Wu, and Rohini Srihari. Feature selection for text categorization on imbalanced datasets. *KDD Exploration, Special issue on Learning from Imbalanced Datasets(to appear)*, 6(1), 2004.

Naive Bayesian Classifiers for Ranking

Harry Zhang and Jiang Su

Faculty of Computer Science, University of New Brunswick
P.O. Box 4400, Fredericton, NB, Canada E3B 5A3
hzhang@unb.ca
http://www.cs.unb.ca/profs/hzhang/

Abstract. It is well-known that naive Bayes performs surprisingly well in classification, but its probability estimation is poor. In many applications, however, a ranking based on class probabilities is desired. For example, a ranking of customers in terms of the likelihood that they buy one's products is useful in direct marketing. What is the general performance of naive Bayes in ranking? In this paper, we study it by both empirical experiments and theoretical analysis. Our experiments show that naive Bayes outperforms C4.4, the most state-of-the-art decision-tree algorithm for ranking. We study two example problems that have been used in analyzing the performance of naive Bayes in classification [3]. Surprisingly, naive Bayes performs perfectly on them in ranking, even though it does not in classification. Finally, we present and prove a sufficient condition for the optimality of naive Bayes in ranking.

1 Introduction

Naive Bayes is one of the most effective and efficient classification algorithms. In classification learning problems, a learner attempts to construct a classifier from a given set of training examples with class labels. Assume that A_1, $A_2, \cdots$, A_n are n attributes. An example E is represented by a vector $(a_1, a_2, , \cdots, a_n)$, where a_i is the value of A_i. Let C represent the class variable, which takes value $+$ (the positive class) or $-$ (the negative class). We use c to represent the value that C takes. A naive Bayesian classifier, or simply naive Bayes, is defined as:

$$C_{nb}(E) = \arg\max_c p(c) \prod_{i=1}^{n} p(a_i|c). \tag{1}$$

Because the values of $p(a_i|c)$ can be estimated from the training examples, naive Bayes is easy to construct. It is also, however, surprisingly effective [10]. Naive Bayes is based on the conditional independence assumption that all attributes are independent given the value of the class variable. It is obvious that the conditional independence assumption is rarely true in reality. Indeed, naive Bayes is found to work poorly for regression problems [7], and produces poor probability estimates [1].

Typically, the performance of a classifier is measured by its predictive accuracy (or error rate). Some classifiers, such as naive Bayes and decision trees, also

J.-F. Boulicaut et al. (Eds.): ECML 2004, LNAI 3201, pp. 501–512, 2004.

produce the estimates of the class probability $p(c|E)$. This information is often ignored in classification, as long as the class with the highest class probability estimate is identical to the actual class. In many applications, however, classification and error rate are not enough. For example, a CS department needs a ranking of its students in terms of their performance in various aspects in order to award scholarships. Thus, a ranking is desired.

If a ranking is desired and only a dataset with class labels is given, the area under the ROC (Receiver Operating Characteristics) curve [18, 15], or simply AUC can be used to evaluate the quality of rankings generated by a classifier. AUC is a good "summary" for comparing two classifiers across the entire range of class distributions and error costs. Bradley [2] shows that AUC is a proper metric for the quality of classifiers averaged across all possible probability thresholds. It has been shown that, for binary classification, AUC is equivalent to the probability that a randomly chosen example of class − will have a smaller estimated probability of belonging to class + than a randomly chosen example of class + [9]. Thus, AUC is actually a measure of the quality of ranking. The AUC of a ranking is 1 (the maximum AUC value) if no positive example precedes any negative example.

Some researchers believe that AUC is a better and more discriminating evaluation method than accuracy for classifiers that produce class probability estimates [11]. Since AUC is a different, probably better, evaluation method than accuracy for machine learning algorithms, the next natural question is: What is the performance of traditional learning algorithms, such as naive Bayes and decision trees, in terms of AUC?

It has been shown that traditional decision tree algorithms, such as C4.5, produce poor probability estimates, and thus produce poor probability-based rankings. Substantial work has been done in improving the ranking quality of decision tree algorithms (see next section for detail).

It is also well-known that naive Bayes performs surprisingly well in classification, but has a poor performance in probability estimation. What is its performance in ranking? In this paper, we argue that naive Bayes also works well in ranking.

The rest of the paper is organized as follows: Section 2 reviews the related work in improving traditional learning algorithms to produce accurate rankings. Section 3 describes an empirical study showing that naive Bayes outperforms a sophisticated decision tree learning algorithm that has recently been developed for generating accurate rankings, which provides empirical evidence that naive Bayes has good performance in ranking, just as in classification. Section 4 explores the theoretical reason for the superb performance of naive Bayes in ranking. The paper concludes with a summary of our work and discussion.

2   Related Work

The ranking addressed in this paper is based on the class probabilities of examples. If a learning algorithm produces accurate class probability estimates, it certainly produces an accurate ranking. But the opposite is not true. For example, assume that E_+ and E_- are a positive and a negative example respectively, and that the actual class probabilities are $p(+|E_+) = 0.9$ and $p(+|E_-) = 0.4$. An algorithm that gives class probability estimates: $\hat{p}(+|E_+) = 0.5$ and $\hat{p}(+|E_-) = 0.45$, gives a correct order of E_+ and E_- in the ranking, although the probability estimates are poor. In the ranking problem, an algorithm tolerates the error of probability estimates to some extent, which is similar to that in classification. Recall that a classification algorithm gives the correct classification on an example, as long as the class with the maximum posterior probability estimate is identical to the actual class.

Naive Bayes is easy to construct and has surprisingly good performance in classification, even though the conditional independence assumption is rarely true in real-world applications. On the other hand, naive Bayes is found to produce poor probability estimates [3]. Some work has been published to improve its probability estimates. Zadrozny and Elkan [19] propose using a histogram method to calibrate probability estimation. A more effective and straightforward way to improve naive Bayes is to extend its structure to represent dependencies among attributes [8]. Most of the extensions, however, aim at improving the predictive accuracy, not at better probability estimation or ranking. Lachiche and Flach present a method that uses AUC to find an optimal threshold for naive Bayes, and thus improves its classification accuracy [6]. An interesting question is, what is the performance of naive Bayes in terms of ranking (AUC)?

Decision tree learning algorithms are one of the simplest and most effective learning algorithms, widely used in many applications. Traditional decision tree learning algorithms, such as C4.5, are error-based, and also produce probability estimates. In decision trees, the class probability $p(c|E)$ of an example E is the fraction of the examples of class c in the leaf that E falls into. How to build decision trees with accurate probability estimates is an interesting question.

Unfortunately, traditional decision tree algorithms, such as C4.5, have been observed to produce poor estimates of probabilities [14, 16]. According to Provost and Domingos [17], the decision tree representation, however, is not (inherently) doomed to produce poor probability estimates, and a part of the problem is that modern decision tree algorithms are biased against building the tree with accurate probability estimates. They propose the two techniques to improve the AUC of C4.5: smooth probability estimates by Laplace correction and turning off pruning. The resulting algorithm is called C4.4 [17]. They compared C4.4 to C4.5 by empirical experiments, and found that C4.4 is a significant improvement over C4.5 with regard to AUC.

Ling and Yan proposed a method to calibrate the probability estimate generated by C4.5 [12]. Their method does not just determine the class probability of an example E by the leaf into which it falls. Instead, each leaf in the tree contributes to the probability estimate. Ferri, Flach and Hernandez-Orallo present a novel algorithm for learning decision trees, which is based on AUC, rather than entropy. The resulting decision trees have better AUC without sacrificing accuracy [5].

However, to our knowledge, there is no systematical study of the performance of naive Bayes with respect to ranking, measured by AUC. By a systematical study, we find that naive Bayes actually performs well in ranking, just as it does in classification. In this paper, we present empirical experiments and the theoretical analysis for this observation.

3   Comparison Between Naive Bayes and Decision Tree

In this section, we present an empirical comparison between naive Bayes and C4.4, and give some explanation of the experimental results.

3.1   Experiments

We conduct experiments to compare naive Bayes with C4.4, and AUC is used as the evaluation criterion. We use 15 datasets from the UCI repository [13], shown in Table 1. In our experiments, the average AUC has been obtained for both C4.4 and naive Bayes by using 10-fold stratified cross validation. C4.4 has been implemented in Weka [20] and compared to existing Weka implementations of naive Bayes. Since Laplace correction has been used in C4.4 and significantly improves the AUC [17], we also use it in naive Bayes. The experimental results are shown in Table 2.

Table 1. Description of the datasets used in the experiments.

Dataset	sizes	num. of attributes	missing value
Breast cancer	286	9	Yes
Vote	435	16	Yes
Chess	3196	36	No
Mushroom	8124	22	Yes
Horse Colic	368	28	Yes
Wisconsin-breast-cancer	699	9	Yes
Credit Approval	690	15	Yes
German Credit	1000	24	No
Pima Indians Diabetes	768	8	No
Heart-statlog	270	13	No
Hepatitis Domain	155	19	Yes
Ionosphere	351	34	No
Labor	57	16	No
Sick	3772	30	Yes
Sonar	208	61	No

We conduct a paired two-tailed t-test by using 95% as the confidence level to see if one algorithm is better than the other. Figures in Table 2 are indicated in boldface whenever the observed difference of the AUCs between naive Bayes and C4.4 is significant. We can see that naive Bayes outperforms C4.4 in 8 datasets,

Table 2. Experimental results on AUC.

Dataset	C4.4	Naive Bayes
Breast cancer	59.42 ± 10.94	**70.43 ± 15.94**
Vote	**100.00 ± 0.00**	95.26 ± 1.10
Chess End-Game	100.00 ± 0.00	100.00 ± 0.00
Mushroom	**98.13 ± 2.19**	97.97 ± 2.01
Wisconsin-breast-cancer	98.33 ± 2.29	99.57 ± 1.45
Credit Approval	88.47 ± 4.39	**92.43 ± 3.26**
German Credit	69.88 ± 5.83	**79.63 ± 5.48**
Pima Indians Diabetes	73.76 ± 5.74	**82.43 ± 5.29**
Heart-statlog	82.82 ± 9.84	**91.36 ± 4.39**
Hepatitis Domain	82.42 ± 11.84	**89.23 ± 9.94**
Ionosphere	92.34 ± 4.65	94.95 ± 3.94
Horse Colic	**86.38 ± 8.82**	84.23 ± 6.85
Labor	70.67 ± 28.18	**95.73 ± 16.93**
Sick	**99.84 ± 1.12**	96.23 ± 2.18
Sonar	76.24 ± 9.94	**85.95 ± 11.01**
Average	85.25	90.36

ties in 3 dataset and loses in 4 datasets, and that the average AUC of naive Bayes is 90.36%, substantially higher than the average 85.25% of C4.4. Considering that C4.4 is the state-of-art decision tree algorithm specifically designed for high AUC, we believe that this presents evidence that naive Bayes has some advantage over decision trees in producing better rankings.

3.2 Comparing Naive Bayes with Decision Trees from Representational Capacity

The experiment in the preceding section indicates that naive Bayes has some advantage over the decision tree algorithm C4.4. What are the reasons behind the experimental results? In this section, we give some intuitive explanation, and we will analyze the ranking performance of naive Bayes theoretically in Section 4.

In decision trees, the class probability of an example is estimated by the proportion of the examples of that class in the leaf into which the example falls. Thus, all examples in the same leaf have the same probability, and will be ranked randomly. This weakens substantially the capacity of decision trees in representing accurate rankings. That is because two contradictory factors are in the play at the same time. On one hand, decision tree algorithms, such as ID3 and C4.5, tend to build small decision trees. This results in more examples in leaves with more reliable probability estimates of the leaves. However, smaller trees imply a smaller number of leaves, thus more examples will have the same class probability. This limits the discriminating power of the tree to rank examples. On the other hand, if the tree is large, not only may the tree overfit the data, but the number of examples in each leaf becomes small, and thus the probability estimates would not be accurate. This would also produce bad rankings.

Let us assume that all attributes and the class variable are Boolean, and that we have n attributes. Then, for a given decision tree T, each leaf represents only one class probability $p(C = +|E)$ $(p(C = -|E) = 1 - p(C = +|E))$. Assume that T has L leaves, then the maximum number of the possible distinct class probabilities is L. A full decision tree, in which each attribute occurs once on each path from the root to a leaf, can represent at most 2^n distinct class probabilities. Obviously, such full decision trees are rarely meaningful, since decision tree algorithms tend to construct small trees, and the number of training examples is normally much less than 2^n. Therefore, in reality, L is much less than 2^n. In a small decision tree, however, the number of distinct class probabilities that it can represent, i.e., the number of its leaves, is also small. Thus, it is very possible for many examples to have the same class probability. This is an obvious disadvantage for generating an accurate probability-based ranking. That is why Provost and Domingos [17] recommend turning off pruning for better ranking.

That contradiction does not exist in naive Bayes, which calculates the class probability $p(c|E)$ based on $p(a_i|c)$, as showed in Equation 1, where a_i is the value of attribute A_i of example E. Although naive Bayes has only $2n + 1$ parameters, the number of possible different class probabilities can be as many as 2^n. Therefore, intuitively speaking, naive Bayes has an advantage over decision trees in the capacity of representing different class probabilities.

4   Theoretical Analysis on the Performance of Naive Bayes in Ranking

Although naive Bayes performs well in classification, its learnability is very limited. In the binary domain, it can learn only linearly separable functions [4]. Moreover, it cannot learn even all the linearly separable functions. For example, Domingos and Pazzani [3] discover that several specific linear functions are not learnable by naive Bayes, such as conjunctive concepts and m-of-n concepts. In other words, naive Bayes is not optimal in learning those concepts. We find out, however, that naive Bayes is optimal in ranking in both conjunctive concepts and m-of-n concepts. Here the optimality in ranking is defined as follows.

Definition 1. *A classifier is called locally optimal on example E in ranking,*

1. *if E is a positive example, there is no negative example ranked after E; or*
2. *if E is a negative example, there is no positive example ranked before E.*

Definition 2. *A classifier is called globally optimal in ranking, if it is locally optimal on all the examples in the example space of a given problem.*

When a classifier is globally optimal, the AUC of the ranking produced by it is always 1.

4.1   Conjunctive Concepts

A conjunctive concept is a conjunction of n literals L_i, where a literal is a Boolean attribute or its negation. It has been shown that naive Bayes, as a classifier, is optimal in learning conjunctive concepts if examples are uniformly distributed and the training set includes all the 2^n possible examples [3]. Let $+$ and $-$ denote the class of $C = 1$ (true) and the class of $C = 0$ (false), respectively. In the training set, only one example that has $L_1 = L_2 = \cdots = L_n = 1$ is in class $+$. Thus, $p(+) = \frac{1}{2^n}$, $p(-) = \frac{2^n-1}{2^n}$, $p(L_i|+) = 1$, $p(\bar{L}_i|+) = 0$, $p(\bar{L}_i|-) = \frac{2^{n-1}}{2^n-1}$, and $p(L_i|-) = \frac{2^{n-1}-1}{2^n-1}$. Assume that E is an arbitrary example and m is its number of the conjunction literals being true. Then, the class probability estimates given by naive Bayes are

$$p_{nb}(+|E) = p(+)p^m(L_i|+)p^{n-m}(\bar{L}_i|+)$$
$$= \begin{cases} \frac{1}{2^n} & \text{if } m = n \\ 0 & \text{otherwise,} \end{cases} \tag{2}$$

and

$$p_{nb}(-|E) = p(-)p^m(L_i|-)p^{n-m}(\bar{L}_i|-)$$
$$= \frac{2^n - 1}{2^n}\left(\frac{2^{n-1} - 1}{2^n - 1}\right)^m\left(\frac{2^{n-1}}{2^n - 1}\right)^{n-m}. \tag{3}$$

It is easy to show that naive Bayes will give the correct classification for all examples. Let us consider the ranking produced by naive Bayes. For a positive example E_+, we have $m = n$. The probability $p_{nb}(+|E_+)$ is $\frac{1}{2^n}$. For any negative example E_-, $m < n$, and $p_{nb}(+|E_-) = 0 < \frac{1}{2^n} = p_{nb}(+|E_+)$. That means that naive Bayes never ranks a positive example before a negative example in the class probability based ranking. Naive Bayes is therefore optimal for conjunctive concepts under uniform distribution.

If the assumption that examples are uniformly distributed is removed, naive Bayes gives the correct classification for all the examples in class $-$, given a sufficient training set. However, for a positive example $(m = n)$, the result will depend on the class distribution. If $p(+) < \frac{1}{2^n}$, it is possible that naive Bayes will fail to assign a correct class to a positive example. That means that naive Bayes is not optimal in classification if the example distribution is not uniform.

However, no matter what the value of $p(+)$ is, $p_{nb}(+|E_-) = 0$ and $p_{nb}(+|E_+) = p(+) > 0$. Therefore, naive Bayes is still optimal for conjunctive concepts in ranking, as shown in the theorem below.

Theorem 1. *Naive Bayes is globally optimal in ranking on conjunctive concepts.*

4.2   *m*-of-*n* Concepts

An m-of-n concept is a Boolean function that is true if m or more out of n Boolean attributes are true. Clearly, it is a linearly separable function. Domingos and Pazzani [3] show that for the concept 8-of-25, when the input Boolean attributes have just six or seven 1s, naive Bayes gives an incorrect answer of 1 (instead of 0).

Their result is based on two assumptions: (1) The sampling consists of all 2^{25} examples of the 8-of-25 function, or is the uniform distribution; (2) The threshold for classification is 0.5. That is, an example E belongs to class $+$ if and only if $p(+|E) \geq 0.5$. The corresponding probabilities can then be obtained explicitly [3]:

$$p(+) = \frac{\sum_{i=m}^{n} \binom{n}{i}}{2^n},$$

$$p(-) = \frac{\sum_{i=0}^{m-1} \binom{n}{i}}{2^n},$$

$$p(A_i = 1|+) = \frac{\sum_{i=m-1}^{n-1} \binom{n-1}{i}}{\sum_{i=m}^{n} \binom{n}{i}},$$

$$p(A_i = 1|-) = \frac{\sum_{i=0}^{m-2} \binom{n-1}{i}}{\sum_{i=0}^{m-1} \binom{n}{i}}.$$

Let q denote $p(A_i = 1|+)$. Obviously, $q > 0.5$. The class probability estimate produced by naive Bayes, denoted by $p_{nb}(+|E)$, is:

$$p_{nb}(+|E) = p(+)q^i(1-q)^{(n-i)},$$

where i is the number of attributes of 1.

Now let us consider the ranking performance of naive Bayes in m-of-n concepts. Assume that E_+ is a positive example with k_1 attributes of 1, and that E_- is a negative example with k_2 attributes of 1. Obviously, $k_1 \geq m > k_2$. Then we have

$$p_{nb}(+|E_+) - p_{nb}(+|E_-) = p(+)q^{k_2}(1-q)^{n-k_1}(q^{k_1-k_2} - (1-q)^{k_1-k_2}). \quad (4)$$

Since $q > 0.5$ and $k_1 > k_2$, Equation 4 is always positive. Thus, for m-of-n concepts, the class probability of a positive example is always greater than the class probability of a negative example in naive Bayes. Therefore, the ranking generated by naive Bayes is optimal, as shown in the following theorem.

Theorem 2. *Naive Bayes is globally optimal in ranking on m-of-n concepts.*

4.3   General Optimality of Naive Bayes

The two example problems in the preceding sections are quite surprising, since it has been known that, as a classifier, naive Bayes cannot learn all m-of-n concepts under uniform distribution and cannot learn all conjunctive concepts under some non-uniform distributions. The rankings generated by naive Bayes, however, are optimal in both problems. This provides us evidence that naive Bayes performs well in ranking, in some problems even better than classification.

In our following discussion, we assume that the prior probabilities $p(E)$ of all examples E are equal. Since $p(+|E) = \frac{p(+)p(E|+)}{p(E)}$, thus the ranking is also determined by $p(E|+)$.

Now let us consider the general case. Assume that E_+ is a positive example and E_- is a negative example. Thus, $p(E_+|+) > p(E_-|+)$. Let $p_{nb}(E_i|+)$ denote the probability estimates generated by naive Bayes, $i = +, -$. Let x and y denote the errors of probability estimates on E_+ and E_- given by naive Bayes. That is:

$$x = p(E_+|+) - p_{nb}(E_+|+)$$
$$y = p(E_-|+) - p_{nb}(E_-|+)$$

Naive Bayes generates the correct order for E_+ and E_-, if

$$p_{nb}(E_+|+) > p_{nb}(E_-|+).$$

That is

$$y - x + (p(E_+|+) - p(E_-|+)) > 0. \tag{5}$$

Assuming that x and y are uniformly distributed, we plot a figure in which x any y corresponds to the horizotal and vertical axes respectively, as shown in Figure 1. The shaded area corresponds to the cases in which Equation 5 is true. Since $p(E_+|+) > p(E_-|+)$, naive Bayes is optimal in more than a half of the possible area. It is easy to calculate the area of the shaded area, denoted by A.

$$A = -\frac{1}{2}((p(E_+|+) - p(E_-|+)) - 2)^2 + 4 \tag{6}$$

It is interesting to notice that, the greater difference between $p(E_+|+)$ and $p(E_-|+)$, the greater chance that naive Bayes is optimal. For example, when $p(E_+|+) - p(E_-|+) = 0.5$, the probability of naive Bayes being optimal is 0.78125.

Now let us assume that all the dependences among attributes are complete. An attribute A_i is said to depend on A_j completely, if $A_i = A_j$. If $A_i = A_j$ and all other attributes are independent, the true probablity $p(E|+)$ for an example $E = (a_1, a_2, \cdots, a_n)$ is

$$p(E|+) = p(a_i|+) \prod_{k \neq i,j} p(a_k|+).$$

The probability $p_{nb}(E|+)$ given by naive Bayes is

$$p_{nb}(E|+) = p(a_i|+)^2 \prod_{k \neq i,j} p(a_k|+).$$

Given two examples $E_+ = (a_1^+, a_2^+, \cdots, a_n^+)$ and $E_- = (a_1^-, a_2^-, \cdots, a_n^-)$ belonging to the positive and negative class respectively, we have

$$p(E_+|+) = p(a_i^+|+) \prod_{k \neq i,j} p(a_k^+|+) > p(E_-|+) = p(a_i^-|+) \prod_{k \neq i,j} p(a_k^-|+).$$

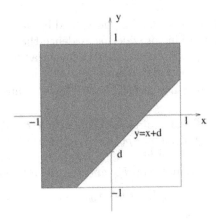

Fig. 1. A figure shows the optimality of naive Bayes in a general case, in which $d = p(E_-|+) - p(E_+|+)$, and the shaded area corresponds the optimal area of naive Bayes.

It is easy to show that, if $p(a_i^+|+) \geq 0.5$, $p_{nb}(E_+|+) > p_{nb}(E_-|+)$. Notice that E_+ is a positive example, it is a reasonable assumption that $p(a_i^+|+) \geq 0.5$. We have a formal definition on the property of such an attribute value.

Definition 3. *A value a_i of attributes A_i is called indicative to class c, if $p(A_i = a_i|c) \geq p(A_i = \bar{a}_i|c)$, where $\bar{a}_i$ is another value of A_i other than a_i.*

For example, for the problem of m-of-n concepts, $p(A_i = 1|+) > p(A_i = 0|+)$ for any attribute. So $A_i = 1$ is indicative to class $+$. If all the attribute values of an example are indicative, naive Bayes always gives the optimal ranking for it, illustrated by the theorem below.

Theorem 3. *Naive Bayes is optimal on example $E = (a_1, a_2, \cdots, a_n)$ in ranking, if each attribute value of E is indicative to class $+$.*

Proof. By induction on i, the number of pairs of attributes with complete dependence.

When $i = 1$, it is true from the preceding discussion. Assume that the claim is true when $i = k$. That is, if there are k complete dependences among attributes and $p(E_+|+) > p(E_-|+)$, then $p_{nb}(E_+|+) > p_{nb}(E_-|+)$, where $E_+ = (a_1^+, a_2^+, \cdots, a_n^+)$ and $E_- = (a_1^-, a_2^-, \cdots, a_n^-)$ belong to positive and negative class respectively. Consider that $i = k+1$. Assume that the new complete dependence is between A_{n-1} and A_n. Then $p(E_+|+) > p(E_-|+)$. Since $A_{n-1} = A_n$,

$$p(E_+|+) = p(E_+ - \{A_{n-1}\}|+) = p(a_1^+, \cdots, a_{n-2}^+, a_n^+|+),$$
$$p(E_-|+) = p(E_- - \{A_{n-1}\}|+) = p(a_1^-, \cdots, a_{n-2}^-, a_n^-|+).$$

Since there are only k dependences among $A_1, \cdots, A_{n-2}, A_n$, according to induction hypothesis,

$$p_{nb}(a_1^+, \cdots, a_{n-2}^+, a_n^+|+) > p_{nb}(a_1^-, \cdots, a_{n-2}^-, a_n^-|+).$$

Thus, we have

$$\prod_{i=1 i\neq n-1}^{n} p(a_i^+|+) > \prod_{i=1 i\neq n-1}^{n} p(a_i^-|+).$$

Since all the attribute values of E are indicative, $p(a_{n-1}^+|+) > p(a_{n-1}^-|+)$. Then, we have

$$\prod_{i=1}^{n} p(a_i^+|+) > \prod_{i=1}^{n} p(a_i^-|+).$$

Therefore, $p_{nb}(E_+|+) > p_{nb}(E_-|+)$.

Theorem 3 presents a sufficient condition on the local optimality of naive Bayes. Notice that even when all the attribute values of an example are indictative, it is possible that naive Bayes gives a wrong classification.

5   Conclusion

In this paper, we argue that naive Bayes performs well in ranking, just as it does in classification. We compare empirically naive Bayes with the state-of-the-art decision tree learning algorithm C4.4 in terms of ranking, measured by AUC, and our experiment shows that naive Bayes has some advantage over C4.4. We investigate two example problems theoretically: conjunctive literals and m-of-n concepts, which were used to analyze the classification performance of naive Bayes in [3]. Surprisingly, naive Bayes works perfectly in both problems with respect to ranking, although it does not perform perfectly in terms of classification. For more general cases, we propose a sufficient condition for the local optimality of naive Bayes in ranking.

Generally, the performance of naive Bayes in ranking is similar to that in classification, in the sense that both tolerate the estimation error of class probabilities to some extent. It is interesting to know which one tolerates error to a higher extent. Our conjecture is that, for naive Bayes, it might be ranking.

References

1. Bennett, P. N.: Assessing the calibration of Naive Bayes' posterior estimates. Technical Report No. CMU-CS00-155 (2000)
2. Bradley, A. P.: The use of the area under the ROC curve in the evaluation of machine learning algorithms. Pattern Recognition **30** (1997) 1145-1159
3. Domingos, P., Pazzani M.: Beyond Independence: Conditions for the Optimality of the Simple Bayesian Classifier. Machine Learning **29** (1997) 103-130
4. Duda, R. O., Hart, P. E.: Pattern Classification and Scene Analysis. A Wiley-Interscience Publication (1973)
5. Ferri, C., Flach, P. A., Hernández-Orallo, J.: Learning Decision Trees Using the Area Under the ROC Curve. Proceedings of the 19th International Conference on Machine Learning. Morgan Kaufmann (2002) 139-146

6. Lachiche, N., Flach, P. A.: Improving Accuracy and Cost of Two-class and Multi-class Probabilistic Classifiers Using ROC Curves. Proceedings of the 20th International conference on Machine Learning. Morgan Kaufmann (2003) 416-423

7. Frank, E., Trigg, L., Holmes, G., Witten, I. H.: Naive Bayes for Regression. Machine Learning 41(1) (2000) 5-15

8. Friedman, N., Greiger, D., Goldszmidt, M.: Bayesian Network Classifiers. Machine Learning 29 (1997) 103–130

9. Hand, D. J., Till, R. J.: A simple generalisation of the area under the ROC curve for multiple class classification problems. Machine Learning 45 (2001) 171-186

10. Kononenko, I.: Comparison of Inductive and Naive Bayesian Learning Approaches to Automatic Knowledge Acquisition. Current Trends in Knowledge Acquisition. IOS Press (1990)

11. Ling, C. X., Huang, J., Zhang, H.: AUC: a statistically consistent and more discriminating measure than accuracy. Proceedings of the International Joint Conference on Artificial Intelligence IJCAI03. Morgan Kaufmann (2003) 329-341

12. Ling, C. X., Yan, R. J.: Decision Tree with Better Ranking. Proceedings of the 20th International Conference on Machine Learning. Morgan Kaufmann (2003) 480-487

13. Merz, C., Murphy, P., Aha, D.: UCI repository of machine learning databases. Dept of ICS, University of California, Irvine (1997). http://www.ics.uci.edu/~mlearn/MLRepository.html

14. M. Pazzani, P., Merz, C., Murphy, P., Ali, K., Hume, T., Brunk, C.: Reducing misclassification costs. Proceedings of the 11th International conference on Machine Learning. Morgan Kaufmann (1994) 217-225

15. Provost, F., Fawcett, T.: Analysis and visualization of classifier performance: comparison under imprecise class and cost distribution. Proceedings of the Third International Conference on Knowledge Discovery and Data Mining. AAAI Press (1997) 43-48

16. Provost, F., Fawcett, T., Kohavi, R.: The case against accuracy estimation for comparing induction algorithms. Proceedings of the Fifteenth International Conference on Machine Learning. Morgan Kaufmann (1998) 445-453

17. Provost, F. J., Domingos, P.: Tree Induction for Probability-Based Ranking. Machine Learning 52(3) (2003) 199-215

18. Swets, J.: Measuring the accuracy of diagnostic systems. Science 240 (1988) 1285-1293

19. Zadrozny, B., Elkan, C.: Obtaining calibrated probability estimates from decision trees and naive Bayesian classifiers. Proceedings of the Eighteenth International conference on Machine Learning. Morgan Kaufmann (2001) 609-616

20. Witten, I. H., Frank, E.: Data Mining –Practical Machine Learning Tools and Techniques with Java Implementation. Morgan Kaufmann (2000)

Conditional Independence Trees

Harry Zhang and Jiang Su

Faculty of Computer Science, University of New Brunswick
P.O. Box 4400, Fredericton, NB, Canada E3B 5A3
hzhang@unb.ca
http://www.cs.unb.ca/profs/hzhang/

Abstract. It has been observed that traditional decision trees produce poor probability estimates. In many applications, however, a probability estimation tree (PET) with accurate probability estimates is desirable. Some researchers ascribe the poor probability estimates of decision trees to the decision tree learning algorithms. To our observation, however, the representation also plays an important role. Indeed, the representation of decision trees is fully expressive theoretically, but it is often impractical to learn such a representation with accurate probability estimates from limited training data. In this paper, we extend decision trees to represent a joint distribution and conditional independence, called conditional independence trees (CITrees), which is a more suitable model for PETs. We propose a novel algorithm for learning CITrees, and our experiments show that the CITree algorithm outperforms C4.5 and naive Bayes significantly in classification accuracy.

1 Introduction

Classification is a fundamental issue of machine learning, in which a classifier is induced from a set of labeled training examples represented by a vector of attribute values and a class label. We denote a vector of attributes by an bold-face upper-case letter $\mathbf{A}$, $\mathbf{A} = (A_1, A_2, \cdots, A_n)$, and an assignment of value to each attribute in $\mathbf{A}$ by a corresponding bold-face lower-case letter $\mathbf{a}$. We use C to denote the class variable and c to denote its value. Thus, a training example $E = (\mathbf{a}, c)$, where $\mathbf{a} = (a_1, a_2, \cdots, a_n)$, and a_i is the value of attribute A_i. A classifier is a function that maps an example to a class label.

There are numerous inductive learning algorithms, such as decision trees, Bayesian networks, and neural networks, that can be categorized into two major approaches: probability-based approach and decision boundary-based approach. In a probability-based learning algorithm, a probability distribution $p(\mathbf{A}, C)$ is learned from the training data, and an example E is classified into the class c with the maximum posterior class probability $p(c|E)$ (or simply class probability), as shown below.

$$C_{pb}(E) = \arg\max_c p(c|E). \tag{1}$$

J.-F. Boulicaut et al. (Eds.): ECML 2004, LNAI 3201, pp. 513–524, 2004.

Various probability-based learning algorithms have been developed, which are different in the way of estimating $p(c|E)$. For example, a naive Bayes classifier (or simply naive Bayes), shown in Equation 2, is a successful one widely used in many applications.

$$C_{nb}(E) = \arg\max_c p(c) \prod_{i=1}^{n} p(a_i|c).$$ (2)

A naive Bayes is based on the crucial assumption that all the attributes are independent given the value of the class variable, called conditional independence assumption and shown in Equation 3. Obviously, this assumption is rarely true in reality.

$$p(\mathbf{a}|c) = \prod_{i=1}^{n} p(a_i|c).$$ (3)

In a decision boundary-based algorithm, an explicit decision boundary is extracted from the training data, and an example E is classified into class c if E falls into the decision area corresponding to c. Decision tree algorithms are well-known as decision boundary-based. While decision trees perform quite well in classification, it is also found that their probability estimates are poor [9]. Building decision trees with accurate probability estimates, called probability estimation trees (PETs), has received a great deal of attention recently [10]. Some researchers ascribe the poor probability estimates of decision trees to the decision tree learning algorithms. Thus, many techniques have been proposed to improve the learning algorithms in producing accurate probability estimates[10].

To our observation, however, the representation also plays an important role. Indeed, the representation of decision trees is fully expressive theoretically, but it is often impractical to learn such a representation with accurate probability estimates from limited training data.

In a decision tree, the class probability $p(c|E)$ is estimated by the fraction of the examples of class c in the leaf into which E falls. Thus, the class probabilities of all the examples in the same leaf are equal. This is an obstacle in building an accurate PET, because two contradictory factors are in play at the same time. On one hand, traditional decision tree algorithms, such as C4.5, prefer a small tree. Thus, a leaf has more examples and the class probability estimates are more reliable. A small tree, however, has a small number of leaves, thus more examples will have the same class probability. That prevents the learning algorithm from building an accurate PET. On the other hand, if the tree is large, not only may the tree overfit the training data, but the number of examples in each leaf is also small, and thus the probability estimates would not be accurate and reliable. Such a contradiction does exist in traditional decision trees.

Our motivation is to extend the representation of traditional decision trees not only to represent accurate probabilities but also to be easily learnable from limited data in practice. Naturally, if an accurate PET is built, its classification accuracy should also be high, since an accurate approximation of $p(c|E)$ is found and can be used for classification. Thus, we use classification accuracy to evaluate learning algorithms in this paper.

The rest of the paper is organized as follows. Section 2 introduces the related work on learning decision trees with accurate probability estimates. Section 3 presents a novel model for PETs and a corresponding algorithm for learning PETs. In Section 4, we present empirical experiments. The paper concludes with discussion and some directions for future work.

2   Related Work

Since traditional decision tree algorithms, such as C4.5, have been observed to produce poor probability estimates of probabilities [9], a substantial amount of work has been done recently on accurate PETs [10]. Provost and Domingos [10] point out that the reason behind the poor estimates of decision trees is not the decision tree representation, but the inductive algorithm. They propose a few techniques to modify the C4.5 learning algorithm.

First, they turn off the pruning and collapsing in C4.5, since they notice that a larger tree tends to have more accurate probability estimates.

Second, they propose to use Laplace correction to smooth probability estimates. The reason is the fragmentation problem: As the splitting process proceeds, the data associated with each descendant node becomes small. Eventually, when the depth of the tree is large, there is very little data with each leaf node [6]. Thus, the probability estimates based on frequency are not accurate. This issue is more serious after turning off the pruning and collapsing mechanism.

The resulting algorithm is called C4.4. They also find out that bagging, an ensemble method, improves the probability estimates of decision trees significantly.

Ling and Yan also propose a method to improve the probability estimates of decision trees [7]. They present a method to generate the class probability of an example, in which an average of the probability estimates from all leaves of the tree is used, instead of only using the leaf into which it falls. Thus, each leaf contributes to the class probability estimate of an example in different degree.

In learning a decision tree, a critical step is to choose the "best" attribute in each step. The entropy-based splitting criteria, such as information gain and gain ratio, have been widely used. There are also other splitting criteria proposed. One is Bayesian approach [3], which searches for a decision tree with the maximum posterior probability given the training examples.

Although decision trees are well-known as a nonparametric and decision-boundary based classifier, each leaf of a tree actually represents a conditional probability distribution. These types of decision trees are called probabilistic decision trees. Jordan [5] analyzes decision trees within a probabilistic framework. A decision tree actually represents a sequence of probabilistic decisions, each conditional on the attribute values and previous decisions. Thus, Bayesian theory can be used in analyzing the performance of the tree. A learning algorithm based on EM (Expectation-Maximization) has been proposed for maximum likelihood parameter estimation in a hidden Markov decision tree.

A questionable point of traditional decision trees (including probabilistic trees) is that only the attributes along the path from the root to a leaf are used in both classification and probability estimation. Since a small tree is preferred by traditional decision tree learning algorithms, many attributes may not be used. This is a more serious issue in learning PETs than classification. Kohavi proposes to deploy a naive Bayes in each leaf, and the resulting decision tree is called an NBTree [6]. The algorithm for learning an NBTree is similar to C4.5. After a tree is grown, a naive Bayes is constructed for each leaf using the data associated with that leaf. An NBTree classifies an example by sorting it to a leaf and applying the naive Bayes in that leaf to assign a class label to it. Actually, deploying a model at leaves to calibrate the probability estimates of a decision tree has been proposed by Symth, Gray and Fayyad [11]. They also notice that every example from a particular leaf has the same probability estimate, and thus suggest to place a kernel-based probability density estimator at each leaf.

Our work is inspired by the works of Kohavi, and Symth, Gray and Fayyad, but from different point of view. Indeed, if a local model that incorporates the attributes not occurring on the path is deployed at each leaf, together with the conditional probability of the attributes occurring on the path, the resulting tree represents accurate probabilities. If the structure of standard decision trees is learned and used the same way as in C4.5, however, the leaf models would not directly and explicitly benefit from the structure, and thus would still play a role of smoothing. Our motivation is how to learn and use the structure of a tree to explore conditional independences among attributes, such that a simple leaf model, like a naive Bayes, gives accurate probability estimates. Then, the resulting model is more compact and more easily learnable, while its representation is still accurate.

3   Understanding Decision Trees from Probabilistic Perspective

Even though there theoretically exists a decision tree with accurate probability estimates for any given problem, such a tree tends to be large and learnable only when sufficient (huge) training data are available. In practice, a small tree is preferred. Thus, poor probability estimates are yielded. Therefore, the representation of a decision tree should be extended to represent accurate probabilities and be learnable from limited training data.

3.1   Probabilistic Decision Trees

Figure 1 shows an example of a probabilistic tree, in which each leaf L represents a conditional distribution $p(C|\mathbf{A_p}(L))$, where $\mathbf{A_p}(L)$ are the attributes that occur in the path from the root to L. For simplicity, the attributes that occur in the path is called the path attributes of L, and all other attributes are called the leaf attributes of L, denoted by $\mathbf{A_l}(L)$.

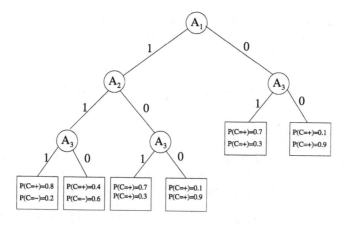

Fig. 1. An example of an probabilistic tree

In practice, $p(C|\mathbf{A_p}(L))$ is often estimated by using the fraction of examples of class C in L, and the classification of a decision tree is based on $p(C|\mathbf{A_p}(L))$. Thus, from the probabilistic point of view, a decision tree can be also viewed as a probability-based classifier, defined as below.

$$C_{dt}(E) = \arg\max_c p(c|\mathbf{a_p}(L)), \tag{4}$$

where L is the leaf into which E falls, $\mathbf{a_p}(L)$ is the value of the path attributes of L, and $C_{dt}(E)$ is the classification given by the decision tree.

Comparing Equation 4 with Equation 1, $p(c|\mathbf{a_p}(L))$ is actually used as an approximation of $p(c|E)$ in a decision tree. Thus, all the examples falling into the same leaf have the same class probability. Due to the fact that traditional decision tree learning algorithms prefer a small tree, a leaf tends to have more examples with the same probability. Therefore, decision trees are prone to be poor PETs.

3.2   Conditional Independence Trees

In a probabilistic tree, a leaf L represents the conditional probability distribution $p(C|\mathbf{A_p}(L))$. If there is a representation of the conditional probability distribution over the leaf attributes at each leaf, called the local conditional distribution and denoted by $p(\mathbf{A_l}(L)|\mathbf{A_p}(L), C)$, then each leaf represents a full joint distribution over all the attributes, as shown in the equation below.

$$p(\mathbf{A}, C) = \alpha p(C|\mathbf{A_p}(L))p(\mathbf{A_l}(L)|\mathbf{A_p}(L), C), \tag{5}$$

where α is a normalization factor.

Definition 1. *A probabilistic decision tree T is called a joint probabilistic tree, if each of its leaves represents both the conditional probability distribution $p(C|\mathbf{A_p}(L))$ and $p(\mathbf{A_l}(L)|\mathbf{A_p}(L), C)$.*

Definition 2. *A joint probability tree T is called a conditional independence tree, or simply CITree, if the local conditional independence assumption, shown in Equation 6, is true for each leaf L.*

$$p(\mathbf{A_l}(L)|\mathbf{A_p}(L), C) = \prod_{i=1}^{m} p(A_{li}|C, \mathbf{A_p}(L)), \tag{6}$$

where $\mathbf{A_l} = (A_{l1}, A_{l2}, \cdots, A_{lm})$ are the leaf attributes of L.

According to Definition 2, the structure of a CITree represents the conditional independences among attributes, and its leaves represent a joint distribution. A CITree is different from a probabilistic tree in the following aspects.

1. A CITree represents a joint distribution over all the attributes, but a probabilistic tree represents only the conditional probability distribution of the path attributes.
2. A CITree explicitly defines conditional dependences among attributes.

Comparing Equation 6 with Equation 3, we notice that the local conditional independence assumption of CITrees is a relaxation of the (global) conditional independence assumption of the naive Bayes. Thus, the local conditional independence assumption is more realistic in applications. In addition, the local conditional independence represented in a CITree is also different from the conditional independence in a Bayesian network. In a Bayesian network, An attribute A_1 is conditionally independent of attribute A_2 given A_3 means that for all the values of A_3, A_1 is independent of A_2. In a CITree, however, the conditional independence is that A_1 is independent of A_2, given a specified value of A_3. The granularity in a CITree is finer than that in a Bayesian network.

It is interesting to notice that, after growing a CITree, if a naive Bayes is deployed on each leaf using only the data associated with it, the naive Bayes, called leaf naive Bayes, represents the actual joint distribution. A leaf naive Bayes in leaf L is shown below.

$$C_{lnb}(E) = \arg\max_{c} p_L(c) \prod_{i=1}^{m} p_L(a_{li}|c), \tag{7}$$

where $p_L(c)$ denotes the probability of examples in L being in c, and $p_L(a_{li}|c)$ is the probability that the examples of class c have $A_{li} = a_{li}$ in L. It is obvious that $p_L(c) = p(c|\mathbf{a_p}(L))$ and $p_L(a_{li}|c) = p(a_{li}|c, \mathbf{a_p}(L))$. So $p_L(c) \prod_{i=1}^{m} p_L(a_{li}|c)$ is proportional to $p(c|E)$. Thus, if the structure of the CITree is found, the naive Bayes is a perfect model for leaves.

Generally, a CITree can be viewed as a combination of a decision tree and a naive Bayes. It is well-known that decision trees are fully expressive with the class of propositional language; that is, any Boolean function is represented by a decision tree. However, a naive Bayes has limited expressive power; that is, it can only represent linear Boolean functions [4]. Interestingly, any joint distribution can be represented by a CITree. According to the product rule,

$$p(A_1, A_2, \cdots, A_n, C) = p(C)p(A_1|C)P(A_2|A_1, C) \cdots P(A_n|A_1, \cdots, A_{n-1}, C).$$
(8)

It is trivial to build a CITree to represent $p(A_1, A_2, \cdots, A_n, C)$. Thus, CITrees are also fully expressive.

The representation of CITrees, however, is more compact than that of decision trees. To show this, let us consider only full dependences among attributes. An attribute A_i is said to fully depend on A_j, if $A_i = A_j$. Notice that if an attribute is conditionally independent of all other attributes, it does not occur on any path. If several attributes conditionally depend on one attribute, only that attribute occurs in the path. In the extreme case that the global conditional independent assumption is true, a CITree has only one node, which is just a global naive Bayes. Assume that there are n attributes. The maximum height of a CITree is $\frac{n}{2}$, which corresponds to that each attributes depends exactly on another attribute. The maximum height of a decision tree is n. Our experiments in Section 4 show that the average size of CITrees is much smaller than that of decision trees.

3.3 A Novel Algorithm for Learning CITree

From the discussion in the preceding section, a CITree can represent any joint distribution. Thus, a CITree is a perfect PET, and the classification based on CITree is accurate. But in practice, learning the structure of a CITree is just as time-consuming as learning an optimal decision tree. However, a good approximation of a CITree, which gives good estimates of class probabilities, is satisfiable in many applications. If the structure of a CITree is determined, a leaf naive Bayes is a perfect model representing the local conditional distributions at leaves.

Building a CITree could be also a greedy and recursive process, similar to building a decision tree. At each step, choose the "best" attribute as the root of the (sub)tree, split the associated data into disjoint subsets corresponding to the values of the attribute, and then recur this process for each subset until certain criteria are satisfied.

Notice as well, however, the difference between learning a CITree and learning a decision tree. In building a decision tree, we are looking for a sequence of attributes that leads to the least impurity in all leaves of the tree. The key in choosing an attribute is whether the resulting partition of the examples is "pure" or not. It is natural, since the most common class of a leaf is used as the class of all the examples in that leaf. However, such a selection strategy does not necessarily lead to the truth of the local conditional independence assumption. In building a CITree, we intend to choose the attributes that make the local conditional independence among the rest of attributes true as much as possible. That means that, even though the impurity of its leaves is high, it could still be a good CITree, as long as the leaf attributes are independent. Thus, traditional decision tree learning algorithms are not directly suitable for learning CITrees.

In learning a CITree, an attribute, given which all other attributes have the maximum conditional independence, should be selected at each step. Thus, we should select the attribute with the greatest influence on other attributes. Our idea is to try each possible attribute as the root, evaluate the resulting tree, and choose the attribute that achieves the highest classification accuracy.

Similar to C4.5, our learning algorithm has two separate steps: growing a tree and pruning. In growing a tree, each possible attribute is evaluated at each step, and the attribute that gives the most improvement in accuracy is selected. The algorithm is depicted below.

Algorithm CITree (**T**, **S**, **A**)
Input : CITree **T**, a set **S** of labeled examples, a set of attributes **A**
Output : a CITree.
    1. Evaluate the current CITree **T**.
    2. For all attributes A in **A**
        – Partition **S** into $S_1, \cdots, S_k$, each of which corresponds to a value of A.
        – Create a leaf naive Bayes for each S_i.
        – Evaluate the resulting CITree.
    3. Choose the attribute A_{opt} with the highest accuracy.
    4. For all values a of A_{opt}
        CITree(T_a, S_a, **A** $- \{A_{opt}\}$).
        Add T_a as a child of **T**.
    5. Return **T**.

Note that we train a leaf naive Bayes by using the examples in this leaf, and the accuracy is the accuracy of classifying those examples using the leaf naive Bayes.

In the algorithm described above, we grow a tree as large as possible until we are out of data or attributes, and then start a pruning process with two steps:

1. Conduct the pessimistic error-based post-pruning in C4.5.
2. Apply pruning based on the accuracy of leaf naive Bayes, in which the children of a node are removed only if the resulting pruned tree (making it a leaf node and deploying a naive Bayes at it) performs no worse than the original tree.

4   Experiments

We conduct experiments to compare our algorithm CITree with C4.5 and naive Bayes. Our algorithm is implemented within the Weka framework [12]. We use the implementation of naive Bayes and C4.5(J48) in Weka. We have chosen 33 datasets from the UCI repository [8], described in Table 1. In our experiment, the average accuracy on each dataset has been obtained using 3-fold cross validation 10 times. Numeric attributes are discretized using ten-bin discretization implemented in Weka[12]. Missing values are also processed using the mechanism in Weka.

Table 2 shows the average accuracy obtained by the three algorithms. The comparison of the three algorithms on these datasets, in which a paired t-test

Table 1. Description of the datasets used in the experiments

dataset	Size	Number of Attribute	missing value	Class
Letter	20000	17	N	26
Mushroom	8124	22	Y	2
Waveform	5000	41	N	3
Sick	3772	30	Y	2
Hypothyroid	3772	30	Y	4
Chess End-Game	3196	36	N	2
Splice	3190	62	N	3
Segment	2310	20	N	7
German Credit	1000	24	N	2
Vowel	990	14	N	11
Anneal	898	39	Y	6
Vehicle	846	19	N	4
Pima Indians Diabetes	768	8	N	2
Wisconsin-breast-cancer	699	9	Y	2
Credit Approval	690	15	Y	2
Soybean	683	36	Y	19
Balance-scale	625	5	N	3
Vote	435	16	Y	2
Horse Colic	368	28	Y	2
Ionosphere	351	34	N	2
Primary-tumor	339	18	Y	22
Heart-c	303	14	Y	5
Breast cancer	286	9	Y	2
Heart-statlog	270	13	N	2
Audiology	226	70	Y	24
Glass	214	10	N	7
Sonar	208	61	N	2
Autos	205	26	Y	7
Hepatitis Domain	155	19	Y	2
Iris	150	5	N	3
Lymph	148	19	N	4
Zoo	101	18	N	7
Labor	57	16	N	2

with a confidence of 95% has been used, are summarized in Table 3. Our observations are summarized below.

1. The CITree algorithm outperforms the naive Bayes significantly: It wins in 7 datasets, ties in 26 datasets and loses in 0 dataset. The average accuracy for CITree is 83.26%, higher than the average accuracy 81.83% of naive Bayes. That fact is understandable, since the conditional independences among attributes have been explored and represented in CITrees. Thus, the class probability estimates of a CITree are expected to be more accurate than those of naive Bayes.

2. The CITree algorithm also outperforms C4.5 significantly: It wins in 7 datasets, ties in 25 datasets and loses in 1 datasets. The average accuracy for

Table 2. Experimental results on accuracy. In this table, the dataset are sorted in a decreasing order of their size

Dataset	CITree	NB	C4.5	CITreeSize	Treesize(c4.5)
Letter	81.17 ± 0.35	69.89 ± 0.65	78.27 ± 0.57	133	8737
Mushroom	99.93 ± 0.12	95.59 ± 0.69	100 ± 0	9	30
Waveform	80.12 ± 1.75	79.56 ± 0.68	71.96 ± 1.36	23	1153
Sick	96.9 ± 0.46	96.9 ± 0.46	97.86 ± 0.42	8	45
Hypothyroid	93.06 ± 0.41	93.06 ± 0.41	93.17 ± 0.23	1	24
Chess End-Game	96.86 ± 0.87	87.95 ± 0.85	99.17 ± 0.25	26	55
Splice	92.5 ± 1.64	95.15 ± 0.73	93.46 ± 0.88	14	214
Segment	91.06 ± 0.79	88.44 ± 0.83	91.48 ± 1.36	12	386
German Credit	75.03 ± 1.25	75.03 ± 1.25	71.68 ± 1.02	8	134
Vowel	79.74 ± 8.16	63.45 ± 3.39	67.61 ± 2.43	22	649
Anneal	94.9 ± 2.28	94.08 ± 1.23	98.72 ± 0.66	5	75
Vehicle	67.36 ± 2.83	60.57 ± 2.3	68.34 ± 2.73	15	412
Pima Indians Diabetes	74.31 ± 3.16	75.35 ± 2.49	74.89 ± 2.03	5	56
Soybean	91.19 ± 1.44	91.36 ± 1.47	88.61 ± 1.26	8	81
Wisconsin-breast-cancer	96.89 ± 0.91	97.14 ± 0.68	94.33 ± 1.16	8	46
Credit Approval	85.03 ± 1.33	84.77 ± 1.3	85.62 ± 1.35	6	42
Balance-scale	89.39 ± 1.2	89.39 ± 1.2	66.54 ± 2.9	1	85
Vote	93.98 ± 1.64	89.04 ± 1.97	95.06 ± 1.28	6	10
Horse Colic	80.6 ± 2.75	79.71 ± 3.57	83.88 ± 1.6	8	15
Primary-tumor	42.09 ± 4.35	48.31 ± 2.36	39.57 ± 1.77	6	83
Ionosphere	89.01 ± 3.39	90.35 ± 2.24	88.34 ± 2.93	9	48
Heart-c	84.27 ± 3.71	84.37 ± 2.73	78.06 ± 2.89	1	49
Breast cancer	72.73 ± 2.86	72.73 ± 2.86	71.92 ± 3.4	2	7
Heart-statlog	82.88 ± 3.61	83.31 ± 2.7	77.64 ± 5.04	1	87
Audiology	70.95 ± 3.99	71.21 ± 4.08	77.03 ± 2.89	1	49
Glass	58.14 ± 4.59	58.55 ± 4.26	58.56 ± 3.95	4	78
Sonar	76.13 ± 2.63	76.69 ± 2.79	66.79 ± 6.25	7	47
Autos	64.6 ± 10.4	61.15 ± 6.3	66.15 ± 6.16	9	145
Hepatitis Domain	81.7 ± 3.81	81.7 ± 3.81	81.71 ± 3.9	1	4
Iris	95.29 ± 3.6	95.29 ± 3.6	95.49 ± 2.45	1	11
Lymph	82.35 ± 3.02	82.92 ± 2.48	77.73 ± 6.57	2	31
Zoo	96.14 ± 2.87	96.14 ± 2.87	92.33 ± 3.52	1	15
Labor	91.25 ± 3.38	91.25 ± 3.38	70.8 ± 6.6	1	6
Average	83.26	81.83	80.69	11	391

decision trees is 80.69%, lower than CITree's. The CITree algorithm builds a tree from a viewpoint different from C4.5's. Since C4.5's good performance in classification is well-known, this comparison provides evidence to support CITree's.

3. The sizes of CITrees are significantly smaller than the sizes of decision trees over all the datasets. Here the size of a tree is the number of nodes. The average tree size for CITrees is 11, and for C4.5 it is 391. This verifies that a CITree is much more compact than a decision tree. However, the efficiency of the CITree algorithm is lower than C4.5. Roughly speaking, the average training time of the CITree algorithm is 10 time slower than C4.5.

Table 3. Summary of the experimental results. An entry *w-t-l* means that the algorithm at the corresponding row wins in *w* datasets, ties in *t* datasets, and loses in *l* datasets, compared to the algorithm at the corresponding column

	C4.5	NB
CITree	7-25-1	7-26-0
C4.5		7-17-9

5   Conclusions

In this paper, we propose a model CITree for accurate probability representation, the structure of which explicitly represents conditional independences among attributes. We show that CITrees are more expressive than naive Bayes and more compact than decision trees. A CITree can be implemented by using naive Bayes at leaves. We present a novel algorithm which builds a tree by exploring the conditional independence among attributes, different from traditional decision tree learning algorithms. Our experiments show that CITrees outperform C4.5 and naive Bayes significantly in classification accuracy. The results provide evidence that a CITree yields more accurate probability estimates.

Our goal of this research is to build accurate PETs. Although accuracy to some degree reflects the quality of probability estimates, it is interesting to know directly the errors of the probability estimates by using artificial data. In our future research, we will also investigate other performance measures that more precisely reflect the errors between the true probability and the estimated probability, such as the area under the ROC curve [2].

References

1. Bennett, P. N.: Assessing the calibration of Naive Bayes' posterior estimates. Technical Report No. CMU-CS00-155 (2000)
2. Bradley, A. P.: The use of the area under the ROC curve in the evaluation of machine learning algorithms. Pattern Recognition **30** (1997) 1145-1159
3. Buntine, W.: Learning Classification Trees. Statistics and Computing **2** (1992) 63-73
4. Domingos, P., Pazzani M.: Beyond Independence: Conditions for the Optimality of the Simple Bayesian Classifier. Machine Learning **29** (1997) 103-130
5. Jordan, M. I., A Statistical Approach to Decision Tree Modeling. Proceedings of the Eleventh International Conference on Machine Learning, Morgan Kaufmann (1994) 363-370
6. Kohavi, R.: Scaling Up the Accuracy of Naive-Bayes Classifiers: A Decision-Tree Hybrid. Proceedings of the Second International Conference on Knowledge Discovery and Data Mining (KDD-96). AAAI Press (1996) 202-207
7. Ling, C. X., Yan, R. J.: Decision Tree with Better Ranking. Proceedings of the 20th International Conference on Machine Learning. Morgan Kaufmann (2003) 480-487
8. Merz, C., Murphy, P., Aha, D.: UCI repository of machine learning databases. Dept of ICS, University of California, Irvine (1997). http://www.ics.uci.edu/~mlearn/MLRepository.html

9. Provost, F., Fawcett, T., Kohavi, R.: The case against accuracy estimation for comparing induction algorithms. Proceedings of the Fifteenth International Conference on Machine Learning. Morgan Kaufmann (1998) 445-453

10. Provost, F. J., Domingos, P.: Tree Induction for Probability-Based Ranking. Machine Learning **52(3)** (2003) 199-215

11. Symth, P., Gray, A., Fayyad, U.: Retrofitting decision tree classifiers using kernel density estimation. Proceedings of the Twelfth International Conference on Machine Learning. Morgan Kaufmann (1996) 506-514

12. Witten, I. H., Frank, E.: Data Mining –Practical Machine Learning Tools and Techniques with Java Implementation. Morgan Kaufmann (2000)

Exploiting Unlabeled Data
in Content-Based Image Retrieval

Zhi-Hua Zhou, Ke-Jia Chen, and Yuan Jiang

National Laboratory for Novel Software Technology
Nanjing University, Nanjing 210093, China
{zhouzh,chenkj,jiangy}@lamda.nju.edu.cn

Abstract. In this paper, the SSAIR (Semi-Supervised Active Image Retrieval) approach, which attempts to exploit unlabeled data to improve the performance of content-based image retrieval (CBIR), is proposed. This approach combines the merits of semi-supervised learning and active learning. In detail, in each round of relevance feedback, two simple learners are trained from the labeled data, i.e. images from user query and user feedback. Each learner then classifies the unlabeled images in the database and passes the most relevant/irrelevant images to the other learner. After re-training with the additional labeled data, the learners classify the images in the database again and then their classifications are merged. Images judged to be relevant with high confidence are returned as the retrieval result, while these judged with low confidence are put into the *pool* which is used in the next round of relevance feedback. Experiments show that semi-supervised learning and active learning mechanisms are both beneficial to CBIR.

1 Introduction

With the rapid increase of the volume of digital image collections, content-based image retrieval (CBIR) has attracted a lot of research interest in recent years [16]. The user could pose an example image, i.e. user query, and ask the CBIR system to bring out relevant images from the database. One of the difficulties here is the gap between high-level semantics and low-level image features, due to the rich content but subjective semantics of an image. Relevance feedback has been shown as a powerful tool for bridging this gap [14]. In relevance feedback, the user has the option of labeling a few of images according to whether they are relevant or not. The labeled images are then given to the CBIR system as complementary queries so that more images relevant to the user query could be retrieved from the database.

In fact, the retrieval engine of a CBIR system can be regarded as a machine learning process, which attempts to train a learner to classify the images in the database into two classes, i.e. relevant or not. Since the classification is usually with different confidence, the learner produces a rank of the images according to how relevant they are to the user query. The higher the rank, the more relevant the corresponding image. Upon receiving the user feedback, the machine learning

J.-F. Boulicaut et al. (Eds.): ECML 2004, LNAI 3201, pp. 525–536, 2004.
© Springer-Verlag Berlin Heidelberg 2004

process uses the newly labeled images along with the original user query to retrain the learner, so that a new rank could be produced which typically puts more relevant images at higher ranks than the original one did. It is obvious that the above is a typical supervised learning process, where only labeled data are used in the training of the learner. In CBIR, since it is not convenient to ask the user to label many images, the labeled training examples given by the user query and relevance feedback may be very small, and pure supervised learning from such a small training set may be hard to obtain good generalization performance.

During the past years, using unlabeled data to help supervised learning has become a hot topic. Considering that in CBIR there are lots of unlabeled images in the database, this paper proposes to exploit them to improve the retrieval performance. In detail, the SSAIR (Semi-Supervised Active Image Retrieval) approach, which employs semi-supervised learning and active learning mechanisms, is proposed. Experiments show that utilizing unlabeled images could greatly enhance the performance of CBIR.

The rest of this paper is organized as follows. Section 2 briefly introduces semi-supervised learning and active learning. Section 3 presents SSAIR. Section 4 reports on the experiments. Section 5 discusses on some related works. Finally, Section 6 concludes and raises several issues for future work.

2   Semi-supervised/Active Learning

Semi-supervised learning deals with methods for exploiting unlabeled data in addition to labeled data to improve learning performance. Such methods include using transductive inference for support vector machines to optimize performance on a specific test set [7], using a generative model built from unlabeled data to perform discriminative classification [6], and using Expectation-Maximization to estimate maximum *a posteriori* parameters of a generative model [13]. A prominent achievement in this area is the *co-training* paradigm proposed by Blum and Mitchell [2], which trains two learners separately on two different views, i.e. two independent sets of attributes, and uses the prediction of each learner on unlabeled examples to augment the training set of the other.

Active learning deals with methods that assume the learner has some control over the input space. In utilizing unlabeled data, it goes a different way from semi-supervised learning, where an *oracle* can be queried for labels of specific instances, with the goal of minimizing the number of queries required. There are two major schemes, i.e. *uncertainty sampling* and *committee-based sampling*. The former methods such as [9] train a single learner and then query the unlabeled instances on which the learner is the least confident. The latter methods such as [1][15] generate a committee of several learners and select the unlabeled instances on which the committee members disagree the most. A recent progress is the *co-testing* paradigm proposed by Muslea et al. [12], which trains two learners separately on two different views as co-training does, and selects the query based on the degree of disagreement among the learners.

3   SSAIR

In CBIR, the user usually poses an example image as the query. From the view of machine learning, such a user query is a labeled positive example, while the image database is a collection of unlabeled data[1]. Let $\mathcal{U}$ denote the unlabeled data set while $\mathcal{L}$ denote the labeled data set, $\mathcal{L} = \mathcal{P} \cup \mathcal{N}$ where $\mathcal{P}$ and $\mathcal{N}$ respectively denote the sets of labeled positive examples and negative examples. Originally $\mathcal{U}$ is the whole database DB, $\mathcal{P}$ is $\{query\}$, and $\mathcal{N}$ is empty. Let $|\mathcal{X}|$ denote the size of a set $\mathcal{X}$. Then the size of $\mathcal{U}$, $\mathcal{P}$ and $\mathcal{N}$ are $|DB|$, 1, and 0, respectively.

In relevance feedback, the user may label several images according to whether they are relevant or not to $query$, which could be viewed as providing additional positive or negative examples. Let $\mathcal{P}^*$ and $\mathcal{N}^*$ denote the new positive and negative examples, respectively. Since the feedback is usually performed on images in the database, both $\mathcal{P}^*$ and $\mathcal{N}^*$ are subsets of DB. Therefore, the relevance feedback process changes $\mathcal{L}$ and $\mathcal{U}$. As for $\mathcal{L}$, its positive subset $\mathcal{P}$ is enlarged to be $\mathcal{P} \cup \mathcal{P}^*$, and its negative subset $\mathcal{N}$ is enlarged to be $\mathcal{N} \cup \mathcal{N}^*$; but as for $\mathcal{U}$, since some of its elements have been moved to $\mathcal{L}$, it is shrunk to be $\mathcal{U} - (\mathcal{P}^* \cup \mathcal{N}^*)$.

After obtaining the enlarged $\mathcal{P}$ and $\mathcal{N}$, in each round of relevance feedback, a traditional CBIR system would re-train a learner which then would give every image in $\mathcal{U}$ a rank expressing how relevant the image is to $query$. It is obvious that such a rank could be more accurate than the one generated by the learner trained with only the original $\mathcal{P}$ and $\mathcal{N}$ because now the learner is fed with more labeled training examples. However, since it is not convenient to ask the user to label a lot of images in the relevance feedback process, in most cases the enlarged training set is still very small.

Inspired by the co-training paradigm [2], SSAIR attempts to exploit $\mathcal{U}$ to improve the performance of retrieval. In detail, SSAIR employs two learners. After obtaining $\mathcal{P}$ and $\mathcal{N}$, both learners are re-trained and then each of them gives every image in $\mathcal{U}$ a rank. Here the rank is assumed to be a value between -1 and $+1$, where positive/negative means the learner judges the concerned image to be relevant/irrelevant, and the bigger the absolute value of the rank, the stronger the confidence of the learner. The most relevant/irrelevant images, i.e. images with the biggest/smallest ranks, judged by each learner are passed on to the other learner as additional labeled positive/negative training examples. Then, both the learners are re-trained with enlarged labeled training sets and each of them produces a new rank for images in $\mathcal{U}$. Note that these additional images won't be moved from $\mathcal{U}$ to $\mathcal{L}$. In other words, they are only temporarily used as labeled training examples, and in the next round of relevance feedback they will be regarded as unlabeled data again.

The new ranks generated by the learners can be easily combined via summation, which results in the final rank for every image in $\mathcal{U}$. Then, images with the top $resultsize$ ranks are returned. Here $resultsize$ specifies how many relevant

---

[1] For simplicity of discussion, here it is assumed that the database contains no annotated images.

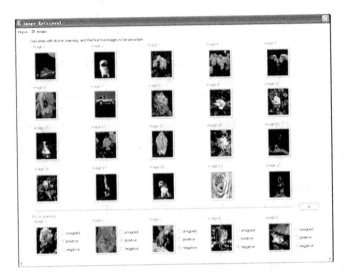

Fig. 1. User interface of a prototype system

images are anticipated to be retrieved. This parameter could be omitted so that all the images in the database are returned according to descending order of the real value of their ranks.

In traditional CBIR systems, the pool for the user to give feedback is not distinguished from the retrieved images. That is, the system gives the user the retrieval result, and then the user chooses some images from the result to label. It is evident that in this way, the images labeled by the user in the relevance feedback process may not be the images that are most helpful to the improvement of the retrieval performance. For example, labeling an image that has already been well learned may be helpless.

Inspired by the co-testing paradigm [12], since SSAIR employs two learners, it can be anticipated that labeling images on which the learners disagree the most, or both learners are with low confidence, may be of great value. Therefore, SSAIR puts images with the bottom *poolsize* absolute ranks into the pool for relevance feedback. Here *poolsize* specifies how many images can be put into the pool. This parameter could be omitted so that all the images in the database are pooled according to ascending order of the absolute value of their ranks.

Thus, SSAIR does not passively wait the user to choose images to label. Instead, it actively prepares a pool of images for the user to provide feedback. A consequence is that in designing the user interface, the retrieval result should be separated from the pool for relevance feedback. For example, the user interface of our prototype system is shown in Fig. 1, where the region above the dark line is for the display of the retrieved images while the region below the dark line is for the display of the pooled images for relevance feedback.

In summary, the pseudo-code of SSAIR is presented in Table 1. Note that the learners used by SSAIR could be implemented in different ways. In this paper we use a very simple model as shown in Eq. 1, where Z_{norm} is used to normalize the

Table 1. Pseudo-code describing the SSAIR approach

SSAIR(*query, DB, L_1, L_2, poolsize, resultsize*)

Input: *query*: User query
   DB: Image database
   L_i ($i \in \{1..2\}$): Learners
   poolsize: No. images in the pool
   resultsize: No. images to be returned

$\mathcal{P} \leftarrow \{query\}$; $\mathcal{N} \leftarrow \emptyset$; $\mathcal{U} \leftarrow DB$
repeat until user is satisfied
   if user want to give feedback
   then
      Getfeedback($\mathcal{P}^*, \mathcal{N}^*$)
      $\mathcal{P} \leftarrow \mathcal{P} \cup \mathcal{P}^*$; $\mathcal{N} \leftarrow \mathcal{N} \cup \mathcal{N}^*$; $\mathcal{U} \leftarrow \mathcal{U} - (\mathcal{P}^* \cup \mathcal{N}^*)$
      for $i \in \{1..2\}$ **do**
         $\mathcal{P}_i \leftarrow \mathcal{P} \cup \{\arg\max_{x \in \mathcal{U}} L_{(3-i)}(x, \mathcal{P}, \mathcal{N})\}$
         $\mathcal{N}_i \leftarrow \mathcal{N} \cup \{\arg\min_{x \in \mathcal{U}} L_{(3-i)}(x, \mathcal{P}, \mathcal{N})\}$
      else for $i \in \{1..2\}$ **do** $\mathcal{P}_i \leftarrow \mathcal{P}$; $\mathcal{N}_i \leftarrow \mathcal{N}$

      for $x \in \mathcal{U}$ **do** $Rank(x) \leftarrow \frac{1}{Z_{norm}} \sum_{i \in \{1..2\}} L_i(x, \mathcal{P}_i, \mathcal{N}_i)$

      $Pool \leftarrow \emptyset$; $Result \leftarrow \emptyset$

      for $i \in \{1..poolsize\}$ **do** $Pool \leftarrow Pool \cup \{\arg\min_{x \in \mathcal{U}} |Rank(x)|\}$

      for $i \in \{1..resultsize\}$ **do** $Result \leftarrow Result \cup \{\arg\max_{x \in \mathcal{U}} Rank(x)\}$
end of repeat

Output: *Result*

---

result to $(-1, 1)$, ε is used to avoid zero denominator, and Sim_i is a similarity measure.

$$L_i(x, \mathcal{P}, \mathcal{N}) = \left(\sum_{y \in \mathcal{P}} \frac{Sim_i(x, y)}{|\mathcal{P}| + \varepsilon} - \sum_{z \in \mathcal{N}} \frac{Sim_i(x, z)}{|\mathcal{N}| + \varepsilon} \right) / Z_{norm} \qquad (1)$$

Since images can be represented as feature vectors after appropriate feature extraction, in this paper the reciprocal of the Minkowsky distance between two d-dimensional feature vectors $\hat{x}$ and $\hat{y}$ is used to measure the similarity between two images x and y, as shown in Eq. 2 where ε is used to avoid zero denominator. Note that for the first learner ($i = 1$) in SSAIR the order of the Minkowsky distance is 2, while for the second learner ($i = 2$) the order is 3. In general, the smaller the order, the more robust the resulting distance metric to data variations; while the bigger the order, the more sensitive the resulting distance metric to data variations. Therefore these two learners could produce different ranks in SSAIR.

$$Sim_i(x, y) = 1 / \left(\left(\sum_{j=1}^{d} |\hat{x}_j - \hat{y}_j|^{(i+1)} \right)^{1/(i+1)} + \varepsilon \right) \qquad (2)$$

Note that other kinds of semi-supervised and active learning paradigms can also be used here to exploit the unlabeled images. SSAIR employs co-training and co-testing like schemes just because this enables semi-supervised learning and active learning be easily and gracefully integrated together. It is worth mentioning that the standard co-training [2] and co-testing [12] require *sufficient but redundant views*, but some recent work [5] shows that using two different supervised learners instead of two attribute sets can also work well, which is really the way SSAIR goes. These issues will be discussed further in Section 5.

4   Experiments

SSAIR is empirically compared with three image retrieval approaches, i.e. RFIR, SSIR, and AIR. The difference between SSAIR and RFIR is that RFIR uses neither semi-supervised learning nor active learning. The difference between SSAIR and SSIR is that SSIR does not use active learning. The difference between SSAIR and AIR is that AIR does not use semi-supervised learning.

Experiments are performed on a set of 2,000 images from the COREL database. These images belong to 20 classes, each of which has 100 images. The features used to represent the images are color histograms. Note that since the purpose of the experiments is to explore whether employing semi-supervised learning and active learning mechanisms are helpful to CBIR, the relative performance of SSAIR against other approaches is more important than its absolute performance. So, here we have not spent much time in trying to use stronger features, although doing so might greatly improve the absolute retrieval performance.

For each compared approach, after obtaining a query, five rounds of relevance feedback are performed. In each round the user could label 5, 7, or 9 images as his/her feedback. The whole process is repeated for five times with different queries, and the average results are recorded.

The evaluation measures used in CBIR have been affected much by these used in common information retrieval [11]. A straightforward while popularly used measure is the *PR-Graph*, which depicts the relationship between *precision* and *recall* of a specific retrieval system. However, since there is a PR-Graph for each class of images after every round of relevance feedback, it is hard to present these graphs in a paper of limited length as this one. Usually, a CBIR system exhibits a trade-off between precision and recall, to obtain a high precision usually means sacrificing recall and vice versa. Considering that in CBIR precision and recall are of the same importance, here BEP (*break-event-point*) is introduced as an evaluation measure. In definition, if the precision and recall are tuned to have a equal value, then this value is called the BEP of the system (Lewis, 1992). The higher the BEP, the better the performance. Through connecting the BEPs after different rounds of relevance feedback, *BEP-Graph* is obtained, where the horizontal axis enumerates the round of relevance feedback while the vertical axis tells the BEP value.

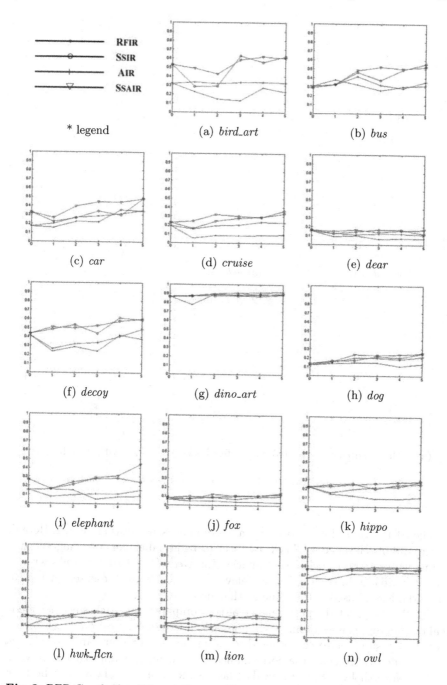

Fig. 2. BEP-Graphs for different classes of images, with 5 feedbacks in each round

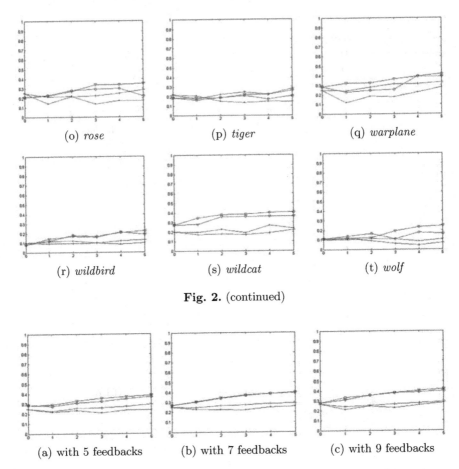

(o) *rose*   (p) *tiger*   (q) *warplane*

(r) *wildbird*   (s) *wildcat*   (t) *wolf*

Fig. 2. (continued)

(a) with 5 feedbacks   (b) with 7 feedbacks   (c) with 9 feedbacks

Fig. 3. Geometrical-BEP-Graphs with 5, 7, or 9 feedbacks in each round

The BEP-Graphs for the twenty classes of images are shown in Fig. 2. Here in each round of relevance feedback, the user provides labels for five images. After averaging across all the classes of images, the *Geometrical-BEP-Graphs* with 5, 7, or 9 feedbacks in each round of relevance feedback are presented in Fig. 3, where the legend used is the same as that used in Fig. 2.

Fig. 2 shows that the performance of the compared approaches are not identical on different classes of images. There are classes such as *car* on which SSAIR is distinctly superior to the other three approaches, but there are also classes such as *dino_art* on which the performance of the compared approaches are very similar. Nevertheless, Fig. 2 reveals that SSAIR is almost always the best or among the best approaches on all these image classes. This finding is supported by Fig. 3(a), which exhibits a clear rank of the performance of the compared approaches, that is, SSAIR > SSIR > AIR > RFIR. This observation tells that introducing semi-supervised learning and active learning into CBIR is beneficial, and the benefit from semi-supervised learning is bigger than that from active learning. This is not difficult to understand because semi-supervised learning enables the utilization of images in addition to these labeled by the user in relevance feedback, although the user feedback process in AIR is more effective than that in SSIR. Moreover, Figs. 3(b) and 3(c) show that when the number of feedback in each round increases, the benefit from active learning decreases so that the performance of SSAIR is very comparable to that of SSIR. This is also not difficult to understand because as the number of feedback increases, the images that the user chosen from the retrieval result to label would have more chances to overlap with the images that the system actively asks the user to label.

Besides BEP-Graph, this paper uses another measure, i.e. *effectiveness*, to evaluate the compared approaches. This measure was proposed by Mehtre et al. [10], and adopted to quantify the utility of relevance feedback mechanisms recently [4]. The definition is shown in Eq. 3, where S denotes the number of relevant images the user wants to retrieve, R_q^I and R_q^E respectively denote the set of relevant images and all images retrieved in the shortlist. The bigger the η_S, the better the performance.

$$
\eta_S = \begin{cases} |R_q^I \cap R_q^E|/|R_q^I| & if \; |R_q^I| \le S \\ |R_q^I \cap R_q^E|/|R_q^E| & if \; |R_q^I| > S \end{cases} \tag{3}
$$

Due to the page limit, here we only present the *geometrical-effectiveness*, i.e. the average effectiveness across all the image classes, as shown in Table 2 where $\bar{\eta}_{200}^i$ denotes the geometrical-effectiveness of the i-th round of relevance feedback with the size of shortlist being 200.

Table 2. Geometrical-effectiveness with 5, 7, or 9 feedbacks in each round

	$\bar{\eta}_{200}^1$		$\bar{\eta}_{200}^2$		$\bar{\eta}_{200}^3$		$\bar{\eta}_{200}^4$		$\bar{\eta}_{200}^5$	
	RFIR	AIR	RFIR	AIR	RFIR	AIR	RFIR	AIR	RFIR	AIR
	SSIR	SSAIR	SSIR	SSAIR	SSIR	SSAIR	SSIR	SSAIR	SSIR	SSAIR
5 feedbacks	30.2	33.6	30.8	35.9	28.8	36.7	31.1	39.9	32.4	41.8
	36.5	37.0	41.4	43.2	43.1	46.2	45.6	48.0	47.0	49.2
7 feedbacks	29.0	34.2	29.5	37.0	30.5	38.1	33.1	40.0	34.9	41.6
	40.7	41.4	43.5	45.3	46.3	46.9	47.7	48.5	49.7	49.9
9 feedbacks	29.0	34.2	29.5	37.0	30.5	38.1	33.1	39.8	34.9	41.6
	43.4	41.5	45.7	47.3	48.7	49.6	49.0	51.3	51.4	52.4

Table 2 shows that except on the 1st round of 9 feedbacks where SSIR is better than SSAIR, SSAIR is always better than SSIR, SSIR is always better than AIR, and AIR is always better than RFIR. The table also exhibits that the gap between the performance of SSIR and AIR is relatively big. These observations verify again that introducing semi-supervised learning and active learning into

CBIR is beneficial, and the benefit from semi-supervised learning is bigger than that from active learning.

5   Related Works

As early as in 1983, Bookstein [3] conjectured that having the user label the top-ranked documents, while desirable from a user interface standpoint, might not be optimal for learning. But until Lewis and Gale (1994) showed that labeling documents with a current estimated probability of relevance of 0.5 could improve effectiveness of a text classifier over labeling top-ranked documents, active learning had not been introduced into information retrieval.

As for CBIR, active learning began to be used only recently. In the SVM_{Active} approach developed by Tong and Chang [17], in each round of relevance feedback, a support vector machine is trained on labeled data and then the user is asked to label the images most close to the support vector boundary. Since the learner used in SSAIR is far simpler than the support vector machine used in SVM_{Active}, SSAIR is more efficient than SVM_{Active}. Moreover, since SSAIR employs semi-supervised learning mechanism while SVM_{Active} does not, SSAIR is stronger than SVM_{Active} in exploiting unlabeled data.

Another work on introducing active learning to CBIR was done by Zhang and Chen [19]. Their system randomly chooses a small number of images to annotate at first. Then, the system starts to repeatedly select the image with the maximum knowledge gain for the user to annotate, until the user stops or the database has been fully annotated. This work is quite different from SSAIR not only because it does not use any semi-supervised learning mechanism, but also because it mainly works on hidden annotation while SSAIR works on relevance feedback. As Zhang and Chen [19] said, relevance feedback does not accumulate semantic knowledge while hidden annotation, on the other hand, tries to accumulate all the knowledge given by the user.

Wu et al. [18] has tried to apply semi-supervised learning to CBIR. They cast the problem of CBIR as a transductive learning problem, and proposed the D-EM algorithm to solve this problem. On a small subset of COREL which contains only 134 images, they reported that their approach had achieved good results nevertheless physical or mathematical features were used. It is worth noting that their approach works in the Expectation-Maximization framework, while SSAIR was inspired by the co-training paradigm. Moreover, their approach does not use any active learning mechanism while SSAIR does.

The standard co-training algorithm [2] requires *sufficient but redundant views*, that is, the attributes be naturally partitioned into two sets, each of which is sufficient for learning and conditionally independent to the other given the class label. It is obvious that SSAIR does not utilize two sufficient but redundant views. In fact, the semi-supervised learning mechanism embedded in SSAIR is somewhat like the algorithm proposed by Goldman and Zhou [5], which uses two different supervised learners instead of two attribute sets. In contrast to Goldman and Zhou's algorithm, SSAIR does not employ time-consuming cross validation technique to determine how to label the unlabeled examples and how to produce the final hypothesis. Therefore, the semi-supervised learning mechanism of SSAIR is more efficient.

The active learning mechanism embedded in SSAIR was inspired by co-testing [12]. In contrast to the algorithm proposed by Muslea et al. [12], SSAIR does not utilize two sufficient but redundant views. Instead, it employs two learners obtained through setting different parameter values of the same model. Since sufficient but redundant views are not often available, the active learning mechanism of SSAIR has better applicability.

6 Conclusion and Future Work

This paper advocates applying semi-supervised learning and active learning together to CBIR. As an example, the proposed SSAIR approach gracefully integrates the merits of these learning mechanisms in exploiting unlabeled data, and experiments show that it could effectively improve the retrieval performance.

Although the utility of SSAIR has been verified by experiments, there is a lack of theoretical analysis. This might have encumbered the exertion of the full power of SSAIR. For example, in current form of SSAIR, in each round of relevance feedback each learner only labels for the other learner two images, i.e. the most relevant/irrelevant images it judged to be. If theoretical analysis on the relationship between the performance of the learners and the possible noises in the labeling process is available, it might be found that letting each learner label more images is still safe, which may help improve the performance of SSAIR. This is an important issue for future work.

Moreover, in this paper images are described by simple color histogram features. Although it is anticipated the retrieval performance could be further improved through utilizing stronger image features, there is a bare possibility that utilizing unlabeled images is not so beneficial when the features are strong. Therefore, investigating the performance of SSAIR facilitated with strong image features is also an interesting issue for future work.

Acknowledgement

This work was supported by the National Outstanding Youth Foundation of China under the Grant No. 60325207, and the Foundation for the Author of National Excellent Doctoral Dissertation of China under the Grant No. 200343.

References

1. Abe, N., Mamitsuka, H.: Query learning strategies using boosting and bagging. In: Proceedings of the 15th International Conference on Machine Learning, Madison, WI (1998) 1–9
2. Blum, A., Mitchell, T.: Combining labeled and unlabeled data with co-training. In: Proceedings of the 11th Annual Conference on Computational Learning Theory, Madison, WI (1998) 92–100
3. Bookstein, A.: Information retrieval: a sequential learning process. Journal of the American Society for Information Science **34** (1983) 331–342

4. Ciocca, G., Schettini, R.: A relevance feedback mechanism for content-based image retrieval. Information Processing and Management **35** (1999) 605–632

5. Goldman, S., Zhou, Y.: Enhancing supervised learning with unlabeled data. In: Proceedings of the 17th International Conference on Machine Learning, San Francisco, CA (2000) 327–334

6. Jaakkola, T., Haussler, D.: Exploiting generative models in discriminative classifiers. In: Kearns, M.S., Solla, S.A., Cohn, D.A. (eds.): Advances in Neural Information Processing Systems, Vol. 11. MIT Press, Cambridge, MA (1999) 487–493

7. Joachims, T.: Transductive inference for text classification using support vector machines. In: Proceedings of the 16th International Conference on Machine Learning, Bled, Slovenia (1999) 200–209

8. Lewis, D.: Representation and learning in information retrieval. PhD thesis, Department of Computer Science, University of Massachusetts, Amherst, MA (1992)

9. Lewis, D., Gale, W.: A sequential algorithm for training text classifiers. In: Proceedings of the 17th Annual International ACM SIGIR Conference on Research and Development in Information Retrieval, Dublin, Ireland (1994) 3–12

10. Mehtre, B.M., Kankanhalli, M.S., Narasimhalu, A.D., Man, G.C.: Color matching for image retrieval. Pattern Recognition Letters **16** (1995) 325–331

11. Müller, H., Müller, W, Squire, D.M., Marchand-Maillet, S., Pun, T.: Performance evaluation in content-based image retrieval: overview and proposals. Pattern Recognition Letters **22** (2001) 593–601

12. Muslea, I., Minton, S., Knoblock, C.A.: Selective sampling with redundant views. In: Proceedings of the 17th National Conference on Artificial Intelligence, Austin, TX (2000) 621–626

13. Nigam, K., McCallum, A., Thrun, S., Mitchell, T.: Text classification from labeled and unlabeled documents using EM. Machine Learning **39** (2000) 103–134

14. Rui, Y., Huang, T.S., Ortega, M., Mehrotra., S.: Relevance feedback: a power tool for interactive content-based image retrieval. IEEE Transactions on Circuits and Systems for Video Technology **8** (1998) 644–655

15. Seung, H., Opper, M., Sompolinsky, H.: Query by committee. In: Proceedings of the 5th ACM Workshop on Computational Learning Theory, Pittsburgh, PA (1992) 287–294

16. Smeulders, A.W.M., Worring, M., Santini, S., Gupta, A., Jain, R.: Content-based image retrieval at the end of the early years. IEEE Transactions on Pattern Analysis and Machine Intelligence **22** (2000) 1349–1380

17. Tong, S., Chang, E.: Support vector machine active learning for image retrieval. In: Proceedings of the 9th ACM International Conference on Multimedia, Ottawa, Canada (2001) 107–118

18. Wu, Y., Tian, Q., Huang, T.S.: Discriminant-EM algorithm with application to image retrieval. In: Proceedings of the IEEE International Conference on Computer Vision and Pattern Recognition, Hilton Head, SC (2000) 222–227

19. Zhang, C., Chen, T.: An active learning framework for content-based information retrieval. IEEE Transactions on Multimedia **4** (2002) 260–268

Population Diversity
in Permutation-Based Genetic Algorithm

Kenny Q. Zhu[1] and Ziwei Liu[2]

[1] Department of Computer Science, National University of Singapore, Singapore 119260
kzhu@comp.nus.edu.sg
[2] Advantech Singapore Pte Ltd, #03-06 Technopark@Chaichee, Singapore 469004
lziwei@hotmail.com

Abstract. This paper presents an empirical study of population diversity measures and adaptive control of diversity in the context of a permutation-based algorithm for Traveling Salesman Problems and Vehicle Routing Problems. We provide detailed graphical observations and discussion of the relationship among the four diversity measures and suggest a moderate correlation between diversity and search performance under simple conditions. We also study the effects of adapting key genetic control parameters such as crossover and mutation rates on the population diversity. We are able to show that adaptive control of the genetic operations based on population diversity effectively outperforms fixed parameter genetic algorithms.

1   Introduction

Traditional genetic algorithms (GA) often suffer from loss of diversity due to premature convergence of the population. As a result, the search is trapped in local optima. Hence, the maintenance of diversity is one of the most fundamental issues of GA. Previous studies on population diversity can be divided into two categories: *diversity measures* and *maintenance of diversity*. A large amount of work has been devoted to diversity measures, which includes early study of variance of fitness [11,3], and uncertainty [3]. Recently, other measures such as evolution history [14], distance [2], epistasis [7] and measures in the phenotype and genotype space [15] have also been introduced. A survey of population diversity measures in genetic programming (GP) can be found in [5]. Work on diversity maintenance includes crowding and preselection [13], self-adapting mutation rates [9], etc. Some studies have been devoted to adaptive GA and population diversity control. A good survey about aspects of adaptive GA can be found in [12]. Parameter control in general evolutionary algorithms is discussed in a recent survey by Eiben, *et al.* [1], which includes references to other works on self-adaptation in GA.

The GA we are concerned with in this paper is one in which individual chromosomes are integer encoded, and the crossover operations are *permutation-based* [10]. In this type of GA, all individuals have the same set of distinct alleles (integers) in all generations. The different permutations of the individuals decode into different fitness values. Permutation-based GA is used to solve Traveling Salesman Problem (TSP) [8], Vehicle Routing Problem (VRP) [4] and its variant Vehicle Routing Problem with Time Windows (VRPTW) [16], and many other problems. TSP can be defined as: given a set

J.-F. Boulicaut et al. (Eds.): ECML 2004, LNAI 3201, pp. 537–547, 2004.

of towns and the distances between them, determine the shortest path starting from a given town, passing through all the other towns *exactly* once and returning to the first town. The objective of VRP/VRPTW is to find routes for vehicles to service all the customers at a minimal cost (in terms of number of routes and total distance traveled), without violating the capacity and the travel time constraints of the vehicles and, in the case of VRPTW, the time windows imposed by the customers. Both classes of problems are in the NP domain.

We define and compare four important diversity measures, namely phenotypes, genotypes, standard deviation of fitness and ancestral ids. These measures represent diversity from different angles, hence the behaviors are also different. We perform a comprehensive empirical study on the effects of genetic operations such as crossover and mutation on the population diversity. A simple adaptive control function is applied to maintain diversity at desirable levels through automatically varying application rates of genetic operators. Benchmarks show that adaptive diversity control is able to strike a balance between global exploration and local exploitation, and outperforms traditional fixed parameter GA's.

2   Canonical Algorithm

The basic algorithm for solving TSP/VRP uses a fixed-length integer-string representation for encoding, and a heuristic to decode the chromosomes into fitness values. The algorithm starts with an initial population of 50 random individuals unless otherwise stated, and selects individuals for reproduction. After reproduction through a number of operations, the new population replaces the whole parent populations to complete one generation. The algorithm runs for a fixed number of generations. We briefly introduce some elements of this algorithm below.

The representation of a solution is a string of distinct integers of length K, where K is the number of customers (cities). The string is known as a *chromosome,* whose length is K. Each *gene* (integer) of the chromosome is a customer's identifier. For example,

$$3 - 2 - 4 - 5 - 9 - 8 - 7 - 10 - 6 - 1 - 12 - 11$$

A problem-specific algorithm [17] is used to decode the string into solutions and to compute the fitness. A binary *tournament selection* mechanism is used in this algorithm. Three commonly used order-based *crossover* operators are applied to the mating chromosomes. They are *Partially Matched Crossover(PMX), Order Crossover(OX)* and *Cycle Crossover(CX)* [10]. Each will be applied independently in our experiments. The probability of applying crossover operator to a pair of mating individuals is denoted by p_c.

We use a *sequence insertion* mutation, which is defined as relocating a subsequence from one position of the chromosome to another position. Mutation rate is denoted by p_m. Besides mutation, we use a *post-recombination* operator called *random immigrants* [6], that randomly generates chromosomes to replace randomly selected existing chromosomes. Random immigrants is applied at a rate of p_r.

The algorithm can be summarized as follows.

GA-1 Initialize the population P with N chromosomes;

GA-2 Decode chromosomes to obtain fitness values in the population. Set crossover rate p_c, mutation rate p_m and random immigrants rate p_r;

GA-3 Create a new population by repeating the following steps:
1. Select two parent chromosomes from a population by Tournament Selection;
2. With a probability p_c, crossover the parents to form two new children, otherwise copy the parents to become offspring;
3. With probability p_m, mutate the new offspring;
4. Place the new offsprings in a new population;

GA-4 Replace the old population with the newly generated population;

GA-5 Do random immigrants if required;

GA-6 If the stop criterion is satisfied, stop; else go to GA-2.

3 Diversity Measures

Four diversity measures, namely, the number of unique *phenotypes*, the fitness *standard deviation*, the total distance among *genotypes*, and the number of unique *ancestral ids*, are compared and studied in this paper. In what follows, P is a set of all chromosome sequences in a population, N is the number of sequences in the population, and K is the length of the sequences in P.

Phenotypes (ptype) The number of unique fitness values in the population, normalized between 0 and 1. The computation takes $O(N \log N)$ time.

$$ptype(P) = \frac{|U| - 1}{N - 1},\tag{1}$$

where $U \subseteq P$, and $\forall f_i \in U$ and $\forall f_j \in U$, $f_i \neq f_j$ if $i \neq j$.

Standard deviation (stddev) The standard deviation of fitness values in a population $(O(N))$:

$$stddev(P) = \sqrt{\frac{\sum_{i=1}^{N} (f_i - \bar{f})^2}{N - 1}},\tag{2}$$

where N is the population size and f_i is fitness of the ith individual.

Genotypes (gtype) The sum of the *edge distances* between any two genotypes (individual strings). Let s be an integer sequence that represents a genotype. We define $A(s)$ to be a set of arcs in s. The edge distance between genotype u and v is defined as:

$$\mathcal{D}_e(u, v) = |A(u) \setminus A(v)|,\tag{3}$$

In other words, edge distance is defined as the number of arcs in u but not in v. Note that this number is equal to the number of arcs in v but not in u. The edge distance here is different from the commonly used edit distance for measuring similarity among sequences. This is because we are trying to measure the similarity in subsequences, which is key in TSP and VRP.

$$gtype(P) = \frac{\sum_{i \neq j} \mathcal{D}_e(P[i], P[j]))}{(K - 1)(N - 1)N},\tag{4}$$

where $P[i]$ and $P[j]$ are the ith and jth genotypes in P. This takes $O(N^2 K^2)$.

Ancestral id (uid) Each individual in the initial population has a unique id. During crossover, two parents produce two children. One of the children inherits the mother's uid and the other inherits the father's uid. One's uid changes when it's mutated or being replaced in random immigrants procedure.

Unless otherwise noted, the benchmark problem used in this paper is R101 from Solomon's 100-node VRPTW problem set [16]. Problem R101 is characterized by randomly distributed customer locations and short time windows for each customer. It is one of "harder" problems in the problem set that have not yielded the optimal solution as far as we know. Extract methods are required to obtain the optimal solution but the cost is prohibitive.

With a fixed, 100% random initial population, and PMX crossover only, the basic algorithm was run 10 times with the parameters: $p_c = 0.6$, $p_m = 0$ and $p_r = 0$. In each generation, the population diversity is recorded by four measures defined above. Fig. 1 through Fig. 4 demonstrate the natural evolution of these measures over 201 generations, without any mutation.

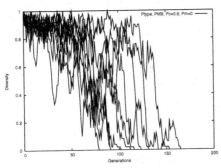

Fig. 1. Evolution of Ptype over generations

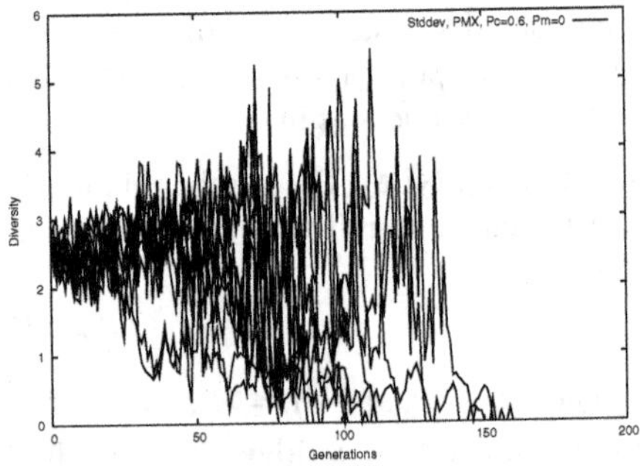

Fig. 2. Evolution of Stddev over generations

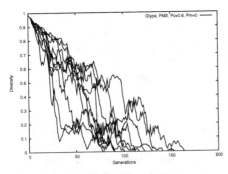

Fig. 3. Evolution of Gtype over generations

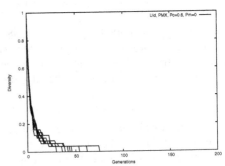

Fig. 4. Evolution of Uid over generations

Both phenotype measure and standard deviation measure displays a rather steep phase transition at about the 100th generation and quickly converges to zero, except stddev is more volatile. These two measures are similar because both are based on fitness values. Standard deviation measure is more sensitive to the variance in the population, therefore the large fluctuation is observed. Genotype decreases more gradually but the descent happens right from the beginning, unlike ptype and stddev. This can be explained because recombination causes convergence at the genotype level first, before such change is reflected in the fitness values. The gradual descent of gtype measure also suggests this measure can be more useful in early prediction and diversity control. The rapid convergence of uid is a certainty because, with no mutation, the number of ids will monotonically decrease. The selection mechanism (in which the fitter individuals are preferred in mating) accelerates the decrease in unique ids.

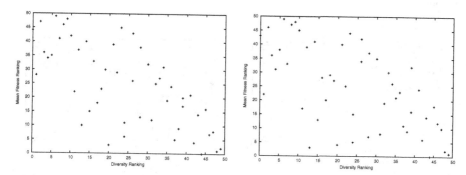

Fig. 5. Ptype rankings vs mean fitness rankings   **Fig. 6.** Stddev rankings vs mean fitness rankings

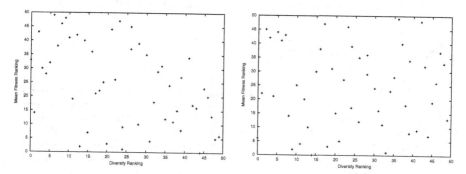

Fig. 7. Gtype rankings vs mean fitness rankings   **Fig. 8.** Uid rankings vs mean fitness rankings

We ran the algorithm to 201 generations for 50 times, and plot the rankings of accumulated diversity over 201 generations against the rankings of the mean fitness at the 201st generation, for every diversity measure in Fig. 5 through 8. Notice in the case of VRPTW, the fitness value is taken to be the total cost of a solution which is a combination of the number of routes and the total distance. In these figures, both diversity and fitness are ranking in ascending order.

Some moderate, "negative" correlation can be seen from all plots except that of uid. In Fig. 5 through Fig. 7, dots are clustered near the upper-left to lower-right diagonal line. In other words, the general trend is: the higher the diversity, the smaller the fitness value, or the better the search quality. The correlation is particularly evident in ptype as it is defined by fitness values only. The randomness displayed in Fig. 8 is again the result of early convergence of uid measure (Fig. 4).

The consistency of the four diversity measures can be estimated by taking the standard deviation of the average diversity over the 50 runs. The standard deviations are $\sigma_{ptype} = 0.1004$, $\sigma_{gtype} = 0.0557$, $\sigma_{stddev} = 0.334$, and $\sigma_{uid} = 0.0068$. Stddev measure values were normalized to 1 before the calculation. Gtype and uid measures appear more consistent than others, because of their low deviation. The very small deviation of uid is due to its very premature convergence. The volatility of the stddev measure shown in the graph contributes to its high variance and it is the least reliable measure of the four.

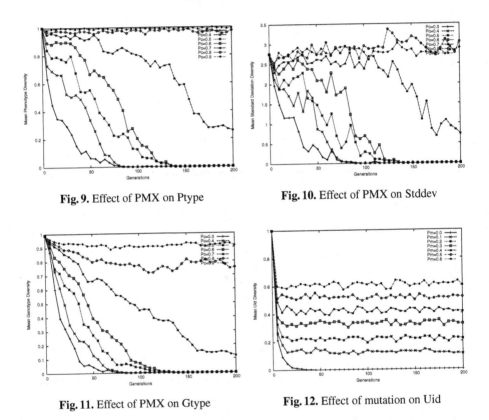

Fig. 9. Effect of PMX on Ptype   **Fig. 10.** Effect of PMX on Stddev

Fig. 11. Effect of PMX on Gtype   **Fig. 12.** Effect of mutation on Uid

4 Effects of Genetic Operators on Diversity Measures

Methods of maintaining population diversity generally come in two categories: methods based on the selection process and those based on genetic operators. In this paper, the second approach is adopted. We hope to control the diversity through the three common genetic operators defined in Section 2. Three sets of experiments with the following

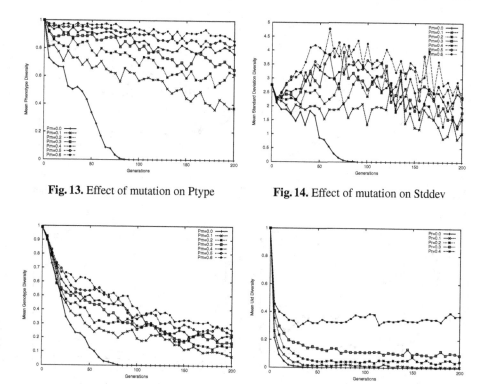

Fig. 13. Effect of mutation on Ptype

Fig. 14. Effect of mutation on Stddev

Fig. 15. Effect of mutation on Gtype

Fig. 16. Effect of random immigrants on Uid

parameters were first conducted to demonstrate the independent effect of crossover, mutation and random immigrants on diversity.

Crossover: $p_c = 0.3 \cdots 0.9$ (PMX), $p_m = 0$, $p_r = 0$ at steps of 0.1.

Mutation: $p_c = 0.4$ (PMX) , $p_m = 0 \cdots 0.60$, $p_r = 0$ at steps of 0.1.

Random immigrants: $p_c = 0.4$ (PMX), $p_m = 0$, $p_r = 0.1 \cdots 0.4$ at steps of 0.1.

Each set of parameters were tested 10 times and the mean diversity at each of the 201 generations was recorded by all four measures. We then plot the convergence graph of the mean diversity for each diversity measure under different parameter settings, and these are included in Fig. 9 through Fig. 19. Uid diversity is only affected by mutation and random immigrants as only these two operators contribute new ids into the system, therefore a plot of crossover effect on uid is not included.

One can observe from these plots that all three operators promote diversity by all measures. With increasing crossover rate p_c (Fig. 9, 10 and 11), The diversity curves are spread out almost evenly, which suggests p_c is a good tool in controlling the diversity. For lower crossover rates (up to 0.8), population eventual converges; for higher p_c, our experiments show that population remains highly diversified even over many more generations. It is noted, however, when diversity drops below certain threshold, crossover alone is not able to reverse the converging trend. This is especially evident in the ptype

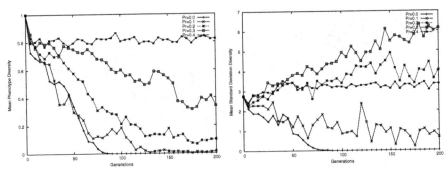

Fig. 17. Effect of random immigrants on Ptype **Fig. 18.** Effect of random immigrants on Stddev

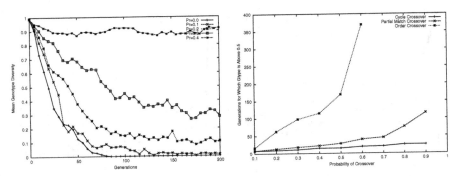

Fig. 19. Effect of random immigrants on Gtype   **Fig. 20.** Comparison of OX, PMX and CX

and stddev measures, where the diversity curve is generally flat in the beginning, and turns down sharply after some transition point.

The effect of various mutation rates on the diversity is visibly different from the crossover. Fig. 12 shows that varying the mutation rate effectively sets the uid diversity at corresponding levels, which is easy to understand, given the definition of uid. Fig. 9 to Fig. 11 show a big jump in the diversity levels (in all three measures) from $p_m = 0$ to $p_m = 0.1$, but the differences become less significant as p_m increases. This is due to the fact that mutation happens in genotype level and the changes are always localized, therefore the effect is limited. Stronger diversifying forces can be seen in Fig. 16 through Fig. 19, except excessive random immigrants can drag down the overall fitnesses of the population uniformly, which causes some anomaly at $p_r = 0.4$ in Fig. 18. It is easy to prove that the population does not converge to uniformity when p_m or p_r is non-zero. We can classify the use of random immigrants, crossover and mutation as diversification at the population, phenotype and genotype levels, respectively. Therefore, a combination of all three operations is expected to give a more balanced and consistent result in promoting diversity.

Fig. 20 shows the comparison among the three crossover operators. OX, PMX and CX are applied to random population at p_c from 0.1 to 0.9, and the number of generations when the gtype diversity reaches 0.5 is recorded for each setting. Apparently, OX is the most effective in boosting diversity while CX is the least effective.

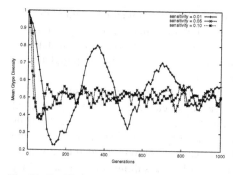
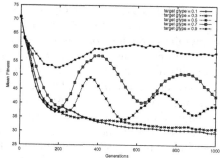

Fig. 21. Oscillation at various sensitivities ($d_t = 0.5$)

Fig. 22. Mean fitness progression under target diversities 0.1 - 0.9 at step 0.2 (OX)

5 Adaptive Control

From the previous sections, the positive correlation of diversity and search quality, along with the fact that genetic operations promote diversity, motivate us to maintain diversity at some healthy level so that more promising regimes in the search space can be explored. One interesting way to control the diversity is to adaptively calibrate the crossover/mutation rates against the changing population diversity. To illustrate the benefits of adaptive control, we apply the following simple adaptive function on the rates of crossover, mutation or random immigrants to maintain diversity at a target level.

$$p' = max(p_{min}, \ min(p_{max}, \ p(1 + \frac{\xi(d_t - d)}{d}))), \tag{5}$$

where p is the current rate of genetic operations, p' is the new rate in the next generation, d is the diversity of current population, d_t is the target diversity, ξ is the control *sensitivity*, and p_{min}, p_{max} are the lower and upper bounds of the rate.

In every generation of the algorithm, the crossover and mutation as well as random immigrants rates are recomputed by (5), and the new rates will be used in the recombination phase of that generation. The choice of (5) is based on the belief that the population is further diversified when genetic operations are applied at higher probability. So when d falls below d_t, the new rate p' is somewhat increased in (5). Contrary to that, if d becomes larger than d_t, probability will be decreased until d comes in line with d_t. A small ξ means gradual change in the rate, and that also translates into *slower* fluctuation of the diversity, also known as the oscillation of the feedback control (Fig. 21). Larger ξ causes the population diversity to follow more closely to the target diversity. The oscillation, instead of monotonic convergence or divergence, allows the population to concentrate on one region to optimize for a while, and then move on to other regions. While (5) may appear simplistic and arbitrary, our experiments below already demonstrate the clear advantage of the adaptive control. The search for better adaptive functions remains an open area of research.

Setting the target diversity d_t at 0.1 to 0.9, and using OX crossover alone, we ran the basic algorithm five times to examine the significance of d_t. The progression of the mean fitness at various target gtype levels is plotted in Fig. 22. When diversity is maintained at low levels, the population converges rather monotonically. When target diversity rises above 0.5, the population mean fitness starts to fluctuate, although such fluctuation appears to subside with time. Because the mean fitness curve approximately portrays the search horizon, a hovering curve essentially represents the traversal across a terrain of peaks and valleys in the solution space. In other words, the population is sufficiently diversified to explore a number of localities.

However, we also observe that the higher diversity levels generally result in higher fitness values or worse search result. This is because our canonical GA has only limited capability of local optimization, as the algorithm traverses across many domains. Thus we propose to use some local search techniques such as greedy descent to exploit the "good areas" further, as a complement to the global exploration provided by diversity adaptive control. Fig. 22 also indicates that the oscillation is diminishing under overly high diversity settings, e.g. $d_t \geq 0.9$. This is undesirable because the algorithm does not have the chance to zoom in to some of the prospective good neighborhood. The optimal value for d_t is problem-specific and needs to be tuned for a class of problems.

In the last experiment, we compare the solution quality of adaptive GA and a fixed-parameter GA which is based on our canonical algorithm. The benchmark problems are the full set of Solomon's VRPTW 100-node problems. Now, a mixed initial population of both random and good solutions is used. The good individuals are obtained from Push Forward Insertion Heuristic (PFIH) [16] and its *2-neighborhood*. We will focus on the gtype diversity as it behaves most consistently and is easy to control. OX is used as the only crossover operator. The initial crossover and mutation rates are 0.77 and 0.1, respectively. These initial rates are obtained from some VRPTW literature and are known to be standard.

We test-ran both the fixed parameter GA and the adaptive GA up to 500 generations, with target diversity $d_t = 0.5$ and $\xi = 0.01$. The reason for selecting $d_t = 0.5$ is to take advantage of the oscillation. In the fixed-parameter GA, $p_c = 0.77$ and $p_m = 0.1$. Our preliminary tests indicate that these settings appear to be the best for fixed-parameter GA.

The average results over 10 runs are compared in Table 1. Columns marked "Fixed" and "Adaptive" record the solutions on the number of routes and total distance traveled, in the two GA schemes tested. The smaller these numbers are, the better the solution. Clearly, with the target diversity at 0.5, our adaptive GA consistently outperforms fixed-parameter GA in terms of the quality of solutions, in all categories of VRPTW. The average execution time, however, is somewhat longer than the fixed algorithm. This is expected as the adaptive algorithm normally traverses more regions in the search space.

Table 1. Fixed parameter vs. adaptive algorithm

Category	p_c/p_m	Fixed	Time	Category	Adaptive	Time
C1	0.88/0.49	10/835.6	72	C1	10/828.9	80
C2	0.89/0.36	3/610.9	804	C2	3/589.9	735
R1	0.85/0.56	13.3/1263.4	131	R1	12.8/1242.7	305
R2	0.84/0.48	3.2/1021.4	1288	R2	3/1016.4	1308
RC1	0.85/0.57	13.1/1437.2	177	RC1	13/1412.0	239
RC2	0.84/0.49	3.9/1249.7	765	RC2	3.7/1201.2	883

References

1. Ágoston E. Eiben, R. Hinterding, and Z. Michalewicz. Parameter control in evolutionary algorithms. *IEEE Transactions on Evolutionary Computation*, 3(2):124–141, 1999.
2. A. L. Barker and W. N. Martin. Dynamics of a distance-based population diversity measure. In *Proceedings of the 2000 Congress on Evolutionary Computation*, pages 1002–1009.
3. M. A. Bedau, M. Zwick, and A. Bahm. Variance and uncertainty measures of population diversity dynamics. *Advances in Systems Science and Applications Special Issue*, I:7–12, 1995.
4. L. Bodin, A. Assad, and M. Ball. *Routing and Scheduling of Vehicles and Crews - the State of the Art*. Pergamon Press, 1983.
5. E. Burke, S. Gustafson, and G. Kendall. A survey and analysis of diversity measures in genetic programming. In *GECCO 2002: Proceedings of the Genetic and Evolutionary Computation Conference*, pages 716–723.
6. H. G. Cobb and J. J. Grefenstette. Genetic algorithms for tracking changing environments. In *Proceedings of International Conference on Genetic Algorithms*, pages 523–530, 1993.
7. C. Cotta and J. M. Troya. Using dynastic exploring recombination to promote diversity in genetic search. In *Proceedings of 6th International Conference on Parallel Problem Solving from Nature - PPSN VI*, pages 325–334. Springer, 2000.
8. G. Dantzig, R. Fulkerson, and S. Johnson. Solution of a large-scale traveling-salesman problem. *Operations Research*, 2, 393–410.
9. M. Glickman and K. Sycara. Reasons for premature convergence of self-adapting mutation rates. In *Proc. of the 2000 Congress on Evolutionary Computation*, pages 62–69.
10. D. E. Goldberg. *Genetic Algorithms in Search, Optimization and Machine Learning*. Addison-Wesley Pub. Co., 1989.
11. D. E. Goldberg and M. Rudnick. Genetic algorithm and the variance of fitness. *Complex Systems*, 5(3):265–278, 1991.
12. F. Herrera and M. Lozano. Adaptation of genetic algorithm parameters based on fuzzy logic controllers. *Genetic Algorithms and Soft Computing*, pages 95–125, 1996.
13. S. W. Mahfoud. Crowding and preselection revisited. In *Parallel problem solving from nature 2*, pages 27–36, 1992. North-Holland.
14. N. F. McPhee and N. J. Hopper. Analysis of genetic diversity through population history. In *GECCO99: Proceedings of the Genetic and Evolutionary Computation Conference*, 1999.
15. R. W. Morrison and K. A. De Jong. Measurement of population diversity. In *5th International Conference, Evolution Artificielle, EA 2001*, pages 31–41. Springer, 2001.
16. M. M. Solomon. Algorithms for vehicle routing and scheduling problems with time window constraints. *Operations Research*, 35(2), 1987.
17. K. Q. Zhu. A diversity-controlling adaptive genetic algorithm for the vehicle routing problem with time windows. In *Proceedings of International Conference on Tools with Artificial Intelligence (ICTAI 2003)*, pages 176–183.

Simultaneous Concept Learning of Fuzzy Rules

Jacobus van Zyl and Ian Cloete

School of Information Technology, International University in Germany,
76646 Bruchsal, Germany

Abstract. FUZZYBEXA was the first algorithm to use a set covering approach for induction of *fuzzy* classification rules. It followed an iterated concept learning strategy, where rules are induced for each concept in turn. We present a new algorithm to allow also simultaneous concept learning and the induction of ordered fuzzy rule sets. When a proper rule evaluation function is used, simultaneous concept learning performs far better than iterated concept learning with respect to rule set size, rule complexity, search complexity, and classification accuracy. We provide empirical results of five experiments on nine data sets and also show that the algorithm compares favourably to other well known concept learners.

1 Introduction

We recently extended the set covering framework to the fuzzy domain, and presented a new algorithm, FUZZYBEXA, that induces fuzzy classification rules [1]. This method compares well with state of the art concept learners. There exists very few fuzzy rule learners that, unlike fuzzy decision trees and fuzzy neural networks, directly induce fuzzy classification rules, and to the best of our knowledge, none that use a fuzzy set covering approach to learning.

The *set covering* approach to concept learning has also been called *sequential learning* [2], because in this approach one rule is learned, the data covered by the rule are removed, and the process iterated, until a disjunctive set of rules for all concepts have been found. Learning multiple concepts generally follow two strategies: (1) For a concept (or class) in the data set, a set of disjunctive rules are induced by repeating the learning procedure for each concept in turn. (2) Multiple concepts are learned by finding a good classification rule for any one of the concepts, and assigning this class as consequent of the rule. The literature, e.g. [2], offers no preference for one strategy over the other. We call the two strategies for this process *iterated concept learning* (learning one class at a time, iterated over all classes) and *simultaneous concept learning* (simultaneously considering all classes by learning one rule at a time for any class, repeated until all data are covered), and abbreviate them as ICL and SCL, respectively. Examples of algorithms following the ICL strategy are FUZZYBEXA, BEXA, and Webb's rule learner, whereas C4.5, CN2, and Neural Networks all follow the SCL strategy [1, 3–5]. Fuzzy classification rules can be extracted from fuzzy decision trees and fuzzy neural networks, and although learning is done using SCL, unordered rule sets are obtained [6, 7].

J.-F. Boulicaut et al. (Eds.): ECML 2004, LNAI 3201, pp. 548–559, 2004.

In this paper we introduce FUZZYBEXAII, that uses SCL to induce classification rules from fuzzy data. The induction process produces an ordered rule set, and we show that in many cases this methodology produces superior results to FUZZYBEXA, i.e. on average better classification performance, radically smaller rule sets, and also less search complexity. We also introduce the fuzzy accuracy function for rule evaluation in SCL, and demonstrate that this function is much better behaved for SCL learning than, for example, the fuzzy entropy function. In the next section we review fuzzy set covering and FUZZYBEXA. In Section 3 we show how to extend FUZZYBEXA to use the SCL strategy, and in the following section we show that the rule evaluation function plays a pivotal role in finding good classification rules. In Section 5 we provide the results of five different experiments on nine data sets for FUZZYBEXA with ICL and SCL using several different evaluation functions, as well as an empirical comparison between FUZZYBEXAII and other concept learners. The following section contains a discussion of the experimental data, and Section 6 concludes our paper.

2   FUZZYBEXA: A Fuzzy Set Covering Framework

Fuzzy instances differ from crisp instances in two fundamental ways. Firstly, fuzzy instances belong to all attributes and attribute values, whereas crisp instances belong to only one attribute value per attribute. Secondly, fuzzy instances belong to attribute values to a certain degree, measured on the scale $[0, 1]$, whereas crisp instances either match an attribute value or not, i.e. their memberships are measured in the set $\{0, 1\}$. The fuzzy instance space is described by a vector of linguistic variables (fuzzy attributes) A_i, $I = \langle A_1, A_2, ..., A_n \rangle$, where each variable is a family of fuzzy sets, $A_i = \langle L_1, L_2, ..., L_m \rangle$. Each L_j is a fuzzy set, i.e. a linguistic term (fuzzy attribute value). Together, all the linguistic terms belonging to the same linguistic variable form the *term set* of that linguistic variable. Linguistic terms and variables are referred to simply as terms and variables. A fuzzy instance belongs to each term to a certain degree, its membership degree. The membership of fuzzy instance i to the term L is given by its membership function to the term, $\mu_L(i)$, and thus a fuzzy instance is of the form, $i = \langle \langle \mu_{11}(i), ...\mu_{1p}(i) \rangle ... \langle \mu_{n1}(i), ...\mu_{nq}(i) \rangle \rangle$, where the first subscript is the variable index and the second the term index of the respective variable. Propositional rules are of the form "IF X THEN Y," where X is called the antecedent and Y the consequent. Contrary to the crisp case, fuzzy instances match antecedents only to a certain degree. Let $\mu_A(i)$ and $\mu_B(i)$ be the membership of a fuzzy instance i, $i \in I$, to the two terms A and B respectively, then the degree to which an instance matches an antecedent is computed using the standard fuzzy operators, $\mu_{A \wedge B}(i) = \mu_{A \cap B}(i)$, $\mu_{A \vee B}(i) = \mu_{A \cup B}(i)$, and $\mu_{\neg A}(i) = \mu_{\bar{A}}(i)$. Instances may belong to antecedents to a very small degree. This may be undesirable, and to avoid such cases we apply an α-cut to the antecedent. The membership of an instance that belongs to an antecedent below the threshold α_a, called the antecedent threshold, is defined to be zero. Only instances that belong to an antecedent with membership α_a or above match the antecedent, and the antecedent is said to cover the instances. The set of all instances within a set S that is covered by an antecedent c is called the extension of the antecedent in S, and is denoted as $X_S(c)$,

$$X_S(c) = \{i \in S | \mu_c(i) \geq \alpha_a\}. \tag{1}$$

As stated above, fuzzy instances belong to terms only with certain membership, and this is also true for the concept. To prevent instances from belonging to a concept to only a small degree, we define instances to belong to a concept only when their membership to the concept is above a_c, the concept threshold.

FUZZYBEXA's description language is a fuzzy version of VL$_1$, called Fuzzy VL$_1$ [1]. Antecedents in Fuzzy VL$_1$ are conjunctions of internally disjunctive expressions, also called conjuncts. Each conjunct may contain terms from only one term set. Consider for example the variables *outlook* and *wind* with term sets $\{sunny, cloudy, rainy\}$ and $\{windy, calm\}$, respectively. An example of a Fuzzy VL$_1$ antecedent is, $[outlook = sunny \vee cloudy] \wedge [wind = calm]$, where the conjuncts are delimited with square brackets. We can also write this expression in short form as $[sunny, cloudy][calm]$, where the conjunction symbol is dropped and the disjunction is replaced by a list of its elements.

FUZZYBEXA performs a top-down general-to-specific search of the hypothesis space starting with the most general conjunction (mgc). The most general conjunction must have the property that it covers all instances. Consider the conjunction $[sunny, cloudy, rainy][windy, calm]$. This conjunction cannot in general cover all instances, since there may exist a subset B, $B \subset I$, such that $B = \{i \in I | \mu_{sunny \vee cloudy \vee rainy}(i) < \alpha_a\}$, and B is therefore not covered. To form the mgc we add to each term set a new term, called its *alpha complement*. The membership of an instance to this term is defined to be zero when the instance belongs to any other term in the term set with membership α_a or greater, and one when the instance does not belong to any other term in the term set with membership α_a or above. Thus, the mgc for the example above is $[sunny, cloudy, rainy, \bar{\alpha}_{outlook}][windy, cloudy, \bar{\alpha}_{wind}]$. This conjunction covers all instances in the instance space, and thus is most general.

FUZZYBEXA consists of three layers. The top layer implements the fuzzy set covering approach to rule induction and is called *CoverConcepts*. It receives a training set T of instances and a list of concepts for which to induce classification rules. For each concept con_i the training set is split into a set of positive instances P and a set of negative instances N. To obtain P, we use Eq (1), $P = X_T(con_i)$, and for N use $N = T - P$. Next, FUZZYBEXA invokes its middle layer to obtain the conjunction that best describes the current concept. It then adds the rule with this conjunction as antecedent and the current concept as consequent to its rule set. Then all the positive instances covered by this rule are removed from the set of positive instances, while the set N remains unchanged. FUZZYBEXA iteratively induces more rules until either all the positive instances are covered, or no "useful" conjunction could be found. It then continues with the next concept until all the concepts are covered.

FUZZYBEXA's middle layer, *FindBestConjunction*, implements a set of search heuristics to guide the search. It first forms the mgc as described above, and then invokes the bottom layer routine to obtain a set of specializations of this conjunction. Each of the conjunctions are evaluated according to an evaluation function. FUZZYBEXA can use any evaluation function that assigns better scores to conjunctions that cover the positive set better than the negative set, where the exact definition of better is defined by the evaluation function itself. Let $M(S,c) = \sum_{i \in X_S(c)} \mu_c(i)$, where S is a set of instances and c a conjunction. In this paper we investigate two functions, a fuzzy evaluation function related to the Laplace estimate, $L(c) = \frac{M(P,c)+.5}{M(T,c)}$, and the fuzzy accuracy function, $A(c) = M(P,c) - M(N,c)$. FUZZYBEXA can perform a beam search of the hypothesis space by choosing the *beamwidth* best conjunctions to specialize further. Conjunctions that are consistent, i.e. that cover no negative instances, are removed from the search process. FUZZYBEXA keeps the best conjunction found thus far in a variable *bestconj*. If the best conjunction found during the search performs no better than the *mgc*, the result "no useful conjunction found" is returned, otherwise, *bestconj* is returned. The middle layer also employs other search restrictions for efficiency and performance measures not discussed here. For more details about FUZZYBEXA, see [1].

FUZZYBEXA's bottom layer, called *GenerateSpecializations*, receives a set of conjunctions and returns the set of refinements of these conjunctions. FUZZY-BEXA can use different specialization models, but for the purposes of this paper we will only consider the exclusion specialization model. The set of terms used to describe conjunction c is called its description set, denoted by $D(c)$. In this set, all the terms are uniquely labeled, e.g. the term *high* of the variable *humidity* and the term *high* of the variable *cost* are different. If necessary, we can rename the terms to *humidity.high* and *cost.high*. Thus, there exists a one-to-one mapping between c and $D(c)$. In the exclusion specialization model, a conjunction is specialized by excluding (removing) one of the terms from its description set, i.e. c_2 is specialized to form c_1 by removing a term from $D(c_2)$, e.g. $[a,b][z]$ specialized forms $[a][z]$ or $[b][z]$. Let c_1 and c_2 be two conjunctions from the set of Fuzzy VL_1 conjunctions for a particular problem. Then $c_1 \preceq c_2$, c_1 *is more specific or equal to* c_2 if $D(c_1) \subseteq D(c_2)$, and $c_1 = c_2$ if $D(c_1) = D(c_2)$. We say $c_1 \prec c_2$, c_1 *is more specific than* c_2 if $c_1 \preceq c_2$ and $c_1 \neq c_2$. Thus, the set C, is partially ordered under the relation $\preceq$, and forms a lattice. Furthermore, if $c_1 \prec c_2$, $D(c_1)$ is formed by excluding one or more terms from $D(c_2)$, and c_1 is therefore a more restrictive description, able to match fewer instances than c_2. In fact, c_1 can cover only a subset of the instances covered by c_2, and $X_I(c_1) \subset X_I(c_2)$. Thus, the extension operator is an order-preserving map from conjunctions to instance sets. FUZZYBEXA's exclusion specialization model therefore results in a general-to-specific, top-down search of the lattice of Fuzzy VL_1 descriptions.

3 FUZZYBEXAII: Induction of Ordered Fuzzy Rules

In this section we introduce FUZZYBEXAII, a novel SCL approach that induces ordered fuzzy rules from a fuzzy data set. Table 1 shows FUZZYBEXAII's *Cover-Concepts* routine. Compared to that of FUZZYBEXA, the SCL top layer routine

Table 1. FuzzyBexaII's CoverConcepts procedure

CoverConcepts
> **Input:** Set of training instances T, Set of concepts to learn C
> **Output:** A rule set describing the concepts
> Set the current rule set to empty
> While T contains instances
> > $best$ = FindBestRule(T, C)
> > Add $best$ to the rule set
> > Remove the instances covered by $best$
> Return the rule set

of FuzzyBexaII is less complex. It starts by initialising the rule set to empty. Then, it iteratively finds the best *rule* for the current set of training examples using the middle layer routine *FindBestRule*–in ICL the middle layer returned the *antecedent* that best covered the concept it was forced to use. For SCL the training set is not split into positive and negative parts, but passed as a whole to the middle layer. The rule found by the middle layer is then added to the rule set, and all instances covered by the rule are removed from the training set. This also differs from ICL, where only the positive instances covered by the rule are removed. We will discuss the implications of this decision later.

FuzzyBexaII's middle layer, see Table 2, implements several heuristics for guiding the search in the hypothesis space. It uses the set *spec* to maintain the set of current conjunctions to consider as rule antecedents. This set is initialized with the *mgc*. The routine functions as follows. A set of specializations of the conjunctions in *spec* is obtained by invoking FuzzyBexaII's bottom layer routine. Then, for each specialization *ant* in *spec*, the concept best described by the conjunction is selected. This is done by dividing the instances covered by the conjunction into groups according to their class,

$$G_i(ant) = \{d \in X_T(ant) | \; \mu_{concept_i}(d) \geq \alpha_c\}. \tag{2}$$

The sigma count or scalar cardinality of each group is then computed,

$$M(G_i(ant)) = \sum_{d \in G_i(ant)} \mu_{ant}(d) \tag{3}$$

and the concept of the group with the highest cardinality is chosen as the best rule consequent. The potential rule is then evaluated according to an evaluation function. This function is fundamental in guiding the search through the hypothesis space, and we will investigate its influence on the search process and overall performance in more detail later. If the potential rule outperforms the current best rule, it replaces the current best rule.

The next step implements an efficiency stop growth measure. This measure is very important to prevent unnecessary exploration of parts of the hypothesis space that cannot yield rules better than the current best rule. Let j be the index of the concept chosen as rule consequent. Assume that in the idealistic

Table 2. FuzzyBexaII's FindBestRule procedure

FindBestRule
  Input: Set of instances, Set of concepts C
  Output: The best rule found during this search
  Set the current best rule to empty
  Add the *mgc* to the set of current conjunctions, *spec*
  While *spec* contains conjunctions
    spec = GenerateSpecializations(T, *spec*)
    For each conjunction *ant* in *spec*
      Let *consequent* be the concept from C best covered by the conjunction *ant*
      If eval(*ant, consequent*) is better than that of the best rule,
        Replace the current best rule with "IF *ant* THEN *consequent*"
      If *ant* can never be better than the best rule, remove it from *spec*
    Retain only the *beamwidth* best conjunctions in *spec*
  Return the best rule found

Table 3. FuzzyBexaII's specialization model

GenerateSpecializations
  Input: Set of instances T, set of conjunctions C
  Output: Set of specializations of the conjunctions in C
  Initialise the set of *spec* to be empty
  For each conjunction c and associated usable term L,
    If $X_T(L)$ and $X_T(c)$ have no instances in common,
      Mark this term as unusable in this conjunction
  For each conjunction c and associated usable term L,
    Create a specialization by excluding L from c
    Add the specialization to *spec*
  Remove all duplicate conjunctions from *spec*
  Return *spec*

case all groups G_i, $i \neq j$, are empty. If even in this case the performance of the potential rule is worse than the best rule, it is futile to continue further exploration of this part of the hypothesis space. This is true since we are specializing antecedents, moving from top to bottom in the lattice of antecedents, and thus subsequent rules can never cover more instances, and therefore cannot increase their cardinality and performance above that of the best rule. Note, this test includes the consistency test as a special case – when an antecedent is consistent no subsequent antecedent can perform better that it. This test is an adaptation of an approach by Quinlan and Cameron-Jones for the crisp iterated concept rule learner by Webb [8, 3]. After all conjunctions were considered, a beam search is implemented by retaining only the *beamwidth* best conjunctions in the set *spec*. The process is iterated until *spec* becomes empty and the best rule is returned.

    FuzzyBexaII's bottom layer routine *GenerateSpecializations*, shown in Table 3, implements the specialization model. The function of this routine is similar to that of FuzzyBexa, i.e. to obtain a set of refinements of the input set of conjunctions. The routine starts by initialising the set of specializations *spec* to be empty. Then follows two loops. The first implements an efficiency measure, and the second performs the specialization. With each conjunction we associate a set of "usable" terms that may be used to specialize the conjunction, and we initialise the mgc to contain all terms in its usable set. The first loop compares the extension of the conjunction and the extension of terms from its usable set. Any term where the two extensions have no members in common, i.e. any term L and conjunction c where

$$X_T(L) \cap X_T(c) = \emptyset \tag{4}$$

is removed from the set of usable terms for this conjunction. Excluding such a term will not change the extension of the conjunction, and therefore make it overly specific. The next loop generates specializations by excluding from each conjunction the terms from its associated usable set in turn. Duplicates may occur if two conjunctions were specialized by excluding the same terms in different order, and are removed. The resulting specializations are returned.

4   The Rule Evaluation Function

The entropy evaluation function is often used for SCL learning, including decision tree and fuzzy decision tree learning [9, 10]. Let r be a rule with a as antecedent and $\{c_1, ..., c_N\}$ the possible consequents of r, then the normalized fuzzy entropy is given by

$$E(r) = \frac{1}{\log N} \sum_{i=1}^{N} \frac{M(a \wedge c_i)}{M(a)} \log \frac{M(a \wedge c_i)}{M(a)}, \tag{5}$$

where $M(x)$ is the sigma count. Since we want an evaluation function that assigns higher scores to better conjunctions, we use the evaluation function $1 - E(r)$. This function has a maximum value of one for rules that cover only one class, and a minimum value of zero for rules that cover each class in the same proportion. However, the entropy function does not favour high coverage, e.g. a rule that covers five instances of one class and none of other classes and a second rule that covers a thousand instances from one class and none of other classes will both have a score of one. The Laplace estimate was suggested as an improvement of the CN2 algorithm that also used the entropy function [5]. In [11] we suggested the fuzzy accuracy function for ICL,

$$A(r) = \sum_{i \in X_P(a)} \mu_a(i) - \sum_{i \in X_N(a)} \mu_a(i), \tag{6}$$

where P is a subset of T containing all instances that belongs to the concept, and $N = T - P$. We adapt the accuracy function for use in SCL by considering each concept in turn, and regard instances belonging to other concepts as members of N. We assign the rule consequent as the concept that results in the highest evaluation, and also assign this evaluation value to the rule. This evaluation function will prefer rules that cover a large number of instances from one concept and few of the other.

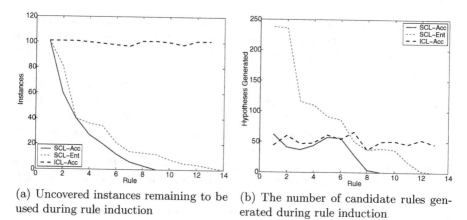

(a) Uncovered instances remaining to be used during rule induction

(b) The number of candidate rules generated during rule induction

Fig. 1. Results for ICL and SCL with different evaluation functions on the Zoo data

5   Experiments

In this section we show experimental results on six real world domains obtained from the UCI machine learning repository. We fuzzified data by assigning membership values from $\{0,1\}$ to nominal attributes, and by using a clustering method to place bell shaped membership functions on the continuous domains of linearly ordered attributes. We will discuss results obtained for FuzzyBexa (ICL) with the accuracy and Laplace evaluation functions, and also for Fuzzy-BexaII (SCL) with the entropy and accuracy evaluation functions. We denote FuzzyBexaII with the entropy and accuracy evaluation functions as SCL-Ent and SCL-Acc respectively, and FuzzyBexa with the accuracy and Laplace evaluation functions as ICL-Acc and ICL-Lap, respectively.

Figure 1 shows results obtained by SCL and ICL on the training set of the Zoo data, where we ignored the variable "animal," and learned the concept "type of animal," e.g. mammal, bird, fish, etc. The different methodologies of SCL and ICL are clearly discernable from Figure 1(a). For most of the rules, ICL considered all the instances during the induction process. This happens since ICL removes only the positive instances covered from the training set for each class, and reinsert these into the training set when the next concept is considered. SCL, however, never reinserts covered instances, and its graphs are monotonously decreasing. From Figure 1(a) one can also see the number of instances covered by each consecutive rule. This is indicated by the difference on the y-axis of two consecutive points. When there is no difference for ICL, it implies that the rule covered all the positive instances. The last seven rules induced by SCL-Ent covered very few instances each. Figure 1(b) shows the number of candidate hypotheses generated for each rule during the search. SCL-Ent started out with a very high number, and then as there were successively fewer instances available, generated successively fewer candidates rules. For the first six rules SCL-Acc and ICL-Acc had similar behaviour. However, for the last two rules of SCL-Acc there were less than 10 instances, and consequently it needed only a few hypotheses to cover them. The use of the accuracy function also resulted in a much smaller rule set for SCL. SCL-Acc had 9 rules and SCL-Ent 14 rules.

Table 4 shows results for five experiments. All results quoted are on test set results from a 10-fold cross validation. For each data set the mean and standard deviation are computed, and the average of the means of all data sets are shown in the last column. The best performance on each data set is set in bold face. The first experiment investigates the accuracy of the induced rule sets. SCL-Ent had the worst overall performance, and did significantly worse on the Colic, Hepatitis and Lymph data sets. It had the best performance on the Zoo data set. SCL-Acc, in contrast, performs very well, and obtained better overall results than any of the other methods. ICL-Acc and ICL-Lap had very similar results, and was overall about 2% worse than SCL-Acc, but 3.5% better than SCL-Ent. The second experiment compares the size of the rule set induced by each method. Here, SCL-Acc is the clear winner. On average its rule sets contained about three times fewer rules than ICL-Acc and ICL-Ent. It also becomes clear that SCL-Ent is not a good method to use, as it induced 12 times more rules than SCL-Acc, and also had worse classification accuracy performance. This result is most likely due to the entropy evaluation function not favouring conjunctions with higher coverage. Thus, a large number of consistent conjunctions covering only small sets of instances are induced.

One obvious observation is that SCL-Acc is able to induce extremely compact rule sets. This behaviour cannot be attributed only to the accuracy function, as ICL-Acc did not perform as well. One big difference between SCL and ICL is that the rules induced by SCL are ordered and that by ICL unordered. Table 5 shows the rule set induced by SCL for the Zoo data. The first rule correctly classifies all mammals. Thus, after the first iteration, all mammals are removed from the data set. Similarly, the second rule removes all birds from the data set. Now consider the third rule, it states that animals with fins are fish. On its own, this rule would incorrectly classify whales and dolphins as fish. However, since the rules are evaluated in order, the first rule would fire for a whale, correctly classifying it as a mammal, and further rules would not be considered.

We believe the aforementioned characteristic is present in many data sets, and is the reason why SCL outperforms ICL on many data sets. After the first few rules took care of macro features that are easily identified, rules found later need not concern themselves with these features, and can distinguish between the special cases. An ordered rule set is a representation of a more complex unordered rule set, and also does not require the arbitration process of unordered rule sets when multiple rules fire. When ICL has to induce a rule for fish, it will have to find a more complex antecedent, e.g. [milk = false][fins = true], i.e. the rule must not fire on any of the macro features, but still differentiate the special cases. Consequently, ordered rule sets can be much smaller than unordered rule sets, while still obtaining high accuracy. ICL often induces many more rules to prevent the covering of macro features while still covering some of the micro

Table 4. Various test results for SCL with the Entropy and Accuracy evaluation functions and ICL with the Accuracy and Laplace Evaluation functions

	Colic		Diabetes		Hepatitis		Iris		Lymph		Zoo		Ave
	Mean	StdDev	Mean	StdDev	Mean	StdDev	Mean	StdDev	Mean	StdDev	Mean	StdDev	Mean
Accuracy of the Rule Set													
SCL, Ent	78.0	6.0	68.2	2.7	76.8	11.2	93.6	6.3	73.6	12.1	**96.0**	**8.2**	81.0
SCL, Acc	84.5	3.3	**74.0**	**4.8**	**86.5**	**6.9**	96.4	5.1	81.1	12.3	**96.0**	10.5	**86.4**
ICL, Acc	**85.3**	**4.7**	71.2	4.1	83.9	10.1	95.7	6.0	81.1	11.5	91.1	11.2	84.7
ICL, Lap	83.4	5.7	71.1	2.8	80.6	7.6	**96.4**	**5.1**	**81.8**	**14.4**	93.1	13.4	84.4
Number of Rules in the Rule Set													
SCL, Ent	88.0	7.8	183.2	16.5	34.0	2.1	9.9	0.3	41.8	3.5	12.7	0.7	61.6
SCL, Acc	**5.1**	**0.3**	4.4	1.7	**3.1**	**0.3**	3.9	0.3	6.5	0.7	7.9	0.3	5.2
ICL, Acc	34.4	2.7	**2.4**	**0.5**	19.3	1.2	4.0	0.0	19.6	1.5	12.3	1.1	15.3
ICL, Lap	34.5	1.6	8.6	1.1	19.0	1.1	4.3	0.5	21.8	1.3	10.6	0.7	16.5
Complexity of the Rule Set Measured in Terms													
SCL, Ent	184.4	20.8	759.2	79.1	56.0	4.3	13.5	1.0	70.0	8.6	12.5	1.1	182.6
SCL, Acc	**14.2**	**2.8**	**5.6**	**2.9**	**4.5**	**1.4**	**3.5**	**0.5**	**12.7**	**1.7**	**10.3**	**1.3**	**8.5**
ICL, Acc	128.0	9.6	6.2	1.9	62.9	5.0	6.0	0.0	67.9	7.2	35.4	3.9	51.1
ICL, Lap	166.7	12.1	36.6	6.0	68.3	5.9	7.0	1.6	76.5	5.3	27.9	2.2	63.8
Number of Conjunctions Generated During Rule Set Induction													
SCL, Ent	53800	5632	24420	2349	11300	744	334	24	8008	722	955	134	16470
SCL, Acc	**2409**	**192**	**355**	**110**	**632**	**74**	**123**	**15**	**907**	**55**	315	23	790
ICL, Acc	10137	637	6780	436	2360	122	196	13	2243	222	601	61	3719
ICL, Lap	12373	1068	5851	306	2592	251	263	27	2719	168	493	38	4048
Average Number of Hypotheses Generated per Rule													
SCL, Ent	610.9	32.4	132.6	2.5	332.0	13.9	33.4	3.1	191.3	15.0	74.5	7.4	229.1
SCL, Acc	472.1	28.1	83.4	11.1	203.7	12.0	31.3	4.0	139.9	11.4	39.5	3.0	**161.7**
ICL, Acc	294.6	11.4	2924.8	579.9	121.8	4.5	48.6	3.4	113.8	5.2	48.3	2.1	592.0
ICL, Lap	357.6	19.5	689.8	101.5	135.9	10.5	61.1	7.4	124.7	8.8	46.0	0.9	235.9

features. The small number of instances available for induction of the last rules in SCL implies that less search is necessary for these rules. This is different for ICL and clearly visible in Figure 1(b), and the overall result is that SCL-Acc requires less search for rule set induction. The rule sets induced by SCL are also not unnatural, as humans also represent concepts such as animal type using an ordered rule set, i.e. reasoning by working with exceptions. The last rule induced by SCL often has the antecedent TRUE. This happens when after the exclusion of instances covered by previous rules, only instances of one class remain. This must not be confused with the default rule used in unordered rule sets. In unordered sets, the default rule fires when no other rule fires, and usually has the majority class as consequent. SCL could also employ such a default rule when the last rule does not have TRUE as antecedent.

SCL in combination with the entropy function did not perform well. This is because entropy does not guide the search in the direction of high coverage. The first rule induced by SCL-Ent, for example, had "bird" as consequent. However, there are 20 bird and 41 mammal instances. Thus, SCL-Acc induced a rule for the class with the most instances since this rule has the highest coverage. On the Colic data SCL-Acc alternated between the classes such that the most instances are covered by each consecutive rule. Subsequent rules should in general cover

Table 5. SCL-Acc induced rule set for the Zoo data

[milk = true] → type=mammal	[eggs = true][backbone = false][legs = $\neg\bar{\alpha}$]
[feathers = true] → type=bird	→ type=insect
[fins = true] → type=fish	[backbone = true][tail = true] → type=reptile
[eggs = true][breathes = false]	[aquatic = false] → type=invertebrate
→ type=invertebrate	TRUE → type=amphibia

Table 6. Results of FuzzyBexaII, C4.5, Layered Search and Exhaustive Search on three data sets. Theory size for C4.5 is measured in tree nodes, in number of test conditions for layered and exhaustive search, and in number of terms for FuzzyBexaII

	Error			Theory Size		
	Diabetes	Hepatitis	Lymph	Diabetes	Hepatitis	Lymph
C4.5	25.4	20.4	21.7	44.0	17.8	N/A
Layered Search	26.9	19.1	18.9	207.4	27.0	30.1
Exhaustive Search	27.2	20.0	19.0	208.7	27.9	30.1
FuzzyBexaII	23.0	13.6	18.9	5.6	4.5	12.7

fewer instances than previous rules, thus rules with stronger support are placed higher up in the rule hierarchy. This can be clearly seen in the shape of the graph for SCL-ACC in Figure 1(a). SCL-Ent in the same figure, however, had subsequent slopes higher than previous slopes, demonstrating its unbiasedness towards high coverage.

The third experiment in Table 4 measured the complexity of rules as the number of terms in the rule set. Here, the good performance of the accuracy function for both SCL and ICL is evident. Again SCL-Acc had the best performance, requiring six times fewer terms than ICL-Acc and seven times fewer than ICL-Lap. The rule sets found by ICL-Acc were about 15% less complex than that found by ICL-Lap. The rule set complexity found by SCL-Acc was on average about 5% of that of SCL-Ent. The fourth experiment shows that, interestingly, SCL-Acc needed to investigate only a very small part of the search space to obtain its results. ICL-Acc was second, but generated 4.6 times more candidate rules, whereas ICL-Lap generated 5.2 times more candidates. SCL-Ent's struggle to obtain good rule sets becomes clear; it generated 16470 hypotheses versus ICL-Acc's 790. The last experiment compares the number of hypotheses generated per induced rule. SCL-Acc again needed the least number of hypotheses. Interestingly though, SCL-Ent generated the second least. However, since the induced rules cover so few instances, many rules were needed making the total search very large. ICL-Acc generated the most hypotheses. However, if we remove the outlier of the Diabetes data, the ICL-Acc would have 125.4, ICL-Lap 145.1, and SCL-Acc 177.3, resulting in ICL-Acc with the smallest search per rule. ICL-Acc induced the smallest and second most accurate rule set for the diabetes data. However, it required 20 times more search than SCL-Acc, and therefore a very large number of hypotheses were generated per induced rule.

We also compared our FuzzyBexaII algorithm (using the accuracy function) with three other concept learners. The results quoted for C4.5, Layered Search and Exhaustive Search were obtained from the literature [8, 12, 4]. The first column shows the average error on the test sets. FuzzyBexaII had similar classification results as the other methods for the Lymph data, better results on the Diabetes data, and significantly better results on the Hepatitis data. It's theory size (complexity) is also significantly smaller in all cases.

6   Conclusion

This paper presented FuzzyBexaII, an algorithm for learning ordered fuzzy rule sets for classification. We also enhanced the method with early stopping efficiency measures, without which the search would be prohibitively big. We further presented five empirical experiments on six data sets, and demonstrated that if the correct kind of evaluation function used, i.e. functions that give preference to rules with high coverage, ordered rule sets are much less complex than unordered rule sets, while at the same time being very accurate. As an example of an appropriate evaluation function we showed how to adapt the fuzzy accuracy function for SCL. We discussed the various reasons for SCL's good performance, and also showed with further experiments that FuzzyBexaII can outperform other learning systems with respect to rule set size and accuracy.

References

1. Cloete, I., van Zyl, J.: Fuzzy rule induction in a set covering framework. (2004) (Submitted).
2. Mitchell, T.M.: Machine Learning. McGraw-Hill (1997)
3. Webb, G.: Systematic search for categorical attribute-value data-driven machine learning. In: Proceedings Sixth Australian Joint conference of Artificial Intelligence, Melbourne, Singapore: World Scientific (1993) 342–347
4. Quinlan, J.R.: Improved use of continuous attributes in C4.5. Journal of Artificial Intelligence Research **4** (1996) 77–90
5. Clark, P., Boswell, R.: Rule induction with CN2: Some recent improvements. In: Proceedings of the Sixth European Working Session on Learning. (1991) 151–163
6. Yuan, Y., Shaw, M.J.: Induction of fuzzy decision trees. Fuzzy Sets and Systems **69** (1995) 125–139
7. Kasabov, N.K.: On-line learning, reasoning, rule extraction and aggregation in locally optimized evolving fuzzy neural networks. Neurocomputing (2001) 25–45
8. Quinlan, J.R., Cameron-Jones, R.M.: Oversearching and layered search in empirical learning. In: IJCAI. (1995) 1019–1024
9. Cios, K.J., Sztandera, L.M.: Continuous id3 algorithm with fuzzy entropy measures. In: Proc. IEEE Int. Conf. Fuzzy Syst. (1992) 469–476
10. Dong, M., Kothari, R.: Look-ahead based fuzzy decision tree induction. IEEE-FS **9** (2001) 461–468
11. Cloete, I., van Zyl, J.: Evaluation function guided search for fuzzy set covering. In: IEEE International Conference on Fuzzy Systems, Budapest, Hungary (2004)
12. Quinlan, J.R.: Bagging, boosting and C4.5. In: Thirteenth National Conference on Artificial Intelligence, AAAI/MIT Press (1996)

SWITCH: A Novel Approach to Ensemble Learning for Heterogeneous Data

Rong Jin[1] and Huan Liu[2]

[1] Department of Computer Science and Engineering, Michigan State University
East Lansing, MI48824, USA
rongjin@cse.msu.edu

[2] Department of Computer Science and Engineering, Arizona State University
Tempe, AZ85287-8809, USA
hliu@cse.asu.edu

Abstract. The standard framework of machine learning problems assumes that the available data is independent and identically distributed (i.i.d.). However, in some applications such as image classification, the training data are often collected from multiple sources and heterogeneous. Ensemble learning is a proven effective approach to heterogeneous data, which uses multiple classification models to capture the diverse aspects of heterogeneous data. If an ensemble can learn the relationship between different portions of data and their corresponding models, the ensemble can selectively apply models to unseen data according to the learned relationship. We propose a novel approach to enable the learning of the relationships between data and models by creating a set of 'switches' that can route a testing instance to appropriate classification models in an ensemble. Our empirical study on both real-world data and benchmark data shows that the proposed approach to ensemble learning can achieve significant performance improvement for heterogeneous data.

1 Introduction

The standard framework of machine learning problems assumes that the available data is independent and identically distributed (i.i.d.), which usually results in a homogeneous distribution. However, in some applications such as image classification, the training data are often collected from multiple sources and thus exhibit a heterogeneous distribution. For heterogeneous data, a single classification model may not be sufficient to describe all the training data very well. One intuitive solution is to divide the heterogeneous training data into a set of homogeneous partitions and train a classification model over each homogeneous partition. To predict the class label for a testing instance, we can first examine which models are most likely to give a correct prediction for this instance and then apply those models to predict the class labels.

The idea of ensemble methods is to create multiple models from a single training dataset and combining them for classification. There have been many studies on this subject [1-3]. The well-known ensemble learning algorithms include Bagging [4], Gaussian mixture model (GMM) [5], and AdaBoost [6]. In this paper, we propose a novel ensemble learning approach that first partitions the heterogeneous data into homogeneous sections and then builds a classification model for each homogeneous

J.-F. Boulicaut et al. (Eds.): ECML 2004, LNAI 3201, pp. 560–562, 2004.

section. Unlike most existing ensemble learning method where different models are combined linearly, the presented ensemble approach introduces a routing 'switch' for each classification model that automatically determine whether the classification model should be applied to input instances. With the switches, a different subset of classification models is invoked for each instance

2 SWITCH – A Novel Ensemble Approach

The new ensemble approach will be described in two parts: model generation and model combination.

Model Generation. Our approach toward model generation is to divide the training dataset into multiple homogeneous sections and create a classification model for each partition. One apparent approach for obtaining the homogeneous partitions is to apply some traditional clustering algorithm to group similar training data together. However, the drawback of this approach is that each partitioned section will only contain a small number of training examples and thus the resulting classification model can severely over-fit the partitioned data. To solve this problem, we combine multiple partitions together for training a single classification model. More specifically, in our experiments, we apply the EM clustering algorithm to divide the training data into 6 different partitions and a different classification model is trained for every two partitions. As a result, there are a total of 15 classification models and each one is trained over roughly 1/3 of the training data.

Model Combination. Let $\mathbf{x}$ be an instance, y be a class label, and $M = \{m_1, m_2, ..., m_n\}$ be the ensemble of n classification models. Our goal is to compute $P(y|\mathbf{x},M)$. Let h_i be the hidden variable that indicates whether model m_i should be used for classifying the instance $\mathbf{x}$. By assuming that the selection of one classification model is independent from the selection of another, likelihood $P(y|\mathbf{x},M)$ can be simplified as the following expression:

$$P(y|\mathbf{x},M) \approx \sum_{i=1}^{n} P(h_i = 1|\mathbf{x})P(y|\mathbf{x},m_i) + Const \tag{1}$$

where models within the ensemble M are combined through another set of models $P(h_i = 1|\mathbf{x})$. Details of derivation can be found [7] In our experiment, a model for estimating $P(h_i = 1|\mathbf{x})$ can be learned as follows: For every classification model m_i in the ensemble, apply it to classify all training data and compare the predicted class labels to the true ones. For every training instance, if the predicted class label is the same as the true class label, mark it with a pseudo class '1'. Otherwise, a pseudo class '0' is assigned to the instance. Then, a 'switch', namely a classifier that is able to determine whether the corresponding model in the ensemble should be used to classify an instance, is trained over all the training instances with their pseudo class labels. The 'switch' will then be used to estimate the conditional probability $P(h_i = 1|\mathbf{x})$. In the experiments below, a Naïve Bayes model is to estimate $P(h_i = 1|\mathbf{x})$ due to its simplicity and reasonable good performance [8].

3   Experiments

Two heterogeneous datasets are used in this experiment: a dataset for indoor classification that contains 2500 examples represented by 190 features and a dataset for outdoor classification that contains 1403 examples represented 126 features. They are used to train image classifiers for identifying indoor and outdoor scenes. The experiments are performed with 5-fold cross validation and the average classification error rates are calculated. Table 1 summarizes the results for the new ensemble approach 'SWITCH' together with the baseline approach and two ensemble algorithms. For all methods, support vector machine is used as the basis model. We notice in Table 4 that compared to the baseline model, SWITCH is the only approach that consistently reduces the classification error significantly over the two datasets. It can be seen that Bagging also slightly outperforms the baseline model consistently over the two datasets. This result indicates that the new ensemble approach is effective for heterogeneous datasets. Italic numbers indicate they are smaller than the baseline error rates; italic and boldfaced numbers indicate the lowest error rates. In addition, more empirical studies of the proposed ensemble approach on both heterogeneous and homogeneous data can be found in [7].

Table 1. Averaged classification errors.

	Outdoor	Indoor
SVM	0.238±0.032	0.463±0.036
AdaBoost	0.240±0.028	*0.442±0.044*
Bagging	*0.233±0.022*	*0.447±0.036*
SWITCH	***0.196±0.028***	***0.407±0.035***

References

1. Dietterich, T.G., An Experimental Comparison of Three Methods for Constructing Ensembles of Decision Trees: Bagging, Boosting, and Randomization. Machine Learning, 2000. **40**(2): p. 139-157.
2. Ali, K.M. and M.J. Pazzani, Error Reduction through Learning Multiple Descriptions. Machine Learning, 1996. **24**(3): p. 173-206.
3. Bauer, E. and R. Kohavi, An Empirical Comparison of Voting Classification Algorithms: Bagging, Boosting and Variants. Machine Learning, 1999. **36**: p. 105-139.
4. Breiman, L., Bagging Predictors. Machine Learning, 1996. **24**(2): p. 123-140.
5. Bishop, C.M., Neural Networks for Pattern Recognition. 1995, Oxford: Oxford University Press.
6. Schapire, R.E. and Y. Singer, Improved Boosting Algorithms using Confidence-rated Predictions. Machine Learning, 1999. **37**(3): p. 291-336.
7. Jin, R. and H. Liu. SWITCH: A Novel Approach to Ensemble Learning for Heterogeneous Data. MSU-CSE-04-24, Dept. of Computer Science and Engineering, Michigan State University, 2004
8. Domingos, P. and M.J. Pazzani. Beyond independence: conditions for the optimality of the simple Bayesian classifier. in Proceedings of the Thirteenth International Conference on Machine Learning. 1996.

Estimating Attributed Central Orders
An Empirical Comparison

Toshihiro Kamishima[1], Hideto Kazawa[2], and Shotaro Akaho[1]

[1] National Institute of Advanced Industrial Science and Technology (AIST),
AIST Tsukuba Central 2, Umezono 1–1–1, Tsukuba, Ibaraki, 305–8568 Japan
mail@kamishima.net
http://www.kamishima.net/
[2] NTT Communication Science Laboratories, NTT Corporation
Hikaridai 2–4, Seika, Soraku, Kyoto, 619–0237 Japan

1 Introduction

Lists of ordered objects are widely used as representational forms. Such ordered objects include Web search results or best seller lists. In spite of their importance, the methods of processing orders have received little attention. However, research concerning object ordering is becoming more common. Some researchers have developed various methods to perform almost the same task: a learning function used for sorting objects from examples of ordered sequences. We call this task the estimation of *Attributed Central Orders* (*ACO* for short). The performance of this task is useful for sensory surveys[1], information retrieval, or decision making. We performed a survey of such methods, empirically compared the methods' properties, and discuss their merits and demerits.

Sections 2, 3, and 4, show the specifications of this task, describe the experimental results, and provide a summary, respectively.

2 Attributed Central Orders

This section describes the estimation task of ACOs. An order is a sorted sequence of objects according to a particular property, such as preference, size, or cost. An example of an order is $O_i = A \succ D \succ C$. These sorted objects are the members of the universal object set X^*. In the case of the figure below, $X^* = \{A, B, C, D, E\}$.

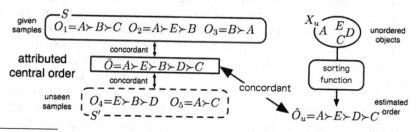

---

[1] The quantification of respondents' sensation or impression

J.-F. Boulicaut et al. (Eds.): ECML 2004, LNAI 3201, pp. 563–565, 2004.

An ACO estimation task can be considered a regression task whose target variable is ordinal. A regression line corresponds to an ACO. Analogous to the case of a regression line, an ACO is estimated so as to be concordant with both given samples S and unseen samples S', to be generated (above figure left). Note that an ACO consists of all the objects in X^*. This task differs from a regression in two ways. First, the target variable is ordinal. Therefore, the discordance is measured by the distance between orders, such as Spearman's or Kendall's distance [1]. Further, an ACO is represented by a sorting function that sorts unordered objects so as to be concordant with the ACO. Second, almost all the samples are incomplete, that is, sample orders consist of subsets of X^*. Hence, there may be objects not observed in given samples (ex., D in the above figure). Such objects should be ranked under the assumption that the neighboring objects in the attribute space would be nearly ranked.

3   Experiments

We tested five methods for estimating ACOs. Cohen et al. proposed a method (Cohen) based on a preference function indicating which of two orders is ranked higher [2]. Kazawa et al. used the Order SVM (OSVM) designed to calculate the cumulative probability distribution [3]. Herbrich et al. proposed the SVM (SVOR) based on the ordered pair of objects [4]. Kamishima and Akaho combined a linear regression method with paired comparison methods [5] (TR), and Akaho and Kamishima [6] extended Thurstone's model to handle attributed objects (ATM).

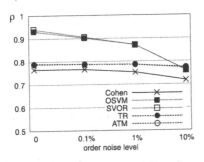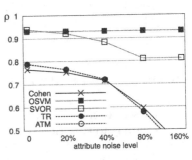

We applied these methods to artificial data. The robustness against order and attribute noise was tested. Order noise is the permutation in sample orders, while attribute noise is the perturbation of attribute values. The left and right figures above show the depression of estimation accuracies in accordance with the increase of order and attribute noise level, respectively. The ρ represents the Spearman's rank correlation, which measures the concordance between the estimated and the true orders. The larger ρ indicates the more accurate estimation. The two SVM-based methods, OSVM and SVOR, were robust against attribute noise, but not against order noise. Order noise more greatly decreased the level of performance, because the interchanged ordered pairs tend to become support-vectors. The perturbation of attribute values does not affect the support-vectors to as great a degree, so these methods are robust against attribute noise. Conversely, the non-SVM-based methods were robust against permutations of orders, but not against perturbation of attribute values. These methods can learn correctly if correct orders constitute the majority of sample orders, thus these methods are robust against order noise. However, any perturbation in attribute values always affects their performance.

4   Discussion and Summary

We first discuss the time complexities. These methods' sorting complexities are comparable. The learning time of the SVM-based methods are slow, the Thurstone-based TR and ATM are intermediate, and the Cohen method is the fastest. Overall, the slower methods show higher levels of prediction accuracy. In the SVM-based case, the number of pairs in samples are limited to $10^5 \sim 10^6$. Though Thurstone-based methods can deal with a greater amount of data, the number of distinct objects in S is limited to $10^5 \sim 10^6$. The two SVM-based methods and the others are robust against different types of noise. Hence, for the data of which orders are permutated, the non-SVM-based methods are preferable, while for the data whose attributes are disturbed, the SVM-based methods are preferable. Prediction accuracy strongly depends on the fitness of the model bias for the target data. The lower bias model can be incorporated into non-SVM-methods, but the time complexity might increase. The SVM-based methods can use kernels of the higher-biases, but it is not feasible to reduce the time complexities. In our next study, we plan to explore the effects of tuning these model biases. In order to evaluate the methods' generalization abilities, we will perform tests involving another real data set in which $|X^*|$ is large.

Acknowledgments. This work is supported by the grants-in-aid 14658106 and 16700157 of the Japan society for the promotion of science.

References

1. Marden, J.I.: Analyzing and Modeling Rank Data. Volume 64 of Monographs on Statistics and Applied Probability. Chapman & Hall (1995)
2. Cohen, W.W., Schapire, R.E., Singer, Y.: Learning to order things. Journal of Artificial Intelligence Research **10** (1999) 243–270
3. Kazawa, H., Hirao, T., Maeda, E.: Order SVM: A kernel method for order learning based on generalized order statistic. The IEICE Trans. on Information and Systems, pt. 2 **J86-D-II** (2003) 926–933 (in Japanese) [An English version will appear in "Systems and Computers in Japan" Wiley Periodicals, Inc.].
4. Herbrich, R., Graepel, T., Bollmann-Sdorra, P., Obermayer, K.: Learning preference relations for information retrieval. In: ICML-98 Workshop: Text Categorization and Machine Learning. (1998) 80–84
5. Kamishima, T., Akaho, S.: Learning from order examples. In: Proc. of The IEEE Int'l Conf. on Data Mining. (2002) 645–648
6. Akaho, S., Kamishima, T.: A statistical approach for learning from order examples linear models. In: Proc. of the 16th Annual Conference of JSAI. (2002) (in Japanese).

Batch Reinforcement Learning with State Importance

Lihong Li, Vadim Bulitko, and Russell Greiner

University of Alberta,
Department of Computing Science,
Edmonton, Alberta, Canada T6G 2E8
{lihong,bulitko,greiner}@cs.ualberta.ca

Abstract. We investigate the problem of using function approximation in reinforcement learning where the agent's policy is represented as a classifier mapping states to actions. High classification accuracy is usually deemed to correlate with high policy quality. But this is not necessarily the case as increasing classification accuracy can actually decrease the policy's quality. This phenomenon takes place when the learning process begins to focus on classifying less "important" states. In this paper, we introduce a measure of state's decision-making importance that can be used to improve policy learning. As a result, the focused learning process is shown to converge faster to better policies[1].

1 Problem Formulation and Related Work

Reinforcement learning (RL) [11] provide a general framework for many sequential decision-making problems and has succeeded in a number of important applications. Let S be the state space, A the action set, and D the start-state distribution. A policy is a mapping from states to actions: $\pi : S \mapsto A$. The state- and action-value functions are denoted by $V^\pi(s)$ and $Q^\pi(s, a)$, respectively [11]. The quality of a policy π is measured by *policy value* [10]: $V(\pi) = \mathbf{E}_{s_0 \sim D} V^\pi(s_0)$. A RL agent attempts to *learn* the optimal policy with maximal value: $\pi^* = \arg\max_\pi V(\pi)$. The corresponding optimal state- and action-value functions are denoted by $V^*(s)$ and $Q^*(s, a)$, respectively.

In this paper, we focus on classification-based RL methods where a policy π is represented as a classifier labeling state s with action $\pi(s)$. Then learning a policy π is reduced to learning a classifier [4, 6, 7, 12]. Recent implementations of this idea have demonstrated promising performance in several domains by learning high-quality policies through high-accuracy classification. It should be noted, however, that in sequential decision-making the classification error is *not* the target performance measure of a reward-collecting agent. Consequently, increasing classification accuracy can actually *lower* the policy value [9]. An intuitive explanation is that not all states are equally important in terms of preferring one action to another. Therefore, the classification-based RL methods can be improved by *focusing the learning process on more important states*. The expected benefits include faster convergence to better policies.

We examine the so-called *batch reinforcement learning* in which the policy learning occurs *offline*. Such a framework is important wherever online learning is not feasible

---

[1] Due to space limitation, only deterministic policy with binary actions are discussed. Details and extensions can be found in [9].

J.-F. Boulicaut et al. (Eds.): ECML 2004, LNAI 3201, pp. 566–568, 2004.

(e.g., when the reward data are limited), and therefore a fixed set of experiences has to be acquired and used for offline policy learning [2, 8]. In particular, we are interested in a special case where the state space is *sparsely sampled* and the optimal action values for these sampled states are computed or at least estimated. The sampled states together with their optimal action values form the training data for batch learning: $T_{Q^*} = \{\langle s, a, Q^*(s, a)\rangle | s \in T \subset S, a \in A\}$, where T is the sparsely sampled state space. The assumption of knowing the optimal action values may at first seem unrealistic. However, a technique called *full-trajectory-tree expansion* [5, 8] can be used to compute or estimate such values. This technique is especially useful in domains where good policies generalize well across problems of different sizes: the agent can first obtain a good policy on problems with tractable state space where the technique is applicable, and then generalize the policy to larger problems.

With the training data T_{Q^*}, the optimal actions can be computed: $\forall s \in T, a^*(s) = \arg\max_a Q^*(s, a)$ and the training data for learning a classifier-based policy are formed: $T_{CI} = \{\langle s, a^*(s)\rangle | s \in T\}$. Finally, the optimal policy is approximated by minimizing the classification error: $\widehat{\pi}^*_{CI} = \arg\min_{\widehat{\pi}^*} \sum_{s \in S} \mathcal{I}(\widehat{\pi}^*(s) \neq \pi^*(s))$, where $\mathcal{I}(A) = 1$ if A is true and 0 otherwise. The subscript CI (*cost-insensitive*) is in contrast to its *cost-sensitive* counterpart that will be introduced in the next section.

2 Batch Reinforcement Learning with State Importance

In contrast to the cost-insensitive algorithm outlined in the previous section, a novel RL algorithm based on *cost-sensitive* classification is proposed, which uses the state importance values as misclassification costs. As a result, the learning process focuses on important states thereby improving the convergence speed as well as the policy value.

Intuitively, a state is important from the decision-making point of view if making a wrong decision in it can have significant repercussions. Therefore, the *importance* of a state s, $G^*(s)$, is defined as: $G^*(s) = Q^*(s, a^*(s)) - Q^*(s, \bar{a}(s))$, where $a^*(s)$ is the optimal action and $\bar{a}(s)$ is the other (sub-optimal) action [2]. Similarly, the *importance of state s under policy π*, $G^*(s, \pi)$, is defined as: $G^*(s, \pi) = Q^*(s, a^*(s)) - Q^*(s, \pi(s))$. Clearly, if $\pi(s) = a^*(s)$, then $G^*(s, \pi) = 0$; otherwise, $G^*(s, \pi) = G^*(s)$.

It is desirable for the agent to approximate π^* by agreeing with it at important states. One way is to use the state importance values as the misclassification costs: $\widehat{\pi}^*_{CS} = \arg\min_{\widehat{\pi}^*} \sum_{s \in S} \left(G^*(s) \cdot \mathcal{I}(\widehat{\pi}^*(s) \neq \pi^*(s)) \right)$. Then learning the policy is reduced to cost-sensitive classification where s is the attribute, $a^*(s)$ is the desired class label, and $G^*(s)$ is the misclassification cost. Thus, given the training data T_{Q^*}, the agent can first compute $G^*(s)$ for all states $s \in T$ to form a training set: $T_{CS} = \{\langle s, a^*(s), G^*(s)\rangle \mid s \in T\}$, and then compute $\widehat{\pi}^*_{CS}$ using cost-sensitive classification techniques.

A question of both theoretical and practical interest is whether it is preferable to solve $\widehat{\pi}^*_{CS}$ as opposed to $\widehat{\pi}^*_{CI}$. It is shown [9] that: (i) the policy value is lower-bounded in terms of the cost-sensitive classification error of $\widehat{\pi}^*_{CS}$; however, (ii) if the cost-insensitive classification error of $\widehat{\pi}^*_{CI}$ is not zero, then no matter how small the error is, the resulting policy can be arbitrarily close to the worst policy in terms of policy value. Empirical support was gained from experiments on a series of 2D grid-world domains.

---

[2] NB: Such a definition of $G^*(s)$ is similar to the *advantage* introduced by Baird [1].

3   Summary and Future Work

Classification-based policy acquisition is an interesting development in RL that attempts to gain a better policy by increasing the classification accuracy. However, the correlation between policy value and classification accuracy is non-monotonic as the states are not equally important. We then proposed a measure of state's decision-making importance and outlined a way to utilize such values in a class of RL problems. Advantages of such a method are supported both theoretically and empirically. The promising initial results open several avenues for future research. First, when computing resources are limited, it is possible to focus learning only on the more important states by ignoring the others. However, the extent to which such an *a priori* pruning may lead to overfitting needs to be explored. Another area for future research is an investigation of the extent to which this approach depends on the cost-sensitive classifier. In particular, it would be interesting to investigate the benefits of applying modern cost-sensitive classification techniques (e.g., cost-proportionate example weighting [13] and boosting [3]) in focused learning.

Acknowledgments. We thank Rich Sutton, Dale Schuurmans, Ilya Levner and Greg Lee for helpful discussions and other forms of help. The research is supported by the Alberta Ingenuity Center for Machine Learning, the University of Alberta, and NSERC.

References

1. Leeman Baird. Advantage updating. Technical report, Wright-Patterson Air Force Base, 1993.
2. Thomas G. Dietterich and Xin Wang. Batch value function approximation via support vectors. In *Advances in Neural Information Processing Systems 14*, volume 14, 2002.
3. Wei Fan, Salvatore J. Stolfo, Junxin Zhang, and Philip K. Chan. AdaCost: Misclassification cost-sensitive boosting. In *Proc. of the 16th Int'l Conf. on Machine Learning*, 1999.
4. Alan Fern, SungWook Yoon, and Robert Givan. Approximate policy iteration with a policy language bias. In *Advances in Neural Information Processing Systems 16*, 2004.
5. Michael Kearns, Yishay Mansour, and Andrew Ng. Approximate planning in large POMDPs via reusable trajectories. In *Advances in Neural Information Processing Systems 12*, 2000.
6. Michail Lagoudakis and Ronald Parr. Reinforcement learning as classification: Leveraging modern classifiers. In *Proc. of the 12th Int'l Conf. on Machine Learning*, 2003.
7. John Langford and Bianca Zadrozny. Reducing T-step reinforcement learning to classification. In *Proc. of the Machine Learning Reductions Workshop*, Chicago, IL, 2003.
8. Ilya Levner and Vadim Bulitko. Machine learning for adaptive image interpretation. In *Proc. of the 12th Innovative Applications of Artificial Intelligence Conf.*, 2004.
9. Lihong Li. Focus of attention in reinforcement learning. Master's thesis, Department of Computing Science, University of Alberta, Edmonton, Alberta, Canada, June 2004.
10. Andrew Y. Ng and Michael Jordan. PEGASUS: A policy search method for large MDPs and POMDPs. In *Proc. of the 16th Conf. on Uncertainty in AI*, 2000.
11. Richard S. Sutton and Andrew G. Barto. *Reinforcement Learning: An Introduction*. MIT Press, Cambridge, MA, March 1998.
12. SungWook Yoon, Alan Fern, and Robert Givan. Inductive policy selection for first-order MDPs. In *Proc. of the 18th Conference on Uncertainty in AI*, 2002.
13. Bianca Zadrozny and John Langford. Cost-sensitive learning by cost-proportionate example weighting. In *Proc. of the IEEE Int'l Conf. on Data Mining*, 2003.

Explicit Local Models:
Towards "Optimal" Optimization Algorithms*

Jan Poland

IDSIA, Galleria 2, CH-6928 Manno, Switzerland
jan@idsia.ch

Abstract. We use Hutter's AIXI theory, which concerns optimal rational agents in unknown environments, in order to establish a theoretical background for model-based optimization. This implies recommendations for the design of practical optimization algorithms.

In the recent past, a considerable amount of research has been devoted to model-based optimization algorithms, i.e. algorithms that use techniques from Machine Learning. Despite the efforts and considerable practical successes, there is no general theory which is both mathematically satisfying and practically relevant. We won't close this gap completely: We will present Hutter's AIXI theory which is general and mathematically neat, but not of direct practical relevance. Yet this theory yields practical recommendations for the design of model-based optimization algorithms.

In principle, any optimization algorithm might be termed "model-based" as soon as it stores and uses the information gained by function evaluation. However, it is common to call only those algorithms model-based which incorporate fairly advanced Machine Learning methods. Any use of information aims at reducing the number of function evaluations needed. Looking closer, we can distinguish two different reasons for models in optimization algorithms: (1) *Models as surrogates for expensive functions.* This has been one of the major motivations for the use of models in the past, in particular in evolutionary computation. (2) *Models for facilitating the optimization.* This includes all techniques rendering the optimization more efficient than random sampling. Cleverly chosen models may represent just the features of the objective function which are essential for optimization, neglecting all others. Examples are Quasi-Newton methods for functions on $\mathbb{R}^d$, where a quadratic model is maintained, or the Bayesian Optimization Algorithm (BOA) on bit strings, which approximates the distribution of good solutions using a Bayesian network. Also noise filtering methods fall in this category. It is desirable for an algorithm to cover *both* aspects. Our aim is to give guidelines for the design of such algorithms, particularly but not only for continuous real-valued functions on $\mathbb{R}^d$. In general, global optimization is infeasible unless the dimension d is very small ("curse of dimension"). It is therefore often agreed that *local* optimization is sufficient.

---

* This work was supported by SNF grant 2100-67712.02.

J.-F. Boulicaut et al. (Eds.): ECML 2004, LNAI 3201, pp. 569–571, 2004.
© Springer-Verlag Berlin Heidelberg 2004

Answering the question of how a (hypothetical) optimal agent would behave in an unknown environment, Hutter [1, 2] proposed the AIXI theory. Consider a decision-maker or agent, which may choose actions $x_t \in \mathcal{X}$ in discrete time $t = 1, 2, \ldots$. After each action, a probabilistic observation $y_t \in \mathcal{Y}$ is received from the environment. That is, an environment μ is specified by a distribution on $\mathcal{Y}$ for a given history (sequence of past actions and observations): $\mu(y \mid x_1 y_1 x_2 y_2 \ldots x_{t-1} y_{t-1} x_t)$. In the general case, the output $\mathcal{Y}$ usually consists of an informative part and a *reward*. The goal of the agent is maximizing the total future reward up to some time $T > 0$, the *horizon*. For optimization we may immediately make some important simplifications [2, Sec.7]. The environmental distribution only depends on the *current* input, i.e. $\mu(y \mid \ldots) = \mu_f(y \mid x_t)$. Here, $f : \mathcal{X} \to \mathcal{Y}$ is the objective function (without noise, we therefore have $\mu_f(y|x) = \delta_{f(x)}(y)$). The output without the reward is defined as $\mathcal{Y} = \mathbb{R}$. For noiseless functions, we could define the reward for example as $\text{Reward}(x_T) = -f(x_T)$ and $\text{Reward}(x_t) = 0$ for $t < T$. If the function evaluation is noisy, then an appropriate specification of the reward is not clear. Since we will not try to maximize the reward in the above form, we leave this question unanswered.

The agent works with a (in theory at most countable) class $\mathcal{M}$ of environments, also called *model class*. For optimization, it is natural that $\mathcal{M}$ consists of *explicit functions* rather than (implicit) properties of functions, e.g. distributions of good inputs as in the BOA. Assume for the moment that the objective function f is known and not noisy. Then trivially the optimal action is letting $x_T = \arg\min f$, but of course this does not solve the optimization problem. So we will require that $\mathcal{M}$ *contains only models which are easier to optimize than* f. Thus using the models actually saves computational resources. This may be given if f is expensive to evaluate, or if the graphs of the models are relatively simple compared to the graph of f, in particular if the models are only defined *locally*. Local models also result in a smaller model class, reducing computational costs. They are sufficient for a local optimization. On the other hand, $\mathcal{M}$ will not contain the objective function f. This is the price one pays for the applicability, while theoretical guarantees are usually based on the assumption $f \in \mathcal{M}$.

If the true environment μ is not known ("black-box optimization"), then we may estimate it using the Bayes mixture $\frac{\sum_{\mu \in \mathcal{M}} \mu(y|x_t) w(\mu) \prod_{i=1}^{t-1} \mu(y_i|x_i)}{\sum_{\mu \in \mathcal{M}} w(\mu) \prod_{i=1}^{t-1} \mu(y_i|x_i)}$, where $w(\mu)$ is the prior weight of μ. The Bayes mixture does depend on the past, in contrast to each single μ. In a Bayesian sense, it is optimal to estimate the true environment by the Bayes mixture and then choose the current action in order to *maximize its total expected future reward*: this is the definition of the AIXI agent [1]. That is, the agent should perform a *multi-step lookahead* and consider the complete relevant future. In contrast, the sampling strategy of most common optimization is *greedy*. However, evaluating the expectimax-tree generally involves a huge computational effort, and approximation is not trivial. This has a counterpart in machine learning, namely in active learning: There, the agent tries to sample in order to maximize the information gain by each function evaluation. Although this equally requires the evaluation of a tree, asymptotical analysis and empirical evidence suggest that here the greedy strategy is already quite good [3]. For optimization, a pure active learning approach maximizing only information gain and ignoring the objective value is unacceptable in general. However, combined with *local models* we can justify it: Sampling and evaluating serves for improving the local model, while the domain of the model is shifted towards the optimum. Of course, this heuristic procedure does not answer the problem of how to optimally do multi-step lookahead.

Evaluating a Bayes mixture is computationally hard in most cases, too. The exact expression is usually intractable, and Monte Carlo methods may be expensive. Therefore a maximum a posteriori (MAP) estimator is often used instead, which has worse performance in general. In optimization, there is a particular caveat: Models may tend to have "false optima", more generally even small model errors may heavily mislead the optimization process. If the model space contains several local optima (e.g. for feed-forward networks if the domain $\mathcal{X}$ is continuous), this can lead to further instability. It is thus favorable to choose a model class which always provides an *unambiguous* MAP estimator, for continuous domain e.g. a linearly parameterized class. Then the estimator is even unbiased (under Gaussian noise). False model optima are probably the main argument against explicit models and in favor of estimation-of-distribution algorithms as BOA, which are less prone to this problem.

We have obtained some guidelines for the design of model-based optimization algorithms: One should use *explicit local models* and perform a multi-step lookahead, approximating the objective function by a Bayes mixture. If this is computationally too expensive and a MAP estimator is used instead, one should choose the model class in order to assert unambiguous estimators. From the algorithms known on continuous domain, the derivative free optimization (DFO) methods [4] are somewhat closest to these recommendations. However they use an interpolation model which is not appropriate for noisy functions. We implemented an algorithm with a local quadratic regression model instead. It is significantly faster in terms of function evaluations compared to other algorithms, such as the Evolution Strategy with Covariance Matrix Adaptation (CMA-ES, [5]). For nicely behaving benchmark functions as Rosenbrock, our algorithm uses $1/4$ of the function evaluations of CMA-ES on average, achieving the same quality of optimum. Moderate noise almost does not affect our algorithm. We conclude with an open question: It is not obvious how to build good explicit local model classes on discrete domain.

References

1. M. Hutter. Towards a universal theory of artificial intelligence based on algorithmic probability and sequential decisions. *ECML*, pp. 226–238, 2001.
2. M. Hutter. A theory of universal artificial intelligence based on algorithmic complexity. Technical Report cs.AI/0004001, München, 62 pages, April 2000.
3. David A. Cohn. Neural network exploration using optimal experiment design. *NIPS*, pp. 679–686, 1994.
4. A. R. Conn, K. Scheinberg, and Ph. L. Toint. Recent progress in unconstrained nonlinear optimization without derivatives. *Math. Progr.*, 79(3):397–415, 1997.
5. N. Hansen and A. Ostermeier. Completely derandomized self-adaptation in evolution strategies. *Evolutionary Computation*, 9(2):159–195, 2001.

An Intelligent Model for the Signorini Contact Problem in Belt Grinding Processes

Xiang Zhang, Bernd Kuhlenkötter, and Klaus Kneupner

University Dortmund, Department of Assembly and Handling System
Leonhard-Euler-Strasse 2, 44227 Dortmund, Germany
xiang.zhang@uni-dortmund.de

Abstract. A bottleneck in the real-time simulation of belt grinding processes is the calculation of the force distribution between the workpiece and the grinding wheel, which can be simplified by the Signorini contact problem. The Finite Element Method (FEM) is the conventional way of solving such a contact problem, but too computationally expensive to meet the real-time requirement. This paper demonstrates a new approach to model the Signorini contact problem based on learning. This new model approximates the FEM model so that it is not necessary to execute optimization for each contact in run time; hence the calculation time is dramatically reduced.

1 Background

The key link in the real-time simulation of belt grinding processes is to get the removals on the workpiece surface in time [1]. The different removals on the workpiece surface result from the different local contact forces between the workpiece surface (hard) and the elastic grinding wheel (soft).

A contact problem between an elastic body and an idealistically rigid body is named the Signorini contact problem. According to this theory the elastic body deforms in a way that tends to minimize its strain potential energy when in contact with the rigid body, requiring that some initial and boundary conditions are satisfied. Once the strain field (deformation) is known, the force distribution can be easily obtained by Hooke's law. Blum and Suttmeier [2] worked out a FEM model that considers this contact problem as the Signorini contact problem. Although having adopted an optimized mesh discretization, it still requires about 15 minutes for doing the subjected optimization of one contact situation. The calculation of the force distribution becomes a bottleneck in the real-time simulation flow.

To accelerate the calculation two branches are under research nowadays. The first branch is to optimize the mesh division; another one is to improve the convergent rate and the stability of the optimization algorithm. Both cannot avert doing the iteration steps each time when a new contact situation is presented. To overcome this a learning machine is introduced in this paper to approximate the well-established FEM model. Although an optimization process is also necessary in the training phase, it can finish the calculation of one contact situation in a

J.-F. Boulicaut et al. (Eds.): ECML 2004, LNAI 3201, pp. 572–574, 2004.

very short time because the time-consuming transaction is put into the training phase and no longer in the run time. The Multi-Layer Perceptrons (MLP) and Support Vector Regression (SVR) are tested as the learning machines because both methods are capable of multi-dimensional regression problems.

2   Data Representation and Numerical Experiments

The input of the Signorini problem is the initial boundary condition that can be digitized in terms of the geometrical data of the workpiece. For simplification the contact area is limited to a $50mm \times 50mm$ square area and is discretized into a 50×50 mesh evenly spaced with $1mm$ interval. Thus the initial boundary condition can be written as a height matrix $\mathbf{H}$, in which each elements represent the vertical distance between the workpiece and the grinding wheel. It is not a good idea to impose all elements of the matrix $\mathbf{H}$ directly as the input to learning machine, just like what is done by FEM, because one cannot expect good results or generalization with such a high input dimension (2500). According to one assumption the contact problem can be localized to reduce the input dimension. The assumption is that *The force on one mesh point is affected only by the contact situation (heights) of its surrounding points inside a finite size area (function area).* The force of the center point is determined only by the heights in the function area, which is normally a partial contact area. Obviously, if the function area is large enough, or is the whole contact area, the assumption is undoubtedly correct. The small function leads to a low input dimension, but weakens the correctness of the assumption. Thus the function area size must not be too small to guarantee the assumption's correctness. Through training experiments the best function area size is $11mm \times 11mm$. Therefore, the learning machine takes 121 heights in the function area as input and the force on the center point of the function area as output. One contact point generates one input/output pair for training and testing. 180 characteristic contact situations are defined for training and 64 for testing and there are over 100,000 contact points in the training situations and about 50,000 in the testing situations.

Two methods can be used to further reduce the input dimension. One is the Partial Point Selection (PPS); the other one is the classical Principle Component Analysis (PCA). The PPS, as its name implies, takes only a couple of points in the function area instead of all points with preferences. PPS can easily lower the input dimension without losing much information because the workpiece surface is assumed to be continuous in every direction and varies smoothly, not sharply. Only 41 points, which locate on four (vertical, horizontal and two diagonals) lines, are selected out from all 121 points in the $11 \times 11mm^2$ function area.

For MLP, one hidden layer is used because more than one hidden layer didn't show any advantages in experiments. Only the RBF kernel is considered in the SVR. Table 1 shows the best results of different batches of training pairs. All models are managed to simulate the 64 contact situations after they are trained. The mean relative simulation error in table 1 indicates an average simulation error of 64 testing contact situations. The best result of SVR is 6.5%, which

Table 1. One model for all training sets

MLP			SVR		
Training Pairs	Neurons	Mean Relative Simulation Error	Training Pairs	nSV	Mean Relative Simulation Error
1570	10	10.5%	5160	606	8.8%
3140	11	10.2%	6880	675	6.5%
4710	15	10.8%	10264	880	8.2%

is still a little high. A training set classification strategy is applied in order to get higher precision. The training sets (contact points) are divided into 16 categories according to the relative position of contact points and the function area in a physical manner and then train a model for each category. However, the results in the adjoining area may be not as smooth as wanted. This can be overcome by an overlapping training strategy. That means that the contact points in the adjoining area of different categories should be involved in training all these categories for smoothness. There are two advantages of this classification strategy. The first one is that the learning machine can converge to a smaller error, another is that the number of neurons or support vectors is less than only one model with the same error endurance, which indicates a faster calculation. By this classification strategy the mean relative simulation error of testing situations reaches 4.1% using the SVR compared to 4.9% using the MLP. Additionally, the force distribution given by the SVR looks smoother than that by the MLP. However, the MLP model conducts the calculation much faster than that of the SVR model.

3   Conclusion

This paper demonstrates a new way to model the Signorini problem using the SVR and MLP to learn non-linear mapping rather than solving the optimization problem each time when a new contact situation is given. The experiments show that both SVR and MLP can approximate the traditional FEM model with an error below 5%. The SVR has a relatively better approximating precision than the MLP, but a longer calculating time. The calculating time is reduced to about 1 second compared to 15 minutes of original FEM model. This makes it possible to real-time simulation of belt grinding processes.

References

1. Zhang, X., Cabaravdic, M., Kneupner, K., Kuhlenkoetter, B.: Real-time simulation of robot controlled belt grinding processes of sculptured surfaces. International Journal of Advanced Robotic Systems 2 (2004) 109–114
2. Blum, H., Suttmeier, F.T.: An adaptive finite element discretisation for a simplified signorini problem. Calcolo 37 (2000) 65–77

Cluster-Grouping:
From Subgroup Discovery to Clustering

Albrecht Zimmermann and Luc De Raedt

Institute of Computer Science, Machine Learning Lab, Albert-Ludwigs-University
Freiburg, Georges-Köhler-Allee, 79110 Freiburg, Germany
{azimmerm,deraedt}@informatik.uni-freiburg.de

Abstract. The problem of **cluster-grouping** is defined. It integrates subgroup discovery, mining correlated patterns and aspects from clustering. The algorithm CG for solving cluster-grouping problems is presented and experimentally evaluated on a number of real-life data sets. The results indicate that the algorithm improves upon the subgroup discovery algorithm $CN2\text{-}WRACC$ and is competitive with the clustering algorithm $CobWeb$.

Keywords: clustering, subgroup discovery, correlated pattern mining.

1 Problem Specification and Context

The problem of cluster-grouping integrates subgroup discovery, mining correlated patterns and aspects from clustering. Subgroup discovery [1] aims at finding groups in the data that are over- or under-represented w.r.t. a specific target attribute; correlated pattern mining [2] is a form of association rule mining, which aims at finding rules whose condition part correlates strongly with its conclusion part w.r.t. a statistical evaluation criterion (e.g. χ^2 or entropy); and clustering [3] aims at identifying groups that are homogeneous w.r.t. an evaluation criterion such as *category utility*.

Although these three techniques are perceived as being quite different in the literature, it turns out that they are an instance of the more general problem of cluster-grouping that we introduce below. The cluster-grouping problem is concerned with finding rules $b_1 \wedge \ldots \wedge b_c \rightsquigarrow h_1 \vee \ldots \vee h_d$ (over boolean variables) that score best w.r.t. an interestingness function σ and set $\mathcal{E}$ of instances. We call d the dimension of the rule.

More formally, the *cluster grouping* problem can be defined as follows:

- **Given**
  - a set of rules $\mathcal{L}$ (the hypothesis space)
  - a set of instances $\mathcal{E}$ (i.e. boolean variable assignments)
  - an convex interestingness measure $\sigma : \mathcal{E} \times \mathcal{L} \mapsto \mathbb{R}$
  - a positive integer k
- **Find** the k rules in $\mathcal{L}$ that have the highest score w.r.t. σ and $\mathcal{E}$.

J.-F. Boulicaut et al. (Eds.): ECML 2004, LNAI 3201, pp. 575–577, 2004.

Subgroup discovery (as studied by [1]) is the special case of cluster-grouping where the conclusion part of the rules in $\mathcal{L}$ is a fixed boolean attribute and σ is *weighted relative accuracy (WRAcc)*; correlated pattern mining (as studied by [2]) allows for rules of dimension 1 and employs convex interestingness measures (such as χ^2 and entropy); and conceptual clustering can be regarded as the problem of finding k rules (whose condition part defines the clusters and whose conclusion part defines the d boolean variables of interest) w.r.t. a measure such as *category utility*.

2   The *CG*-Algorithm

The *CG*-algorithm for cluster grouping is an extension of Morishita and Sese's algorithm [2] for correlated pattern mining. Whereas Morishita and Sese coonsidered only rules of dimension 1, *CG* allows for rules of arbitrary dimension d. *CG* is similar to the correlated pattern mining algorithm of [2] in that it employs a branch-and-bound algorithm to search for the k best patterns w.r.t. the interestingness measure σ. The key idea underlying the algorithm is that for *convex* functions it is possible to compute an upper bound $u(r)$ on the quality of a rule r and all its specializations.

The *CG* algorithm works as follows. It initializes the queue of candidate solutions Q with the most general rule. It then repeatedly deletes the best candidate c from Q and evaluates its refinements w.r.t. u and σ. If a refinement is among the k best patterns already encountered, it is added to the current list of solutions. If a refinement's upper bound u scores worse than that of the worst element on the current list of solutions, it is discarded. All other refinements are added to the current list of candidates. The search continues until the list of candidates becomes empty.

To compute the upper bound, Morisha and Sese introduce the concept of a *stamp point* $\langle x, y \rangle$ with x denoting the coverage of a rule and y denoting the number of true positives. Correlation measures are then treated as functions defined on stamp points. While the *actual* future stamp points for specializations of the rule cannot be known in advance, the current stamp point constrains the set of *possible* future stamp points S_{poss}. The upper bound mentioned above is calculated by evaluating the correlation measure on the points lying on the convex hull of S_{poss}. We have extended this technique to arbitrary dimension d, allowing it to be used in clustering (in which the behavior of a rule with regard to all attributes is used as guidance in the search). For rules of dimension 1, the convex hull is a parallelogram, for dimension d one has to consider a hyperbody. In determining the vertices of that body, additional restrictions have to be observed preventing a simple recursion of the two-dimensional technique.

3   Experiments

We performed experiments on a variety of UCI data sets. We compared our approach to *CobWeb* [3] for clustering and to *CN2-WRAcc* [1] for subgroup discovery.

For clustering we applied *CG* to the initial data set, mining the rule with the highest *category utility* and used the condition part of the resulting rule as a splitting criterion. *CG* was then applied on the resulting subsets. In this way we construct a hierachical clustering. For comparison we computed the *category utility* of *Cobweb*'s solutions (averaged over 10 randomized orderings) and *CG*'s solutions and also the agreement between the respective solutions using the *Rand Index*. The resulting *category utilities* are shown in the left-hand table below.

Dataset	CU CG	CU CobWeb	Data set	CG	CN2-WRAcc
Breast-w	0.62	0.6496 ± 0.0001	Car	44.5 ± 38.8	84.75 ± 9.2
Breast-w-equal	1.088	$1.147 \pm 1.95 * 10^{-5}$	Zoo	1531 ± 1980.1	2133.6 ± 27.7
Credit-a	0.379	0.374 ± 0.0178	Nursery	82.6 ± 108.1	141.4 ± 13.1
Credit-a-equal	0.6241	0.6243 ± 0.00067	Breast-W	95.5 ± 6.4	529
Glass	0.301	0.291 ± 0.0125	Voting	36 ± 4.2	301
Hepatitis	0.446	0.459 ± 0.0142	Mushroom	196.5 ± 34.7	1806 ± 4.2
Iris	0.5369	0.5321 ± 0.0083			
Sick	0.2132	$.2077 \pm 0.0171$			
Voting	1.362	1.468 ± 0.0001			
Zoo (6 clusters)	0.6398	0.6349 ± 0.005			
Zoo (5 clusters)	0.7187	0.7196 ± 0.004			

Some of *CobWeb*'s solutions had lower *category utility* than the *CG* solution. While *CobWeb* also found solutions having higher *category utility*, those could not easily be described by conjunctive rules. In general the agreement between the *CobWeb* and *CG* solutions is very high (93.2% ± 5.3%).

For subgroup discovery we used *CG* to compute all rules achieving optimal value. We compared those rules to *CN2-WRAcc*'s solutions w.r.t whether the rules with highest *WRAcc* value were found and whether all such rules had been found. In the right-hand table above the average number of candidate rules considered during the search process are shown for *CN2-WRAcc* with beam size 1 and for *CG*.

CN2-WRAcc fails to always find the highest-scoring rules as *CG* does. This is the case even for beam sizes in excess of 10 and up to 50. Additionally *CN2-WRAcc* considered more candidate rules during the search even for small beam sizes.

The results presented above show that *CG* is a valid alternative to *CN2-WRAcc* and *CobWeb*.

References

1. Todorovski, L., Flach, P., Lavrac N. Predictive Performance of Weighted Relative Accuracy. *Proceedings of the 4th European Conference on Principles and Practice of Knowledge Discovery in Databases.* Lyon, France. September 2000
2. Morishita, S., Sese, J. Traversing Itemset Lattice with Statistical Metric Pruning. *Proceedings of the 19th ACM SIGACT-SIGMOD-SIGART Symposium on Principles of Database Systems.* Dallas, Texas, USA. May 2000
3. Fisher, D.H. Knowledge acquisition via incremental conceptual clustering. *Machine Learning, Volume 2, Number 2,* 139-172, Kluwer Academic. 1987

Author Index

Lecture Notes in Artificial Intelligence (LNAI)